Art and
Creative Development
for Young Children, Fifth Edition

Join us on the web at

EarlyChildEd.delmar.com

Art and Creative Development for Young Children

FIFTH EDITION

Robert Schirrmacher

THOMSON

DELMAR LEARNING

Australia Canada Mexico Singapore Spain United Kingdom United States

THOMSON

DELMAR LEARNING

Art and Creative Development for Young Children, Fifth Edition
Robert Schirrmacher

Vice President, Career Education SBU:
Dawn Gerrain

Director of Editorial:
Sherry Gomoll

Acquisitions Editor:
Erin O'Connor

Developmental Editor:
Patricia Osborn

Editorial Assistant:
Stephanie Kelly

Director of Production:
Wendy A. Troeger

Production Manager:
J.P. Henkel

Production Editor:
Joy Kocsis

Production Assistant:
Angela Iula

Technology Project Manager:
Sandy Charette

Director of Marketing:
Wendy E. Mapstone

Channel Manager:
Kristin McNary

Marketing Coordinator:
David White

Cover Design:
The Drawing Board

Composition:
Graphic World Publishing Services

For permission to use material from this text or product, submit a request online at http://www.thomsonrights.com

Any additional questions about permissions can be submitted by email to thomsonrights@thomson.com

Library of Congress Cataloging-in-Publication Data

Schirrmacher, Robert
   Art and creative development for young children/Robert Schirrmacher.—5th ed. p. cm.
   Includes bibliographical references and index.
   ISBN 1-4018-7261-1
   1. Art—Study and teaching (Early childhood)—United States.   2. Creative ability—United States. 3. Child development—United States.   4. Creative activities and seat work.   5. Curriculum planning—United States.   I. Title.

LB1139.5.A78S35 2005
372.5'044—dc22
                                                    2005043065

NOTICE TO THE READER

Contents

Section Three
**Art and
Aesthetics**

Section Four
**Providing Art
Experiences**

Section Five
Roles and Strategies

Appendices

Preface

Art education and artistic processing help children understand their world. When children look at art, they learn to make meaning of symbols that communicate ideas, experiences, and feelings that can be shared. Of course art is fun, but it is also mentally engaging. The art of young children may not resemble anything in the real world. With older children, art begins to approximate reality more closely. Young children, art, and creativity are very compatible. Young children can be noisy, active, and messy. Art too can be noisy, active, and messy. Art can also be quiet and meticulous like a child who sits motionless while small fingers try to glue together pieces of paper, yarn, and ribbon. Art allows children to experiment and explore, to see what they can create. Their creative self-expression enhances their self-esteem.

The Fifth Edition of *Art and Creative Development* is written for early childhood educators and those preparing to work with children in a public or private preschool, child care, and kindergarten through third grade settings. Sound principles and basic art media are appropriate regardless of the age of the artist. The book will take you back to your own childhood to help you move toward your future as a professional early childhood educator who will help young children reach their creative and artistic potential.

Based on developmentally appropriate practices, this new edition continues to reflect an art focus, emphasizing child-directed (opposed to teacher-directed) activities and outlining an art center approach. It is full of ideas and activities for all children to enjoy integrating creative experiences in music, dance, dramatic arts, and literature into the early childhood curriculum.

CONCEPTUAL APPROACH

The book is written from three different perspectives attempting to synthesize the author's training and experience as an artist, teacher of young children, and teacher educator. It is neither a cookbook of activities nor a review of theory and research; it subtly blends theory and research with practical application. It is based on the developmental perspective that knowing what and how to provide for an art activity is as important as knowing why. The teacher plays a key role as facilitator within a recommended art center approach, maximizing creative expression, responsible freedom, decision-making, and discovery.

ORGANIZATION

There are 16 chapters clustered around five main sections: Creativity, Young Children as Artists: A Developmental View, Art and Aesthetics, Providing Art Experiences, and Roles and Strategies. Each section contains three or more chapters using photographs and questions to introduce chapters that follow. The addition of sections connects the material, helping the chapters to flow and develop cohesively. Each chapter begins with an opening section providing a photograph and several thought-provoking questions to stimulate critical thinking, foster group discussion, and motivate the reader. In addition, each chapter provides objectives, an Introduction, a Summary, a list of Key Terms, Suggested Activities, and a Review of the chapter.

SPECIAL FEATURES

Abundant class-tested activities are throughout the book. Age ranges are provided for many activities; however, these should be regarded as guidelines only. A teacher's knowledge of a particular child's developmental level must be the main guide in determining the appropriateness of any activity.

The following icons are used to indicate the age appropriateness of art activities as follows:

T = Older toddlers and two-year-olds

P = Preschoolers or three- and four-year-olds

K = Kindergartners or five-year-olds

S = School-age children or five- through eight-year-olds

A new icon to feature art instruction is added to highlight recommended activities.

The NAEYC guidelines for Developmentally Appropriate Practices (DAP) have been expanded to focus on art practices. They are listed in the front inside cover. Guidelines for DAP are cross-references throughout the text. The icon to the left indicates a statement supported by the NAEYC position paper on Developmentally Appropriate Practices.

Consider This boxes present information for the student to stop and think about various possibilities.

Reflection boxes contain content that allows the student to step back and reflect upon their own experiences and apply to the content at hand.

Hints provide helpful suggestions for teachers to save time by providing 'short cuts' as well as other helpful hints.

Quality literature suggest recommendations for music and movement, art therapy, special needs, artistic elements, cultural diversity, story songs, and art in general.

NEW TO THIS EDITION

- A new Chapter 14 "Art Experiences through Technology" discusses the impact of technology on teachers and children providing activities to support art experiences for young children.
- Over 100 new full color photographs integrated throughout the chapters depict toddlers, preschoolers and school-age children engaged in art as well as their finished products.
- Children's Art has been expanded to include Computer Art.
- A new multicultural icon honors children's different cultural art experiences.
- *Special Needs* boxes identify characteristics of young gifted children.
- A new Appendix H provides information on The National Standards for Arts Education.
- A new Appendix I provides suggestions for Multicultural Picture Books.

Updated and new information has been added to the following chapters:

Chapter 1 "Understanding Creativity"

- A new discussion of the creative/artistic Process vs. Product controversy.

- The work on Multiple Intelligences is expanded to include the possibility of other intelligences.
- Individual intelligences are matched to the realm of art.
- Implications of Multiple Intelligences to one's work with children is also presented.

Chapter 2 "Creative Thinking"

- Brain functioning and brain preferences, as they relate to student learning, and adult teaching is discussed.

Chapter 3 "Creative Experiences"

- The work of Vygotsky is applied using specific teacher-child examples.
- The concept of literacy is expanded to multiple literacies including visual and media literacy with an emphasis on the contribution of picture books to visual literacy.
- Additional information on music and movement including teacher's role and musical experiences for infants and toddlers.

Chapter 4 "Art and the Developing Child"

- A discussion on the use of art to celebrate holidays.

Chapter 7 "Aesthetics"

- Criteria for selecting art prints and suggestions for their placement in childhood settings.
- A 3-part strategy for engaging children in a discussion and appreciation of the art of picture book illustration.

SUPPLEMENTS

An *Instructor's Manual to Accompany Art and Creative Development for Young Children* will include answers to the chapter review questions at the end of each chapter as well as additional suggestions for instructional activities and resources.

The fifth edition features a NEW Online Companion™ that is a useful supplement to the book and provides instrumental resources and activities, in addition to what the book provides. Such resources and activities include:

- Samples of children's artwork to illustrate the developmental stages of drawing
- Samples of children's artwork illustrating the various elements of visual art (line, shape, texture, space, etc.) to provide students opportunities to practice appropriate teacher responses

- Sample lesson plans to provide examples of developmentally appropriate visual art production and appreciation activities in an early childhood classroom
- Suggested laboratory activities to build student knowledge and dispositions toward visual art and music
- Web sites for teachers and children to further expand their resources and learning
- Annotated bibliography of arts-related trade books

The Online Companion™ icon appears at the end of each chapter to prompt you to go online and take advantage of the many features provided.

You can find the Online Companion™ web site at www.EarlyChildEd.delmar.com.

A Computerized Test Bank is NEW to this edition with a variety of questions such as multiple choice, short answer, true and false, and matching to customize exams and quizzes.

ABOUT THE AUTHOR

Robert Schirrmacher is a full-time Instructor with the San Jose/Evergreen Community College District. The author received his Ph.D. in Early Childhood Education from the University of Illinois. His experience includes teaching preschool, kindergarten, and first grade at undergraduate and graduate levels. He has assisted in Montessori schools and directed programs for young children. He continues to serve as consultant to parent groups and public and private early childhood programs. As an advocate for developmentally appropriate education and quality care for young children, the author is actively involved in professional organizations at the local, state, and national levels.

ACKNOWLEDGMENTS

Children and parents with whom I have worked in Michigan, Illinois, Florida, Alabama, and California, including all former and present students of child development and early childhood education who have helped me refine my thinking on children's art.

Faculty, staff, parents, and children at our two child-development centers: San Jose City College and Evergreen Valley College.

A special thanks to the staff and children of PS27 c/o Schuyler Elementary School, Schenectady Country Community College, Astor Services, Community Family Development, and Battery Park City Day Nursery in making this book special and unique.

CONTRIBUTORS

Jill Fox, Ph.D.
Associate Professor
Virginia Commonwealth University
Richmond, VA

REVIEWERS

Deb Ahola, M.S.
Associate Professor
Schenectady County Community College
Schenectady, NY

Linda Aiken, M.A.
Associate Program Director
Southwestern Community College
Sylva, NC

Carol Anderson, M.S.
Adjunct Professor
Colorado Community Colleges Online
Denver, CO

Elaine Camerin, Ed.D.
Program Manager
Daytona Beach Community College
Daytona Beach, FL

Pamela Davis, Ph.D.
Professor
Henderson State University
Arkadelphia, AR

Jill Fox, Ph.D.
Associate Professor
Virginia Commonwealth University
Richmond, VA

Linda Gamble, M.Ed.
Coordinator of Special Projects and Adjunct Faculty
University of Maine at Farmington
Farmington, ME

Section One

Creativity

The author believes so strongly in creativity that it will be explored as a separate aspect of development in Chapter 4. Others would include creativity under cognition, because creativity depends on thinking. What is creativity? Can you give an example? Creativity is an elusive term; although we all would agree that it is important, we may not all agree on what it is. Because creativity peaks during the early years, it seems fitting that Chapter 1, Understanding Creativity, should contain extensive discussion on the nature of creativity.

Look at the preschoolers in the photograph. What are they doing? Is anything creative happening? The teacher has carefully planned a dramatic play center around the theme of picnicking. This was prompted by an informal discussion in which children mentioned their interest in going with their families to the park for a picnic. Birthdays, holidays, and other family events were often celebrated with a picnic. The teacher believed it wise to start with a theme that children knew and enjoyed. The children are using the play food and other props to dramatize or represent what a picnic means to them. The play is rich with language and social interaction. It is also open-ended in that there is no one right way to go on a picnic.

Chapter 2, Creative Thinking, identifies the components of creative thinking, also called divergent production, and activities that easily can be incorporated into small or large group times.

Besides art, how else can children express their creativity? Chapter 3 identifies Creative Experiences in the areas of play, language, music, and movement that incorporate creative expression throughout the day.

Chapter 1

Understanding Creativity

Children can be creative with just about anything. They do not need fancy or expensive toys. What do you see going on in this photograph? The teacher has planned an art activity that will allow the children to be creative. The activity was well thought out. She provided a smock to keep the child's clothes clean as well as different colors of paint and enough brushes. She was also very resourceful in recycling bubble wrap, the clear plastic type used for shipping. It is best when children are able to use the colors they select and paint their bubble wrap as they see fit. Some children cover their entire pieces; others do not. Some use only one color; others enjoy using and mixing many colors. Some children use their painted bubble wrap to make a print by gently pressing it onto another sheet of paper. When carefully lifted off, a print results.

The child appears to be actively engaged and focused. How simple yet how creative! Can you think of any other uses for bubble wrap in the early childhood classroom? How about letting the children pop the bubbles or walk on the bubble wrap? If the ideas sound unusual, try to suspend judgment and go with the creative flow.

Objectives

After reading this chapter, you should be able to:

- Explain creativity as an attitude, process, product, skill, set of personality traits, and set of environmental conditions.
- Compare and contrast creativity with conformity and convergent thinking.
- Discuss the relationship between creativity and intelligence.
- Discuss ways adults can facilitate children's creative expression.
- Explain the concept of multiple intelligences and their relationship to art.
- Identify characteristics of gifted and talented children.
- Discuss the implications of brain research.

INTRODUCTION

What or with whom do you associate with **creativity?** Do you think of architecture by Frank Lloyd Wright, a play by Shakespeare, a painting by Georgia O'Keeffe, Henry Ford's Model T, or the *Nutcracker Suite?*

These are classic examples of the creative works of some very creative individuals. You probably had other examples. Children were not included in this list. Were they included in yours? Let us focus on creativity and see how it specifically relates to young children.

Consider This...

Having converted their spacious basement into several play spaces, the Cliffords are involved in family child care. Today, Mika has put a hair roller on each one of her fingers, saying, "See my rings, me pretty." Yoshi has taken a spare roll of toilet paper and is wrapping up the dolls. He says, "Got hurted, fix." Rhonida is putting the teddy bear counters into a bowl atop the play stove saying, "Mmmm, hot soup: it's good for you. Sit and eat." Cassie has found an empty shoe box and is planning to make a boat for the small plastic family. She says, "They are rich and famous movie stars and live on one of those yok [yacht] things on the ocean, and way up in the mountains." The Cliffords do not dismiss these episodes as humorous but unimportant. They see these playful behaviors as indicators that the children in their care are developing creatively. The children are fortunate to have adults like the Cliffords who accept, value, and plan for their creative expression.

BEGINNINGS OF CREATIVITY

Creative expression begins early in life (see Figure 1–1). Babies manipulate toys, explore space, discover their body parts, test hunches about their immediate world, and even solve problems. For example, Lea wants a toy rattle that she has accidentally kicked to the foot of her crib. Through trial-and-error behavior she discovers that she can get the toy by tugging at the blanket it rests on.

Figure 1-1 Creative expression begins early in life.

Yani: Art Prodigy

According to Newman (1990), Wang Yani can be considered an art prodigy. Yani, the daughter of Chinese oil painter Wang Shiqiang, began painting when she was only two and had her first exhibit at age four. Two years later she had completed some 4,000 paintings. Her works have been exhibited throughout the world. Perhaps you have heard about her or viewed an exhibition of her work.

Yani began painting like most children, smearing paint and making unrecognizable shapes. Yani's father credits her success to her drive, not to talent. Frustrated and annoyed that her pictures bore so little resemblance to her mental images, at age three Yani proceeded to cram many years of artistic development into several months. She painted for hours on end, improving her skills through trial and error. Although Yani believed she was just having fun, her father believes she was refining her craft (Newman, 1990).

Yani's art is filled with delightful creatures. Her favorites are monkeys, and many people believe that Yani identifies monkeys and their antics. By age six, however, Yani had expanded and began painting birds, flowers, landscapes, and people. Monkey antics gave way to children and landscapes of the scenic region of Southern China where Yani lives with her family.

Is Yani naturally talented or was she taught? Yani's father claims he did not teach her the way art is typically taught in Chinese schools. He gave up his own painting in oils so as not to influence her style. Instead, Yani's father guided her into developing her sense of perception and into discovering techniques for controlling her brushes, ink, and water.

The steps to Yani's rapid development as a gifted artist appear so simple that one wonders why there are not more child art prodigies. Yani had the concentration, drive, determination, and motivation to master painting and to develop her own technique. She received support from her artistic father, who provided space, materials, and encouragement. Still, one cannot dismiss the role of natural talent and teaching in cases involving child prodigies.

There are many examples of creativity in adults and young children. Merely identifying examples, however, does not help us understand the nature of creativity. Just what is creativity? How will we know if something or someone is creative? One way to attempt to understand creativity is by defining it.

CREATIVITY

There are many ways to define creativity. Perhaps this has added to the confusion, misunderstanding, and mystique surrounding it. People have different definitions for the same term. How would you define creativity?

Some generally accepted definitions are

- the ability to see things in new ways.
- boundary breaking and going beyond the information given.
- thinking unconventionally.
- making something unique.
- combining unrelated things into something new.

How does your definition compare with these? Torrance (1963a), a pioneer in creativity, has chosen to define creativity as the process of sensing problems or gaps in information, forming ideas or hypotheses, and communicating the results. For example, two five-year-olds, Missy and Eric, want to build a school, but they have no blocks or pieces of wood. They consider using shoe boxes, which are fairly durable and stackable, for a base. Gardner (1993a) offers a second definition with four key parts. He sees the creative individual as a person who regularly solves problems, fashions products, or defines new questions in a domain in a way that is initially considered novel but that ultimately becomes accepted in a particular cultural setting. First, Gardner believes that a person must be creative in a domain, rather than across all domains. This directly challenges the concept of an all-purpose creative trait that underlies tests of creativity. Second, he believes that creative individuals regularly exhibit their creativity as opposed to a once-in-a-lifetime burst of creativity. Third, he insists that creativity can involve the fashioning of products or the devising of new questions as well as the solution of problems. This greatly expands more traditional definitions that emphasize the making of products. Fourth, he believes that creative activities are only known as such when they have been accepted in a particular culture. The crucial point is that nothing is creative in and of itself. Creativity is inherently a cultural judgment.

Although our attempts to define creativity may provide us with some general feel for the concept, there are other ways to better understand and explain creativity.

EXPLAINING CREATIVITY

Although there is no single definition of creativity, there are different ways to explain it. Creativity can be explained as a(n)

1. attitude.
2. process.
3. product.
4. skill.
5. set of personality traits.
6. set of environmental conditions.

Creativity Is an Attitude Not an Aptitude

For young children it may be more helpful to view creativity as a way of doing things. Creativity is a special and different way of viewing the world in which there are no right or wrong answers, only possibilities. Think of creativity as an attitude rather than an aptitude. Children demonstrate a creative attitude when they

- try out new ideas and different ways of doing things.
- push boundaries and explore possibilities.
- manipulate and transform ideas and materials.
- take things apart and put them back together in different ways.
- physically play with objects.
- imagine, engage in fantasy, or just daydream.
- solve problems or try to figure things out.
- ask questions or challenge accepted ways of thinking or acting.

Creativity As a Skill

Although all children are capable of creativity, the potential to create remains dormant without practice. With practice, the potential to create becomes a reality. For example, the skill of playing tennis is quickly lost without practice. Good tennis players practice frequently. So, too, the skill of creativity requires exercise to grow. Without practice, the ability to write,

Figure 1-2 Creative processing with play dough.

Creativity: Process or Product?

This question often revolves around a discussion of young children's creative pursuits. Which is more important—the process or product? The question remains the same whether the activity is play, music and movement, or art. Both sides of the process vs. product debate or answers to the question need to be explored. Is the process or the "how" more important than the "what" resulted or the finished product?

Young children play for the sake of playing. They may stack blocks for the sheer joy of stacking with no regard for what results. They may make up their own words to songs and may dance about creatively just for the pleasure in doing so. For art, the process involves the active, hands-on doing, exploring, trial-and-error experimenting, trying out, and manipulating of sensory-rich "messing about" with artistic tools and media. Processing is serious work and a means and end in itself. Young children see what they can make happen with paint, glue, and collage materials. Processing honors the unexpected and provides opportunities for problem solving, including how to keep wet paint from running or smearing. In all creative pursuits, the focus is often on processing with little or no regard for what may result as a finished product. Through experimenting and processing, children are totally caught up in creative activity. Often, they abruptly terminate their processing with little concern that they have not officially finished by making something. So it may be pointless to ask a process-oriented child "What is it?" or "What did you make?" when the intent was pure processing. To do so is to impose a product-oriented mindset. These children did not set out to make something so there is no need to show a product. For young children, processing is enjoyment and completion in and of itself. The here and now in the present engagement replace a need to "make something." The reward and pleasure are in the doing—whether it be singing, dancing, playing, or engaging in art. It is not necessary to make something which could be recognizable to others or even rewarded with a compliment such as "Oh how pretty, look what you made—a house." With the processing approach, there will not be anything

to display on the wall or take home to post on the refrigerator. Processing does not need to culminate in a finished product to validate its importance. The worth is in the doing. Edwards (2002) calls this process approach experiential, in that children engage in the process of art without knowing or maybe even caring what the steps will be along the way or what will turn out. Nor do these children know or care what the outcome will look like or if indeed there even is an outcome or product.

The processing side of the debate views art as more verb than noun. The process of doing art could be called "arting." According to Edwards (2002) and Isbell and Raines (2003), in the early years "arting" or artistic processing is more important to the young child than the act of creating a finished art product or outcome. According to Cherry and Nielsen (1999), the important goals of early childhood art are the involvement, the movement, and the discovery of self-accomplishment. In other words, the process, not the product.

The product stance argues the importance of making something and that processing steps are secondary to the finished product. Adult artists sell their finished products, not the process. According to Isbell and Raines (2003), some children become interested in the product as they become more skilled in the use of varied art materials and techniques. For them, the art product is important, but it is self-imposed and not demanded by the teacher. Often they have an idea in mind of what they want to make. This drives their artistic processing. They get excited when they successfully execute their plans and something turns out the way they wanted. Often, they will repeat the process to make more than one artistic product. They may take delight when others recognize their products as what they set out to make. One major concern needs to be raised surrounding the product approach. Children may be tempted to bypass creative processing for the sake of just making something, especially if done for adult recognition, approval, and reward. For example, a child may hastily draw a flower to hear a teacher say, "Oh, how beautiful. I just love flowers." The concern is

(continued)

Creativity: Process or Product?   (continued)

that the child has bypassed his or her own creative processing to make a product that pleases someone else. This is not the nature of art. Children and adults create to express themselves and leave a mark that is personally expressive and meaningful.

In summary, artistic processing and product making do go hand in hand. A product is created out of processing, but even adult artists engage in endless processing before achieving an acceptable finished product. If the finished product did not turn out, back to more processing. Still, artistic processing should be at the heart of early childhood art activities. Value children's processing without expecting a finished product. In turn, accept the interest of some children, often older, to want to make a finished

product. Isbell and Raines (2003) propose an interdependent progression in the process vs. product discussion. They believe that the creative process begins while exploring and playing with tools and materials. After many experiences, children move on to the next step by focusing on a particular approach. Once an approach is chosen, children use this method in the production level. The last step involves stopping, evaluating, or even reworking. These authors add that it is difficult to pinpoint when one step ends and another begins in the visual arts. The very young child often spends more time in the exploratory stage, whereas the more experienced child may spend more time at the production level. Each step, however, is intertwined and important for the developing child.

make music, sing, dance, and paint would be lost. Creativity as a potential and skill requires exercise. Sternberg and Lubart (1995) believe that creativity, like intelligence, is something that everyone possesses in some amount. Moreover, creativity is not a fixed attribute. One's level of creativity is not carved in stone at birth, and like any talent, it is something virtually anyone can develop to varying degrees.

When a discussion of creativity arises, many adults are prone to state, "I'm just not creative." Everyone seems to have a friend or relative who is creative, but not all people believe themselves to be creative. In part, this relates to the old idea of a creative elite and a product explanation for creativity. Still, all people evidence some degree of creativity, whether in writing, sewing, cooking, making crafts, pursuing hobbies, home decorating, or even teaching! It is important to find a creative outlet and practice the process or skill involved. What is your creative outlet?

Still, why do some adults feel themselves uncreative when by contrast young children are considered highly creative? What has happened between early childhood and adulthood? Research on creativity suggests that the child reaches a peak of creative functioning during the early childhood years. Torrance (1965) plots the degree of creative functioning versus age. Creativity often peaks at about four to four and a half years of age and is followed by a sharp drop upon entrance into elementary school. Perhaps the push for conformity, accountability, and academics in elementary school accounts for this sharp drop. Yet this drop

is not inevitable. Environmental conditions and practice can keep the spirit of creativity alive.

Creativity As a Set of Personality Traits

The personality approach attempts to identify the personality profile of highly creative individuals. Researchers have identified highly creative individuals and have attempted to identify personality traits that these individuals share. Some of these include:

- an openness to the new and unexpected.
- a tolerance for ambiguity.
- a willingness to experiment and take risks.
- impulsivity.
- curiosity.
- a preference for complexity.
- being highly intuitive.
- sensitivity.
- flexibility.
- introversion.
- individualism.
- nonconformity, daring to be different.
- independence.
- playfulness.
- a sense of humor.
- preference for being alone, may be unsocial or very social.

The list of personality traits is extensive, and not every highly creative individual will possess all the traits. Also, the list of personality traits will vary de-

Profile of a Gifted/Talented/Highly Creative Child

Think of a child that you have observed or worked with whom you would call creative. What words would you use to describe this child? While the following traits describe creative children, no one child will perfectly match this tentative profile. Creative children tend to be

1. original, imaginative, spontaneous, resourceful, and uninhibited.

2. sensitive to sensory stimuli and have heightened awareness. They are open to new ideas, see things afresh, and are intuitive.

3. curious, alert, impulsive, risk taking, adventurous, and into everything.

4. independent in thinking and social behavior. They can appear aloof and may prefer older peers and adults to friends their own age.

5. developmentally advanced, precocious, fast learners. They have good memories, extensive vocabularies, and are interested in books, often learning to read by themselves at an early age.

6. perfectionists with a good sense of humor; they ask "why" questions.

7. persistent, with a long attention span; they can stick with a plan or idea.

8. nonconforming and unconventional; they question or challenge the status quo.

9. inventive and innovative, and good at solving problems.

10. not overly concerned with being neat or prompt; they may be easily bored with routine and mundane tasks.

---

pending on the researcher. Torrance (1962) identified the following seven indicators of creativity that may be useful in identifying and explaining the behavior of the highly creative young child.

Curiosity.   The child's questioning is persistent and purposeful. Curiosity can be either verbal: "What is that?" or "Why?"—or nonverbal: manipulation and active exploration.

Flexibility.   If one approach fails, the creative child will try a variety of different approaches.

Sensitivity to Problems.   The child is quick to see gaps in information, exceptions to the rules, and contradictions in what is seen and heard.

Redefinition.   The child sees hidden meaning in statements that others accept at face value. New uses are found for familiar objects. The child sees connections between things that appear unrelated to others.

Self-Feeling.   The child has a feeling of self-importance and individuality. Self-direction permits the child to work alone. Merely following directions or conforming results in boredom.

Originality.   The child has surprising, uncommon, interesting ideas.

Insight.   The child has access to realms of the mind that the less creative visit only in their dreams. Much time is spent toying with ideas and possibilities.

Identifying the one typical personality pattern of the highly creative individual may be impossible. There is too much variation among creative individuals. Still, a set of global traits may provide some assistance in identifying these individuals and understanding the nature of creativity.

Creativity As a Set of Environmental Conditions

If creativity is an inherent potential, there must be things that can be done to enhance or retard its development. Environmental conditions include people, places, objects, and experiences. Children do not create out of a vacuum. They need a source of inspiration or an experiential background from which to draw. For example, a child who has never visited an airport or been aboard a plane will have difficulty discussing these concepts or incorporating them into block play, dramatic play, movement, art, and other creative activities. By contrast, a child who has visited an airport and flown on a plane will be able to discuss these experiences and use them as pivots for creative expression. Parnes (1967) draws an analogy between a kaleidoscope and creativity. The more numerous and colorful the pieces in the drum of a kaleidoscope, the greater the variety of resulting shapes, colors, and patterns. Likewise, in creative expression, the greater one's background of experiences with people, places, and objects, the greater the range of possibilities to draw from in creative activity.

Home Environment.   Obviously, the home environment is a critical factor in a child's development of creativity. Is there a home environment that optimizes the development of creativity?

According to Healy (1994) parents who produce creative children share the following characteristics. They

- show them how to be problem finders as well as problem solvers.
- have full lives themselves and do not depend on their children to meet their emotional or achievement needs.
- are not in awe of their child and do not defer to his or her demands or feel compelled to entertain him or her.
- tolerate divergent ideas and mistakes made "in the service of learning."
- provide discipline and structure to give children security to explore.
- set realistic standards and encourage pride in achievement.
- show active interest in a child's thoughts and creative efforts.
- encourage a close, nurturing relationship as well as freedom of physical expression.
- give children early responsibility for making choices and taking appropriate responsibility for their own decisions.
- permit children to have solitude and develop imaginative thinking by daydreaming.
- show children how to be curious and observant.
- allow honest expression of emotions.
- encourage children to feel intuitively as well as think logically.
- do not put pressure on school for "competency" that excludes intellectual creativity.
- expose children to a broad range of artistic and intellectual pursuits.

The above factors and behaviors can be practiced in home and school settings to foster children's creative development.

The Creativity Equation

Children will be creative on their own, but there are conditions or factors that nurture creativity. They can be combined into the following equation:

Unconditional Love from
Significant Adults
Acceptance, Encouragement,
and Nurturance

+

Autonomy and Freedom

↓

Competence and Self-Esteem

↓

Risk Taking and Creativity

Children need unconditional love, acceptance, encouragement, and nurturance from adults who are significant in their lives. These include family members, relatives, friends, and teachers. Children need adults who empower them to exercise responsible freedom to do things on their own and to make things happen. In turn, this develops competence and enhances their self-esteem. Competence and self-esteem are reciprocal. Making something on their own makes children feel good about what they accomplished. Good feelings about themselves motivate children to keep trying new things and become even more competent. In turn, children will feel safe to take risks and trust their creative impulses to venture out and dance to the beat of their own drummers.

OBSTACLES TO CREATIVITY

Just as a stimulating environment and family factors can enhance creativity, negative conditions can restrict it. Four environmental conditions that provide potential obstacles to creativity are

- parents.
- school.
- sex roles.
- society, culture, and tradition.

Parents

Parents often have certain expectations for their children. Unfortunately, creative children may not conform to these expectations. Highly creative children often question authority, limits, adult logic, and explanations. These children act and behave differently. Parents may view these creative behaviors as misbehavior. They may perceive and treat their creative child as odd, immature, abnormal, or naughty. Parents may need to be informed and educated about the nature of creativity through classroom observation, readings, and informal sessions in which they discuss creativity and engage in creative processing themselves.

School

The teacher may not understand, encourage, or value the creative child. Too often the creative child must operate in a school situation based entirely on conformity and **convergent thinking.** The child is taught that black is the color of night when he or she has experienced it as purple-blue or licorice. With the current emphasis on academics in early childhood education, there is a concern that little time if any will be spent on creative activities. It is also possible that some children feel confined in noncreative classrooms and "shut down" or rebel to protect their creative integrity. It is important for teachers to understand, value, and encourage creativity by providing an abundance of curricular activities that foster it.

Sex Roles

Sex roles limit boys and girls to certain types of behavior on the basis of gender. Creative functioning, however, transcends sex role barriers. Forcing children to conform to stereotypical sex roles denies them their optimal development as individuals. We do children a disservice when we expect boys to be active, independent, and rugged, and girls to be passive, dependent, and gentle. If sex roles were to dictate, boys would be denied access to quieter expressive activities and girls would be denied access to reactive manipulative experiences. Either way someone loses, because both types of experience are vital to creative processing.

Society, Culture, and Tradition

Society, culture, and tradition are distinct concepts, but each dictates a certain set of behaviors, values, and attitudes. These are transmitted to children at a very early age in the form of expectations. Unfortunately, creative children may operate with a different agenda. Problems arise for highly creative children in a milieu where adults have all the answers and children are expected to fit into a rigid behavioral mold or pattern. Often, the rationale includes, "That's the way it's done in our family" or "If it was good enough for me, it's good enough for you." It is important to respect, reinforce, and uphold the expectations of society, tradition, and one's culture without sacrificing individuality in the process.

ACEI Position Paper on Children's Right to the Arts

The Association for Childhood Education International (Jalongo, 1990) believes that children have a right to the expressive arts. In order to reaffirm the importance of the expressive arts in school, educators must accept the following beliefs.

1. Every child has a right to opportunities for imaginative expression.

2. Educating the child's imagination is education for the future.

3. The educated imagination is the key to equity and intercultural understanding.

4. Children's creative productivity is qualitatively different from adults'.

5. Creative expression should permeate the entire curriculum.

6. Imagination is the key to artistry in teaching and excellence in our schools.

7. We must refashion our schools for the twenty-first century.

CHILDREN NEED ADULTS WHO FACILITATE CREATIVE EXPRESSION

The following strategies send a message to children that their creative expression is valued.

1. Celebrate Creativity

Help children identify with creative heroes. For example, bring in telescopes or visit a planetarium on Galileo's birthday. Read books about creative individuals. Discuss their accomplishments. Ask, "What if we didn't have lights?" Turn off the lights and light candles. Discuss the importance of the lightbulb. Point out creativity when you see it: "A Velcro lunch box, now that's a creative idea." Accept and celebrate your own creative side.

2. Value Children's Creativity

View creative development as a vital component of the whole child. Allow them the freedom to think and act differently. Accept their uniqueness. Accept their attempts at creative processing that might not result in a finished product. Advocate on behalf of creativity and inform others. Discuss the importance of creativity with children, parents, staff, and administrators. Speak up against budget cuts for the arts or attempts to replace play with academics.

3. Be a Creative Partner

Empower children by making yourself available to enter their creative worlds. Be a play partner who follows the lead of children rather than imposing your own plot, sequence, and script (see Figure 1–3).

4. Provide Time and Space for Creative Expression

Children need plenty of space to lay out materials and work alone or together to give form to their ideas. Time and space should be fluid and flexible. Tables, chairs, and movable units may need to be arranged to meet the demands of the activity at hand. Creativity may entail noise, excitement, movement, and clutter. Perhaps this is why young children and creativity are so compatible. An excessive concern for constant cleanliness or neatness inhibits creative "messing about."

Figure 1-3 Being creative with a parachute.

5. Provide Toys and Materials Conducive to Creativity

Let children creatively use and transform toys and materials. Accept the fact that small building blocks from the manipulative center will be transported to the house area and used as food or money. Clean smocks from the art center may find their way into the dress-up area where they will be used as capes for superheroes. Provide props for pretend and fantasy play as well as recycled junk. Do not feel that you must impart a specified purpose or use. Children will turn safe and clean trash into creative treasures. In choosing and providing toys and materials, **open-ended** items are more conducive to creative expression than **closed-ended** ones. Open-ended materials are loosely structured and do not require one right or correct way to work. They have multiple rather than single outcomes. For example, water, sand blocks, play dough, and building pieces are open-ended in that they empower children to use them in creative ways. There is no one preset right way to build with blocks or play with water. By contrast, a puzzle is an example of a closed-ended material in that it is designed with a single outcome or correct purpose, to fit the pieces together in a predetermined pattern. Although one can use puzzle pieces creatively, for example, as food or money, that is not their intent. A comparison and contrast of open- and closed-ended toys and materials is found in Table 1–1.

Toys and play materials can also be categorized as simple and complex. Simple toys and materials foster some degree of creative expression, whereas complex toys and materials extend the potential for creativity. Toys and play materials that offer some degree of creativity can be made complex. For example, blocks

Table 1-1 Comparison of Open-Ended and Closed-Ended Materials

OPEN-ENDED	CLOSED-ENDED
are conducive to creativity	are conducive to conformity
have multiple outcomes	have single outcomes
have many uses	have a singular use
are multipurpose	have only one purpose
are used in many "right" ways	are used in only one "right" way
are flexible: have a use and purpose determined by child	are inflexible: have a use and purpose predetermined by adult
reflect unlimited range of possibilities or options	reflect very limited range, only one possible way

alone are considered simple in that they can be creatively combined. Block play can be made more complex by adding props, including small containers, vehicles, and animals. The same is true for water and sand play. Adding kitchen containers to water and sand play expands the creative possibilities.

6. Provide a Psychological Climate Conducive to Creativity

Children flourish in a psychologically safe setting that respects, trusts, and empowers them to act autonomously without the fear of criticism, rejection, failure, or pressure to conform. Children need to make choices and decisions and to do things on their own in their own ways. By providing an array of materials and activities from which to choose, the environment can be set up to foster children's autonomy. An overly structured day revolving around teacher-directed activities impairs children's creative development. They quickly learn to override their drive for creativity and autonomy and instead become dependent on others for right answers or solutions.

7. Weave Creativity and Creative Expression Throughout Your Curriculum

Creativity should not be approached as an isolated skill that must be scheduled into an already overcrowded day. Children cannot magically turn on their creativity to fill a half-hour time slot on alternating Fridays. The curricular areas provide ample opportunities for children to use both sides of the brain. For example, children may need to learn about the food

groups and making healthy choices, but there are also creative ways to plan menus and make posters for healthy eating. A resourceful teacher will find ways to integrate creativity into the curriculum.

COMPARING AND CONTRASTING CREATIVITY

Another way of attempting to understand and explain creativity is through comparison and contrast. One way to learn about a concept is by comparing and contrasting it with other concepts that are either similar or different.

Creativity vs. Conformity and Convergent Thinking

Convergent thinking (noncreative) and behavior based on conformity are built into our educational system and reflected in our school goals. There are facts and bodies of knowledge that we want all children to possess. For example, children need to know that up is the opposite of down, that a triangle has three sides, that wheels are round, that STOP on the traffic sign does not mean to run, and that there are five pennies in a nickel. This type of knowledge involves memory and convergent thinking in that all children are expected to come up with the one right answer. Beyond this, conformity in school often entails behaving in a certain way, with an emphasis on sitting still, speaking only when spoken to, obeying, not challenging authority, not questioning, compliance, and doing what is generally expected. Obviously, conformity is important if groups of people are to get along, whether in school or in the wider society. When it is carried to extremes, however, an emphasis on conformity and convergent thinking can kill the creative spirit.

Creativity vs. Intelligence

Creativity can also be compared and contrasted with intelligence. It has sometimes been erroneously assumed that a high IQ is needed to be creative. Research, however, indicates that high scores on tests of creativity are not correlated with high scores on IQ tests. A high IQ says something about intelligence, but it cannot guarantee high creativity. This is easy to understand, because answering items on an IQ test requires remembering bits and pieces of factual information and involves convergent or noncreative thinking. Thus, it is possible for a child with a high IQ to be quite uncreative compared with other children of average intelligence. It does seem, however, that some basic level of intellectual functioning and an average IQ near 100 is required for creativity. For example, a child must have some basic knowledge of the properties of a milk carton and transportation before he or she can creatively transform an empty milk carton into a moving van. Therefore, using tests of intelligence to screen highly creative children must be done judiciously. Such tests are merely one of many tools, including teacher observation and parental reports, that can be used. According to Torrance (1962), if we were to identify children as gifted solely on the basis of IQ tests, we would eliminate approximately 70 percent of the most creative. In summary, although some amount of intelligence is a prerequisite for creativity, a high IQ does not guarantee high creativity. In turn, average intelligence does not necessarily mean mediocre creative ability. Intelligence is merely one factor influencing creativity.

Because children's thinking is a vital concern of early childhood educators, it may be interesting to pursue further the relationship between intelligence and creativity. It appears that the profiles for the highly intelligent child and that for the highly creative child do not match. Nor does the profile for the child of low intelligence match the profile for the child of low creativity. Wallach and Kogan (1965) studied the interplay of intelligence and creativity in school-age children. Four patterns emerged.

1. High intelligence and high creativity—These children were flexible and could be serious at one time and playful at another. They could easily adapt to different learning environments. They were very self-confident and displayed high attention and concentration for school tasks. They

also engaged in attention-getting and disruptive behavior.

2. Low intelligence and high creativity—These children were frustrated and had a difficult time in traditional schools. This probably tended to make them feel unworthy and inadequate. They were cautious, lacked self-confidence, and engaged in disruptive behavior.

3. Low intelligence and low creativity—These children did not appear to understand what school was all about. They spent their time in either intense physical activity or passive retreat.

4. High intelligence and low creativity—These children were devoted to achieving in school. They had high attention spans and high self-confidence. They were unlikely to act up in school and were well liked by their teachers.

Teachers were later asked to identify their ideal pupil from these four profiles. Which one would you select? Teachers overwhelmingly selected children characterized as highly intelligent but low on creativity. The behavior problems that could arise from creativity (or its stifling), as in 1, appear to outweigh any advantages or assets. It may be understandable why teachers in this study favored high intelligence over high creativity. Highly intelligent children follow directions, work independently, listen, pay attention, obey, and conform. On the other hand, the highly creative child is often viewed as a problem requiring individual attention. According to the general personality profile, highly creative children tend to be daydreamers, independent, nonconforming, impulsive, outspoken, challenging, and questioning individuals who test limits. It comes as no surprise that Getzels and Jackson (1962) also found that teachers favored high IQ but less creative children because they were easier to manage.

Gardner (1993b) cautions against the use of creativity tests to measure and/or predict creativity because their validity has never been adequately established. A valid test is one that contains items that reflect the nature of the concept or skills being tested. So creativity tests contain items that are not directly related to the construct being tested, creativity. Instead of using tests of creativity Gardner would favor assessing creativity in real life (as opposed to artificial testing situations) where children are engaged in creative pursuits and their creative processes and products are documented. This line of thinking provides the rationale for using portfolio assessment discussed in Chapter 16.

Creativity may or may not be a characteristic of children identified as **gifted and talented.** Children who are considered gifted and/or talented show high performance in one or more of the following areas: general intellectual ability, academic aptitude, creative thinking or production, leadership ability, talent in visual and performing arts, and physical ability, such as athletics. According to Safford (1989), the early identification of gifted and talented children is difficult because certain groups of children, including those from low-income families, minorities, and those with special needs often do not fit traditional patterns or demonstrate their abilities in traditional ways.

Characterizing gifted and talented children can be challenging because their development across domains may be uneven. Generally, young gifted and talented children may

- be curious and inquisitive.
- have a good sense of humor.
- be unusually aware of their surroundings.
- be able to think quickly and at higher, abstract levels.
- have an extensive and mature vocabulary.
- ask thought-provoking questions.
- have a long attention span.
- be able to sustain concentration.
- have a developmental lag between their physical and intellectual domains, with fine motor skills lagging behind their cognitive skills.
- have a developmental lag between their social and intellectual domains that may lead them to be intolerant of less-advanced peers.

Gifted and talented young children are most often found in mainstream early childhood classrooms (Safford, 1989). Because of their unique needs and characteristics, they present special challenges and opportunities for their teachers. Programs and approaches that provide challenge, nurture diversity and divergent thinking, and enable children to learn at their own pace and in multiple ways provide a good match for gifted and talented children. Enrichment activities to supplement their mastery of core curriculum will challenge their gifts and talents. Mixed-age grouping is recommended, because a child who exhibits one or more gifts may not excel socially. Open-ended art activities (see Chapter 10) and the art center approach (see Chapter 13) provide creative challenges for gifted and talented children.

Multiple Intelligences. Not all researchers view intelligence as a single and solitary concept. They view intelligence in the plural not singular. For Sternberg (2002), intelligence is how children solve real-life problems, not how they have done on intelligence tests. Intelligence consists of analytic, practical, and creative forms that allow people to deal with situations that range from automated, well-known tasks to highly novel, problem-solving ones. Analytic intelligence comprises the skills emphasized in school. Creative intelligence may show itself in highly original work in a particular field of interest or talent or when applied to coming up with new ideas and different answers. Sternberg (2002) believes it is important that children develop creative intelligence if they are to deal successfully with a rapidly changing world. Practical intelligence is the ability to function successfully in one's environment. These different ways of being "smart" may explain why those who are academic stars in school are not always the most successful in life, and vice versa. Schools that value only abstract, analytic learning at the expense of the arts, practical experiences, and personal development fail to see the big picture. According to Gardner (1993b), there are many ways of demonstrating one's intelligence. Gardner (1993b) defines intelligence as the capacity to solve problems or make things that are valued by one's culture. Gardner believes there are eight criteria for identifying an intelligence. Wilkens (1996) explains these as the following:

1. Each of the intelligences can potentially be isolated by brain damage or degenerative disease. A true intelligence will have its function identified in a specific location in the human brain. This means it is possible to destroy the ability in one sector while leaving the others intact.
2. Each of the intelligences exists in exceptional people, including idiot savants and prodigies. Examples include Mozart, who was able to perform at the piano at the age of four, and Dustin Hoffman's *Rain Man* character, with his knowledge of specifics and details. As witnessed in the previous examples, difficulty in interpersonal or daily living skills may also be involved. There is no guarantee of competence across all the intelligences.
3. Each of the intelligences has a process of developing during normal child development and has a peak end-state performance. For example, verbal-linguistic intelligence presents itself in early childhood while logical-mathematical peaks in adolescence and early adulthood.
4. Each of the intelligences is evident in species other than human beings. For example, birds make music and rhythm while bats use visual-spatial intelligence to navigate.
5. Each of the intelligences has been tested using various measures not necessarily associated with intelligence. Although IQ tests may be used they are by no means the only measure.
6. Each of the intelligences can work without the others being present.

7. Each of the intelligences has a set of identifiable operations. Gardner compares this to a computer needing a set of operations in order to function.

8. Each of the intelligences can be symbolized or has its own unique symbol or set of symbols. For example, Interpersonal intelligence uses gestures and facial expression.

Multiple intelligences include **bodily-kinesthetic, musical-rhythmic, interpersonal, visual-spatial, verbal-linguistic, logical-mathematical, intrapersonal,** and **naturalistic.** We all have some of each intelligence as well as particular strengths. Everyone can be characterized as smart in one or more of the intelligences. The multiple intelligences, related "smarts," and corresponding strengths and interests are depicted in Table 1–2.

While identifying the eight multiple intelligences identified in Table 1–2, Gardner (1998, 1999) has speculated that others may exist. The possibilities include a spiritual and existential intelligence as well as a moral intelligence. Spiritual intelligence, while not equated with religion, enables one to grasp cosmic and transcendent truth, achievement of a state of being, and one's effect on others. A discussion of spirituality, however, is controversial within a scientific or academic community in which objectivity is a criterion. Existential intelligence entails the ability to contemplate the meaning of life and death. However, spiritual and existential intelligences remain theoreti-

cal because their origin in the brain has not been identified. Moral intelligence involves making value judgments. However, because intelligence is value-free, the existence of a moral intelligence remains speculative. Spiritual, existential, and moral have not been officially endorsed as intelligences.

How do art skills and process match up with the eight different intelligences? How are multiple intelligences strengthened through art? Refer to Table 1–3.

Both Sternberg and Gardner have provided a wider view of intelligence. What are the implications? The theory of multiple intelligences offers implications for both instruction and assessment to include the following:

1. We must broaden our views of intelligence to incorporate multiple examples from different categories. All intelligences are important, and children come to us with different sets of developed intelligences. Not all children are verbally or mathematically inclined. This does not mean they are not smart. They are just smart in other ways—ways that have been ignored in discussions on intelligence. Traditionally, schooling has focused on verbal-linguistic and logical-mathematical intelligences. Children who excelled in language, reading, math, and logical thinking flourished. They were "smart" or successful in the areas that the school valued and stressed. Unfortunately, children who did not

Table 1-2 Gardner's Multiple Intelligences (1993b)

INTELLIGENCE	"SMART"	STRENGTHS AND INTERESTS
bodily-kinesthetic	body	sports, movement, dance, acting, dramatics, large motor and playground activities
musical-rhythmic	music	singing, dancing, playing a musical instrument, listening to music
interpersonal	people	making friends, socializing, cooperative projects, being a leader, resolving peer conflicts
visual-spatial	pictures	art, looking at pictures, daydreaming, puzzles, maps, charts
verbal-linguistic	words	speaking, reading, writing, listening, telling stories, thinking in words, discussions, memorizing, word puzzles, word games
logical-mathematical	math	math, reasoning, logical and abstract thinking, problem solving, patterns, working with numbers, computers
intrapersonal	self	understands self, knows strengths and accepts limits, works alone, pursues own interests, reflective, self-paced learner
naturalist	nature	recognizes plants, minerals, animals, clouds, rocks, flora, fauna, other natural phenomena

excel in these areas had no outlets to express the different ways in which they were intelligent.

2. The many different ways to be smart must be recognized and respected. It is crucial to plan experiences that include the different intelligences.

Gardner (1999) refers to this as multiple key entry points to content. Not every activity will involve all the intelligences, but the more intelligences involved, the greater the chance that all children will excel.

Table 1-3 Relationship of Multiple Intelligence to Child Art

MULTIPLE INTELLIGENCE	RELATIONSHIP TO ART
1. bodily-kinesthetic	• manipulation of art tools enhances use of large muscles, sensory-motor integration, fine motor skills and eye-hand coordination • involves bodily and kinesthetic movements and multisensory stimulation • different media require different types of processing, involving different physical movements and skills
2. musical-rhythmic	• children can make musical instruments or sound makers • art can be produced in response to music • background music can trigger artistic processing
3. interpersonal	• children talk about and share their art with others • children work together and practice social skills at the art center • children use peers as resources while doing art • children elect to engage in group art projects • as part of the project approach, art involves collaboration • children comply with rules and limits of the art center
4. visual-spatial	• art involves symbolic representation • materials for two- and three-dimensional processing are provided • use art books, art posters, and illustrated children's books that are visually aesthetic and stimulating • children's art work is displayed at their eye level
5. verbal-linguistic	• children talk about their art • encouraging art sharing as part of "show and tell" • read art books to children • engage in art dialogue with children • take art dictation encouraging children to tell and write their own art-related words and stories • teach art vocabulary including the artistic elements • label art materials and supplies • conduct art critique using artistic elements for children to discuss works of art
6. logical-mathematical	• patterning, color mixing, quantifying, problem solving • set up an organized art center in which similar materials are grouped together or classified • children make choices, decisions, and carry out plans
7. intrapersonal	• children work alone and reflect on their processing and results • personal emotions, thoughts, and ideas are expressed • provide multicultural art supplies • plan art activities focusing on the child's sense of self; Art replies to "Who am I?"
8. naturalist	• take nature walks to collect nature specimens for art • provide natural materials for painting, printing, and collage, sculpture, and weaving • children use personally meaningful symbols to represent nature and their surrounding natural environment

3. Using an integrated approach to curriculum development and project method will increase the likelihood that many intelligences will be involved in an activity or course of study.

4. Target the development of specific intelligences through activity centers by setting up stations throughout the classroom with resources related to each intelligence. For instance, a verbal-linguistic center could include books, word processors, and writing tools.

5. Provide students with choices of activities that capitalize on their learning style and brain preference. Dominant intelligences can be reinforced, whereas weaker intelligences are strengthened. Students have opportunities to improve their weaknesses by tapping their strengths.

6. Because all children do not learn in the same way, they cannot be assessed in the same way. Consider creating an intelligence profile for each student. A good approach to assessment is to allow students to explain or document what they know or have learned in their own ways using their different intelligences. View assessment as a collaborative effort with students identifying the criteria by which they will be assessed. Students receive feedback and evaluation from numerous sources including teachers, peers, parents, and self-reflection. Both processes and products are assessed. If warranted, assessment data including that from standardized tests and state assessment measures are analyzed and used to guide student progress. This approach to authentic assessment using a portfolio approach will be discussed in an upcoming chapter.

Brain Research. Early childhood educators have long believed that rich, early experiences and quality time with caring and loving family are critical to a child's development. These implications, however, have become even more important as neuroscience researchers make new discoveries about brain growth in the early years. **Brain research** is a line of study documenting that early experiences have a decisive impact on the architecture of the brain and on the nature and extent of adult capacities. What do we now know? During the early years the brain has the greatest capacity for change. How the brain develops hinges on a complex interplay between one's genes (heredity) and life experiences (environment). The developing brain is malleable, flexible, and plastic and has the ability to explode with new synapses or connections. The brain's neural plasticity allows it to constantly change its structure and function in response to external experiences.

The environment affects not only the number of brain cells and number of connections among them, but also the way those connections are wired. On the positive side, brain growth can be positively stimulated. The brain develops in an integrated fashion over time so an enriched environment addresses multiple aspects of development simultaneously. On the negative side, however, neglect or abuse can impede the child's developing brain functions. If a child receives little stimulation early on, synapses will not sprout, and the brain will make few connections. The harmful impact of stress on early brain development damages overall growth and development, placing the child at much greater risk of developing a wide range of cognitive, behavioral, and physical problems. In some cases, these effects may be irreversible. While traumatic events may significantly influence the behavior of adults, they actually change the *organizational framework* for the brain of a young child. Life experiences are now believed to control both how the infant's brain is architecturally structured and how intricate brain circuitry is wired. Early experiences have a decisive impact on the architecture of the brain and on the nature and extent of adult capacities. Early experiences do not just create a context; they directly affect the way the brain is wired.

In reviewing the literature on the development of the brain Shore (1997) as well as Richey and Wheeler (2000) found that experiences and opportunities afforded to children during the early childhood years are critical to the development of neural pathways that govern cognitive, motor, and socioemotional learning and development. A child's brain at birth has all the brain cells or neurons that it will ever have. Connections among neurons are formed as children explore their environment, play, and develop attachments to family members and providers. Connectivity is a crucial feature of brain development because the neural pathways formed during the early years carry signals and allow one to process information throughout life. Timing is also crucial. Even though learning continues throughout life, there are critical periods, prime times, or windows of opportunity during which the brain is particularly efficient at creating neural pathways or systems that facilitate specific kinds of learning. Experiences children have during these sensitive periods stabilize neural pathways and lay the foundation for optimal development. For example, the window of opportunity for vision and language development appears quite early and is lost by about age 10. If a child is born deaf, the neural pathways remain silent and atrophy. This is not to say that an adult cannot learn a second language. However, it is much more difficult to learn a foreign language after age 10 or so, and the language will probably be spoken with an accent. Lack of experiences during critical periods will result in underdeveloped neural pathways. Thus, the architecture of the brain reflects the presence or absence of a wide range of physical, cognitive, and socioemotional experiences during the early years.

Just as experts have only begun to understand the complexities of the growing brain, the formative task is bridging the gap between neuroscience and early childhood education. In summary, play is a critical element in early childhood because it provides the context for experiences that are vital to the development of neural pathways. Children must have time to practice and master those skills they have learned before moving on to learning new ones, and learning must take place in a meaningful context and in an environment of love and support. A developing brain does not know the difference between an inexpensive set of plastic measuring cups that nest and an expensive toy with an exaggerated claim by the manufacturer. The key is to be responsive. According to Galinsky (1997) being responsive is not about using flash cards or buying expensive toys. It is not one-way stimulation from adult to child like filling an empty vessel with water. Being responsive is engaging in the dance—the subtle give-and-take in which the child leads and the adult follows.

And what about art? In the past there was a tendency to view art exclusively as an affective process. We now know that art is both a cognitive and affective process. Children think and feel when engaged in art. Because making art requires that children think and feel about their experiences or ideas and then find symbols to express them, art is a highly symbolic and meaning-making activity.

All Children Are Creative but Not All Are Labeled Gifted or Talented.
All children have the potential to create but some are more creative than others. What accounts for this difference? First, some children have had their creativity nurtured; others have not. Ways of nurturing children's creative potential are discussed in this chapter as well as in Chapters 2 and 3. Second, intelligence influences creative expression. Children of high intelligence are labeled **gifted.** Children with creative aptitude for art, music, drama, or dance are labeled talented. In some schools children who are considered gifted and/ or talented receive enrichment to challenge them and to supplement their regular courses of study.

CREATIVITY AND CHILD DEVELOPMENT

What is the relationship between creativity and a child's development? Are there any developmental benefits to a child's creative functioning? Whatever

the form that creativity may take, the child develops large and small muscle skills through handling and manipulating the appropriate tools or apparatus. Musical instruments are played, paint is mixed and spread, clay is pounded, and the body moves to music and song. Creative expression can enhance physical development. Socially, it can also help children come to terms with themselves and others. At times creativity involves solitary thinking or grappling with a problem. At other times social skills, including sharing, taking turns, and entertaining other points of view are practiced. Creative expression fosters emotional development and positive mental health by validating the uniqueness of the individual. Juan, age three, made a clay dinosaur with two legs and an oversized head. He was proud of his accomplishment, and it did not matter if dinosaurs had four legs. Juan felt good about himself and the dinosaur he had created. Creativity fosters success and mastery, because there is no one right way involved. In turn, successes accumulate and enhance a positive self-concept. Children feel worthy and competent, knowing that they can have an effect on their environment. Philosopher Mihaly Csikszenthmihalyi (1997) believes there is a strong connection between creativity and happiness based on research showing that being creative stimulates the brain's pleasure centers. Creativity fosters mental or cognitive development. It involves a wide range of higher-level thinking skills, including observation, problem solving, discovery, analysis, hypothesizing, predicting, testing, and communicating, among others (see Figure 1–4). In the school setting, creativity can enhance and reinforce learning in the traditional curricular areas of math, science, social studies, listening, speaking, pre-reading, pre-writing, and other expressive arts. Beyond individual development, creativity

Figure 1-4 Rocky's Rock Restaurant makes a personally creative statement.

advances civilization and society by addressing and attempting to solve the global problems of hunger, poverty, disease, war, and pollution.

SUMMARY

The mystery surrounding creativity was addressed in this chapter. Creativity can be viewed as making a unique product. Children, however, may make or create things that are new or original only to them. These were considered creative on the basis of their creative processing, which may or may not result in a finished product. Creativity was also viewed as a skill requiring practice. Environmental conditions can either foster or hinder creativity, and an optimal home environ-ment was identified. Creativity was also compared and contrasted with conformity, convergent thinking, and intelligence. It was found that a high IQ did not guarantee a high degree of creativity.

Creative children should be viewed as a national asset. We must not allow them to become an endangered human resource. Expect them to wonder, question, and challenge conventional wisdom or traditional ways of doing things. They may enjoy doing their own thing rather than "playing the game of school." The creative traits cluster around a personality that goes beyond the status quo and thrives on daring to be different and nonconformist. And this is exactly the type of person on which the future depends. We need creative individuals who will not settle for givens, but instead strive to fulfill themselves while making the world a better place to live for all people.

Key Terms

bodily-kinesthetic	gifted and talented	naturalistic
brain research	interpersonal	open-ended
closed-ended	intrapersonal	process vs. product
convergent thinking (noncreative)	logical-mathematical	verbal-linguistic
creativity	multiple intelligences	visual-spatial
	musical-rhythmic	

Suggested Activities

1. Identify or develop at least one thing you do creatively. Practice and continue to refine it. Document your own creative development, including setbacks, frustrations, and successes, with a diary or journal.
2. Make a resource list of local businesses and contacts that are good sources of free (or inexpensive) and recyclable materials. Include the name, address, phone number, and contact person.
3. Spend one morning observing a teacher's use of time, space, and curriculum, as well as his or her teaching behavior. List specific recommendations for how each could be modified to further enhance creativity.

4. Write your own definition of creativity. Ask five other individuals to do the same. Note similarities and differences. Are there gender, race, or ethnic influences in the differences?
5. With your fellow students, brainstorm a list of creative individuals. Identify their names and their claims to creativity. Use gender to examine your list. Do you have an equal number of female and male creative individuals? Keep brainstorming until you have five of each.
6. Examine Healy's (1994) portrayal of what families can do to raise creative children. Do the characteristics in the list match your own upbringing? Discuss your answer.

Review

1. What is the relationship among creativity, convergent thinking, and intelligence?

2. Name three different ways of understanding creativity.

3. Pretend that you are speaking to your parent group on creativity. They ask you for important things that they can do at home to enhance their child's creativity. Specifically, what three suggestions do you recommend?

4. List any four major obstacles to creativity.

5. Are young children more process- or product-oriented in their creative expression? Explain your position.

6. Complete the Creativity Equation:

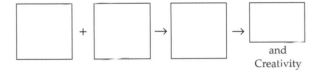

$$\boxed{} + \boxed{} \rightarrow \boxed{} \rightarrow \boxed{}$$
and
Creativity

7. Is intelligence a single concept confined to thinking? Include a discussion of multiple intelligences to justify your position.

8. **Creativity** may be one characteristic of children who are **gifted and talented.** What other characteristics may gifted and talented children exhibit? Discuss the strategies you could use in your classroom to meet the needs of gifted and talented children. Explain why these strategies would be successful.

9. List the eight multiple intelligences. What are three other intelligences that may exist?

10. Explain what the research on brain development means for early development. What are two key implications? Identify and number each.

Chapter 2

Creative Thinking

What do you see happening in this picture? Is this something you would do with children?

Mr. Carey and his group of three-year-olds are playing with water, funnels, and clear plastic tubing. The children are engaged in an informal science activity. The teacher asks open-ended questions to stimulate their language and thinking: "What do you see happening?" "How can we get the water to come out?" "How else can we hold the tube?" "What else can we do to keep the water from coming out?" "How can we make the water come out faster or slower?"

INTRODUCTION

There are many ways of being creative. These outlets or modes of creativity include the following: play; the expressive arts: art, music, movement, dance, drama, and mime; and thought and language. For example, play is an excellent opportunity for creative expression. A young child building with blocks relies on past experiences in transforming pieces of wood into a train, airport, or castle. Putting on an oversized coat helps four-year-old Beth become a business executive, queen, or pilot. Children can use their bodies to creatively move like animals, robots, or astronauts. They can also use paint, markers, clay, and paper to give form to their innermost thoughts and substance to their experiences. Young children also creatively transform standard English. Darrell, age three, felt that "carage" made more sense than garage. Tanya, age four, announced to her preschool class that Santa Claus has a team of "snowdeer," not reindeer. Swiss made no sense to five-year-old Kyle, shopping with his grandmother. He insisted on having "hole cheese" in his sandwiches. Young children also engage in creative thinking, although this particular mode is often given less emphasis and less of a role in the early childhood curriculum.

Just what is creative thinking? Creativity has been identified as a cognitive process or way of thinking. DeBono (1970) identified two types of thinking: vertical and lateral. **Vertical thinking** involves learning more about something or arriving at a conventional, accepted, convergent answer. For example, when Ms. Bell asked her preschoolers, "What time of the day do we eat breakfast?" Lin answered, "In the morning." But if the object is to find unusual, divergent, creative solutions for problems, **lateral thinking** is appropriate. Lateral thinking is the way of using one's mind or

mental processes that leads to creative thinking or products. For example, Katie, who was playing alone at the sandbox, decided to creatively use sticks and twigs to keep her company.

Children Express Their Creativity through Thinking

Art is not the only way to express one's creativity. Being able to think in creative ways is another. Some may believe that creative thinking is abstract and reserved for adults. Creative thinking is not confined to authors, artists, scientists, and inventors. Young children can and should engage in creative thinking. Creative thinking is a skill that not only helps children solve problems in their daily lives, but also prepares them for life in the twenty-first century. If we are to solve social, economic, political, and environmental problems, it will be through efforts at creative problem solving. Using the same old solutions to persistent problems has not worked. Children who grow up valued as creative and original thinkers will have the necessary skills to confront and solve problems facing them in the twenty-first century.

The Child's Right to Creative Thought and Expression

Jalongo (2003) writes on behalf of the Association for Childhood Education International (ACEI) in their position paper on The Child's Right to Creative Thought and Expression. Some of the main points and recommendations are that

- the definition of creativity be enriched and enlarged to be consistent with contemporary theory and research.

- creative expression depends not on talent alone, but also on motivation, interest, effort, and opportunity.
- the creative process is socially supported, culturally influenced, and collaboratively achieved.

By taking this position, the ACEI identifies the following challenges:

1. There is a need to redefine creative teaching and confront misconceptions about creative thinking.
2. Students must be provided with role models of motivation and persistence in creative thought, and better ways of assessing creative processes and products must be found.
3. Educational institutions and the larger societies in which they exist need to reflect deeply on what they hope children will become. The international community needs resourceful, imaginative, inventive, and ethical problem solvers who will make a significant contribution, not only to the information age in which we live, but beyond to an unknown future.

Creativity and the Brain

Creativity can also be discussed as a function of the brain. According to Galin (1976), the human brain houses two separate but interacting thinking systems, or hemispheres. The right and left hemispheres are joined by the corpus callosum, a thick branch of nerves that serves as a communication system between them. The hemispheres have different specializations. The left hemisphere houses the thinking abilities traditionally associated with school: reading, writing, math, and rational and logical thinking. The right hemisphere specializes in nonrational, intuitive thinking and spatial relations—in short, creative ways of processing information. Dominance is not established at birth, and it is imperative that children be provided with experiences that capitalize on and integrate the functioning of both sides of the brain. Although schools are set up to emphasize conformity and convergent thinking, or left-brain functioning, Galin believes that at an early age the right-brain or creative function is dominant. Early childhood educa-

Consider This...

The children we work with today will become the world citizens of tomorrow. If we do a good job of nurturing and educating them, they will thrive. What will life in the twenty-first century be like? What if we were able to rid civilization of all its negative features? What if future children found

- affordable housing instead of homelessness?
- employment and equal opportunity instead of welfare and unemployment?
- peace instead of war and violence?
- lawfulness instead of lawlessness and crime?
- preventive medicine, cures, and affordable health care instead of life-threatening diseases, terminal illnesses, and AIDS?
- love and friendship instead of gangs and hate?
- equality and acceptance of diversity instead of discrimination?
- conservation and environmental protection instead of pollution and depletion of natural resources?
- positive self-esteem and self-respect instead of substance abuse?

This wish list can be a reality if individuals are encouraged to approach these problems in new and different ways using creative thinking. Children can be encouraged to think creatively at an early age. As adults they will be better able to address and solve community and global problems. According to Sternberg and Lubart (1995), intelligence is not enough. There are plenty of "smart" people around, and many of them are failing to realize their life goals because they cannot keep up with a rapidly changing world. These authors believe creativity may be the key to both survival and success in the twenty-first century.

tors are in a key position to open the vistas of thinking for young children by planning experiences that engage both left- and right-brain functioning.

Why Does the Left Brain Have to Be Right? Seen from above, the human brain resembles a walnut. The two halves or cerebral hemispheres, right and left, are connected at the center by the corpus callosum which provides communication between the two hemispheres. The nervous system is connected to the brain in a crossed-over fashion. The **left hemisphere** controls the right side of the body; the left side of the body is controlled by the **right hemisphere.** The two hemispheres of the brain are specialized and process information differently (see Table 2–1). Each side possesses capacities for certain mental processes that are independent of each other. The right hemisphere operates in a mode that is nonverbal, subjective, intuitive, and global. The left hemisphere operates in a mode that analyzes, abstracts, verbalizes, and uses logic.

The old view held that the two hemispheres competed and never worked together to process information. But according to Edwards (1979), the two hemispheres can and do work together in a number of ways. Sometimes they cooperate and divide the task, with each half contributing its special abilities in doing what it does best. The hemispheres can also work singly; one hemisphere dominates and is "on" while the other is "off." The hemispheres may also compete and one may try to do what it knows the other half can do better. For example, Zena is standing at the easel painting a picture. She is trying to paint her family. How may her brain approach this task? The left side of her brain reacts logically telling Zena she needs four figures, two male and two female. If the left side dominates, her father would be painted with his beard and depicted taller than her mother. Zena would plan to paint herself smaller than her older brother. If the right side of her brain predominates, Zena could react emotionally rather than logically. She could become engrossed in mixing colors and making designs to highlight clothing. Or, her mother could be painted larger than life and wearing a crown while her older brother could appear in the background, lacking facial features.

Schools that pay only lip service to creativity are set up according to left-brain functioning. Curricular

Table 2-1 Two Sides of the Brain

LEFT BRAIN	RIGHT BRAIN
thinks concretely	thinks abstractly
plans	spontaneous
systematic, serious	playful, enjoys humor
analytic	intuitive
logical	impulsive
aware of time	unaware of time
sequential and linear	nonsequential, holistic
can break down whole into parts	focuses on whole, not parts
verbal	nonverbal
uses language	uses touch, kinesthetic
mathematical, calculating	recognizes faces, three-dimensional shapes, patterns
responsive to positive moods	responsive to negative moods
can write music scientifically	processes tones and sounds
cognitive, rational	sensory, affective, creative
factual	processes imagery, dreams
reality-bound	fantastical

Table 2-2   Brain Specialties

LEFT BRAIN SPECIALIZES IN	RIGHT BRAIN SPECIALIZES IN
handwriting	spatial relationships
language	shapes and patterns
reading	color sensitivity
phonics	singing, music, dance
locating details and facts	art
following directions	creativity
listening	feelings and emotions
math	visualization

implications based on brain specializations are listed in Table 2–2. In left-brain–oriented schools, teaching is sequenced, and time schedules are rigidly followed. Children sit in desks aligned in straight rows. Teachers reward convergent thinking with letter grades. Reading, writing, and math (the three Rs) form the core of the curriculum. Right-brain pursuits including art, music, and movement do not receive equal time, attention, and funding, and may be the first areas eliminated when the budget is cut. This is unfortunate. Jane Alexander, former chairwoman for the National Endowment for the Arts (1995), advocates restoring arts education to the school curriculum as a means of enhancing students' creativity, helping their development, and curbing violence. She believes that some individuals who do not have a way to express themselves creatively do so violently. Is graffiti one example?

What are the implications for teachers and students with matching or opposing brain preferences? Having identified your own brain preference, see if you can identify your own instructor's brain preference in teaching. Teachers with left-brain strengths generally prefer to teach using lecture and discussion. To incorporate sequence, they put outlines on the board or overhead, and they like to adhere to prepared time schedules. They give problems to the students to solve independently. Teachers with left-brain preferences assign more research and writing than their right-brain colleagues. A reasonably quiet, structured classroom is preferred. The classroom tends to be neat and clean with items in their place. A left-brain teacher is a good match for left-brain students who prefer to work alone. They like to read independently and incorporate research into their papers. They favor a quiet classroom without a lot of distrac-

tion. By contrast, teachers with right-brain strengths generally prefer to use hands-on activities over a lecture format. In concert with the right-preference of seeing the whole picture, these teachers incorporate more art, manipulatives, visuals, and music into their lessons. They tend to embrace the concept of multiple intelligences. They like to assign more group projects and activities and prefer a busy, active, noisy classroom environment. For example, books and materials may be scattered throughout the classroom. Right-brain students prefer to work in groups. They like to do art projects and would, for example, prefer to design and make a representative collage than write a term paper. Is there a match? Do you and your instructor have a "good fit" regarding brain preferences in how you learn and how he or she teaches?

The information on brain functioning provides teaching challenges and opportunities. Students with strong left- or right-brain tendencies much prefer to be taught to their neurologic strengths. If you are a left-brain teacher, try adding at least one right-brain method such as role playing or group projects into your teaching. If you are a right-brain teacher try adding at least one left-brain method such as direct teaching or individual projects. Give your students a variety of assignments from which to choose. Watch children gravitate to their neurologic strengths when given a choice. For example, children can choose to make a collage, write a paper, or put on a play to demonstrate their knowledge of a topic or concept.

Creativity as a Mental Operation

Guilford (1977) was one of the original investigators of creativity as a mental process or operation. He conceptualized a **"structure of the intellect"** consisting of three dimensions: contents, products, and operations. Operations include knowing, discovering, or being aware (cognition); retrieving information from storage (memory); the generation of multiple responses **(divergent production);** coming up with the one right answer **(convergent production);** and judging the appropriateness of information or decisions (evaluation).

Characteristics of Divergent or Creative Thinking

What makes divergent or creative thinking different from uncreative thinking? Creative or divergent thinkers share the following mental qualities. They are

1. *fluent* thinkers who have many ideas and solutions
2. *flexible* thinkers who have different ideas that cross categories or break boundaries
3. *original* thinkers who have unique and unusual ideas
4. *elaborate* thinkers who add details to the ideas

The divergent thinking of creative children is fluent, flexible, original, and elaborate, although not all four qualities appear in each thought or action.

When confronted with a problem, creative or divergent thinkers are able to come up with a long list of possibilities or options. This characterizes **fluency** or fluent thinking. For example, ask children for their ideas on celebrating the upcoming December holidays. Their fluent replies may include baking cookies, playing in the snow, exchanging gifts, making cards, taking a field trip to the mall, singing songs, putting on a play, making presents for family members, parties to celebrate Hanukkah and Kwanzaa, writing letters to Santa, giving a gift to Santa, or giving gifts to needy children. The sheer quantity of responses indicates fluency. They reflect a good job of brainstorming for many ideas, and all ideas should be accepted and respected.

The above responses indicate **flexibility.** Flexibility is the ability to mentally push boundaries, shift categories, and take mental detours. It results in a varied and diverse array of responses. One's thinking can be fluent without being flexible. The children's thinking was fluent in that it generated several party-type suggestions. It was flexible in that their options went beyond the scope of party-type ideas for themselves to include Santa, parents, and the less fortunate. These options reflect flexible thinking.

Giving a gift to Santa is one original idea, especially for a young child. **Originality** refers to uniqueness. Original ideas are uncommon, unusual,

different, and unexpected. By contrast, the other party-type suggestions are not wrong but quite obvious and common.

Creative individuals have elaborate ideas and express themselves in complex ways. **Elaboration** involves a lot of detail and rich expression. For example, in her letter to Santa, Arden merely requested a new doll and did not elaborate. By contrast, Beau was elaborate in requesting a "new robot, it's awesome, with arms and wings that move around and can do things. It has batteries and rockets that shoot out sideways." Beau was able to stretch and expand his thought. Creative children embellish their artwork with colors and decorate their speech with fancy words. Creative children at play build elaborate constructions out of blocks which may be embellished with masking tape for roads and string for power lines.

Edwards and Springate (1995) apply the components of divergent thinking and production to the creative act of finger painting in the following ways. Finger painting allows children to experience fluency between a medium, the child's body, and the child's ideas. The activity is flexible and gives children freedom to experiment and explore with color, motion, design, and physical movement. Because there is no one right way to finger paint, the activity encourages originality. Finger painters elaborate on their paintings by adding new colors, details, or incorporating other materials, such as brushes or combs.

Whole Brain, Whole Learning

Few would argue that schools should not stress conformity and convergent thinking. Still, a better balance is needed between creativity and individuality vs. conformity and convergent thinking. We need to balance left- and right-brain learning. Our educational goals, curriculum, and practices should exercise many modes of learning and different styles of processing information. Certainly, we do not want children to creatively read the word *shoe* as anything other than what it is. Nor would we want children to creatively add 2 + 3 and come up with 32. Still, children should not be spoon-fed knowledge, nor have their left brain overworked and their right brain left to atrophy. The author observed a kindergartner being corrected for stating that the color of the sun was "white hot." It appeared that the teacher was looking for convergent thinking to produce the one acceptable answer of "yellow." Conformity and convergent thinking can be taken to extremes. Over time, children come to reject divergent thinking as incorrect or useless. And as an aside, your right brain is correct; the sun is not yellow.

Not all creative-thinking activities provide the opportunity to assess all four components of divergent production. The following sample item from a test of creativity will help us practice informally evaluating a child's thinking for originality and elaboration. In the following example, children are asked to complete an open-ended drawing similar to the one in Figure 2–1. Obviously, there is no one right way to complete this picture, and many possibilities exist. How would you complete it? Carefully examine the finished product in Figure 2–2. What can you say about this six-year-old's originality and elaboration? The author would rate this low on both originality and elaboration. The completed picture is rather stereotyped, unimaginative, mundane, and not very original. Details are minimal, and the picture lacks elaboration. From only this one sample, the author is not in a position to make a strong statement about this child's level of creativity. It does indicate, however, that this particular child needs practice and encouragement in divergent production. On the other hand, consider a drawing completed by a different six-year-old (see Figure 2–3). What can you say about this six-year-old's originality and elaboration? The author believes that this com-

pleted drawing evidences a high degree of originality and elaboration.

Not every creative activity will or should lend itself to evaluation for fluency, flexibility, originality, and elaboration. Fluency and flexibility may be more appropriate to games of creative thinking. Originality and elaboration can be applied to children's art. The informal rating scale in Table 2–3, adapted from Guilford's 1977 work, can be used to assess divergent production. Again, our intent is not to grade or label creativity, or to include it on a child's report card. Discretionary use of the following instrument will help us keep track of progress as we strive to reach our goal of helping young children to demonstrate fluency, flexibility, originality, and elaboration in their creative processing and production.

Children Need to Engage in Convergent and Divergent Thinking

What is creative thinking? When is thinking creative and what makes creative thinking different from uncreative thinking? Creative thinking can be equated with divergent thinking. Thinking is divergent when

Figure 2-1 Open-ended drawing.

Figure 2-2 Completed drawing by a six-year-old.

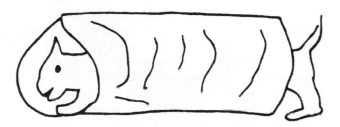

Figure 2-3 Completed drawing by a six-year-old.

LOW	FLUENCY	HIGH
• few different		• many different
	FLEXIBILITY	
• lacks variety		• wide variety
• rigid		• flexible
• limited range		• wide range
	ORIGINALITY	
• stereotyped		• unique
• unimaginative		• imaginative
• common		• unusual
	ELABORATION	
• lacks detail		• very detailed
• unelaborate		• elaborate
• simple		• complex

Table 2-3 Rating Scale

(Source: Guilford, J. P. (1977). *Way beyond the IQ.* Buffalo, NY: The Creative Education Foundation.)

many possibilities or options result. Divergent thinking is open-ended, allowing for an array of possibilities. For example, you can engage in divergent thinking when planning a creative curriculum. Ask yourself, "What can I provide for the children that will enhance their creativity?" There is no one piece of material or specific activity, but rather endless possibilities, including experiences in art, play, language, music, and movement, among others. By contrast, convergent thinking results in one correct answer. Much of what is learned in school requires convergent thinking, especially when taking tests. Convergent thinking is required to produce the one right answer to the following questions:

- Do dogs have puppies or kittens?
- What is the name of the largest dinosaur?
- What comes out at night, the sun or the moon?
- Name the months of the year in proper order.
- What shape is our classroom door?
- What is the opposite of hot?
- How many fingers am I holding up?
- What is the sum of three plus five?
- What is the capital of the United States?

Both modes of thinking, convergent and divergent, are very important. Children who lack opportunities to engage in convergent thinking will lack access to a core body of knowledge needed for school success and academic achievement. Acquiring a body of factual information is not enough, however. Children also need opportunities to engage in creative thinking. Children denied access to creative processing and divergent thinking will become conforming individuals who do not realize their creative potential. The problem arises when conformity and convergent thinking dominate the curriculum at the expense of individual and divergent thinking.

ACTIVITIES FOR CREATIVE THINKING

Sample items taken from tests of creativity (Torrance, 1966) and modified for use with young children provide suggestions for activities to foster creative thinking. Some general guidelines are in order. You may want to try out these activities yourself first. Record and evaluate your responses. Allow yourself and your children plenty of "think time" to grapple with the problem posed. The activities can be conducted with individual children or with small or large groups. Creative-thinking games can be played at any time during the day and can easily become part of one of the following routines: arrival time, opening activity, small

group time, circle time, snack time, story time, transition time, indoor recess, indoor rainy-day activity, and predismissal time, among others. Explain the nature of these creative-thinking games. You are looking for unusual responses, and there will be no one right answer. This may be unsettling to some children. Participation should be voluntary, and some children will feel more comfortable with these activities than others. Try to reward and encourage thinking rather than acceptable answers. Children may get silly, and some answers may bear no relation to the question asked. These children may simply be testing your commitment to creativity and suspending conformity. Initially, the games should be kept short. Stop when the children show signs of restlessness or lack of interest. Because the games are so open-ended, they may create some initial mental discomfort, especially to children who have been led to believe that all questions have one right answer.

Because young children vary in their level of creative thinking and verbal ability, it is difficult to recommend specific age ranges for the following creative-thinking activities. Activities that require some degree of verbal fluency can be successfully used with kindergartners and children in the primary grades. Activities requiring a verbal response can also be used with preschoolers who demonstrate strong oral language skills. Activities requiring a nonverbal response, such as drawing, can also be used with younger children. Older children can be challenged to write their responses, thereby making creative thinking a literacy event. There is no upper age limit on the thinking games.

Finish My Picture

Ask the children to complete one of the pictures in Figure 2–4. The pattern could be drawn on the board at child level or run off as a photocopy. The advantages of using a photocopy are that children may be less prone to copy other children and that later they can share their products with one another. In this way they come to see that there are many, many possible responses.

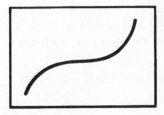

Figure 2-4

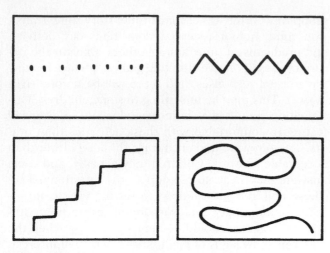

Figure 2-5

Picture Possibilities

Draw one of the line or pattern pictures in Figure 2–5 on the board or on a transparency for the overhead projector. Allow the children time to think about possible meanings. Ask them to give you a possible title or interpretation: "What do you see in this picture?" "What else could it be?"

What Would Happen If?

Ask the children to listen very carefully as you ask them one of the following. What would happen if

- refrigerators ate food?
- bathtubs could talk?
- you could be invisible?
- cars could drive by themselves?
- toys were real?
- dreams came true?
- you never had birthdays?
- pets went to school?

Young children may enjoy using the tape recorder to tape their responses. Print the above sentences on index cards and place them in a learning center.

Unusual Uses

Bring in the following items. Encourage the children to inspect each one carefully and to handle them all. Ask them to think of many things to do with these items.

- shoe
- shoe box
- cork
- juice can
- napkin
- golf tee
- dish
- newspaper
- balloon
- brick
- paper clip
- rubber band

Just Suppose

Ask the children to listen carefully to a short story. Have them "just suppose" an end to your story. Examples could include the following:

- Just suppose you found $1 million. How would you spend it?
- Just suppose you met a moon child in an empty field. What would you say or do?
- Just suppose you could be somebody else. Who would you be?
- Just suppose you could be the teacher. What would you do?
- Just suppose you found a magic flying carpet. Where would you go? Why there?
- Just suppose you could be invisible for one whole day. What would you do, and where would you go?
- Just suppose you could be any animal. Which would it be? Why?

Your Own Book Ending

Assemble a small group of children for story time. Ask them to listen quietly while you read a class favorite. *Where the Wild Things Are* by Maurice Sendak is one possibility. Slowly read the story, stopping just before the end. Close your book. Ask the children to think up a different way to end the story. Some children may insist on giving back the predetermined ending. Encourage them to come up with their own even though it will be different from the book ending. As children gain experience at supplying their own endings, you can stop reading earlier in the story and require them to supply a greater part of the creative ending.

Tell Me about My Picture

Seat a small group of children in a close circle. Hold up an interesting picture you have clipped from a magazine. Try to find pictures that are vague and have a variety of possible meanings. Ask the children to examine the picture carefully and

- give different names or titles for the picture. What else could we call it? What else could this story be about? What happened to cause this? What could happen next?
- tell their very own stories about this picture.

Beginning writers can be encouraged to dictate or even print their own story lines. Individual children may enjoy taping their own story at a learning center.

How Many Ways

Seat a small group of children in a close circle. Ask them to listen very carefully as you ask the following questions. How many different ways can you

- celebrate your birthday?
- scare your brother or sister?
- get into trouble?
- make a new friend?
- be happy?
- go on a vacation?
- spend Saturday?
- surprise Grandma or Grandpa?
- earn some money?
- do a good deed?

Descriptives

Seat a small group of children in a close circle. Hold up one of the following objects. Encourage each child to inspect it carefully as it is passed around the circle. Ask the children to tell you many different words that describe a

- flag.
- umbrella.
- cereal box.
- key.
- toy.
- sock.
- gerbil.
- lunch box.
- pencil.
- coin.

Encourage children to use descriptive terms, including references to color, shape, size, use, form, texture, weight, composition, and so on.

Make Up a Story

Seat a small group of children in a close circle. Ask the children to listen very carefully to the beginning of a story. Then, ask them to finish your story. Three very simple story starters are as follows:

- Once upon a time there was a little girl who wanted her very own horse. But her Mommy said there was no money to buy one. So one day the little girl . . .
- One morning Marco was waiting for the school bus. He waited and waited, but it did not come. So Marco decided to . . .
- Kitten wanted to go to school. But Billy said, "Kittens don't go to school. They stay at home." So one day Kitten . . .

Figure 2-6

Encourage children to make up their own beginnings to share with their friends.

Picture Guess

The open-ended designs in Figure 2–6 can be sketched on the board one at a time. Ask the children to study the shape carefully. Allow plenty of think time, and do not encourage quick shouting out Have the children tell you many different things each of the pictures could be.

Make It Better

Seat a small group of children in a close circle. Hold up a familiar toy, such as a stuffed animal or race car. Encourage each child to inspect it carefully as it is passed around the circle. Ask the children these questions.

- How could we make it a better toy?
- What could we do to make it more fun to play with?

What Would . . . If It . . . ?

Seat a small group of children in a close circle. Ask them to listen very carefully to your question and then think up their own answers. Here are some sample questions.

- What would taste better if it were sweeter?
- What would be more fun if it went faster?
- What would be scary if it were bigger?
- What would be happier if it could escape?
- What would be funny if it were alive?

What Things . . .

Seat a small group of children in a close circle. Ask them to think of many things that

- are round.
- make noise.
- sink.
- are wet.
- smell.
- have horns.
- shine.
- roll.
- are green.
- hurt.
- are square.
- stick.
- squeak.
- ring.
- fly.

Pretend

Seat a small group of children in a close circle. Ask them to carefully listen to a "Pretend . . ." sentence. Examples could include the following:

- Pretend you did not have a paintbrush. What else could you use to paint the walls?
- Pretend you did not have a present. What else could you take to a friend's birthday party?
- Pretend you did not have a friend to play with. What else could you do?
- Pretend you did not have any money for your play store. What else could you use?

FACILITATING YOUNG CHILDREN'S CREATIVE THINKING

Although children will act and think in creative ways without prompting, adults can facilitate the process by providing time, space, and resources, as well as setting the stage.

Provide a Psychological Climate Conducive to Creativity

Children flourish in a psychologically safe setting that trusts and empowers them to act autonomously without the fear of criticism, rejection, or failure. Expectations for children's behavior are positive yet appropriate. Autonomy involves exercising one's freedom, or acting freely but in responsible ways. Children need to act autonomously by making choices and decisions, solving problems, and making things happen on their own. By providing an array of materials and activities from which to choose, the environment can be set up to foster children's autonomy. An overly structured day, in which choices regarding activities are made for the chil-

dren, impairs their creative ability. They quickly learn to override their creative impulses and autonomous drive while becoming overly dependent on others for answers and solutions.

Creative Thinking Takes Time

Children need large blocks of time to engage in activities that involve thinking. Exploring and exhausting possibilities take time. Time should be viewed as fluid and flexible. Your daily schedule should be divided into a few large blocks of time rather than several short blocks. Larger blocks provide enough time to think, plan, and try out possibilities, and then to leave, return, and begin again. Children who are rushed are not only denied adequate time to think and do but may also resist by misbehaving. Children need time to daydream and reflect, at times to do nothing but sit and think. Let creativity and creative thinking permeate your day. Engage children in creative-thinking activities throughout the day. Use individual and small group times, snack, transition, and early morning/ late afternoon to play games requiring creative thinking. Sometimes creativity is unpredictable and will evolve into something unplanned requiring additional time. The flexible teacher is able to flow with the "teachable moment" as well as to bring closure when warranted.

Children Need Space in Which to Be Creative

Children need plenty of space to lay out materials and to work alone or together to complete their plans. Like time, space should also be fluid and flexible. Creative thinking may require private, enclosed, solitary space for private thinking and daydreaming. Other creative activities may require larger open spaces for group involvement. Tables, chairs, and movable units may need to be arranged to meet the needs of the activity at hand. Creativity may entail noise, excitement, movement, and clutter. An excessive concern for constant cleanup or neatness inhibits creative "messing about." Perhaps this is why creative expression and young children are so compatible.

STRATEGIES TO FACILITATE CREATIVE THINKING

The following strategies will help children feel that their attempts at creative thinking are valued.

1. Build Creative Thinking into Your Program

Provide a variety of ways for children to think creatively. Integrate your curriculum. Avoid an overemphasis on conformity and convergent thinking. Children who are led to believe that there is only one right way or correct answer will have their creativity stifled. Expect that creative children will question and challenge your ideas and ways of doing things. Provide opportunities for children to explore creative options and possibilities, to play with their ideas.

2. Model Creative Thinking

According to Sternberg and Lubart (1995), the best way to foster creativity is to provide creative role models. If you want children to be creative, you can prescribe no course or set of exercises that will help them more than being a role model of creativity yourself. Children learn to take sensible risks and to fight obstacles by watching others doing these things. Be a creative thinker and model the process. Share your creative solutions to problems. For example, you promised the children that they will be able to finger paint in the morning. You promised, however, before discovering that there is no more paint. You announce the problem and model how you engaged in creative thinking to come up with a solution: "We ran out of paint so I thought of what else we could use. I'll put shaving cream into each of these four trays and we can use that for finger painting." Also share your frustration and setbacks. Let children know it took you several tries to find a way to keep the door closed so the classroom pet would not escape at night. Try new ways of doing things. Let children know that if one way does not work out, you simply think again and try another.

3. Recognize, Encourage, and Value Creative Thinking and Problem Solving

Reward the process of thinking creatively rather than the idea itself. In the previous classroom pet cage example, the teacher should also recognize her accomplishments by saying, "I like my idea of an open padlock and it seems to be working. It took some good hard thinking." This is not the same as boasting or bragging. Encourage children to be creative thinkers. In the former shaving cream example, Carlos gets the liquid watercolor and says, "Let's make colors." Reply,

"Carlos wants to add coloring to our shaving cream. Good thinking."

4. Help Children Value Their Own Creative Thinking

Help them stand up for their ideas in the face of criticism and peer pressure. Say, "That was your idea and it's OK if your friend doesn't agree with you." For example, what if the children do not like Carlos's idea and say, "No, that's yucky." The teacher could say, "I think Carlos has an idea. If you don't want color just say so." "Carlos, it's OK if your friends don't like your idea." In turn, help children respect the ideas of others. Help them see that it is OK to be different and to have different ideas.

5. Pose Problems Requiring Creative Solutions

For example, to a group of school-age children who want to go on a field trip, say, "How can we raise money to go?" Look for many and different ideas. Help children build on each other's ideas. Provide ample think time during which you remain silent and wait for them to reply. Defer judgment and evaluation. Avoid saying, "That won't work," or "Let's think of a better idea." Resist the temptation to step in too soon and shield children from manageable amounts of frustration and even failure at times. Help children test out their hunches and rethink possibilities. Encourage critical thinking. Discuss the pros and cons of the ideas generated.

6. Engage Children in Critical Thinking

For example, once again Miss Tina finds herself reading the story of *Goldilocks and the Three Bears* to a small group of preschoolers. It is a favorite and she always provides puppets, stuffed animals, costumes, character headbands, and a set of felt pieces for children to use later, retelling the story in their own words. She approaches today's reading with a different goal in mind—**critical thinking.** Before reading she asks the children to listen carefully and decide who is good or nice as opposed to who is bad or naughty. Devlin says the bears are bad, especially Papa Bear because he scares the little girl and she has to run away. Afi thinks that Mama Bear is good because she cooks for her family and will not let them eat the food if it is too hot. Rosa thinks that Baby Bear is bad because he woke up Goldilocks. She adds that she gets into trouble at home if she wakes up her new baby sister. Kalmir disagrees.

He believes Goldilocks is naughty because she broke Baby Bear's chair. Nan adds that Goldilocks ate the porridge and that was not right because she did not ask first. Sergio says that Goldilocks is the "baddest" because she walked right into the house; the bears could call the police and take her to jail. The children are thinking critically about the characters in simple terms such as good vs. bad and naughty vs. nice that they easily understand. Miss Tina was able to help the children look beyond the labeling and see the bigger issue of safety and intent. She agreed that Goldilocks did something that could be called bad or naughty because it was unsafe and very dangerous. She asked the children if it is okay to go into a stranger's house. Fay said it would be okay if she knocked first. Miss Tina asked the other children what they thought. And so the critical thinking continued.

7. Ask Open-Ended Questions

Open-ended questions are worded in such a way that there is no one correct answer. They invite an array of possible responses. They require children to engage in divergent or creative thinking and to operate at a higher mental level in formulating answers. Examples of open-ended questions include:

- When reading a story, ask, "What do you think will happen next?"
- When solving a peer-related problem, ask, "Well, what do you think we can do to solve this problem?"
- When frustrated with blocks that will not stack up or nature items that will not stay glued, ask, "How else could you get that to work?"

- When listening to sounds or looking at partially covered magazine pictures, ask, "What else could it be?"
- When planning a walk around the block, ask, "What are some things we need to think about to make sure we have a safe trip?"
- When keeping a roof on a block building from caving in, ask, "Who can show us a different way?"
- To a child who wants to snatch a prized toy from another, ask, "What else could you do instead of grabbing the toy?"

By contrast, closed-ended questions aim for one right answer. Either you know it or you do not. Closed-ended questions require low-level or convergent thinking based on recall. Answers to closed-ended questions are stored in memory as bits and pieces of unrelated information. Examples of closed-ended questions include:

- What color is the sun?
- If you have two pennies and I give you two more, how many pennies will you have all together?
- What shape is the clock on the wall?
- How many wheels are there on a tricycle?

See Table 2–4 for comparison and contrast of different types of questions.

Let's apply our study of questioning to Miss Tina's reading of *The Three Bears*. If she wanted children to engage in low-level thinking and give back factual information she could ask the following closed-ended questions:

- How many bears were there in our story?
- What was the name of the little girl?

Table 2-4 Types of Questions

CLOSED OR CONVERGENT QUESTIONS	OPEN OR DIVERGENT QUESTIONS
seek the one right answer or correct response	seek many possible answers
invite a quick response	take time to think about and formulate a response
require low-level thinking, e.g., names and facts	require higher level thinking, e.g., reasoning and problem solving
require answers previously stored in child's memory	invoke child's imagination, and are actively constructed
involve simple answers and responses	involve complex answers and responses
involve answers known to adults	involve responses unknown to adults
ask what, who, when, and where	ask how, why, or tell me about

Creativity and the Early Childhood Education Curriculum

It would be fair to say that a general misunderstanding pervades the concept of creativity and its role in the curriculum. With the present emphasis on accountability, basic academic skills, testing, reform, and budget cuts, creativity may be eyed suspiciously by parents, taxpayers, and even teachers, who often report that they believe creativity to be important yet find little time to encourage it. The elusive nature of creativity merely complicates the issue. Reporting to parents that their child is reading at level *X* may convey more information than saying their child is highly creative. Some believe that doing well in math is a more marketable skill than high creativity. At a parent meeting, one father asked, "If creativity is so important, why doesn't it appear on my child's report card and school record?" He went on to state that he did not recall creativity being part of his school career and felt he had become a success in spite of it. His point may reflect wider public opinion. This is another reason why parent education, teacher education, and arts advocacy are critical.

- Why was she called Goldilocks?
- What did Mama Bear cook in the morning?
- Where did Baby Bear find the girl?
- Why did the bears go for a walk?
- Did they find the girl upstairs or downstairs?
- How many bowls were on the table?
- What got broken?

She knows that these questions will be easy for her children and will not engage them mentally. By contrast, children will be engaged in higher-level thinking as they actively construct answers to the following open-ended questions:

- Let's give the bears first names. What could we call them?
- Let's change the story. Who can share a different ending?
- Why do you think Goldilocks ran away from the bears' house?
- What do you think about going into a stranger's house?
- How could we help Baby Bear and Goldilocks become friends?
- What else could Mama Bear cook for breakfast?

Asking open-ended questions led to an involved discussion with most of the children wanting to contribute different ideas. It is also important to provide think time. Children need time to reflect on the question while mentally and verbally formulating one or more answers. Do not become impatient and answer your own question. This disrespectful practice sends a negative message to children. It tells them you will not invest the time in waiting to hear what they have to say. They may interpret this to mean that you really do not care about them or their ideas.

SUMMARY

There are many ways to express one's creativity. Play, the expressive arts (art, music, movement, dance, dramatics, and mime), language, and thought are just a few that are relevant to early childhood. Creativity, or divergent production, was viewed as a thinking skill or mental operation within Guilford's (1977) "structure of the intellect." Creative thought and production are characterized by fluency, flexibility, originality, and elaboration. A rating scale and sample activities were provided for the adult reader to use with young children.

Key Terms

close-ended question	elaboration	open-ended question
convergent production	flexibility	originality
creativity	fluency	right hemisphere
critical thinking	lateral thinking	structure of the intellect
divergent production	left hemisphere	vertical thinking

Suggested Activities

1. Do several of the creative thinking activities. Record your own responses. Use the rating scale to informally evaluate your divergent thinking and production. Record your strengths and weaknesses in fluency, flexibility, originality, and elaboration.

2. Do one of the creative-thinking activities with a small group of young children. Record their responses. Practice using the rating scale to evaluate their creative thinking.

3. Check out tests of creative thinking from the library and review them. Begin a card file of creative-thinking activities. Be creative and modify the test items rather than merely copying them.

4. Observe in a kindergarten, first, second, or third grade classroom. Select a time when the teacher is engaged in direct teaching. Record the questions the teacher asks. Are they more closed/convergent or open/divergent? Do you feel the teacher's questions effectively accomplished the purpose of the activity? Explain your answer.

Review

1. List the five major mental operations. Which one is generally equated with creativity?

2. List the components of divergent thinking and production.

3. Match each term with its description.
   - a. elaboration   coming up with many possibilities
   - b. originality   the uniqueness of an idea
   - c. flexibility   making an idea rich or complex
   - d. fluency   coming up with very different responses

4. Name five specializations for each side (left and right) of the brain.

5. List five ways adults can facilitate children's creative thinking.

6. Identify the two types of questions. Compare and contrast them. Which type of question is reflected in the following: "Children, I want each of you to think of what it means to be a friend." Justify your answer.

Chapter 3

Creative Experiences

What do you see in this picture? Is this child at work or is she "just playing"? Are art and play the same? Why or why not?

The teacher has provided easels that extend her art area. She believes in organization and plans so children have their own defined work space when doing art. Individual pieces of chalk are provided in the cells of an ice cube tray. The girl is free to use the chalk and draw as she pleases. Drawing when seated provides a different physical experience than painting while standing at the easel. Although the artist seems quite wrapped up in her drawing, double-sided easels could allow for social interaction. Rather than drawing a picture, the girl enjoys using linear vertical and horizontal chalk marks on her paper. In this chapter the reader will be introduced to a variety of mark-making activities.

Objectives

After reading this chapter, you should be able to:
- Explain how children express their creativity through play.
- List at least three criteria that characterize play.
- List the five different types of play.
- Discuss multiple literacies.
- Discuss how young children use language creatively.
- Develop creative experiences in music and movement.
- Discuss three different ways adults can facilitate children's creative expression.
- Engage children in mark-making activities.

INTRODUCTION

Chapter 1 introduced the reader to creativity in its widest sense. Chapter 2 focused the discussion on creative thinking. This chapter begins our discussion of various art media by examining the process of mark making, as well as some activities to help children make creative marks. It also outlines other ways that children express their creativity. These include play, language, and music and movement.

CREATIVITY ENHANCES CHILDREN'S DEVELOPMENT

Creativity and creative expression, whether demonstrated through art, thinking, play, language, music, or movement, foster the development of the whole child, including the physical, social-emotional, cognitive, and creative domains. For example, Tearra wants to use the unit blocks to make a house for her doll family. Physically, she must lift, carry, manipulate, and position the blocks. Her eyes and hands work together as her small fingers carefully stack and straighten the large blocks. Initially, Tearra works alone. Creativity respects the child's right to privacy. Later, she invites Portia to help. Socially, they work together practicing cooperative skills, including turn taking and sharing. They practice language skills as they talk and listen to each other. Planning a house to accommodate four dolls takes much thinking and planning. At first they make a wall around their dolls but become dissatisfied saying it looks more like an animal cage. They want separate rooms for each doll. The problem is posed and they

think of some different solutions—they are problem solving. They are proud of their joint accomplishment which enhances their self-esteem. Although their house lacks sides and a roof, their compartmentalized structure is their own creative idea. They run to get their teacher, who takes two photographs that will be added to their portfolios.

MODES OF CREATIVE EXPRESSION

Our discussion of creativity in the first two chapters sets the stage for creative expression discussed in Chapter 3. It is important to remember that art or visual art is merely one aspect of the arts. What is included in the term "the arts"? According to Edwards (2002) "the arts" include literature, drama, music, dance, and the visual arts. Edwards (2002) provides subcategories for each of the five arts as follows:

Literature: poetry, illustrations, writing, books, storytelling, reading, and speaking

Drama: creative dramatics, pantomime, improvisation, play production

Music: sound, pitch, rhythm, singing, playing musical instruments, musical games, listening, and creative movement

Dance: body awareness, movement, and creative expression

Visual Arts: self-expression, visual and tactile art, print and craft media, artistic analysis, and interpretation; both two-dimensional (drawing, painting, printing) and three-dimensional (modeling, sculpting, construction)

Why are the arts important? According to Wright (2003), the arts involve a unique form of knowing—thinking with the body that fuses thought, emotion, and action. Through the arts, children are involved in a special kind of literacy in which they turn action into representation. Because artistic thinking involves meaning and understanding, Wright (2003) recommends ample time in the curriculum for young children to experience the arts, their specific modes of expression, and related processes. This helps develop an understanding of the artistic components: processes, discipline-based forms of expression, elements, and concepts. What are the goals of art education for young children? The National Standards for Arts Education provides recommended skills and abilities for children from kindergarten through fourth grade. See Appendix H.

Our discussion of the modes of creative expression incorporate literature and drama in a section entitled Language. Music and dance are incorporated in a section entitled Music and Movement. The visual arts will be discussed in the chapters that follow. While not considered one of the arts, a discussion of Play begins the section on modes of creative expression. Play involves both creative expression and symbolic representation.

CHILDREN EXPRESS THEIR CREATIVITY THROUGH PLAY

Balke (1997) sees similarities in children's play and art. She believes that play's expressive elements are what make it similar to the work of the artist. Children play with toys just as artists play with their media. Although neither art nor play is necessary to survival, she questions what life would be like without art. She asks, "How could we have culture without art?" Similarly, "What would childhood be like without play?"

What is **play?** Play is a difficult concept to understand because it lacks a precise definition. One person may define play as children's work, while another defines play as frivolous activity lacking purpose. A variety of behaviors can be labeled play, ranging from what infants do with their bodies and toys to games, hobbies, sports, recreational pursuits, and creative activities such as art, music, and dance. Although play cannot be precisely defined, perhaps it can be contrasted with work. Historically, play has been viewed as the opposite of work. It was the Puritan work ethic that gave impetus to this work-play dichotomy. Adult work was considered earnest, serious, worthwhile,

Consider This...

Margo is a first-year kindergarten teacher in a suburban school. She has spent the last few weeks of summer meeting with the kindergarten and primary teams. Personally, she believes she will fit in and be able to get along. Professionally, however, she has some concerns. Margo is trying to reconcile what she learned in her classes about developmentally appropriate practices. Her co-teachers tease her about her "book learning" and remind her that although preschoolers can spend their days playing, kindergarten means work. She becomes even more concerned as the kindergarten reading-readiness and math workbooks arrive. Margo found blocks, a water table, and dramatic play props in storage. She would like to set up centers but wonders where, because tables and chairs take up most of the space. She asks herself, "What is the role of play and creative expression in programs for young children, kindergartners in particular?"

This chapter explores the concept of play, contrasting it to work, and identifying criteria that characterize play. Play takes many forms, and this chapter examines physical play, constructive play with blocks, dramatic play, play with natural materials, and games (see Figure 3-1). Language and the components of music and movement are two other major ways that children express their creativity. Ideas for setting up centers in these curricular areas along with recommended materials and suggested activities are also presented. Chapter 3 closes with a review of ways teachers can enhance and facilitate children's creative expression.

Figure 3-1 A center for creative play.

productive activity. By contrast, children's play was viewed as idle, frivolous fun bordering on evil. The present impact of this thinking is evident when a child is said to be "just" playing. The qualifying *just* connotes a lack of purpose and worth. Rarely does one complain about a child who "just" reads or behaves, because these behaviors are valued. This negative attitude toward play is reflected by the parent, or educators such as Margo's peers, who feel that children must work rather than play if they are to learn. The following example, however, shows that work and play are not opposites. The young child thoroughly absorbed in carefully stacking blocks to build a tower displays the same careful precision and effort of the adult builder at work. The positive qualities associated with work are also found in play. A further distinction between work and play examines the process and product of each. Generally speaking, play is process oriented while work is product oriented. One plays for the sake of playing; one works for the end product of one's endeavors. Examples of creative processing through play include:

- building with blocks, stacking or fitting them together.
- playing with empty boxes.
- filling and emptying containers with water.
- using kitchen tools and containers to scoop, sift, and mold sand.

- pounding and hammering nails into soft wood; sawing and gluing wood pieces together.
- pretending to serve lunch to the baby dolls using pretend food.
- making up a new version of tag, hide-and-seek, hopscotch, or jump rope.
- using poker chips as money at the outdoor fast-food drive-through.

So, what is play? Garvey (1990) identifies the following five criteria that define play.

1. Play is pleasurable and enjoyable. Children play because it is fun.
2. Play has no extrinsic goals. Children are intrinsically motivated to play. They play because they want to and in the absence of any tangible reward.
3. Play is spontaneous and voluntary. Play empowers children to make decisions about what to play, who to play with, where and how to carry it out, as well as when to start and finish.
4. Play involves some active engagement on the part of the player. Young children are active learners and play is an active process. Play can be intense and captivating, thereby disproving the myth that children have short attention spans and cannot stay with an activity for a long period of time.
5. Play is linked with nonplay areas. Play fosters the development of the whole child and fosters learning in the early childhood curricular areas. During play, children are physically and mentally active, socializing and talking with their peers and feeling good about what they have playfully made happen. Because there is no right or wrong way to play, children are creative and successful at play, and their self-esteem is enhanced. Play also allows children to express and master their feelings and emotions. They think and form concepts while playing.

According to Elkind (2003), play is as fundamental a human disposition as loving and working. Play is characteristic of children at all times and places. We play because we are programmed to play. It is part of human nature.

In reviewing the literature on the benefits of play, Berk (1994) found:

1. Make-believe play strengthens a variety of specific mental abilities.
2. Language is greatly enriched by play experiences.
3. Make believe also fosters young children's ability to reason about impossible or absurd situations—a finding highly consistent with Vygotsky's (1986) emphasis that fantasy play assists

Become a Play Advocate

Stone (1995) encourages educators to advocate for play in the primary grades. She believes that even at the kindergarten level there is an erosion of quality playtime. Some educators unwittingly sacrifice play in their quest to reach prescribed academic goals. She believes that even teachers who know the importance of play to a child's development find themselves on the defensive when questioned about play in their classrooms. Stone states teachers have become too embarrassed to give playtime a place because of "more important" curricular priorities. Hence, play is reduced to recess time, hidden in the curriculum, or tagged as miscellaneous "free time."

What can be done? Knowing what play is, the types of play, and the benefits of play alone is not enough. To be a true advocate of children's play, a teacher must be able to verbalize knowledge about the values of play to parents and colleagues. Stone feels play is important because it significantly affects the development of the whole child—

physically, socially, emotionally, and cognitively. Further, she believes that play creates a natural learning environment in which children construct knowledge of their world and make meaning. It affords young children the opportunity to think, develop concepts, symbolize, think divergently, and solve problems. When playing, young children practice language, social skills, physical skills, and express their creativity. Can you relate the above examples to our concept of the whole child?

Along with knowing about play and verbalizing its developmental significance, we can add the importance of documenting learning when children are playing. For example, teachers can display or photograph evidence of things children have made coupled with anecdotal records capturing those moments when children are learning through play. See Chapter 16 for a detailed discussion of documentation and assessment of children's learning through the use of portfolios.

children in separating meanings from the objects for which they stand.

4. Young children who especially enjoy pretending or who are given encouragement to engage in fantasy play score higher on tests of imagination and creativity.

In sum, fantasy play contributes to social maturity and the construction of knowledge. For people who have questioned whether play activities, so natural and absorbing to children, must be curbed in favor of more *productive* activities or whether play constitutes a powerful zone of proximal development, the findings reviewed clearly grant play a legitimate and fruitful place in children's lives.

Creative Play with Boxes, Cartons, and Accessories

Children can be creative with just about anything they find. Play materials need to be safe, clean, and sturdy, but need not be expensive to foster creative play. Commercial toys that are costly may not enhance creativity, despite their labeling. Empty cardboard boxes and containers are great props for fostering creative play because they

- are safe, sturdy, and durable.
- are lightweight and easy to move about.
- are recycled items.
- are free and can be discarded without a financial loss.
- can be personalized using tape, paint, crayons, or markers.
- come in a variety of sizes and shapes.
- can be many things depending on what the children decide.
- are versatile and can be used indoors or outdoors.

Large appliance cartons can easily become structures, such as a house, school, castle, restaurant, store, or hospital, as well as vehicles such as a rocket ship or bus. Turning the carton on its side converts it into a tunnel or a cave. Cut doors and windows for the children, but do not suggest what the box should become. Let the children impart their own meaning while you serve as a resource to the project. Children may want to paint or decorate the interior and exterior. Providing an array of boxes and cartons in different sizes will help children see possibilities and make connections; they may use the small boxes for furniture or control panel instruments. Problems may arise if you provide only one carton to a large group. Providing more than one large appliance carton fosters small group cooperative play in which individual children have space and a part to play. Play with boxes requires supervision. Some children do not like being enclosed in a small area. Help children see that segregating play with one carton for the girls' house and another for boys only is discriminatory and not fair. Your commitment to anti-bias will prohibit exclusion based on gender. It also violates your classroom rule for playing together without hurting others. Adding props or accessories such as old sheets and a steering wheel increases the range of creative possibilities. Use cartons to enhance your language and literacy program. A carton decorated like a house sets the stage for dramatizing classic books such as *Goldilocks and the Three Bears*. A carton-turned-bridge facilitates the acting out of *The Three Billy Goats Gruff*.

Creative Play with Plastic Pipe

Children enjoy constructing with lengths of plastic pipe and several of the following fittings:

- elbows, pipes which come in 45- or 90-degree bends
- couplings, short pipes that join two other pipes in a straight line
- tees, *T*-shaped joints with three openings
- crosses, *X*-shaped joints with four openings

Children impart meaning to the materials; the connected pieces become whatever the children decide. Buy lengths of plastic pipe (PVC). Precut lengths are inexpensively priced, or lengths can be cut with a saw. Buy a variety of fittings that allow children to assemble lengths or connect pieces into angles. Connectors without internal threads are easier to assemble. Pieces are priced according to diameter, and it is important to purchase all pieces in the same diameter. Adults may want to consider using plastic pipe to make a puppet stage or a four-sided structure that can be suspended from the ceiling with fishing line.

Types of Play

Play takes many shapes and forms. These overlapping categories include:

1. physical play.
2. constructive play with blocks.
3. dramatic play.
4. play with natural materials.
5. games.

1. Physical Play

As its name implies, **physical play** involves motor activity and movement. Physical play entails both gross motor (large muscle) and fine motor (involving the small muscles and eye-hand coordination) activity. Outdoor play activities such as running, climbing up and going down a slide, riding tricycles, and jumping involve gross motor or large muscle activity. Large muscle play can occur indoors but limited space may restrict it. Still, indoor climbing structures do provide for gross motor activity, especially on days when the weather keeps children inside. Activities such as stringing beads, pegs and PegBoards, parquetry and design blocks, puzzles, small blocks, sewing and lacing cards, and table toys that lead to sorting or being taken apart and put back together involve fine motor or small muscle activity as well as eye-hand coordination. These are referred to as manipulatives. Because young children are physical beings, physical play is a high priority. Infants grasp and release soft toys and shake rattles. For a toddler, physical play means repeatedly filling and dumping toys into a plastic bucket while wandering about the room. Preschoolers enjoy fitting Lego® blocks and bristle blocks together. Whether they actually make something is secondary to the process of fitting together and taking apart. Kindergartners have mastered puzzles with many pieces and may build complex structures with connecting blocks while dramatizing with small people and vehicles. School-age children who have mastered running, catching, throwing, and skipping may progress to competitive games involving races and tests of physical prowess.

Physical Play on the Outdoor Playground.

Rarely does one have enough outdoor space or equipment for outdoor play. Space is often at a premium and some sites have only a blacktop or small yard with which to work. Others must share space with different age groups or have inherited outdated equipment. Quality playground equipment is expensive. If children were to have their say, however, they would probably allocate most of the annual operating budget and daily schedule to playing outdoors (see Figure 3–2). Your input regarding the design, modification, or improvement of a children's playground may be sought at some point in your professional career. Assuming that space is not restricted and cost is not an issue, what outdoor play areas would you like to see? Suggested areas and recommended materials are listed below.

- water: water table, dishpans or tubs, kitchen gadgets, and containers

Figure 3-2 Creative play outdoors.

Figure 3-3 Block play.

- sand: sandbox or sand table, dishpans or tubs, kitchen gadgets, and containers
- water + dirt or sand = mud!
- carpentry or woodworking table with sturdy tools, goggles, lightweight woods
- flexible, multipurpose, multilevel climbing equipment for an array of large muscle activities like climbing, jumping, and sliding
- riding vehicles (simple and complex, one- and two-passenger) and a clearly defined one-way path, traffic cones and signs
- art materials on an art cart and easels that are freestanding or attached to a fence
- music and movement materials, including dance props, rhythm instruments, recorded music and player
- pets or small animals and cages
- garden and gardening tools
- playhouse, dress-up clothes, bridge, stage, elevated platform or other structure for dramatic play

- shady area for looking at books or listening to and telling stories
- obstacle course stations to jump on and off, crawl through, etc.
- construction materials: large and small blocks, barrels, boards, planks, lumber, old sheets, crates, cardboard boxes, appliance cartons, large sheets of cardboard, tires, tree stump, etc.
- assorted props: balance beam, balls in a variety of sizes, jump ropes, bean bags, hoops, ring toss, parachute, flat wooden ladder, cargo net, low basketball hoop and net, etc.
- storage shed or area that can be locked

2. Constructive Play with Blocks

Building with blocks is a good example of **constructive play.** Children are not only physically active as they build with blocks but may also dramatize. In Figure 3–3 children are using blocks to build a farm and dramatizing with related props. Blocks serve all facets of a child's development, as seen in the play of Tearra and Portia. Physically, blocks are lifted and carried about, enhancing development and coordination of small and large muscles. Socially, children may choose to interact and talk with others as they build. This involves cooperative group effort and social give and take. Emotionally, children feel good about what they have successfully created. Destruction may bring emotional release and more joy than construction. Cognitively, children think, plan, and learn about balance, height, shape, space, cause and effect, architectural forms, and even gravity when tall towers give way to an unsturdy base. Because block play is open-ended, it fosters a child's creative development.

Types of Blocks. There are several types of blocks: unit, large hollow, cardboard bricks, and miscellaneous, including smaller table blocks and those made of soft foam. Wooden blocks, including unit and large hollow, are an expensive but sound investment. If properly cared for, they should last many years. Wooden unit blocks are built to scale, e.g., square or half unit, unit, double unit, and quadruple unit, so children encounter mathematical concepts as they compare blocks by length. There are also an array of block shapes, including curve, ellipse, switch, triangle, ramp, column, buttress, arch, and pillar that supplement the lengths of unit blocks. Older block builders may rely on some of the additional shapes but do not feel obligated to purchase multiples of each and every shape, especially for younger and beginning block builders.

Block Center. Block play requires ample space and protection from foot traffic. Building on a carpet reduces the noise level. Blocks require storage and should never be randomly placed in a box or storage bin. This damages the finish, edges, and corners. Blocks should be arranged on low open shelves according to size, length, and shape so they are easily found and put away. Reserve a bottom shelf for the heavier pieces with lightweight props on the top. Providing an outline of the block shape will help in matching and cleanup. Trace the shape of the block onto colored contact paper, cut it out, and attach it to the back of the appropriate shelf. Provide props such as animals, small dinosaurs, small people, vehicles, and traffic signs to enrich block play, as well as small sheets for roofs, boards for ramps, blue construction paper for water, Plexiglas®, and masking tape for streets or sidewalks. Similar props such as cars and trucks can be kept together in clear tubs or baskets. Remember to rotate block props and to include items that reinforce what you are studying. For example, be sure to include toy fish and blue fabric when studying sea life. There is nothing more frustrating to young builders than having their construction "accidentally" knocked down. This can be avoided by reminding children not to build too close to each other or too close to the storage shelves. To make cleanup less chaotic, remind children to only take a few blocks out at a time and then use them before going for more. Also, dismantling buildings from the top down eliminates unnecessary noise and accidents.

Whereas unit blocks stress fine motor and eye-hand coordination, large hollow blocks provide a gross motor and large muscle challenge. They also allow children to build larger, child-proportioned structures. Be sure to include steering wheels for children who make child-sized vehicles. Smaller unit blocks encourage children to build in miniature, which is why small props are provided. Blocks foster active play and you may need to set guidelines regarding safety issues like how high children can build. Children may also need this reminder: "Blocks are for building, not throwing. They are heavy and can hurt." These printed words can appear as signs in your block centers. Keep a camera loaded with film and ready to photograph individual or group block constructions. Take dictation or encourage children to write if they have words that accompany their building. The dated photo can be included in the child's portfolio. Children may need your assistance in making signs such as "Please do not knock down" or "Keep up." Reserve a shelf in your block area for books on construction and building, along with papers and writing instruments. This will connect block play with literacy. Along with labeled shelves, include photographs of multicultural homes and neighborhoods as well as males and females involved in block-play–related pursuits like construction, farming, and transportation.

Cardboard bricks are a third type of block. They are inexpensive and not sturdy. They are large but lightweight, which inhibits complex building such as making high towers and may frustrate the skilled builder. On the positive side, they make less noise when they tumble. On the negative side, children enjoy walking on them, which quickly destroys them. Cardboard bricks are a good choice for the very young, who can later graduate to heavier wooden blocks. Make your own blocks by covering shoe boxes or milk cartons with contact paper. Other types of blocks include rubber, foam, and small table blocks. Rubber and foam blocks are lightweight, inexpensive, and recommended for young and beginning block builders. Table blocks, which are smaller than unit blocks, involve small muscle control and eye-hand coordination and result in construction on a smaller scale. Different types of blocks can also supplement each other during constructive play.

3. Dramatic Play

Dramatic play is also referred to as play that involves fantasy, imagination, or make-believe. Children engage in dramatic play alone or with others and usually with props. A child who is dressing a baby doll is engaging in dramatic or symbolic play. Toddlers learn that the doll symbolically represents a real baby. A preschooler may use a box as a table. Children who engage in dramatic play have attained representational ability. Children practice language and social skills, as well as planning and decision-making skills, in dramatic play. They can rehearse family roles and learn about community helpers. Children re-create what they know through dramatic play. A child who has been loved and nurtured will act out this scenario in dramatic play. A child who talks harshly to or even spanks a baby doll tells you something very different about what he or she knows or has experienced. Children will also use dramatic play to work through emotional issues such as sibling rivalry, fear of abandonment, or impending hospitalization. In contrast to dramatic play, **sociodramatic play** is a more organized, cooperative type of fantasy play engaged in by older preschoolers, kindergartners, and young school-age children in which roles are divided and players have different parts. For example, in playing house, there may be a mommy, a daddy, twin babies, and a pet dog. Each child has a role, function, and speaking part to play.

Dramatic Play Center. In Vygotsky's (1978) sociocultural theory (see Chapter 4) play was given a major role in children's development. Play serves at least four major purposes.

Celebrating Diversity through Dramatic Play

To make your dramatic play area diverse be sure to include the following tools, props, and clothing for children to explore race and ethnicity, culture, gender, and special needs. Always begin with the diversity represented in your classroom and expand from there to other groups in your community. These props include:

- stage rooms of the house other than the kitchen. Include male and female clothing, pictures of both boys and girls, men and women, and pictures and books that show a diversity of family composition.
- tools and equipment for people with special needs. Examples include wheelchairs, walkers, braces, hearing aids, ramps, thick eyeglasses, books written in Braille, crutches, canes, and magnifiers.
- fake food, for example plastic or rubber, representative of different cultural groups.
- food containers, boxes, and tins representing items from different cultures and with labels in different languages.

- bags and baskets for shopping.
- clothing, shoes, hats, scarves, and belts that represent both everyday wear and holiday attire from a variety of cultures.
- multiracial dolls and dolls with adaptive equipment for a range of disabilities.
- eating utensils from different cultures including Chinese soup spoons, chopsticks, wooden, tin, and plastic bowls, dishes, cups, and ladles.
- cooking utensils from different countries including saucepans, kettles, steamers, strainers, wok, garlic press, tortilla press, grater, tea balls, fry pans, whisks, etc.
- cushions, pillows, mats, small area rugs, and placements from traditional cultures decorated with representative colors, patterns, and designs.
- a variety of infant carriers including basket, stroller, infant sling, and Native American cradle board.
- a variety of beds and bedding for dolls including blanket, cradle, hammock, and futon.

1. Play, and representational play in particular, create a zone of proximal development, within which children advance to higher levels of psychological functioning. Through play children not only repeat concepts and skills already learned but they challenge themselves to learn new, higher level ones.
2. Representational play helps children learn roles and rules for it is driven by rules for behavior that children must follow to successfully act out a play scenario. Make-believe play does not only serve the preschool years but evolves into games with rules during middle childhood.
3. In representational play young children create an imaginary situation that permits them to cope with unrealizable desires and develop the capacity to renounce impulsive action in favor of deliberate, self-regulatory activity.
4. Fantasy play helps children in separating meaning from objects for which they stand. Play is a vital preparation for the later development of abstract thinking.

An indoor dramatic play center can be located next to the block area because both invite loud, active, imaginative play. Similar items should be organized, grouped together, and labeled. Providing furniture that resembles a home, including table and chairs, cooking and eating equipment, kitchen appliances, food, multiethnic dolls and clothing, stuffed animals, mirror, cash register, microphone, camera, puppets, walkie-talkies, and telephones sets a familiar and comfortable stage. Props enhance dramatic play by expanding the realm of creative possibilities. Be sure to include clothing that represents what both men and women, as well as uniformed community helpers, wear in your locale. Children are learning about their social world, so expect boys to try on half-slips and jewelry and girls to play being the daddy. Providing open-ended props like a sheet or a length of rubber hose will challenge older preschoolers.

Connect dramatic play to your curriculum. Providing "money," such as Styrofoam™ pieces or strips of green construction paper, facilitates counting; grouping food in the grocery store builds classification skills. Include books on multiethnic families and the occupations under study. Children can only re-create what they know so they will have difficulty dramatizing being a banker, astronaut, travel agent, or circus performer. Make sure that they have directly

Sociodramatic Play

Smilansky (1968, 1971) views sociodramatic play as an advanced form of dramatic play. Sociodramatic play revolves around a theme with children engaging in behaviors that support the theme. For example, Figures 3-4, 3-5, 3-6, and 3-7 document sociodramatic play around a medical theme. What are the characteristics that qualify make-believe as sociodramatic play? According to Smilansky these include:

role playing—Children assume make-believe or pretend roles involving talk and action. What are the roles that you see played out in Figures 3-4, 3-5, 3-6, and 3-7?

make-believe with objects—Children use make-believe objects to represent real ones. What make-believe objects are visible in Figures 3-4, 3-5, 3-6, and 3-7?

make-believe with actions or events—Sociodramatic play incorporates situations or events related to the

theme. What actions or events are happening in Figures 3-4, 3-5, 3-6, and 3-7?

verbalizations—Verbal expressions are related to the play theme. What could the children be saying in Figures 3-4, 3-5, 3-6, and 3-7?

social interaction—At least two players are engaged in sociodramatic play. Is this criterion met in Figures 3-4, 3-5, 3-6, and 3-7?

persistence—The play episode engages children for more than five minutes. Although it may not be evident from examining Figures 3-4, 3-5, 3-6, and 3-7 this particular sociodramatic play episode lasted much longer than five minutes with children leaving and returning periodically.

experienced what you want them to act out. Invite in a mother who is a dentist and then set the stage for dental play in your dramatic play corner. Or go on a field trip to a local supermarket. Set up your own version with clothing and props upon your return. Encourage socio-dramatic play by building prop boxes for dramatic play around a theme (see Figures 3–4 through 3–7). For example, collect clothing and props related to a veterinary hospital and place in a large box labeled with symbols (e.g., pictures of animals and the words *Veterinarian* or *Animal Doctor*). Keep an inventory of the contents taped to the inside lid. For instance, include the following: stuffed animals, lab coats, surgical gowns and masks, and red-cross armbands for doctors and nurses; lab coats for office workers and dress-up clothes for pet owners; doctor tools and medical bag, Band-Aids, and gauze or lengths of white fabric; boxes, baskets, bowls, and brushes for sick pets. Introduce your prop box with a book or better yet a field trip or class visit by a vet. Connect your prop box and dramatic play area to literacy. Include writing instruments, clipboards, stamps, papers, envelopes, cook-books, and magazines. Specific literacy props for dramatizing a veterinary hospital include an appointment book, old X rays, a prescription pad, a doctor's In/Out sign, magazines for the waiting room, empty medicine containers, and books on animals, first aid, or veterinarians. Including papers and writing materials will encourage children to write letters, lists, receipts, and to send and receive mail.

Favorite books and stories can be acted out in the dramatic play area. This will work better with children who have interacted together in sociodramatic play. Start with a simple nursery rhyme such as "Humpty Dumpty," moving on to short stories with a few characters, simple plots, and manageable speaking lines. Provide simple costumes and props to ease children into the role. For example, Humpty Dumpty may wear a fancy bathrobe and a simple crown, and horses may hold simple masks. Girls can play the part of the king's men and take creative liberty to change the rhyme to include "all the king's women."

4. Play with Natural Materials

Adults who appreciate a walk on the beach, splashing in the waves, soaking in a bathtub, or smelling and feeling sawed wood will understand how play with water, sand, and wood appeal to young children. **Play with natural materials** is sensory-rich, soothing, and therapeutic. Because our world is made up of water and sand, children gradually develop concepts about bodies of water such as oceans and land forms such as deserts. Although water is wet and sand is dry, both hold great sensory appeal and lead children to similar discoveries; for example, both can be poured and measured. Children can also discover that water, sand, and wood have unique properties. Unlike sand, water can freeze and melt. Wood can be sawed into small pieces and attached with either glue or hammer and nails. Natural materials are open-ended and pro-

Figure 3-4

Figure 3-6

Figure 3-5

Figure 3-7

vide unlimited creative possibilities, while also supporting physical, social, emotional, cognitive, and language development. Along with the obvious physical challenge, carpentry and woodworking foster children's verbal and social interaction. They develop skills in observation, problem solving, measurement, and hypothesizing.

Water/Sand Play. Water and sand need large containers that will provide ample room for small group play. Water/sand play tables with lids are commercially available and a sound investment. They tend to be large enough to accommodate four children and come with a drain plug. Alternatives include:

- dish pans or baby bathtubs.
- shallow flat containers such as photographic developing trays.
- a shallow wading pool or plastic sandbox.
- a plastic boat.
- a large tractor or truck tire.

Place your table near the sink and cover surrounding floor area with a vinyl shower curtain or old towels that can be thrown in the dryer when wet. Cleanup equipment for mopping up water or sweeping up spills should be kept on an adjacent storage shelf along with accessories. Provide waterproof smocks and remind children to roll up their sleeves. Children should also keep a change of clothing in their cubbies. Limit the number of children based on the size of your water or sand table. Discuss guidelines and limits and set them in positive terms: "We play with sand and water and keep it in the table. Splashing water gets our friends wet." "Throwing sand is dangerous and can hurt the eyes." Give children a choice of either upholding the guidelines or playing somewhere else. Remind children that part of the cycle of playing with water and sand is cleaning up.

Water/sand play can occur both indoors and outdoors. Some teachers prefer to have an indoor sensory table that rotates contents between water (with and without soap bubbles), sand, shaving cream, nature specimens such as shells, pebbles, stone, or flower petals, snow, shaved ice, aquarium gravel, marbles, sawdust, birdseed, or cornstarch and water. It is of foremost importance that children experience the tactile quality of the contents. Later, add props and accessories to supplement tactile exploration. Choose those that are appropriate for contents. Eliminate glass, sharp or rusty items, and those that are breakable, or are too small and tempting to put in one's mouth.

Water/sand play accessories include:

- animal figures, aquarium nets.
- balloons, bicycle pump, blocks, boats, bowls, brushes (e.g., bottle, spray, squirt, shaving), bulb basters, buttons, buckets, berry baskets.
- clothespins, colanders, combs, condiment bottles, containers (with holes and without in graduated sizes), cookie cutters, corks, cups, cars, construction vehicles, craft sticks.
- dish detergent, dish mops, dolls and clothes.
- egg beaters, egg cartons.
- film cans, fishing bobbers, funnels (alone or attached to ends of plastic tubing).
- golf balls and tees.
- hose with spray nozzle.
- ice, ice-cream scoop, ice-cube trays.
- Jell-O® molds.
- kettle.
- ladles, liter bottles (with holes punched around the base to create a fountain).
- magnets, margarine tubs with lids, marbles, measuring cups and spoons, medicine droppers, milk cartons, muffin tins.
- natural items (e.g., rocks, pinecones).
- nesting cups.
- pail, pans, paintbrushes, people figures, pie tin, Ping-Pong® balls, pitchers, plastic eggs, plastic hoses and tubes, plastic straws, Popsicle® sticks, pots, plastic containers, pipe cleaners.
- rocks, rolling pin, rubber washers.
- salt shakers, scoops, scrub brush, shells, sieve, sifters, slotted spoons, small boats, snow, soap (bar), sponges (e.g., alphabet and numeral), spools, stones, strainer, Styrofoam™ packing, syringe, shovels, spray bottles.
- teapot, thermometers, thimble, tinfoil (flat pieces and balls), tongs, tongue depressors, toothpicks, tubing, Tupperware®.
- vehicles.
- water wheels, watering can, whisk, wood scraps, wooden blocks, wooden spoons.

Activities for water play include:

washing—Provide shells, paintbrushes, small furniture, vehicles, bar soap, scrub brush, and washboard. Discuss how items look before and after washing.

dish washing—Periodically have children wash the dishes and play with food in the dramatic area.

doll washing—Provide dolls of color along with bar soap, washcloths, and brushes. Help children see that dark skin does not equate with dirty. Skin color is a given and constant that does not change with washing. Dirty baby dolls with light skin stay light skinned, but clean, after washing; dirty baby dolls with dark skin stay dark skinned, but clean, after washing.

measurement—Provide measuring cups and container of water. Encourage children to discover how many small containers are needed to fill a larger container.

magnetism—Provide small fishing poles and magnetic fish.

melting—Place a block of ice, ice cubes, snow, or shaved ice in a container outdoors in the sun. Encourage children to see what happens over time. Does one form melt faster than the others?

temperature—Engage in play with water of different temperatures. Leave the water out in the sun before playing. Later, add ice cubes. Discuss the similarities and differences.

absorption—Provide Q-tips®, paper towels, sponges, and an array of nonabsorbent materials. Encourage children to discover which ones absorb water.

evaporation—Provide large paintbrushes, house painter's gear and buckets of water. Encourage children to paint the sidewalk, building, windows, and clean the riding vehicles. Observe what happens to the painted-on water over time.

evaporation—Have children wash doll or baby clothes and hang them on a clothesline outdoors to dry. Or use several wet sponges—alphabet and numerals are good choices because they connect water play with literacy. Encourage them to check back over time. What happened and why?

freezing—Children pour water into ice-cube trays. Place one in freezer; leave others in the room or in the sun. Have children notice any differences. What happened and why?

freezing—Have children wash doll or baby clothes. Place in freezer and check over time. What happened and why?

coloring water—Provide eye droppers and place drops of food coloring or liquid watercolor into water. What change takes place? What if different colored waters are mixed? Begin by providing one or two primary colors at a time.

coloring water—Have children place strips of crepe paper or tissue paper in clear plastic tumblers. Note what happens to the water.

coloring water—Add colored ice cubes to a container of water and watch what happens.

dissolving—Provide materials including Jell-O®, salt, sugar, dirt, pebbles, marbles, paper scraps, etc. Have children place each in water and observe which ones dissolve.

sink and float—Provide an array of objects that sink (e.g., marbles, pebbles, nuts, bolts) and items that float (e.g., corks and twigs). Encourage children to predict and then test out their hunches by placing the objects in water.

sink and float—Provide materials such as wooden craft sticks, small wooden scraps, or sheets of tinfoil for making boats.

sink and float and dissolving—Place bars of soap in water. Observe what happens over time. Have children observe the size of the soap and consistency of the water.

mixing—Have children make mud pies by combining water with sand or dirt.

mixing—Add liquid soap to water and provide rotary egg beaters.

making music—Assemble eight identical glass tumblers or bottles. Fill the containers with water at varying levels. Gently strike each with a rhythm stick or pencil and listen.

conservation—Provide containers that hold the same volume or amount but are of different sizes and shapes. Encourage children to fill and compare but do not verbally impose adult logic. Avoid saying, "See, it's still the same amount."

Although water may be more versatile in terms of potential activities, children can also use sand in the above activities involving measurement, absorption (of water), coloring (with chalk), mixing, (with paint), and conservation. Wet sand is good for sculpting; children can use their fingers to practice printing their name or favorite letters in dry sand.

Carpentry or Woodworking. The thought of carpentry or woodworking and young children concerns some educators. It may be a safety issue or one's own discomfort level based on a lack of knowledge and skills in using tools. Tools empower boys and girls as well as provide opportunities in refining large muscle and fine motor skills as well as eye-hand coordination. Carpentry and woodworking also allow for emotional release. An angry child who has difficulty verbalizing his or her feelings can hammer or saw them out. This does not address the heart of the problem but it does relieve pent-up anger. Tools must be individually introduced through modeling, with children practicing the correct way to hold and use a tool. Safety is a foremost consideration. Carpentry or woodworking takes very close supervision with a maximum of four chil-

dren participating at a time, one per corner. Children should wear aprons and safety goggles. Provide real tools in smaller sizes as opposed to toy tools which can easily bend and snap. Tools can be displayed on the Peg-Board with the outlines of each drawn around it. Tables can be commercially purchased but a handyperson could easily make one to your specifications, or simply cut the legs off a wooden kitchen table. Sawhorses with a sturdy plank or old door that has been securely attached can also be used. Height is very important—the bench should be waist-high to the children, neither too high nor too low. Along with a sturdy workbench, recommended tools include:

- claw hammers (12-ounce weight)
- C-clamps (to hold the wood steady while sawing)
- vises mounted at opposite corners of the workbench (to hold the wood steady while sawing)
- pliers
- screwdrivers: slotted and Phillips
- hand drill, brace, and bit (better for older children because it involves downward pressure with one hand while other hand turns a circle)
- saws: crosscut with 10–12 teeth per inch (10- or 12-point) and 16- to 18-inch blade
- nuts, bolts, washers, screws, and nails
- wood scraps (soft woods including fir, white pine, and balsa)
- wood craft sticks
- doweling
- wood glue
- large Styrofoam™ pieces
- sandpaper and sandpaper blocks

Young children will approach carpentry or woodworking activities with a process orientation. They want to see what they can do with tools, wood, and fasteners. Sawing wood and hammering nails are pleasurable in and of themselves. Older children will be more interested in making something and may even plan their finished product in advance. Encourage them to make blueprints or simple sketches of what they plan to make. Invite children to

- hammer nails into layers of cardboard that have been glued together.
- hammer nails into a tree stump.
- hammer golf tees into Styrofoam™.
- hammer nails into Styrofoam™.
- hammer nails into a jar lid.
- hammer nails into a block of plasticene or clay.
- tighten screws on toys, tricycles, and furniture.
- use sandpaper on rough edges of blocks of wood or on old wooden toys and blocks.
- use tools to make block props.
- glue wood scraps into a wood collage.

Hint: Help children use a hammer by showing them how to hold it. Young children tend to grasp the hammer near the head. Holding the handle farther back, however, provides greater leverage and pressure. You may want to tap a nail to help children begin hammering. Or push the nail through an index card or sturdy strip of paper with the child holding the end of the card or paper as they strike the nail. This way fingers and thumbs stay clear of the hammer. When the nail is adequately pounded, they can pull the paper away.

Hint: Provide nails that are short with broad heads. Roofing nails work well. Longer nails take too long to hammer in and often bend in the process.

Hint: To help children use a saw, secure wood in vise or C-clamp. Help the child hold the saw at a 45-degree angle and use light pressure to rhythmically move the saw downward in a back and forth motion.

Hint: Reserve the hand drill for use with school-age children. It is difficult to operate since one hand applies downward pressure while the other makes it go around. Also, young children tend to make it turn backward, which only loosens the drill bit.

Hint: Make a game out of cleanup. Provide whisk brooms and dustpans for sweeping up sawdust. Magnets work well for picking up fallen nails, nuts, bolts, and screws. Always match up tools to their outline on the Peg-Board. Tools lying around pose potential safety problems.

Games. Think back to your own childhood and reflect on the games you played. Do you remember playing tag, hide-and-seek, or an informal game of ball? Do you recall winning or never getting picked for the team? Have you ever observed a teacher trying to play "Duck, Duck, Goose" with a group of young children? They play out of turn and often do their own thing. Young children have difficulty playing games. Their egocentric side may keep them from waiting, taking turns, and playing by the rules. They may change and break the rules at whim to make it work for them. This is not cheating, but rather reflects their inability to hold to rules that protect others and may keep them from winning. With years of social interaction, older children see how rules protect the rights of all individuals and may ostracize a child whom they believe is cheating. **Games** are competitive, usually resulting in a winner and loser. This may be difficult for even older children to face. Depending on your group it may be wise to modify games. For example, in "Musical Chairs," the play is ongoing but no chairs are removed so there are no losers; everyone gets to play every round of the game. School-age children, however, become socially competitive as they test their mental prowess with card and board games, involving memory, strategy, or chance. They compare their physical abilities such as aiming, racing, chasing, or hiding, and in sports such as baseball, soccer, basketball, and kickball. You may want to introduce them to cooperative games that foster team building and working together rather than winning at the expense of others.

Let's apply Vygotsky's theory to play and young children. Our focus will be on understanding the child's zone of proximal development and scaffolding. A teacher can find out where a child is developmentally through anecdotal records and reflective observation. What is the child's present level of functioning? Play interests? What is the child capable of doing? What does this child know? This key developmental information provides access into the individual child's range of proximal development. Do not be scared off by Vygotsky's terms. Like Piaget, he wrote in a language other than English that had to be translated. Based on one's observations, teachers can facilitate learning and development through play using the strategy of scaffolding. For example, Kimber-Lee is a preschooler with Down syndrome who loves to play. You have observed that she enjoys standing in the dramatic play center smiling at her peers but without joining in. They neither include nor exclude her. The more you observe, the more you reflect on the possibility that her delayed language and minimal social skills keep her from participating. Although other children seem more confident in approaching and joining in, Kimber-Lee appears not to know how. What is the next step? What is an optimal match for this child? A teacher could scaffold this in different ways. What would you do? Perhaps you decide to play alongside her and help her join in. You will model the words "Can I play too?" and work with her peers to include Kimber-Lee in their play. You suggest that because she enjoys holding and rocking the baby dolls that she could be the big sister who is babysitting. All parties agree on this role and that it fits into and extends their play scenario. Kimber-Lee's participation in play is successful. By getting into her zone of proximal development and using scaffolding you have facilitated her success in play.

CHILDREN EXPRESS THEIR CREATIVITY THROUGH LANGUAGE

The profile of the creative child reminds the author of two famous characters in children's literature. First, like the little boy in *The Emperor's New Clothes*, creative children are able to see what others do not. They are also able to stand up for their beliefs and not yield to social pressure, whereas others may change their opinions to conform and not appear different. Second, like the Ugly Duckling who becomes the beautiful swan, children can trust their creativity to help them become the unique individuals they are destined to be. Help children acknowledge and accept their creative uniqueness by identifying with characters in literature.

The early years are a time of rapid language development. Language is caught rather than taught. Children learn an extensive collection of words or vocabulary which helps them communicate with others. The infant who says "bobba" will be given a bottle by an adult who knows the infant is asking for a bottle. Saying "bobba" will not get a ride in the car although saying "go" may. Much of language development entails learning that words refer to specific objects and actions. Children also creatively invent their own words as evidenced in the following examples:

- Sahid calls his brother's convertible a "top-down car."
- When served pancakes for breakfast, Jocelyn exclaims, "Oh good, flat cakes; my favorite."
- Gabrielle asks her teacher for some "cutters" as she points to the empty scissors rack.
- Daryl asks his mother if he can talk to his grandma on the "hello phone."
- Amira walks with a doll in the stroller as she announces, "I'm getting a baby pusher like this for my birthday."
- During lunch Cory argues that they are drinking "cow juice," not milk.

- Mrs. Lo is doing a food activity with her small group. She passes around an uncut pineapple. When it is Orin's turn he remarks, "Oh, Christmas-tree fruit."
- Scott puts on his jacket but does not get it fastened. While pointing to the Velcro® fasteners he asks, "Can somebody stick me together?"
- McKenzie's parents pack a slice of pepperoni pizza in her lunch box. Her friends look on with envy as she exclaims, "Oh, cold meatzza for lunch again!"
- Vui is proud of her new umbrella. She says, "See my new rain-brella."
- In our lunch room one boy opened his sandwich and removed the slice of cheese, saying, "I hate hole cheese."
- "Daddy, why didn't you park the car in the 'carage'?" asks Lee.
- Mother asks, "Did you get in trouble today at school?" Skeet answers "Nunce. No even once!"
- Emily reminds her grandma to take the God book (Bible) to church with her.
- While at the beach Carmen ran to get her parents to come see the "walking shells" (hermit crabs).

Language is actively constructed. Children will invent words and creatively err when forming plurals or verb tenses. They are constructing the rules of language and may overgeneralize in the process. Knowing that you add an *s* to the end of words to form plurals leads children to talk about "geeses" and "fishes." Because *ed* is added to the end of a word to signify past tense, children proudly announce, "I wented home," or "I goed to school." Adults who have learned English as a second language will testify that English is a complex language with more exceptions than regularities. Express interest as children creatively construct and invent words that work and make sense to them. There is no need to correct. Instead say, "Meatzza—that's a clever name for meat pizza." In this way McKenzie learns that her creative expression through language is valued but that conventional alternatives also exist.

Informal Creative Language Activities

A child's waking day offers a wealth of opportunities for fostering language development (see Figure 3–8). Children in school learn language while interacting with peers and adults. Consider these two recommendations. First, children who are vertically grouped with a range of ages are exposed to a wider array of vocabulary and language patterns than children who are grouped by identical chronological age. Second,

Figure 3-8 Using words to describe what I made.

Figure 3-9 Keara learned about her name.

Figure 3-10 Christian wrote his own story.

Figure 3-11 Jay wrote his own story.

teachers must model and provide opportunities for speaking, listening, reading, and writing. Some informal creative language activities include the following:

- Provide oral language props including puppets, telephones, and walkie-talkies. These props help shy children and those beginning to learn English.
- Tell stories in novel ways using unusual props. Invite children to tell you stories or "read" the pictures in books.
- Make storytelling props like felt or Pellon® (interfacing) pieces available to children. Tell

them how much you enjoy being at the receiving end of a good story.

- Take creative liberty with traditional and contemporary literature. Add, change, or delete characters. For example, invent new wild things for *Where the Wild Things Are*.
- Take dictation. Ask children if there are words or a story to go along with their artwork. Carefully listen, write, and read it back. Encourage the child to read along with you (see Figures 3–9, 3–10, 3–11).
- Observe opportune times to get involved and facilitate children's play. For example, children who are simply sitting in the dramatic play area may be waiting for a good idea. Facilitate play by suggesting that the babies appear hungry and may want to go out to eat before their afternoon nap. Stay involved as long as necessary

but without dominating or imposing your way of doing things.

Using Literature to Facilitate Children's Creative Expression

There are many examples of children's books that foster creative expression. Following are some good books and creative activities to extend the stories.

- After reading *The Napping House* by Audrey Wood, ask the children to come up with their own napping story. Change the location to create a napping story set on a farm, at a zoo, or in outer space.
- *Pretend You're a Cat* by Jean Marzollo is a good lead-in to a creative movement activity. Have the children move or make noises like the animals in the story. What other noises or movements does each make? Pretend you are an animal that does not appear in the story. What noise or movements does it make? What else could it say or do?
- After reading *Imogene's Antlers* by David Small, have the children brainstorm for other possible uses for Imogene's antlers.
- In *Bearymore* by Don Freeman, Bearymore, a performing circus bear, is told by the ringmaster to come up with a new act. What could it be? Ask the children to help Bearymore think of new and different ways to perform.
- Discuss the dilemma in *Doctor DeSoto* by William Steig. How can the mouse-dentist treat his wolf-patient without being eaten in the process?
- After reading *A House Is a House for Me* by Mary Ann Hoberman, ask the children to identify things that could be a house for something else. For example, a Band-Aid could be a house for a cut. What could be a house for a butterfly? Try to have the children come up with many different possibilities.
- After reading *Can I Keep Him?* by Steven Kellogg, have the children identify unusual pets and brainstorm potential problems with keeping that animal for a pet. For example, an alligator might be a good pet but it would have too many teeth to brush.
- After reading *When Sophie Gets Angry—Really, Really Angry* by Molly Bang, encourage children to discuss what makes them angry. Ask, "What gets you angry, really, really angry?" Be prepared to take dictation to accompany their angry pictures. Or, children can contribute to a Mad Mural featuring things that get them mad.

- After reading *It Looked Like Spilt Milk* by Charles G. Shaw, encourage children to make their own shapes using white fiberfill. Inexpensive fiberfill is available at fabric and craft stores. Children can glue their white "cloudy" creations to a piece of dark construction paper for contrast.

Literacy and Multiple Literacies

The term **literacy** means knowing how to read and write. Emergent literacy explains the spontaneous and early unfolding of reading and writing in the early years. Children are meaning makers. They construct meaning from the spoken and printed word. As with intelligence, the single definition of literacy is being questioned. There are many ways to be literate. Broadly speaking, being literate means being well-educated. As with multiple intelligences there are **multiple literacies.** The new concept of multiliteracy acknowledges multimodal ways of thinking. According to Wright (2003), a multiliteracy approach to education views children as remakers, transformers, and reshapers of knowledge who use a range of representational resources and multiple modes of thinking. The early experience of young children with the computer gives credence to the concept of technologic literacy including computers, the Internet, and digital media as well as hypertext, Web pages, and e-mail messages. The same holds true for mathematical and scientific literacies. A case can also be made for the development of artistic literacy because art is a complex form of object and imagery. Constructing insightful meaning from art requires time, focus, reflection, effort, and analysis. In summary, there are many ways to be competent and literate in our postmodern, rapidly changing, technologic world. Visual and media literacy will be discussed in the next section. Our ever-shrinking world and commitment to anti-bias recognize the need for cultural literacy.

Visual Literacy

From a very early age children are immersed in a visual culture composed of a multitude of visual images that bombard their senses at an alarming rate given the hours of television viewing and time spent on the computer. Children are surrounded with visual images whether it be the picture of a new toy in a shopping catalog or logo on a cereal box. Based on the idea that visual images are a language, **visual literacy** can be defined as the ability to understand and produce visual messages. Children become visually literate by the practice of visual encoding and decoding. Visual encoding involves expressing one's thoughts and ideas in visual form. Visual decoding involves translating and understanding the meaning of visual imagery. Visual literacy is an emerging area of study of increasing importance with the ever-expanding proliferation of mass media in society. Children live in an information environment saturated with visual images. As more and more information and entertainment are acquired though nonprint media such as television, videos, movies, video and computer games, and the Internet, the ability to think critically and visually about the images presented becomes a crucial skill.

Media Literacy

Older children need to become not only educated producers but also critical consumers in a wide variety of media. The goal of media literacy education is to help children become able to read, analyze, evaluate, and produce communications in a variety of media. According to Hesse and Lane (2003), **media literacy** extends the traditional concept of literacy defined as the ability to read and write to electronic media. Recommended picture books that facilitate a discussion of media literacy include:

Brown, M., & Brown, L. K. *The bionic bunny show.*
Novak, M. *Mouse TV.*
Winn, C. M., & Walsh, D. *Box-head boy.*

Positive aspects of the media can be identified, such as prosocial behavior, whereas media messages of hate, violence, prejudice, discrimination, consumerism, rejection or intolerance must be discussed to help develop critical awareness. Useful Web sites for media literacy include:

www.childrennow.org—Children Now: Children and the Media Program
www.kff.org—Kaiser Family Foundation: Entertainment Media Studies and Public Education Partnerships
www.lionlamb.org—The Lion and the Lamb Project
www.mediafamily.org—National Institute on Media and the Family
www.medialit.org—Center for Media Literacy

The study of visual literacy is approached from a range of disciplines including a study of the physical processes involved in visual perception, use of technology to represent visual imagery, and the intellectual strategies used to interpret and understand what is seen. For example, the swastika is a visually encoded symbol made up of a series of lines—at a purely visual level nothing more than a simple visually encoded form that resembles the convergence of four "Ls." What does it mean to you? Through visual decoding, its underlying meaning can be perceived as disturbing and emotionally charged in that it rep-resents the hateful terror of Nazi Germany's Third Reich and horrific images of torture and concentration camps.

Picture Books and Visual Literacy

Picture books develop children's visual literacy. A picture book is any book in which the message depends upon pictures as much if not more than the text. The pictures must be accurate and synchronized with the text to give the reader key information regarding the written text. A storyline, however, is not required as is the case with ABC, counting and single concept books. Wordless picture books usually do tell a story, but they have no text. A picture book conveys its message through a series of sequential images. What is the relationship of picture books to literacy? Because of early exposure to picture books as first reading experiences, children do not think only in written language but in visual images as well. It is the pictures young children see along with the words they hear that help them develop a sense of story. Pictures are the story. They give meaning to words. The child must decode visual messages in pictures and encode them into oral language. When children begin to retell stories from books, their words are guided by their individual "reading" of the illustrations. Beautifully illustrated children's picture books provide a context for the development of reading, writing, and oral language.

CHILDREN EXPRESS THEIR CREATIVITY THROUGH MUSIC AND MOVEMENT

Music and movement begin early in life when parents sing lullabies and dance with infants in their arms. Children may grow up with grandparents who sing to them and older siblings who dance about the house. They learn that people use music and movement to communicate. In turn, they sing when happy, often repeating TV jingles and familiar songs. They will sing while at play, in the bathtub, on the potty, or when falling asleep. They will creatively make up their own words to familiar tunes. See Table 3–1 for Pica's (2003) Developmental Stages of Musical Experiences.

Music and movement complement the developing child who is naturally talkative and constantly in motion. A child's singing and body movement indicate mood. A happy child will sing and actively move his or her body. An overly quiet, sullen child with halting, limited movements may signify a different mood, such as an off-day or possible problem. As with art, there is

Table 3-1   Developmental Stages of Musical Experiences

As with motor development, every child progresses through the stages of musical development at his or her own pace. Although the sequence of developmental stages remains the same for all children, the ages at which they reach and pass through each stage can vary from child to child.

MUSIC EXPERIENCES FOR INFANTS AND TODDLERS

According to the National Association for Music Education (MENC) (1991) infants and toddlers experience music by hearing it, feeling it, and by experimenting with musical sounds and vocalizations. Very young children should experience music daily while receiving caring, physical contact. Strategies for enhancing the musical development of infant and toddlers include:

- singing and chanting to them; using a diverse selection of songs and rhymes.

- imitating the sounds infants make.

- exposing the very young to a wide variety of vocal, body, instrumental, and environmental sounds.

- providing exposure to selected live and recorded music.

- rocking, patting, touching, and moving with the children to the beat, rhythm, patterns, and melody of the music they hear.

- providing safe toys that make musical sounds that the children control.

- talking about music and its relationship to feelings and emotions.

MUSIC EXPERIENCES FOR TWO-, THREE-, AND FOUR-YEAR-OLDS

According to MENC (1991), preschoolers need an environment that includes a variety of sound sources, selected recorded music, and opportunities for free improvised singing and the building of a repertoire of songs. An exploratory approach, using a wide range of appropriate materials, provides a rich base from which conceptual understanding is gradually constructed. A variety of individual musical experiences is important for preschoolers, with little emphasis on activities that require children to perform together as a unit. As a result of their experiences with music, four-year-olds should initiate both independent and collaborative play with musical materials. They should also demonstrate curiosity about music. For children in kindergarten through fourth grade, National Standards for the Creative Arts are contained in Appendix H.

TWO-YEAR-OLDS

- Use their bodies in response to music, often by bouncing up and down.

- Can learn short, simple songs.

- Show increasing ability to follow directions in songs.

- Respond enthusiastically to favorite songs, often asking to hear them repeatedly.

- May sing parts of songs (often not on pitch), but seldom sing with a group.

- Enjoy experimenting with sounds, with everything from household objects to musical instruments.

- Can discriminate among songs.

THREE-YEAR-OLDS

- Have greater rhythmic ability.

- Can recognize and sing parts of familiar tunes, though usually not on pitch.

- Make up their own songs.

- Walk, run, and jump to music.

- Enjoy dramatizing songs.

(Continued)

Table 3-1 Developmental Stages of Musical Experiences *(continued)*

FOUR-YEAR-OLDS

- Can grasp basic musical concepts like tempo, volume, and pitch.
- Show a dramatic increase in vocal range and rhythmic ability.
- Create new lyrics for songs.
- Enjoy more complex songs.
- Love silly songs.
- Prefer "active" listening (singing, moving, doing fingerplays, accompanying music with instruments).

FIVE- TO SIX-YEAR-OLDS

- Can reproduce a melody.
- Begin to synchronize movements with the music's rhythm.
- Enjoy singing and moving with a group.
- Enjoy call-and-response songs.
- Have fairly established musical preferences.
- Can perform two movements simultaneously (e.g., marching and playing a rhythm instrument).

SEVEN- TO EIGHT-YEAR-OLDS

- Are learning to read lyrics.
- Can learn simple folk dances taught by adults.
- Enjoy musical duets with friends.
- May display a desire to study dance or play an instrument.
- Can synchronize movements to the beat of the music.
- Can compare three or more sounds.

(Courtesy of Pica, R. [2000].)

a human need to make music and move to it. This need crosses time and culture. People have been making music and dancing since day one in caves and may one day do the same in outer space. Music and movement are lifelong pursuits. Adolescents appear addicted to music and dance while adults are known to hum, whistle, sing in the shower or while driving, play an instrument, and dance. The interest and love for music and movement compensate for any perceived lack of innate talent or ability.

Why Music and Movement Are Important

Why is music important? According to the position paper by the National Association for Music Education (MENC) (1991), music is a natural and important part of young children's growth and development. Early interaction with music positively affects the quality of children's lives. Successful experiences in music help children bond socially, emotionally, and cognitively with others through creative expression in song, rhythmic movement, and listening experiences. Music in early childhood builds a foundation upon which future music learning is built. Encourage children to become active music makers rather than passively watching others perform for or entertain us with their music. Music empowers young children. They can make their own music and construct their own meaning from their musical experiences. Both music educators and early childhood educators agree strongly that music should be a valued and ongoing part of children's experience and learning. Two areas of research that support the importance of music include the idea of a musical intelligence were identified by Howard Gardner and the research on brain development. Music facilitates brain growth and development. Multisensory musical behaviors that involve oral, visual, and tactile movements are concurrent with critical growth spurts in the brain. Multisensory behaviors of singing, moving, playing musical instruments, and listening activate both hemispheres of the young child's brain and optimize learning. If music is vital to brain growth and development, is the force so powerful as to increase intelligence? This is the question surrounding the so-called "Mozart effect." The media have given much attention to the notion of increasing intelligence by playing classical music such as the works of Mozart. Although lacking in supporting research, claims suggest that listening to Mozart for even a few minutes on a regular basis can increase intelligence and subsequent performance on tests of intelligence. The claim appears simplistic and too good to be true. In reality, music may simply serve as a tool for warming up or getting the brain ready to engage with and process information.

What should an early childhood music program entail? According to the position paper by MENC (1991), music education for young children involves a developmentally appropriate program of singing, moving, listening, creating, playing instruments, and responding to visual and verbal representations of sound. The content of such a program should represent music of various cultures in time and place. Music is an inclusive activity in that everyone joins in at his or her level of comfort and competence. Musical activities can include all children in meaningful ways when they are designed to offer varied levels of participation. According to Humpal and Wolf (2003), music offers varying levels of engagement ranging from listening or observing to joining in as an active participant. For example, a child with autistic-like behaviors may be comfortable listening and sitting near other children who are singing but without direct participation.

Creative experiences in music and movement serve two major purposes. First, they meet the needs of the whole child: physically, socially, emotionally, cognitively, creatively, and in the area of language. Second, they help integrate and enrich the early childhood curriculum. When moving to music, children are involved in physical activities—stretching, bending, reaching, hopping, crawling, and leaping, to name a few. Small muscle and fine motor control as well as eye-hand coordination are needed to play musical instruments. Socially, young children may choose to sing and dance with others. This involves taking turns, cooperating, and sharing musical instruments—all important social skills. Multicultural songs and dances extend children's social horizons and help them see the universality among people—all people everywhere sing and dance. An acceptance of how children sing and move fosters their self-acceptance and promotes positive self-esteem. Emotionally, they are also able to express their feelings. Music can have a calming effect on an upset child or provide an outlet for feelings of frustration or anger. For example, children can sing in mad voices or use their bodies to show how mad they are feeling. Cognitively, music helps children develop concepts of fast-slow, high-low, colors, animals, shapes, the alphabet, and numbers, as in counting songs. The patterns heard in music prepare the child for the patterning that underlies math and reading. Learning about themselves and their world can be done in developmentally appropriate ways through the use of music and movement, as opposed to a didactic academic approach. Adults who accept children's attempts at singing and dance send a message that there is no right or wrong way. In turn, this nurtures children's creative development. The language arts, speaking, listening, reading, and writing, are also enhanced through music and movement. Because singing is speech set to music, children's oral language development is also enhanced. Children practice listening and auditory skills like discrimination and memory when learning the words to new songs or attending to music's repetition, rhythm, and rhyme. Music is intimately connected to a young child's emerging literacy. Children can compose and even draw-write their own songs or dance steps. They may also want to write their own books about a favorite song. Song charts based on simple repetitive favorites such as "There Were Ten in the Bed" can facilitate word recognition, reading, and math.

Components of Music and Movement

There are four vital components to a comprehensive music and movement program. These include listening to music, singing, playing instruments, and moving to music.

1. Listening to Music

The previous section on language stressed the distinction between hearing and listening. Although most children are able to hear, not all listen. Hearing is physical in that it involves receiving auditory input. Listening involves the brain's perception of musical input and making sense out of what was heard. Listening is a learned skill. Music contributes to its development and enhancement. Listening involves three related auditory skills: awareness, discrimination, and sequencing. An example of each skill follows. Children demonstrate auditory awareness when they attend to quiet background music played during naptime. Discriminating between and sound made by a drum and a bell reflects auditory discrimination. Children can identify which musical instrument made which particular sound. Children practice auditory sequencing when they repeat a pattern or rhythm clapped out or played by the teacher.

Teachers should discuss music just as they discuss books and art prints. Teachers can ask children to describe what they hear, for example, is it fast or slow? How does it make them feel? Which instruments were used? Do you like this piece of music? As with art and language, music can lead into other activities. For example, children may want to make their own guitar after listening to a guitar solo. They can also extend their musical experience by representing it through art by forming a clay model or painting a picture that captures the musical mood. They can perform their own dance or dramatic rendition of a musical piece such as "The Nutcracker."

Listening to a song is a good preparation for singing. It allows children to learn the words and rhythm. Provide a variety of music for children to listen to. Play music throughout the day. Music with an upbeat tempo will facilitate cleanup. Lullabies by Brahms will set a quiet relaxed tone for rest. Provide more than just children's songs. Introduce children to folk music, jazz, classical music, and music from different cultures. Provide a tape recorder with a jack and multiple headsets for more than one child to use at a time. Color-code instructions (e.g., green dot on play and red dot on stop) to foster children's independent use. Include children's songbooks on tape. Children will enjoy having their individual or small group singing recorded for future playbacks. By listening to a variety of music, children come to learn that music

- can be fast or slow, just like when they walk as opposed to run.
- has tempo, as they compare a lullaby with a march.
- can be loud or soft (they can also sing in a loud or soft voice).
- has a beat, like a clock or their heart.

Stages of Musical Development

MENC (1991) identifies four stages children of musical skills development that parallel those of language development. Music and language have similar roots. First vocalizations such as cries, coos, and babbles are the precursors of song and musical understanding just as they are the precursors of speech and language. The musical stages include awareness, exploration and inquiry, and utilization. First, at the musical awareness stage, children use their senses to touch, manipulate, and gain an initial awareness of musical sound. They do this by playing with a variety of sound sources including musical toys and objects that make noise. Second, the musical exploration stage, children's musical play behaviors include moving, listening, playing rhythm instruments, and singing. This includes singing isolated song fragments and "chime in" phrases. Children perform rhythm patterns and a steady beat. They begin to discriminate basic musical ideas including same/different, loud/soft, fast/slow, and high/low. Third, at the musical inquiry and utilization stages, children begin to translate musical understandings through singing, moving, and playing rhythm instruments. They also can follow song pictures and puzzles and begin to verbalize the elements or characteristics of music such as melody and rhythm. They engage in more complex problem solving processes involving music and music making as well as translating familiar musical ideas to unfamiliar context.

2. Singing

Wolf (1994) believes that children progress from listening to tagging on, which is followed by joining in, and culminates in independent singing. According to this framework, children learn to sing by first listening to songs sung to them. Toddlers soon start to "tag on" to songs that they hear and like. They may echo bits and catchy parts while at play. Preschoolers join in singing as part of a group. Eventually most young children not only enjoy singing with a group but are equally comfortable singing alone. This usually occurs by kindergarten. Children can sing alone, with others, or while listening to a record or tape. Because music and movement are closely related, choose songs that are accompanied by activity. For example, children enjoy hammering with their fists while singing "Johnny Works with One Hammer" and the finger and hand motions that accompany the "Itsy Bitsy Spider" or "Wheels on the Bus." It is not required that the teacher be a gifted singer. Children are more interested in an enthusiastic model who loves to sing. Children are not critical if you cannot sing well, because they have a very limited singing range (a few notes above middle C) and often sing off-key when notes are too high or too low. Begin by learning the song well before presenting it to the children. When introducing a new song, sing slowly and clearly, repeating the song. Then invite the children to sing along. Select songs that you like and ones based on your children's interests, abilities, and developmental stage. Young children enjoy songs that are silly and involve body actions or their names. Select short, simple, active songs with a limited musical range, repetition, and simple rhythms. Examples include "Do You Know the Muffin Man?" and "If You're Happy and You Know It." Each of these allows for creative improvisation. Have parents teach you songs in other languages and help translate songs learned in English into a second language. Sing throughout the day during transitions and routines like arrival time, group time, play time, cleanup time, and departure time. Continue singing when outdoors. Plan for music but also allow for spontaneity. Break into a song when it begins raining or when welcoming back a child who has been hospitalized. Sing familiar songs but encourage children to creatively invent their own. Work with small groups in creatively changing the words to familiar songs just for fun or to fit a routine or transition. For example, to the tune of "Are You Sleeping, Brother John?" try singing "Are you cleaning, are you cleaning, Jay and Kate, Leslie and Don?" Or, "This is the way we clean up our room, clean up our room, clean up our room. This is the way we clean up our room on Monday morning." Become familiar with a host of child-oriented popular recordings but do not restrict children's musical diet to pop music, simple finger plays, and rhymes. Certainly, it is a good familiar start, but definitely not enough. Children need a well-balanced and diverse musical menu. Young children will respond to the music of great composers including Mozart, Bach, Chopin, Beethoven, Strauss, Grieg, Ravel, Tschaikovsky, and Prokofiev. Why classical music? It is not only soothing but there is some indication that classical musical has an effect on brain development. Find your favorite composers and identify selections for your children. Visit a children's bookstore where tapes and CDs feature classical selections that have been specifically chosen for use with young children. Edwards (2002) recommends playing classical music along with traditional favorites that include:

- Hap Palmer.
- Ella Jenkins.
- Greg and Steve.
- Pete Seeger.
- Lisa Atkinson.
- Sharon, Lois, and Bram.
- Bob McGrath.
- Jose Luis Orozco.
- Raffi.
- Thomas Moore.
- Woody Guthrie.
- David Jack.
- Peter Alsop.

- Linda Arnold.
- Burl Ives.
- Sesame Street.
- Barney.
- Wee Sing.
- Disney.
- Rosenshontz.

Two recommended sources for purchasing music include:

Educational Record Center
888-372-4543
www.erckids.com

Kimbo
800-631-2187
www.kimboed.com

Categories for selecting children's music include traditional and folk songs, nursery rhymes, lullabies, and finger play and body action songs. You may remember some of the traditional and folk songs from your own childhood. The same holds true for lullabies. Some readers may have used lullabies to soothe or help a baby fall asleep. Because nursery rhymes are steeped in Anglo culture, we cannot assume that all children are familiar with them. Finger plays are just that. Children make finger motions to accompany a rhyme. They use other parts of their bodies to make actions for the rhymes. Given the context of traditional nursery rhymes, the words may be abstract and/or controversial. A teacher has the option to change the objectionable wording, avoid using the selection or use the selection as written along with an explanation and critique.

Traditional and Folk Songs:
- "This Old Man, He Played One"
- "Miss Molly Mack"
- "Three Blind Mice"
- "One For the Money"
- "The Farmer in the Dell"
- "One, Two, Buckle My Shoe"
- "ABC Song"
- "Old MacDonald Had a Farm"
- "Hot Cross Buns"
- "Rain, Rain Go Away"
- "Happy Birthday"
- "How Much is That Doggie in the Window? "

Nursery Rhymes:
- "Here We Go Round the Mulberry Bush"
- "London Bridge"
- "Twinkle, Twinkle Little Star"
- "Mary Had a Little Lamb"
- "Jack and Jill"

- "Humpty Dumpty"
- "Little Miss Muffet"
- "Hickory Dickory Dock"
- "Old Mother Hubbard"
- "Baa, Baa Black Sheep, Have You Any Wool?"
- "Jack Be Nimble"
- "Little Boy Blue"

Lullabies
- "Rock-a-Bye Baby"
- "Are You Sleeping?/Frere Jacques"

Finger Plays and Body Action Songs
- "Eency Weency Spider/Itsy Bitsy Spider"
- "Row, Row, Row Your Boat"
- "The Hokey Pokey"
- "Head, Shoulders, Knees and Toes"
- "Teddy Bear, Teddy Bear"
- "Where is Thumbkin?"
- "Let's Go on a Bear Hunt"
- "The Wheels on the Bus"
- "Five Green Speckled Frogs"
- "I'm a Little Teapot"
- "There Were Ten in the Bed"
- "Five Little Ducks"
- "If You're Happy and You Know It"

How to choose? According to Wolf (1994), look for in-tune singing, children's voices, easy-listening adult vocals, and simple instrumentation. Songs can integrate and extend into other curriculum areas. Singing "Old MacDonald Had a Farm" can tie in with a discussion of animals or life on a farm. "The Wheels on the Bus" can introduce a unit on transportation or vehicle safety. "Mary Had a Little Lamb" can lead to a discussion of rough and soft with children decorating their own lambs with cotton balls. This activity extends a music-based book into the realm of art. A book-based curriculum connects literacy with the creative arts.

Story Songs. Rhythm is important to **story songs** because it provides structure. Creative teachers can take familiar songs and change words or ideas to match their curriculum. Singing is also paired with movement or visual aids that can foster multisensory learning and the use of multiple intelligences. Begin by modifying or borrowing elements such as the tune from an existing tune. For example, sing the words of the book *Polar Bear, Polar Bear,* by Bill Martin Jr. to the tune of "Twinkle, Twinkle, Little Star." What is the advantage of this strategy? When a teacher sings with the children, as opposed to playing recorded music, she or he can adjust the speed and volume to suit the group. This is an effective strategy for use with children with language delays, hearing loss, cognitive deficits, or for those learning English as a second

language. Some examples of favorite story songs include:

Cabrera, J. Over the meadow
Goodhart, P. Row, row, row your boat
Hoberman, M. A. The Eensy-Weensy Spider
Hoberman, M. A. I know an old lady who swallowed a fly
Hoberman, M. A. The lady with the alligator purse
Hoberman, M. A. Miss Mary Mack
Hoberman, M. A. Skip to my Lou
Martin, B. Brown bear, brown bear
Martin, B. Polar bear, polar bear
Raffi: "Baby beluga"
Raffi: "Down by the Bay"
Raffi: "Five Little Ducks"
Raffi: "Shake my Sillies Out"
Raffi: "The Wheels on the Bus"
Westcott, N. B. Peanut butter & jelly: A play rhyme
Sweet, M. Fiddle-i-fee: A farmyard song for the very young
Williams, S. I went walking

3. Making Music with Rhythm Instruments

Children love to make music, as evidenced by the popularity of banging on pots and pans. Do not overlook the body as a musical instrument. Children enjoy clapping hands, shaking body parts, stamping feet, slapping thighs, and snapping fingers to music. There are different types of musical instruments that are commercially available. Include both rhythm and melodic instruments in your selection. Drums, tambourines, sticks, triangles, maracas, cymbals, and sandpaper blocks are examples of percussion instruments that make a single sound and can be used to make and keep a beat. Children can play a tune on melodic instruments including a xylophone, a piano, a keyboard, and tone bells. Be sure to include other items that make sounds, including kitchen gadgets, keys, musical toys, music boxes, a metronome, or sound containers. Although commercially available, rhythm instruments can be inexpensively made. Music is integrated with art when instruments are creatively decorated. Instructions for how to make a few simple instruments follow.

rattles—Place dry gourds on a windowsill, turning them every few days. After a few weeks the seeds inside will dry and fall away from the inner skin.

drums—Children can rhythmically pound any of these: milk cartons, coffee cans, oatmeal boxes, wooden bowls, pots, pans, empty house-paint cans, stainless steel mixing bowls.

shakers—Put beans or pebbles between two paper plates and staple the edges together. Or fill a margarine tub (or any plastic container with a removable lid), paper bag, or plastic stocking eggs with beans or pebbles.

maracas—Place rice or gravel in an empty, clear plastic shampoo or detergent bottle.

rhythm sticks—Children can rap together two pencils or dowel rods.

spoons—Use any two metal spoons.

bells—String jingle bells on a piece of elastic and tie the ends. Wear on wrists or ankles. Or attach to plastic six-pack rings, or through holes punched in toilet paper tubes. Bells can also be sewn onto ribbon strips.

cymbals—Bang together two pot lids or pie tins.

banjo—Stretch several different-sized rubber bands over the bottom of a shoe box and strum.

sand blocks—Glue sandpaper to two wooden blocks.

baton—Roll up a newspaper to make a drum major or orchestra conductor's baton.

gong—Hit an old license plate with a toy mallet.

Children need experience with rhythm if they are to use rhythm instruments successfully. Having young children listen to music and clap out the beat with their hands or tap it out with their feet is a good introduction to rhythm instruments. Provide ample experiences in clapping rhythm patterns to their names, simple poems, and nursery rhymes. For example, Ida's name involves two claps: I (clap) da (clap). When introducing a rhythm instrument, first listen to the music for its rhythmic patterns and then match the beat with the instrument. It is wise to have multiples of rhythm instruments and introduce them one at a time—for example, four tambourines in a small group. This prevents children from just creating noise by playing a group of unrelated instruments together with no regard for rhythm. Children also enjoy having a parade or playing in a band. Children can take turns using the baton to lead the orchestra. Sing "Old MacDonald had a band, ee-i-ee-i-o. And in that band he had a (add instrument)." Or sing "The Farmer in the Dell" with the instruments choosing each other, or "This is the way we play our bells," etc.

4. Moving to Music

**N
A
E
Y
C**

What are movement skills? According to Pica (2004), movement involves three major skill categories: locomotor, nonlocomotor and manipulative. Locomotor skills involve moving the body as whole from one point to another. Walking, running, skipping, galloping, sliding, crawling, and climbing are examples of locomotor skills.

Nonlocomotor or stability skills are executed in place as the axis of the body rotates around a fixed point. Twirling, spinning, stretching, turning, twisting, bending, and stooping are examples of nonlocomotor skills in which children work on balance.

Manipulative skills involve either the large or small muscle groups as well as a combination of both. Bouncing a basketball, throwing, catching or kicking a ball and striking with a bat involve the large muscles. Manipulative skills are usually associated with playing games. Manipulative skills are more difficult than locomotor or nonlocomotor. Because of this Sanders (2002) recommends frequency and repetition as key ingredients in an early childhood movement program.

Children need movement experiences and activities on a daily basis. They also need to revisit and practice core skills to attain mastery. Knowledge of one's body and body parts is also a necessary component to movement exploration. Children need to be aware of their body and what they can make it do along with understanding their relationship to objects and others in their immediate space. As with art, movement also has its own set of concepts or musical elements. These include space, time, and energy or force. Simply put, children move through space with varying degrees of speed and with different levels of force. Children can travel through space both indoors and outdoors. They can also move by remaining fixed in their own personal space. They wiggle their bodies fast or move it slowly (time). They can tiptoe about lightly or stomp their feet (energy or force).

Large motor actions like walking, hopping, swaying, marching, and galloping can be paired with music. Children enjoy moving like animals, vehicles, or characters in a favorite story. Model movement and dance. You need not be a gifted dancer. It is more important to share your love of music and the way your body moves to music. Props help the unsure or shy child. Include hoops, crepe paper streamers, scarves, hats, crowns, fancy costumes, ribbons, magic wands, grass skirts, fans, soft batons for leading the band, pompoms, and lengths of sheer fabric. Streamers taped to outstretched arms make dancing wings. **Creative movement** gives children an outlet for their physical energy, encouraging them to express their feelings and creativity in nonverbal ways. Creative movement activities can be either totally open-ended or teacher-guided. In open-ended activities, children move in ways that are individually meaningful. For example, a teacher can play a tape of *Swan Lake* and watch the children dance, however the music moves them (see Figure 3–12). In teacher-guided activities, the adult provides the stimulus or frame which subtly structures the movement activity. Examples include asking children to move

- like a familiar animal or pet.
- like a familiar vehicle, e.g., motorcycle.

Figure 3-12 Creative movement.

ties, keep developmental appropriateness in mind. It will be impossible for a child to move like a helicopter or an elevator if he or she has never directly experienced one. Remember that images of helicopters or elevators in books or on TV are symbolic images. The symbolic images of cows in books are small, flat, mute animals who do not smell. As such, these vicarious experiences do not advance a child's knowledge of cows. You will be more successful if you structure movement experiences around things children know and have experienced. Children living in rural areas may have well-developed concepts of farm animals, whereas city children may not.

Children also need ample space, including their own personal space in which to move. By extending their arms out around them, children can define their personal space, which others must respect. Remember to move with the children without telling or showing them how to move. There is more than one way to move like a snake. Above all else, remember to provide a psychologically safe environment in which children feel comfortable to trust their creative impulses and move in ways that make sense to them. As with singing, respect the right of children to refrain from participation, especially for those who are shy or unsure.

- like a familiar community helper, e.g., fire fighter or truck driver.
- creatively, like a flying car.
- in ways that enact a nursery rhyme like "Jack Be Nimble" or a simple story like "The Three Little Pigs."
- in pantomime to waking up, getting dressed, eating, or falling asleep.
- in ways that are angry, sad, happy, scared, or surprised.
- as if they were trees swaying in the wind, toast in a toaster, clothes in a dryer, water going down the bathtub drain, or food in a blender.
- with imaginary wings and fly away.
- by making their body grow very tall or shrink very small.
- by staying in one spot and wiggling all over and then becoming perfectly still.
- by moving around hula hoops in slow and quiet ways.
- by using their hands and arms to make rainbows in the sky.
- by becoming very crooked or very soft and squishy.

Solicit children's input in other ways to move. They will tell you ways they know how to move, for example, wiggly. They will suggest concepts, like dinosaurs, for movement. In planning movement activi-

Moving with a Parachute in Creative Ways. A parachute is a good investment and a piece of movement apparatus that has many uses. Get a small parachute; if unavailable, use a tablecloth or sheet. Tie knots at the corners and midpoints to signify places and something to hold. Use with a small group of children to reinforce spatial, directional, and temporal concepts. Some parachute activities include having the children

- hold the parachute high (above their heads) or low (down on the ground).
- lift their arms and parachute as high as possible, release, and then watch as it floats to the ground.
- move the parachute slowly and then very fast.
- bounce lightweight objects like balloons or balls on top of the parachute (either try to keep them on or try to have them bounce off).
- make the parachute get small by walking to the middle and then get big by walking back to their places.
- walk to the right and then to the left while holding the parachute waist high.
- run under the parachute without getting caught.
- extend arms upward and while still holding on, turn around and sit on the ground while the parachute covers them up.

Other recommended props for movement include:

- balance beams.
- balance boards.
- balls: foam, rubber and plastic, different sizes for different purposes.
- bats: plastic or foam.
- beanbags.
- can walkers.
- carpet squares.
- traffic cones.
- crawl-through shapes.
- hockey sticks: foam.
- hoops with small diameters.
- jump ropes.
- launch boards.
- mats.
- music: records, tapes, CDs and DVDs.
- paddles: foam.
- parachutes.
- punchball balloons.
- rhythm sticks: wooden or plastic.
- ribbon sticks.
- scarves.
- bowling pins: plastic or two liter plastic soda bottles.
- scoops or plastic milk jugs that have cut away.
- stilts.
- streamers.
- wedges: foam.

Music and Movement Center. Provide a soft, comfortable place for children to listen to and make beautiful music as well as move and dance. See Figure 3–13. Location is crucial. Select an area where children making noise will not disturb those involved in quiet activities. If inside space is very limited you may want to think about an outdoor music and movement center. A music cart allows you to take your music program outdoors on good weather days. Include:

- record player and records.
- tape players which are designed for children, and easy to operate along with a jack box, and several head phones.
- tapes labeled with title and picture. Remove the tabs from the tops of cassettes so tapes cannot be recorded over.
- CD player and CDs for older children.
- piano (highly recommended but not always available).
- rhythm instruments: both percussion and melodic. Percussion include maracas, tambourines, castanets, finger cymbals and rhythm sticks. Melodic include bells, small keyboards, tone bars, xylophones, and piano (if available). Hang your rhythm instruments on a pegboard. Draw an outline around each to show children where to store them. Cup hooks under a shelf are good for hanging small items like castanets and triangles. Include homemade rhythm instruments.
- materials for making their own instruments.
- a small selection of papers and writing tools for children to make their own songbooks or sheet music. Blank staff paper, pencils, and markers will encourage older children to write their own music.
- books on music, musicians, and musical performances. Include other visuals such as songs on charts.
- multicultural picture books of the country where the music and instruments come from.
- Plexiglas® mirrors so children can watch themselves move and dance.
- props including scarves, streamers, and lengths of fabric.
- a prop box of fancy dress-up clothes that facilitate movement and dance, such as a tutu.
- a small selection of mark making materials to encourage children to combine drawing with music.
- pictures of children and adults singing, dancing, playing instruments, and listening to music. Include male and female dancers and musicians from many cultures.

Provide ample time for children to discover and make music. To round out your music and movement program, take children on field trips where they can hear music and see dance performed. If not possible, invite in family members and community volunteers

Figure 3-13 A creative place for music and movement.

who sing, dance, or play musical instruments. This is a good way to have family members share their cultures' music and dance.

Teacher's Role. Recommended strategies and aspects of the teacher's role include the following:

- Set up a physically and psychologically safe environment in which children can be free to express themselves creatively through music and movement.
- Value music and recognize that an early introduction to music is important in the lives of children. All children have the potential to be music makers and music appreciators.
- Model an interest in and use of music in daily life.
- Model an interest in music. Be an active participant not a passive spectator. Your positive attitude and enthusiasm will be contagious. Interest and enthusiasm are key attributes.
- Recapture your own "musical child" and sing, move, play, and dance without inhibition. Be confident and lose yourself in the musical moment. Take a musical risk and let yourself get caught up in the musical aesthetic. Children will follow your lead.
- Accept and validate children's creative musical expression by smiling, nodding, and joining in.
- Be confident in one's own level of musical ability. Children are looking for a music partner, not a trained singer, dancer, or musician.
- Be willing to improve your musical skill and stretch your musical tastes.

- Seek assistance in acquiring and using appropriate music resources. Invite parents to share aspects of their musical heritage.
- Use developmentally appropriate songs, rhymes, chants, singing games, and musical books, and rhythm instruments.
- Encourage spontaneous music by singing, dancing, and making music with them.
- Use developmentally appropriate musical materials and teaching techniques.
- Find, create, and/or seek assistance in acquiring and using appropriate music resources.
- Create a musical learning environment. Structure the indoor and outdoor learning environment to include music/movement.
- Be sensitive and flexible when children's interests are diverted from your original plan.
- Sing with the children, do fingerplays, and take an active music part during transitions, center time, and group/circle time.
- Expose children to a variety of musical forms and compositions including folk, classical, jazz, and alternative.
- Base activities on children's interests. Empower them. Let children choose their own partner, select the songs to be played, and change the way to use props or play a game.
- Weave music throughout your day and curriculum. Extend children's ongoing projects by adding music and movement to their theme.
- Provide opportunities for different levels of participation to include all children.
- Provide adequate time for sustained practice and repetition of key skills while slowly introducing new ones.

Teacher's Role in Children's Play: A Delicate Balance

According to Balke (1997), the younger the child, the more important the adult's involvement in their play. Yet what exactly should that role be? Jones (1993) says the teacher's role in children's play should be nondirective. She believes that adults who take over or monopolize play are denying children their need to invent or construct it for themselves. Because children do benefit from adult input into their play, Jones recommends the following five strategies.

1. setting the stage

2. adding props and dramatic ideas

3. helping with problem solving

4. observing and talking with children about their plans and ideas

5. helping children invent new plans or rework old ones based on their observations of children at play

She identifies the importance of adults sharing and modeling their own playfulness without overwhelming children or performing for them. Herein lies the delicate balance.

To make your music and movement program culturally responsive be sure to

• integrate music from other cultures into your daily program.

• learn and sing songs from different cultural groups.

• play and display musical instruments used by various cultural groups.

• learn the dances and rhythmic movements of cultural groups represented in the wider community.

Suggested multicultural rhythm instruments include:

Agogo bells (Africa)

Ankle/wrist bells (Native American)

Balaphon xylophone (West Africa)

Cactus rain sticks (Chile)

Coconut shells and strikers (Caribbean)

Den den drum (Japan)

Djembe tone drum (West Africa)

Floor tom-tom (Native American)

Steel drum (Trinidad)

Wood guiro and scratcher (Mexico)

Wood maracas (Cuba)

Zulu mariba/thumb piano (Africa)

Neely (2002) recommends the use of musical conversations in which teachers speak musically to children. They sing, speak rhythmically, more expressively, and play instruments throughout the day. They also comment, foster decision making, provide choices and suggest option and facilitate problem solve. These scaffolding strategies help children construct meaning from their musical experiences.

Examples of these music-based teachable moments include:

* modeling expressive and rhythmic speech as children with transitions, group or circle time and choice time.

* encouraging children to sing, move, dramatizing stories, or adding instruments as they bring to life words in a story or poem.

* improvising or making up new songs or changing familiar ones. Sing high, then low; soft, then loud. Change the words of a familiar song and/or change the melody. Play with songs just as you would experiment with clay: pinching, pulling, flattening it. There is no one right way to play with clay. The same holds true for a song.

FACILITATING CHILDREN'S CREATIVE EXPRESSION

Teachers can build on children's creative drive by implementing the following strategies.

1. Provide ample blocks of time for creative expression. Children need large blocks of time to create and re-create. Being hurried or pressured to begin or finish works against the creative impulse. Children also need time to start, change, and return to their creative processing.

2. Provide ample space indoors and outdoors for children to express their creativity. Space should be fluid and flexible allowing for spontaneous activity which may extend between learning centers. For example, block building may extend into dramatic play.

3. Provide resources including open-ended toys, props, materials, and creative junk. Children cannot create from workbook pages.

4. Set the stage for creative expression by providing a psychologically safe environment. Be accepting of children's processing. Give them permission to be different and to do things their way, as long as their health and safety are not at risk.

5. Play a variety of roles. Observe and record individual children as they create. Be a player and participant in children's play, without taking over.

6. Comment on and interpret the content and processes of children's play. Provide emotional support and facilitate negotiation and problem solving. Expand play activities by offering suggestions and questions. Extend play into all areas of your curriculum. Scaffold children's play to foster growth and development. Match your observations with well-timed interventions that skillfully combine children's present level of functioning with an optimal challenge or next step.

ART MARK MAKING

Mark making is a term used to refer to the variety of artistic marks that young children make. Young children begin by making scribbles or unrecognizable marks and progress to recognizable shapes and forms. Scribbling is important both in itself and as practice for later printing, writing, and drawing. Scribbling is to drawing and printing or writing as babbling is to talking and crawling is to walking. Most young children will have some experience with using crayons, pencils, markers, or pens at home.

Children need large sheets of paper to make movements with the entire arm. Later, they will develop hand coordination and fine motor control. Crayons are recommended for the beginning mark maker. Colored pencils are too long and thin and have a soft point. They are hard to control, and the points break easily. The advanced mark maker can be given colored pencils for making precise drawings. Scribblers need crayons, but not a wide array of colors. Often, one dark color is enough for making marks. Their interest will be in making marks and strokes rather than using a variety of colors. Crayons will be peeled, sucked, and broken. Actually, scribblers need peeled crayons so that they can use both the tips and the sides and bottoms to make a variety of marks.

There is no one best position for mark making. Older infants and toddlers enjoy sprawling on the floor on their tummies and marking with crayons on a large piece of paper. This setup can accommodate four mark makers at any one time, one at each side of the paper. Others may enjoy kneeling on the floor while marking. Easels are not just for painting. Some children may be most comfortable standing while making marks. Others will prefer to stand or sit at a table (see Figures 3–14, 3–15). The seated position is most appropriate for the older, experienced mark maker, since it requires more-restricted small muscle movement. Standing, reclining, and kneeling permit greater whole body involvement and movement while marking.

Children make marks with a variety of tools

- pencils
- crayons
- chalk
- markers

Pencils

colored—for advanced mark makers

drawing—#2 for making marks

erasers—to be used sparingly, not in striving for perfection

grips—three-sided pencil holders, more important for printing than for artistic mark making

lead—#2 for making marks

primary—thick; may be too heavy for smallest hands

Chalk

chalkboard—good for marking with long, sweeping strokes

colored—for marking on chalkboard and on black, white, and colored construction paper

pastels—leave a soft, smooth, velvety line; not recommended for beginners. Use to draw on cloth or paper but not chalkboard. Pastels provide the best of

chalk and crayons. They are powdery but do not rub off like chalk. They are not as hard as crayons but are just as colorful and brilliant.

white—for marking on chalkboard and on black and colored construction paper

> **Hint:** Chalk can be used wet or dry. Chalk is messy, and older children will enjoy blending colors made with chalk. Chalk needs a fixative. Brushing liquid starch or buttermilk on the paper first will help the chalk adhere. Chalk can also be dipped into either of these fixatives and then applied. Children tend to dislike the smell of buttermilk. Spraying with hair spray will also help the chalk adhere. Use hair spray outdoors and sparingly.

Figure 3-14 Being creative while seated at an art table.

Figure 3-15 Making marks with chalk.

Hint: Chalkboard paint is available at hardware stores. You can paint on your own chalkboard surface.

Hint: Like crayons, chalk will quickly break, especially if loosely thrown into a box. A piece of foam rubber can make a chalk holder. Use a scissors point to carefully bore small holes or openings into the foam rubber. Insert one piece of chalk into each hole. Make sure that the chalk fits tightly in an upright position.

Crayons and Accessories

Chunk-o-Crayon—a small, square stick of heavily pigmented color; comes in primary colors, black, and a rainbow of colored specks; good for wide strokes and rubbings

Cray Away—washable crayons, water-soluble. Or dip in water for watercolor effects.

crayon melter—commercially available

crayon sharpener—save the colored shavings!

Easy-Grip or Chubbi Stump—look like small ice-cream cones and fit tiny hands

Easy-Off—can be removed from washable surfaces, e.g., walls; good for use at home

fabric—for marking directly on cloth, or use on paper and then transfer to fabric with a hot iron

fluorescent—bright, vibrant colors

food-warming tray—for special melted-crayon activities

grater—for shaving crayons

hexagonal—six-sided crayons; will not roll and are a good size for little hands

jumbo or extra large—may be too big and heavy for youngest

nonroll—for children working on slanted surfaces or who find the major use of crayons is for rolling

So Big—first crayons for older infants and toddlers

standard size—thin and prone to break with pressure

thick or large—sturdier than standard

triangular—long, three-sided, good for wide, sweeping strokes

Hint: Young children do not need large boxes of crayons with every color under the sun. Colors, shades, and tints can be made by using the basic set. Children or parents assume that more and bigger is necessarily better. This is not the case with crayons.

Hint: Some children enjoy keeping their own basic set of eight crayons in a cigar-box-type container in their cubbies. However, some teachers feel that it is important to provide a mass of crayons and encourage children to share. Add exotic and metallic colors such as silver, gold, copper, and bronze.

Hint: Never throw away a broken crayon. They can be melted down and made into new ones. Place several small, peeled, broken crayon pieces into a nonstick muffin tin resting in a skillet of boiling water. Or line metal muffin tin openings with tinfoil to eliminate sticking. The skillet rests on a hot plate. Colors can be kept separate or creatively combined in the muffin tins. Remember the principles of color mixing. Mixing purple and brown will yield a dark color. Let cool. Carefully remove and use as a fat crayon. Remember, never melt crayons directly over heat; they are highly flammable. Or place the muffin tin in the oven at 250° F until the crayons have melted. Turn off the oven when crayons are completely melted. Remove the muffin tin when the oven is cold. Remove crayon cookies by pushing on the bottom of the muffin tin. Remind children that these tempting cookie-type creations are made of wax and are not to be eaten.

Layers of different melted colors can also be poured into a film container or pill bottle. Carefully pour from a muffin tin or use an old pot, making sure to wipe it clean between color meltings. Let harden between layers of color. Put it in the refrigerator to hasten hardening. Gently tap the bottom to remove, or quickly dip in hot water to loosen. The result will be a lipstick-shaped crayon that produces stripes and rainbow colors when used on its side. Or broken crayons can be slowly melted together in a plastic egg carton placed on a cookie sheet in the hot sun. Or pour melted crayon wax into a sturdy paper cone. Wrap several layers of sturdy paper into an ice-cream cone shape. Tape securely. Pour in layers of colored wax. Carefully unwrap the paper when the colored cone is hard. Small colored cones will fit nicely into small hands. Remind children that these are special crayons and not food.

Hint: To make a crayon egg, carefully poke a pin through both ends of an egg. Blow out the yolk and white of the egg. Place in the egg carton. Enlarge the opening on the top of the egg so you can pour melted crayon wax into the empty egg. To melt wax, place unwrapped, broken crayons or stubs in an empty coffee can. Place the can in a pan of boiling water. When melted, pour into the egg mold. (Do not do this part with children.) When crayon wax has hardened, peel off the eggshell.

Hint: Children will inevitably break crayons to hear the pleasurable popping noise and peel the paper off. It is a way for them to exhibit their power over objects. They can break a crayon in two with their own bare hands! Thicker crayons are harder to break, but are also more difficult to manage. Removing the paper allows children to use the sides in wide, sweeping strokes. Many parts of a crayon other than the pointed tip can be used. Children may also quickly discard the box, because fitting the crayons back in once they have been removed is difficult and frustrating.

Hint: There is no one best way to store crayons. Maria Montessori could have advocated grouping a mass of crayons by color and sorting each in its own container—for example, all the reds together. She would most likely have provided only the primary colors and encouraged children to mix these basic three to get all others.

Hint: Children who use vigorous hard strokes when coloring with crayons can have their colorful marks polished. Use a paper towel over a

pointer finger and polish the crayon marks until they smear together, blend, and sparkle.

Hint: Peeled, broken crayon stubs can be recycled into crayon creatures. Cover the bottom of one to six cookie cutters with two layers of heavy-duty tinfoil to prevent leaking of melted crayon. Place on a cookie sheet. Fill each cookie cutter with peeled, broken crayon bits and pieces. Mixing colors is an option. Place the cookie sheet in a warm oven for about 10 minutes or until crayons melt and float but are not totally liquid. Place the entire cookie sheet with cookie cutters into the freezer for about 30 minutes. Carefully remove crayon creatures from cookie cutters. Use like crayons. Wash cookie cutters with hot soapy water.

Hint: Soap crayons can be made using mild powdered laundry soap, food coloring or liquid watercolor, and water. Add 1 cup of laundry soap to bowl. Add several drops of color. Slowly add water by the teaspoon until soap is liquid. Stir well. Pour into ice-cube trays. Set in sunny, dry spot for a few days. Allow crayons to harden. Great for writing on sinks or bathtubs.

Markers

Markers are popular mark-making tools for young children, because they can make bright strokes with little pressure. They come in a variety of colors and tip styles and are indispensable to any early childhood art program. Some drawbacks are their relative expense compared with crayons and the fact that they dry out and must be replaced.

Hint: Markers and their tops or caps get easily separated. A marker cap keeper will also help very young children or those with physical disabilities who may have trouble pulling off the caps. To make a marker cap keeper, collect deep plastic meat trays and fill them with plaster of parls (inexpensively purchased from hardware and building supply stores). While it is wet, press in about eight markers, caps down. If the caps are smooth, try wrapping rubber bands around them first. Let dry. This creates a keeper for the markers, makes it easier for children to use them, and avoids the problem of lost tops.

Items to accompany mark-making tools include:

* ruler.
* stencils.
* pencil compass.
* protractors.
* lids and tops (to trace).

Here are some activities for mark making.

Scribbling

Older infants, toddlers, and preschoolers scribble. They make marks for the sheer joy of moving a tool across paper and seeing what happens. They need a variety of mark-making tools and large sheets of paper.

Crayons. Crayons are a preferred medium. They are colorful, responsive to children's movements, and fairly inexpensive. They are always ready for use and do not require mixing or special preparation. Most young children will have experience with them and will automatically be drawn to them. Young children will have their color preferences. Vibrant colors, such as silver, gold, and hot pink, will quickly lose their pointed tips. Young scribblers do well with only the basic primary colors. Yellow is difficult to see when used on white paper.

Crayons are composed of pigmented wax. Dark crayons contain more wax, are softer, and will leave an opaque mark. Light crayons contain less wax, are harder, and will leave a transparent mark. The older mark maker discovers that if you color dark over light, e.g., brown over yellow, the lighter color will not show. The younger mark maker, however, will not be that concerned with color mixing and planning.

Marking with crayons or scribbling will progress in stages. Young scribblers push, pull, and drag their crayons across the paper, resulting in horizontal, vertical, diagonal, and circular marks. The crayons will not be lifted off the paper, and the resulting marks will be continuous, with little or no variation. Beginning scribblers will often look away while marking, being more interested in the muscular activity itself than in the finished product. Details and small marks will be largely absent because of limited fine muscle development and control. With time, practice, and control, shapes and symbols begin to be included. De-

tails and variations appear. Some variations on the use of crayons include:

* scribbling with a crayon in each hand.
* marking with a crayon in the nondominant hand—for example, a righty uses a crayon with left hand.
* using two or more crayons that are tied together with a rubber band.
* making notches or grooves in a peeled crayon and using it in a sideways, swirling, or up-and-down motion.
* mixing colors by blending or overlaying crayons on white paper.
* using crayons on colored construction paper.
* varying the pressure on crayons, coloring heavily or lightly, and noticing the effects of pressure on the types of marks.
* polishing crayon marks by rubbing them with a tissue to make a shiny surface.
* using all sides of the crayon: the point for small dots; the flat end for larger round circles; the side for sweeping, wide strokes; and holding the crayon in the middle and rotating it to make bows or large circles.
* using only dots made with a crayon to form a picture, outline, or design.

Musical Scribbling

Children also enjoy scribbling or mark making to music. Make a mark or stroke that shows how the music makes you feel. Most of the previous suggestions also apply to musical scribbling. Make a simple doodle to music. Stop and turn the paper in a different direction. Attempt to continue the design or to complete a picture that the doodle suggests. For example, a mass of looping lines might suggest a snake. A tail and head could be added. Or it could be spaghetti, with the child drawing a fork and plate.

Drawing or Sketching

Older children develop from random scribbling to more purposeful drawing or sketching that is often systematically planned out in advance. Some children may enjoy drawing or sketching

* each other.
* objects in the room.
* a very simple display, such as two stuffed animals.
* school or center experiences, such as a field trip or outdoor play.
* people, places, and things at home.
* numbers, letters, and words.

- using only geometric shapes.
- a new animal made up of two very different ones, for example, a "turtlephant" with a turtle's head and an elephant's body.
- items brought for show-and-tell.

Chalk and Pastels

Older children will appreciate the possibilities of marking with chalk. It is messy, but the colors produced are beautiful, and the possibilities for blending are endless. Children can mark

- with light chalk on dark paper, such as white on black for a snow scene.
- with colored chalk on white paper.
- with dry chalk on wet paper.
- with wet chalk on dry paper.
- with the tip and/or side of the chalk.
- by rubbing or blending chalk dust on a cotton ball (scrape with a dull knife or popsicle stick).
- on rough, textured paper that responds to chalk.
- by dipping the chalk in liquid starch before marking.
- with chalk sticks soaked in a solution of ⅓ cup sugar to 1 cup water for five to 10 minutes before use. The colors will appear more brilliant and tend to resist smudging.
- on paper wet with buttermilk or a combination of canned milk and liquid starch, to add sparkle.
- outdoors on sidewalk and blacktop (it washes away with rain).
- with pastels, which provide a compromise between crayon and chalk. They are fairly solid and come in brilliant colors, but are slightly expensive.

Recipe for Sidewalk Chalk

1 cup of plaster of paris (do not pack)
about ½ cup of cool water
liquid tempera paint
Pour plaster into a disposable margarine container or large paper cup. Stir in most of the water. Add 2 to 3 tablespoons of liquid tempera. Mix well, especially at the bottom. Add a little more water as the mixture thickens. Stir well and pour into small paper cups. Peel paper off when the chalk is dry. Use to mark on sidewalks.

Mural

Making a mural involves many social skills and decision making. How will we share the entire mural space? Who will make what, and where? Murals can revolve around a theme, such as outer space. Young children, however, often depart from the theme. There may be three planet Earths in the mural or animals floating about in space. Often, there will be a second bottom baseline at the top of the mural. This is to be expected. Murals can be the focus of a group story or dictation. Provide a long strip of paper. Place it on the floor in an out-of-the-way spot and encourage each child to make his or her unique contribution. Letters, names, numbers, and words can also be added to the art picture story.

Fence Mural

A fence mural is a good outdoor art activity when weather permits. Several child artists can make their marks at the same time on the same piece of paper. Begin by securing a long, wide, heavy length of paper to a fence. Use lots of strong tape so the paper will not tear, blow away, or fall down. Place containers of markers at intervals on the ground along the base of the fence. Free end rolls of heavy paper are often available from newspaper printers.

Me Marks

Most young children are interested in talking and learning about themselves. This can be part of social studies or a unit on "me." Some related mark-making activities include:

- a self-portrait.
- drawing, making marks, or making self-sketches that show being happy, angry, sad, scared, hurt, lonely, or silly.
- a "me" book that shows things that make me feel one of the previous ways—for example, a separate page with *happy* on it.

A wall mirror will help children notice details, including eye and hair color, clothing, and the presence or absence of freckles and front teeth. Still, even though young children can visually see, they will not necessarily represent realistically.

Object Trace-Over

Much of the artistic junk (see Appendix A) will have a characteristic shape and outline, often geometric in nature. Lids, tops, caps, boxes, and containers can be traced over. The shapes can be creatively combined. Some can be repeated in a sequence or pattern. Some children may prefer to make something out of their traced objects. For example, a series of traced-over circular lids could suggest a caterpillar or wheels on a bulldozer.

Architect's Art

You will need a ruler, pencil, and protractor. Older children can make a number of lines with a ruler and pencil by tracing the arc of a protractor. An interesting design with lines, circles, and arcs will result. Children can add their own designs.

Graph Paper Cube Design

Buy graph paper with large squares or make a series of 1-inch squares on a sheet of paper and photocopy it. Children can be encouraged to think of an object that has a square or rectangular shape or is composed of small boxes. For example, it would be more difficult to make a round swimming pool than a rectangular skyscraper. Sketch out the exterior outline. Fill in the individual squares to complete the picture.

Run, Mark, Run

Children will enjoy using markers on paper towels or thin fabric on which they will blend and run. Place newspaper or cardboard underneath.

Sandpaper Art

Children can use crayons to make heavy marks or a design on a small 4- to 6-inch square of sandpaper. Use fine or medium grade rather than coarse. Press hard, and make solid-colored forms. When the sandpaper is fairly well covered with crayon marks, it can be heated in a warm oven at 250° F for 10 to 15 seconds until the crayon melts. The crayon wax will harden and produce an interesting effect. Also, this activity can be a good tie-in to discussing the effects of heat and temperature change. What happens if we leave our crayons in the sun or on the heater? Will the same thing happen to our pencil? Who knows why?

Glue Design

Make a design using a bottle of liquid white glue on wax paper. Make thick masses, shapes, or forms. Let dry until hard and clear. Decorate the dried glue with thin or fine-line felt-tip pens. The dried and decorated shapes can be carefully peeled off, laced with thread, and hung overhead or worn as jewelry.

Crayon Shavings

Old, broken crayons can be recycled for this activity. Carefully scrape a dull plastic knife or Popsicle stick along the crayon and catch the shavings. Place them on a piece of wax paper and arrange them into a design. Add glitter, ribbon, tissue paper, and a piece of string if a hanging is desired. Place another piece of wax paper on top. An adult can press with a warm iron to melt the wax and seal it. Cut the excess wax paper off or snip it into an interesting shape. Use black construction paper for the outer frame. Hang it over the window and let the light shine through.

Coffee Filter Art

Crayon shavings can also be placed on a flattened paper coffee filter. Place a sheet of construction paper on top. An adult can press with a warm iron. You will get two pieces of art. The heat will melt the crayon wax, and you will have a colored design on a round white background. You will also get a print of that design on your piece of construction paper (see Figure 3–16).

Iron Art

Fold a sheet of drawing paper in half. Mark or color dark and solid on one half. Refold the paper with the colored design inside. An adult can press with a warm iron to make a print. Open. A colored image or print will appear on the other half.

Fabric crayons can be used in a similar way. Mark with fabric crayons on white paper. Color heavily. Place the paper face down over fabric. An adult can transfer the picture onto the fabric by ironing the paper with a warm iron. The wax will melt, and the heat will set the colors into the fabric.

Fabric crayons are designed to be used with fabric. Locate some material scraps—prewashed muslin, an old T-shirt, or white sheet. Staple a small square of old sheet or muslin to cardboard to keep the fabric from slipping. Use the fabric crayons to make heavy marks or a design. Place paper on top and press with a warm iron. The heat will melt the colored wax and set the design. Individual squares could be sewn together into a quilt.

Crayon Etching

Probably everyone has done at least one crayon etching. Older children can fill up a piece of manila paper with a crayon design. Leave no space empty. Polish with a paper towel to help the layer of color adhere. Next, using black crayon, color darkly over the entire surface. Polish again. Last, use a popsicle stick to etch out a design. A fairly thick etched line will reveal a rainbow of colors beneath. This activity is recommended only for older children who have the patience

Still, children need to discuss the dangers and take precautions. Place a large sheet of paper on the warming tray. Children can slowly draw a picture or design. Remind them to keep their hands and arms off the warming tray. The heat from the warming tray will melt the wax, leaving a melted impression. This activity is not dangerous but needs supervision.

Rub-a-Dub-Rub

Rubbing a marking tool over a textured surface produces an interesting rubbed effect. Some people do this over gravestones while studying family or local history. Visitors make rubbings of family and friends whose names are listed on the Vietnam Memorial. Crayons are recommended for children, although chalk could also be used. Hold a piece of paper in place while rubbing. Possible textured surfaces include:

- wood grain.
- tree bark.
- fabric.
- cement and concrete.
- flocked wallpaper.
- leaves and other flat nature specimens.
- screens and grills.
- brick.
- signs with raised letters.
- comb.
- sandpaper.
- mosaic tile.
- leather.
- buttons.
- paper clips.

Some of the author's favorite textured surfaces are:

- embossed greeting cards.
- keys.
- license plates.
- coins.
- corrugated cardboard.
- paper lace doilies and Valentine's Day placemats.

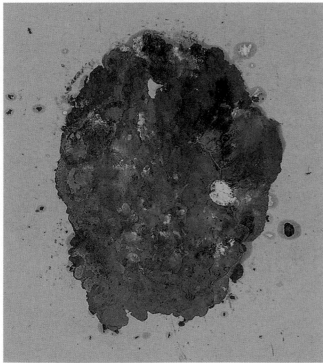

Figure 3-16 Coffee filter art and print.

and muscular strength to color dark over an entire sheet of paper and stay with this activity through its several steps.

Crayon Melt

Crayon-melting activity needs a food-warming tray. The tray will remain warm but not dangerously hot.

Bingo Marker Art

Bingo markers are large markers used to mark off cards at bingo games. Unlike markers with a narrow pointed tip, bingo markers have larger round heads. Their surface is fragile and can easily be ruined if children pound with them. Show children how to gently push down. Bingo markers come in a variety of colors. Use them on coffee filters, paper towels, or paper doilies for an interesting effect.

Lazy Susan Art

Find a base that revolves. Place a round sheet of paper on the round turntable or base. Gently spin the base while holding a marker on the paper. Children will discover that too much pressure will stop the turntable. This is recommended for older children with good coordination because it involves doing two things at the same time. Children can also work in pairs with one spinning and the other marking, and then change jobs.

Record Player Art

An old record player can be used with close adult supervision. Place a paper plate on the turntable and turn on the record player. Have the child hold a marker on the plate as it turns around. The marker can be moved about to create interesting line designs. The child may want to change colors or use more than one marker at a time, perhaps one in each hand. A windup toy record player would be a good alternative to an electric one.

Kaleidoscope Art

Accordion-fold any white absorbent paper such as coffee filters, white tissue paper, or one-ply paper towels. Then fold in half. Use markers to color along the edges and then dip in water. Squeeze out excess moisture. Let dry first before attempting to unfold and open.

Doorknob Hangers

Draw and cut out several basic hanger shapes similar to the ones found on hotel room doors requesting privacy or maid service. Encourage children to use markers to customize their own with pictures or designs. Discuss the concept of privacy, personal space, and ownership. Older children may write messages like "Do Not Disturb" or "Keep Out," especially if they have siblings.

Paper-Bag Backpacks

Make your own backpack using a large brown grocery sack, cut down and folded over at the top several times for strength. Use the strips that are cut off the top as shoulder straps. Staple them firmly in place. Children can use markers to decorate their backpacks. If a backpack tears and cannot be repaired, a new one can be easily made. Miniature versions of the backpacks for dolls and teddy bears can be made using brown paper lunch bags.

Sun Visors

Use a cloth tape measure and find the children's average head size. Measure approximately two-thirds of the way around the forehead, for this is the area that holds the visor. Create a *U*-shaped visor pattern in this size and trace and cut individual visors out of poster board. Visors can be decorated using markers. Cut a piece of elastic about 10 inches long. Staple one end to the visor. Adjust it to fit each child's head snugly. Staple the other end to the visor. Trim away excess elastic or visor. This is a good activity on a hot day or a summer field trip.

Pass-It-On Picture

Fold a piece of white paper into quarters with the top fourth folded down and the bottom fourth folded up. One child uses the top to draw a head. The paper is turned over and passed to a second child who draws the middle. The third child uses the unused portion to draw legs. When the paper is opened, a creative combination of head-middle-bottom appears. Children may need to practice this activity a few times to understand the process.

Magnet Marker

You will need a marker, nut, ½-inch washer, duct tape, clear Plexiglas®, magnet, and blocks for elevation. Place uncapped marker through nut. Place nut and marker on top of washer so that the tip of the marker is exposed. Secure marker, washer, and nut together with duct tape. Place Plexiglas® on top of blocks to make a bridge. Plexiglas® needs to be elevated high enough for child's hands to move easily underneath. Tape a piece of paper to Plexiglas®. Stand marker up on paper. Make sure the washer lies flat against the Plexiglas®. Slowly and carefully move magnet underneath the Plexiglas® to begin mark making on paper.

Tile Marking

Children can make marks with permanent felt markers on a piece of ceramic tile. In turn, these can become holiday gifts. The tiles can be used as paperweights or trivets. Free tiles can be collected from building contractors who have leftover tiles. You can also contact home improvement stores for tile samples or surplus. Choose white or a light solid color. Begin by covering your work surface and have children wear a smock since permanent felt markers will stain. Children should be encouraged to carefully and quickly make their design since the ink in permanent markers dries quickly.

SUMMARY

This chapter continued our discussion of creativity and introduced the reader to three major modes of creative expression other than art. These included play, language, and music and movement, which was further broken down into listening to music, singing, making music with instruments, and moving to music. Play was examined as an elusive term; it was not easily defined. Nor could it be simply contrasted with work, for children work very hard at their play. Instead, criteria for characterizing play were identi-

fied. A discussion of play in its many forms covered physical play, constructive play with blocks, dramatic play, play with natural materials, and games. Ideas for creative play using cardboard boxes, cartons, and accessories, as well as plastic pipe, were suggested. As with play, information on centers, materials, and activities in the curricular areas of language and music and movement were also provided. The chapter closed with suggested ways adults can facilitate and enhance children's creative expression by providing space, time, and resources, along with setting the tone and playing different roles.

Key Terms

constructive play	media literacy	play with natural materials
creative movement	modes of creative expression	sociodramatic play
dramatic play	multiple literacies	story songs
games	physical play	the arts
literacy	play	visual literacy
mark making		

Suggested Activities

1. Observe children at play. Capture a creative episode by writing down what transpired. Use words to record words and actions objectively. Analyze your observation and justify why this episode was creative.

2. Work with a small group of children in implementing one of the following creative activities discussed in this chapter:
   a. boxes, cartons, and accessories
   b. plastic pipe (PVC)
   c. parachute

3. Implement one of the water play activities discussed in this chapter with a small group of children.

4. Work with a partner and implement one of the movement activities discussed in this chapter. This can be done informally during play time or large group time.

5. In small groups, discuss your early childhood memories. Think back to the types of play you engaged in and play materials used. Were your play experiences similar or different from others in your group? Now, think about what children play today. Has play changed since you were a child? How so?

6. Refer to the mark-making activities in this chapter. Select one and provide the necessary materials for a small group of children to engage in a mark-making art activity.

Review

1. List three modes of creative expression other than art.

2. Identify at least three criteria that characterize play.

3. Name five different categories or types of play.

4. List the four components of music and movement.

5. Discuss three different ways adults can facilitate children's creative expression.

6. Stone (1995) identifies three things teachers need to know or be able to do to become play advocates. Identify and briefly explain each.

7. Play was given a major role in children's development according to Vygotsky's (1986) sociocultural theory. Explain four major purposes that play serves.

8. Discuss the concept of multiple literacies. Include a discussion of picture books and visual literacy.

For additional art and creative development resources, visit our Web site at
www.EarlyChildEd.delmar.com

Section Two

Young Children As Artists: A Developmental View

What do you see happening in the picture? A young girl has chosen to visit the easel area. She is painting by herself, although a friend will later join her. The teacher has placed the easels together to encourage verbal and social interaction. The girl in the picture is free to paint whatever she wants and will paint her rainbow with the colors she selects. She may take freedom with her choice and placement of colors—it is her rainbow. That is the essence of creativity.

Why is art important for young children? Is there more to art than just enjoyment? Pretend you are teaching and a parent complains that there is too much emphasis on art in your program. You show her your schedule reflecting an array and balance of activities, but she is still not satisfied. Although her daughter loves art, the mother asks, "Why is art so important?" How would you respond?

Let us review what we know about the developing child and connect this to art. What is the relationship between art and child development? Does art foster the development of the young child physically, socially, emotionally, cognitively, and creatively? Chapter 4, Art and the Developing Child, attempts to answer these questions. Although the child is fragmented into developmental pieces for individual analysis, the focus is on an interactive model of the whole child. Always remember that each child is unique, and our job is to recognize, accept, value, and nurture each child's uniqueness.

Chapter 5, Children's Artistic Development, attempts to explain art by examining different theories and stage sequences. Theories provide explanations for the how, what, and why of children's art. Stages provide a sequence or progression in children's artistic development. Over time, beginning scribbles become more controlled, shapes are combined and detailed, and pictures become recognizably realistic.

Chapter 4

Art and the Developing Child

What do you see happening in the opening picture? What activity has the teacher prepared? It appears that this girl has taken creative liberty at the easel. She found that she could use both her brush and hand to apply the paint. There is no right or wrong way to paint, and this girl has been creative in discovering a new way. The girl featured is developing creatively just as she is growing and developing physically, socially, emotionally, and cognitively.

Objectives

After reading this chapter, you should be able to:

- Discuss how art fosters child development.
- Discuss how art supports development across the developmental domains.
- Identify the benefits of art activities for children with special needs.
- Use an art example to portray a holistic model of development.
- Discuss the developmental progression in a child's use of scissors and how to meet the needs and abilities of young cutters.
- Identify at least 10 different items commonly used in children's art activities that compromise their health and safety.
- Discuss constructivism and constructivist education.
- Recognize the importance of cultural influences on children's learning and classroom interactions.
- Identify three types of knowledge.
- Discuss Vygotsky's sociocultural theory.
- Critique the use of food in art activities.
- Provide experiences for children to process with art materials and tools.

▶▶ INTRODUCTION

N A E Y C

This chapter provides a developmental overview of the young child: physically, socially, emotionally, cognitively, and creatively. According to our **holistic model of child development,** these aspects influence and are influenced by one another. Ideally, we can act on this knowledge in planning art activities. Our present analysis attempts to answer the following question: How does art foster the development of the whole child? Our purpose is twofold: first, to help understand how art can foster a child's development; and second, to use what we know about art and child development in planning our art program and justifying it to ourselves and others. Providing a justification is more than giving a defensive reply: "Art is important, and that's why we spend a lot of time doing it!" If art is important (and it is), we should be able to provide a rationale for studying it. Relating art to a child's development provides one rationale.

DEVELOPMENTAL MODEL

One way to get a working knowledge of young children is to build a model for studying development in the following areas:

physical—including large muscle or gross motor, small muscle or fine motor, perceptual-motor or eye-hand coordination, and sensory development, good health, self-care

social—including a development of the self and relations with others (see Figure 4–1)

emotional—including feelings about self and emotional expression as well as personality and temperament

Figure 4-1 Art can be a physical and social experience.

cognitive—including thinking, problem solving, discovery, language, curiosity, reasoning, and learning

creative—including original thinking, imagination, and verbal and nonverbal expression

This model of development is depicted in Figure 4–2. Still, this neat division or separation is too simplistic. A pie or pizza can be neatly cut into five pieces or slices, but a child's development cannot. Aspects of development interact; they are interdependent and interrelated. It is impossible to study a child's physical development in isolation. Physical development is influenced by and also directly influences social, emotional, cognitive, and creative development. For example, five-year-old Joey has been included mid-year in a regular kindergarten classroom. Muscular

dystrophy has left him confined to a wheelchair. This influences what he can and cannot do physically, but it is not the only influence on his overall development. Joey's physical state affects and is also affected by his social, emotional, cognitive, and creative functioning. Initially, Joey was treated as an outcast. He was shunned by his peers and was misunderstood by his teacher. Slowly, he withdrew. Emotionally, Joey began feeling sorry for himself, wishing he was like his peers. His self-concept suffered, and he began to doubt his personal worth. Cognitively, he began to avoid school tasks, shunned class discussion, and refused to work. Creatively, however, Joey channeled his energies into making original pictures of outer space. Interestingly, Joey always drew himself as the space captain, with

Children With Special Needs and Inclusion Classrooms

In the past, educators referred to children with special needs by using the terms *handicapped* or *disabled*. Both these terms promote negative images and stereotyping. The term *disabled* connotes *not* abled. Currently, the preferred term is *differently abled*. Other acceptable terms include *exceptional children* and *children with special needs*.

Since the passage of the Americans with Disabilities Act (ADA) in 1992, it is against the law for public early childhood programs to refuse to serve a child with special needs. The following terms are often used in discussions about children with special needs in the public schools:

Least restrictive environment: describes a setting that is appropriate for the child and provides the most contact possible with children without special needs

Mainstreaming: the placement of children with special needs in programs having a majority of children who do not

Full inclusion: an approach in which children with special needs are placed in the same programs or classrooms and receive individualized and appropriate services alongside their peers who have no special needs

Full inclusion is very important during the preschool and elementary school years. The underlying assumption is that all children belong together, and children with special needs should be served in the same programs they would have attended if they did not have such needs. A single inclusive system of care, intervention, and education is considered best for all children and their families. Inclusive settings adapt the environment with modifications to welcome children with special needs. Special educators provide services in the regular classroom alongside their regular education colleagues. Advocates of full inclusion believe that the pull-out system of serving students with special needs raises issues. Children are labeled and stigmatized, their programming is fragmented, and regular educators assume little or no ownership for children with special needs.

Inclusion is the law. Still, according to Allen and Schwarz (1999), there are a number of concerns about inclusion. One expressed by parents and teachers is that the requirements of children with special needs may not be adequately met in an integrated program. A second concern is that typically developing children will receive less than their than their fair share of attention. A third concern is that typically developing children will learn inappropriate and bizarre behaviors from atypical children. How do you feel about these concerns? Allen and Schwarz concluded that the advantages of inclusion for both typically developing young children and those with special needs are numerous and well documented in the research literature. However, other questions still need to be addressed. Will teachers have the training, resources, specialists, services, administrative support, and the open, unbiased, diversity-embracing attitude required to make inclusion happen?

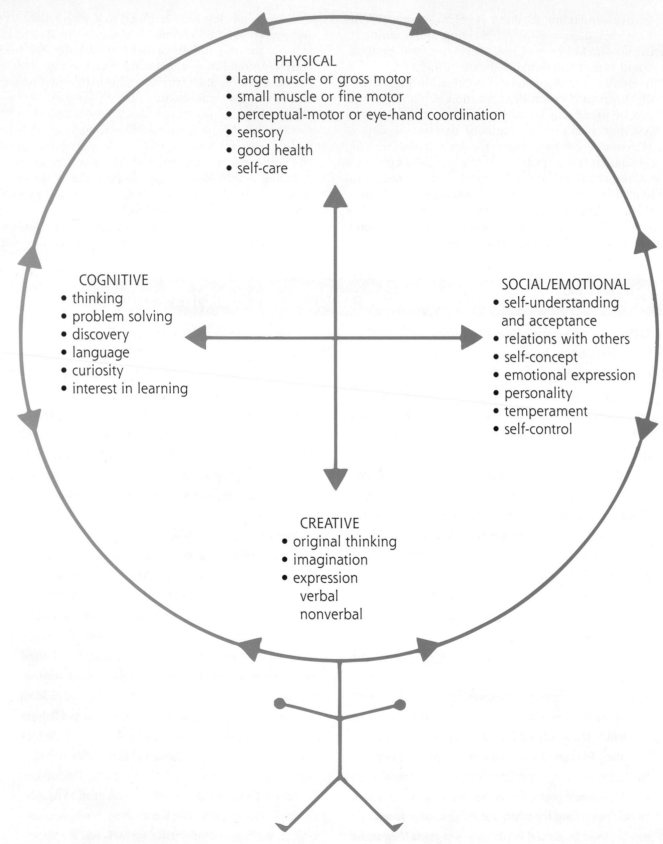

PHYSICAL
- large muscle or gross motor
- small muscle or fine motor
- perceptual-motor or eye-hand coordination
- sensory
- good health
- self-care

COGNITIVE
- thinking
- problem solving
- discovery
- language
- curiosity
- interest in learning

SOCIAL/EMOTIONAL
- self-understanding and acceptance
- relations with others
- self-concept
- emotional expression
- personality
- temperament
- self-control

CREATIVE
- original thinking
- imagination
- expression
  verbal
  nonverbal

Figure 4-2 Holistic model of child development.

massive, powerful legs and strong arms. As in Joey's case, child development is uneven, reflecting developmental spurts and lags. Fortunately, Joey's teacher recognized the problem and her lack of knowledge and enrolled in a course on inclusion. She worked closely with Joey, his mother, his peers, and his resource teacher. The students openly discussed special needs and how all people have strengths and weaknesses, assets and limitations. Over time, the children accepted Joey and welcomed him into their activities. In fact, they became overprotective, and Joey regressed to an earlier stage of helplessness. Continual discussion, support, and encouragement helped Joey become more independent. He began to show improvement in his schoolwork and eagerly reported to his mother what he was learning. Joey became very well liked by his peers, and his self-concept improved.

DEVELOPMENTAL PROFILE

Providing a detailed description of child development is beyond the scope of the present chapter. Instead, a general overview of a young child's physical, social, emotional, cognitive, and creative development will be presented.

Physical Development

Young children are physical beings characterized by much activity and energy. Physical development depends on adequate rest, exercise, sleep, and good nutrition. Young children are intrinsically motivated to effect their environment. They do this primarily through motor activity and sensory exploration.

Infants develop prehension, or grasping, and a pincer grasp that allows them to hold objects between their fingers and opposing thumb. Older infants can hold a stubby crayon and be guided into making marks on paper. Young children are more adept with large muscle or gross motor skills than with small muscle or fine motor skills. They will master easel painting with large brushes before they can use a small brush with watercolors. By age three, most preschoolers can hold a crayon with their fingers, as opposed to the earlier clenched-fist grip. Young children are good doers, talkers, and movers. They have difficulty sitting still, listening, and remaining silent.

Art and Physical Development. Art activities provide experience and practice in developing and refining gross motor or large muscle skills. Art involves physical and manipulative activity. While easel painting, children use their entire arms and upper torsos in

making large, sweeping motions with paintbrushes. Large, long-handled, wide-bristle brushes facilitate this movement. The muscles of the hand are developed while working with clay—tearing, rolling, twisting, coiling, pounding, pinching, and flattening it. Whole hand and arm motions are involved in hand painting, with paint spread and worked with the fingers, whole hand, nails, knuckles, fist, palm, and back of the hand. These gross motor or large muscle skills are perfected before fine motor or small muscle skills. Using the smaller watercolor brush with its shorter handle and narrow point involves greater precision and fine motor control. All the manipulative movements involved in art help develop the hand and finger muscles that are needed to properly hold and use a pencil. Although making children into early printers or writers is not the main purpose of art, art does facilitate the development of this skill.

Scissoring is another physical activity that involves a patterned *open-close* rhythmical movement. Cutting with scissors on a line fosters eye-hand coordination and visual acuity, with the eyes and scissoring hand working together. Children do not develop this important skill without some guidance and practice. See the following page for guidelines.

Practice in developing and refining gross and fine motor skills makes art activities valuable for all children, including those with physical disabilities. The tactile and visual qualities of art activities make them ideal for blind or deaf children. Through art, children can communicate their ideas to others without being dependent on either oral language or strictly visual symbols. For children with fine or gross motor disabilities, most art activities can easily be adapted for their full and enthusiastic participation. Some general guidelines for tailoring art for children with special needs include the following:

1. Visual
   * Verbally describe materials and the ways they may be used.
   * Engage in art activities along with the child while verbally describing your actions.
   * Encourage children to manipulate items as you talk. For example, finger paint may feel cold and repulsive if the child is not prepared for the experience and has no visual cues.
   * Keep art tools within reaching distance.
   * Use the buddy system and pair up sighted and blind children.
2. Auditory
   * Model the process. Demonstrate in precise ways, especially if several steps are involved.
   * Face the child when speaking and use facial gestures for emphasis.

- Communicate with children about their art using sign language, lip reading, and other signals and gestures they understand.
- Combine verbal, visual, and physical cues. For example, say, "I'm painting while moving a brush in an up-and-down motion at the easel."

3. Physical

- Allow for using materials in different ways, such as lying on the floor over a bolster.
- Tape a group of crayons or markers together for easier grasping.
- Apply nonskid tape, sandpaper, or corrugated cardboard to marking instruments to ensure a better grip.
- Tape the child's paper to the work surface to prevent sliding.
- Encourage paper tearing or provide precut shapes for children who are unable to use scissors.
- Provide finger paint and soft play dough for easier manipulation.
- Allow the child to hold the brush in his or her mouth instead of the hand if preferred.
- Model the process for the children.
- Gently guide the child's hand when manipulating an art tool.
- Put the child in control by asking how he or she wants the tool to move.

According to Karnes (1993), the value of art activities for children with special needs cannot be overempha-

sized. However, because art may be a new experience for some children with special needs, a good beginning is talking about the art media and modeling how to use the materials. As with all children, the aim is to first make them feel comfortable and successful. After this, provide time and space for them independently to explore, discover, and create. Remain a resource and consultant to them, offering assistance as needed.

Art Safety. No discussion of physical development or child development would be complete without a discussion of health and safety. Growing up healthy and safe is a major component of physical development. The following guidelines ensure art experiences which do not compromise a child's physical health and safety.

glitter—Glitter is not recommended. The small pieces are sharp and can easily scratch the eye. Children often have glitter on their fingers and then rub their eyes. If you decide to use glitter, provide ample supervision and use with children aged four and older. Provide shakers for dispensing glitter onto glue rather than using their fingers. Remind children to wash their hands thoroughly when finished using glitter.

knives or sharp objects—Children should not use knives, sharp scissors, or objects such as a compass.

An Artist With Special Needs

French Expressionist artist Henri Matisse was an artist with special needs. When this painter became ill, he found it too painful to stand and paint at an easel. Rather than give up his art, Matisse modified and adapted his artistic medium and technique. Confined to his bed or wheelchair, Matisse began to make collages with shapes he cut from paper. His art products were collaborative efforts in that his assistants painted the cut shapes. Matisse is a good role model for young artists with special needs. Read books with photographs of Matisse as well as samples of his art, including the following:

Boutan, M. (Ed.). (1996). *Art activity packs: Matisse.* San Francisco: Chronicle Books.

De Paola, T., & Lear, E. (1991). *Bonjour Mr. Satie.* New York: Putnam.

Flux, P. (2002). *Henri Matisse.* Portsmouth, NH: Heinemann.

Hyde, M. E. (1996). *Matisse for kids.* New York: Pelican.

Laden, N. (1998). *When Pigasso met Matisse.* San Francisco: Chronicle Books.

LeTord, B. (1999). *A bird or two: A story about Henri Matisse.* Grand Rapids, MI: William B. Eerdmans.

Merberg, J., & Bober, S. (2002). *Magical day with Matisse.* San Francisco: Chronicle Books.

O'Connor, J., & Hartland, J. (2002). *Henri Matisse: Drawing with scissors.* New York: Grosset & Dunlap.

Raboff, E. L. (1991). *Henri Matisse.* New York: HarperCollins.

Sturm, E., & Hoena, B. (Eds.). (2003). *Matisse (Masterpieces: Artists and their works).* Mankato, MN: Capstone Press.

Venezie, M. (1997). *Henri Matisse.* New York: Scholastic.

Cutting with Scissors

Cutting with scissors is a difficult developmental task for many young children (see Figure 4–3). Using scissors gives children a feeling of power and mastery. Scissors, once a taboo or "no-no," now become an acceptable tool if used properly. Some guidelines for helping children cut and for selecting proper equipment include the following:

NAEYC

1. Tearing paper is a good starting point for young children. Torn pieces can be pasted on paper or cardboard to form a collage, as seen in Figure 4–4. Tearing paper is itself an important skill that need not be eliminated when a child learns to cut.

2. Cutting thin, pliable play dough is a good introduction to using scissors.

3. Snipping or fringing paper is a beginning step in using scissors with paper. Give children a narrow $\frac{1}{4}$- or $\frac{1}{2}$-inch-wide paper strip. Show them how to make a single cut or snip into the paper. Children enjoy snipping off small pieces that can be pasted. Small snips into a wider 1-inch strip will produce fringe. Hole-punched computer paper sides are ideal for snipping and fringing. Paper ribbon has more body than paper and is easily cut into confetti.

4. With practice, the young child will be able to make repeated snips in a sequence or line. Draw a thick, straight line on paper, and show children how to follow it while cutting. It does not matter if children stray from the line. The aim is to help them coordinate repeated snips into a continuous cutting action.

5. Advanced cutters can practice cutting wavy, bending, or angular lines. Children can also practice cutting out geometric shapes.

6. Cutting along interior lines, such as the eyes in a mask or paper-bag puppet, is too difficult. It is also potentially dangerous, because children are prone to begin the hole by poking with the point of the scissors.

7. Rules for the proper use of scissors need to be established, discussed, and posted in words or pictures or both. Rules include:

- Scissors are used only for cutting paper.
- Walk when carrying scissors. Running with scissors is very dangerous. If you fall while running with scissors, you or someone else could get poked or stabbed.
- There is a right way to hold and pass scissors. Hold the closed points in your own hand, pointed down, when carrying scissors or passing them to someone else.

8. A scissors rack provides safe storage for scissors and makes scissors easy to get and return to their upright position. Metal stands are commercially available at a modest cost. Scissors that are merely placed in a box tend to tangle together. An egg carton or a coffee can with a plastic lid can substitute for a metal scissors rack. Over time, however, the holes will tear from repeated use, and the makeshift rack will need to be replaced.

9. Various types of scissors are commercially available. Blunt scissors have rounded ends. Clip-type scissors have one pointed and one rounded end. Sharp scissors have two pointed ends. There are different scissors for different cutting needs and abilities. For example, smaller 4-inch scissors with rounded tips are safe for use by young children. Their blades are fairly dull, but their metal handles may pinch or irritate the skin.

- Scissors with rubber-coated finger holes are more comfortable and will not hurt.
- Plastic safety scissors are lightweight, inexpensive, comfortable, and easy to use.
- Squeeze-type scissors have an easy-grip, continuous-loop handle. A gentle squeeze with two hands, the fingers and palm of one hand, or the thumb and fingers of one hand will cut. The two blades are blunt and fairly small. They are good for snipping and fringing. Extensive cutting will take more squeezing and hand activity than when using scissors with longer blades.

(Continued)

Cutting with Scissors (continued)

10. Some young children, including those with special needs and/or poor fine motor coordination, have more difficulty learning to cut than others. Merely observing someone else cut or trial-and-error practice may not be enough. Try using double-handled training scissors with four rubber-coated finger holes. The teacher and child cut together as one. Over time, these children may graduate to using a single pair of scissors.

11. Both right- and left-handed scissors should be made available. It is very difficult and frustrating for a "lefty" to hold and cut with scissors designed for a "righty."

12. Children's 5-inch pointed metal scissors are longer, heavier, and sharper. The more-skilled cutters in

kindergarten and the primary grades may prefer these.

13. Some young children have difficulty holding scissors in the air and working both blades. Children who find scissors heavy or awkward can rest the bottom blade on the table and let only the top finger do the work.

14. Some papers are easier to cut than others. Very lightweight papers, including tissue and cellophane, are flimsy, difficult to cut, and will tear. Cardboard, posterboard, and wallpaper are too thick and resistant for most children's strength and scissors. Manila, butcher paper, newspaper, newsprint, and drawing paper are recommended for beginning cutters. Skilled cutters can move on to construction paper.

Figure 4-3 Cutting with scissors can be a physical challenge.

Figure 4-4 Tearing paper is an alternative to cutting with scissors.

electricity—Young children should not use appliances that are plugged in to the wall and generate heat. Examples include a hot plate, electric skillet, or iron. These could be used with older school-age children provided there is one adult supervisor for each child in the activity.

hot glue gun—Liquid glue is preferred because it is difficult for a child visually to determine when a glue gun is hot enough to use. Glue guns can be used with older school-age children provided there is one adult supervisor for each child in the activity. Glue guns with a "cool" setting are also

recommended but still require supervision because electricity is involved.

rubber cement—Rubber cement is often misused as an inhalant and should not be provided.

balloons—Balloons are very dangerous for toddlers and other young children who tend to put things in their mouths. Pieces of popped balloon are very inviting and may resemble candy or chewing gum to children with strong oral needs.

powder paints—Paints in powder as opposed to liquid form pose a threat. The fine powder granules may either promote an allergic reaction or trigger a respiratory condition such as asthma. They also pollute the air. Children should neither mix nor directly use paint in its powder form. Adults should use a mask when mixing and use up all powder paint at each mixing.

nature items—Some flowers and leaves are poisonous if ingested. Nature items can be used in art projects provided there is ample supervision.

meat trays—Recycled meat trays serve many uses in early childhood programs. They can hold collage items or become the background for a junk collage. They can be used as paint containers if lined with paper towels for a printmaking activity. They also make great frames.

It is now believed that plastic foam trays that once held any kind of raw meat or fish may carry bacteria that cause illness. Plastic foam meat trays are very porous and hold more bacteria and juices than clear plastic trays.

Why put the children at risk? What should be done? You can eliminate most of the bacteria by cleaning the trays antiseptically. The trays should be washed with soap and hot water, rinsed in a solution of two teaspoons of chlorine bleach per quart of water, and then rinsed again in warm water to remove the bleach residue. Or it might be simpler to use trays that held fruit, vegetables, or baked goods.

crayons—Tests conducted show that three major brands of crayons scribbled with and nibbled on by millions of children worldwide contain asbestos. The asbestos is most likely a contaminant of the talc that most companies use in crayons as a strengthener for the paraffin and coloring agents. The dangers of asbestos are well known. Tens of thousand of miners, shipyard and construction workers, and their family members have died of asbestos-related diseases. The amount of asbestos found in crayons was far lower than the exposures received by workers, but studies have shown that infants and children are far more susceptible to toxins and carcinogens than adults. Toxic material has been found in crayons before, and 11 brands of crayons, all produced overseas, were ordered off store shelves because lead was found in the pigments. Lead has been proven to cause brain damage in infants and young children. The response to the findings has ranged from denial and disbelief to grave concern with a commitment to further investigation.

Art Poisoning. Many art supplies used by young children can be toxic. Examples include rubber cement, permanent felt-tip markers, pottery glazes, enamels, spray paints, lead-based supplies, and wheat wallpaper paste, among others. These toxic materials can be inhaled, ingested, or absorbed through the skin. Young children are at high risk for many reasons.

1. They are still growing and have a very rapid metabolic rate. They will absorb toxic materials into their bodies more readily than an adult.
2. Their brain, lungs, and nervous system are still forming and thus are at risk.
3. Young children have lowered body defenses.
4. Their lower body weight puts them at high risk, because a given quantity of a toxic material will be more concentrated in their bodies.
5. Young children may be impulsive, engage in thumb sucking and nail biting, have frequent hand-to-mouth contacts, and neither understand nor follow the necessary precautions.

Art Safety Guidelines. Art can be a safe and pleasurable experience if guidelines are established and followed. Suggested guidelines for teachers follow.

1. Use judgment in providing staplers, staples, sharp scissors, tin cans, glitter, spray paint, toothpicks, hot plate, needles, pins, knives, and so on. Some young children are responsible and can be trusted to use these items at an early age with some supervision. Others may be too young (in developmental age or maturity) to understand the need for proper handling.
2. Take the time to discuss any potential hazards and dangers. Be honest and positive without dwelling on all the fatal possibilities. Focus on educating rather than frightening children.
3. Try out the art activity in advance. Is it safe? Can your particular group of children properly use the tools involved?
4. Demonstrate and model the proper way to use the tools: "This is the way to use a hole puncher. Sally, now you show me how to use it." "Good, you used it the safe way."
5. Supervise all art activities. Aides and parent volunteers can assist in supervision. Some activities will require closer and more direct supervision than others. Remember to anticipate the level of supervision needed when planning.
6. The Art and Crafts Materials Institute has developed a voluntary program designed to promote safety in children's art materials. Look for and purchase those art products bearing their labels: AP for Approved Product or CP for Certified Product.
7. The label *nontoxic* is very misleading. According to present criteria, only materials that are acutely toxic merit labeled toxic. Therefore *nontoxic* embraces a wide range of dangers from

Safety Tips

- Read the label!
- Always use products that are appropriate for the individual user. Children in grade six and lower and adults who may not be able to read and understand safety labeling should use *only nontoxic* materials.
- Do not use products that have passed their expiration date.
- Do not eat, drink, or smoke while using art and craft materials.
- Wash up after use—clean yourself *and* your supplies.
- Never use products for skin painting or food preparation unless indicated that the product is meant to be used in this way.
- Do not transfer art materials to other containers—you will lose the valuable safety information that is on the product package.

Additional procedures to follow
when using products that have cautionary labeling:

- Keep products out of reach of children.
- Keep your work area clean.
- Vacuum or wet mop dust; do not sweep it.
- Do not put your brush, pen, etc., in your mouth.
- Keep your work area well ventilated; make sure you have a system that takes out old air *and* brings in new air.
- Avoid skin contact and eating these materials. Keep materials out of your eyes and mouth.
- Use any and all protective equipment specified on the label, such as gloves, safety glasses, and masks.
- Use a mask or gloves that are impermeable to whatever product you are using; the wrong type of equipment could do as much or more harm than using no equipment at all!
- Protect any cuts or open wounds by using the appropriate gloves, etc.
- Mix and handle certain dry materials in a locally exhausting hood or sealed box.

- Spray apply certain materials only in a locally exhausting spray booth with filters.
- Do not mix different food-safe glazes together because the balance of ingredients in the mixed glaze will be disrupted and the resulting mixture may not be dinnerware safe.
- Carefully follow suggested disposal methods.

Procedures to follow when a product
has a flammability warning:

- Do not store or use product near heat, sparks, or flame.
- Do not heat above the temperature specified on the label.
- Use explosion-proof switches and an exhaust fan with an explosion-proof motor, if specified on the label.

Products that are hazardous require the following
on their labels:

- a conformance statement to ASTM D 4236, unless impractical and then at the point of sale (This requirement also applies to nontoxic products.)
- a signal word, such as *Warning* or *Caution*
- a listing of the ingredients in the product that are at a hazardous level
- a listing of how the product may hurt you if not used properly (may cause lung cancer, may cause harm to the developing fetus, etc.)
- instructions on how to use the product properly and safely (do not eat, drink, or smoke; use a respirator; wear gloves; etc.)
- an appropriate telephone number, usually the telephone number of the manufacturer or importer
- a statement that the product is inappropriate for use by children

(Reprinted with permission: The Art & Creative Materials Institute, Inc. Hanson, MA.)

minimally to acutely toxic. Tests to determine toxicity are done on adult animals. A product considered nontoxic when tested on an adult rat may provoke a very different reaction in a young child.

8. Refuse donated art supplies unless the ingredients are known.

9. Do not use old art supplies. Older materials may be highly toxic. They may have been produced when ingredients were not listed on the label and criteria for toxicity were absent.

10. Insist that children clean up and wash their hands after doing art.

11. Food and drinks remain at the snack table or kitchen area and are not taken to the art center.

12. Children with open cuts, sores, or wounds that are not properly covered should not do art activities that involve potentially toxic supplies.

13. Parents of children with allergies, asthma, and other medical problems should consult their pediatrician regarding any limits on their child's use of art supplies.

14. Post the number of your local or state poison control center. Call your local hospital for the number. Have the product in hand when you dial so that you can quickly read the ingredients from the label and take prompt action.

What Makes an Art Material "Safe"? Knowledge of materials and their proper use makes them safe. Be sure to read the label on all products you use so you will know they have been evaluated and are nontoxic or need special handling to avoid possible health hazards from misuse. Look for the ACMI seals so you will know the product has been evaluated by a qualified toxicologist for *both acute and chronic* hazards. Or, you may see other indications that the product conforms to ASTM D 4236, the chronic hazard labeling standard that is now part of the U.S. labeling law. Follow all safe use instructions. Purchase only products with the ACMI Non-Toxic Seals (CP, AP, and HL [Non-Toxic]) for young children, those with special physical or mental needs, and any persons who cannot read or understand the safety labeling on product packages. Observe good work habits and teach them to others. Some of these good habits are outlined on the following pages.

Although the safety precautions on the following pages are not necessary with ACMI-certified nontoxic products, they are good habits to learn and practice with any art material use. Above all, purchase art materials that have been evaluated with your safety in mind, and read and follow any label directions to safely enjoy rewarding art, craft, and other creative activities.

Social Development

Infants begin life as asocial, egocentric beings with little regard for the needs of others. Through socialization they are introduced to a wider arena of family, relatives, and significant others. Their individual desires are slowly curbed in response to the needs of others. Young children are egocentric and may need assistance in learning how to share; wait patiently; take turns; listen to others; and respect the property, rights, and ideas of others. They can also express empathy in appreciating the plight of others hurt or in trouble.

According to Erikson (1963), it is important for parents and caregivers to help

- infants develop a sense of trust rather than mistrust.
- toddlers develop a sense of autonomy rather than doubt or shame.
- preschoolers develop a sense of initiative rather than guilt.

Young children struggle with their freedom. At times they will be independent and autonomous. At other times they will be dependent, seeking comfort, security, and reassurance. Young children are talkers and socializers. They learn language and social skills from interacting with others, observing significant models, and witnessing the effects of their behavior upon others. For example, a young child who constantly snatches toys from others may find that they refuse to include her in their play. Young children are interested in themselves: who they are, what they look like, what they know, and what they can do. Their interest also extends to their peers and the immediate community. They enjoy being part of a social group other than their family.

Art and Social Development. Art helps children learn about themselves and others. Children validate their uniqueness by making a personal statement through art. "This is my chalk mark," says Deidra. It is a part of her, an extension of her self, and unlike others. Art helps children become comfortable with themselves, learning what they like and dislike and what they can and cannot do. Missy finds out that she prefers using clay to pasting. She likes to work intently alone, away from noise and social interaction. Missy is independent. Yet Missy rarely has the art center all to herself. The classroom is a social setting, and she is learning how to interact positively with others. The art center has rules that protect the welfare of both the group and the equipment. In turn, children learn responsibility for cleanup and proper return of materials to their rightful place. This is difficult for

Missy, who is an only child and is used to getting her own way at home. Slowly, she is learning to share materials, take turns, and wait patiently.

Clemens (1991) views art as a form of positive child guidance. She sees artwork as a preventive measure, a benign alternative to letting children express themselves in destructive ways. Art is offered because it makes survival in the classroom more likely. Controlling children is not the issue. If you give children interesting choices, your class will run more smoothly. For these reasons, Clemens believes that art should take a prominent place in one's daily program.

Emotional Development

Most young children like themselves—who they are, what their name is, what they look like, and what they can do. It is our job to help them continue to feel good about themselves. The concept of one's self is in a very formative stage during early childhood. Young children need an abundance of opportunities to experience mastery, success, and acceptance and to witness their own competence: "Look, teacher, I did it all by myself. Good for me!" Young children may transfer their parental attachment to their teacher or caregiver. They may express love and affection and be overly possessive. They may be jealous of their peers and expect or demand a caregiver's total time, interest, attention, and praise.

Art and Emotional Development.
Art is an emotionally pleasurable experience. Most children express happiness, joy, and pride in their art. This results in positive mental health and an expression of feelings. Young children are emotional beings, and art allows intense involvement. Merely thinking that there may be a connection between art and emotional development, however, is simplistic and intuitive. For more than three decades Coles (1992) has investigated the inner lives of children through their expressive words and pictures in a variety of settings including hospitals, clinics, homes, schools, and places of worship. He has concluded that children disclose their deepest convictions, feelings, and dreams with crayon, paint, and pencil. Art helps children nonverbally express those objects, ideas, people, places, experiences, events, and feelings that are emotionally significant. Often, a child is unable or unwilling to verbally discuss highly emotional topics or feelings about self, family, and friends. Art, however, allows these feelings, fantasies, fears, and frustrations to surface and be expressed (see Figure 4–5). It allows children the opportunity to represent in fantasy what cannot happen in reality. Negative feelings and impulses can be

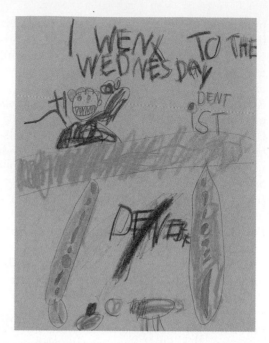

Figure 4-5 Through art, children can represent and master unpleasant experiences.

released in a positive, acceptable way through art. For example, anger against another cannot be physically expressed in the classroom, but it can be portrayed and expressed through art. "Show me in your picture how angry you are right now" (see Figure 4–6).

Art enhances a child's self-concept and feelings about self. Because art guarantees success, children experience mastery, which further enhances a positive self-concept. It is important for young children to have a positive self-concept, because it is a prerequisite to learning. Children who do not feel good about themselves do not learn. Their energy and attention are focused on fear of failure and self-doubt. It is a lot wiser to focus our attention on developing a positive self-concept in the early years as a preventive measure rather than attempting to remediate a negative self-concept in older children who may have given up on themselves, learning, and life.

Children with attention deficits or behavioral issues often suffer from low self-esteem. Their feelings of frustration and insecurity may emerge as negative social interactions with peers or adults. Participation in art activities provides a positive avenue for expressing their emotions and a low-stress setting in which they may develop positive social skills. The teacher can facilitate their participation in art activities by the following:

- Provide children with their own materials and ample workspace. Avoid making children to wait for a turn in using materials.

Figure 4-6 Art allows children to express how they feel.

- Allow children to explore the properties of the materials and to make multiple products if they choose.
- Provide materials such as play dough that can be actively used to release energy and feelings.
- Provide child-centered, open-ended activities in which children can be successful. Avoid teacher-directed activities that involve following directions or multiple steps.
- Limit children to a few choices rather than overwhelming them with permission to use anything and everything in the art center.

Cognitive Development

The early years are a time of very rapid cognitive development. By age two, the brain has reached 75 percent of its adult weight. By age five, the brain has attained 90 percent of its adult weight. The early years provide an opportunity for mental stimulation and challenge. Young children are self-motivated, curious explorers who are eager to learn about themselves, others, and the world. They need concrete materials to manipulate; problems to solve; people, places, and events to experience; and a time to discuss and ask questions. Books and the media may provide important vicarious, second-hand information, but they are no substitute for direct experience.

Art Therapy

When art materials are used effectively by art therapists it is because they were trained to understand not only the art process, but also the processes of normal and abnormal human development as well as theories of personality. According to Dunn-Snow and D'Amelio (2000), art teachers have access to students' nonverbal communications, and sometimes those graphic expressions speak louder than words. Alerting a counselor, teacher, or parent about a child's verbal or graphic expression that is disturbing may be the first step in discovering and helping to solve the problem or at least address the issue. Art, play, music, dance, literature, dramatics, and puppetry are vehicles for psychotherapy. Art therapy is the psychotherapeutic use of art for emotional understanding and healing. Although therapy with adults is largely verbal, children profit from nonverbal forms.

Qualified therapists look for some of the following in art

- An expressive use of colors. Red, bright orange, or black may be used repeatedly to symbolize objects of emotional importance. Black may be used to represent fear or death, red for rage or love.
- Personal meaning behind the repeated use of a symbol. Art therapists try to "crack the code," or discover the link between the artistic symbol and the unconscious. What meaning lies behind a child's repeated portrayal of a charging horse, a monster, a knife, or blood?
- An exaggeration, distortion, or overemphasis of objects reflecting emotional significance. Perhaps this is why young children first draw themselves as a large head with protruding arms, mounted on stick legs. They like their faces and how they look, so they draw them big.

(Continued)

Art Therapy (continued)

Arms and legs help them do things and get around, so they are also emphasized. Refer to the self-portrait (see Figure 4-7) drawn by a four-year-old. Note the "wound" on the face. At the time she had a bruise from a fall and was very vivid in pointing it out, representing and exaggerating it in her self-portrait.

- The omission or underemphasis of objects also provides emotional clues. For example, children with low self-concepts often omit themselves or make themselves tiny by comparison with others. Children with intense sibling rivalry may simply omit that sibling when drawing the family. Art allows children to accomplish in fantasy what they cannot do in reality. For a child with sibling rivalry, it may mean the elimination of that sibling, at least on paper.

- Placement provides clues to emotional significance. Objects that are drawn large and in the center of the paper are important. Children with low self-concepts may draw themselves off in a corner or in the far background. They may also be hidden behind larger objects of emotional significance placed in the center foreground. Painful, fear-evoking content may also be reduced in size and safely tucked away in a far corner of the picture.

- Defense mechanisms that protect the ego appear in art. Harmful or painful thoughts and experiences that are repressed in reality may be safely uncovered and expressed through art. The child who has been abused may portray herself with unusual colors or designs on her body. Identification may be reflected in a child's repeated use of a symbol with which to identify. The aggressive child identifies with the soldier or the marauding tiger. The fearful child becomes the scared witch on paper.

The concept of art therapy can be applied to children's art rendered around the events of 9/11. Teachers began to see images of destruction and pain reflected in the art of children. It was their way of trying to make sense out of a seemingly senseless act. Art helped them cope and work through their fears and anxieties. Some books that help children understand 9/11 include:

Cart, M. (Ed.) *9/11 The book of help.*

Frank, M. *Understanding September 11.*

Gerstein, M. *The man who walked between the towers.*

(2004 Caldecott Medal winner).

Goodman, R., & Fahnestock, A. *The day our world changed.*

Heard, G. *The place I know.*

Kalman, M. *Fireboat.*

Patel, A. *On that day.*

Poffenberger, N. *September 11th, 2001.*

There are inherent difficulties in the use of art therapy. First, it requires extensive training. Second, one needs many samples of a child's artwork over a long period of time to recognize patterns, rather than making a snap judgment or rash interpretation. For example, it would be naive to assume that a child's preoccupation with the color red indicates a fixation with blood, violence, fire, or rage. There are many possible explanations. Red may simply be the child's favorite color, the nearest color, or the only one available. Even early childhood educators who are untrained in art therapy, however, can use art to help children nonverbally express their feelings and emotions. Our aim is to provide a vehicle for emotional expression and release rather than analysis or interpretation.

Constructivism

Piaget's (1962, 1971) theory goes by many names including cognitive-developmental, transactional, interactionist, and constructivist. Let us examine each of these terms. Piaget's focus is on thinking and his developmental stages explain how young children's thinking or cognition changes over time. Changes in a child's cognitive development result from transactions or interactions with people, places, and objects in the environment. Children are active agents in their own development. They construct knowledge based on their actions on objects and their interactions with peers and adults. Children test new information against what they already know. As a result, mental constructs are revisited, reworked, and refined. Therefore, a basic premise of **constructivism** is that

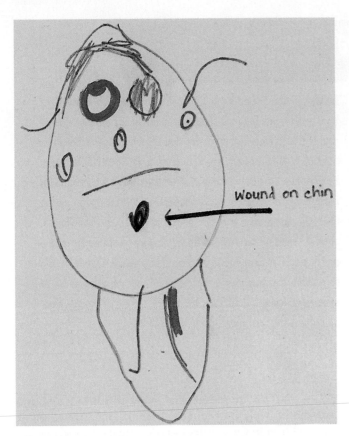

Figure 4-7 Children include, distort, and exaggerate what is personally meaningful to them.

wound on chin

children must actively construct knowledge. It cannot be given to them through direct teaching. The process is similar to constructing a building. Workers lay brick and cement on top of each other. Over time, a building takes shape. Similarly, the child lays brick after brick in constructing a house of knowledge. Some bricks fit; others must be refashioned or discarded. The process takes time (and hard work). Piaget's work leads teachers to critically examine the role of direct instruction in children's learning. According to Piaget, much of what children learn cannot be verbally transmitted through direct teaching, which involves too little work from the child.

Types of Knowledge

According to Piaget, there are three different **types of knowledge:** physical, social-conventional, and logical-mathematical. Each approaches learning and teaching in a different way. **Physical knowledge** includes discovering the physical properties of objects. This includes the external reality and observable properties such as form, weight, and function. Physical knowledge is best acquired through direction interactions

and sensory motor experiences with various objects along with reflecting on the results. **Social-conventional knowledge** refers to information about daily living accepted by society. It includes manners, acceptable behaviors, and customs, along with the names of the days of the week, months of the year, numerals, and alphabet letters. Social-conventional knowledge can be taught and is best learned through social interaction. **Logical-mathematical knowledge** is constructed around the relationships of objects to one another. Children form mental concepts about the relationship between objects. Logical-mathematical knowledge is actively constructed as children sort, classify, group, seriate, count, compare, and contrast objects. They are forming mental constructs of the relationships between objects.

How do the types of knowledge affect art? Children construct physical knowledge when they discover the properties of art materials and media. For example, they explore the properties of paint and a paintbrush and what they can do with them. You can try to tell a young child that paint is wet and sticky, but most will prefer to learn this on their own. Adults facilitate a child's social knowledge when, for example, they provide the names and labels for art tools such as *paintbrush* and *paint.* The same holds for the names of colors. Although children can discover that paint is wet and sticky, they will not "discover" that the paint is called *turquoise.* Wet and sticky are physical properties that can be discovered; turquoise cannot. It is an arbitrary and abstract term. It is easier and appropriate to simply tell children the color name. Logical-mathematical knowledge is constructed when a child compares two paint containers and sees, for example, that one is more full than the other. This relationship is constructed by the child. More full and less full are not inherent in either of the containers. Paint can be wet, sticky, and turquoise but the child's comparison of the amount of paint in each container constructed this more/less relationship. One container is only *less full* when the child actively (mentally) compares it to another which holds *more* paint.

So, assume a *hands-off* teacher role and a *hands-on* student role when you want children to discover the properties of objects (physical knowledge). Encourage them to reflect on the results of their actions on objects: "What do you see happening?" Teach children in developmentally appropriate ways when they are learning information that is arbitrary, culture-bound, and cannot be discovered (social-conventional knowledge). Provide children with sets of materials and objects and encourage them to construct relationships between objects such as grouping and classifying (logical-mathematical knowledge).

Constructivist Education: Putting Constructivism into Practice

DeVries and Zan (1995), along with Chaillé and Britain (2003), wed Piaget's theory with developmentally appropriate practices, resulting in constructivist education. A constructivist approach views young children as theory builders. They focus on physical knowledge and are social beings who need support to develop autonomy. The learner is actively constructing knowledge rather than passively taking in information. Learners do not acquire knowledge that is transmitted to them; rather, they construct knowledge through their cognitive activity. Children take ownership for how and what they learn. Rather than just a set of activities, constructivist education is an approach based on the belief that children construct their own knowledge, intelligence, and personality, as well as social and moral values. A misconception about constructivist education is that because it values play, it does not include academics. This is not true, for constructivist teachers are serious about children's construction of knowledge about literacy, numeracy, science, social studies, and the fine arts. According to DeVries and Zan, the problem for the constructivist teacher in approaching academics is to distinguish what must be *constructed* from what must be *instructed*. Piaget's differentiation of types of knowledge aids the teacher in making this distinction.

According to Piaget, young children's thinking is action oriented and largely nonverbal. He believed that thinking precedes the development of language. Language enhances thinking, but is not its source. Children understand and know more than they can verbalize. Likewise, what a child can say or discuss may not be an accurate indicator of intelligence. A young child's understanding and representation of the world proceed through stages.

Overview of Piaget's Stages of Development

During Piaget's **sensory motor stage** (birth to age two), infant thinking is limited to sensory impressions and motoric behaviors. A toy rattle is something to be held, shaken, dropped, stared at, listened to, smelled, and tasted. There is no thinking about the rattle apart from these sensory and motoric actions.

Toddlers attain significant cognitive achievements as they leave the sensory motor stage (birth to age two) and enter the **preoperational stage** (ages two through seven). Representation frees toddlers from a reliance on action-based thinking. They can now form mental images, symbolize, and think about their world in the absence of direct action.

Preschoolers in Piaget's preoperational stage (ages two through seven) are using symbols, including play, art, and language, to represent their world. They continue to construct and refine their concepts of time, space, classification, seriation, and number. Preschool-

ers in Piaget's preoperational stage think in ways that are qualitatively different from adult logic or reason.

Children in the primary grades have entered Piaget's stage of **concrete operations** (ages seven through eleven). An operation is an internalized action. Older children have attained several important cognitive operations, including reversibility, conservation, classification, and seriation, as well as addition, subtraction, multiplication, and division, that help them think in more logical terms. Their thinking, however, is still bound to the concrete. They are unable to think abstractly.

Vygotsky

There has been a renewed interest in the work of Lev Vygotsky, a Soviet developmental psychologist. Both Piaget and Vygotsky studied how children learn and develop. Like Piaget, Vygotsky believed that children actively construct knowledge. He also believed that development cannot be separated from its social context. Vygotsky's **sociocultural theory** advocated the position that learning can lead development. He also believed that *language* plays a central role in cognitive development. Vygotsky's theory is similar to Piaget's in that both believe in the importance of play and that learning is actively constructed. A major difference is Vygotsky's emphasis on the role of language and direct instruction in learning. Unlike Piaget, he also does not propose a universal series of developmental stages. Instead, Vygotsky believes that development and learning are embedded in a child's family and cultural context. Adults teach socially valued skills at a very early age. Children's learning is influenced by what their social world values.

Vygotsky's theory challenges Piaget's ideas of language and thought. According to Vygotsky, language plays a critical role in the formation of a child's mind because it is a major vehicle for communication. Language serves as a means by which a child's social experiences are mentally represented. So, language, even its earliest forms, is socially based. Rather than Piaget's concept of young children's speech as egocentric or immature, Vygotsky saw it as connected to what children are thinking. Young children talk aloud and later this **self-talk** becomes internalized so that children act without having to talk aloud. Vygotsky believed that children speak to themselves for self-guidance and self-direction. The **private speech** that helps children think about their behavior and plan for action is also critical to self-regulation.

Because learning is considered essentially an interpersonal and dynamic process, teachers must develop comfortable and cooperative relationships with children. Children need adults who act as **intellectual mediators** readily available to observe, pose a question or problem, challenge, model, give information, or facilitate a child's learning by referring a child to a more knowledgeable or skilled peer. Teachers must know each child's **zone of proximal development (ZPD).** This construct refers to a range of skills, tasks, or abilities that a child cannot yet do alone but can accomplish with adult and peer assistance. **Cooperative learning** and **group projects** are highly recommended. There are upper and lower limits to the ZPD. The lower limit would include those skills, tasks, or abilities that are already in the child's repertoire. The child can perform certain tasks by himself or herself and without assistance. The upper range refers to those tasks that are within a child's reach with some degree of assistance. Again, assistance can range from observing a more skilled peer to direct teaching. **Scaffolding** is an important strategy for teachers working within a child's zone. For example, a young child has been exploring with the three primary colors and is able to accurately name red, blue, and yellow. Let us place this accomplishment at the lower range of color learning. Knowing this, a teacher is able to *scaffold* and help the child on to the next step. What could that be? With the information that a child knows about primary colors, how could a teacher scaffold, or help this child to learn more about colors? Would you encourage that child to mix two primary colors and discuss the results? Name the secondary color? Probably. It appears within the child's

zone and an assisted step that will enhance the child's learning about color. Our discussion of scaffolding continues in Chapter 10.

Art and Cognitive Development. Eisner (1976) makes one of the strongest cases for the relationship between art and thinking, learning, and overall academic performance. Art reflects what a child knows about the world. Children who have directly experienced a wide variety of people, places, and objects will have an array of things to choose from when doing art. Children who have neither been to a zoo nor been exposed to pets will probably not include animals in their art. One must know about something before one can re-create it through art (see Figure 4–8).

Translating ideas, concepts, and experiences into art involves many thinking skills. One must decide what to represent and how to execute it. "To make a dinosaur, should I use clay, markers, or paint?" thinks Nate. He must plan, organize, and make choices. Art involves concentration, staying on a task, and seeing it through to completion—all important work skills and habits. "What steps are involved and how should I go about it?" ponders Nate. He decides to draw an outline with pencil, trace over it with thick marker pen, cut it out, and then paint it at the easel. Art involves problem solving. Nate needs dark paint when only the three primary colors are available. He decides to mix all three together into a muddy color that he thinks is just the right color for

Figure 4-8 A field trip to the zoo prompted one child to make this elephant.

a "beast." Nate becomes upset when the muddy color runs into the white of the dinosaur's eye. Using too much water has thinned down the paint. Nate has learned about cause and effect. He hypothesizes and gets a crumpled paper towel to gently blot it out. It is impossible to document all the thinking that is going on in Nate's head while he is doing art. By the way, Nate is a bright four-year-old who is largely nonverbal. Art provides an opportunity for him to symbolize what he knows but cannot and will not discuss. Over time, he may. Through art, Nate can communicate with himself and others. "Yes, Nate, I see how hard you worked to get the eye just right," says his teacher. The thinking cycle moves from planning to implementing, evaluating and reworking, if necessary. The author believes that the thinking side of art has been neglected in favor of identifying physical, social, emotional, and creative ends. The major benefits of art may very well be cognitive in nature.

Through art, children learn about the concepts of color, shape, size, line, texture, and other artistic elements. For example, Beth knows her basic geometric shapes. She discovers that squares combine to form a rectangle. Painting red over yellow makes orange. Lines that intersect form an X or cross shape. White added to blue lightens it and makes it the perfect color for Beth's sky. Difficult spatial concepts, including right, left, up, down, over, beside, through, next to, on top of, between, and under, are represented in art. These spatial concepts will be vital to reading comprehension at a later time.

Art serves as an index of a child's thinking. We can look at children's artwork, particularly painting and drawing, and find out what they know about their world, what they consider important, and how they choose to represent it. Detailed artwork indicates that a child knows much about that particular subject. Children who can express what they know about their world will be at an advantage later when they are expected to write and read about it. Signs (words) spoken or in print must have some referent. Art gives children the opportunity to symbolize that referent and serves as a bridge between object and sign (see Figure 4–9).

Participation in art activities may be particularly valuable to children with special needs whose patterns of thinking and ways of communicating differ from those of other children. Through art, children with special needs may communicate their thoughts and emotions through their own visual symbols. They can participate in art activities with their peers to receive positive feedback and practice social skills. Teachers can support the participation of children with special cognitive and communications needs by:

Figure 4-9 Young children are concrete learners. Art helps them symbolize their experiences.

- providing verbal directions slowly and clearly and adding visual cues.
- providing close supervision.
- providing child-centered, open-ended activities to guarantee success.
- breaking multistep activities into small steps.
- building various levels of difficulty into activities, for example, allowing children to use pre-cut paper shapes or to cut their own shapes in a collage.
- encouraging children to talk about their art, or to dictate words or sentences to share to accompany what they have created.
- encouraging children to talk while doing art and to share their thoughts and feelings about their artistic experiences.

Creative Development

Creativity begins during infancy as babies invent solutions to problems and engage in novel actions. According to Torrance (1965), young children are at their peak of creative functioning, which declines with age. Young children are highly imaginative. Imagination is strongly related to creativity. Rewarding a

Figure 4-10 Art fosters creative expression.

child's sense of autonomy and initiative enhances creative functioning (Erikson, 1963).

Art and Creative Development.

As seen in Figure 4–10, art allows children to express their own creativity, originality, and individuality. Children's artistic expressions may be vaguely similar yet still significantly different from all others. Art is the perfect medium for young children, who are so highly imaginative. Their fantasy can be given form through art. Art is an open-ended activity that encourages discovery, exploration, experimentation, and invention. All of these skills are vital to creativity. Gene thinks about what will happen if he uses two paintbrushes at a time. He tries it out and is pleased with the double-stroked result. He asks his teacher to help him tie a rubber band around three paintbrushes. Through active experimentation, he invents a new way to paint.

Individual Differences

A working knowledge of child development can be a very useful tool for early childhood teachers. Knowing the needs, interests, and abilities of young children at a given age or stage can help us design developmentally appropriate art activities. Knowledge of child development, however, will give us only a general pattern of what is *normal, typical,* or *average*. Few children conform to the norm or can be considered typical or average. Children are unique individuals. Their physical, social, emotional, cognitive, and creative development will reflect **individual differences** resulting from both heredity and environmental influences. Individual differences make teaching young children both fascinating and challenging. Within any one age group

there will be a wide range of commonalities in terms of physical, social, emotional, cognitive, and creative needs, interests, and abilities. There will also be significant individual differences. Obviously, it would be much simpler to work with a group of three-, four-, or five-year-olds with similar, if not identical, developmental characteristics. However, the aim of early childhood education is to foster the development of unique individuals, not to mass produce automata.

Differences in development and learning that result from heredity or environment or their interaction are expressed in the following ways:

background: race, culture, and social class

family: family size, siblings, birth order, divorce and remarriage, parental educational and occupational levels, nutrition, parental teaching style, and child abuse or neglect

individual: gender, personality and temperament, motivation, learning style, and personal interests

 ## Cultural Influences

Children's backgrounds are composed of racial, ethnic, and cultural differences. Racial differences are expressed in skin color and other physical characteristics. Cultural differences are expressed in foods, celebrations, and dress, but more importantly, in language, customs, and values. Racial and cultural differences extend, enhance, and enrich early childhood classrooms and society in general. Early childhood teachers have the responsibility of integrating perspectives, activities, traditions, and values from multiple cultures into the curriculum for two reasons. First, it is important that each child recognize that he or she is a valued member of the classroom community; cultural influences on learning must be recognized and honored so that each child learns and develops to his or her full ability. Second, early childhood teachers are models for their students. Children will imitate their teacher's attitudes toward and interactions with other individuals and cultures. The following guidelines can help early childhood teachers structure learning activities and their interactions with children and families:

1. Accept the child as is, unconditionally, including **culture.** Treat all children equally. Guidelines, rules, and rewards should apply equally to all children.

2. Value, accept, respect, and encourage the child's native language and culture as strengths and expressions of unique individual difference.

3. Help the child feel comfortable in school. The sights, sounds, and surroundings may be

unfamiliar and overwhelming to some children who have nothing with which to compare them.

4. Discuss the study similarities and differences among people. It is important for children to focus on human similarities as a framework for the individual differences resulting from culture and ethnicity. Some examples include the following: What are some things that all people need? We all need housing and food. Where he came from, Lin lived on a houseboat with his parents and grandparents. What do you think it would be like to live on a boat? Now, Lin lives in an apartment. How many of you have ever lived in an apartment? I did while I was going to school. So even though Lin talks differently from us, he is still a lot like us. He has his own language and a place to live, just as we do. We are going to help Lin learn our language, and he will teach us his.

5. Involve parents. Some immigrant parents may have great reservations about school. Some may be embarrassed about their lack of standard English. Others may be ashamed of their minimal level of education. Some will place great value on their child's education and have unrealistically high expectations. All will be proud of their culture and willing to share their ethnicity if encouraged and invited. Help them feel comfortable. Let them know that they would have something very special that the children and you would like to know more about. For example, Lin's mother was invited to cook a rice dish with the children for a snack. Others could come dressed in native costume or bring in cultural artifacts. Their presence and participation will make their child feel good about being in school.

6. Help immigrant children to be successful and experience mastery. Many of them are experiencing *culture shock.* They are aware of their language and cultural differences. They need an abundance of things they can do successfully rather than an endless of things they need to remediate.

7. Understand that cultural differences may underscore a child's reluctance to participate in art activities. Give children time to observe and feel comfortable. Children who have not been encouraged to be independent and autonomous may seek direction, instruction, and specific assistance during art activities. They may want you to guide their hands or do it for them.

8. Learn key art words in the languages your children speak. Ask parents to translate the names of colors, words such as *art, paint,* and *play,* and phrases like "Do you want to . . . ?" and "Do you like that?" in the children's home languages. Use the phrases to talk the children about their art activities.

CONTEXT: INTERACTION OF CHILD DEVELOPMENT AND ENVIRONMENTAL INFLUENCES

Our developmental profile neatly dissected the whole child for the purpose of analyzing the different aspects of development one at a time. The truth is that children are much more than the sum of their developmental parts. Physical + Social-Emotional + Cognitive + Language = Whole Child. Development is not this simplistic and does not occur in isolation.

Art and the Holidays

In early childhood programs, holidays should be observed simply and with sensitivity to children's ethnic and cultural backgrounds. Young children are often overexposed to traditional "mainstream" holiday observances. For children whose families celebrate these holidays, the anticipation and excitement can lead to emotional overstimulation and even physical exhaustion. For children whose families celebrate other holidays, or none at all, the emphasis on traditional holidays can leave these children feeling left out and uncomfortable. Many teachers have used the traditional "mainstream" holiday motifs, symbols, decorations, and activities while excluding those that are traditional in other cultures. This may create bias in children's thinking and view of the world. Cherry and Nielsen (1999) recommend enriching all children's lives by encouraging open-ended, creative art experiences that reflect all the cultures present in your classroom and community.

Children develop within a context, and this wider setting must be studied to understand the impact it makes upon a developing child. Children's development is influenced by home, community, and environmental influences. For example, children will be influenced by family changes, poverty, and socioeconomic variables, including neighborhood crime. The influences are mutual and reciprocal—children also influence their home, community, and environment. For example, children who are under stress as a result of divorce may regress and become dependent. In turn, parents may change their parenting techniques, providing extra comfort and reassurance. The wider context of children's development is depicted in Figure 4–11.

Figure 4-11 The context: interaction of child development and environmental influences.

ART ✏ PROCESSING WITH ART MATERIALS AND TOOLS

Very young children **process** with art materials long before they purposely decide to make an art product. They enjoy tearing and taping paper, smearing and spreading paste and glue, and using scissors and staples. Some very simple activities include the following:

- tearing paper
- cutting with scissors
- pasting and gluing
- taping and sticking
- stapling
- punching holes in paper

Each of these is not only enjoyable by itself but is also a necessary skill for other art activities.

Scissors and Cutters

There are many different tools for cutting, including the following:

blade cutter—for cutting mats

blunt—steel scissors; blunt is fine, as long as they still cut

comfy or cushie grip—with rubber-coated finger holes

crinkle-cut scissors

Fiskars®—cut most things. They come with comfort-molded universal ring handles for right or left hand

Fiskars Paper Edgers®—can be used left- or right-handed and cut papers in six different designs.

hole punchers

Krazy Kut® scissors—cut papers in little and big wave, lightning, zigzag, scallop, and zipper patterns

lefty—designed specifically for left-handed children

paper cutter—for cutting paper into a variety of shapes and sizes, as well as paper strips

paper punchers—assorted shapes

pinking shears—jagged edge on paper and fabric adds variety

safety—lightweight plastic for right- and left-handed cutters

scissors rack—metal or wood for safely and neatly storing scissors

sharp—steel, in right- and left-hand models, for experienced four-year-olds and five-year-olds

snip loop or easy grip scissors—recommended for beginning cutters or for children with limited motor control

teacher's straight shears—very sharp; for teacher's use only!

Food for Thought: Food for Art?

Opinion is divided on the use of food in art projects. Breakfast cereal and macaroni are often strung on string or yarn for necklaces. Beans and popcorn are glued on paper. Rice is used in collage. Younger children enjoy hand painting with pudding, frosting, or whipped topping. Infants and toddlers like to use applesauce. The above activities are enjoyable and may serve important developmental and sensory ends. The author, however, advises against the use of food in art for several reasons.

1. Food is expensive. If parents want to donate, they can bring in junk recyclable materials, ingredients for cooking, or other more crucial and perhaps costly supplies such as wooden blocks, books, or puzzles.

2. Food is a precious commodity that many take for granted and waste.

3. There is such a pressing need for food in developing countries that the casual use of food in art can be questioned on moral and ethical grounds.

4. The number of homeless people has increased dramatically in recent years. In times of economic recession, some middle-class families may find themselves homeless as a result of job loss. Families with children represent a large segment of our homeless population. Some areas have a severe shortage of food targeted for the homeless. It may be difficult to justify stringing O-shaped pieces of breakfast cereal when one knows that many local children will go to bed hungry.

5. The use of food in an art activity may offend some cultural groups who use that food item for religious or ethnic celebration.

6. Foods such as frosting, pudding, and whipped topping are highly caloric and contain an abundance of sugar.

7. Adults should never use food in art activities with toddlers because they are developing self-regulatory skills and must learn to distinguish between food and other objects that are not to be eaten (Bredekamp, 1987).

In summary, there are many sound alternatives to the use of food in art. Small drinking-straw sections can replace macaroni for stringing. Sand rather than rice can be glued. Styrofoam squiggles can replace beans in a collage activity. Be creative in identifying alternatives to food in art activities.

---

training—double-handled with four rubber-coated finger holes; teacher and child cut together
X-Acto® knife—for cutting mats

Hint: Regardless of the type selected, scissors must cut. There is nothing more frustrating to a young cutter than a pair of scissors that snag, tear, or clog up with paper but do not cut it.

Hint: Mix water, white glue, and food coloring or liquid watercolor for the very young paster. Toddlers would also enjoy placing pieces of precut or pretorn papers onto a piece of construction paper with glue. Glue can be mixed with water to both extend it and eliminate its crusty appearance when dry. Mix water and white glue in equal parts, for example, ½ cup white glue to ½ cup water.

Hint: Add liquid watercolor to clear glue to get a colored glue that is richer in color than colored white glue.

Hint: Tap-N-Glue® cap, a relatively new product, has taken the mess and waste out of gluing. Young children can easily turn the bottle upside down and gently tap. The special cap makes the glue come out in small drops. There is no opening and closing of tops and no clogs or leaks. Special caps fit bottles of white glue. Tap-N-Glue® caps are inexpensive and make gluing an economical art activity that can be offered on a daily basis. Call 1–800–992–9018.

Adhesives: Glue, Paste, Tape, and Accessories

The following list suggests many different adhesives:

cloth tape—for color coding

colored tape—for taping and sticking

E-Z-up® clips—held with wax to the wall; claims to stick to any surface; holds artwork; reusable

glue sticks—no drips or mess

masking tape—for taping and sticking

paste—individual containers with applicators for bonding paper

paste brush—rather than using fingers

paste cups—with lids; small margarine tubs are ideal

paste refill—pint, quart, or gallon

Plasti-Tak®—reusable, no-mar adhesive for displaying art on walls

Popsicle® sticks—make good paste spreaders

roll-on glue—same as glue stick, no drips or mess

School Glue Gel®

Scotch or clear tape—for taping and sticking

Tap-N-Glue® caps—no mess or waste

wall clips—same as E-Z-up® clips; for displaying artwork on wall

white liquid glue—good all-purpose adhesive; buy individual small bottles and large refill. Good for paper, wood, Styrofoam®, nature specimens, and most junk.

> **Hint:** Some young children enjoy eating paste, given its smell and touch. Provide a damp sponge or paper towel and encourage periodic wiping of fingers before the big gob of paste gets too tempting.

> **Hint:** Since paste dries out very fast, it is important to replace the lids. Children will forget. Try gluing a small piece of wet sponge to the inside lid to keep the paste moist. Use baby food jars with lids, margarine tubs, or other small, covered containers.

> **Hint:** Small bottles of white glue are easy to hold and use. Also, some children feel obligated to use up a whole bottle. A smaller bottle may satisfy this need to empty the container without wasting paste.

> **Hint:** Some teachers prefer to pour small amounts of white glue into a small plastic bowl

or lid. This bypasses the use of individual bottles, which dry out very quickly because children often forget to twist the tops shut.

> **Hint:** Some children enjoy spreading the liquid glue with their fingers. Small sponges can also be used to dab the glue and apply it. A special glue stick is easy to make. Wrap a piece of netting twice around a Popsicle® stick and secure it with a rubber band at one end. The weave in the netting holds the glue until the child is ready to apply it.

Glue Recipe

Watered-Down Glue

white liquid glue

water

Slowly add water to glue. Stir thoroughly. Add more water if too thick. Use this to coat strips of paper.

Tearing Paper

Young children should not feel excluded from art activities just because they cannot use scissors. Very young artists can tear paper. Tearing paper is a good activity for developing the hand and finger muscles. Begin with very thin papers like newspaper, scrap tissue, or old phone directories. The individual pieces can be pasted or glued to each other or onto a piece of paper.

Torn-Paper Picture

Torn-paper pieces can be arranged and pasted or glued onto a piece of paper to form a torn-paper picture. Older children may enjoy using construction paper. Being able to use scissors does not mean that one has outgrown the interest in tearing paper for art activities. The author observed a classroom where kindergartners were making a Halloween mural out of torn-paper shapes. Torn shapes with rough, jagged edges are ideal for this activity. One witch's hat had a long, exaggerated point, and so did her nose!

Cutting with Scissors

Recall this chapter's discussion of the developmental sequence for using scissors. Successful cutting with scissors is a developmental landmark. Some children will cut for the sheer sake of cutting, with little regard for the pieces cut. Some will want to take their individually cut pieces home in a bag. Others will enjoy pasting the pieces that they have cut onto paper. You may want to tape a paper bag to the table to catch the cut paper snips as they fall, rather than attempting to pick up or sweep them off the floor later.

Folding and Cutting

Children can fold a thin piece of paper and use their scissors to snip out a piece. Refold the paper in a different direction and continue cutting and snipping. Open up the paper and glue it against a colored piece of construction paper for a background. This will help the cutout design stand out.

Pasting and Gluing

Very young children enjoy smearing paste or dripping glue for the sheer pleasure of it. They enjoy the smell, cold feel, stickiness, and texture of solid paste. It has a thick, crumbly feel and sticks to the fingers. Liquid white glue has a very different wet feel to it. Children enjoy squeezing glue onto paper. Bottles filled to the brim may be quickly emptied. You may want to add food coloring to your paste and glue to enhance its visual appeal for beginning pasters and gluers. Very young children may not be interested in gluing or pasting anything in particular. Older children will combine pasting and gluing with tearing and cutting. Papers that have been cut or torn or both can be pasted or glued onto an art surface.

Paste and glue serve different purposes. Paste will hold lightweight papers together, but glue is needed to bond heavier objects, including boxes and wood. Rubber cement is meant for adhering paper but should not be used with children because of its misuse as an inhalant.

Stapling

Staplers and stapling fascinate young children. Stapling is more a fine motor skill than an artistic process. A hand-held stapler requires a squeezing motion with one hand, while a large stapler involves a gentle pounding, stamping, hammering, or pushing action. The miniature stapler may be too small for children to activate and control. Using a stapler is noisy, but older children thoroughly enjoy it and the activity exercises their finger and hand muscles. They will staple just to get a group of staples attached to paper. Sometimes the staples will form a design or pattern on colored paper. At other times they may use a stapler in place of paste or glue for attaching small pieces of paper, fabric, or collage material to each other or a background.

Sprinkle a Picture

Children can make a picture or design with paste or glue on paper. They can carefully sprinkle

- confetti
- paper dots (from a hole punch)
- small balls of cotton (on dark paper)
- small shells
- seeds
- pine needles
- pieces of broken jewelry
- sand
- Styrofoam® chips or squiggles
- glitter

Hint: To make colored sand, place sand in plastic bag. An adult can use an ice-cream stick to scrape colored chalk dust into bag. Shake well. Some teachers use a few drops of food coloring or liquid watercolor, but this is messier and involves drying overnight. Powdered tempera can also be used.

Hint: Children under four, however, should not use glitter, according to the Society for the Prevention of Blindness. When it sticks to fingers and children rub their eyes, the glitter can damage the eye by actually cutting it. Older children should be closely supervised when using glitter.

Carefully slide the excess off the paper and back into the container. Some teachers use salt, sugar, popcorn, cornmeal, or rice in shakers for this activity. The author advises against the use of food in art activities for reasons previously stated.

Taping and Sticking

Very young children enjoy sticking tape. Teachers can provide plastic tape in a variety of colors, widths, and lengths. Place cut or torn pieces of tape on a nonstick surface. Children will enjoy lifting them off and placing them on paper. Pieces of torn or cut paper can also be taped onto an art surface.

Lick-and-Stick Art

Children enjoy licking and sticking the colorful labels and gummed papers available from office supply and stationery stores. Items include:

- paper reinforcements
- gummed stars and labels
- stickers
- price tags
- colored dots
- book club stamps
- seals

These can also be licked and placed in a visual arrangement.

Hole and Paper Punch Art

Older children will have the muscular strength to work with a hole punch using either one or both hands. They seem fascinated with the process. Provide strips of paper from which to punch holes. They may want to save the punched holes. Punched holes can be used for gluing. Children can also make a design outline or picture with punched holes and paste this onto another paper. For example, a design could be punched out of white paper and glued to a piece of colored construction paper for a greeting card. New versions of hole punches come in smaller squares which provide a variety of paper shapes when punched. There is also a Dial-A-Design 6-in-1® paper punch. Simply turn the wheel to choose either a tulip, star, heart, cat, dinosaur, or musical note to punch out by pressing the button.

Stringing Art

Stringing objects is not only a good activity for improving eye-hand coordination but is also a way to creatively string together items. Use a shoelace or sturdy yarn with a plastic needle. Knot the far end of the yarn or shoelace to keep the objects from sliding off. Children will enjoy stringing

- spools
- paper reinforcements
- hole-punched paper
- tinfoil
- egg-carton cups
- sections of plastic straws
- pieces of colored paper
- sections of toilet-paper rolls
- plastic paper clips
- Styrofoam® pieces
- buttons
- washers
- soda-pop rings
- pipe cleaners twisted into circular shapes

Items that have been strung can be tied into a necklace, bracelet, or belt and proudly worn. Although the author advises against the use of food in art, children can string nutritious breakfast cereal and eat it throughout the morning as breakfast or a snack.

Contact Paper Art

Provide various collage materials, including colored tissue paper, yarn, paper scraps, and other flat objects. Cut clear contact paper at least 6 inches in diameter for each child. Remove the backing and place sticky side up on art table. This eliminates the need for paste or glue. Tape four corners with masking tape to secure. Very young children will enjoy placing objects on contact paper and seeing them magically stick. When done, place a larger sheet of construction paper over the contact paper to frame.

Sand Pendulum

See Figure 4–12. Punch a small hole in the center of the bottom of the inside of a paper cup. Make three evenly spaced holes in the rim of the cup. Cut three pieces of string and run them through the three holes. Tie the three ends into a knot. Set up two matching chairs back to back and about three feet apart. Place a pole, e.g., yardstick, thick dowel rod, or broomstick between the top of both chair backs. Secure with duct tape. Cut a piece of string long enough to reach from the pole to the floor. Tie one end of this long string to the pole and the other end to the knot in the cup's string. Cover the floor with newspaper. Lay black construction paper on top of the newspaper beneath the cup. Cover the hole in the cup with one finger while filling the cup with sand. The child can gently swing the pendulum while you let go of the cup. As the sand pours from the cup, it will make a design on the black paper. Children can apply glue to their black paper first if they want to save the design. If not, simply refill the cup with the contents on the black paper.

Figure 4-12 Sand pendulum.

Glue Stickers

Tacky and flexible when dry, glue stickers' transferable designs will cling to most flat plastic, glass, and metal surfaces, including windows, refrigerators, sliding glass doors, and mirrors. Place a piece of clear plastic kitchen wrap on a table. Apply white or colored glue to the plastic wrap and make a design using finger, brush, or craft stick. Add food coloring or liquid watercolor to color the glue. Allow sticker to dry at least 24 hours. Check to see if child's sticker needs more drying time by carefully lifting the clear wrap off the table and looking under the sticker. Lighter color spots means sticker needs more time to dry. To remove sticker, gently peel away from clear wrap.

Rainbow Glue

Add liquid watercolor to clear (not white) glue for more brilliant colors. Place in shallow bowls or squeeze bottles. Children can also use their fingers or small brushes.

> **Hint:** A new adhesive is School Glue Gel®, manufactured by the same company that makes white glue. It is less messy than white glue because it will not run or drip.

Puffy Paint

This is an economical alternative to store-bought puffy paint. In a bowl, mix equal parts (e.g., 1 cup each) of flour, salt, and water. Add food coloring or liquid watercolor. Mix thoroughly. Pour into condiment squeeze bottle. Make sure tip has an opening that will allow contents to exit when squeezed by children. Repeat process if more colors are desired. Experiment by varying the size of the holes in your squeeze bottles. Look for color-coded or clear squeeze bottles so contents are identifiable. Cover small cardboard squares with tinfoil. Puffy paint will squeeze out like toothpaste and sparkle. Spatulas can be provided for smearing the puffy paint. Let dry overnight and it will harden on the tinfoil in three-dimensional relief. Puffy paint cannot be saved, and containers must be cleaned after use before contents mold or harden.

Starch and Yarn Art

Pour liquid starch into small bowls. Discuss that although starch is a pretty blue color it is not to eat or drink because it could make you sick. Cut different colors and lengths of yarn. Provide a clean Styrofoam®

tray or sheet of wax paper for each child. Children can dip their yarn in the starch and lay it on the surface to create a design. Closely supervise. Provide wet sponges or paper towels for children to wipe off their fingers before touching their faces.

Bleeding Art

This is a good outdoor activity. Each child needs a squirt bottle filled with clear water and a large sheet of white paper. Provide scraps of tissue paper and crepe paper. Have the children place the paper scraps on the white paper in an interesting design and then squirt with water. The colored papers will begin to "bleed" and the colors will run and mix. The wet scraps can be removed and discarded. Place in the sun to dry. If done indoors, place white paper in a large box lid to contain children's squirting. You can eliminate the squirt bottles by putting the papers outside on a rainy day. This combines art and science as children discuss what happened and how it happened.

SUMMARY

We have moved from an overview of holistic child development to links between art and a child's development. This chapter explained how art fosters a child's physical, social, emotional, cognitive, and creative development. Art was viewed as a developmentally appropriate and important activity. Knowledge of a young child's physical needs and abilities suggested strategies and materials for helping the child learn to cut with scissors. Although art is pleasurable and multisensory, potential art hazards do exist. Guidelines for identifying toxic art supplies and suggested alternatives are provided in Appendix F. Although art fosters emotional expression and release, it was recommended that art therapy not be attempted without adequate training. The relationship between creativity and art has long been recognized, but the link between art and thinking may be as strong. Although the use of food in art activities appears to be creative, objections were raised. It was recommended that the teacher seek alternatives to the use of food in art.

Books Focusing on Young Children With Special Needs

Sharing books with young children is a good way to help them understand, and respect special needs. Some recommended books include the following
Brown, T. *Someone special, just like you.*
Bunnett, R. *Friends at school.*

Fassler, J. *Howie helps himself.*

Heelan, J. R. *Rolling along: The story of Taylor and his wheelchair.*

Lears, L. *Ian's walk: A story about autism.*

Maguire, A. *Special people, special ways.*

Meyer, D. J. *Views from our shoes: Growing up with a brother or sister with special needs.*

Millman, I. *Moses goes to a concert* (sign language.)

Rogers, F. *Let's talk about it: Extraordinary friends.*

Shriver, M. *What's wrong with Timmy?*

Stuve-Bodeen, S. *We'll paint the octopus red.*

Watson, E. *Talking to angels.* (autism.)

Willis, J. *Susan laughs.*

Key Terms

art therapy

concrete operations

constructivism

constructivist education

cooperative learning

culture

differently abled

group projects

holistic model of child development

inclusion

individual differences

intellectual mediators

logical-mathematical knowledge

physical knowledge

preoperational stage

private speech

process

scaffolding

self-talk

sensory motor stage

social-conventional knowledge

sociocultural theory

types of knowledge

zone of proximal development (ZPD)

Suggested Activities

1. Observe a young child actively involved in an art activity. Record what the child says and does. How did this art experience help the child physically, socially, emotionally, cognitively, and creatively?

2. Observe children aged three, four, and five using scissors. Using the guidelines in this unit, what recommendations can you make for each with respect to tools, paper, activity, or teacher input?

3. Arrange to work with a difficult or troubled young child. Ask the child to draw or paint how he or she is feeling. Encourage the child to talk about the picture. Encourage emotional expression without formally attempting art therapy.

4. Conduct an art safety inspection of an early childhood art center. Identify items which compromise the health and safety of young children.

5. Plan and carry out an open-ended art experience in which children process with art materials and tools.

6. In the open-ended art experience you planned and carried out earlier, consider ways you might adapt the experience and/or the materials for children with limited vision or hearing? For children with special cognitive or communicative needs?

7. Visit an early childhood classroom just to observe the children. How many expressions of *individual differences* do you see and hear? Discuss those differences and the ways in which the teacher meets the needs of individual children.

Review

1. List the five aspects of a child's development.

2. At your midyear open house, a few parents wonder why so much time is devoted to art in your preschool program. Using the holistic model of child development, what could you say to justify your art program?

3. A parent is alarmed because her five-year-old is always drawing ghosts and graveyards. She fears that her child is abnormal or emotionally disturbed. What are some possible explanations for this child's art?

4. Suggest a nonfood art activity for each of the following:

   a. printing with cut vegetables

   b. gluing breakfast cereal on a self-portrait for facial features

   c. sprinkling powdered gelatin over white glue for sparkling lines

   d. making ice cream for a snack and then finger painting with it

5. Identify 10 art materials that are potentially unsafe or unhealthy for children.

6. Discuss constructivism and constructivist education.

7. Identify and briefly explain three types of knowledge.

8. Discuss Vygotsky's sociocultural theory.

For additional art and creative development resources, visit our Web site at
www.EarlyChildEd.delmar.com

Chapter 5

Children's Artistic Development

What can you tell about the child who created this picture? How old could this child be? How does this piece of art compare with the human figures you have seen children make?

Children share many similarities. They all scribble before they engage in controlled drawing. They play with colors before they paint recognizable pictures. Children also draw what is familiar to them. They use what they know as the basis for their art. This is a self-portrait drawn by a South African boy.

Objectives

After reading this chapter, you should be able to:

- Discuss and critique the different explanations for the development of children's art.
- Match the corresponding artistic accomplishments with Kellogg's and Lowenfeld and Brittain's stages.
- Overview artistic development from birth through age eight using the author's sequence.
- Provide children with experiences in painting.

INTRODUCTION

Children's art has a mysterious quality to it. The flow of lines, shapes, colors, and overall design may make more sense to the child artist than to the adult observer. Why do children scribble? What does their art mean? Why do they draw stick figures when they know people do not look that way? Theories and stages attempt to provide answers to these questions. This chapter surveys and critiques a physical, emotional, perceptual, cognitive, general developmental, and cognitive developmental explanation for children's art. The author has used the stages identified by Kellogg and by Lowenfeld and Brittain in proposing one general sequence to account for the development of art from birth through age eight.

EXPLAINING CHILDREN'S ART

Appreciating children's art may be easier than understanding it or attempting to explain it. Beyond the sheer enjoyment, adults have been trying to make sense out of children's art for decades. Researchers, teachers, parents, art educators, and those interested in child development are concerned with the content, motive, process, and product. Their interest focuses on the following:

- What children choose to include or represent (content)
- How children create (process)
- Why children create (motive)
- What they create as a result (product)

The **content** refers to the subject matter or object being represented. This could include a pet animal, person, feeling, mood, wish, dream, or impulse. The content of children's art is often very personal or idiosyncratic. For example, a wide stroke of black paint may represent a tree trunk. On the other hand, it may represent a child's creative exploration with paint and brush and not be intended for public communication. Too often, adults are prone to search for public meaning where there is none. The **process** refers to the actions and skills involved in creating an art product—cutting and tearing paper, rolling clay, painting, or marking with crayons. Not all art processing results in the creation of a finished art product. Many young children process for its own sake. The **motive** refers to the reason underlying a child's art. For example, adults may explore why a child filled a paper with wide strokes of black paint. Does the child's preoccupation with the color black signify some underlying emotional problem? Is the mark characteristic of a lack of maturation? Does the solitary mark represent social isolation? Or is the child representing the concept of one? The **product** refers to the final outcome. Examples include black paint smeared across a paper, a clay dinosaur, a paper-bag puppet, or a geometric design done in watercolor. The finished product may or may not bear any resemblance to the content or subject matter.

In analyzing the what, why, and how of children's art, there is a risk of misinterpretation or of reading too much into the art. After studying children and their artwork for an extended period of time, however, trends and patterns do emerge. A skillful observer can note these trends and patterns and begin to make some generalizations about what, why, and how children create.

THEORIES OF ARTISTIC DEVELOPMENT

Theories of artistic development attempt to explain what, why, and how children create. The theories are similar yet different. All theories of artistic development attempt to do the same thing—explain a child's artistic development. Each, however, takes a different slant, perspective, or focus. Some theories do a better or more complete job of explaining than others.

Why does one need a theory of artistic development? A theory provides the overall structure or foundation for what we do with children. Different theories suggest different educational practices. For example, there is much debate about the roles of theory and practice in the preparation of early childhood educators. We all want teachers who are competent practitioners. Someone who is long on theory but short on practice would not do a good job in the classroom. Our aim is to translate theory into practice. A theory can be our blueprint or road map, steering us to sound, developmentally appropriate practice. Theory can also help us justify how, why, and what we do with children.

There are numerous theories and explanations that attempt to explain the development of child art. They can be grouped into the following six categories.

1. physical
2. emotional
3. perceptual
4. cognitive
5. general developmental
6. cognitive developmental

1. Physical Explanation for the Development of Child Art

A **physical** explanation for the development of child art holds that the content, process, product, and style of children's art are indicative of their limited physical development. The young child has limited eye-hand coordination, fine motor control, small muscle development, manual dexterity, and visual acuity. Young children mark aimlessly, scribble, and draw unrecognizable shapes because they are physically incapable of anything else. Young children's drawing often appears immature and unintelligible to some adults.

It is obvious that the physical development of a young child does affect artistic expression. For example, one cannot expect a toddler to draw a detailed still life in realistic fashion. Yet, a child may simply choose to scribble or explore with the media, just as an adult may choose to doodle. Accomplished artists who have mastered the techniques of realism often opt for an impressionistic, expressionistic, or abstract style. Adult primitive art, with its simplistic quality, conveys purposeful intent rather

than limited physical development and lack of coordination.

2. Emotional Explanation for the Development of Child Art

An **emotional** explanation for the development of child art holds that the content and style of children's art is indicative of their emotional makeup, personality, temperament, and affective state. Objects, emotions, people, and events of significance are often emphasized in children's drawings and paintings through an exaggerated, distorted, and expressive use of color, size, shape, line, texture, and overall treatment. For example, when a child draws her father as a "Superman" caricature with bulging muscles, a huge red heart, and a wide smile, this may signify her love, respect, admiration, and identification rather than distortion due to faulty vision or limited physical development.

3. Perceptual Explanation for the Development of Child Art

A **perceptual** explanation for the development of child art holds that the content and style of children's art reflects their perceptual development. A perceptual explanation is not identical to a physical one, because perception is not synonymous with vision. Vision, the mechanistic recording of reality, involves projecting images upon the retina. Perception is influenced by the neurophysiological structure, personality, and prior learning. The perceptual explanation holds that a child draws what he or she perceives rather than what he or she sees. The task of art is to create the structural equivalent of the perceived three-dimensional object on the two-dimensional canvas. This can be a monumental task for the artist, regardless of age.

The development of child art provides support for a perceptual explanation. The young child's first attempts at drawing are scribbles with a minimum of line and shape; they gradually increase in complexity and clarity. Some children, however, draw or paint less than they actually see. For example, a child may choose to paint the stripes of a tiger with wide, sweeping strokes, and ignore the head or other extremities. It is also possible that the medium can limit one's expression of the perceptual image. For example, using a wide-bristle brush dipped in watered-down paint might limit the number of details that appear in one's painting. The size of the paper also places constraints on what can be fit into the picture.

4. Cognitive Explanation for the Development of Child Art

A **cognitive** explanation for the development of child art holds that the content and style of children's art is indicative of general intelligence and a function of conceptualization. Children can draw or paint only what they know. One's concept of an object will determine how that object will be represented. For example, when one draws an apple, one's concept of an apple is determined by one's experiences with its color, taste, size, shape, and smell and by related experiences in picking apples, polishing apples, planting apple seeds, climbing apple trees, paring apples, bobbing for apples, mashing apples for cider, and baking and eating an apple pie. Observation of young children involved in art supports a cognitive explanation. Young children rely on memories, images, experiences, and concepts when they draw or paint. Detailed drawings will reflect concepts with which the child has had extensive experience. For example, it would be expected that an urban child will have a less-developed concept of a silo, tractor, and barn than a child living on a farm. The differences will appear when each child draws or paints a farm scene. One would expect the child living on a farm to execute a picture with greater detail and elaboration (see Figure 5–1).

Goodenough (1975) devised the **Draw-A-Man test,** a nonverbal measure of intelligence. It has been revised to Draw-a-Person test. It is assumed that the child's drawing of the human figure is a reflection of that child's concept of a man. Indices of conceptual maturity include appearance of limbs and location, size, and relationship of body parts (see Figure 5–2). If a child has a well-defined concept of a man, reflected in an accurate drawing with properly located body parts, this would indicate a high level of intelligence on the Goodenough measure. The problem with this normative approach is its neglect of individual differences, experiences, and motivational, attitudinal, and environmental factors that can either foster or inhibit concept formation. Ears may be particularly relevant to a young girl with pierced ears. A child living in an area where both sexes sport long hair may be oblivious to ears. A related problem with the human figure drawing test is that some children choose to omit body parts out of whim rather than lack of knowledge. The human figure drawn without ears may be simply the result of creative expression and personal preference. It is also possible that the child may have run out of paint, patience, or interest. Test reliability and validity are concerns.

Concept formation and perceptual analysis are reciprocal processes. Knowledge of an object can improve one's ability accurately observe its details to. In turn, careful observation can lead to increased knowledge of the object.

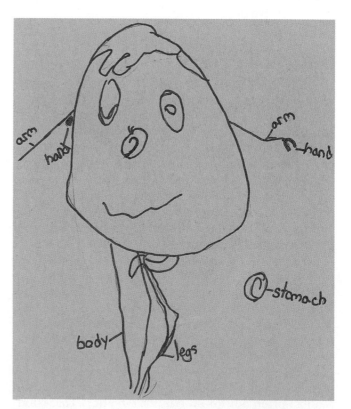

Figure 5-2 The young artist is not concerned with proper placement of body parts.

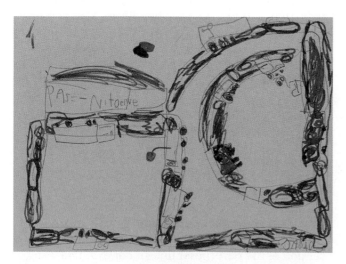

Figure 5-1 Children draw the world as they know and interpret it.

5. General Developmental Explanation for Child Art

A fifth explanation for the development of child art is more global. It provides a **general developmental** explanation that incorporates social, cultural, personality, and environmental factors as well as elements of former explanations. General developmental explanations make use of a stage sequence approach in attempting to explain the artistic expression of the child in holistic fashion.

Theories have given us ages and stages to help understand a child's artistic development. Like theories, there are many stage sequences for the development of children's art. Knowing stages will help us

- understand where a child is developmentally.
- set appropriate but flexible expectations, neither too high nor too low.
- plan a developmentally appropriate art program.
- serve as a framework for evaluation and for conferences with parents.
- appreciate the process and products of art during the early years.

NAEYC Like all development, artistic expression follows a predictable sequence, shifting and changing as the child grows. Development, however, is fluid, meaning that children may move back and forth between stages. Development is also individual, and children move at their own rate and pace.

Kellogg (1969) has amassed over a million paintings and drawings of children from the United States and 30 other countries over the past few decades. Her stages appear in Figure 5–3.

According to Kellogg, some 20 basic scribble patterns make up the first stage of development. These basic **scribbles** are the foundation for future graphic art, pictorial and nonpictorial. As the child proceeds from scribbling to picture making, he or she passes through stages: placement, shape, design, and pictorial. More specifically, the 20 basic scribbles are subsequently drawn according to some 17 different placement patterns by the age of two. By the age of three, these **diagrams** or *gestalts* contain shapes, including the circle, cross, square, and rectangle. One basic diagram, the **mandala** (or **mandaloid**), dominates the child's visual thinking at this time and serves as a basic artistic referent in future drawing. Children use mandalas to draw people, flowers, and **sun figures.** Gestalt psychology has shown the mandala, a crossed circle, to be a universal pattern that the brain is predisposed to utilize in all visual perception (see Figure 5–4).

With the ability to draw diagrams or mandalas, the child moves into the design stage. Two diagrams are put together to make **combines,** or structured designs (see Figure 5–5). Three or more united diagrams constitute an **aggregate.** Between the ages of four and five, most children arrive at the **pictorial stage,** in which their structured designs or aggregates begin to represent objects. Kellogg likens the development of stages in child art with primitive art. Her normative approach supports the position that all children everywhere draw the same things, in the same way, at the same age. The development of artistic ability in the individual appears to recapitulate the artistic development of the human species.

Kellogg's (1979) stages in drawing a human figure are depicted in Figure 5–6.

Lowenfeld and Brittain (1987) are interested in the creative and mental growth of children. Their theory and stages of artistic development are widely recognized and accepted. Their ages, stages, and characteristics appear in Table 5–1.

▶▶ Art Moves from Manipulation to Representation
NAEYC

Children's art does become more realistic over time, and it appears that there is a general sequence or progression to their artistic development. Very young children are in a manipulative stage. The younger the child the greater the reliance on processing, exploring, making, doing, or playing with crayon, marker, paintbrush, or play dough. Actions on objects are repeated and there is little concern for making something. For example, a child may simply squeeze play dough between her fingers without trying to use the play dough to symbolize something else. Older children, kindergartners, and school-age children, in particular, are very concerned that their art resembles something. They are in the stage of representation and work hard at making their artistic symbols look realistic and recognizable to others. They may become disappointed and avoid art if they cannot produce realistic art.

In sum, the developmental explanations, including Kellogg and Lowenfeld, use some form of stage sequence to account for the development of child art. In viewing the child as a whole, they also recognize physical, social, emotional, perceptual, and cognitive factors that influence artistic expression. Yet a general developmental explanation must also account for cultural, religious, individual, and environmental factors in tracing the development of child art. A child's culture and religion may affect his or her drawing ability depending on whether or not the culture values art. A

SCRIBBLE STAGE

There are 20 basic scribbles

1. dot ●

2. single vertical line

3. single horizontal line

4. single diagonal line

5. single curved line

6. multiple vertical line

7. multiple horizontal line

8. multiple diagonal lines

9. multiple curved lines

10. roving open line

11. roving enclosed line
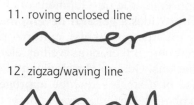

12. zigzag/waving line
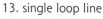

13. single loop line

14. multiple loop line

15. spiral line

16. multiple-line overlaid circle

17. multiple-line circumference circle

18. circular line spread out

19. single crossed line

20. imperfect circle

Figure 5-3 Kellogg's stages.

Two–three-year-olds: PLACEMENT STAGE

Scribbles become more controlled and the child becomes
concerned with placement. There are 17 different placements.

Some include:

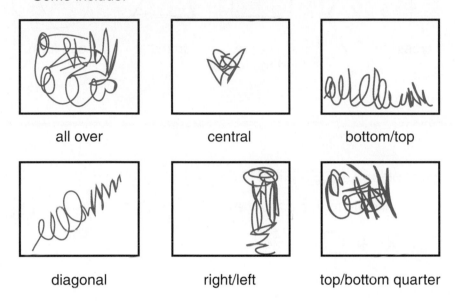

all over	central	bottom/top

diagonal	right/left	top/bottom quarter

Three-year-olds: SHAPE STAGE

Former scribbles drawn at two produce overall *gestalts* or
forms. These gestalts or forms contain the following
implicit shapes:

Later, the above implied shapes are drawn as single outline
forms called *diagrams*.

Figure 5-3 (continued)

Three-year-olds: THE SIX DIAGRAMS include:

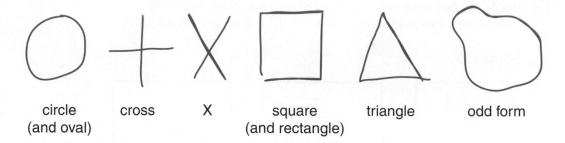

| circle (and oval) | cross | X | square (and rectangle) | triangle | odd form |

Three–four-year-olds: DESIGN STAGE

Two diagrams are united to form a *combine*

For example:

Some *combines* include:

Three or more diagrams are united to form an *aggregate*

For example:

Some *aggregates* include:

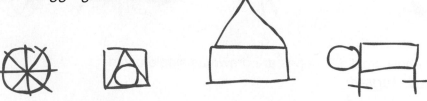

Figure 5-3 (continued)

Four–five-year-olds: **PICTORIAL STAGE**

Their structured designs begin to look like objects that adults can recognize. The *pictorial stage* **can be divided into two phases:**

1. early pictorial
2. later pictorial

Figure 5-3 (continued)

child with an unfulfilled need for acceptance may draw realistic pictures in order to win the praise of a teacher who dislikes abstract art. Environmental factors include home and family, who may constantly punish a child for manipulating, experimenting, exploring, and getting messy. A normative comparison could label this child uncreative or developmentally delayed in artistic expression without allowing for environmental effects.

6. Cognitive Developmental Explanation for Child Art

It would appear that an explanation that incorporates the best of cognitive and general developmental expla-

nations would account comprehensively for the development of child art. Because early childhood educators have been educated in Piaget's theory, it would seem feasible to see whether this theory can be applied to the realm of art. A comprehensive theory that explains all sectors of child development would be more useful than separate theories that explain different behaviors.

Piaget on Child Art

What can Piaget tell us about children's art? His theory and stages of intellectual development claim to be comprehensive, encompassing, and universal. Artistic expression is, at least in part, a cognitive activity. It

Figure 5-4 An early mandala figure, or mandaloid.

Figure 5-5 Shapes combined into designs become mandala figures or mandaloids.

follows that a **cognitive developmental** theory such as Piaget's should explain the development of child art. The task, however, is a difficult one, because Piaget himself believed that it is more difficult to establish regular stages of artistic development than of mental functions. He notes that general development is one of progression, whereas artistic development is one of retrogression. The artwork of the young child appears more creative than that of the older child. In reviewing the theories of children's artistic development, it appears that Piaget accounts for physical, emotional, perceptual, cognitive, and individual factors within his cognitive developmental framework.

Piaget's theory is cognitive in that his interest was in how children think. It is developmental in that his focus was on how children's thinking changed over time. He believed that all children progress through four major stages of development, which proceed in invariant sequence. Cognitive development proceeds from sensory motor, concrete activity to symbolic, higher-order conceptual functioning.

Piaget holds drawing or the graphic image to be a form of the semiotic or symbolic functions and as such a representational activity that is considered to be halfway between symbolic play and the mental im-

age. It is like play in its functional pleasure and autotelism (assimilation) and like the mental image in its effort at imitating the real (accommodation). The first spontaneous attempts at artistic expression can be seen as a series of endeavors to reconcile the tendencies inherent in symbolic play and those that characterize adapted behavior. Through drawing, the child attempts to simultaneously satisfy the need for assimilation and to adapt himself or herself to objects and others through accommodation. According to Piaget and Inhelder (1969), the very first form of drawing does not seem imitative but is more like pure play. It is this play of exercise or scribbling that toddlers do when given a pencil, crayon, or marker. Soon, however, the young child realizes forms in these aimless scribbles and tries to repeat them from memory. There may be little or no likeness between these scribbles. As soon as this intention exists, Piaget and Inhelder believe, drawing becomes imitation and image.

Lowenfeld and Brittain's stages of artistic development appear to parallel Piaget's stages of cognitive development. A comparison of Piaget with Kellogg and Lowenfeld and Brittain is found in Table 5–2.

Gardner on Art

Howard Gardner (1980), an insightful observer of children's creative development, wondered what happens to the spontaneity of early creativity during the elementary years. Further, he asked what would promote continued artistic development. Years of study and observation convinced him that creativity has distinct forms and different needs during three different developmental phases which extend into adulthood.

1. Scribbling:

2. Drawing a single shape:

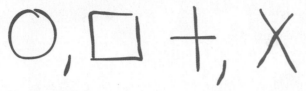

3. Combining single shapes into designs:

4. Drawing mandalas, mandaloids, and sun figures:

5. Drawing a human figure with limbs and torso:

Figure 5-6 Kellogg's stages in drawing a human figure.

Table 5-1 Stages of Artistic Development by Lowenfeld and Brittain

AGE	STAGE AND CHARACTERISTICS
1½–4 years:	**I Scribbling: The Beginnings of Self-Expression**
	Scribbling is a developmentally and artistically important kinesthetic, manipulative, and expressive behavior.
1½–2½:	**Substage IA: Disordered and Random Scribbling**
	• large muscle, whole arm movements
	• kinesthetic pleasure, pure processing
	• whole-hand grip on marking tool
	• may not look at paper while marking
	• accidental, random motoric mark making
	• haphazard lines
	• swing of arm coming in contact with paper results in mark
	• uses shoulder motion
	• may scribble beyond confines of paper
	• exploration—what can I do by moving these tools on paper?
	• lines made with simple movements
	• tight grip with rigid wrist position
	• minimal movement with fingers in marking
2, 2½–3:	**Substage IB: Controlled Scribbling**
	• smaller marks, better control and organization
	• marking motions are repeated
	• uses wrist motion with greater control
	• stays within drawing area of paper
	• variety of lines and direction appear
	• better visual and motoric control over where to make lines
	• watches intently while scribbling
	• more-intricate loops and swirls appear
	• wider range of scribbles
3, 3½–4:	**Substage IC: Named Scribbling**
	• spends more time mark making
	• gives names to scribbles
	• relates scribbles to things in environment
	• name of scribble may change in the process
	• holds marking tools with fingers, better fine motor control

Table 5-1   Stages of Artistic Development by Lowenfeld and Brittain   *(continued)*

AGE	STAGE AND CHARACTERISTICS
3, 3½–4:	**Substage IC: Named Scribbling** *(continued)*

- greater variety of lines
- increased concentration
- more-intentional placement of marks
- awareness and intentional use of empty space
- scribbles not matching the name or label given except to child artist
- moving from sheer physical expression to making marks that stand for something else by giving them a name

4–7 years:	**II Preschematic**

A schema is a generalized symbol that represents a specific concept. For example, a child's stick-figure drawing is used to represent all people.

- child's first representational attempts
- symbolic representation built up from former scribbles
- appearance of recognizable geometric shapes
- placement and size random and out of proportion
- random floating spatial arrangement
- may turn or rotate paper while drawing
- distortion and omission of parts in human figure drawing
- head-feet representation of human figure as in Figure 5–7
- head-feet representation of human figure
- over time, arms, body, fingers, toes, clothes, hair, and other details appearing
- objects drawn as isolated entities; no relationship
- art as personal self-expression rather than for public communication
- very personal idiosyncratic symbols
- can copy a square at age four, triangle at five
- relative size appearing at end of stage
- child learning that what is known or experienced can be symbolically represented by mark making
- children drawing how they feel or think about an object, leading to omission, exaggeration, and distortion
- color used randomly, not realistically
- schemas or symbols beginning to be recognizable to others
- children enjoying talking about their art
- drawing things that are important, relevant, or personally meaningful, e.g., family, pets, or friends
- objects drawn facing forward

(continued)

Table 5-1 Stages of Artistic Development by Lowenfeld and Brittain *(continued)*

AGE	STAGE AND CHARACTERISTICS
7–9 years:	**III Schematic: Achievement of a Form Concept**
	• form concept developed and repeated
	• drawing reflecting a child's concept, not perception of an object
	• bold, direct flat representation
	• two-dimensional spatial representation
	• baseline appearing to portray space
	• skyline possibly also appearing at top
	• drawing reflecting what a child knows
	• subjective portrayal of space
	• X-ray drawing appearing simultaneously, showing exterior and interior view
	• representation of space showing a frontal and aerial view depicted simultaneously
	• human figure made up of geometric shapes repeated and refined
	• detailed and decorative
	• move to greater conformity or stiffness in drawing things the way they should be
9–12 years:	**IV Dawning Realism: The Gang Age**
	There is a greater awareness of details. Older children are more self-conscious about their art. The plane replaces the baseline. Objects are drawn smaller and less distorted.
12–14 years:	**V Pseudonaturalistic/Realistic Drawing**
	Young adolescents are very self-critical of their drawing. Detailed human figures with sexual characteristics appear. Cartoons, caricatures, and action figures are also popular. Depth and proportion appear. End of spontaneous art.
14–17 years:	**VI Artistic Decision: Adolescent Art**
	For some adolescents, natural artistic development does not extend beyond the former stage unless they are given further instruction. Some pursue naturalistic style, while others use art for a personal statement. They may copy an artistic style in forming their own personal style.

In the first stage, preschoolers are instinctively creative, delighted in music, art, drama, and language. Gardner (1980) observed that the expressiveness of their paintings and drawings had much in common with those of talented adults using ideas or images in fresh, unusual ways. A child begins making marks during the second year of life. The child of two grabs a marker and scribbles enthusiastically on every surface. A three-year-old produces a vast array of geometric forms including circles, crosses, rectangles, and triangles. The child is establishing a vocabulary of lines and forms, the basic building blocks of a graphic language. The four- and five-year-old cease-lessly creates and re-creates representations of objects, often recognizable to others. The *tadpole man* appears. The child's drawing of a person represents a tadpole with two legs emanating from a large head. The preschooler evolves fixed patterns, or schemas, e.g., house = square with triangle on top. A summit of artistry is achieved at the end of the preschool years. Drawings by preschoolers are characteristically colorful, balanced, rhythmic, and expressive. The drawings of young schoolchildren are often their most striking creations: vibrant, expressive, exhibiting a strong command of form and considerable beauty. Gardner adds that children's drawings can be said

Figure 5-7 Preschematic art: head-feet representation of the human figure, or a sun figure according to Kellogg.

without exaggeration to undergo a complete life cycle of their own.

During the second stage, around age seven however, the pattern shifts. Children's imagination appears to get stuck and they stop engaging in creative processing in favor of a preoccupation with language, games, or peers. Free graphic expression is replaced by a strong determination to achieve photographic realism in drawing. Gardner observed eight- through 10-year-olds searching for literal meanings rather than metaphors. Many prefer to copy or collect pictures rather than create their own.

What has happened in the course of a few years? Some blame schools and families for the strong message children receive to conform and think convergently. There is another explanation. The period of literal thinking with its emphasis on following the rules is also operating at this time. After engaging in imagination during the early years, children in this second phase think differently. Because art is a cognitive pursuit, one would expect that the nature of their art production would also change.

The third stage, around ages 15 to 25, brings a convergence of the abilities to plan a creative project, implement, and evaluate it. While most people are mastering fixed information or skills in a chosen field,

Schirrmacher's Stages: A General Overview of Artistic Development

A General Overview of Artistic Development (Birth to Eight)

The author has attempted to combine the different stages of artistic development suggested by Kellogg, Lowenfeld and Brittain, and others into one workable general sequence. The levels or stages are overlapping, and ages are approximate. Schirrmacher's sequence of early childhood art follows.

I. Manipulating the Media: Scribbling and Mark Making (one-two years)

Very young children's first art experiences are purely sensorimotor actions resulting in scribbles. They approach crayons, markers, and play dough with the intent of exploring their properties and discovering what they can make them do. What happens if the crayon is mouthed, swung, and then accidentally strikes the paper? What an

interesting thing, thinks the toddler. The very young child lacks fine motor control and eye-hand coordination. Scribbles or vague marks will appear random and haphazard to the adult but wonderfully creative to the young artist who accomplished this feat. Scribbling is nonverbal self-expression. Scribbling and mark making are to drawing as babbling is to speech and crawling is to walking. Scribbling has sensory appeal in that children see the mark they make as they move the tool across the paper. So much the better if the paper tears or the crayon breaks. Look what I made happen, thinks the young artist. Toddlers move from random scribbling to making scribbles which are more controlled, deliberate, and pronounced. Circular strokes are repeated and crayons are moved horizontally or vertically back and forth, making lines which cross and intersect. Some lines and circles are repeatedly traced

(Continued)

Schirrmacher's Stages: A General Overview of Artistic Development (continued)

over. Scribbles become more purposefully placed rather than extending beyond the paper and onto the table or easel. Scribbles may be named, although there may be no connection between the verbal label and graphic symbol (see Figure 5-8).

II. Making Shapes, Outlines, Designs, and Symbols That Have Personal Meaning (two–four years)

Young preschoolers work at refining their circles, ovals, lines, and attempted geometric shapes. Lines cross or enclose space forming squares, triangles, and rectangles. A cross enclosed by a circle forms a mandala. Children progress from mandalas to suns to stick figures. Single and repeated round and linear marks become a circle which may represent the sun. A sun with facial features, including eyes and mouth, becomes a face. A circle or sun-face with radiating lines develops into a person with arms and legs radiating out from the round face. The potato person is born. Because infants are intrigued by the human face, it is no surprise that the human figure is first drawn as all face. This stick figure is a schema, a generalized symbol or form concept that will be used to represent any and all human figures, regardless of age, sex, or build. Animals develop from this human figure. They are vertically or horizontally portrayed as the human with a tail or animal ears. A square becomes a schema for any and all buildings. A circle atop a vertical line is the "lollipop" schema used to portray trees and flowers. Eisner (1976) would call these examples of pictographs, or simplified flat, two-dimensional shapes. The child adds, omits, distorts, exaggerates, or streamlines these very personal symbols. The result is an abbreviated form with little concern for actual color, shape, or size. Spatial arrangement is random, and the child may simply rotate the paper to fit objects in. The very personal symbol or design may not be recognizable to the observer. Children in this stage are still very much process oriented. They delight in playing with colors, shapes, and forms. They enjoy talking about their creations but may walk away from or discard their products, indicating their relative love of processing.

III. Pictorial Art That Is Becoming Recognizable to Others (four–six years)

Older preschoolers and young school-age children become concerned with creating art that looks like something. They may plan their art in advance and use details to polish their products. Pictorial art is a stage in the development of children's art when their art is becoming recognizable to others although color, shape, size, placement, proportion, and perspective are arbitrary. A purple dog may dwarf a green cow, both of which appear to be floating in the sky. Color is used emotionally, reflecting their relationship to the symbols rendered. Triangles and squares mastered in the prior stage are now combined into houses which appear to float in space. Later they will rest at the bottom of the paper or on a drawn baseline. Over time, houses are decorated with geometric shapes, including a rectangular door, square windows with parted curtains, and a smoking chimney drawn parallel to the roof line, defying gravity. Facial features, body parts, and clothing are added to the human figure. Some personally important parts like the head, eyes, smile, and belly button tend to be exaggerated. If a child's father has a beard, he may be given one in the picture. Figure 5-9 appears distorted as a claw is used to symbolize hands and feet. Some children will choose to simply eliminate body parts such as the neck and shoulders. During this stage some children become interested and even obsessed with producing multiple products. They will draw a favorite subject over and over again. Their desire to simultaneously portray the inside and outside of objects, for example, the exterior of a plane in a storm and interior with pilot and passengers, leads them to make "X-ray drawings" reflecting what the child knows rather than how it appears in reality. Children in this stage lack the control, coordination, and skill necessary to realistically represent their three-dimensional world on a two-dimensional canvas.

Schirrmacher's Stages: A General Overview of Artistic Development (continued)

IV. Realistic (school-age five-eight years)

School-age children want things to look right, to draw and paint things the way they appear in reality. They strive for photographic realism (see Figure 5-10) and seem dissatisfied making abstract or nonrepresentational art. Nonrealistic art is relegated to younger children who scribble. School-age children work on size placement, shape, color, perspective, proportion, depth, shading, and the use of details to capture reality. Rather than floating in space, a house rests on a lower baseline and the sky and sun inhabit a top baseline. Things in the distance are drawn smaller and set back, giving the illusion of depth and perspective. School-age children develop, re-peat, and refine symbols which can often be categorized by gender. Generally, boys draw male superheroes, race cars, vehicles, army and war scenes, and sports events. Generally, girls draw female superheroes, princesses, horses, fair maidens, and unicorns. With increasing age, children become self-critical and succumb to peer pressure, internalizing hurtful comments that focus on their artistic shortcomings. The few who receive guidance and specific instruction will continue to engage in art. Others pursue impressionistic, expressionist, and nonrealistic art. Unfortunately, too many will close the door on their short-lived artistic and creative career, concluding they are uncreative and untalented in art.

Figure 5-8 Scribbling and mark making produce very personal symbols and designs.

Figure 5-9 Early attempts at representing the human figure.

the creative individual stands out as one who continues to take risks, attempt new projects, and preserve individuality. By ages 30 to 35, these patterns are even more evident.

Gardner (1980) speaks of a **U-shaped curve** in artistic development. This means that some important aspects of artistry emerge early in a child's life only to go underground during a period of middle childhood. It is during this period that decisions are made by the individual either to move forward and grow artistically through specialized training or refinement of an individual style, or to forgo art altogether.

Figure 5-10 The older artist strives for realism.

 **PAINTING**

Painting is a pleasurable, messy, and creative art activity. It also allows children to plan; to make decisions about what to paint, colors, and placement; and to work on their own. Not all children will have had experience painting before coming to school. Painting will be a popular activity. For these reasons, painting should be made available throughout the day every day. Some children panic when they see only one or two easels and fear that they will never get a turn if painting is allowed only once a day for a short period of time (see Figure 5–11).

Generally, painting involves the use of tempera or watercolor paints. Tempera paints are opaque and give a smooth, flat covering of intense color. They are

Table 5-2 Stages of Art Compared with Piaget's Stages of Cognitive Development

PIAGET'S STAGE	KELLOGG'S STAGE	LOWENFELD AND BRITTAIN'S STAGE
Sensory Motor (0–2)	Scribbling (2)	
Preoperational: (2–7)		
• Preconceptual (2–4)	Placement (2–3)	Scribbling (2–4):
		• disordered and random
		• controlled
		• named
	Shape (3):	
	• gestalts	
	• diagrams	
	Design (3–4):	
	• combines	
	• aggregates	
• Intuitive (4–7)	Pictorial (4–5)	Preschematic (4–7)
	• early	
	• late	
Concrete operations (7–11)		Schematic (7–9)
		Dawning realism (9–12)
Formal operations (11-adult)		Pseudorealism (12–14)
		Artistic decision (14–17)

Figure 5-11 Easel painting with a friend.

Figure 5-12 The young painter at work.

water-soluble, and adding water will dilute them and dull their intensity. Tempera paints come in both liquid and powder form. The liquid form is more expensive but comes ready to use. The powder form is more economical but must be mixed with water. Also, powdered tempera paints are not recommended for children under 12 (see Chapter 4). Powdered tempera colors create inhalable dusts, and some colors contain toxic pigments, preservatives, and additives. Wear a mask when preparing the powder, and do not mix in the presence of children. When your supply of powdered tempera is deple-ted, switch to liquid tempera for the sake of child safety.

Watercolor paints are transparent and allow for a layering of colors. Children should have experience with tempera before graduating to watercolors. Still, children never outgrow their interest in tempera painting. There are many different painting arrangements, including:

standing at an easel—This position allows for whole-arm strokes and total body involvement. It allows for the use of long-handled brushes. Easel painting, however, does have its drawbacks. Given the slant or angle, paint tends to run and drip down. This frustrates some children who expect liquid paint to defy gravity and stay put where they place it. They expect it to act like a marker or crayon. On the positive side, easels encourage verbalization and socialization between painters, especially if the easels are placed side by side (see Figure 5–11).

seated at a table—Children can also paint on a flat surface while seated at a table (see Figure 5–12). This placement keeps paint from dripping and allows layers of paint to be built up. Usually a table can accommodate a few painters at one time. Children can use shorthandled brushes, as in wa-

tercoloring. Paint will be more controllable, but the amount of arm and body movement will be restricted.

standing at a table—This position allows for whole body movements while painting on a flat surface. Whereas four children can sit down and paint at the same time, only one can stand and paint at each end of the table. This position is highly recommended.

on the floor—Painting on the floor provides a flat surface, although this position also restricts whole body movement. It is hard to involve the bottom torso when one is kneeling. Children, including those who are physically challenged, enjoy sprawling on the floor and will find this position comfortable. Standing for a long period of time while painting tires and bores some young children.

outdoors—Use any of the above indoor arrangements to paint outdoors.

Although painting while standing at a table or easel is highly recommended, it is wise to give children experience painting at a variety of different angles and placements.

Paints and Painting Accessories

brushes—see the later section on brushes

condiment bottles—squeeze ketchup and mustard bottles with pointed tips make good paint dispensers

cotton swabs—for dabbing paint

dispensers—bottles for squeezing paint

drying rack or line—to let pictures dry undisturbed

extender—a bulking powder that extends paint without losing its brilliance

finger paint—good for hand painting, given its thick, chunky texture fluorescent, water-, or tempera colors—for the advanced child artist

food coloring—added to water makes a fast paint

funnels—to avoid waste when pouring powder paint and for printing

glass—pane of glass or sheet of Plexiglas® for monoprinting

ice-cube trays—for color mixing

ink—one bottle of black is standard

kitchen gadgets—for printing with paint

liquid laundry starch—add to tempera to make finger paint

magic brush set—paint, water, and brush are combined into one magic brush tube. A cross between a marker and a paintbrush. The set is commercially available.

media mix—add to tempera to make finger paint; it claims to intensify colors

messless sign caddy paint system—a complete rainbow assortment of nontoxic water-soluble paints in squeeze bottles, used with special felt brushes. Spillproof containers available. Pretty colors but expensive.

muffin tin—for paint palette

no-spill paint cups—hold paint and resist tipping

paint pots—with lids; fit snugly in a tray

paint stirrers—Popsicle® sticks, tongue depressors, or coffee stirrers will do

paint tumblers—with snap-on lids to keep paint from drying out

plastic dryer—a hanging dryer with pinch clips for holding wet pictures. Available in housewares at discount stores.

plastic spoons—for mixing paint

poster paint—brighter and more expensive than tempera. Good for making signs, posters, or banners on poster board.

pumps—fit gallon paint containers; one pump yields one ounce

spatula—to mix paints in bulk

splatter screen—for spatter printing

sponges—for printing

spoon rest—to hold brush with paint

squeeze bottles—good for dispensing tempera paint. Some companies offer liquid tempera in squeeze bottles.

sweater dryer—wire screen or net for spatter printing

syrup dispensers—good for storing mixed paint and for use with art palette method of painting

tempera cakes or color paint cakes—concentrated tempera; use like watercolor, comes in tray, refills available, no spilling or mixing involved, more expensive than liquid and powder

tempera liquid—more expensive than powder but saves on measuring and mixing. Colors more brilliant than powder.

tempera powder—most economical but requires mixing

watercolor—individual sets of eight are recommended

Hint: Remember to buy and use only lead-free, nontoxic paint.

Hint: Buy red, blue, yellow, black, and white in bulk. These can be mixed to produce other colors, shades, and tints. Start beginning painters with the primary colors.

Hint: Add liquid dishwashing detergent to tempera paint. It will make it bubbly and easier to wash off hands and out of clothes. It will also help paint adhere to slick or glossy surfaces, such as glass, plastic, metal, tinfoil, and waxed cartons. Detergent also keeps paint from cracking when it dries.

Hint: Add a drop or two of oil of cloves or oil of wintergreen to prevent spoilage if you mix paint days in advance.

Hint: Add coffee grounds, salt, or sand along with white glue to paint to give it a rough, coarse, gritty texture. Adding sugar will give it a sparkling appearance when dry. Adding sawdust will give it a thick, lumpy texture. Adding white glue to paint thickens it.

Hint: Finger paint can be made by

- adding liquid laundry starch to tempera or food coloring.
- mixing wheat paste (wallpaper paste), water, and tempera paint until smooth.
- mixing liquid starch, soap flakes, and tempera paint.
- adding small pieces of finely ground colored chalk to paste. Add a few drops of water if too stiff.

Hint: To mix powder paints:

Pour powder through a funnel into a paint container. Mix with enough water to form a thick, creamy liquid. Aim for the consistency of yogurt. Test on paper. It should not run. Add more water if too thick, more powder if too thin and runny. A recommended ratio is 2 parts tempera powder to 1 part water. Add a few squirts of liquid dishwashing detergent to aid cleanup. Shake or mix well until smooth and creamy.

Hint: To mix liquid paints:

Place a spoonful in a container. Slowly add water. Test on paper. Add more water if still too thick, more liquid paint if too thin and runny.

Hint: Individual jars or bottles of paint can be stored in a plastic tub to keep them from tipping over. You can also make a paint holder out of a plastic egg carton. Use only the top section, and discard the individual egg holders. Trace three circles using the jars, milk cartons, or juice cans that will later hold the paint. Carefully cut out the three holes. Insert the containers and fill each with paint and one brush. A shoe box could also be used because it is deep and sturdy.

Hint: Tall plastic cups or see-through containers are recommended. Juice cans or small milk cartons are an ideal size but do not allow the child to see the color within. Painting the outside of the container the same color as the paint it will hold will solve the problem.

Hint: Biocolor® paint is made from natural ingredients and cosmetic pigments, ensuring a completely nontoxic and environmentally safe product. Unlike other tempera paints, Biocolor® will not crack, flake, or fade. It is economically priced so it can be used as everyday high-quality tempera paint. It is available from Discount School Supply. See Appendix D.

Hint: An extender such as bentonite reduces paint cost and gives the desired consistency. It also can be added to tempera to make finger

WARNING

The reader has been previously warned about using tempera powder with young children. It is important to use up remaining bottles of tempera powder and order only liquid paint in the future.

paint. Other extenders can be made by mixing flour or cornstarch with water; cornmeal will produce a different texture. Soap or detergent powder will also thicken paint.

Hint: Liquid starch makes the paint creamy and results in a glossy finish. Too much starch causes flakiness when the paint dries.

Hint: Keep a tight lid on paint containers and store in a cool place. Refrigerate if milk is used in the recipe.

Hint: The following procedure is recommended when children paint at the art table: Place an absorbent paper towel at the bottom of a Styrofoam® tray and add paint. The towel works as a blotter, absorbing the paint but providing just enough color when touched by a brush. It also facilitates cleanup.

Hint: Make your own no-spill paint containers. Trace the top of a small empty juice can onto a sponge. Cut out the inside circle. Slide juice can through sponge. Cut sponge to snugly fit inside easel tray. The sponge secures the paint container and catches paint drips.

Paint Recipes

Salt Paint

½ cup liquid starch
2 cups salt
1 cup water
tempera powder or food coloring

Thoroughly mix liquid starch, salt, and water. Slowly add food coloring or tempera powder. Use as paint. Pictures will sparkle when the salt paint dries.

Easel Paint

In a tall container, mix:
1 cup liquid starch
½ cup soap
1 cup powdered tempera
Stir gently until all the powder is dissolved into the liquid. Let stand for one hour. Stir again, breaking up any large lumps—pour into empty tempera jar, cover tightly and shake. Consistency improves overnight. Shake gently before using.

Whipped Soap Paint

soap flakes
warm water
food coloring (optional)
Pour soap flakes into a bowl. Slowly add water. 1 cup soap flakes to ½ cup water is a good ratio. Beat with rotary eggbeater until frothy but not stiff. Use as paint on black construction paper. Good for making winter snow scenes. It has a thick, heavy texture that adds a three-dimensional effect. Or add food coloring and use on white or other colors of paper.

Special Paint

1 part glycerin (available at drugstore)
1 part water
1 part white glue
tempera paint (powder or liquid)
Mix to the consistency of cake icing. Add tempera slowly. Stir well. Cover with lid and let set for a few days. Use with foam-head paintbrush. See the section on special painting and special painters in the activity section in this chapter.

Brushes

There are many different types of brushes recommended for painting. Long-handled brushes with flat bristles are called flats. They produce wide strokes. Brushes with rounded and pointed bristles are called rounds. They produce narrow lines and strokes. Be sure to include a wide array of brushes for painting, including:
bath brush—for easel painting
bowl brush—new, not used, for easel painting
detergent dispenser—fill with paint and use as brush
dish pom-pom—for a novel paintbrush (see Figure 5–13)
easel—long-handled for painting while standing at the easel

Figure 5-13 Dish pom-pom painting.

feather duster—for interesting effects while easel painting
foam-head brush—for innovative painting
hairbrush with plastic spikes
household brushes—an array of inexpensive household and paintbrushes found at discount stores is also recommended
makeup brushes—provide nice variety for the older artist
nail brush
paste brush—for spreading paste
pastry brush—for painting while seated
scrub brush—for large, vigorous, sweeping strokes
shaving brush—stubby handle is easy to grip
short-handled brush—for painting while seated or close up at easel
silverware sorter or tray—to sort and store brushes
spoon rest—for holding wet brush while painting
stencil brush—short-handled with stiff bristles for dabbing and small strokes when making a stencil
toothbrush—for general painting, stencil, and spatter printing
varnish brush—wide, inexpensive, found at discount stores
vegetable brush—for general painting
watercolor brush—short and thin, with pointed bristles
whisk broom

Hint: Brushes come in a variety of sizes, shapes, qualities, and prices. Long-handled brushes are good for easel painting, when a child stands a short distance from the paper. Short-handled brushes are often used for painting while seated at a table, where the distance between artist and paper is minimal. Buying flats, rounds, and both short- and long-handled brushes will encourage a variety of paint strokes. Brush tips are made of red sable, camel hair, bristle, natural, or synthetic materials. A moderately expensive brush with stiff bristles is a good investment. The bristles will hold up to thick paint and will not fall out with the first washing. Never use a brush to mix paint. Instead, use a stick or spoon.

Hint: Brushes need to be washed soon after each use, preferably before the paint has become dried and crusty. Rinse out excess paint. Add a small drop of liquid detergent and gently wash the bristles. Rinse thoroughly with warm but never hot water (hot water will melt the glue that holds the bristles in place). Squeeze out excess water. Reshape bristles to their natural shape (e.g., twirl a watercolor brush into a pointed shape). Let air dry. Always store brushes with their handles down and bristles up. Tall, thin potato chip cans are ideal for brush storage.

Hint: Brushes can be homemade. Clamp a small sponge with a pinch-type clothespin and use as a brush. A wad of cloth tied to a pencil makes a good paintbrush. Cotton swabs can be tied with string or yarn and used for dabbing paint.

Hint: Trim the edges of inexpensive foam paintbrushes into shapes and designs.

Hint: Bristles on brushes will split and spread over time. Carefully use a razor blade to trim jagged edges or stray bristles.

Hint: Insert a small paintbrush into a hair roller or ball of clay. This will provide a larger, graspable surface for the child with limited fine motor coordination and control.

Other Painting Tools

A brush is not the only tool for painting. Also, there is no reason to use only one brush at a time. Children can paint with a brush in each hand or with two brushes tied together. Other recommended painting tools include:

- balloons
- fingers and hands
- string (6 inches in length) attached to pinch-type clothespin
- eyedroppers
- cotton swabs or cotton balls
- straws
- sponges
- combs
- Popsicle® sticks or tongue depressors
- feathers
- toothpicks
- sticks, twigs, bark, weeds, ferns, hay, straw, or pine needles
- string
- rags
- assorted kitchen gadgets
- powder puffs
- spatulas
- kitchen shakers
- empty plastic razors
- wads of cloth tied to thick pencils
- small paint rollers for trim
- pipe cleaners twisted into unusual shapes
- shoe-polish applicators

Painting Surfaces

Children do most of their painting on paper. It is important to provide paper in a variety of colors, shapes, sizes, and textures. Children can explore painting on papers that are wet as well as dry. Painting on damp paper will provide an effect similar to that of watercolors. The colors will bleed and blend. The edges will be soft, with many creative accidents as paint runs together to form unusual shapes. Allow time before adding too many colors, which may all run together and form a dark blot. Some other things to paint on include:

- glass or windows
- Formica® or tabletops
- cardboard
- boxes
- wood
- wallpaper
- paper bags
- newspaper
- tinfoil (over cardboard)—add liquid detergent to paint
- bubble wrap
- smooth stones
- paper plates
- plastic

Easel and Art Surfaces

art storage and easel—a long, double-sided easel with room for four children and shelves for storage. Commercially available, but fairly expensive.

chalkboard—for use with chalk

double- or triple-sided easel—self-standing with paint rack

easel clips—two clips to hold the upper corners; large paper clips or clothespins will do. Make sure children can work them.

messy tray—a plastic self-contained area for one finger painter. A large cookie sheet will also do.

see-through easel—acrylic, plastic or Plexiglas®, transparent, see-through, wipe-off surface

wall easel—a board attached to the wall that swings out when in use and stores flat against the wall the rest of the time. A real space saver and a good project for a volunteer parent/grandparent/carpenter.

Hint: Easels are expensive but a good investment. Standing easels allow for whole arm sweeping strokes. Make sure the easel is at the child's height. Paper should be placed in front of the child's chest and within easy reach, neither too high nor too low. Saw off the legs of the easel if necessary. Actually, a minimum of two easels should be provided for a large group of children. Having too few easels makes children anxious and concerned that they will never get a turn.

It is also possible to construct a homemade tabletop easel out of a sturdy cardboard carton. Two pyramid-shaped tabletop easels can be made by cutting the carton diagonally. Cut two slits at the top for inserting clothespins or clips to hold the paper. Two identical hardwood panels can be hinged together to make a more durable tabletop easel. Add a small chain between the panels to keep the easel stationary when it is open.

Hint: There is another way to make a homemade tabletop easel. Find a large wallpaper sample book. Remove the pages and save the cover. One book makes a double-sided easel. Find a shallow carton lid that the book can rest on. Select your angle and cut notches on the book covers. Insert the carton into the notches. Use clothespins or clips at the top to hold paper.

Hint: Remember to use easel clips or clothespins that the children can work by themselves. Some teachers prefer to place several pieces of paper at each easel in the morning. This eliminates the continual taking down of the completed painting and hanging up of the clean sheet. Also, remember to place some form of covering under the easel. Newspaper is easy to come by and disposable. An old washable throw rug, however, will not only protect the floor but also be more attractive and comfortable to stand on.

Painting Precautions

Remember to roll sleeves up, remove sweaters, and use a smock. Provide one brush or painting tool for each color. Do not fill paint jars full. Full jars only add to the dripping and mess. Instead, fill jars less than half full and add paint as needed. Try to use a clear container so that children can easily see the color of the paint. Glass jars are clear but also potentially dangerous. Fairly large, see-through plastic cups or containers are ideal. Or paint a tin can the color of the paint it will hold. Encourage children to keep the paints and brushes to their left and paper to the right. This will reinforce the left-to-right progression so crucial to later reading and writing.

How many colors should be provided? Some believe that beginning painters need only one color until they have learned the basic processes involved in holding a brush, dipping for paint, wiping excess, positioning on paper, and making strokes. Others begin with two. The author recommends providing the three primary colors. Additional colors will appear on the canvas through accidental or purposeful mixing. They can also be mixed using the palette method. Containers of white and black will help children lighten or darken colors. There is no one right answer to the opening question. Those who stress the technical skills involved will recommend using only one color. Those who stress the importance of color mixing and creative expression would provide two or more. Five would be maximum. More is not necessarily better when providing colors of paint. The same holds true for the number of crayons in a box. Children can be as creative with the basic eight as they can with an overwhelming sixty-four.

Painting is a messy activity. Remind children to scrape the side of the brush on the inside rim of the jar before they remove it from the paint. This will help eliminate the dripping of excess paint on table, floor, smock, and paper. Encourage children to replace the brush or painting tool in the one designated container. Mistakes will happen. Be sure to rinse brushes thoroughly to avoid unwanted mixing of paints. Children should wash their hands before taking off their smocks. This will avoid smearing of paint on skin, hair, and clothing.

Paint Palette

Children who have had some experience in color mixing can be introduced to painting with a palette. An aluminum pie plate, frozen dinner tray, or plastic lid is recommended. Children take blobs of mixed paint and mix their own colors, shades, and tints on their palette. Always have the primary colors and white and black available. Children need their own brushes for color mixing on the palette. They also need a cup of water for cleaning the brushes between color mixings.

Here are some activities for painting.

Hand Painting

Finger painting is an activity that is not usually offered in the home. Still, most young children have had some experience spreading soap on the sides of the bathtub or food on the tray of their high chair. *Finger painting* is not an accurate term. The activity, which involves much more than merely spreading paint with the fingers, should more accurately be called hand painting. Often, adults approach hand painting by neatly dabbing their forefingers with their pinkies gracefully up in the air. The whole hand and arm should be involved. Some teachers allow children to paint with their feet. Hand painting is messy but developmentally appropriate. Children make direct contact with the medium. There is no brush to separate the artist from the paint. Children enjoy the cool, slimy texture. It gives young children the opportunity to get messy without fear of reprimand. It is an activity that should be provided on an ongoing basis. Some children will be reluctant. They may fear that their clothes will get dirty or that their parents will be angry with them for making a mess. They will need time and gentle reassurance. Seeing the other children and their teacher engaging in hand painting may reassure them. A child should not be forced to do hand painting against his or her wishes.

When hand painting, children should be encouraged to get fully involved by using the following:
front or palm of the hand—for wide strokes
back of the hand—for wide strokes
side of the hand—for long, thin strokes and zigzags
fingertips and joints of the fingers—for dabbing marks
fingers, front and back—for long marks
thumbs—for round marks
knuckles—for a series of marks

fingernails—for fine lines that etch through the paint
fists—for massive marks and round swirls
wrists—for massive marks
hand with fingers spread wide—for hand prints
whole arms, toes, and feet—best done outdoors on a warm day

As with brush painting, sleeves need to be rolled up and sweaters removed to encourage freedom of movement, and smocks should be worn. Hand painting while kneeling or sitting on the floor restricts movement. Hand painting while standing at a table is recommended. It allows children to use their large arm muscles more freely, reach all over their papers, and have a better view of what they are doing. Standing up also keeps one's smock from dangling in the wet paint.

Music sets the mood for finger painting. Slow music encourages lazy, smooth strokes. Fast music encourages rapid, swirling lines.

Shaving cream can be used with older children. It is thicker than most finger paints, and children enjoy the texture. Remind them that it is not whipped cream and is not edible. Squirt a glob for each child and spray water to dilute.

Hand painting should be done on paper with a glossy or glazed surface. Finger paint paper is commercially available but fairly expensive. Slick cardboard, shiny shelf paper, gift boxes, magazine covers, or a nonstick baking sheet can also be used. Add liquid detergent to the paint and do hand painting directly on a Formica® tabletop. Lay a sheet of paper over the table, rub gently, and take a print of the hand painting. This will please those children who want to save what they made. Adding some vinegar to the wash water will help clean the tables.

Begin by giving each child a piece of paper. The papers can be laid out glossy side up and sponged down with water first or occasionally squirted with a pump sprayer. Begin with the primary colors. Add one glob or teaspoon of paint. Paint that is applied too heavily will crack or chip off when dry. It is difficult to manage hand painting with a large group. The first child may finish before you have given paint to the last child. It may be easier and less stressful to do hand painting in shifts with fewer children. This allows you to observe and interact rather than merely dispense.

Encourage children to use both hands in thoroughly spreading the paint. Squirt with water if the paint becomes dry. Add a second color. Over time the colors will become thoroughly mixed. Mixing red and blue will make purple. This may be the time to stop. You may want to add yellow or white to lighten it up if the children are still interested and want a third color. Placing the paper flat on newspaper to dry will result in a curled picture. When the picture is thoroughly dry, turn it over and press it flat with a warm iron. Or place the paper on a larger piece of newspaper before painting. Some paint will stick the paper to the newspaper, resulting in less curling when dry.

Etched Hand Painting

Objects such as a comb, a paper clip, a fork, a key, or a notched piece of cardboard can be pulled and swirled through the wet hand painting. This will produce an interesting etched design. Still, these are merely accessories and do not replace the active processing with both hands.

Hand Painting Print

Children who are process oriented may not need expensive finger paint. They can finger paint directly on a tabletop, tray, or cookie sheet. If they choose to save what they have created, slowly lay a sheet of paper on top and gently lift up. A print of their finger painting results. This saves on the cost of buying expensive finger paint paper. It also cleans the table.

Hint: Provide thin disposable plastic gloves for children with sensitive skin.

Shaving Cream Hand Painting

Using shaving cream is an alternative to finger paint. Please see precautions discussed in the Hint that follows. Be sure to dampen the tabletop or finger paint paper first to facilitate movement. Make sure the glossy side of the paper is facing up. The adult can squirt a mound of shaving cream and let the children first explore its tactile properties. Add a few drops of liquid watercolor. Avoid food coloring because it stains the hands in concentrated form. Children would enjoy using squirt bottles with plain water or liquid watercolor with their mound of shaving cream.

Hint: Shaving cream is not recommended for children under the age of three because it can be harmful when ingested or rubbed in the eyes. Only an adult should handle the can of shaving cream. Because children may confuse shaving cream with whipped topping, provide close supervision and discuss safety precautions. Always avoid mentholated shaving cream because its fumes can be harmful if inhaled. Children with skin conditions can wear clear disposable gloves.

Shaving Cream Print

Follow the directions for making a hand painting print. Black paper makes a good contrast for white shaving cream.

Finger Paint Recipes

Cornstarch Finger Paint

½ cup cornstarch
4 cups boiling water
cold water
food coloring or tempera powder
Dissolve cornstarch in small amount of cold water. Gradually add boiling water. Stir constantly. Cook until mixture is clear. Continue stirring. Glycerine can be added to remove stickiness and provide a smooth texture. Add food coloring or tempera powder. Scents can also be added. Cool.

Detergent Finger Paint

liquid dishwashing detergent
water
food coloring or tempera
Add water slowly to detergent until you get a pasty mixture. Add coloring. Easy to clean up.

Flour and Water (Paste) Finger Paint (cooked)

½ cup flour
½ cup cold water
1½ cups boiling water
2 teaspoons alum
food coloring or tempera powder
extract, e.g., peppermint, lemon, or perfume (optional)
Mix flour and cold water. Stir in boiling water and bring mixture to a boil. Stir constantly. Remove from heat. Add alum and coloring. Add extract if children are able to enjoy the smell without tasting. Finger paintings done with this recipe tend to dry flat.

Liquid Starch Finger Paint

1 cup liquid starch
1 teaspoon tempera powder
Slowly add tempera to liquid starch until you reach the color desired.

Paste Finger Paint (uncooked)

flour
water
food coloring

Mixing flour and water provides a very economical paste. Add food coloring to it and use it as finger paint. Add water to flour until you get a paste consistency, easy to spread around but not too thin or runny. Paint on tabletop or cookie tray for easy cleanup.

Starch Finger Paint

2 cups instant laundry starch
1 quart water
3 cups Ivory® flakes
¾ cup talcum powder
1 teaspoon oil of cloves
food coloring
Dissolve starch in water and mix. Slowly add soap flakes. Add talcum and then oil of cloves. Continue mixing until thick and it forms peaks. Add food coloring to water before mixing.

Wheat Paste or Wallpaper Paste Finger Paint

wheat paste or wallpaper paste
lukewarm or cold water
food coloring or tempera powder
oil of wintergreen (available at drugstore)
Slowly add water to paste to get a creamy texture. Stir until smooth. Add coloring. A drop or two of wintergreen will disguise the odor if children find it unpleasant. Check to make sure paste ingredients are nontoxic.

Easy-to-Clean Finger Paint

⅛ cup water
½ cup dry laundry starch (chips or powder)
½ cup mild soap powder
coloring (optional)
Combine all ingredients. Beat until thick. Add liquid watercolor if desired.

Soap Flakes Finger Paint

2 cups soap flakes (not liquid)
2 cups warm water
coloring (optional)
Add soap to water. Beat with mixer until reaching consistency of whipped egg whites. Spray with liquid watercolor if desired.

Flour and Salt Finger Paint

1 cup flour
1½ cups salt

¾ cup water
coloring (optional)
Mix first three ingredients. Add liquid color if desired. This paint has a grainy quality and provides a different tactile experience.

Water Painting: Where Did My Picture Go?

Children need something to put on their painting tools, but not necessarily paint. Most young children enjoy painting with water. They may have done it at home in the bathtub or sink or on the pavement. It is a good introduction to using a brush and is highly recommended as an outdoor art activity. Provide old household brushes and plastic pails of water. Painting caps and old painting clothes, e.g., coveralls, may help ease them into the role of painter. Children can paint cement, brick, trees, outdoor nonrusting equipment, and windows. Food coloring can be added, but it will streak the surface being washed.

Whipped Soap Painting

Whipped soap is thick and good for making snow scenes on black construction paper, white hearts on red, or on wax paper. Follow the Whipped Soap Paint recipe in this chapter. A few drops of food coloring or powder paint can also be added.

Roll a Line Design

Find a lid from a box. Cut a paper to fit in. Mix paints. Find items that roll, including:

- toy cars
- small balls
- marbles
- beads

Carefully dip them in paint and place them in the box lid. Encourage the child to tilt, tip, and move the lid to get the items rolling in different directions. Dip them in more paint if needed. The result will be a crisscrossed linear effect.

The author prefers doing this with a frisbee, pie tin, or cake pan. The round frame provides a strong contrast to the linear design. Cut a circle out of paper. Make sure that it fits into the bottom ridge. Use light paints, including white, yellow, and light blue, if working on black construction paper.

Roll Painting

Children can use a rolling pin or brayer to make their paintings. Use a spoon to add different globs of paint on one half of a large sheet of paper that has been folded and opened. Refold. Roll over it with the rolling pin or brayer. Roll gently from center to sides. This will distribute the paint in different directions. Carefully reopen. Add additional colors. You will have a painted design on both sides, each a mirror image of the other.

String Painting

Fold a sheet of paper in half. Open it and spread it flat. Place globs of paint on one half. Place a footlong piece of string curled up on one inside half before refolding. Make sure one end of the string is sticking out. Gently pull on the string while holding the folded paper in place with the other hand.

Straw Painting: Blow a Blot

Children enjoy blowing through a straw to spread blobs of paint. Young children will need to practice holding and blowing through a straw in preparation for this activity. Perhaps they could blow bubbles for a science exploration. Paint should be fairly thin. Place paint in the middle of the paper with a small spoon. Encourage children to hold their straws close to but not touching the paint. Blow out, not in. Move the paint from the middle to the sides of the paper. Add other colors. Blow the colors into each other. Rotate the paper if necessary. The result will be an interesting design composed of mixed colors, weblike patterns, and intersecting lines.

> **Hint:** Cut a notch near the top of the straw. If children suck in, the paint will exit the notch rather than entering their mouths. Remind children to use only their own straws.

Special Painting with Special Painters

Children enjoy using sponges and foam as painters. Sponges or foam of various widths can be cut into different shapes and inserted into pinch-type clothespins. A Popsicle® stick can also be gently inserted and glued in place. Use a razor blade, X-Acto® knife, or scissors to cut the top edge into a pointed, grooved, forked, notched, or wavy pattern. This will result in a different type of stroke when painting. Encourage children to use the special painters in different ways. They can make dots and dabbing motions, twirls to make circular shapes, and long strokes, either up and down or sideways. See the recipe for Special Paint in-

cluded in this chapter. Remember to have the painter slightly wet before using special paints.

Squeeze and Dribble Painting

Pour paint into squeeze bottles, old liquid glue bottles, meat basters, or mustard and ketchup dispensers. Children can squeeze and dribble a design on paper. Paint can also be squeezed from a small hole in a thick plastic bag.

Shake a Painting

Fill kitchen shakers with different colors of powder paint. Make sure the holes in the shakers are large enough for the powder to shake out easily. Wet the paper with a sponge or squirt bottle. Shake different colors onto the wet paper. Mix with a Popsicle® stick or paintbrush.

Drip Drop a Painting

Children can use a medicine or eyedropper to make a painting. Provide different colors. One eyedropper can be used if the child remembers to clean it out between colors. Paint can be squeezed up into the eyedropper and slowly dropped in a design on a white paper towel, a coffee filter, or white drawing paper.

Etch a Painting

Place tinfoil over a piece of cardboard. Tape it on the back. Children enjoy working with tinfoil. Add Ivory® flakes to the paint to help it adhere to the slick surface. Use only one color of paint to paint over the tinfoil background. Let the paint dry. Use a Popsicle® stick to carefully etch or scratch a picture through the dried paint. Etching too hard will tear through the tinfoil. The result will be an outline of a picture in shiny silver.

Dot Painting

Encourage children to dip the end of the paintbrush handle in paint and make a picture composed of circular dots of paint. One finger could also be used to produce the same effect.

Sensory and Texture Painting

Vary the texture of paints you provide at the easel or painting table. Offer very thick paint one day and thin and runny the next. Try mixing one or more of the following to your paint:

- sand
- sawdust
- liquid starch
- crumbled nature items, including leaves and flower petals
- powdered laundry soap
- coffee grounds
- shaving cream
- herbs or spices
- baby powder
- baking soda
- glitter
- shaved ice

Encourage children to use words to describe what they see and feel as they paint.

Painting in a Bag

An alternative to the mess (and tactile experience) of hand painting is to paint in a bag. Provide each child with a sturdy zip-lock bag filled with about 4 tablespoons of finger paint or liquid tempera. Glitter could be added. Shaving cream could also be used. Release extra air and secure with duct tape. This is a good alternative for shy children or those with sensitive skin.

Magnet Painting

You will need a piece of Plexiglas®, a strong magnet, metal objects (such as washers, paper clips, nuts, bolts), and two blocks. Place Plexiglas® across two blocks forming a bridge, allowing enough room underneath for a child's hand to move freely. Tape a piece of paper on top of the Plexiglas®. Metal objects can be tied together using embroidery thread. Dip the metal objects into paint and place on paper. Have the child hold the magnet under the Plexiglas® and move the magnet about. The magnetic pieces will spread paint on the paper, creating a design. Children discover a science concept while doing art.

Vehicle Tracks Painting

Locate cars, trucks, planes, and other toy vehicles with two or more wheels. Provide low but ample containers of paint. A child can roll their vehicle in paint and then onto paper. Driving their vehicle creates a design. This activity reinforces a discussion on modes of transportation.

Ice-Cube Painting

Fill an ice-cube tray with colored water. Use liquid watercolor rather than food coloring. Insert a craft stick

in each cube. Sticks do not need to be inserted vertically. Freeze overnight. Children enjoy rubbing their ice-cube painters across slick paper. Use finger paint or shiny freezer wrap. Children love to watch the ice melt, spreading color. This is a good activity to do outdoors on a warm day. This activity extends a discussion about the sun or seasons.

As a variation, provide clear ice cubes and tissue paper pieces. Freeze clear water and do not add coloring. Children can cut or tear their own pieces of tissue paper. Pieces can be laid on a white piece of paper. Children can paint over the colored pieces with their ice-cube painter. They can watch as the colors from the tissue paper bleed onto the white paper.

Mirror Painting

Provide handheld or full-length mirrors. Children can use tempera paints and brushes to paint facial features and clothing. They could also draw with water-based markers. When done, children can wash the mirror, using warm soapy water, and towel dry for the next person.

Roll a Can Painting

Find coffee cans with lids. Measure the inside circumference and depth. Cut papers accordingly. Provide paint and items that roll, including marbles and golf balls. Curl and position paper inside can. The child places one or more rolling objects dipped in paint into the can. Securely attach lid. Place on floor and gently roll. Remember to create a path that makes it safe to roll without bumping others.

Paint Pendulum

This activity is similar to the sand pendulum discussed in Chapter 4 (see Figure 4–12). Find a paper cup with a pointed bottom. Punch a small hole at the point. Make three evenly spaced holes in the rim of the cup. Cut three pieces of string and tie them through the three holes. Tie the three ends into a knot. Set up two low matching chairs back to back and about 3 feet apart. Place pole, thick dowel rod, or broomstick between the seats or tops of the chairs. Secure with duct tape. Cut a piece of string long enough to reach from the pole to the floor. Tie one end of this string to the pole and the other to the knot in the cup's string. The cup should be 6 to 12 inches above ground. Cover the large area under and around chairs with newspaper. Lay paper between the chairs. Tape over the hole in the cup and add thinned liquid tempera. Show the child how to gently swing cup. Remove tape. Paint will drip an interesting design as it swings back and forth.

Oil and Water Painting

Mix one color of paint in a cup until thin and watery. Mix a second color of paint with cooking oil in another cup. Place a sheet of paper in a baking pan or small tray. The child uses an eyedropper or spoon to drip spots of the thinned paint onto the paper. Use another eyedropper or spoon to drip spots of the oily paint on top of the watery paint. Tip pan back and forth to mix. Observe and discuss what happens. Oil and water do not mix and the oily paint floats on the water to create unusual effects. Children are artists and scientists with this activity.

Runaway Paint

This is a good activity for children to observe the effects of their actions on objects. Place a large piece of white paper on a cookie sheet. Secure the corners of the paper with tape. Mix three different colors of liquid paint. Add enough water to get a thin consistency so that the paint will run. Place a spoon in each color and encourage the child to spoon one color onto the paper. Have them tip the cookie sheet to make the color run across the paper. Repeat using different colors. Encourage the child to tip the cookie sheet in different directions. Note how the colors run into each other and mix.

Mural Painting

This is a good outdoor group activity. Tape a long, wide, heavy length of butcher paper to a fence. Use plenty of masking tape so the paper will not tear or fall down. Place containers of paints and brushes at intervals along the length of the fence. Small tables or sturdy cardboard boxes work well as paint stands. This activity allows for the participation of many children at the same time. A variation of this activity is to provide small paint rollers instead of brushes.

Ramp Painting

This is another good outdoor group activity. Secure or build a ramp. The ramp could be the end of a wide slide or a large piece of wood or sturdy cardboard that is elevated at one end. Provide containers of liquid

paint as well as a collection of objects that roll, e.g., spools, toy vehicles, pinecones, or balls. Tape a large sheet of paper to the ramp. Place a row of blocks to catch the objects after they have rolled down the ramp. Children will enjoy dipping their object in paint and rolling it down the ramp.

Painting with Tissue Paper and Glue

Mix equal amounts of white glue and water. It will look milky but will dry clear and shiny. Each child will need a piece of tin foil, placed shiny side up. Children can tear colored tissue paper into pieces. Provide brushes and children can paint the glue mixture onto their piece of foil. Encourage them to lay pieces of tissue paper down, then brush more glue over it. The tissue papers will soak up the wet glue and works as your paint. Pieces can be overlapped. Children will create new colors where the tissue paper overlaps. Repeat the process by adding layers of tissue and glue.

SUMMARY

Children's art has a fresh, spontaneous quality that is easier to appreciate than to explain. Theories have attempted to explain what, why, and how children create. Different theories have different explanations for the content, motive, process, and product of children's art. A physical explanation holds that young children scribble and draw unrecognizable marks because they lack motor coordination and control. An emotional explanation states that children distort, add, omit, and exaggerate through art those things that have high emotional value to them. A perceptual explanation holds that children rely on their perceptions when drawing. Young children's perceptions lack clarity and refinement, and their artwork will reflect this. A cognitive explanation holds that children draw what they know. Children who lack experience and sensory involvement with people, places, and things will have little to include in their art. A general developmental explanation using a stage sequence approach incorporates the former explanations while addressing the whole child and individual differences. Kellogg's stages move from scribbling to placement, shape, design, and pictorial. Lowenfeld and Brittain's stages include scribbling, preschematic, schematic, dawning realism, pseudonaturalism, and artistic decision.

Key Terms

aggregate

cognitive

cognitive developmental

combine(s)

content

diagrams

Draw-A-Man test

emotional

general developmental

mandala (mandaloid)

motive

painting

perceptual

physical

pictorial stage

process

product

scribbles

sun figures

theories of artistic

development

U-shaped curve

Suggested Activities

1. Collect several art samples from children (later infancy to age eight). Attempt to sequence them according to Kellogg's, Lowenfeld and Brittain's, and the author's general sequence. Which system works best for you? Why?

2. Recall the physical explanation for children's art. Check out books on art history. Note the similarities and differences between children's art and adult abstract and "primitive" art.

3. Collect several samples of art from one young child over an extended period of time. Note patterns or growth over time. Attempt to explain the what, why, and how of this child's art using different theories of artistic development.

4. Ask children aged two, three, four, five, and six to draw a picture of themselves using crayons or markers. Ask their permission to keep or borrow the pictures. Try to sequence them according to Kellogg's stages in the development of human figure drawing. Do your data support her stages?

5. Observe a child painting at either an easel or seated at a table. Carefully record how the materials are used and the results. Refer to the six theories that explain children's artistic development. Which theory or theories best explains what you observed? Discuss your answer.

6. Provide a painting activity for one or more young children.

Review

1. Match the artistic term with an appropriate example:

____ product   a.   "I get so mad sometimes, and that's why I make scribbles all over my paper."

____ content   b.   Jim looks in the mirror and smiles. He runs back to the easel and works on his self-portrait.

____ motive   c.   Amy folds, tears, and staples a sheet of scrap paper. She crumples it up and tosses it in the wastebasket on the way to lunch.

____ process   d.   Keely paints several lines and shapes. She says, "See my pretty, pretty design."

2. Identify the six major theories or explanations for children's art.

3. Match the age range with its appropriate stage according to Lowenfeld and Brittain.

   a. 1½–2, 2½ ____ Named scribbling

   b. 2, 2½–3 ____ Schematic

   c. 3, 3½–4 ____ Pseudonaturalistic/realistic

   d. 4–7 ____ Disordered and random scribbling

   e. 7–9 ____ Preschematic

   f. 9–12 ____ Dawning realism

   g. 12–14 ____ Controlled scribbling

4. Identify the author's general stages of artistic development:

   1–2 and up _____

   2–4 and up _____

   4–6 _____

   5–8 primary grades and up _____

5. Discuss Gardner's overview of artistic development. What does he mean by a *U*-shaped curve in artistic development?

For additional art and creative development resources, visit our Web site at
www.EarlyChildEd.delmar.com

Section Three

Art and Aesthetics

What do you see in this picture? The child is trying to tell you a story in pictures. Some things are drawn in the foreground while others fade into the background. The teacher has also printed the child's accompanying words. Do you get a sense of how tall the hotel is? Can you feel the waves of the ocean as they wash onto the sand? What about the flags? Using words and pictures is one way for this child to represent a personally meaningful and beautiful experience.

Chapter 6, The Elements of Art, identifies the building blocks that all artists use when making art. Artists use line, color, shape or form, mass or volume, design or composition, pattern, space, balance, and texture. Adult artists may strive for a particular effect by consciously using one or more of the artistic elements. Young children are less deliberate and more spontaneous as they process with the media. This does not mean, however, that their artwork lacks the artistic elements. Think of scribbling as nothing more than a series of colorful lines and shapes in space.

Chapter 7, Aesthetics, focuses on helping children experience and appreciate the beauty in their world. A discussion with Aline D. Wolf should facilitate the reader's understanding of aesthetics and art appreciation in the early years.

Chapter 8, Sensory Experiences, is a resource of activities for the visual, auditory, tactile, olfactory, gustatory, chromatic, thermic, sterognostic, baric, and kinesthetic senses. Providing sensory stimulation helps children have aesthetic experiences. An aesthetically pleasing classroom environment makes good use of all available space.

Is early childhood art ever more than just letting children experiment and explore? Is there something more to art than scribbling, handling play dough, smearing paint, and gluing things onto a collage? Chapter 9, The Complete Early Childhood Art Program, provides the bigger picture. A complete art program provides children with ample time, space, and materials to make art; experiences for the senses; an introduction to art, artists, and their styles; and aesthetic involvement.

Chapter 6

The Elements of Art

Children learn that their world is made up of colors, lines, and shapes. In turn, they use color, line, and shape to make pictures. Repeating certain shapes produces a pattern. The young girl in the picture has produced a pattern of repeated shapes. The activity is printmaking. The girl has made a print by dipping a piece of apple in paint and pressing it on paper to make a print. Printmaking is the art activity featured in this chapter. The reader will be provided with a set of printmaking activities using an array of common objects that make interesting impressions.

Objectives

After reading this chapter, you should be able to:

- List and briefly explain the artistic elements.
- Discuss the categories and physical properties of color.
- Devise an art activity that will help children learn about the artistic elements.
- Help children make prints.

INTRODUCTION

Some people have difficulty separating whether a work of art is good or bad from how they feel about it. Liking a work of art does not make it good. Although artistic tastes and preferences are personal, we can use accepted criteria to talk about, analyze, and critique art. The artistic elements are one accepted criterion. They include line, color, shape, mass or volume, design or composition, pattern, space, balance, and texture. A work of art can be critiqued in terms of how successfully the artist has used one or more of the artistic elements. Art activities to help children learn about, appreciate, and use the artistic elements will be provided in this chapter.

AESTHETIC CRITERIA

What does one look for in an aesthetic experience? How does one analyze, let alone critique, a dance, musical score, or work of art? The various expressive arts have their own criteria. In dance, one could match up an individual dancer's movement with the music. Do the movements flow? Evaluating a musical score on the basis of rhythm, tempo, and one's emotional response is appropriate when listening to music. The visual arts have their own criteria or **artistic elements.** These include:

1. line
2. color
3. shape
4. mass or volume
5. design or composition
6. pattern
7. space
8. balance
9. texture

Each of these will be explained and illustrated with activities. Some are discussed further in Chapter 8, Sensory Experiences. Please refer to Appendix E for books on the artistic elements—line, color, and shape in particular.

1. Line

What is a line? A **line**

- is a visible mark made by an artistic tool, such as a crayon, moved across a surface, such as paper.
- is a continuation of a dot.
- usually suggests direction, movement, rhythm, or form.
- does not exist in nature. Nature produces edges. Artists produce lines to represent edges.
- helps the artist define shapes and contours or represent edges.
- is something we use to make letters, words, numbers, symbols, and signs.

Lines can be used in many different ways. Lines have their own dimensions, including size, direction, length, width, and weight. They also have their own personality. Lines can be

- long or short (length).
- tall or short (height).
- thick, fat, heavy; or thin, skinny, light (weight). Heavy lines may convey a feeling of force, weight, boldness, or strength. Thin lines may add a delicate, light, or timid touch.
- big or little (size).
- horizontal, vertical, or diagonal (direction). Horizontal lines suggest calm, quiet, and a sleeping, restful position. Vertical lines suggest stability and strength. Think of the lighthouse in the middle of the sea, an upright steel girder, or a rocket blasting off. Diagonal lines suggest

tension and activity, as in climbing uphill or skiing downhill.

- up or down (direction).
- forward or backward (direction).
- to the right or to the left (direction).
- continuous; or broken, dotted.
- open or closed.
- jagged or smooth.
- patterned or irregular.
- straight or curved, zigzag or wiggly. Curved lines suggest graceful movement, as in a dance or in nature. Zigzag lines suggest energy, as in a bolt of lightning.
- controlled, or uncontrolled and spontaneous.
- dark or light.
- parallel or perpendicular, intersecting or crossed.
- fast or slow.
- plain or fancy.
- sharp or soft.

Here are some art activities that will help children learn about lines.

Line Design

Children can make abstract line designs using string and a frame. Secure a wooden picture frame. Hammer small nails a few inches apart around the frame. By pulling the string taut from nail to nail, the child can create a line design. Different colors of yarn will add the element of color to the linear design. A cardboard frame can also be used. Cut 1-inch-long slits on all four sides. Encourage children to connect the slits with yarn. The result will be a line design.

Dancing Lines

This activity is a variation of drawing to music. Play a short passage of music and ask the children to respond by making a line with a marker, brush, or paint. For example, a march could suggest a forceful, patterned up-and-down line. A waterfall could suggest thick vertical lines, whereas water dripping from a faucet could suggest a vertical dotted line. What kind of a line is suggested by the following taped sounds?

- water boiling
- rocket blasting off
- siren blaring
- sawing wood
- ice-skating music
- a polka
- thunder
- hopping on one foot
- jumping rope
- a creaking swing in motion

Line Art

Children can make their own line art by dipping cut pieces of string into a small bowl of white glue. Gluey string can be creatively arranged in a linear design on a black sheet of construction paper. Colored yarn can be glued onto white drawing paper. Let dry.

Squeeze and Sprinkle

Children can be encouraged to make a linear design using a small bottle of white glue. Before it dries, have them sprinkle sand, glitter, or crushed eggshells to highlight their line design. Let dry.

Lots of Lines

Children can cut line strips out of construction paper. Encourage them to make some thick, thin, wide, fat, short, and long. Provide cut strips of paper for very young children who lack scissoring skills. Children will enjoy arranging their cut-paper lines into a design and gluing them onto a piece of colored construction paper.

Stick Art

Children can make line designs using toothpicks, Popsicle® sticks, or pipe cleaners. Each of these can be spread with glue and pressed onto cardboard or sturdy paper. The arrangement will be a linear design with angles. Children may bend the pipe cleaners into nonlinear forms. This is to be expected. Arrange and let dry.

2. Color

A world ablaze with color provides a beautiful backdrop for our daily lives. What is color? **Color**

- is based on the passage of light. It is the visual sensation of light caused by stimulating the cones of the retina. As the light source changes, so does the color. With no light there is no color.
- comes from the sun. We see colors because of the way certain objects reflect color rays to our eyes. For example, we see a banana as yellow because the banana absorbs all the color rays except yellow and reflects the yellow rays back to our eyes.
- makes each of us respond with feeling. Some of us have favorite colors. Children develop their color preferences and palettes early in life.

These influence the colors that we use to select articles of clothing, home furnishings, and cars, and to do art.

Colors can be categorized as:

1. **Primary**

   Red, blue, and yellow are the three **primary** colors. They are called primary because they are used to produce the other colors.

2. **Secondary**

   Mixing two primary colors in equal amounts results in a **secondary** color. For example,

   red + yellow = orange
   yellow + blue = green
   red + blue = purple/violet

3. **Intermediate**

   Mixing an adjoining primary and secondary color in equal amounts results in an **intermediate** color. For example,

   yellow + orange = yellow-orange
   red + orange = red-orange
   red + violet/purple = red-violet
   blue + violet/purple = blue-violet
   blue + green = blue-green
   yellow + green = yellow-green

4. **Complementary**

   Complementary colors are opposite each other on the color wheel. They provide a dramatic visual contrast. Examples include red and green, yellow and purple, and blue and orange.

5. **Neutral**

   Neutral refers to pigments that do not have a particular color. Black and white are considered neutrals.

Please refer to the Color Wheel (on the back cover), which identifies colors as primary, secondary, and intermediate.

Colors have recognizable physical properties, including:

1. **Hue**

   Hue refers to the color name. Hue is color in its pure, unmixed form. For example, red and blue have different hues.

2. **Value**

   Value refers to the relative lightness or darkness of a hue. It refers to the amount of light that a surface reflects back to the eye. For example, the value of a hue such as yellow is lighter than that of a darker hue such as purple. Red and blue can have the same value (dark) but different hues.

3. **Intensity**

   Intensity refers to the purity of light reflected from a surface. Terms like bright and dull refer to color intensity. Pure colors are most intense or bright, and mixing a color with others dulls its intensity.

4. **Tint**

   Adding white to any color lightens its value and results in a **tint**. For example, adding white to red makes pink.

5. **Shade**

   Adding black to any color darkens its value and results in a **shade.** For example, adding black to red makes maroon.

Colors also have **thermal qualities** that have a psychological impact on the viewer. Colors make us feel. Colors can

1. be **warm.**

   Warm colors, including red, yellow, and orange, remind us of hot or warm objects, such as the sun or fire.

2. be **cool.**

   Cool colors, including blue, green, and purple/violet, remind us of cold or cool objects, such as water, ice, grass, and shade.

3. give the illusion of size and space.

   Light colors make objects appear to be larger than they actually are. Dark colors make objects appear to be smaller than they actually are. For example, painting a room off-white will make it look larger. Painting the same room a dark tan will make it look smaller. Light colors make objects look closer. Dark colors make objects look farther away.

Adult artists are consciously concerned with how the viewer will be affected by their choice of color. An artist may use red, yellow, and orange to convey the sense of heat in painting a Fourth of July picnic. Blues and greens could be used to paint a ship adrift at sea. Light colors would be used to paint a portrait. Dark colors may be used to hint at the presence of crowds in the far background. Color has many possibilities and personalities. Some of these are

- light or dark (value).
- bright or dull (intensity).
- warm or cool (thermal quality).
- opaque (oils, acrylics, thick tempera) or transparent (watercolors, thinned tempera).
- primary, secondary, or intermediate.
- pure or mixed.

Here are some activities for color. Others will be presented in the sections on the visual and chromatic sense in Chapter 8.

Color Sort

Children enjoy sorting different objects by color. Provide a muffin tin or egg carton. Very young children can use only a few openings. Older children can be challenged with a dozen openings. Cut circles of different colors and place one in the bottom of each opening. Use pieces of construction paper, small yarn balls, or pom-poms for the children to sort. Children can use metal tongs to pick up the yarn balls or pom-poms and place them in the matching opening.

Wheel of Colors

Use a round, clean pizza cardboard. Glue on pie-shaped wedges of different colors. Find as many pinch-type clothespins as you have color wedges. Use markers to color each clothespin a corresponding color. For example, a red pie wedge will have a clothespin marked with red. Encourage children to clip each clothespin to the matching color. Older children may enjoy using a separate set of clothespins that have color names written on them. The color names can be matched with the corresponding colors.

Color Cooking

Sweet snacks should be the exception rather than the rule. When used, however, they can be turned into an educational experience. Children can learn the principles of color mixing by frosting cookies, graham crackers, or cupcakes. Begin with clear icing or vanilla frosting in three small bowls. Put blue, red, or yellow food coloring into one of the bowls. Children can frost some of the goodies with the primary colors. Mix any two of the primary colors to get purple, orange, or green frosting. This can be done in conjunction with holidays.

- red and green during Christmas
- pink, white, and red for Valentine's Day
- green for St. Patrick's Day
- purple and yellow for Easter
- orange and black for Halloween
- red, white, and blue for the Fourth of July
- orange, brown, and yellow for fall and Thanksgiving

A recipe for a drink that reinforces color:

Orange Drink

6-ounce can of concentrated orange juice
1 cup milk
½ cup water
10 to 12 ice cubes
1 teaspoon vanilla
Pour in blender. Blend until frothy.

A recipe for a snack that reinforces color:

Edible Color Blocks

1 envelope Knox® gelatin
⅓ cup cold water
1 small box Jell-O® (experiment with colors and flavors)
1 cup boiling water
Dissolve Knox® gelatin in cold water. Dissolve Jell-O® in boiling water. Mix everything together. Pour into rectangular pan. Cool. Cut into shapes.

Color Mixing

Children will enjoy experimenting with mixing colors. Find six baby food jars. Six sections of a plastic egg carton can also be used. Fill three with several drops of water. Add one of the primary colors of food coloring to each. This leaves three empty for color mixing. An eyedropper can be used to mix equal parts of any two colors. What new color do you get? Repeat the process using two different colors.

A variation on this task includes additional materials. Provide a color-mixing directions card as follows:

red + blue   =
blue + yellow =
red + yellow   =

Provide a separate eyedropper for each of the primary colors. Label three jars red, blue, and yellow. Label three other jars red + blue, blue + yellow, and red + yellow. Young children need directions using actual color swatches rather than the color words. Older children can do the color mixing by reading the color names.

Hand Painting

Finger, or more appropriately, hand painting, is a good opportunity to learn about color mixing. Provide one primary color, and encourage the children to use their entire hands in moving the paint about. Next, add a second primary color. What happens when they mix? What color did you make? This may be enough color mixing at one sitting for young children. At a different time, repeat the above process using the primary color that was not originally involved.

Color Clay

Teachers can use one of the recipes for homemade clay or play dough listed in Chapter 11. Start with three uncolored balls. Add a few drops of food coloring of one of three primary colors to each ball. Knead. Divide the primary-colored balls in half. Use half to experiment with color mixing. What happens if balls of red and blue, blue and yellow, or red and yellow are mixed together? What new color of clay do we get? The result will be different-colored clay balls.

Made in the Shade

Children can learn to make tints and shades of a color. Individual finger paint sets or tempera paints can be used. Begin with the three primary colors. Add a small dab of white to each. What happens? What color did you get? Is it lighter or darker than the one you started with? Mix the three secondary colors and repeat the process. Repeat the process adding a very small dab of black. Adding white will produce tints of red, yellow, blue, and the secondary colors. Adding black will produce shades.

Color Helpers

Discuss with children how community helpers often wear a certain color. Fire fighters wear red. Police officers wear blue. Doctors, nurses, veterinarians, ambulance drivers, paramedics, and hospital workers wear white or green (in surgery). Cooks and chefs also wear white.

Color Day

Declare a day of the week to have a specific color. For example, every Friday is color day. This Friday's color will be green. Encourage children to wear something green. Activities, songs, stories, and snacks can be focused on the color green. Some color-coordinated snacks are

- red: apples, cherries, strawberries, ketchup.
- yellow: bananas, scrambled eggs, mustard.
- green: grapes, celery, lettuce.
- orange: carrots, cheese, pumpkin bread.
- purple: grape juice, grapes.
- brown: whole wheat bread, peanut butter, chocolate milk, or pudding.
- blue: blueberry muffins.
- white: cottage cheese, milk, plain yogurt, rice, mayonnaise.

Color Stories

Please see Appendix E for a list of art-related books. Slobodkina's *Caps for Sale* is an excellent one to read

and act out. Children will enjoy stacking the red, blue, brown, and gray caps. They can take turns being the peddler or the monkeys.

3. Shape

Shape is an appropriate criterion for critiquing two-dimensional art that has length and width. Specifically, what is a shape? Shape

- refers to the outside form of an object.
- is the edge of an enclosed space.
- is defined by a line or outline, or by contrasting color or texture in the surrounding area.
- represents positive space or figure.
- is created by connecting lines.

Shape has its own qualities and personalities. Some characteristics are

- simple or complex.
- circular or angular.
- geometric, including circle, square, rectangle, or triangle; or nongeometric, including irregular, free-form, organic, or amorphic.
- active or quiet.
- clearly defined or vaguely defined.
- tall or short.
- big and large, or small and little.
- open or closed.
- solid, heavy, massive; or open, light.
- proportional or nonproportional.
- concave or convex.
- transparent or opaque.
- hard or soft.
- abstract or realistic.
- symmetrical or asymmetrical.
- precise or vague.

Here are some activities that help children learn about shape.

Sandpaper Shapes

Geometric shapes, including circles, squares, triangles, rectangles, diamonds, and so on, can be cut out of pieces of sandpaper and mounted on sturdy cardboard. Children will enjoy using their fingers and hands to feel the shapes. Older children can progress to feeling only the outlines of shapes done in sandpaper.

Beanbag Shapes

Children will enjoy manipulating and tossing beanbags that have been cut into geometric shapes. Shape beanbags can vary in size, shape, and color. They can be sorted and classified as well as tossed in a basket or dropped in a pail.

Puzzling Shapes

Geometric shapes can be carefully drawn with a ruler on poster board. Use a different color for each shape for younger children. Older children will not need the color clue. Cut each shape into a number of pieces. Color code the pieces on the back if necessary. Laminate the individual pieces and trim the excess. Match the number and sizes of the pieces with your age group. For example, a square cut in half diagonally may challenge a toddler but might bore a kindergartner.

Sew a Shape

Trim the raised edges off plastic foam meat trays. Cut each into a different geometric shape. Sturdy cardboard could also be used. Use a hole punch to carefully punch an inner outline of the shape. Encourage children to sew the shape by following the line of holes that outlines the shape. They can use a shoelace or thick yarn rather than thread. Use a large plastic needle or tape the beginning end to get it through the holes. Tie a large knot, button, or bead at the end so that it will not pull through. Some children will sew with an over-under, in-and-out motion as one would do with needle and thread. Others may prefer to loop or lace around the edge. Either of these is preferred to randomly connecting the holes without any notice of shape.

A piece of Peg-Board® with the outline of a shape drawn through the holes could also be used. The children could use golf tees rather than yarn to complete the outline of the shape.

Safety Shapes

An awareness of shape serves many purposes beyond mere aesthetic beauty. Different shapes are used on signs that help people live, walk, and drive safely. The same is true for colors. Even if one cannot read a sign, the shape and color tell us what to do. Take a short neighborhood walk and look for safety signs, such as STOP. Safety shapes include the octagon, triangle, diamond, and circle. Children may want to make red, green, and yellow circles and paste them in proper order against a black background to make a traffic light.

Shape Stamps

Children enjoy placing objects on an inked stamp pad and stamping that impression on a piece of paper.

Find items that have round, square, rectangular, and triangular shapes. The round edge of a plastic hair roller is ideal for a round shape. Find hair rollers in different sizes. Encourage children to creatively combine the shapes into a design or picture.

Shape Spatter Paint

Cut geometric shapes out of sturdy cardboard. Place a sheet of paper into the lid of a box. Place one shape on the paper. Place a thin screen over the top. Dip an old toothbrush in paint. Carefully brush across the screen, making sure that the paint is spattering around the edge of the shape. Remove the screen and carefully lift up the shape. The outline of the shape will appear on the paper. Repeat the process, creatively combining shapes at a different sitting as a separate activity.

There are many standard activities that are appropriate for learning about color as well as shape. Some are described here.

Signs

Signs or displays of colors and color names as well as shapes and their corresponding names help children learn these concepts. A color caterpillar can have a body made up of different-colored sections. Each circular ball of the body is a different color. A shape train can have a regular locomotive but cars of different geometric shapes. The names can be neatly printed above or below the items in each. Remember to post these at children's eye level rather than high up at adult level.

Manipulative Games

Traditional games can be specifically designed and adapted to learn about shapes and color. Recommended examples include the following:

- bingo
- lotto
- dominoes
- card games, including old maid, rummy, hearts, and fish

Browse through the aisles of a toy store or the pages of a toy catalogue, noting board games and manipulative materials. Then creatively adapt your own version.

Match and Memory

Make pairs of colors or shapes on index cards. Encourage children to match pairs. Older children enjoy turning all the color or shape cards over and trying to remember where the pairs are. If the two cards that are turned up match, the player gets another turn.

Classify 🅟 🅚

Children can be challenged to find different ways to classify an array of cards. Index cards can be grouped on the basis of color, shape, and size. Older children will enjoy playing with a total deck of twelve cards per color. For example,

Red: circle, square, rectangle, triangle; small, medium, large

If you use this formula for each of the three primary colors, you will end up with a total of 36 cards.

Gone Fishing 🅟 🅚

Draw an outline of a fish on a series of index cards. Add a color or shape to each. Staple a paper clip at the mouth of each fish shape. Find a paper towel roll to use as a fishing rod. Tie a length of string to one end and a small magnet at the other. Spread the fish out on the floor on top of a piece of blue construction paper for the water. Encourage children to catch a fish and name the color or shape.

Partner Match 🅟 🅚

This is a good activity for the entire group. Give each child an outline of a geometric shape or color to hold. Older children may enjoy working with shapes of different colors. Gather children in a circle, holding up their shapes. Have them carefully look around to find someone who is holding the same shape, then take turns finding the partner whose shape matches. Exchange and repeat.

Flip-Flop Books 🅟 🅚

Find a small book of index cards that are bound with spiral wire binding. Neatly cut each card in half. Actually, you will have too many cards, so you may want to carefully remove some. Or you can use the book to cover color, shape, and other concepts. Open up the book to any page. You will have a top and bottom section on the right and left sides, four index-card sections. For example, for the red page in the color book, find or draw something red in the upper half of the right page. Carefully print the word *red* in red marker on the bottom half of the right page. Find or draw something else that is red, but carefully divide it up between the top and bottom halves of

the left side. Encourage children to flipflop through the various pages, top and bottom, until they find a match. For example, the red balloon (top right) with the word in red (lower right) matches the completed picture of a red apple on the left.

4. Mass or Volume

Mass and **volume** are appropriate criteria for critiquing three-dimensional art, which has height, length, and width. What a circle is to two-dimensional shape, a sphere is to three-dimensional mass or volume. What is mass or volume? These are terms that refer to a solid body. An artist such as a sculptor can portray mass or volume in many different ways. Mass or volume can be portrayed as

- open or closed.
- heavy, bulky, massive; or light, delicate.
- solid, impenetrable, blocklike; or open, penetrable.
- opaque or transparent.
- geometric or organic.
- static or dynamic.
- angular or curved.
- hard or soft.
- large or little, big or small.
- stationary or moving.

5. Design or Composition

Throughout this book, the term *design* has been used to describe anything and everything young children create in art. A scribble of lines, a splash of colors, and an array of shapes have been referred to as designs. Adult artists use design in a different sense, as in overall composition. **Design** or **composition** is the overall mark of success, the standard of achievement, and the frosting on the cake. Design and composition as artistic criteria attempt to address the following questions.

- Did the artist accomplish what he or she originally set out to do? Was the artist successful?
- Do line, shape, color, texture, and form blend and work together as a unified whole? Is the arrangement of these artistic elements pleasing and satisfying?
- Does the finished work impart a sense of overall order, coherence, equilibrium, and organization?
- Did the artist strike a balance between monotony and chaos or unity and variety?

- Is there a focal point, emphasis, center of interest, or dominant spot that attracts and holds attention? Does it make the viewer want to return and admire again and again?

With a good design or composition, the answer to the above questions would be yes. Adult artists walk a fine line among unity, variety, and contrast. It is difficult to create a unified work that hangs together while adding novelty, variety, contrast, and an element of surprise to make it interesting. Child artists, who are less concerned with their finished products, may have little concern for design and composition. We can, however, use the principles of design and composition to talk about works of art and make children aware of the planning and energy that often accompany the making of art.

Overall design and composition, although less directly relevant to early childhood art than some of the other criteria, do form an arch or backdrop for the other criteria.

6. Pattern

Pattern surrounds us. Fence posts, steps, rungs of a ladder, railroad tracks, and spokes on a wheel all suggest a repetitive pattern. Patterns not only appear in art and skills in patterning also facilitate learning in the curricular areas of math and reading. Pattern

- refers to the treatment given to a surface.
- suggests flow, rhythm, motion, or movement.
- suggests regularity and repetition.
- can be made with forms, shapes, lines, colors, textures, or symbols that move across a surface in a recurring sequence.

Patterns have their own identity. They can be

- ornate and fancy, or plain.
- regular or irregular.
- symmetrical or asymmetrical.
- sequenced or alternating.

Here are some activities for learning about pattern.

Sponge Painting

Cut different geometric and abstract shapes out of household sponges. Encourage children to identify a pattern, e.g., circle-square-circle, and repeat that pattern on their paper. The pattern can be arranged in horizontal, vertical, or diagonal fashion (see Figure 6–1).

Figure 6-1 Making shapes with sponges dipped in paint.

Pattern Printing

Provide an array of items to print with. Examples include cookie cutters, lids, corks, and bottle tops. Encourage children to identify a pattern and repeat it on their papers. Encourage them to come up with different ways to repeat their patterns horizontally, vertically, or diagonally by dipping their items in paint and making a pattern.

Pattern Picture

Shapes cut out of wallpaper, fabric scraps, or gift wrap can be glued or pasted in a repetitive sequence. For example, a pattern could consist of scraps of white burlap, foil, gift wrap, and white burlap glued in a row. A different pattern sequence could follow below, or the same pattern could be repeated.

String a Pattern

Children can use wooden beads and a shoelace to create a pattern and series of repeated patterns. Children may enjoy repeating a pattern that a teacher begins. Others enjoy making a pattern as it appears on an index card. Remember to tie a large knot at one end. The lacing end should be pointed and reinforced with tape.

7. Space

An artist's ultimate **space** is determined by the size of the canvas, be it paper, cardboard, wood, or a shoe box. Within the overall space, the artist must deal with the problem of arranging elements. How many shapes or symbols will be used? Where will they be placed? How much room will be left? How much blank space will remain? Basically, there are two types of space:

1. **Positive space**
   Positive space is the space taken up with lines, colors, shapes, and forms. Subject matter, content, and design occupy positive space.
2. **Negative space**
   Negative space is the space left between or surrounding subject matter, symbols, or shapes.

Positive space refers to the shape, and negative space is what is left empty. In Figure 6–2, the white star occupies positive space and the black background represents negative space.

Artists use space in different ways. Some artworks are completely filled with vibrant colors and exciting designs (positive space), with little white paper (negative space) showing. Other works may highlight one object or symbol by surrounding it with much negative space.

Some of the different ways artists can use space include:

- positive or negative.
- unoccupied, empty, sparse; or occupied, filled, dense.
- vertical, horizontal, or diagonal.
- symmetrical or asymmetrical.
- ordered or random.
- balanced or unbalanced.

The following activity is for helping children learn about space.

Stencil

A stencil can be cut out of cardboard. Use an X-Acto® knife or safety razor blade to cut out a simple shape, for example, a star. The cutout star is positive space. The surrounding area is negative. Children can hold the star securely on a piece of paper. They can use their drawing or printing hands to mark around the star, using chalk, crayon, or paint. Chalk is preferred because of its ability to combine with other colors. Also, it does less damage to the stencil than paint. Children can also

use the surrounding piece that the star was cut from. Instead of chalking away from the star stencil, they now stroke inward.

8. Balance

When the forms appear to be in proportion to each other, the picture is said to have **balance,** equilibrium, or harmony. Balance involves how an artist uses positive and negative space (see Figure 6–3). Basically, there are two ways of achieving balance:

1. **Symmetrical (formal)**
   With this type of balance, the shapes are evenly or equally balanced around some point, e.g., up or down, right or left, horizontally, vertically, radially, or diagonally. Think of two children of the same weight balanced on the two ends of a seesaw. This is **symmetrical** or **formal** balance. Symmetrical balance is often evident in the artwork of children. For example, a house painted on the right side symmetrically balances a large tree on the left. This type of balance is not bad or wrong; it is merely obvious, and gets boring with repeated use.
2. **Asymmetrical (informal)**
   With this type of balance, the objects are not evenly or equally balanced from a point. For example, a house painted near the upper left cor-

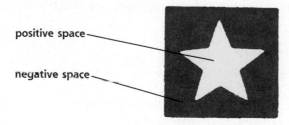

Figure 6-2 Example of positive and negative space.

Figure 6-3 A mask made from a stencil.

ner can be **asymmetrically** balanced with half of a large tree emerging from the right edge of the paper. The balance is unusual and intriguing.

There are many ways to achieve balance. A dark color may balance lighter ones. A massive shape may be balanced with a few smaller ones.

9. Texture

Texture refers to the surface quality of a work of art. How does it feel? Layers of paint, dried finger paint, and a fabric collage all have texture or a certain feel to them. Texture is a term that is appropriate to discussing and critiquing collage, construction, assemblage, and other three-dimensional art activities. Texture can be actual or implied. Young children work with actual textures. Adult artists use both. Implied texture involves technical proficiency in skillfully using the medium to suggest wood grain or peeling rust that does not actually exist on the canvas.

Some terms that relate to texture in art are as follows:

- rough, bumpy; or smooth
- hard or soft
- coarse or fine
- wet, sticky, or dry
- raised or lowered
- flat or layered
- dull or shiny
- pebbled
- granular
- rubbery
- slippery, slick
- spongy
- furry, fuzzy
- sharp

The element of texture will be explored further in Chapter 8. Here are two art activities to help children learn about texture.

Texture Collage

Provide an array of textured objects. Encourage children to glue or paste an array of textured items onto a piece of sturdy paper or cardboard. See Appendix A for artistic junk to include. Because nature items have such a variety of textures, they can be included.

Texture Rubbings

Go on a texture hunt with the children. Both indoor and outdoor environments offer a wealth of textures. For example, placing a piece of white paper over the bark on a tree and rubbing with the side of a crayon will produce an impression or rubbing. The same thing will happen if you rub over cement, wood grain, coins, a license plate, corrugated cardboard, or an embossed greeting card. Encourage children to overlap and creatively combine their rubbings. Older children may enjoy sketching a very simple picture containing large objects, such as a house and a tree. Later, they can finish their picture with rubbed areas. For example, one could rub with a dark crayon over bark in the area sketched for a tree trunk.

ART · MAKING PRINTS

Most young children have had experience making **prints** at home. Rubbing a food-stained mouth on a white bath towel or napkin will leave a print. Muddy shoes will leave a print on the kitchen floor, and touching a wall with dirty hands will leave fingerprints. Many children arrive in the morning with a print of Mom's lipstick on their face from a kiss.

Printing is an extension of painting. Painting involves making movements with a brush or other painter across a surface. Printing involves stamping paper with an object dipped in paint. Printing involves less whole-arm activity and greater concern for placement and overall design. Discuss and show examples of patterns in wallpaper, brick wall, windows, fabric, gift wrap, flowers, and nature when introducing printing. Tempera paints should be fairly thick for the printed impression to show up. A variety of papers can be used.

Young children may approach printing activities as an extension of painting. They may use printmaking tools as things to paint with. In turn, they may smear objects all over the paper, resulting in a paper covered with paint but not clear prints. This tendency reflects a process approach to making art and should not be interpreted as a lack of success at teaching printmaking.

Here are some printing activities.

Hint: Place a thick stack of newspapers under the printing paper. The thickness will help make a good clear print.

Hint: To make a print pad, place a few paper towels on a flat plate. Pour on some tempera paint. Press the printing items on the wet pad. This will cover them evenly with paint.

Monoprint

A pane of glass, sheet of Plexiglas®, acrylic cutting board, or any nonporous surface, such as a Formica® tabletop, can be used. Children can paint their picture or design right on the surface. Use fairly thick paints. Place a larger piece of paper over the painted area. Rub gently with brayer or hand. Carefully lift up. As the term *monoprint* suggests, you will produce one print off the painted surface. Designs can also be etched into a solid mass of paint before the print is taken. Children will also enjoy hand painting on the surface and having a monoprint taken.

Ink-Pad Print

Children enjoy placing their fingers on an ink pad and making a stamped impression on a piece of paper. Ink pads come in colors other than black. What does the fingerprint impression suggest? Children may want to use fine-point markers to make their basic fingerprints into something else by adding body parts, wheels, and details.

Small objects with interesting shapes and textures include the following:

- corks
- coins
- paper clips
- buttons
- seashells
- caps and bottle tops
- nuts and bolts
- carved wooden blocks
- eraser tops on pencils
- spools
- hair rollers
- Styrofoam® pieces and squiggles
- plastic tops from milk containers
- embossed guest soaps
- erasers in different shapes

These can also be printed as described earlier. Re-ink with liquid ink when the print appears dull. Several thicknesses of heavy paper towels or an old washcloth soaked with tempera paint can also serve as a stamp pad.

Sponge Printing

Sponges can be creatively cut into an array of shapes and sizes. Encourage children to dip the shapes in paint and make a stamped print. Geometric shapes can be arranged to form a picture. Or children can repeat a sequence or pattern of printed shapes. Provide

one or more shapes for each color. Wash out a sponge if it is accidentally dipped in a different color (see Figure 6–4).

Loofah Prints

Loofah sponges have an interesting texture and design. Inexpensive loofahs can be purchased from dollar or discount stores. Those with handles will cost more, although you can easily fashion a handle out of a stick. Children can apply paint to the end of their loofah and press down on paper to make print. They can also stand at an easel using a loofah with a handle. The process is the same. Apply paint on the end of the sponge and gently press onto easel paper while holding onto the handle. Young children may decide to use the loofah sponges for painting rather than printmaking.

A Corny Print

Painting an ear of corn and rolling it like a rolling pin on a piece of paper makes a very good print.

Roller Printing

Printing with an ear of corn is one example of roller printing. Other examples of rollers that can be used for printing include the following:

- a hair roller—insert a pencil to hold when rolling
- a long bottle, dowel, or plastic tumbler wrapped with a yarn or string design
- a toilet paper roll with shapes cut out
- a cardboard paper towel roll with shapes cut out

Figure 6-4 Sponge prints.

- a brayer with raised shapes glued onto it
- a rolling pin with raised shapes and designs or flocked wallpaper glued onto it
- a spool with lines and designs carved or etched in—insert a pencil to hold when rolling
- a tin can with yarn or string glued to it

Roll the roller in a low dish, pan, or large plastic foam tray of paint. Roll on paper.

Kitchen Gadget Printing

An array of kitchen gadgets is listed in the section on Paints and Painting Accessories in Chapter 5. Others include the following:

- plastic or nylon utensils
- slotted spoon and fork
- spatula
- pie slice lifter
- wire whisk
- funnel
- potato masher
- pancake flipper
- cookie cutters
- plastic forks
- pie tin (bottom)
- embossed lids and bottoms of jars
- plastic scourer and scrubber with knob handle

These can be dipped in paint and printed on paper. Encourage children to combine and overlap printed shapes creatively to form designs or pictures (see Figure 6–5).

Recycled Junk Print

Actually, many of the items mentioned in the sections on printing with a stamp pad and with kitchen gadgets

could fit in here. See Appendix A for a list of artistic junk. Look for objects with different textures and uneven surfaces. Some items that can be recycled into a printing activity include these:

- corks
- spools
- combs
- hairbrushes with plastic spikes
- bottle tops and jar lids
- pill bottles and vials
- Styrofoam® pieces
- corrugated cardboard
- hair rollers
- keys
- toy cars
- crumpled paper
- bars of soap with raised letters or design
- license plates
- embossed ceramic tiles

Apply paint to the object and place it down on paper. Carefully remove (see Figure 6–6).

Plastic Foam Tray Print

Trim the raised edges off small plastic foam trays. You should have a flat piece to work with. Draw or etch a picture or design into the plastic, using a

Figure 6-5 A print made with kitchen gadgets.

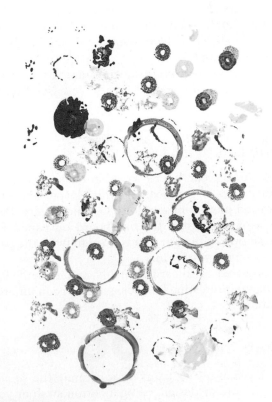

Figure 6-6 Recycled junk print.

Popsicle® stick. Press in without breaking through. The incised line will remain white when the tray is covered with ink or paint and printed. Ideally, a brayer is dipped in ink and spread across the tray. Paint can also be brushed on. Paint over the etched surface with a single color of paint. Press a piece of paper over the tray and gently rub with your hand over the entire surface. Carefully lift the paper to see your print. A second print can be taken immediately if paint is left on the tray. Children can make a series of prints this way. Wash the tray before changing colors.

Nature Print

Items collected from a nature walk can be inked and printed. Look for leaves, pinecones, and other nature specimens with interesting textures and surfaces.

String Printing

Find small blocks of wood or small, sturdy gift boxes. Dip string in white glue and wrap it around the block or box in an interesting design. Or arrange the gluey string in a design on only one side. Let the glue dry. Dip the best side of the block in ink or paint. Place it on paper and gently push down to make an impression. Carefully remove the block to see the print. Repeat and make a continuing series or pattern. Stay with the color chosen rather than trying to wash the printer. Small wood blocks or boxes could also be stamped in an ink pad.

Pieces of dense foam in sheet or tape form can also be cut, built up into raised layers, and glued onto a printer.

Cardboard Print

Secure sturdy cardboard for the background. Cut smaller pieces of cardboard or thick paper and build up a raised picture or design. Glue and let dry. Paint over the design. Press the cardboard on paper. Rub gently all over with your hands. Carefully lift the cardboard to reveal your print.

Corrugated cardboard is highly recommended for building up interesting line designs that go in different directions.

Ceramic Tile Print

Roll a layer of ink or paint on a ceramic tile square. Etch a picture or design, using a cotton swab or your finger. Place a small piece of paper over the tile. Rub

gently. Carefully remove the paper to reveal your print. A tile with raised or embossed surfaces will have a prepared surface ready for printing.

Game Piece Print

Dominoes, checkers, game tokens, bingo markers, and magnetic letters and numbers make interesting designs when dipped in paint and used as stampers to make a print.

Bubble Print

Fill a shallow container with water and tempera paint or liquid watercolor to which dishwashing detergent has been added. Two parts tempera paint to one part liquid dishwashing soap is recommended. Stir. Cut out notch near top of straw. Blow bubbles over the rim of the container using a straw. Place white paper on top of the bubbles to get a print. The result will be a print made up of circular designs that can serve as a background for collage, drawing, or other art activity.

Push-Up Stick Print

Ice-cream bars and Popsicles® come on a push-up stick. Save the push-up sticks. Cut a design or shape out of Styrofoam® and glue it onto a push-up stick. Dip the Styrofoam® in paint or on an ink pad and press it on paper.

Crayon Sandpaper Print

Children can draw a picture or design with crayons on a piece of sandpaper. Encourage them to press hard and fill up the sandpaper. An adult can place a piece of white paper over the colored sandpaper and press with a warm iron. The heat will melt the wax from the colored sandpaper and transfer the design or picture to the paper.

Glue Print

Use white liquid glue to draw a design or picture on a piece of cardboard. Make sure the outline or impression is fairly thick. Let the glue dry. Spread the design with ink or paint. Gently press paper on it. The paint or ink will adhere to the raised dried glue outline. Or glue a picture cut from a magazine to your piece of cardboard. Trace the outline with white liquid glue. Repeat the steps involved in making a glue print. This time you will get a print that resembles the picture cut out of the magazine.

Berry Basket Print

Collect an array of plastic produce baskets with different patterns. Children can use brushes to paint over the bottom design of the baskets or dip in print pads, then apply the baskets to paper.

Balloon Print

Adult should blow up balloons, but not so full that they could pop. Encourage children to handle balloons carefully. Balloons can be dipped in paint and gently pressed onto paper. Replace after a few children have handled them, to avoid popping. This activity is recommended for older children. Provide close supervision if used with young children, making sure they do not put balloon pieces in their mouths.

Windup Toy Print

Find windup or battery-operated small toys such as cars and trucks. Cover a large table or floor space with butcher paper. Brush paint on wheels, activate, and release on paper. Colorful tracks will appear as the vehicle moves about.

Watercolor Tablet Print

Instead of using the brush provided, children can wet their fingers with water and press them into the watercolor tablets. Gently press fingers onto paper, making oval designs or a combination of creative shapes.

CD-Case Print

Collect clear compact disc cases. Child can paint on the top surface. Carefully place a piece of paper on top and gently lift off a print.

Caster Print

Locate round spiked caster cups used under furniture to protect carpets. Provide containers of paint. Encourage children to dip the caster into paint and gently push down on the paper. Lift to see a dotted or spiked print.

Baby Shoe and Sneaker Print

Collect old, small shoes with textured soles. Ask families for donations because once painted and washed, they cannot be worn again. Use a brush to apply paint to the sole rather than dipping shoe into paint. Care-

fully rock entire shoe from heel to toe or vice versa onto paper. Encourage children to overlap and combine shoe shapes creatively.

Make-It-Yourself Stamp Print

Foam shoe inserts are a good material for making your own stamps. The foam can be easily cut into various shapes. An adult can use a glue gun or rubber cement to mount the shapes onto a stamper such as a spool, jar lid, or wood block. Use with ink pads and provide small sheets of paper. Small stamped impressions get lost on a large sheet of paper. Children can push stamps into a pad and gently stamp on paper. Remind them they need not pound to get the stamp to work. Rubber inner tubing also works well as stamping material. Tempera paint can be substituted for ink pads.

Paraffin Block Print

Paraffin blocks are sold inexpensively at grocery and craft stores. They are easy to carve, providing more than one side for printing. Children can carve in their own designs using a pointed tool such as a craft stick, key, or linoleum cutter. Remind children that letters will come out backwards. Use brush or brayer to spread paint over carved block. Press paper over the block and gently rub the surface with the hand. Then lift off the print. Paper can first be folded in half or quarters to make greeting cards or stationery.

Handprint Mural

Using the hand to make a print is one of the most basic printmaking activities. Children dip their hand in paint and gently press it onto a piece of paper. They can also use a brush to apply paint to one hand before making a print. Prints can be repeated and children will observe how their handprint fades with repeated prints. This activity also lends itself to a group project. Rather than providing individual pieces, provide a large sheet of paper and encourage each child to add his or her print. Each child can make a contribution to the handprint mural (see Figure 6–7).

Feet Print

Toy dinosaurs, dolls, and even children's feet can be used. Children will enjoy doing this with their bare feet, outdoors on a warm day. Roll out a length of butcher paper. Pour liquid tempera into shallow containers large enough to accommodate one child's foot. Encourage the children to step in the paint and

Figure 6-7 Handprint mural.

then press his or her foot to leave a print. Repeat with other foot. Remind children that moving about with painted feet is dangerous. Have handy a bucket for washing feet and towels to dry. This activity is best done one-on-one.

Fold a Print 🅿 🅚 🆂

Encourage children to fold their sheets of paper in half. They can use a spoon to drop one or more colors of liquid tempera onto one side of their paper. Slowly fold over and gently press down, using the hand to rub all over. Carefully open up to see the mirror-image print. Older children can paint half of their desired image near the fold but only on one side. For example, a child who paints half a yellow circle next to the crease will have a sun emerge when the paper is folded and then opened back up.

Leaf and Glue Print 🅚 🆂

Collect an array of leaves and ferns. Children can cover one side of the leaf with glue and press it down on paper, leaving a glue print. Carefully lift off leaf. Sprinkle glitter from shaker or small confetti onto glue print.

Scraped Print 🅚 🆂

Children can paint inside a plastic tray. Using a pointed tool like the handle of a paintbrush, scrape a design or picture into the paint. Before dry, put a piece of paper over the paint using hands to rub all over the surface. Carefully lift to see the scraped print. Remember that scraped letters will appear in reverse on the print.

Oil Paint Print 🆂

Mix tempera paint and cooking oil in a cup until creamy. Set aside. Fill a round cake pan half full with plain water. Spoon a few drops of the oil paint mixture on top of the water. Use a fork to gently swirl. Next, have child lay a piece of white paper on top of the swirl. Let the paper float for about a minute. Carefully lift the paper out holding on to two corners. Place the print elsewhere to dry. Glitter can be added by shaking from a container. Use this process to design greeting cards or stationery, by first folding white paper in half or quarters.

Press and Twist Print 🆃 🅿 🅚 🆂

Use a nonporous work surface such as a table or countertop. Fill squeeze bottles with tempera paint and encourage children to gently squeeze one or more small drops of paint onto the work surface. You may want to use masking tape to clearly define children's work area. Place a piece of paper on the drops of paint. Children can gently press down and twist the paper, keeping their fingers wide and stretched open. Carefully lift the paper to reveal the design. Children can continue experimenting with other colors and different ways of twisting their paper. Keep sponges and soapy water nearby to clean the work surface between children. For a more sensorial activity forego the paper and encourage children to press and twist the paint with their bare hand. Be adventurous and do the same outdoors with bare feet on a warm day.

Simple Sun Print 🅿 🅚 🆂

This activity is best done in the morning of a day that promises to be sunny. A simplified version of this activity is to have children collect small rocks and flat leaves. They can arrange their leaves on a large sheet of construction paper outdoors in the direct sun. Place one rock on each leaf on top of the paper. Rocks secure the leaves and must be smaller than the leaves. Keep in direct sun for at least one hour. Carefully remove items and look for outlines and differences in color. The sun will bleach the surrounding area while the part under the leaf (and hidden from the sun) will remain darker. Experiment with shapes other than nature items. These could include toys, puzzle pieces, stencils, keys, utensils, as well as alphabet letters and numerals. For example, children can use magnetic letters to make their name.

Bubble Wrap Print

Popping and stepping on bubble wrap are active sensory experiences. Bubble wrap also makes a good painting surface and provides a textured surface for making a print. Toddlers enjoy painting on the bubble wrap. Provide each child with a square foot of unpopped wrap. Provide wrap with different sizes of bubbles. Preschoolers and older children can make a print in one of two ways. Either they can lay paper on top of their painted bubble wrap and lift their print, or they can carefully lift their painted bubble wrap square and gently press it onto another piece of paper. Rolling out a length of bubble wrap outdoors leads to a mural-making activity. Remember to recycle by rinsing and drying the sheets for repeated use.

Fly Swatter Art

This activity is best done outdoors on a day when children have a lot of excess energy that needs to be productively redirected. Just as adults use fly swatters to swat flies, children enjoy swatting blobs of paint. The result is more of physical release than artistic expression. Still, children witness the effects of their actions on objects. Applying gentle force or swatting the blob of paint makes the paint spread and take on the design of the fly swatter. Begin by spreading a roll of butcher paper on the pavement. Provide smocks and several fly swatters. Squirt blobs of paint approximately the size of a quarter. Children will need ample personal space and should be reminded to keep their fly swatter on the paper. Encourage children to gently swat their paint blobs and observe the mark it leaves. Avoid referring to the blobs as bugs or children will get the mistaken notion that it is okay to kill bugs aimlessly.

Plunger Art

This activity should be done outdoors. Roll out a length of butcher paper on the cement. Provide smocks and several new plungers, one for each container of paint. Plungers with short handles are preferred. Fill shallow containers with paint. The container should be large enough for the head of the plunger to fit. Encourage children to stand and dip their plunger in paint. Next, carefully press it onto the paper. If necessary, remind children that the plungers are art tools and not toys or weapons. The activity works best if children keep plungers with their original color. If children want different colors, have them use different plungers rather than mixing one plunger into different colors.

Bounce-a-Print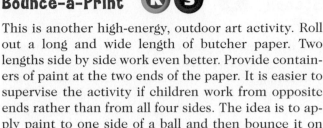

This is another high-energy, outdoor art activity. Roll out a long and wide length of butcher paper. Two lengths side by side work even better. Provide containers of paint at the two ends of the paper. It is easier to supervise the activity if children work from opposite ends rather than from all four sides. The idea is to apply paint to one side of a ball and then bounce it on the paper to make a painted trail. Tennis balls as well as basketballs work for this activity. Children could also simply dip their ball into the shallow container of paint. Remind children that only unpainted balls are for throwing or playing catch.

Nylon Bag Print

You will need several old pair of pantyhose or nylon hose for this activity. Cut off the excess above the ankle leaving the foot. Fill each with small items such as sand, aquarium gravel, pebbles, or marbles. Tie securely making sure there is some extra nylon. Provide containers of paint. Encourage children to dip their nylon bag in the paint and then carefully press onto a sheet of construction paper. Gently lift and observe the print. Prints will be different depending on the contents of the nylon bag.

Salad Spinner Art

Locate one or more salad spinners, which are used to rinse and dry a head of lettuce. Remove the top and measure the size of the inside round bottom. Draw a master pattern on cardboard and cut it out. The adult or child can trace individual round shapes on paper and cut out. Place paper inside salad spinner along with one or more marbles dipped in paint. Close and secure lid. Children will need some hand strength and control to rotate the knob. This turns the inside paddle, thereby moving the marbles, which create a design. Ask parents for an old salad spinner or try garage sales and secondhand stores.

STENCIL, SPATTER, AND SCREEN PRINTING

Stencil, spatter, and screen printing are fairly involved activities that require some amount of instruction and special tools. It is unlikely that young children will discover on their own how to make a stencil, spatter, or screen print.

Stencil

A stencil can be cut from sturdy cardboard or thick paper, including tagboard or poster board. It can also be torn out of construction paper. When you cut a stencil, you actually get two. Recall our discussion of positive and negative space. The shape cut out occupies positive space and is called the positive stencil. The remaining frame or background occupies negative space and is called the negative stencil. Each type of stencil has its own process. Hold the stencil with one hand and use the other hand to stroke from the piece out when using the positive stencil. Hold the background or frame and stroke inward when using the negative stencil.

Stenciling can be done with crayons, paint, or chalk. The author prefers chalk dust dabbed on with cotton balls because of its ability to blend. It also does less damage to the stencil than paint. Paint can be gently dabbed on with cotton balls, a small sponge, or a brush. Short, stiff-bristle brushes used with an upright gentle dabbing motion are recommended for the skilled stenciler. Whatever is chosen to stencil with, do not saturate it with paint. Be careful that the paint, chalk, or crayon does not get under the stencil, causing smears.

It may be difficult for very young children to cut their own stencil out of cardboard. Perhaps it could be drawn by them but cut out by an adult. Encourage children to design a very simple picture with a minimum of fine detail. An X-Acto® knife can be used to cut out a stencil. Remember not to cut through the frame to get to the inside. Very young children can tear out an abstract shape that will work very well in a stencil activity.

Stencils can also be painted with spray paint or sprayed from a sprayer, such as a bug sprayer filled with liquid tempera. This method is best done outdoors. Place the paper in the lid of a large box. Tape the back of the stencil in place. Spray with paint. Let dry. Carefully remove the stencil.

Paper Plate Stencil

Put a paper plate down on a piece of thick paper and trace around it. Cut out the circle and fold it into a small wedge. Cut bits out of the folds to make a stencil. Unfold the stencil and put it back on the paper plate. Dip a sponge in tempera paint and gently blot paint on the stencil, transferring the design onto the paper plate.

Spatter Printing

You will need a large but not too deep box, a screen or mesh wire (e.g., a window screen, kitchen grease guard, or metal strainer), and an old toothbrush. Cut or tear a stencil out of paper. Or items with interesting shapes, such as coins, a comb, cookie cutters, keys, and nature specimens, can be used as positive stencils and placed on a sheet of paper inside the box. Dip your toothbrush in paint and gently move it across the screen, releasing a mist of paint. Dark colors will show up best on white paper. The paint will spatter and outline the stencil or objects. The space taken up with the positive stencil or objects will remain white or the color of the background paper. Carefully move the stencil or objects and repeat with a different color. Switch stencils and work with the negative stencil.

Young children will need to use a large box covered with a fairly large spatter screen. Older children may be able to use a small, handheld food strainer and move it around the stencil. They can carefully rub chalk across the food strainer at the same time. A small spatter screen can also be made by carefully cutting the top and bottom off a sturdy small box. Attach wire or screen to the top. Use with small stencils. Or fasten plastic mesh or screen into an embroidery hoop. If no screen is available, scrape the bristles of the toothbrush toward you with a stick. If you scrape away from you, the spray will spatter you. The thumb can also be used to scrape bristles.

Printing

Silk-screen printing is actually a stencil method of printing. Paint is forced through a piece of stretched mesh fabric that has been prepared with a design. The paint is printed onto fabric or paper. Silk screen is a way to create several prints of the same image and is therefore recommended for making greeting cards or stationery. First, a screen must be prepared.

An embroidery hoop, an old picture frame, or a frame cut from the lid of a shoe box can be used for screen printing. Use an old nylon stocking or a piece of silk, organdy, dotted swiss, or cheesecloth for the silk-screen material. Cut it larger than your frame, pull it tight, and secure it with tacks, tape, or nails. Cut a stencil and place it on paper. Put the silk-screen frame over the stencil. Use a brush, tongue depressor, or cardboard strip to gently spread thick paint on the silk screen, which will cover the stencil. Carefully lift your silk-screen frame. Thoroughly rinse the silk screen after each application of paint. Add different colors if desired. Repeat the pattern while overlapping or creatively combining pieces from different stencils.

SUMMARY

Artistic elements are the building blocks of artist expression. Artists process with line, color, and shape until these elements are successfully combined into a harmonious design or overall composition. Children go through the same steps, but on a more informal and often unplanned basis. These elements are the criteria for making, understanding, appreciating, and critiquing art. Our intent is not to turn children into art critics. That would be developmentally inappropriate. It is our intent, however, to use the vocabulary of the artistic elements so that children can learn to value and directly participate in the arts. They will come to know good art when they see it and will be able to use the artistic elements in justifying their evaluation.

Key Terms

artistic elements	line	shape
asymmetrical (informal)	mass	space
balance	negative space	symmetrical (formal)
color	neutral	texture
complementary	pattern	thermal qualities
cool	positive space	tint
design (composition)	primary	value
hue	prints	volume
intensity	secondary	warm
intermediate	shade	

Suggested Activities

1. Visit an art museum or check out books with art reproductions. Use the artistic elements in analyzing a work of art.
2. Implement an art activity involving one or more of the artistic elements.
3. Facilitate a printmaking experience with children.
4. Complete the following Color Clock activity.
   a. Get white paper.
   b. Use watercolors.
   c. Draw a large circle
      —black-in center
      —blob of paint
   d. Fill-in (with blob of paint)
      12 = yellow (primary)
      4 = red (primary)
      8 = blue (primary)
   e. Mix (secondary colors)
      12 + 4 = 2 (add blob and name of color to clock)
      4 + 8 = 6 (add blob and name of color to clock)
      8 + 12 = 10 (add blob and name of color to clock)
   f. Mix (intermediate colors)
      12 + 2 = 1 (add blob and name of color to clock)
      2 + 4 = 3 (add blob and name of color to clock)
      4 + 6 = 5 (add blob and name of color to clock) P. S. Mathematically incorrect!
      6 + 8 = 7 (add blob and name of color to clock)
      8 + 10 = 9 (add blob and name of color to clock)
      10 + 12 = 11 (add blob and name of color to clock)
   g. Let dry.
   h. Refer to back cover of this book.
   i. Turn in to instructor.

Review

1. List the nine major artistic elements discussed in this chapter.

2. Complete the following color equations:
   a. red + _____   =   orange
   b. yellow + blue   =   _____
   c. _____ + _____   =   purple

3. Put the proper color term in front of each color:
   P for Primary
   S for Secondary
   I for Intermediate
   N for Neutral

   _____ yellow-orange   _____ blue

   _____ green   _____ blue-green

   _____ yellow-green   _____ orange

   _____ red   _____ red-violet

   _____ black   _____ yellow

   _____ red-orange   _____ white

   _____ blue-violet   _____ purple/violet

4. Match the following columns related to color.
   a. the colors that are used to produce all other colors   ____ neutral colors
   b. orange, green, and purple   ____ complementary colors
   c. mixing a primary and a secondary color results in this   ____ secondary colors
   d. these colors are opposite each other on the color wheel   ____ primary colors
   e. black and white are examples   ____ warm colors
   f. a pure, unmixed color   ____ hue
   g. lightness or darkness of a color   ____ value
   h. brightness or dullness of a color   ____ intensity
   i. adding white will produce this   ____ tint
   j. adding black will produce this   ____ shade
   k. red, yellow, and orange are examples   ____ cool colors
   l. blue, green, and purple are examples   ____ intermediate colors

5. Match the following columns related to artistic elements.

a. has hue, value, and intensity   ____ texture

b. can be symmetrical or asymmetrical   ____ balance

c. can be positive or negative   ____ space

d. a recurring, repeated sequence   ____ pattern

e. refers to the integrated whole   ____ mass/volume

f. refers to three-dimensional art   ____ design/composition

g. a visible mark made by moving an artistic tool across a surface   ____ shape/form

h. refers to the surface quality of a work of art   ____ color

i. refers to two-dimensional art   ____ line

Chapter 7

Aesthetics

Many young children spend much of their waking day in an early childhood facility. Whether a large center or small home, teachers try to make it a place where children will want to spend their time productively. The physical environment should beckon and invite children in; it should call out to and engage them. It should also be visually appealing, without being overstimulating. There can be things to stimulate the senses without overloading them—a vase of flowers, a display of artwork, and soothing background music. These aesthetic touches can transform a room into an aesthetically pleasing environment. Wall displays also add an aesthetic touch. In the featured photo, the teacher cut children's paintings into the shape of flowers. She asked children's permission and let them choose which flower shape they wanted. Easter grass was added for a three-dimensional effect. The result was a wall display featuring spring flowers. If you were the teacher, what could you do to modify, improve, or extend this display?

Objectives

After reading this chapter, you should be able to:

- Define and provide a rationale for aesthetics in early childhood education.
- Discuss the aesthetic attitude, process, experience, response, and value.
- Discuss the teacher's role in aesthetics.
- Apply criteria for the selection and placement of art prints.
- Discuss developmental stages as they relate to children's understanding of art and their critical judgment of art.
- Compare and contrast the Reggio Emilia experience with visits to American early childhood settings.
- Provide experiences using watercolors and ink.

INTRODUCTION

Think of a time when you found yourself in a beautiful place. Maybe it was inside a cathedral or atop a mountain. How did it make you feel? Full of awe and wonder? Relaxed and comfortable? These positive feelings can also happen in your classroom when you make it an awesome, beautiful place to be. Although taste is individual, adults and even children appreciate beauty and beautiful things. Working in a pleasing environment will accomplish four goals. First, being surrounded by beauty and having beautiful experiences will help children's aesthetic development and enrich their lives. Second, it will make the environment a pleasant place for you and the children to be for a large amount of the day. Third, you will feel good about being there while reducing your stress level. Fourth, it will subtly influence children's behavior in positive ways.

What is aesthetics and why should it be addressed in early childhood? This chapter attempts to answer these two basic questions. Our concern for the young child's aesthetic development and education stems from our wider concern for the whole child. Young children are aesthetic experts. They demonstrate the aesthetic attitude in their spontaneity, wonder, and amazement at things that adults may take for granted. What is the teacher's role in aesthetics? Teachers can be aesthetic models in the way they dress, behave, and communicate. The indoor and outdoor environment can also be aesthetically pleasing and stimulating.

AESTHETICS

Aesthetics is an abstract concept that means "perception" in Greek. Although we may feel it is important that children learn something about aesthetics, we may not be quite sure what the term entails. Aesthetics is not synonymous with art. Aesthetics includes art, and the other expressive arts like music and dance, but it also goes beyond them. Just what is aesthetics? Aesthetics

- is a nondiscursive and metaphorical way of knowing and experiencing.
- involves the love and pursuit of beauty as found in art, movement, music, and life.
- is an awareness and appreciation of the natural beauty found in nature and one's surroundings.
- is a basic human response to life.
- means being a beholder of beauty and savoring beautiful things in the world around us.
- involves being connected with one's experiences.
- links knowing and feeling, the cognitive and affective.

For purposes of art education, Lankford (1992) defines aesthetics as a group of concepts for understanding

Early Childhood Art Education (R. S.)

The following is a discussion between the author (R. S.) and Aline D. Wolf (A. W.), who is the founder of the Pennsylvania Montessori Academy in Altoona, Pennsylvania. She is the author of *Mommy, It's a Renoir* and four volumes of accompanying art postcards entitled *Child-Size Masterpieces*.

R. S. Some critics believe that art education and aesthetics are too advanced and abstract for young children. What is your response?

A. W. I disagree. Young children are constantly absorbing stimuli from their environment. It follows that we should put beautiful things in their environment for them to absorb. For example, pretend you are planning to use pictures of animals as part of your unit of study or theme. What do you use as resources? There are many beautiful art prints depicting animals which could be used. Examples include Durer's *Hare* and Franz Marc's *Red Horses*. When studying the circus, remember that Renoir, Picasso, and Chagall have all painted pictures on this theme.

  With three-year-olds my goal is for them to look and enjoy. I am not concerned with teaching them the title or artist's name. Over time they begin to note details while developing good taste. Aesthetics is not something you can schedule once a week for thirty minutes. You need to expose children to beautiful things on an ongoing basis.

R. S. Could you clarify Montessori's views on art and aesthetics in the early years?

A. W. Actually, Maria Montessori was a pioneer in addressing the importance of aesthetics in the environment of young children. She insisted that children's surroundings be beautiful. She succeeded in bringing beauty into the Children's House by insisting, first of all, on cleanliness and order. On the walls and shelves she used light-colored paint, which never clashed with the bright colors of her materials. She accented this harmonious, peaceful setting with plants, fresh flowers, a beautiful shell collection, or even fragile china dishes, which she allowed the children to use. The walls were hung with attractive pictures, carefully chosen and representing simple scenes which would interest children. Since children absorb from their environment, children placed in a beautiful and aesthetically pleasing environment would absorb good taste.

  For Montessori, art appreciation begins at a very early age. Materials including the metal insets, color tablets, and geometric shapes foster an indirect preparation for art in that each trains the eyes and hands. Montessori did not devise materials which would specifically foster appreciation. That's why I devised my art postcards.

R. S. Some critics believe that Montessori programs provide too little emphasis on creativity and free expression. They believe there are too few open-ended materials and too little creative messing about. What do you say?

A. W. I disagree. In my visits to Montessori classrooms across the United States I have seen easels and clay provided for free expression. This has been the norm rather than the exception. Other Montessori programs include a wider range of art activities and materials for free expression.

R. S. Aline, I visited one Montessori classroom where only one color of paint was set out at the easel. There was no opportunity for color mixing. Other children were pasting precut shapes onto a sheet of black construction paper. Is this typical?

A. W. No. Montessori never recommended that children paint with only one color. I would need to know more about the children. Perhaps this particular child would benefit from using only one color. Maybe the children were very young and being introduced to paint and painting for the very first time.

Early Childhood Art Education (R. S.) (continued)

R. S. Tell us about your art postcards.

A. W. We know that children learn best by touching and handling. Montessori herself said that the hand was the child's chief teacher. Yet fine art is something we have put out of children's reach or say "Don't touch!" In doing so we deprive them. My art postcards try to reconcile this. They uphold Montessori's principles regarding the importance of visual stimulation while encouraging the use of the hands. The result is a much deeper dimension of learning.

I developed the art postcards so that all children could firsthand experience the beauty of fine art. The cards work in any classroom. One need not be a Montessori teacher to use them. They are inexpensive, small, lightweight, and ready for use individually or in small or large groups.

I also developed the art postcards to combat so much of the ugliness in our world. Offhand I think of lunch boxes, binders, and children's clothing that depict monsters and creatures. Why? We should be giving our children the best. Fine art need not be reserved for the affluent or those living close to art museums. Art postcards bring the museum to the children. With them, all children can know beautiful art while holding it in their hands.

I also suspect that some teachers who do not have a background in art may be uncomfortable with this strategy. I believe that teachers and parents learn about art as they use these materials with children. That is how I learned about art. If readers want to learn more about my materials they can write: Parent Child Press, P. O. Box 675, Hollidaysburg, Pennsylvania 16648-0675.

Art postcards can also be purchased at museum gift shops. It is a good idea to include postcards of paintings in local museums so that children are familiar with the painting when they visit the museum to see the originals.

R. S. Share some other strategies you have either used or observed.

A. W.
- Give children one or two of their favorite art postcards to keep in their own folder at school.
- Encourage children and families to collect art postcards.
- Encourage children to collect art postcards as souvenirs of their trips to art museums.
- Have children mail art postcards to the school and recognize their donation by displaying their name as donor.
- Hang lovely art prints in the classroom. For example, display one at child's eye level on the door.
- Encourage parents to hang a child's favorite art print on their bedroom door or wall.

the nature of art. Aesthetic concepts address virtually all aspects of art from process to product to response. Aesthetic inquiry may be defined as the process of clarifying and answering questions about the nature of art.

Some examples of aesthetic experiences are

- touching the sparkling design of frost on a window.
- viewing the translucent silkiness of a spiderweb.
- watching the movements of leaves and branches on a windy day.
- seeing and touching the delicate petals of a rosebud.
- listening to and moving to the beat of an ethnic folk song.
- stopping to savor the aroma of freshly baked bread.
- sitting in wet sand and splashing in the waves on the shore.

- slowly sipping hot cider while marveling at all the different colors crackling in a campfire.
- admiring the linear design and pattern in a skyscraper.
- noticing the wood grains in a row of blocks.

The type of beauty that aesthetics pursues is the type taken for granted in our everyday lives, rather than the artificial Hollywood-type definition of beauty.

RATIONALE

Why are aesthetics and aesthetic education important in early childhood? There are five reasons. First, our humanistic concern for the whole child motivates us to provide for all aspects of child development. Second, it is our belief that children who marvel at beauty in the world around them will be able to appreciate the beauty of letters, words, numbers, stories, poems, formulas, books, symbols, and people of other cultures. Third, children with the aesthetic sense will develop into adults who know and value good design and can use this as wise consumers in choosing vehicles, clothing, home furnishings, and entertainment as well as on a wider level in planning cities, highways, and attempting to solve problems of pollution, war, poverty, and urban blight. Fourth, it is important for children to value the arts and directly participate in a variety of the arts. Fifth, aesthetic experiences foster concept development.

Aesthetics is a branch of philosophy concerned with an individual's pursuit of and response to beauty. Aesthetics involves the following:

1. attitude
2. process/experience
3. response

1. Aesthetic Attitude

The **aesthetic attitude** involves

- openness or childlike freshness.
- spontaneity.
- intense focusing on the here and now.
- a sense of joy, wonder, marvel, or excitement.
- willingness to perceive as if experiencing something for the very first time.
- commitment or willingness to "stop and smell the roses."

Young children constantly demonstrate the aesthetic attitude. They are sensory gluttons who need to look at, listen to, touch, smell, and taste everything they come in contact with. This may prove embarrassing to some adults: "Nina, please don't touch the daisies." Over time, Nina may decide not to wonder at flowers. She may learn to take them for granted. Or, as her mother told her, "If you've seen one, you've seen them all." Unfortunately, Nina's mother has lost the aesthetic attitude. The author observed a preschool field trip to the library. The children were stopping to watch and listen to the sights and sounds at a construction site. The teacher was hurrying them up, urging them to walk faster to get to their destination. A rich sensory experience was lost. We live in a too-fast-paced world. We rush from home to work. In the process we may ignore rainbows in the sky, colorful patterns in rain puddles, or daisies growing alongside the freeway. The aesthetic experience takes time. It means being frozen for the moment and totally caught up in the here and now.

2. Aesthetic Process/Experience

The **aesthetic process/experience** is intrinsically motivating. Children sense and perceive for the sheer joy of it. The aesthetic process involves active engagement rather than passive taking in. It means using all the senses to ravish an object or experience, getting completely lost or totally consumed. Examples of the aesthetic process include:

- listening attentively to music rather than merely hearing a song.
- visually exploring or quietly contemplating a work of art rather than merely glancing at it.
- manipulating and feeling a peacock's feather rather than quickly touching it.

Aesthetic processing takes time and a commitment to flow with the experience. Children are more aesthetically proficient than adults. They thoroughly examine their world with all their senses. Adults can learn much more about aesthetics from watching children explore the world.

3. Aesthetic Response

The aesthetic attitude and process result in an appreciative reaction or **aesthetic response** on many different levels. Our affective response may involve a sense of wonder, appreciation, surprise, a feeling of being moved or touched, awe, exhilaration, or being carried away. We may get lost in the aesthetic experience and totally caught up or consumed for the instant. At the physiological level, our response may result in a smile, grin, laugh, perspiration, shiver, chill, heavy sigh, or even goose bumps.

Our reactions will also entail a mental response in the form of a decision, judgment, or evaluation. One may ask these questions:

- Was this personally enjoyable, and why?
- Is this work of art, music, or dance good, and why?
- Do I like it, and why?

Our intent is to help children apply simple criteria to discuss and critique works of art. They can learn to separate what is good or bad from what they like or dislike. For example, a young child may not like ballet, but can still appreciate the beauty and grace of the movements. Over time, children will slowly construct their own personal preferences and tastes. They need not follow the crowd in believing that what is popular or current must be good. They will come to identify with and value the arts. One hopes that they will grow up reading good books, listening to a variety of music, and with tolerance for different artistic styles. Life will offer them more than being passively entertained by television.

Eaton (1998) believes the difficulty with understanding the very nature of aesthetic activity, experience, and judgment demands explaining how communication is possible when key words such as *beauty* or *art* seem to mean such different things to different people. To the author's list of the three components of aesthetics, Eaton would add **aesthetic value.** Aesthetic value arises from a positive response of a person or group of people toward something. It is obvious that unless someone feels positively inclined toward a thing or event, it cannot have aesthetic value. It is the value a thing or event has because of its capacity to evoke pleasure that is recognized as arising from features in the object traditionally considered worthy of attention and reflection. The aesthetic in art depends upon the traditions and culture in which we share beliefs about what is valued.

There are stages in children's artistic development. Are there developmental stages children go through in their understanding of art? Gardner and Winner (1976) conducted interviews with 121 children to identify developmental stages of understanding art. Questions focused on the following: the source of art, the production of art, the medium, style, art and the outside world, formal properties of art, and evaluation. They concluded that children pass through three distinct developmental phases in their understanding. The age and characteristics include the following:

4 to 7 years—Very young children have a simplistic understanding of art; the making of art is an easy, mechanical activity and judgments about the artistic quality of a work are all equally acceptable. Some children say that authorities including parents determine what is good. Young children emphasize the technical aspects of a work of art, often believing that anyone can make art—including animals. They believe that decisions involved in making art are governed by physical limitations rather than aesthetic concerns. For example, they would say the picture is finished when the paper is filled.

10 years—In the middle elementary years, children believe art should be a precise rendering of reality. They believe there are criteria for judging quality in works of art; the more real it looks, the better it is.

Adolescence—Teens are more sophisticated in their understanding of art. They realize one's opinions and values vary and that judgments in art are relative and that their opinion is valid.

Gardner and Winner (1976) add that children will remain in an arrested state of development in their understanding of art unless their naive opinions about art are challenged.

Rosenstiel, Morrison, Silverman, and Gardner (1978) sought to identify developmental stages of critical judgment in art. They interviewed children ranging in age from six to 16 with questions related to how one makes judgments regarding art. They identified the following developmental characteristics in children's critical judgment:

first graders—Children are limited to identifying subject matter and colors. They use terms such as *good* or *pretty* when critiquing art.

third graders—Along with subject matter and color, children now comment on the details, designs, and shapes in the work. Third graders consider realism *good* because it is difficult to achieve.

sixth graders—Responses parallel those of third graders. Sixth graders tend to use a few more terms from art history in their comments.

tenth graders—Adolescents are far less likely than children in the former three groups to make contentless statements. They tend to cite a variety of factors when selecting and justifying their responses to works of art. They also tend to mention formal properties, use terminology from art criticism, and mention and recognize work from certain periods in history and specific artists' names.

Rosenstiel and colleagues (1978) concluded that younger children may be able to make finer aesthetic distinctions when viewing works of art but that their verbal responses were confined to their limited vocabulary.

Expose, Not Impose

As early childhood educators, our task is to expose rather than impose. Expose children to a wealth of sensory experiences and variety in each of the arts. Encourage them to critique, develop personal preferences, and value art, music, movement, dance, and literature. Children can use accepted criteria, including the artistic elements, as standards in developing their own preferences. Expose children to a wide variety of art forms and styles without imposing your own preferences. For example, a teacher may not like abstract art, but that does not mean that it is junk or bad, or that realistic art is better. Help children see that art can be good in terms of design or composition even though one may not like it (see Figure 7–1).

Dobbs (1998) views children's understanding of aesthetics as residing along a continuum. For example, for young children, a developmentally appropriate activity may be to learn the distinction between expressing preference and making a judgment. They can be assisted in understanding that although one may like a particular work of art, there are others who may not. Aesthetics is not about uttering subjective preferences, but about the thinking and effort involved in figuring out why we make such choices and how best to support and justify them. Dobbs uses the example of flavors of ice cream, asking children which one they like best. There is no right or wrong answer, nor is it even a question of aesthetics. Instead, it is simply a matter of individual preference. However, to assume that anyone else would value one's choice of ice cream requires a set of reasons supporting a judgment of its goodness. Here one needs to provide a rationale for one's choice, to make a reasoned judgment capable of meeting some external standard or criterion other than one's own preference. This is the idea of objectivity. Aesthetics involves teaching students how to create such argument, how to talk about artworks in a manner that validates the judgments they have made about those works of art.

Aesthetic discussion conducted with younger children should be consistent with their level of cognitive development and mastery of language. Although younger students may discuss issues about art in a less advanced way than older students, and without using technical jargon, they can engage in aesthetic discussion. Simply learning to talk and construct a reasoned argument is an important exercise, not only for aesthetics and art education, but for the general educational goal of schooling.

TEACHER'S ROLE IN AESTHETICS

What can early childhood educators do to foster aesthetic development? Aesthetics does not come neatly packaged in a kit, series of books, text, unit, or set of materials to purchase. Still, it is important and within our reach. There are guidelines for making the teacher, children, and classroom aesthetically alive. Some of these are discussed here.

Teacher as Aesthetic Model

It is important that the teacher personally invest the time to become aesthetically responsive. Teachers can model their own aesthetic awareness and sensitivity. The way one dresses is an aesthetic statement. One need not dress like a fashion model, however, to make this statement. First and foremost, clothing should be neat, comfortable, and appropriate for stooping, moving, playing, and sitting on the floor. We can reflect an appreciation of color and color harmony in choosing articles of clothing and accessories. For example, a young girl is proudly showing off her new sweater. Her teacher asks her to identify the colors. Nikki replies, "It has red and blue." Her teacher replies, "My dress has red and blue in it, too. And I wore my white earrings. I wore the same colors that are in our flag." Or, "Jim, you mixed blue and yellow in your picture and

Figure 7-1 Exposing children to a variety of art forms and styles.

made green. I wore blue slacks with a yellow blouse and my green belt. We match."

Teacher's Inner Beauty

The teacher's inner beauty can be demonstrated by positively relating to all children and valuing their uniqueness. Find something unique and beautiful in each child, and let that child know. Convey beautiful messages. Children appreciate being talked to in regular tones. There is no need to raise the pitch of one's voice artificially and speak in a syrupy sweet manner. Refer to oneself as *I* rather than as *Miss Jones* or *Teacher,* as in, "Miss Jones doesn't like it when the children are not paying attention," or "Teacher will just have to get some more apple juice for snack, won't she?" Talk to children in a natural voice rather than in a condescending or patronizing tone.

Provide for a Wide Variety in the Arts

Children can be exposed to different examples within a variety of the arts. For example, different types of music can be informally introduced throughout the day: slow lullabies or waltzes during rest, classical as background music during snack, and a march or rock-and-roll during cleanup.

Aesthetic Classroom

The classroom can be an aesthetically pleasing and sensory-rich environment (see Figure 7–2). Do a beauty check of your room. Cartoon characters in bright competing colors can be removed from the walls and replaced with aesthetically pleasing artwork, wall hangings, tapestry, weavings, posters, stained glass panels, or prints. Signs on the doors of the classrooms or learning centers can be tastefully constructed, with care taken in the choice of color, material, placement, and printing (see Figure 7–3). Utilize windows and take advantage of the natural light. Hang up objects that play with the light, including mobiles made of cellophane papers and children's art. Items suspended near windows create interesting patterns that move and change throughout the day. Adding mirrors gives a feeling of openness and reflects all the beauty in your room. Mirrors can be placed in different centers and even on the ceiling for an interesting perspective. Have the children grow plants indoors. An outdoor flower garden provides flowers to display throughout the room. Think quality rather than quantity. Did you ever get the feeling of clutter when visiting some antique shops, model homes, or furniture showrooms that appear to fill every inch of living space with prized objects? More is not always better when decorating with beautiful objects.

Aesthetic centers for experiencing art, music, and movement can be arranged. Aesthetically pleasing displays can be set up with:

- beautiful things around a given color, shape, pattern, texture, or design theme, such as things that are square, yellow, checkered, or soft (see Figure 7–4).

Figure 7-2 An aesthetically pleasing use of classroom space.

Figure 7-3 A multilingual classroom sign.

- flowers, plants, nature specimens, or seasonal fruits and vegetables such as harvest corn (see Figure 7–5).
- machine and appliance parts, gears, tools, and mechanical things.
- musical instruments.
- postcards and souvenirs.
- ethnic costumes and artifacts.
- antique kitchen gadgets and farm tools.
- special collections of postage stamps, cookie cutters, baskets, ceramic animals, stuffed animals, license plates, fans, hats, coins, music boxes, arrowheads, minerals, rocks.
- an array of artwork, including drawings, paintings, pottery, ceramics, sculpture, weaving, stitchery, batik, collages, watercolors, and prints.
- art: books, postcards, prints, posters.

Epstein (2001) recommends placing art reproduction in locations where they relate to the children's interests and activities. For example, hang a painting of mothers and children by Mary Cassat in the house area. Add one of Van Gogh's sunflower paintings in the science center. A three-dimensional recycled junk sculpture could be placed in the block area. An example of abstract art such as one of Jackson Pollock's drip paintings could be displayed in the art center.

Szekely (1990) views children's picture books as works of art. Illustrators, like artists, use different media to visualize their thoughts and words. A precise sketch in ink or a realistic painting may work for one book, while a collage or abstract watercolor may work for another. In sharing a beautifully illustrated book with children, you can treat each picture as an artistic creation. Children can freely explore the works in books, in contrast to works in a museum, perhaps carefully running their clean fingers over interesting details. By commenting on the illustrator's use of color, shape, and other artistic elements, art teachers can use books to enhance children's art appreciation skills.

Artists who illustrate their own works are in a special position to find the visual image that best reinforces their words. The following is an incomplete list of popular authors who write children's books. They

Figure 7-4 The classroom should be a beautiful and touchable environment.

Figure 7-5 An aesthetic touch.

Selecting Art Prints

Choose art prints that are high quality but simple for children to understand and relate to. Yenawine (2003) believes that young children are satisfied with finding, naming, listing, counting, and discussing as well as making up stories about what they see in an art print. Images should be simple and recognizable so as not to overwhelm or confuse. Appropriate content includes children, families, pets, animals, familiar objects, actions, and expressions. For example, it would be easier for young children to relate to a print of a smiling clown holding a puppy than a lost herder guiding a camel in a desert storm. Stick with the familiar, and avoid art with levels of hidden meaning or requiring a knowledge of history to understand and appreciate.

Tokonoma

Based on his visits to Japan, Spodek (1993) offers an example that can be translated into an aesthetic display. The tokonoma is an alcove in the tatami room that is found in traditional Japanese homes and inns. The rooms themselves, their floors covered with straw mats or tatamis, are sparsely furnished. On one wall there is usually a small alcove that is devoted to the display of something beautiful—a scroll, a flower arrangement, a piece of pottery or ceramics, for example. The display adds beauty to the surroundings. Spodek suggests that early childhood educators could establish their own tokonoma or beauty area, just as they would have a science or nature display. An art reproduction or a vase of flowers could be tastefully displayed in this area. Children could observe the display on their own and the teacher could engage them in discussions about the display and why it is considered beautiful. The concept of an aesthetic display in the classroom is nothing new. They were found in British Infant Schools during the height of the informal or open education movement when children's self-expression and aesthetics were highly valued.

each have several titles to their credit and use different styles of illustrating their books.

Children can be introduced to the artistic elements by noting illustrations in picture books. Some examples include the following:

Line

Fox, M. *The straight line wonder.*
Green, R. G. *When a line bends . . . a shape begins.*
Isadora, R. *Ben's trumpet.*
Johnson, C. *Harold and the purple crayon.*
Sendak, M. *Where the wild things are.*
Spier, P. *Noah's ark.*
Yenawine, P. *Lines.*

Color

Bank, M. *Yellow ball.*
Burningham, J. *Colors.*
Carle, E. *Hello, red fox.*
dePaola, T. *The legend of the Indian paintbrush.*
DeRolf, S. *The crayon box that talked.*
Grifalconi, A. *Kinda' blue.*
Jonas, A. *Color dance.*
Joose, B. *I love you the purplest.*
Perrault, C. *Cinderella.*
Spinelli, E. *In my new yellow suit.*
Stinson, K., & Betteridge, D. *Those green things.*
Walsh, E. S. *Mouse magic.*
Walsh, E. S. *Mouse paint.*
Whitman, C. *Bring on the blue.*
Whitman, C. *Ready for red.*
Whitman, C. *Yellow and you.*

Shape

Burns, M. *The greedy triangle.*
Grifalconi, A. *The village of round and square houses.*
Grover, M. *Circles and squares everywhere!*
Hoban, T. *Circles, triangles & squares.*
Hutchins, P. *Changes, changes.*
Lionni, L. *Frederick.*
Lionni, L. *Swimmy.*
Snape, C., & Snape, J. *The boy with squares eyes.*

Mass or Volume

Please refer to the section on clay and play dough.

Pattern

Chocolate, D. *Kente colors.*
Robertson, J. *Oscar's spots.*

Space

Getz, D. *Floating home.*
Jenkins, S. *Looking down.*
Jonas, A. *Watch William walk.*
Van Alsburg, C. *Jumanji.*
Wood, A., & Wood, D. *The napping house.*
Yolen, J. *Owl moon.*

Balance

Peek, M. *The balancing act.*

Texture

Hoban, T. *Is it rough? Is it smooth? Is it shiny?*
Saxe, J. G. *The blind men and the elephant.*
Van Alsburg. *The polar express.*
Williams, G. *The rabbits' wedding.*

Visit your local public library and check out books by these and other authors. Share these books with young children. Have children notice the way illustrators use different art media to illustrate their books. Encourage children to use a variety of art media when they illustrate their stories and books. Develop your own list of favorite children's authors to add to the above list.

The Art of Picture Book Illustration

Beautifully illustrated children's picture books are works of art. Many emergent readers do not naturally and automatically focus their attention on the subtle aspects of illustrations. Visual literacy skills can be developed by prompting emergent readers to carefully examine story book illustrations in the following ways:

1. Encourage children to discuss what they see in the illustrations. Asking "What do you see in the picture?" is a good beginning. Use the artistic elements to frame the discussion. Help children to see how the illustrator used color, shape, and line to make a visual statement.

2. Identify and discuss type of artistic media used. Illustrators use a variety of art media including painting, woodcut, linoleum block printing, collage, photography, and drawing. For example, Eric Carle used cut paper collage to illustrate his classic book, *The very hungry caterpillar.* He could have used paint or photographs, but the impact would have been different. Marguerite Davol used collage to illustrate *The paper dragon.* Painting was the choice of Huy Voun Lee to illustrate *At the beach,* while Molly Bang used paper to tell her story of *The paper crane.* The illustrator's choice of media is key to understanding and appreciating a story.

3. Identify the genre or artistic style used by the illustrator. Illustrators also use different artistic styles. For example, Robert McCloskey's *Make way for ducklings* and *Alexander and the terrible, horrible, no good, very bad day* by Judith Viorst both reflect a realistic style of illustration. In both *Anno's journey* by Anno Mitsumasa and *Mr. Rabbit and the lovely present* by Charlotte Zolotow, an impressionistic artistic style is used to illustrate.

This information helps to supply information that is pivotal to understanding stories. Older readers can be guided to compare and contrast illustrations. Show how one illustrator can use the same or different techniques and how a book about families can be illustrated in a variety of ways. Encourage children to illustrate their own stories/books using a variety of media. The chapter on aesthetics continues our discussion of the beauty and aesthetic appeal for children's picture books.

Let us apply what we have learned about the importance of picture book illustrations to literacy with their aesthetic analysis and appreciation by using *Tar beach* by Faith Ringgold (1991). Ringgold's work is particularly noteworthy because she combines narrative text with fabric to weave a rich story to be read both visually and verbally. Begin by providing a visual reproduction of the art work. Ask children to describe what they see and how it makes them feel. Help them identify and discuss artistic elements including colors, shapes, borders, textures, and patterns. Next, read the picture book in its entirety. Ask the children to compare the art print with the picture book version. Discuss the authors' style of illustration. At the end of the discussion, tell the children about the author and artist. Faith Ringgold grew up in Harlem in the 1930s. The author personally experienced the prejudices that existed toward African-Americans during this time. This can generate a discussion of prejudice and exclusion. The author was confined to her home because of childhood asthma. Rather than a hardship, she used this opportunity to spend time with her mother, a fashion designer, who taught her how to sew and to be creative with art and fabrics. The result is a series of story quilts. Each section written on the quilt is a page. In *Tar beach,* the child in her art symbolizes a little girl's dream of flying and changing circumstances for her family. It is a message of optimism, hope, and love. The children learn that Ringgold is a prominent American artist who creates not only quilts but murals, paintings, abstract works, masks, and soft sculptures. This personal history prompts the children to reread the book, this time focusing on the interplay of words and art as they reflect the details and meanings of the author's life and work.

Art Visitors

Invite professional artists, musicians, dancers, craftspeople, volunteers, and parents who have some interest and skill in one of the arts. Remember to include this when you survey parents at the beginning of the year concerning any interests and skills that they might volunteer. Get to know the artists, musicians, and dance companies in your area. Remember to provide brief

The Reggio Emilia Experience

This section is based on the writings of Malaguzzi (1993), Bredekamp (1993), Gandini (1993), Edwards, Gandini, and Forman (1993), Katz (1990), and New (1990, 1993). Recently there has been a sustained interest in the Reggio Emilia schools reminiscent of the fervor of open education and the British Infant Schools during the 1970s. In our quest for developmentally appropriate practices, an examination of the Reggio Emilia experience should provide inspiration, insight, and direction.

The Reggio Emilia school of northern Italy reflects a longstanding commitment (over 30 years) to quality education for children and support for families. Loris Malaguzzi, founder of the Reggio Emilia schools, was influenced by the works of Rousseau, Pestallozi, Froebel, Dewey, Piaget, and Vygotsky, among others. His philosophy and ideology are shared by contemporary American counterparts. Learning is viewed within an interactive-constructivist framework. It is something that children do, not something done to them. Based on Dewey's concept of progressive education, schools should promote children's natural curiosity and creativity as well as active interaction with their community. Children are active learners—exploring, inquiring, problem solving, and representing their experiences in a number of ways.

Gandini (1993) identified the following points which capture the Reggio Emilia experience.

1. A positive image portrays children as competent, curious learners with prior knowledge and much potential. This contrasts a negative image viewing the child as deficient, disadvantaged, egocentric, and needy. Bredekamp (1993) makes an interesting point. Viewing children as needy permits adults to do the very least for them, while recognizing children as competent requires that we provide them with the best environments and experiences possible. Children are trusted and respect is mutual.

2. To understand and work with children, they must be viewed within a social context or system which includes teachers, peers, parents, and the community.

3. Children, parents, and teachers form an important triad. All have needs as well as rights. Children have a right to the best education possible.

4. Parent participation is an essential component. It is an ongoing process taking many forms.

5. The school is viewed as amiable in that it is designed to foster communication and social interaction. Since children learn from their peers, activities are done in small groups. This facilitates problem solving, negotiating, and verbal give-and-take. Each child has a communication box in which letters and notes written by children are exchanged. This gives new meaning and function to cubbies.

6. Time is fluid, not rigidly set by the clock. Children stay with the same teachers and peers for three-year cycles (infancy to three and three to six). Each year the group changes environments.

7. Teachers are active partners and co-constructors in the learning process. Their role is to observe, participate, and serve as resources to children.

8. Cooperation and organization form the foundation of the educational system. Teachers work in pairs as equals. Cooperative efforts between staff and families facilitate the attainment of goals set by the Reggio Emilia schools.

9. Rather than being planned in advance, the curriculum is emergent, based on teachers' observations of children at play. Ideas for projects and possible learning experiences emerge from these observations.

10. Children are encouraged to pursue themes and projects. This project method originated with Dewey and is currently advocated by Lilian Katz. Ideas for short- and long-term study originate with the children and not from curriculum how-to or idea books.

11. The atelierista, or artist in residence, operates within an atelier or art studio. See Chapter 13 for a discussion of art centers. The art studio is stocked with art materials, in transparent containers on open shelves

(Continued)

The Reggio Emilia Experience (continued)

and in bountiful supply. This enables children to autonomously pursue their interests. Children's two- and three-dimensional art is attractively displayed throughout the school.

12. Teachers take seriously their work as observers and researchers. Documenting what children do is an ongoing process taking many forms. Tape recorders are everywhere. This strategy resembles authentic assessment in which teachers assemble individual portfolios.

Two more aspects that can be added to Gandini's (1993) list include aesthetics and the use of space, and the concept of one hundred languages.

Reggio Emilia schools believe the arrangement of classroom space influences social interactions and facilitates creative expression. Aesthetically pleasing features include big windows, see-through space with glass walls, portholes, and glass partitions for easy supervision. Inside there are glassed-in courtyards; outside caves are built into playgrounds. Lofts and tiered risers provide varied spatial viewpoints. There

are mirrored structures and fountains. There are tablecloths on the tables in the eating area. What a beautiful setting to spend much of one's day.

The metaphor of one hundred languages is a metaphor for the child's ability to symbolize what he or she is learning in a variety of ways. Multisymbolic representation includes drawing, painting, clay modeling, talking, using numbers, moving, singing, dramatizing, and using puppets, among others. Absent from the list are paper-and-pencil tests, which are developmentally inappropriate ways of finding out what children know and can do.

In summary, the Reggio Emilia experience does not come with a set of tricks or tips to make it happen painlessly overnight. The American school experience operates within a very different social and family structure and its own geopolitical and cultural context. Reading about, discussing, and observing the Reggio Emilia experience, however, can lead practitioners to reflect upon their own teaching and begin to improve their classroom settings.

---

training just as you would with any volunteer. Some may feel more comfortable answering questions or modeling their art or craft. Others may enjoy working directly with the children.

Art Trips

In addition to having visitors come into the classroom, it may be possible to take children on a field trip. Art abounds in nature, and a simple outdoor walk qualifies as a recommended field trip. Most communities have at least one of the following to visit.

- museum
- art gallery
- exhibit
- concert
- play
- children's theater
- ballet
- recital
- performance
- planetarium
- artist's studio
- arboretum

It is wise to first attend by yourself to make sure that your particular group will profit from this experience. Field trips involve a great deal of planning, energy, and often expense, and they need to be well thought out.

In arranging the field trip, try to match what the experience has to offer with your group's developmental needs, interests, and abilities. For example, most toddlers would not sit still through an hour of chamber music. See if there is someone on the staff who has experience in giving tours to young children. Some museums have special children's rooms and exhibits. Others may have collections that they loan out. Many libraries have art prints that may be rented or checked out.

Sensory Literacy

Help the children become sensory literate. This can be done in two ways. First, help them to stop, sense, and heighten their awareness of the experience at hand. For example, ask the mother of a newborn to let the children at least look and listen. Touch may come weeks later with a supervised bath. Second, stimulate their senses. An array of **sensory literacy** experiences appears in the following chapter.

Figure 7–6 depicts a school corridor celebrating the beauty and sensory quality of children's art.

Figure 7-6 A beautiful display of children's art.

In a sense, the teacher and classroom quietly whisper, "Beauty, it is all around you. Together we will take the time to get involved."

WATERCOLOR AND INK

Tempera painting is a prerequisite to painting with watercolor or ink. Using watercolor and ink requires coordination and fine motor control. These media will frustrate the very young artist. They are used with smaller brushes that are harder to manage.

Watercolor

Watercolors tend to be wet, runny, and transparent. Often, they produce very unintended results. The wet colors may bleed when the child artist is trying to make facial features. The writer recommends that children begin using watercolors to make lines, colors, shapes, and abstract designs rather than attempting realistic, detailed art. Watercolors come in their own small sets with individual semimoist cakes. Buy a medium grade. The brushes that come with the cheapest sets will have bristles that fall out after the first washing.

Watercolors can be used on either wet or dry paper. Watercolors put on wet paper will run and bleed into very interesting patterns and designs. Papers can be wet with a sponge or from a pump spray bottle. A small sponge allows children to blot up excess water or unwanted runs. Special spots can be saturated with water dropped from an eyedropper. The author observed one child doing just that in making a bull's-eye effect or rainbow of blended colors.

Because there is only one brush for several colors, it is important that children wash their brushes each time before changing colors. They will need individual water containers, which should be emptied every time

they appear muddy. When they are done, excess watercolor paint in the set should be carefully blotted up. A careful rinse under the sink will remove excess paint. Be careful not to merely rinse away the unused paints. Let the set air dry. Sets that are closed when wet tend to get gummy. Children find them unappealing.

Hint: Liquid watercolors, of which one brand name is Liquid Watercolor®, are nontoxic and less expensive than food coloring. They produce a range of secondary colors and shades that cannot be matched by food coloring. Liquid watercolors wash out of most fabrics. The colors are intense so they can be used in small amounts or diluted as a liquid dye. Liquid watercolor is available from Discount School Supply (see Appendix D).

Watercolor paper is very expensive if purchased separately by the sheet. Purchased in tablet form, it is still moderately expensive. White drawing paper is acceptable. The author finds that onionskin or good bond typing paper has a good texture for watercolor. An office with outdated letterhead stationery may have a surplus of this. You could easily trim off the letterhead.

Tissue Paper Water Coloring

Tear tissue paper into 1-inch squares and separate by color. Fill clear containers with water. Add squares and use a brush to mix. The dye from the paper will bleed into the water. Children discover that adding more squares of the same color strengthens the intensity of that color. Children can also creatively mix colors. You may want to begin by providing the three primary colors. Children can paint with the colored water that results (see Figure 7–7).

Spray Bottle Watercoloring

Collect child-sized clear spray bottles with a trigger-type release. Fill each with water and add a few drops of liquid watercolor. Show the children how to pump the release while aiming only at their papers. Provide large pieces of paper and art smocks. This is a good activity to do outdoors. Use clothespins to attach the papers to a fence or tape them to the cement.

Coffee Filter Creations

Provide containers of water to which liquid watercolor has been added. Children can fold a coffee filter and

Figure 7-7 Tissue paper watercolor.

Figure 7-9 Aesthetic display.

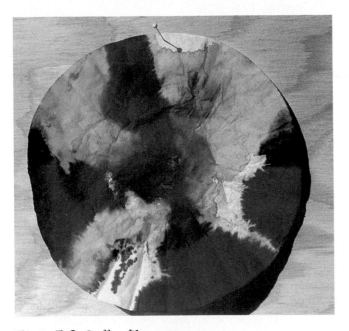

Figure 7-8 Coffee filter art.

dip into one color, squeeze, and select other colors if they choose. Open the coffee filter and lay out flat to dry on newspaper. Indicate child's name on masking tape near his or her filter. When dry, provide a pipe cleaner for those children who want to fashion their filters into flowers, butterflies, bows, or creative creations. Vary the activity by providing absorbent paper towels (see Figure 7–8).

Crystal Watercolors

Encourage children to paint with clean water on white paper. Provide construction or drawing paper. Next, children paint using liquid watercolors. Colors should

spread, blend, and bleed together. Children can also use spray bottles filled with clear water to keep their designs wet and mixed. When done, give child a sheet of clear plastic wrap that is twice the size of his or her white paper. Demonstrate how to crumple and place gently down on top of wet painting. Set in a safe place to dry. Pull plastic wrap off when dry. This produces a very interesting textured effect. Try tinfoil, wax paper, bubble wrap, and nature items in place of plastic wrap.

Brush and Roll

Provide shallow containers of water to which liquid watercolor has been added. Children use small foam brushes and small paint rollers to make creative designs on drawing paper or watercolor paper.

See Figure 7–9 for a collection of watercolor paintings done by children and displayed in an aesthetically pleasing way.

Ink

Even young children can appreciate the beauty of Chinese pen and ink drawings that capture nature with a minimum of lines. **Ink** comes in colors other than black and tends to be fairly expensive. One bottle of black may suffice for use with older children. Ink can be economically used on small sheets of paper with a thin brush. It is appropriate for making linear drawings and designs with a minimum of line and ink. Ink can also be used in printing and stencil activities. It is not recommended for use at the easel or for general painting.

Ink Blots

Children can drop ink on a piece of paper. Carefully fold the paper in half and open. Change colors and repeat the process. Cut around the ink blots and mount them on colored paper.

Dye (Water-Based)

Traditionally, dye activities involve the use of food colors which tend to be expensive, limited in color range, and stain hands and clothing. Liquid watercolors avoid the above pitfall and can be used whenever food colors are needed.

Dribble Dye

Provide each child with a heavyweight, white paper towel. Encourage him or her to fold it into squares. Provide small bottles of food coloring or liquid watercolor. The children can very carefully squeeze small dots or dabs of different colors on the corners, edges, or middle section. Use just enough to bleed through. Open up to reveal a colorful design. Let dry.

Dip and Dye

Provide a white, heavyweight paper towel for each child. You will also need different colors of dye. Place a few drops of food coloring or liquid watercolor in a small dish or container of water. Adding more drops will make colors darker. Different colors can be poured into the different openings in a muffin tin. Encourage children to fold their paper towels into squares. Different folds (horizontal, vertical, diagonal, and random) will produce different effects. Carefully dip the corner or edge into one color. Gently squeeze out the excess. Dip a second small area into a different color. Colors can also be mixed. For example, dip the towel in yellow and then in red. Orange will result. Dry on layers of newspaper. These can be taped over windows for a colorful effect. They can also be care-

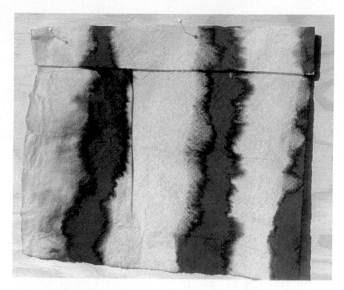

Figure 7-10 Dip and dye.

fully taped together to form a quilt, banner, or backdrop for a bulletin board (see Figure 7–10).

SUMMARY

Aesthetics and young children go hand in hand. Babies begin by exploring and marveling at their world. Over time, children will internalize adult "don'ts" and learn not to look, listen, touch, taste, or smell. They will take their senses and the world of lines, shapes, colors, and design for granted. Our task was identified as a multipurpose one. We need to stimulate their senses; be an aesthetic model in dress, behavior, and communication; and set up a sensory-rich and appealing learning environment. Our discussion focused on a rationale for including aesthetics in early childhood. First, it was seen as a part of a child's holistic development. Second, it will help children see the beauty of line and shapes in the world of letters, words, and numbers they will encounter. Third, it was believed that children who grow up with the aesthetic sense will become wise consumers and concerned citizens who will advocate for beauty in the community and workplace. Fourth, it will help children understand and appreciate a wide range of arts. Fifth, sensory data fosters thinking and concept formation.

Key Terms

aesthetic attitude
aesthetic process/experience
aesthetic response
aesthetic value

aesthetics
atelierista
ink
Reggio Emilia

sensory literacy
tokonoma
watercolors

Suggested Activities

1. Reflect on your most recent or vivid aesthetic experience. Sketch it or attempt to put it into words. Describe how you felt and your reaction.
2. Critique the use of indoor classroom space for its aesthetic appeal. Make specific recommendations.
3. Set up an aesthetically pleasing display of objects that have sensory appeal.
4. Arrange an aesthetic experience through a simple field trip such as a nature walk.

5. Begin a collection of photos depicting beautiful learning environments. Note aesthetically pleasing learning centers and displays. This will serve as a resource of ideas for when you have your own classroom.
6. Select a children's picture book. Use the three steps from Chapter 7 to engage in a discussion of illustrations.
7. Facilitate a watercolor or ink activity with children.

Review

1. Explain aesthetics as an attitude, process/experience, and a response.

2. List five aspects of the teacher's role as it relates to aesthetics.

3. List and briefly discuss the role of art in the Reggio Emilia experience.

4. Identify the developmental stages in children's understanding of art.

5. Identify the developmental stages in how individuals come to make a critical judgment of art.

6. Explain what the author meant by "Expose, not impose" as it relates to children and art.

For additional art and creative development resources, visit our Web site at
www.EarlyChildEd.delmar.com

Chapter 8

Sensory Experiences

Do the children appear to be enjoying themselves? What can children do at this sensory table? In what ways are they actively involved? How many of their senses are being stimulated? Pretend you are supervising this activity. Along with making sure that children have an ample supply of shaving cream, what could you say to help children reflect on what they are seeing, touching, and smelling?

The sheer amount of shaving cream allows for a rich multisensory experience. What props could you add to enhance the creative potential of this activity? Would liquid color, plastic containers and utensils, or squirt bottles filled with water be appropriate?

Objectives

After reading this chapter, you should be able to:

- Discuss the relationship among sensing, perceiving, feeling, thinking, and concept development.
- List and briefly explain the different senses.
- Construct a multisensory activity.
- Identify three major learning styles and select the one(s) that best describe the way you learn.
- Discuss the relationship between learning style and teaching style.
- Provide a rationale for including field trips in an early childhood program.
- Provide art activities based on the process called *resist*.

INTRODUCTION

Young children use all their senses to process their aesthetic experiences. They are sensory gluttons who are intrinsically motivated to look, touch, listen to, taste, and smell everything they come into contact with. They respond on both affective and cognitive levels. For example, they not only experience pleasure in looking at and smelling a flower but also enhance their concept of what a flower is. One hopes that young children with the aesthetic sense will grow up to be wise consumers and planners for a better future that includes beauty and peace.

FROM PERCEPT TO CONCEPT

Perception is the ability to receive sensory impressions from one's surroundings and relate them to what one knows. Sensing, perceiving, thinking, and developing concepts are closely related. The aesthetic experience merges the cognitive with the affective response. Thinking and feeling come together. For example, when they hear bells chime in a church for the first time, young children may perceive the sound, smile with amazement, think about it, and relate it to the doorbell or clock chimes at home. The process can be depicted as

SENSE	+ PERCEPTION	+ FEELING	+ THINKING	= CONCEPTS
visual	look	enjoy	compare	color
auditory	listen	marvel	contrast	tone
tactile	touch	joy	analyze	texture
olfactory	smell	happy	classify	scent
gustatory	taste	amazed	describe	flavor

The world has much to offer. A child with a sensory special need or deficit may miss stimuli. Often, such children develop strengths in other areas. For example, blind children often develop a strong sense of touch or hearing. A child who does not invest the time in perceptual activity or who lacks sensory stimulation is also at a disadvantage. For example, a child who has never touched, looked at, smelled, or listened to an elephant will be at a loss when asked to discuss or read about elephants.

►► MORE THAN FIVE SENSES

Children use their senses to thoroughly explore their environment. Traditionally, the five senses are as follows:

1. visual
2. auditory
3. tactile
4. olfactory
5. gustatory

To this basic list Montessori (1967) would also add the following senses:

6. chromatic
7. thermic
8. sterognostic
9. baric
10. kinesthetic

Each of the above senses will be explained and exemplified with activities. Appendix E contains an incomplete list of books on the senses.

CHILDREN'S LEARNING STYLES

Young children use their senses to discover their world. They also have one or more preferred sensory modalities. This means that children favor either their visual, auditory, or tactile-kinesthetic sense. In turn, they are referred to as visual, auditory, or tactile-kinesthetic learners.

Children with a **visual** strength tend to be holistic thinkers. They learn the big picture and not the individual pieces. They prefer visual images such as pictures to words. Photos, charts, and graphs provide them visual clues. They like to read, write, or draw about what they are learning and are very interested in the finished product.

Children with an **auditory** strength think analytically and are good at speaking and listening. They enjoy discussing what they know and learn from listening to others. They easily follow directions and move sequentially from task to task.

Children with a **tactile-kinesthetic** strength prefer using their hands and bodies to learn. They are holistic learners who thrive on hands-on activity to get the big picture. They are animated, learn by doing, and dislike sitting still and listening to someone try to teach them verbally. For example, during math they may move around while thinking, relying on their fingers and manipulatives.

Adult Teaching Styles

Teachers, in turn, use their own preferred learning style when teaching. One's individual learning strength becomes one's **teaching style.** We teach in ways that are compatible and consistent with how we learn. For example, a teacher who is a visual learner will use books and printed information to teach. Children will be required to read and write. A teacher who is an auditory learner will rely on teaching verbally and engage children in discussion. A teacher who is a tactile-kinesthetic learner will use manipulative materials, role playing, creative dramatics, and hands-on activity to facilitate children's discovery learning.

Matching Adult Teaching Styles with Children's Learning Styles

What are the implications? First, recognize that children learn in different ways and discover children's preferred learning style. Are they visual, auditory, tactile-kinesthetic, or a combination of these? Second, recognize how one's adult teaching style is influenced by one's own learning style. Third, capitalize on how individual children learn and teach to their preferred learning style. Fourth, teach in ways that honor a variety of learning styles. For example, teaching children about earthworms would include a verbal discussion, visual display, and providing real worms for a multisensory experience (see Figure 8–1). Fifth, help children develop competence in their weaker sensory modalities.

Art and Children's Learning Styles

How does our discussion of learning styles and teaching styles pertain to children's art? Children who are visual learners will be drawn to the visual arts, whereas auditory learners may prefer music. Tactile-kinesthetic learners will thoroughly enjoy art activities such as smearing their hands in finger paint or using their fingers to squish play dough or shaving cream. Visual learners will have no trouble imagining pictures in their head which they will draw upon as content for their art. They will work on the totality of their picture rather than focusing on component parts. For example, in making a house they would focus on the entire shape and then add details. These children are very interested in their finished artistic product. Auditory learners do not rely on the pictures in their head. They will sequentially make a picture by mastering the individual parts and pieces. For example, they would make a house by working on parts and details like a door, windows, and chimney. The individual pieces would make up the complete house.

What can be done for children whose learning strength does not predispose them to seek out art? When possible, invite these children to participate in activities that are *outside* their sensory strength. For example, the child with an auditory strength who avoids the art table could be invited to make a picture

Figure 8-1 Learning about worms.

Field Trips Are Multisensory Experiences

Field trips are good opportunities for children to use all their senses. For example, pretend it is the end of summer. How could you begin planning for the upcoming change of season and fall holidays? For some, thoughts turn to the harvest and images of pumpkins come to mind. There are wonderful books, songs, flannel board stories, and finger-plays available. For art, some teachers provide large sheets of pumpkin-shaped paper and have children paint them orange to resemble pumpkins. But are these activities the best introduction? First, one should ask just what children really know about pumpkins. Perhaps they have seen pumpkins at the store and think that is where they somehow "live" or are raised. They may even be able to tell you that a jack-o'-lantern is a pumpkin that has been carved. The question remains, What do children really know about pumpkins? So what is the best way to begin?

The photo in Figure 8-2 documents a field trip to a pumpkin patch. Here, children got a firsthand look at where pumpkins are grown. Based on the photos, what opportunities might children have for using their visual, auditory, and tactile sense on this field trip?

Yes, the children got to look at and touch the pumpkins on the vines. They listened to the sounds of the wind rustling in the patch and smelled the damp soil. Later, in the classroom, they were involved in carving and cleaning pumpkins. Pulp was scooped and seeds were separated. Seeds were baked and tasted along with pumpkin foods including bread, pudding, and pie. Now, all the books, songs, flannel board stories, fingerplays, and art activities about pumpkins will make much more sense to them. The multisensory field experience was a concrete and developmentally appropriate starting point for their study of pumpkins.

Figure 8-2 A field trip provides first-hand experience.

related to a book he or she has listened to on tape or to express visual images related to a favorite song.

Multisensory Experiences

Most experiences involve more than one sense. Cooking is a good example of a **multisensory experience.** Making popcorn involves looking at and touch-ing the kernels before, during, and after popping; listening to the sound of popcorn popping; smelling the scent of melted butter being poured over hot popcorn; and eating the popcorn in big handfuls. Children would also enjoy moving like popcorn popping, starting off as small, compact "kernels" that slowly expand and puff up as they get hotter. A coconut has a distinctive color, shape, covering, texture, and taste. Children can look at the outside of a coconut and discuss its color, size, shape, and covering. "What do you hear when you shake it? What do you think is inside? What can we do to find out? How can we open this coconut? What words describe how it looks and feels? Does it smell? I also have a bag of shredded coconut. How are the two similar? How are they different? Let's cut the coconut in half and look inside. Now what do you see and smell? Scrape off a piece of the white inside. How does it taste? Does it taste the same as the flakes of coconut in the bag?" The line of questioning, discussing, and experiencing is endless. The same process could be done with an artichoke, melon, pineapple, or when baking cookies (see Table 8–1).

1. Visual

The visual sense involves looking and seeing. Ideally, it involves a thorough visual exploration rather than a

Table 8-1 Sensory Experiences at a Glance

SENSE	RECOMMENDED
Visual—to look at	multicultural and anti-bias pictures
	beautifully illustrated children's books
	book covers displayed on walls
	posters
	displays of children's artwork
	art prints
	photographs of children and their families
	printed labels, words, signs, recipe cards, and charts
	objects with interesting visual qualities
	artifacts and souvenirs
	collections of shells, gems, and nature specimens
	media: check movies, filmstrips, and videotapes for quality
	vases of flowers
	potted plants
	classroom pets
	wall hangings, weavings, tapestries
	mobiles
	rebus, poem, song, chant, experience, recipe, and story charts
	changes in food during cooking
Auditory—to listen to	variety of music
	poetry
	rhymes
	fingerplays and body action rhymes
	storytelling with or without props
	books read aloud
	taped sounds and asking, "What could have made that sound?"
	stories on tape and following directions and playing "I Spy"
	informal conversations
	songs
	musical and rhythm instruments
Tactile—to touch	objects and identify them without looking
	rough and smooth sandpaper and fabrics
	objects with different textures including fruits, vegetables, and nature items

(continued)

Table 8-1 Sensory Experiences at a Glance *(continued)*

SENSE	RECOMMENDED
Tactile—to touch *(continued)*	tubs filled with shaved ice, cold, cool, or warm water
	mitts covered with various textured fabrics
	foods during food preparation activities
Olfactory—to smell	flowers
	scents
	aromas
	spices and extracts
	foods
	potpourri
Gustatory—to taste	variety of nutritious foods from different cultures
	healthy snacks children helped make
Kinesthetic—to move	in creative movement activities
	through obstacle courses

passing glance or quick look. Vision and discriminating between letters and words will be required for reading.

The indoor classroom should be a visually rich, appealing environment with nature specimens, artifacts, and objects to visually explore. Samples of children's art as well as art posters or prints can be displayed on the walls. A science center or discovery table can display a collection of seashells, antique kitchen items, or postcards to visually explore.

Some recommended materials to encourage visual exploration include the following:

- prism
- magnifying glasses: handheld and three-legged stool or stand
- safety mirrors: both handheld and full-length
- lenses: concave and convex (making things bigger or smaller)
- microscope and slides
- telescope
- kaleidoscope
- binoculars
- camera
- cellophane color paddles
- sunglasses
- flashlight
- viewer and round picture reels

Water play with bubbles is a simple visual activity. Provide a tub of water, liquid dishwashing soap, and rotary eggbeaters. Food coloring is optional, and children love the effect. A related activity is blowing bubbles outdoors. Children enjoy trying to catch them. Encourage them to note the transparent quality of bubbles as well as the rainbow of colors present. A simple recipe for homemade bubbles follows.

Iridescent Soap Bubbles

1 cup of water
2 tablespoons of liquid dishwashing detergent
1 tablespoon of glycerine (available from drugstore)
½ teaspoon sugar
Here are some other visual activities.

New View

Encourage children to view their indoor and outdoor environment from new perspectives. What do you see when you

- lie on the floor and look up?
- lie on the floor on your right or left side?
- lie on your back outdoors on the grass? What appears in the sky? What shapes do you see in the clouds?

- climb to the top of the jungle gym and look down or up?
- balance on your hands and stand on your head?
- are swinging on the swing? What colors and shapes appear?

Nature Walk

Take magnifying glasses when going on a nature walk. Look for interesting shapes and designs in nature. Stop to

- look at moss, berries, insects, fungus, mushrooms, nests, tree stumps, shadows, birds, spiderwebs, ant hills, or the pattern in rust on a building.
- listen to birds chirping, leaves rustling, wind blowing, dogs, cats, squirrels, twigs cracking, and acorns or nuts falling.
- touch tree bark, damp moss, dry leaves, sand, and cold mud.
- smell evergreen trees, pinecones, pine needles, damp earth, dry leaves, and crisp, cold air.

Collect interesting specimens to bring back to the science table. Some teachers may prefer to leave the natural environment intact and not remove bugs, leaves, or twigs.

Focus Scopes

It is sometimes difficult to notice design and detail in an environment that is alive with color, shape, sound, and movement. Children may need help focusing their visual sense. This is why magnifying glasses, cameras, binoculars, and telescopes are recommended. An empty tissue roll makes a very good focus scope. The outside can be decorated or covered with contact paper to enhance its appeal. Encourage children to examine the indoor and outdoor environment by very slowly exploring with the focus scopes. Pay attention to small things that might be missed by just looking. Focus scopes can also be covered with cellophane at one end and used like color paddles. Children can also join their fingers to make a frame to focus their vision.

Peek Frames

Find an interesting picture in a magazine. Look for color and design and cut off any words. Find sheets of construction paper that are the same size or larger than the picture. Peek frames can be used in many ways. Neatly cut a 1-inch round hole out of your sheet of construction paper. Place this sheet over your picture. Ask the children, "What do you see through my little window? Let's think of many different things that the picture might be." Peek frames can have more than one opening. The hole can also be torn into and slowly peeled larger to foster continued guessing and heighten suspense. This activity forces children to focus their visual sense on a small area of design, color, or shape. The idea is not to guess the one right answer but to use the visual clues to come up with many possibilities.

Look and Match

Children enjoy matching objects or pictures that are the same. Find pairs of some of the following:

- magazine pictures
- fabric scraps
- wallpaper samples
- tile or linoleum samples

Younger children will enjoy matching pairs that are quite distinct. Older children can be challenged with subtle variations in color or design, such as those found in wallpaper sample books.

Masterpiece Match

Children would enjoy matching pairs of art postcards. Art postcards are available from art museums. See Appendix C for other sources. Try to find pairs of postcards that are similar but not identical—for example, a family done in realistic and abstract styles. The subject matter may be the same, but the treatment is different. Older children may also enjoy playing a memory game with the postcards. You will need at least six pairs of postcards. Arrange them face up on the floor. Turn them over. Older children may not need to see them turned right side up. Next, encourage children to turn over a pair. If they match, the child gets another turn. If one child gets all the pairs correct in sequence, this might indicate that there are too few pairs.

I Spy

This activity involves both looking and listening and can be played with a large group. Focus on an item in the room that has a distinct color or shape. "I spy something in the room that is bright red. What could it be?" Children may need additional clues. "It is bright red only on the front. The back side is white. What could it be?" Or, "I spy something on the wall that has a triangle shape. What could it be?" Children enjoy being the leader for this activity. Encourage them to use color or shape clues rather than merely

Art Postcards

Wolf (1988, 1990) has applied the Montessori skills of matching, pairing, sorting, using control cards, and using a time line to art appreciation. The steps involved in using her art postcards are:

Step 1. Match identical paintings. The child matches three identical pairs. Pairs are gradually added until the child can match six identical pairs.

Step 2. Pair similar paintings by an artist. Children pair companion paintings, two paintings by the same artist that are not identical but are similar in subject matter and style. An example would be two paintings of birds by Audubon.

Step 3. Group paintings by an artist. Children begin grouping four paintings by each of three different artists. For example, they begin with highly contrasting subjects–four still lifes by Cezanne, four abstract works by Kandinsky, and four paintings of people by Goya.

Step 4. Children refer to control cards to match the last name of artists with their paintings. After repeating the exercise several times, the children attempt to match the name cards to the paintings without using the control cards.

Step 5. Control cards are used to learn the names of famous paintings.

Step 6. Children are introduced to paintings grouped according to schools of art.

Step 7. Children put paintings into rows corresponding to the school of art to which they belong.

Step 8. Use of the time line. A large number of paintings of one subject, children for example, are placed beside a time line according to their dates. When completed, the line graphically illustrates the development of painting through the centuries.

---

saying, "I spy the round clock on the wall that ticks. What is it?"

Watch the Waves

Capture a wave in a bottle. Find a large plastic bottle. Add mineral oil and some water that has been colored with blue food coloring. Cover tightly. Tilt, tip, and watch the waves.

2. Auditory

The auditory sense involves hearing and listening, which are two very different processes. Children who hear do not always listen. Our world is noisy, with people talking, appliances, stereos, traffic, and televisions. Children are exposed to much auditory stimulation and learn at a very early age to tune much of it out. Casual hearing is appropriate much of the time. Music, literature, or teacher's directions warrant concentrated listening. Our aim is to help children know when to switch from passive hearing to active listening. Recommended objects that foster active listening include the following:

- stethoscope
- tape recorder with tapes of stories, rhymes, and poems
- record player with music and story records
- rhythm instruments
- tuning fork
- music boxes
- bells
- metronome

Some activities are described in the next sections.

Quiet Time

Quiet Time can be used as a relaxation technique after a noisy activity. It is a good routine to quiet the children. Gather children and have them sit quietly. They may giggle at first but will improve with practice. Encourage them to close their eyes and listen. "What do you hear? Think about the sounds but do not talk yet. Let's keep on listening to the noises inside our bodies and around the classroom." Wait a few seconds or minutes, depending on the group. Children may hear their heart beating, blood flowing, stomach grumbling, throat swallowing, lungs breathing, or classroom pet moving about.

Sounds around Us

Tape-record distinct sounds, for example:

- toast popping out of a toaster
- clock ticking
- whistle blowing
- vacuum cleaner in operation
- horn honking
- bell ringing
- blender or electric mixer in operation
- running water
- toilet flushing
- water going down the drain
- animal sounds
- traffic sounds
- telephone ringing
- alarm clock ringing
- door slamming
- siren wailing
- baby crying
- ball bouncing
- someone jumping rope

Some more difficult sounds may include these:

- sticks or twigs cracking
- someone walking on leaves
- a match being struck
- a refrigerator door being closed
- tape pulled off a dispenser
- coins being dropped
- wind blowing
- car ignition being turned on and off

Pause between sounds. Play the sounds back and encourage the children to quietly listen (not just hear) and guess what made the sound. Children may want to close their eyes to help focus exclusively on the sounds without any distracting visual stimuli. Younger children who know but cannot verbalize may enjoy hearing the sound and pointing to a corresponding picture or sketch that you provide.

Sound Detectives

Encourage children to close their eyes and listen very quietly while you perform some action. They must actively listen and attempt to guess what you have just done. Some actions include the following:

- clapping hands
- jumping

- snapping fingers
- rubbing hands together
- blowing a kiss
- yawning
- stamping feet
- bouncing a ball several times
- stapling papers
- dropping a pencil
- writing on the chalkboard
- whistling
- opening and closing a book
- walking on tiptoe
- shutting a door
- turning on a water faucet

Children enjoy taking turns being the leader in this game. Encourage them to think up new actions, not merely repeat what was just done.

Sound Containers

Active listening involves being able to discriminate among sounds. Auditory discrimination involves listening to sounds and deciding which ones are similar and which are different. Hearing similarities and differences will help children with speaking, phonics, and reading. Find a matched set of at least six opaque boxes or containers. Small milk cartons or soda pop cans are fine. Plastic toy eggs or egg-shaped pantyhose containers are also recommended. Cover half of the set in one color and half in another, such as three red and three blue. Because the cues can only be auditory, it is important that the children cannot see what is inside. Separate your set into three, four, five, or six pairs. Fill each pair with an equal amount of one of the following:

- marbles
- salt
- rice
- cotton balls
- paper clips
- wad of papers
- toothpicks
- string
- pennies
- tacks
- ribbons

First, test the items chosen to make sure each pair has identical sounds. Pairs must be significantly different from each other. For example, a pair filled with salt and a pair filled with sugar will probably sound identical. With very young children or those with auditory problems, limit the set to two or three very distinct pairs. Slowly add to your collection as the children begin to master the task. Inconspicuously mark or code the pairs on the bottom to foster a quick check.

Water Sounds

Children can listen to sounds and make music in containers filled with water. Find a set of at least three identical glass bottles or jars. Fill one to the top with water, another halfway, and the third a half inch from the bottom. Different amounts of water will make sounds of different pitch when the bottle is struck with a metal spoon. Practice making sounds that vary in volume (soft and loud) depending on how lightly you strike. Which makes the highest pitch? Which makes the lowest pitch? Encourage children to seriate the sounds from low to high or vice versa. The children will enjoy playing music on the bottles. They may want to incorporate their water sounds with music made on other rhythm instruments. Additional bottles with different water levels can gradually be added.

Listen Along

Children enjoy being read to. Reading to them is one way to encourage an interest in and love of reading. Get animated and stress words and phrasing. Encourage children to hear words that rhyme in poems. Storytelling with props, such as puppets or a flannel board, allows you to get dramatic with the story line while making continual eye contact. It also allows the children to become involved.

3. Tactile

The **tactile** sense involves feeling and touch. For our purposes the tactile sense may operate in conjunction with the visual sense. Activities that involve touching and feeling textures will be categorized as tactile. Those involving touching to identify, recognize, and name an object without looking will be categorized as sterognostic and covered in a later section.

Sandpaper Feel

Different grades of sandpaper, from rough/coarse to fine/smooth, can be used in this activity. Make a pair of strips for each grade of sandpaper. Start with fine and very coarse and add in-between gradations as the children master this activity. Cut the sandpaper into 2-inch-wide strips about 4 inches long. Mount the sandpaper strips on sturdy cardboard or a piece of wood. Encourage children to trace down the strip with

an index finger and feel the texture. Ask them to find another strip of sandpaper that feels the same. What word describes how it feels? Is it rough or smooth? Older children may enjoy seriating the sandpaper strips from smooth to rough or vice versa.

Fabric Feel

Children can wear blindfolds or agree to close their eyes for this activity. Provide identical pairs of some of the following:

- burlap
- velvet
- silk
- netting
- corduroy
- denim
- cotton

- gauze
- fur
- terrycloth
- vinyl
- wool
- carpet

Remember to make the sizes the same so that the only clues will be tactile. Encourage children to discuss their matched pairs. How do they feel? What word tells us? Are they soft, smooth, rough, wrinkly, or bumpy?

How Does It Feel?

Discuss with children how different things feel hard or soft (see Figure 8–3). Encourage them to give examples. Neatly print *hard* and *soft* on separate sheets of paper. Encourage children to say the words after you. Place a picture of something hard and something soft on the corresponding papers. Encourage children to put the following items under the proper heading.

- cotton
- velvet
- stone

Figure 8-3 How does it feel?

- coin
- feather
- plush stuffed animal
- wet sponge
- dry sponge
- powder puff
- sandpaper
- rubber squeeze toy
- tree bark
- cactus
- yarn ball
- plastic
- emery board
- tinfoil (over cardboard)
- plastic wrap (over cardboard)
- steel wool

Young children will enjoy sorting the actual objects. Older children will enjoy cutting pictures of hard and soft objects out of magazines and pasting them onto the corresponding sheet. They may also expand their tactile vocabulary to include rough, smooth, slick, bumpy, prickly, fuzzy, furry, porous, and coarse.

Texture Collage

Children enjoy pasting or gluing objects with varied textures into a collage. The group can also work on a thematic collage containing both pictures from magazines and actual objects that are rough, smooth, sharp, fuzzy, or furry. Provide sturdy cardboard for the background when pasting or gluing heavy objects.

4. Olfactory

Although animals rely heavily on the sense of smell, people do not. We use our sense of smell on a very limited basis, to smell food or perfume or cologne, or to react to unpleasant odors. Children use their sense of smell more than adults. For example, they enjoy scratch-and-sniff stickers. Still, they may refuse to try a food solely on the basis of its smell or color (visual cue). Green, yellow, and orange vegetables hold little **olfactory** or visual appeal for some children. Some activities to stimulate the olfactory sense are described here.

Scent Bottles

Find a set of identical bottles or containers with lids or tops. Pill vials, empty spice bottles, or film containers are ideal. Make two, three, four, five, or six pairs. Color code the lids in each set, for example, six green and six orange. Place a ball of cotton in each pair if you are using liquid scents or extracts. Make air holes in the lids if solids are used. Pieces of nylon stocking can be placed over the opening and secured with rubber bands. Fill each pair with one of the following:

- cinnamon
- mustard
- garlic
- coffee
- pepper
- sawdust
- baby powder
- perfume
- bath crystals or bath salts
- vanilla
- lemon peel
- pine
- tea
- onion
- cloves
- peppermint
- talcum

Cotton balls soaked in clear liquids or extracts provide no visual clues. Scents need to be fresh and will have to be replaced from time to time. Remind children to replace the lids or tops after use. Items like coffee or tea cannot be used in clear containers, because the cue will be visual rather than **olfactory.** Remind children to smell without inhaling or tasting. Match up pairs that smell the same. Use a word to describe how each one smells. Is it sweet, sour, spicy?

It Smells Good Enough to Eat

The olfactory and gustatory senses work together. In general, foods that smell good taste good. This activity can be done with a small group as a lead-in to snack time. Encourage children to close their eyes while you hold a piece of food on a toothpick under their noses. Pause long enough for them to get a good sniff without making skin contact. A piece of banana is one example. Next, hold a different food, such as a pineapple chunk. Do they smell the same or different? Encourage children to match an array of fruits or vegetables on a plate in front of them with your standard. The finale to the activity is being able to eat the samples for snack.

The classroom can also be an olfactory-rich environment. Teachers can add scents and aromas. A bowl or dish of rose petals, pine needles, sachet, incense, dried orange rinds, scented soaps, or potpourri provides a lovely fragrance. Flowers such as roses, mums, and carnations, as well as scented candles and perfume samples also encourage children to stop and smell. The following recipe can be used to produce a cinnamon scent in your room:

Soak several whole cinnamon sticks in cinnamon oil. Dry. Tie together with dried flowers in a bundle. Add a pretty ribbon or lace. The fragrance of cinnamon should last for months.

A Sensory Table Makes Good Sense

A sensory table can be filled with items that involve more than one sense, for example, looking and touching. Fill with items that have tactile and visual appeal. Rotate the contents over time. Possibilities include the following:

- buttons and beads
- rice
- cornmeal
- beans
- sand
- dirt or mud
- water (plain or colored), with or without ice cubes, shaved ice, or snow
- wood shavings
- Styrofoam® pieces/packing peanuts
- marbles
- pebbles and stones
- aquarium gravel
- counters, e.g., teddy bears
- birdseed
- pom-poms
- golf balls
- shaving cream
- nature specimens, e.g., grass, weeds, hay, leaves, pinecones, flower petals
- shredded paper
- confetti

Although toddlers enjoy exploring at the sensory table, small marbles may be problematic for those who insist on putting everything in their mouths. Provide close supervision and use only larger items for the very young. There is no need for an expensive sensory table. Use a wading pool, baby bathtub, or large basin. Depending on the contents, add dinosaurs, small people, vehicles, and animals, as well as kitchen utensils and a variety of containers to foster complex sensory play (see Figure 8-4).

Figure 8-4 Sensory table.

To make a simmering stove-top potpourri mixture, follow this recipe:

Combine whole allspice, whole cloves, cinnamon sticks, and pieces of dried orange peel. Put a tablespoon or two in 3 cups of water and place in a pot. Bring to a boil on the stove and simmer. Add more water as needed.

Children enjoy sticking whole cloves into oranges that have been pierced with holes. Tie with pretty ribbon and hang. They can also be taken home as gifts if the children have had a good deal of input into making them.

More important, the classroom should be free of stale, musty smells. Spraying with a disinfectant spray or air freshener may eliminate or mask stale odors. Fresh air and a routine airing out are essential.

5. Gustatory

Eating and quiet time spent enjoying home-cooked meals have become a luxury in many households. Many children may never see their parents cook a meal. Meals are now quickly eaten on the run or even skipped. Convenience foods may be bland, precooked, or low in nutritional value. Eating occurs out of habit and routine rather than for its **gustatory** or taste appeal. Eating may be something that is done at different times by different family members, perhaps in front of television, or merely something children do before getting ready for bed. Perhaps this is why most early childhood educators value snack time and cooking as a time to talk, socialize, and share food and experiences. Here are some recommended gustatory activities.

Snacks and Cooking

These two activities are vital in any early childhood program. Snacks should be more than crackers and sugary juice. Although they are moderately expensive, nutritious snacks provide their own characteristic look, color, shape, texture, taste, smell, and sound when eaten. Recommended snacks include these:

- banana slices
- pineapple wedges
- peanut butter

- orange slices
- carrot sticks
- apple wedges
- cheese chunks
- celery stalks
- grapes
- melon balls
- pear halves
- grapefruit sections
- cauliflower
- cucumber slices
- sunflower seeds, raisins, and nuts
- strawberries

Cooking experiences using nutritious ingredients with much child input are also highly recommended. For example, children can be actively involved in making fruit salad: washing and dividing the fruit, reading the recipe, mixing, and measuring ingredients. Baking bread is another multisensory cooking activity that involves learning across many, if not all, of the early childhood curricular areas. To bake bread, one must read a recipe and measure ingredients. Children are actively involved in kneading dough. Is it magic or science that makes the dough rise? Bread baking has a wonderful aroma, and the bread has an equally good taste when it is topped with homemade butter. Cooking with apples provides unlimited possibilities for learning and eating. Apples can be cut, peeled, pared, or baked, or the slices can be spread with peanut butter or dipped in melted cheese. The following recipes suggest more uses for apples.

Apple Juice

½ cup seeded apples
1 cup water
1 teaspoon sugar
Put ingredients in blender and blend thoroughly. Chill and serve. Will serve two, so vary recipe given the size of the group.

Applesauce

Cut several apples. Place in electric frying pan or covered skillet. Cover apples with cider. Put lid on pan and bring to a boil. Reduce heat and simmer until apples are soft. Let cool. Take turns grinding in a food mill. Add sugar and cinnamon to taste.

Dried Apples*

Peel and core several apples, and cut them into rings or slices. Place them in salted water for 15 minutes. Dry for 2 weeks.

*Dried grapes become raisins using this recipe.

Taste Party

Children can sample an array of foods and classify them as sweet, sour, hot, cold, or salty. Bitter, bland, and spicy may be difficult for young children. They can be added as children master the basic tastes. Each child will need his or her own spoon. Using an eyedropper, place a drop of a sweet substance, e.g., sugar water, onto each child's spoon. Encourage them to think about the taste before guessing. They should wipe their spoon and take a drink of water from their own cup between tests. Repeat the procedure using salt water. Sample tastes include the following:

- sugar water
- salt water
- chocolate syrup
- cinnamon
- nutmeg
- brewed tea
- orange juice
- lemon juice
- honey
- vinegar water
- maple syrup

Solids can also be introduced at a taste party. Try using these:

- chocolate chips
- carrot cubes
- apple squares
- banana slices
- cheese chunks
- cinnamon candy
- cottage cheese
- melon balls

Remember to check for food allergies before any taste test or food experience.

6. Chromatic

Montessori views the **chromatic** sense as a subset of the broader sense of vision. The chromatic sense involves the ability to identify, match, and discriminate among colors. The following are some activities for the chromatic sense.

Color Matching

Very young children enjoy matching colored shapes cut out of construction paper (see Figure 8–5). Begin with red, blue, and yellow and add more colors as children master this task. Or glue colored shapes in a vertical column on a sheet of cardboard or a file folder. Draw an outline of an identical shape next to each color. Cut out a second set of colored pieces. Encourage children to place the second set next to its match. Paint samples obtained from hardware or paint stores can also be used. Select bright enamels rather than pale pastels. Older children may enjoy matching color names. Later they can match a color name printed on an index card with a color cue.

Figure 8-5 Cutting colored shapes for matching.

Color Seriating

Not all colors are created equal. Colors come in different shades, tints, tones, intensities, and values. Black added to red will turn it into a darker shade, perhaps scarlet. White added to red will turn it into a lighter tint, such as pink. To make a color game for seriation, first find color charts or paint strips that have variations in tint or shade. Begin with very obvious gradations: light green, medium green, and dark green. Glue an identical set to a piece of cardboard or a file folder and let children first match the shapes in order. Later, they can lay them out in a trainlike array from darkest to lightest. Gradually increase the number of colors or add more difficult gradations in color as children become more proficient. This seriation activity can also be made self-correcting or self-checking. For example, place each of the five shades of red on its own index card. The cards can be coded 1 through 5 or A through E in small numbers or letters on the back side. Or, a simple picture, such as a caterpillar, can be drawn on the back. When the colors are put in proper sequence, the picture will be complete when the cards are turned over. The caterpillar should appear whether the cards are seriated from darkest to lightest or lightest to darkest.

Color Our World

Viewing objects through pieces of cellophane will distort their color. Color paddles are sturdy pieces of cellophane or translucent plastic. They are commercially available, or it is easy to make a set. Individual sheets of cellophane wrapping paper or term paper covers can be mounted or framed in cardboard to form a sturdy holder. Provide at least the primary colors. Color paddles can be used individually or together.

For example, viewing the room through red over blue will make it look purple.

Create Colors

Provide round pieces of tissue paper in the three primary colors for each child. Tissue paper is difficult to cut, and you may have to provide precut pieces for younger children. Cut a large piece of wax paper for each child. Children can arrange any two pieces of tissue paper on the wax paper. Make sure the two primary colors have some overlap. Add the third colored circle, making sure it overlaps the other two. Carefully place a second sheet of wax paper on top. Press with a warm iron. Older children should be able to press their own provided they have direct supervision. The heat will melt the wax and seal the round shapes. Hold the picture up to the light or display it on the window. Notice how purple appears where red and blue overlap, orange where red and yellow overlap, and green where blue and yellow overlap. What color appears in the very center, where red, blue, and yellow overlap?

Color Show

You will need an overhead projector for this activity. Project on a blank wall or white sheet. Find a flat glass dish and place it on the illuminated projector. Add several drops of water. Add a few drops of food coloring. Start with one primary color. Wiggle the dish and swirl the beads of food coloring with a toothpick. Add a second primary color. Repeat the process and watch the colors mix. What has happened? Continue with your color show by adding new colors or starting over with a different combination of primary colors. A squirt of black ink will also make an interesting pattern in water. Adding a very small drop of black ink to food coloring will make shades.

As a variation on this activity, fill three zip-lock plastic storage bags with water. Add a different primary food color to each. Do not fill them to the top or bulging. Lock securely. Hold them up and let children view their surroundings through different colors.

7. Thermic

The **thermic** sense deals with one's perception of temperature. How do things feel: hot, cold, warm, lukewarm, or tepid? Our thermic sense responds when we touch a hot stove, eat frozen ice cream, or take a cold shower. Recommended materials include a thermometer and barometer. Here are some activities for the thermic sense.

Fingers Swim

Fill three shallow or low bowls with water. One bowl should contain hot water; a second cool, or room-temperature water; and a third cold, or melted ice water. The bowls of water should look the same but feel very different. Encourage children to put one or two fingers into one bowl and tell you how it feels. Is the water hot or cold? Pairs of bowls can also be used. Can you find water in another bowl that feels just the same as the water in this one? Since the bowls are open, the hot and cold water will return to room temperature very quickly. Encourage children to discuss which feels like the water they use in the bathtub, to swim in, to water the lawn, to drink on a hot day, or in soup.

Temperature Jars

This activity must be prepared fresh each time. It works best with a very small group. Locate three pairs of identical glass jars. Spice jars are ideal. Fill each pair with equal amounts of one of the following:

- hot (but not scalding) water
- cold or melted ice water
- tepid/lukewarm or room-temperature water

Begin by having children hold one of a pair in one hand. Ask them, "How does it feel? What word describes it? Is it hot, warm, cold, or cool?" Encourage them to use their other hand to find a match that feels the same. Remember that this activity must proceed fairly quickly, because the water in all the jars will quickly return to room temperature. As children master this activity, intermediate temperatures, including finer grades of warm and cool, can be added.

How Does It Feel?

Encourage children to discuss how they feel when they directly experience some of the following:

- being in snow
- being out in the rain
- being in front of an air conditioner or fan
- being near the stove or oven
- being near the fireplace
- taking a bath
- having their hair washed and rinsed
- when opening the door of the refrigerator or freezer
- walking barefoot on sand at the beach in the summer
- playing outside in summer with the sun shining

- walking barefoot in mud
- splashing in the waves at the beach
- having their hair dried with a hair dryer
- fanning a piece of paper in front of their faces
- sucking on a Popsicle®
- holding an ice cube

Encourage children to use thermic terms such as hot, warm, cold, freezing, cool, and burning when discussing their reactions.

Thermic Moves

Encourage children to use their bodies to show what happens to water under different temperature conditions.

- Pretend you are a drop of water in the ocean. Someone picks you up with her shovel and carries you home in her sand pail.
- She leaves you outside, and it is getting colder and colder. Winter is coming, and soon it will snow.
- It is freezing cold, and you turn into an ice cube. Someone picks you up and rolls you in the snow. He keeps rolling you until he gets a big ball of snow. He makes two more big balls and stacks them into a snowman. You are up near the snowman's head, and you are very proud.
- Slowly, the sun starts to shine. It is getting warmer and warmer. You are beginning to melt, slowly, very slowly.
- All that's left of the snowman is a big puddle of water.
- Someone scoops you back into the sand pail and brings you inside. She pours the water into a pot and puts it on the stove. She turns the heat on. It feels good being warm inside. The water comes to a boil, and you start to jump around because it is so hot.
- She pours you into the dishpan, and you help make bubbles and clean the dishes.

Thermic Cooking

There are many simple cooking experiences that include heating or freezing ingredients. Here are two simple ones.

Popsicles®

1 cup of hot water
2 cups of lemonade
1 package Jell-O® (any flavor)

Mix and pour into ice-cube trays. Insert a toothpick or Popsicle® stick in each. Freeze. Children and adults enjoy these because the Jell-O® slows down the melting process and eliminates much of the mess.

Snow Sherbert

Snow (fresh, clean, and white)
1 egg
½ cup sugar
1 teaspoon vanilla
1 cup milk
Mix ingredients. Slowly add snow. Stop when it reaches the consistency of sherbert.

8. Sterognostic

Being able to recognize objects through tactile-muscular exploration without the aid of vision is the **sterognostic** sense. Touching and feeling a pinecone involve the tactile sense. But closing one's eyes while touching and handling a pinecone to identify it involves the sterognostic sense. Whereas the tactile sense usually involves visual clues, the sterognostic sense does not. Below are activities for the sterognostic sense.

Feely Bag

Place a margarine tub at the bottom or toe of an old, large sock. Children enjoy working an arm through the sock to find the object in the tub. Use objects made of wood, metal, paper, plastic, cloth, cork, glass, rubber, and leather. Encourage children verbally to describe

- how the object feels: Is it rough, smooth, or bumpy?
- the size of the object: Is it big or little?
- the shape of the object: Is it round, square, triangular, flat, or solid?
- what the object is made of: Is it made of wood, paper, rubber, glass, or metal?
- the length of the object: Is it long or short?
- the weight of the object: Is it heavy or light?

Children can also guess the object's

- color.
- function or purpose: What is it used for?
- name: What is it called? What do you think it is?

As with all questioning, it is important for children to attempt to justify their answer. Asking them, "How do you know?" or "Why do you think so?" encourages them to go beyond random guessing. For example, "I

think it's money 'cause it's round, small, and feels like a penny."

Young children may prefer to match the object they touch with its picture or a sample of the actual object. Toddlers will enjoy merely putting things in and out of the Feely Bag.

Blindfold Game

Children can be blindfolded or agree to keep their eyes closed. The child can be given an object—for example, a doll—to thoroughly touch and feel without the aid of vision. The child can use these sterognostic cues to guess what the object is. Young children do tend to peek or tell each other the answer. This is to be expected.

9. Baric

Recognizing objects as heavy or light and gradations in between involves the **baric** sense. Here is an activity for the baric sense.

Weight Jars

Find a set of six large plastic spice jars and spray paint the insides the same color or cover them with identical wrap. Separate them into pairs—for example, three brown and three yellow—and fill one of each pair with plaster of paris or some other self-hardening and weighted substance

- to the very top.
- to the middle.
- one-half-inch full.

Encourage children to hold one jar in one hand and find another jar that weighs the same. Children should be encouraged to use both hands like a balance scale, with one jar in each hand. Put the matched pair aside. Keep going until the children have decided that the three pairs weigh the same. Subtly coding each matching pair on the bottom will aid in checking. Encourage children to talk about weight. Which pair is heavy/light? Which pair is the heaviest/lightest? Children can order or seriate from heaviest to lightest or vice versa. Older children may enjoy using a set of ten with finer gradations in weight.

10. Kinesthetic

The **kinesthetic** sense involves a whole-body, sensorimotor muscular response. When we talk about children learning by doing or being actively involved, we are referring to their kinesthetic sense. For example, young children learn about animals by observing, listening, smelling, touching, and using their body to act like them. Moving on all fours like a tiger will help the child form a strong concept of that animal, which is necessary for talking about, reading, or making art objects related to tigers. Some activities for the kinesthetic sense follow.

Musical Moves

Record on tape or find albums of different types of music, including these:

- jazz
- classical
- waltzes
- calypso
- lullabies
- reggae
- rap
- Latin rhythms
- rock-and-roll
- Irish jig
- polka
- marches
- electronic
- tango
- Broadway show tunes
- country
- soul
- Hawaiian
- African
- zither
- Mexican hat dance
- flamenco
- any and all ethnic

Each piece of music has its own characteristic mood, tempo, and rhythm. Therefore, each will suggest a certain type of bodily expression through movement. This activity combines listening with the kinesthetic sense of body movement. Play different samples of music, and encourage children to move the way the music makes them feel. The teacher may want to model and move along with the group. However, encourage children to come up with their own way of moving rather than imitating the teacher's moves. Turning the lights off may help set the tone. Moving with the aid of scarves or pieces of fabric may help some children. Other shy or insecure children may prefer to merely watch, not participate. Reassure them, but also encourage their eventual participation. Over time and with repeated practice, children will become more comfortable and confident in their creative movement.

Listen and Move

Children can also move in response to taped sounds. Tape record some of the following:

- a waterfall
- birds chirping, soaring, or flapping their wings
- feet marching
- a jet soaring
- sounds of laughter
- animals growling
- waves pounding against rocks
- popcorn popping
- a car engine trying to start on a cold day
- toast popping out of a toaster
- a chainsaw starting up
- skating on ice
- people swimming in a pool
- water coming to a boil
- teakettle whistling
- jumping off a diving board

This movement activity is more sophisticated than the former. It will take more thought on the part of older children to translate what they know about a waterfall into bodily movement.

Shapes Movement

Young children will enjoy crawling through openings of different shapes. Find a large cardboard appliance carton. Cut a large geometric shape out of each side. Use a circle, square, triangle, and rectangle. Make sure that each shape is large enough for your biggest child to fit through easily. Mark and reinforce the edges of each cut-out shape with different-colored cloth tape. Children can take turns listening to your directions and crawling through the appropriate shape; for example, "Go in the square and come out the triangle." This activity involves listening, sequencing, shape recognition, and body movement. Make the directions longer and more difficult for older children; for example, "Go in any four-sided figure, come out a red shape (marked with colored cloth tape), and walk around all the shapes two times."

Squeeze, Mash, and Taste

Children will enjoy the movement and physical activity needed to

- squeeze oranges, lemons, limes, or grapefruits on a reamer for juice.
- mash apples for cider.
- mash tomatoes for juice.
- mash carrots for cookies or cake.

- mash strawberries for natural ice cream.
- mash bananas for yogurt.

The finished products can be sampled for snack. Juices that look the same do not always taste the same. Adding sugar to lemon juice changes it from sour to sweet.

Artistic Dramatic Play

Children may enjoy pretending that they are artists. Think of what an artist might wear and do. Items to include would be an old white shirt, a beret, an easel, an art supply box (perhaps an old suitcase), a palette, brushes, goggles, and a sketchbook. Place these in the dramatic play center.

Keep on Movin'

Find a large open space and help children locate their own personal space in which they can move without touching another child. "Today, we are going to pretend that our room is filled up with some very different things. Listening and thinking about the different things will help us move. For example, what if the room was filled from the floor to the ceiling with balloons and we had to move? How would we do it? Show me with your body how you would move. How would it feel on your body?" Ask children how they would move to get through these:

- Jell-O®
- snow
- mashed potatoes
- sand
- ice
- water
- peanut butter
- honey
- frozen yogurt
- ice cream
- cotton candy
- syrup
- glue
- rubber tires
- pillows
- jelly beans

Gingerbread Children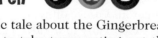

Read the children's classic tale about the Gingerbread Boy. Encourage children to take turns acting out the different parts. Cooking can also be coordinated.

Gingerbread Children

1 box butterscotch pudding mix
½ cup shortening
½ cup brown sugar
1 egg
1½ cups flour
1½ teaspoons ginger
½ teaspoon cinnamon
½ teaspoon baking soda

Cream shortening and sugar. Add egg and let children take turns mixing well. Add dry pudding mix, flour, and spices. Mix well. Distribute individual balls to children. Roll thin and flat, and cut with cookie cutter. Or, mold like clay into gingerbread child. Bake on greased cookie sheet at 350° F for 10 minutes. Will make about a half dozen.

A dried design or picture will **resist** a second liquid put on top. The process of resist is a fascinating one that intrigues children. They do one picture, put a second covering over it, and end up with a totally different effect.

Here are some resist activities.

Crayon Resist

Children can make a picture or design with crayons. It is important to press hard and color fairly dark. Although much of the paper is covered, some empty space should be left. The colored picture can be covered with

- watercolor.
- ink—producing a pitch black, midnight background.
- hand painting.
- Magic Marker®.
- shoe polish.
- tempera paint.

Whichever of these is used for the second coating, the crayon wax will resist the liquid. The liquid will fill in the remaining white negative space. It may also bead up on the colored wax to produce an interesting textured effect.

Paste or Glue Resist

Children can paint a picture or design by making thick marks with paste or glue on white paper. Or apply adhesive to paper and fold the paper in half to get a mirror image. Quickly open up the paper. Let dry thoroughly. Later, paint over the entire paper with

- watercolor.
- ink.
- tempera paint.

The paste or glue will resist any of these liquids. The background will fill up with color, and the dried adhesive will leave a crackled white picture. Let dry thoroughly.

Ink Resist

Children can paint a picture with tempera. Be sure to leave some space white. When the paint is dry, they can cover the entire sheet of paper with black or colored ink. The effect is striking. Black provides a good background for night scenes or Halloween. Blue ink is effective for underwater or sky scenes.

Wax Paper Resist

Place a piece of wax paper over a sheet of white paper. Secure it with tape or paper clips. Use a Popsicle® stick to etch a thick line, design, or picture heavily. The pressure will transfer the wax to the paper. Discard the wax paper. Paint over the entire sheet of paper with watercolor or ink. The lines drawn with the Popsicle® stick will remain white. This activity takes much patience and fine motor control and is recommended for older children.

Embossed Greeting Card Rubbing

This is a good activity involving families by recycling their greeting cards. Remove fronts of cards, saving those with embossed or raised words and pictures. Remove papers from crayons and also provide chalk. Have the child place the card on the table with the embossed side facing up. The child lays thin paper on top and rubs with crayon or chalk. Onionskin paper works well, and construction paper is too heavy. Remind the child to use the sides of crayon or chalk rather than the tip. The card can be taped in place if it moves about. Allow the child to use one card or mix and match several cards.

Masking Tape Resist

Cut different widths and lengths of masking tape and place on table or surface with one end freely unattached for easy removal. Have the child pick off and place masking tape onto white paper, making a design. Some children may want to stop here, and that is OK. Others may want to paint liquid watercolors or tempera over their taped designs. The watercolor will bead up on the tape, leaving an interesting effect. When dry, if children choose to remove the tape carefully, they will see the white paper underneath contrasting with their painting.

Liquid Shoe Polish Resist

Provide sponge-tip applicator bottles containing liquid shoe polish. Children can first draw a picture on white paper using crayons. Remind them to press firmly. Next they can paint over their pictures using dark shoe polish. When the bottle is empty, check to see whether it can be refilled with liquid watercolor or tempera.

Puzzle Pieces Rubbing

Locate puzzles with flat pieces. Provide thin paper. Have the child select a puzzle keeping the pieces in the frame. Lay a piece of thin paper on top of the puzzle. Using the side of a peeled crayon or chalk have the child gently rub all over the paper. Upon removing the paper, the child will see how the outlines of the individual pieces form the puzzle.

Black Magic Pictures

The secret of these pictures is using fluorescent crayons that glow brightly through a wash of black paint. Encourage children to press hard with their crayons and do thick coloring. Provide black poster or tempera paint. Dilute your paint so it is thick enough to color the paper but thin enough to let the colors show through. Have the children brush their pictures using broad sweeping strokes. The fluorescent crayons resist the paint so the picture stands out brightly against the black background.

Name Savers

Write the child's name in white wax crayon before he or she begins painting at the easel. Encourage the child to paint over your white marks. Magically, his or her name appears.

White Crayon Resist

Remove the white from boxes of crayons and set them aside for resist activities. Provide white crayons and white paper. This may frustrate children who want to see what they are doing. Have them persevere and paint with tempera or liquid watercolors to reveal their marks.

Secret Message

Kindergartners and school-age children will enjoy writing secret messages with white crayons on white paper. They can pass their notes to a friend, who then paints it with liquid watercolor or tempera to reveal the message. Remind children that secret messages must be positive and not hurtful or offensive.

White Wax Candle Resist

Provide children with white wax candles. They can be used for drawing or coloring on paper. When done, children can use liquid watercolor or tempera to wash over their marks. The wax resists the paint, leaving the marks intact. You can also do this resist activity on a piece of white cloth. Press down very hard with the white wax candle. The child can brush undiluted liquid watercolor or liquid tempera over the cloth. The fabric remains white where the candle left white marks.

Spray Bottle Resist

Provide clear child-sized spray bottles with trigger-type handles. Fill each with diluted liquid watercolor. Locate flat objects like keys, combs, craft sticks, and puzzle pieces from an incomplete set. This activity is best done outdoors. Roll out a long piece of butcher paper. Have the child choose and arrange shapes on the paper. Teach the child how to use and aim the spray bottles to squirt the objects. The child can remove the objects when dry. The shapes resist the watercolor, leaving their impression. Provide a bucket of water and towels so children can wash and dry their objects for the next child.

Textured Tabletop Resist

This activity is recommended for three reasons. First, it allows for group participation. Second, it can be left up and children can return to it thereby continuing and extending their participation. Third, it fosters whole-arm movement and upper body control. Begin by randomly arranging a variety of textured items on the top of a table. Make sure the items are fairly flat. Recommended examples include yarn, cardboard shapes, fabric scraps, craft sticks, and paper clips. Place a large sheet of butcher paper over the table as if it were a tablecloth. Secure the sides and corners of the paper with tape. This will prevent the textured items from sliding around. Peel the paper off several jumbo size crayons. Encourage children to rub the length of their crayon carefully across the surface while observing the interesting textured shapes that appear. See whether children can guess or match items with their marks.

SUMMARY

Sensory stimulation was viewed as involving more than the five senses. Experiences in sensory stimulation can begin in infancy. Montessori identified the chromatic, thermic, sterognostic, baric, and kinesthetic as vital senses. Materials and activities for each of these senses were provided. Senses, however, do not operate in isolation, and a multisensory approach was advocated. The relationship between sensing, perceiving, feeling, thinking, and concept formation was identified.

Key Terms

art postcards	kinesthetic	sterognostic
auditory	multisensory experience	tactile
baric	olfactory	tactile-kinesthetic
chromatic	perception	teaching style
field trips	resist	thermic
gustatory	sensory table	visual

Suggested Activities

1. Select one of the sensory activities from this unit and implement it with young children.
2. Plan and implement a multisensory cooking experience.
3. Observe in a Montessori classroom. Focus on the sensory materials and how children use them.
4. Stock a sensory table and use with young children.

5. Identify at least three sites in your community which would serve as good field trip experiences for young children. Put vital information including name, address, phone, directions, cost, hours of operation, etc., on an index card. Attach printed information if available. Keep in your professional portfolio.
6. Provide a resist art activity for one or more young children.

Review

1. Match the sense with its key descriptive terms.

_____ auditory	a. touch
_____ olfactory	b. smell
_____ chromatic	c. weight
_____ visual	d. color
_____ gustatory	e. hearing
_____ kinesthetic	f. looking
_____ baric	g. temperature
_____ thermic	h. tactile-muscular
_____ tactile	i. movement
_____ sterognostic	j. taste

2. Use the example of a young child eating cotton candy for the first time to explain the following equation:

Senses+Perception+Feeling+Thinking
=Concept Formation

3. Identify three major learning styles.

4. Discuss the relationship between learning style and teaching style.

5. Pretend you are teaching kindergarten. You would like to take your children to the local Christmas tree farm sometime in December. You have checked everything out in advance and await your principal's approval. She questions your request and asks for your verbal justification. What would you say to convince her of the benefits of this field trip?

For additional art and creative development resources, visit our Web site at
www.EarlyChildEd.delmar.com

Chapter 9

The Complete Early Childhood Art Program

Juanita has found that some of her four-year-olds make derogatory comments about each other's art. "That's no good" or "That's dumb" or "That's not how it's supposed to look!" How would you handle this?

At times Juanita decides simply to ignore it and let her children attempt to work it out. At other times she empowers children by encouraging them to talk about how comments hurt their feelings. "I don't like it when you say my picture's ugly 'cause I worked hard." Juanita came up with a third strategy. She looked at her art program to see whether something was missing. Did she set too-high standards? Did she expect realistic art that the children could not produce? Juanita decided to help her children see that art comes in a variety of forms. She did this by assembling a series of art prints. She laminated each to avoid damage. She helped the children see that art could be nothing more than crossing lines, or it could portray a mother and her baby. Both are valid as art.

Does this strategy sound like something you could use with your children both to expose them to a wide variety of artistic styles and to validate the way they make art?

Objectives

After reading this chapter, you should be able to:
- Describe and give an example of each of the four components of a complete early childhood art program.
- List and explain the three major divisions for categorizing artistic styles or movements.
- Use the art critique to discuss a work of art.
- Discuss the importance of art education in the early years and how national standards relate to early childhood art education.
- Explain how *Project Zero* views art education.
- Contrast *DBAE* with an approach that is based solely on child-centered, creative self-expression.
- Provide collage activities.

INTRODUCTION

Although making art is a first priority, it is only one of the four major components of a complete early childhood art program. It is also important for young children to engage in sensory experiences; learn about art, artists, and their styles; and pursue beauty through aesthetics. This unit will focus on constructing a total or complete early childhood art program.

THE IMPORTANCE OF ARTS EDUCATION

According to the National Standards for Arts Education (Consortium of National Arts Education Associations, 1994), knowing and practicing the arts disciplines are fundamental to the healthy development and are inseparable from the very meaning of what it means to be *educated*. Other reasons include:

1. The arts are worth studying simply because of what they are. Their impact cannot be denied. Throughout history, all the arts have served to connect one's imagination with the deepest questions of human existence: Who am I?
2. The arts are used to achieve a multitude of human purposes: to present issues and ideas, to teach or persuade, to entertain, to decorate or please.
3. The arts are integral to daily life. The arts are all around us from the design of the cereal box at breakfast to the format of the late-night talk show.
4. The arts offer unique sources of enjoyment and refreshment for the imagination. They explore relationships between ideas and objects and serve as links between thought and action.
5. There is ample evidence that the arts help students develop the attitudes, characteristics, and intellectual skills required to participate effectively in today's society and economy. The arts

teach self-discipline, reinforce self-esteem, and foster the thinking skills and creativity so valued in the workplace. They teach the importance of teamwork and cooperation.

6. Arts education benefits the student because it cultivates the whole child, gradually building many kinds of literacy while developing intuition, reasoning, imagination, and dexterity into unique forms of expression and communication.

ART STANDARDS

The educational success of our children depends on creating a society that is both literate and imaginative, both competent and creative. The **National Standards for the Arts** (1994) addresses competence in the arts as well as providing a firm foundation for connecting arts-related concepts and facts across the art forms as well as across disciplines such as the sciences and humanities. The result has been a set of capabilities that will help students arrive at their own knowledge, beliefs, and values for making personal and artistic decisions. By the time they have completed secondary school, students should be able to do the following:

1. Communicate at a basic level in the four arts disciplines: dance, music, theatre, and the visual arts. This includes knowledge and skills in the use of the basic vocabularies, materials, tools, techniques, and intellectual methods of each arts discipline.

2. Communicate proficiently in at least one art form, including the ability to define and solve artistic problems with insight, reason, and technical proficiency.

3. Develop and present basic analyses of works of art from structural, historical, and cultural perspectives, and from combinations of these perspectives.

4. Have an informed acquaintance with exemplary works of art from a variety of cultures and historical periods, and a basic understanding of historical development in the arts disciplines, across the arts as a whole, and within cultures.

5. Relate various types of arts knowledge and skills within and across the arts disciplines. This includes mixing and matching competencies and understandings in art making, history and culture, and analysis in any arts-related projects.

What does this mean for early childhood education? In kindergarten through grade four, young children should experiment enthusiastically with art materials and investigate the ideas presented to them through visual arts instruction. They exhibit a sense of joy and excitement as they make and share their artwork with others. Creation is at the heart of this instruction. Students learn to work with various tools, processes, and media. They learn to coordinate their hands and minds in explorations of the visual world. They learn to make choices that enhance communication of their ideas. Their natural inquisitiveness is promoted, and they learn the value of perseverance.

EARLY CHILDHOOD ART: STUDIO-ORIENTED OR DISCIPLINE-BASED?

The approach to art advocated throughout this book is mainly but not exclusively a studio-oriented approach. This approach holds that young children should be left free to experiment with creative materials. The **studio-oriented** approach has dominated teacher training and influences current thinking and practice with respect to early childhood art. Art education theory has shifted from a child-centered, creative self-expression approach to a discipline-based subject approach. It has provided a framework for curriculum development such as in **Discipline-Based Art Education (DBAE),** an approach advocated by the Getty Center for Education in the Arts. According to Dobbs (1998), DBAE is a comprehensive approach to instruction and learning in art, developed primarily from grades K–12. It is designed to provide exposure to, experience with, and acquire content from several disciplines of knowledge, but especially four fundamental art disciplines: art making, art criticism, art history, and aesthetics. Education in these disciplines contributes to the creation, understanding, and appreciation of art, artists, artistic processes, and the roles and functions of art in cultures and societies. DBAE programs may differ in emphasis, but there is a core of basic characteristics they have in common including a written plan, systematic organization, engagement with works of art, balanced content from the four art disciplines, and developmentally suitable and age-appropriate activities. ArtsEdNet is a Web site originating from the Getty Center for Education in the Arts designed for educators interested in discipline-based art education. It can be found at <http://www.artsednet.getty.edu>.

The author's child-centered approach has been somewhat comprehensive in that it stresses a studio approach while going beyond mere art production in building a complete early childhood art program. This complete program also includes aesthetics and learning

Project Zero Approach to Art Education

Gardner (1993a) has been studying the nature of human symbolization with particular reference to those forms of symbolizing that are key to the arts. He is interested in how children become musicians or poets or painters, why most of them do not, and how these and other artistic capacities atrophy within our own and other cultures. The resulting Project Zero was the implementation of this interest on the nature of artistic knowledge and education. For over three decades researchers at Harvard have participated in Project Zero, a program of research embracing the nature of thinking and its relationship to human development, the arts, and education. To function well in society people must learn to read and write with the various symbols of their culture. Gardner and his associates in Project Zero have worked toward synthesizing research into a descriptive scheme of artistic development in children. Children in the primary grades typically enjoy making and looking at art. They also appreciate artworks in personal and concrete ways. For example, "I like the picture because it's purple and that's my favorite color." Or, "It shows animals and I like animals. I want to be a vet when I grow up." Young children's grasp of artistic symbol systems is too limited to allow them to engage in complex aesthetic inquiry. Upper elementary students can learn to recognize and manipulate certain visual conventions, that is, they can apply studio techniques to accomplish specific visual effects. They form judgments about artworks, are aware that art can express ideas and emotions, and can ponder artistic motives. Adolescents are especially concerned with the way their own and others' artworks convey meaning. They recognize artistic styles and relate art forms to historical and cultural contexts. Abstract thinking is present; they can create and interpret symbols for abstract concepts like love and democracy. They can compare and contrast ideas, speculate about origins and consequences, make inferences, consider alternatives, and raise and deliberate about questions concerning broad issues in art.

Gardner (1993a) makes the following points regarding Project Zero:

1. Particularly at younger ages (below 10), production activities ought to be central in any art form. Children need to work directly with materials and media.

2. Perceptual, historical, critical, and other *periartistic* activities should be closely related to, and emerge from the child's own products. Rather than being introduced in an alien context to art objects made by others, children should encounter such objects in relation to the particular artistic products and problems with which they are themselves engaged.

3. Arts curricula need to be presented by teachers or other individuals with a deep knowledge of how to *think* in an artistic medium. For example, the visual arts must be introduced by someone who can think visually or spatially.

4. Whenever possible, artistic learning should be organized around meaningful projects. See Chapter 11 for a discussion of projects.

5. In most artistic areas, it will not be profitable to plan a K 12 sequential curriculum. Such a formula may sound attractive, but it flies in the face of the holistic, contextually sensitive manner in which individuals gain mastery in crafts or disciplines. Curricula need to be rooted in a *spiral* aspect of artistic learning in which children receive continuing exposure, at various developmental levels to certain core-concepts.

6. Assessment of learning is crucial in the arts (see Chapter 16).

7. Artistic learning does not merely entail the mastery of a set of skills or concepts. Emotional exploration and personal reflection are also imperative.

8. In general, it is risky and unnecessary to teach artistic taste or value judgments directly.

9. Art education is too important to be left to any one group, even if that group is designated as art teachers.

10. Would rather have a student well versed in one of the arts rather than have the student acquire a smattering of knowledge across the lively arts.

about art, artists, and their styles. Sensing and experiencing, not included in the Getty Center's components, are included in this program. Although the Getty Center did not focus on early childhood education, the author believes these are vital components for the early years.

WHAT TO INCLUDE IN AN EARLY CHILDHOOD ART PROGRAM

It is important that children have ample opportunities to make art. However, although it is basic, processing with the media to make art is only one of four key components of any complete early childhood art program. A complete program provides

1. sensory experiences.
2. beautiful and creative experiences.
3. time, space, and materials for making art.
4. an introduction to the world of art, artists, and a variety of art forms and styles.

The first three components should be emphasized during the early years, and the fourth component gradually introduced. Actually, the four components are interrelated, and the separation exists only for the present analysis. For example, making art is dependent on sensing and experiencing.

1. Sensory Experiences

Children do not magically create out of a vacuum or in isolation. Art has an origin. It originates from something personally experienced, an idea, object of importance, event, feeling, or person. A child's daily experiences provide a potential bank of things to include in art. For example, Joshua's idea for painting a farm did not just automatically happen. It was related to spending the weekend at his grandparents' farm. Field trips are crucial because they extend a child's personal range of experiences to the wider community. For example, taking a trip to the fire station provides new content for art.

Sometimes the term *disadvantaged* is used to refer to children who lack these basic environmental experiences. They may be uncomfortable discussing and being tested on things they have never directly experienced. It is dangerous to assume that all children have experienced and know about libraries, hospitals,

Celebrating: Nonwestern Art

Often, people know more about Western than non-Western art. When outlining historical styles, periods, and artists in the European tradition, specific dates and names can generally be identified. There are a number of reasons why this may not be the case when examining the art from non-European cultures. Many cultures do not view the making of arts a separate, autonomous activity. Aesthetic products may be intimately tied to ritual objects, dress, and body ornamentation. An artifact may be intended for daily utilitarian use and its maker anonymous, because the product is something that everyone makes and its existence is not considered to be anything special. For example, people make beautiful baskets to carry items to and from the market. Or the culture in question maintains a verbal, rather than a written record of its history.

It is important to widen one's perspective when learning about art. Take a global perspective, and become familiar with the art made by Asian, Egyptian, Native American, and African-American artists.

Some notable African-American artists include the following:

- Jacob Lawrence (painting)
- Horace Pippin (painting)
- Henry O. Tanner (painting)
- Elizabeth Catlett (sculpture and printmaking)
- Romare Bearden (painting and collage)
- Samella Lewis
- William Pajaud
- Selma Burke (sculpture)
- Edmonia Lewis (sculpture)
- Louis Mailou Jones (painting)
- Allan Crite

Visit museums that specialize in exhibits of nonwestern art. Add samples, books, and reproductions to your collection. Include these in your art teaching and aesthetic displays. Enlist the help of parents and community members in your quest to honor nonwestern art.

airports, stadiums, skyscrapers, elevators, cathedrals, post offices, seashores, or museums. Encourage parents to take their children places and discuss what they have experienced. This will help the children form concepts and will serve as a backdrop for future learning. For example, an informal trip to the hardware store can be a simple but sensory-rich experience filled with the sound, smell, and touch of cut wood or tools classified according to form and function.

Young children are sensory gluttons. Infants and toddlers are fascinated by pattern and detail. They will follow a bug crawling across the floor or marvel at water dripping from a melted icicle. Unfortunately, adults may take these experiences for granted and need to recapture some of this childlike wonder and awareness. Young children will need practice in keeping it alive.

According to Piaget, children come to know their world through their senses and actions. Our role is to help children note details and use all their senses to build rich object concepts. For example, smelling and tasting are appropriate when visiting a bakery, whereas looking and listening are warranted during story time in the library. Objects such as nature specimens can be brought in for focused sensory exploration. "Let's look at the empty hornet's nest. Carefully touch the sides. How does it feel? Do you hear anything when you put your ear to the opening? Let's wrap papier-mâché around a balloon and see if we can make our own hornet's nest."

2. Beautiful and Creative Experiences

Aesthetics is the study of beauty—not the Hollywood view of glamour, but beauty in color, form, and design. In a time of mass production with little concern for effort and quality craftsmanship, the quest for beauty is difficult. Still, there is a human need to make sense out of and appreciate one's self and one's environment, just as there is a basic need to create.

Celebrating: Female Artists

According to Lankford (1992) feminist critics, philosophers, and historians have revealed and denounced patriarchal bases of art and culture which have had the effect of denying women opportunities for participation and recognition in the art world. Historically, women have been poorly represented in the art market, galleries, museums, and art history books. Some notable female African-American artists have been listed in the section on nonwestern art. The following are just a few of the many more women who have made a significant contribution to the world of art

- Dorthea Lange (photography)
- Margaret Bourke-White (photography)
- Louise Nevelson (sculpture)
- Faith Ringgold (quilting and painting)
- Betty LaDuke (painting)
- Helen Frankenthaler (painting)
- Mary Cassatt (painting)
- Judith Leyster (painting)
- Georgia O'Keeffe (painting)
- Barbara Hepworth (sculpture)
- Eva Hesse (sculpture)
- Frida Kahlo (painting)
- Joan Mitchell (painting)
- Berthe Morisot (painting)
- Elizabeth Murray (painting)
- Suzanne Valadon (painting)
- Kathe Kollwitz (printmaking and drawing)

Art forms especially associated with women, such as quilting and weaving, have been devalued as *crafts* rather than *fine art*. Countless paintings, prints, and sculptures have portrayed women as primarily sensual in character and as socially subservient. Feminists attempt to correct negative sexist discrimination through positive social action, and by raising social consciousness about issues of sexual stereotyping, exploitation, and separatism. Feminist content may reflect feminist concerns and feminist artists often work collaboratively, promoting a sense of community and interdependence in contrast to the concept of artist as independent.

Learn about the types of art produced by women. Visit museums that specialize in women's art. Add samples, books, and reproductions of works by women to your collection. Include these in your art teaching and aesthetic displays. Enlist the help of female artists in your program and wider community to share their skills and art products.

Beauty can be found in nature, in one's surroundings, and in everyday objects. Children can use their senses and their bodies in their pursuit of beauty. The eyes can visually explore art, and the ears can listen to sounds and music. Three-dimensional artworks can be touched, scents can be smelled, foods can be tasted, and the body can respond through movement and dance. Young children can learn to appreciate and have beautiful experiences.

Children need to take the time to perceive the beauty in their everyday environment. Classrooms or centers can be aesthetically pleasing places and models of beauty. The room should be clean, bright, and colorful without being chaotic, cluttered, and gaudy. It should appeal to the senses and have things to look at, listen to, touch, smell, and taste. Flowers, plants, animals, soft pillows, a rocking chair, and a piece of sculpture add an aesthetic touch to the room.

Displays are places that children can visit to refine their senses and build aesthetic appreciation. Aesthetic displays can include nature specimens, a postcard collection, items of different textures, art books, antique tools or gadgets, machinery parts, pottery, fabric, postage stamps, foreign currency, or items of a given size, shape, or color. Centers or areas for art, music, and movement give children opportunities actively to represent beautiful images, thoughts, feelings, and concepts through art, music, rhythm, and dance.

Aesthetics is not confined to the interior environment. Beauty abounds in nature and the community. Children can also visit exhibits of beautiful things in museums, churches, and galleries, and they can attend concerts and performances. Artists, dancers, and musicians also can be invited to perform for and work with the children.

3. Time, Space, and Materials for Making Art

Young children need to be personally expressive and creative and to experience success through art. Teachers can help children see the relationship between art and experience. For example, a child may ask, "Teacher, what should I draw?" or "I don't know what to make." A teacher can help a child refer to significant people, places, and things: "What did you watch on TV?" or "How did you celebrate this past holiday?" or "What do you remember about our story today?" Teachers can encourage children to give artistic form and substance to their ideas, urges, wishes, dreams, fears, or interests. The bulk of this book continues our discussion of making art (see Figures 9–1 and 9–2).

4. An Introduction to the World of Art, Artists, and a Variety of Art Forms and Styles

Children may wonder: What is art? Who are artists? Why do they make art? Art is a basic human need. People make art to reflect and symbolize their existence. Children's interest in and study of community helpers can extend to artists. Children can learn that while some artists make art for a hobby, others do it

Figure 9-1 Young artists.

Figure 9-2 Making art.

as a career. Some work at home, outdoors, or in studios. Some artists exhibit and sell their works in galleries. Famous artists have their works exhibited in museums.

Children can also learn that artists work in different media. Although not all artists paint, all do have a pressing need to communicate. They use brush strokes, color, content, form, and the artistic elements to get their points across. Helping children accept and value their own artwork will enable them to appreciate and value the artwork of others. Our intent is to expose children to their rich artistic heritage rather than teach art history. Children can learn that people everywhere and from the beginning of time have made art. It is part of a culture and tells us something about people: who they were, what they looked like, how they lived, what they wore, where they lived, and what they liked to do. A discussion of the major artistic styles and movements follows.

Some books that introduce young children to the world of art include the following:

Laden, N. *When pigasso met mootisee.*
Mayhew, J. *Katie and the Mona Lisa.*
Mayhew, J. *Katie meets the Impressionists.*
Micklethwait, L. *A child's book of play in art.*
Sortland, B., & Elling, L., *Anna's art adventure.*
Walker, G., & Minnerly, D. B. *Molly meets Mona and friends: A magical day at the museum.*
Wellington, M. *Squeaking of art: The mice go to the museum.*

ARTISTIC STYLES

Prehistoric or Primitive Art

Era: 25,000 years ago during the Paleolithic or Old Stone Age
10–15,000 years later during the Neolithic or New Stone Age
Artists:
Unknown cave artists

People have been doing art for many years, way back to the days of when humans first appeared. Just as we have artists' pictures hanging on our walls today, people decorated the walls of their caves with pictures. Cave artists mixed their own paints out of plants, berries, and other foods as well as earth, mud, and clay, most likely mixed with animal blood. They used sharpened sticks to draw and etch pictures. Cave artists liked to draw simple stick-figure people and animals, including leaping bison and deer, using only a

few lines. Outlines were bold, and pictures were decorated with geometric patterns and designs. Proportion was correct. Cave people drew what they knew: themselves, others, and wild animals. That is what their life was about: survival, hunting, food, and safety from wild animals. Primitive people viewed art as magic. To symbolize something meant to somehow capture or control it.

An activity based on this style could be to have children paint a person or animal of their choice on a fairly large, smooth stone.

Naturalistic or Realistic Art

Era: 1700–1800s (Naturalistic)
Artists:
Honore Daumier
Francisco Goya
Rembrandt
Era: Nineteenth century on (United States)(Realistic)
Artists:
John James Audubon
Winslow Homer
Edward Hopper
Georgia O'Keeffe
Norman Rockwell
James Whistler
Grant Wood
Andrew Wyeth

Although **Naturalism** and **Realism** are somewhat different terms, we will use them interchangeably. Both terms emphasize the artist's attempt to make art objective and like the actual object. During the 1700s and 1800s painters attempted to portray life exactly as it was. This was a reaction against a neoclassic and romantic view of the ideal life. Naturalists chose to depict life as it was, often sordid and evil, and people as they were, overweight, ill, and less than beautiful. For example, a still life with flowers and fruit could include bugs and decaying food.

Naturalism and Realism also became popular in the United States in the nineteenth century. Landscapes, birds, farms, the wilderness, and people represented the struggle and simplicity of early American life. Children can examine naturalistic or realistic art and appreciate all the time, effort, skills, and talent needed to make a photographic likeness.

An activity for older children could be to set up a very simple arrangement, for example, a stuffed animal and a doll. Encourage the children to try to draw or paint the two toys just as they are. They will need to examine them repeatedly for color, detail, and shape. This activity may prove frustrating, so it should be offered as an option.

The Folk Arts

Folklife or folklore is an integral part of social life because it describes the beliefs, customs, values, behaviors, and practices common to a particular cultural group of people. The folk arts are the expressions of members of a cultural group. They are produced by individuals for the use of their own folk group members and made by hand rather than mass produced. The folk arts are a universal cultural element and a common way for communities to share their experiences. The folk arts encompass all of the arts. They are a tangible way for children to learn about diversity and about the commonalities across cultural groups. Examples include handicrafts, dances, music, songs, musical instruments, wood carvings, leather works, metal works, pottery, clothing and accessories, jewelry, weavings, quilts, toys, and cooking utensils, among others. When selecting samples to share with children remember that items should be authentic to the group. Family and community members are an excellent source of folk arts. Not only do most families have a collection of sample folk art pieces, but often family members are good craft makers. They may be pleased to come to your classroom and share their experiences.

More specifically, American folk art refers to a movement of American folk artists who lived in New England, New York, and Pennsylvania in the late 1700s to mid-1800s. American folk artists continue to work at their art form or craft today. Two examples are Grandma Moses and Charles Wysocki. American folk art, for example a painting or quilt, can be identified by its bold, simple designs, vivid colors, and simplistic handling of light, proportion, and perspective. Generally, American folk art makes a social, political, or religious statement. Often, common objects and events such as flowers, going to market, or getting married are depicted. It is this "homey" quality that accounts for much of its appeal.

Impressionism

Era: late 1800s to early 1900s
Artists:

> Mary Cassatt
> Paul Cézanne
> Edgar Degas
> Eugène Delacroix
> Raoul Dufy
> Paul Gauguin
> Édouard Manet
> Claude Monet
> Berthe Morisot
> Camille Pissarro
> Pierre Auguste Renoir
> Henri de Toulouse-Lautrec
> Vincent van Gogh

Impressionism is an artistic style in which artists painted what they perceived rather than what they knew to be there. Impressionists were fascinated with color, sunshine, contrasts, light, reflection, and shadow. They were concerned with making only a quick sketch of an object to capture its essence. Later they rapidly filled in their crude outline with intense patches of pigment. They used color and light to represent the artist's impression. Impressionists painted what they saw rather than what they knew to be there. They preferred painting outdoors with natural light. Landscapes were popular subject matter. When viewed from up close, Impressionist paintings depict a vibrating brilliance of colors, pure and unmixed. When viewed from a distance, however, the eyes fuse these neighboring color patches, constructing form and perceiving movement.

An activity could be to make an outdoor painting by dabbing paint with an index finger. Encourage children to place separate dabs rather than mixing them. Or children could use bright fluorescent crayons in making their strokes.

Pointillism

Era: late 1800s to early 1900s
Artist:

> Georges Seurat

Pointillism, an offshoot of Impressionism, involved a concern for color and an innovative technique for representing it. Pointillists worked on large canvases, spending as much as a year or more on one canvas. Small dots or points of pure color were used instead of Impressionist dashes or strokes. Pointillists were concerned with the complementary relationship between colors. They did not mix colors, but instead required that the observer fuse neighboring colors. For example, pointillists would represent water as composed of neighboring dots or points of green and yellow. When viewed from up close, the observer would see only green and yellow dots. From a distance, however, the eyes would blend the yellow and green and perceive blue water.

An activity could be to use crayons or markers to make a picture composed entirely of different-colored dots. Encourage children to use dots rather than lines at all times. Or children can make a picture by dipping the eraser end of a pencil into red, blue, and yellow paint and making a print in the shape of dots. This activity is recommended after children have had an opportunity to do color mixing. For example, if they want to make a purple car, they can use the pointillist technique of alternating red and blue dots in printing. Dots are placed close together with white space between. Younger children who do not have a command of color mixing should be encouraged to merely make a picture or design with colored dots.

Expressionism

Era: late 1800s to 1900s
Artists:
Paul Gauguin
Wassily Kandinsky
Piet Mondrian
Edvard Munch
Emil Nolde
Diego Rivera

Expressionism is an artistic style based on an expression of the artist's emotions and feelings. Expressionists, reacting against Impressionism, searched for emotional expression in their artistic statements. Expressionists purposely altered space, form, line, and color to make an emotional statement that was expressionistic rather than realistic, naturalistic, or impressionistic. The actual subject matter was often lost in the colorful and even violent play of color, line, shape, contrast, and movement. Expressionists distorted reality to express their own views and moods. Because this movement was popular at the time of World War I, it is easy to see how the art reflected contemporary culture. Much of the artwork at this time was violent, depressing, and highly emotional.

An activity could be to let children finger paint to mood music. Music that conveys sorrow, joy, and anger could be played. Encourage children to paint how they feel.

Abstract

Era: late 1940s
Artists:
Elaine de Kooning
Willem de Kooning
Hans Hofmann
Jackson Pollock
Mark Rothko

Abstract artists were intrigued with color and the physical qualities of paint: "What can I do with paint on canvas?" Abstract expressionism began after World War II. Jackson Pollock is a good example of an abstract expressionist who practiced action or gesture painting by dripping, dribbling, spraying, pouring, throwing, and splashing paint. Design was often left to chance or accident. These painters worked on very large canvases with no concern for capturing reality or shape or for telling a story through pictures.

An activity could be to put globs of paint on paper and let children use a soda straw to blow the paint around. The straws should be held close to the paint but not make contact with it. Remind children to exhale or blow out and not inhale or suck in. Children may also like to work outdoors on a group mural. Children can take turns dripping paint, using squeeze bottles or carefully trickling paint from a paper cup.

Fauvism

Era: 1910s
Artists:
André Derain
Raoul Dufy
Paul Gauguin
Henri Matisse
Amedeo Modigliani
Georges Rouault

Fauvism is an offshoot of Expressionism. Fauvists experimented with pure, bright colors in daring and innovative ways to represent positive emotions, including joy, pleasure, comfort, love, and happiness. Often there was little concern for the naturalistic or realistic use of color. Fauvists were not always concerned with mixing the proper color for skin. Human skin could be painted pink, green, or whatever, depending on the artist's mood. In this way, Fauvists believed that they could use color to make an emotional statement. Objects were characterized with bold outlines and abstract lines. An emotional use of color was of primary concern.

An activity could be to make a picture depicting a positive emotion or feeling, such as joy, love, hope, happiness, or caring. Encourage children to select and use the crayons that they believe best capture their feeling, with little or no concern for the naturalistic or realistic use of color. What does *happy* mean to you? Let's find a *happy* colored crayon to make our happy picture. "No, Sara, your happy picture doesn't have to look like anything!"

Cubism

Era: 1900s
Artists:

Georges Braque	Fernand Léger
Paul Cézanne	Piet Mondrian
Marcel Duchamp	Pablo Picasso
Juan Gris	Georges Rouault

Cubism is the source of all twentieth-century abstract art. It seeks an intellectual conception of form and shape. Cubists attempt to break everything down into its component geometric or architectural shapes. How can three-dimensional form, including the back side and bottom, be represented on a two-dimensional flat canvas? To do this, Cubists abandoned traditional treatment of space and form and instead focused on the use of the cylinder, sphere, and cube. For example, a Cubist might represent a tree by simultaneously depicting its top, sides, back, insides, and bottom. Intellectually, we are shown the entire tree. There is little concern for color, depth, or proper perspective. Objects appear flat, with little concern for background or foreground. They may be repeated in an overlapping sequence to suggest motion and movement. Cubists introduced the art form of collage.

An activity could be to make a collage using only geometric paper shapes, either cut or torn. Because a collage often has letters embedded in it, children could search through magazines and add letters to their own collage.

Kinetic Art

Era: 1920s
Artists:

Alexander Calder
Marcel Duchamp

Why must art be flat and motionless? **Kinetic art** attempts to incorporate physical movement by using levers, gears, and movable parts. Kinetic art invites participation. People interacting with kinetic sculpture cause it to move or change. Wind also causes the hanging objects on a mobile to move.

An activity could be to have children make a mobile. Or older children could attempt a moving junk sculpture or assemblage. For example, a robot could be constructed using fasteners, yarn, string, wire, nuts and bolts, and rubber bands, which would facilitate movement.

Surrealism/Dadaism

Era: 1900s
Artists:

Marc Chagall	René Magritte
Salvador Dali	Joan Miró
Jean Dubuffet	Meret Oppenheim
Max Ernst	Man Ray
Raoul Hausmann	Henri Rousseau
Frida Kahlo	Ben Shahn
Paul Klee	

Surrealism means superrealism. It attempts to create a magical, dreamlike world that is more intense than reality. Dreams, images, fantasies, and the subconscious are chosen as subject matter and portrayed either realistically or abstractly. Objects, space, symbols, size, perspective, time, and shape may be distorted, transformed, or superimposed. For example, a fish with a human head may fly through a rock-laden sky. The viewer may appear shocked and ask, What is it? What is it supposed to be? What does it mean? The artist has been successful in causing the viewer to stop, observe, and emotionally respond.

An activity could be to encourage children to represent their dreams, wishes, fantasies, nightmares, and innermost thoughts and feelings. Encourage children to make a personal statement that may not always be pleasant, pretty, or intelligible.

Pop Art

Era: 1950s
Artists:

Jasper Johns	Nam June Paik
Roy Lichtenstein	Andy Warhol

Pop art (Popular art) makes a social statement or critique of contemporary American culture. Pop artists chose subject matter that was familiar to everyday life—soup cans, soft drink containers, movie stars, cartoons, and other examples of advertising art. The common, taken-for-granted product becomes art. Although obvious in subject matter, these objects were represented, often in repeated fashion, with painstaking, realistic detail. Again, photographic realism was attempted and attained. There was no intent to make an emotional statement beyond the satire of the commercialism of contemporary culture.

An activity could be to have older children design their own package or wrapper for a candy bar, cereal, or soft drink. Or children could attempt to draw their own or a group cartoon strip with finepoint markers. Four or five frames may be sufficient.

Op Art

Era: 1960s
Artists:

> Frank Stella
> Victor Vasarely

Op art (Optical art) was an artistic style that developed in the psychedelic 1960s. Op artists were intrigued with the effects of black and white, color, figure-ground relations, and depth. They used the principles of optics and perception to create optical illusions with shapes, lines, and patterns. Wiggly and concentric lines and patterns suggested movement and form in the eye of the beholder.

Op art is a style that demands much in the way of technical proficiency and does not easily translate into an early childhood art activity.

Different artists use different styles. The same artist may use different styles at different times or periods. Children also have their own artistic styles. There is no one right or best way. Different styles are appropriate depending on the artist and what he or she is trying to say through art. Exposing children to the major artistic styles or movements serves two purposes. First, it shows children that there are many possible ways to make art. Second, it shows the similarities between their own styles and the styles that artists have used in the past and continue to use today. For example, children's art resembles both prehistoric art and modern abstract art.

A very simplistic breakdown of the major artistic movements includes these:

- realistic or naturalistic
- abstract
- nonobjective

Realistic or naturalistic art attempts to represent people, places, and objects exactly as they appear. There is an emphasis on objectivity, detail, and photographic realism. Children who aim for photographic realism in their art will be disappointed because developmentally they lack the necessary perceptual, physical, and cognitive ability. Realism or naturalism is merely one of many styles. Many adult artists are successful and satisfied in spite of their inability to produce realistic or naturalistic art.

Abstract art bears only a partial resemblance to the object being represented. The object is somehow streamlined or distorted. An example would be a child's drawing of a box on two wheels to represent a race car.

Nonobjective art involves a creative play with color, shape, line, and design. It is abstract art pushed to the limits. What is produced bears no resemblance to any actual object. For example, a child could paint racing swirls of paint to represent the speed and exhaust fumes associated with a race car rather than abstractly capturing its overall shape.

Art Critique. Even young children can be taught to critique a work of art. First, a teacher provides some background information about the particular piece: who made it, what the artist was like, what the world was like at the time. Young children are egocentric and may be more interested in their own art than in the artwork of others. Cognitively, they will be unable to empathize fully with the lives, plights, and historical times of famous artists. Still, an introduction to the foundations of good art and our artistic heritage is warranted.

Langer (1957) wrote that in order for effective art criticism to occur, three components are necessary: a communicator, the artist; a medium, the artwork; and a receiver or viewer who accepts, interprets, and incorporates what the artist has communicated. Cole and Schaefer (1990) add a fourth component, a facilitator. A teacher who guides the encounter between artwork and child by carrying on an art critique is acting as a facilitator. The role of the teacher as facilitator or enabler will be discussed in detail in Chapter 14.

The **art critique** can focus on the following five points:

1. What is it?
   Is it a painting, drawing, batik, weaving, or print? What are its physical properties? Is it big, small, square, round, solid, moving, or framed? What is it made out of? Did the artist use paper, paint, metal, clay, or yarn?
2. What do you see when you look at this work of art? Encourage children to focus on the artist's use of line, color, shape or form, mass or volume, design, pattern, space, balance, and texture. How are these artistic elements used? What shapes do you see? What colors were used? Can anyone find lines?
3. What is the artist trying to say?
   Try to put the artist's picture into words. What is the message? Pretend that this is a book with

pictures. What words go along with the picture the artist has given? Discuss what you see: people, animals, buildings, or events.

4. How does it make you feel?

Do you feel happy, sad, angry, scared, or funny? What does the artist do to make you feel this way?

5. Do you like it?

Why or why not? What is it about the work of art that makes you like or dislike it? How would you change it?

Questions 4 and 5 will evoke very different responses. Our aim is to help children acquire artistic appreciation and make judgments based on accepted standards, including the artistic elements.

 COLLAGE

A **collage** is a picture composed of different shapes or elements. A collage can be two-dimensional and composed of flat pieces of paper, or it can be three-dimensional and made with Styrofoam® chips and raised layers of fabric. Pieces of paper that are torn, cut, pasted, or taped can be creatively arranged into a collage. Although the activities are listed separately, there is no reason that materials used in one activity cannot be included in another. There is an endless variety of papers that can be used in collage. Some include the following:

- junk mail
- postage stamps
- postcards
- greeting cards
- gift wrap
- wallpaper samples
- travel brochures
- magazines
- newspapers
- coupons
- tinfoil

A collage is not limited to paper. There is an infinite supply of collage materials (see Figures 9–3 and 9–4). The key is quality and organization. Not all junk will have artistic value or potential. Items that are dirty or damaged may hold little aesthetic appeal. A pile of unorganized junk may trigger little creative transformation. It is important to organize collage materials according to some scheme—for example, papers in one bin; ribbon, lace, and yarn in another; magazines in a neat stack on the shelf; and so forth. Children need some basic order to help them see artistic possibilities.

Geometric Shapes Collage

Younger children who lack scissoring skills may enjoy pasting precut geometric shapes into a design or picture. Provide an array of different colors, sizes, and shapes. Older children who have scissoring skills can

Figure 9-3 A valentine collage.

Figure 9-4 Recycled junk collage.

draw and cut their own geometric shapes. Encourage children to place their shapes into some arrangement before gluing or pasting them. Or a rough sketch or outline can be drawn first and later filled in with geometric shapes.

Corrugated Cardboard Collage

Corrugated cardboard has an interesting texture and linear look. Older children can cut different shapes or pieces out of it and make a collage. Encourage them to note how the ridges can go in different directions. This is what gives a corrugated cardboard collage its visual appeal. Corrugated cardboard, with its raised ridges and neutral color, provides a striking contrast when it is used with flat or colorful papers or fabric.

Tissue Paper Collage

Colored tissue paper can be torn or cut. Because it is so thin, it may frustrate the young cutter. Provide small bowls of liquid starch and sponge squares or small brushes for spreading. Encourage children to note both the transparent quality of tissue paper and the possibilities for creating new colors by overlapping and building layers.

Or form a tissue paper collage on a piece of wax paper. Lay another piece of wax paper on top. An adult can gently press with a warm iron. The heat will melt the wax and seal the collage.

Or use thinned white glue to paste tissue papers inside the plastic lid of a coffee can. This will provide a ready-made frame. Carefully punch a hole at the top, lace with yarn, and hang.

Magazine Picture Collage

Magazines offer a wealth of letters, words, and pictures just waiting to be torn or cut out and pasted or taped to paper (see Figure 9–5).

Montage

Montage refers to a collage built around a theme, such as love, friendship, family, pets, or helping. Words and pictures related to the theme can be included. A montage around the theme of vehicles could include pictures of cars, trucks, bikes, airplanes, boats, motorcycles, stop signs, and traffic lights.

Collage Mural

A collage can also be a group project correlated with a unit or concept under study. Some examples include these:

* color
* shape
* size
* initial consonants
* people
* community helpers
* other classes, concepts, and categories

Children can search through magazines looking for samples or examples of the concept. A collage mural can be an extended activity; it need not be completed in a short period of time. It could be set up as a center, with children adding to it from time to time over a period of a few days.

Magazine Mix-Ups

Children have a silly sense of humor. They may enjoy making a picture out of unrelated parts—for example, an animal with a human head or the front of a car with

Figure 9-5 Magazine picture collage.

the tail of an airplane. One teacher introduced this activity by providing part of a picture for each child. The pieces, cut from a magazine, were different for each child. Examples included a cat's head, a person's body, the trunk of a tree, and a diving board with no steps. Children were encouraged to look through their magazine and find a part that would finish their mixed-up picture by adding a silly top, bottom, head, body, or side as needed. There was no need to finish the picture correctly.

A collage does not always have to be done on paper. Be creative, provide the following:

• cardboard	• plastic foam
• paper plates	• meat trays (sanitized)
• box lids	• egg cartons
• wood	• containers

Nor does collage entail only the use of paper. Look through your artistic junk for a variety of materials that can be pasted, glued, stapled, or taped, such as these:

fabric scraps	gauze
felt	sawdust
feathers	wool
Styrofoam® scraps and pellets	game pieces
	emery boards
dried grass	sequins
leaves and twigs	bias tape
bottle caps	broken egg shells
tinsel	rubber bands
cotton balls	electronics parts
tongue depressors	paper scraps
washers	lace
coffee filters	

computer junk including
   resistors, wafers,
   carriers, etc.
rickrack
yarn
curling ribbon
stars and stickers
cornhusks
paper baking cups
jar lids
broken toys
coffee grounds
hair rollers
zippers
burlap
excelsior
shoelaces
toothpicks
beads
wire
ribbon
string
pipe cleaners
pinecones
wood scraps
straws
foil

gravel
flat wooden spoons
bolts
wool
bones
Easter grass
berry baskets
paper cups
checkers
cork
paint-chip samples
buttons
shells
flowers
seeds
cotton swabs (Q-tips®)
spools
acorns
fur
jewelry
chains
keys
foam rubber
nature items
hardware
springs

Figure 9-6 Nature collage.

Nature Collage

Nature specimens can be carefully glued onto paper or sturdy cardboard. (see Figure 9–6)
   Some examples include these:

- leaves
- ferns
- grass
- petals
- weeds
- flowers

Other examples of nature items are listed in Appendix A. Some prefer to first press their nature specimens for about a week between layers of newspaper with heavy objects on top to get them flat. Or they can be arranged on wax paper with a second sheet on top and pressed with a warm iron.

Fabric, Felt, or Material Collage

Children enjoy using materials other than paper in their collage. Provide small scraps of fabric, felt, or material for the young child to paste or glue. Older children with fairly sharp scissors and good cutting skills may be able to cut out or tear their own pieces (see Figure 9–7).

Figure 9-7 Fabric collage.

Figure 9-8 Texture collage.

String or Yarn Collage

A collage can be composed of string or yarn. Each can be dipped in glue and creatively arranged on an art surface. Remind the children to squeeze the excess glue out before placing the string. Obviously, string or yarn should be incorporated with other collage material.

Texture Collage

Most of the collage activities mentioned involve textures. A collage can also specifically focus on textured papers, including these:

- sandpaper
- flocked wallpaper
- tissue paper
- newspaper
- magazine pages

or a variety of textured fabrics and materials, including these:

- wool
- cotton
- velvet
- burlap
- netting
- foam rubber

A variety of textured nature specimens, listed under nature collage, earlier, and in Appendix A, can be included (see Figure 9–8).

Sandwich Bag Collage

Children create their own design inside a plastic sandwich bag. The advantage is that no glue or paste is needed. The disadvantage, however, is that an adult will need to use a warm iron to melt the plastic and seal in the collage. Children will need their own plastic sandwich bag, tray, and array of small collage items. Flat items including ribbon, lace, stickers, stars, confetti, nature items, and assorted papers such as tissue and magazine pictures are recommended. Children should place the bag on their tray and arrange the items inside their bag leaving some plastic area uncovered to facilitate sealing when ironed. When finished, children can bring their tray to an adult who can put their bag between two sheets of tinfoil and press with a warm iron. Peel away the tinfoil and return the collage to the child.

SUMMARY

This unit focused on building a comprehensive early childhood art program. Recommended program components included experiences in sensing; beautiful experiences; making art; and learning about art, artists, and their styles. Although young children need not become art historians, it was recommended that they be introduced to the major artistic movements. These were identified as realistic or naturalistic, abstract, and nonobjective. Individual styles and artists within each general category were identified. A format for conducting an art critique was also provided.

Key Terms

Abstract	folk arts	Op art (Optical art)
art critique	Impressionism	Pointillism
collage	Kinetic art	Pop art (Popular art)
Cubism	National Standards for the Arts	Project Zero
Discipline-Based Art Education (DBAE)	Naturalism	Realism
	Nonobjective art	studio-oriented
Expressionism	non-Western art	Surrealism
Fauvism		

Suggested Activities

1. Arrange to visit an art gallery, exhibit, or museum. Try to identify works of art that belong in each of the three major artistic movements or styles. If possible, visit a location that features nonwestern art and works by female artists.
2. Use the art critique to analyze and discuss a work of art. Research the artist and era.
3. Begin a collection of art postcards, photographs, prints, posters, or books. Visit thrift shops, used book stores, and library sales. Look for reproductions of non-Western art and works by female artists.
4. Arrange to accompany a group of young children on an informal field trip to a local art museum, gallery, or artist's studio. Visit in advance to know what is available.
5. Arrange for an artist to come in, model art processing, and informally work with the children.
6. Set up a collage center and help children create.

Review

1. List the components of a complete early childhood art program.

2. Identify and briefly explain the three major artistic movements.

3. List the five major points or questions for conducting an art critique.

4. The National Standards for Arts Education lists what six reasons for the importance of arts education?

5. The National Standards for the Arts identified a set of competencies. How do they relate to early childhood art education?

6. Discuss the role of art in Project Zero.

7. Discuss DBAE.

For additional art and creative development resources, visit our Web site at
www.EarlyChildEd.delmar.com

Section Four

Providing Art Experiences

It is time to translate what you have learned about art, creativity, and child development into curriculum. What is curriculum? A simple definition is that curriculum is what happens in the classroom—both the planned and unplanned. Our focus will be on planning art activities and turning the unexpected and unplanned into meaningful learning experiences. Chapter 10, Child-Centered Art vs. Teacher-Directed Projects, provides criteria or guidelines for selecting activities that have artistic merit as opposed to nonart activities that rely on patterns and much adult input. Chapter 11, Planning, Implementing, and Evaluating Art, focuses on the role of the teacher as curriculum developer. The chapter also offers different approaches to curriculum development. Chapter 12, Integrating Art across the Early Childhood Curriculum, makes a connection between art and the curricular areas. Activities are provided to show how art can support academic learning by being part of experiences in mathematics, science, literacy, social studies, and the expressive arts. Chapter 13, The Art Center, provides criteria for setting up an art area in your classroom.

What do you see in this photograph? It appears the teacher has planned an art activity in which children make a frog puppet. First, she read a frog story and then had children go to the art table to make their own. How much of the activity was done by the child? How much was done by the teacher? How do you feel about the way the child made his puppet? Is it *right* or *correct*? Did the child do a "good" job? How would you rate this activity in terms of creativity? What if when the mother came to pick up her preschooler she said, "No baby, that's wrong; that's not how a frog looks." If you were the teacher what could you say or do?

Chapter 10

Child-Centered Art vs. Teacher-Directed Projects

What do you see in this photograph? What does Amber's face tell you? Does she appear to be a bit unsure about art?

Amber has not had a lot of experience using paint, crayons, or markers. She watches what other children do with the media. At times, art can be messy. This confuses Amber because her family expects her to stay clean at school. Amber's parents also expect her to create beautiful pictures that look like something recognizable. Her family values art. As Amber's teacher, however, you sense that Amber is not ready to create realistic art. You want to let Amber observe and creatively process and explore.

You also feel pressure from her parents to teach Amber how to make art that looks like something they know.

What should you do? What kinds of art experiences are appropriate for young children like Amber?

Objectives

After reading this chapter, you should be able to:

- Use the continuum of approaches to identify three different ways to teach art.
- Discuss the teacher's role as a facilitator in early childhood art.
- State the criteria or guidelines for early childhood art activities.
- Apply the criteria or guidelines for early childhood art activities in critiquing photocopied or mimeographed sheets, coloring books, crafts, and holiday gifts.
- Identify alternatives to activities masquerading as creative art.
- Distinguish child-centered art from teacher-directed projects.
- Provide art activities using paper.

INTRODUCTION

There are many different ways to approach the teaching of art. This chapter will identify and critique teacher-directed, guided, and child-centered approaches. What is the teacher's role in children's art? Adults can stimulate children to make art by being a model and participant. Adults can model creativity in their daily lives and actively participate in art activities themselves. Although it is important to be an art specialist and to know about art, an adult does not need to be a talented artist to provide creative art experiences for children.

The different approaches to working with young children reside along a continuum. Teacher direction and child-centered are two opposite points along the continuum. See Figure 10–1. Both points are valid at certain times for certain children and certain activities. The role of facilitator or guide is a compromise and midpoint position between these two opposite roles.

A facilitator or guide is readily available without directly monopolizing the activity, as is the case with direct instruction. A facilitator or guide is a keen observer who knows when to subtly step in, intervene, ask a question, or pose a problem. Children who need assistance know that their teacher is a resource person who is available to share facts, knowledge, skills, abilities, time, and attention.

Children's art fascinates adults. Although they may not understand it, parents are proud of their chil-

dren's art. Early childhood educators also value children's art and allow ample time for it in the daily schedule. Although most young children are neither interested in nor ready for formal academics such as reading, virtually all young children are interested in and ready for art.

Most of us recognize the importance of early childhood art, but not everyone would agree about what it entails. Is scribbling art? Can coloring in a coloring book be considered art? This unit provides criteria or guidelines for determining the creative merits of an activity or approach to art. Traditional teacher-directed and product-oriented art activities will be critiqued. Activities masquerading as creative art will be identified, and alternatives will be suggested.

What is art? The great philosopher Susanne Langer believed that humans are born with an urgent biological need to create art. Art helps us put our life experiences into symbolic form. We are then able to stand back and clarify, critically examine, and share our experiences. But how is this done? There are many ways to express one's experiences artistically. Some of these are as follows:

- literature
- drama
- music
- visual arts: plastic and graphic

For our purposes, we will focus on how young children use the visual arts to represent their life experiences.

Teacher-directed	X Guided	Child-centered
• direct instruction	• facilitation	• complete freedom
• teacher intervention		• nonintervention
• structured		• unstructured

Figure 10-1 Continuum of approaches.

The plastic, or three-dimensional, arts include sculpture, ceramics, and architecture. The graphic, or two-dimensional, arts include painting, printmaking, and drawing.

APPROACHES TO TEACHING ART

The major approaches to teaching are also applicable to teaching art. The three approaches are the following:

- teacher-directed
- child-centered
- teacher-guided

Some art projects are structured and **teacher-directed.** The teacher has an idea of what to make and how to go about it. Specific directions are given to ensure a recognizable product. Often, there is little input from the children. For example, a teacher distributes a piece of paper with an outline of a tree. The children are instructed to use a dark color, such as black or brown, to color in the trunk and green for the top. They also cut or tear small circles from red construction paper. These are pasted onto the green top. The completed apple trees look nearly identical. Generally, this approach is used when art is approached with the entire group or small groups of children. Most craft projects are teacher-directed. Seefeldt (1995) critiques teacher-directed art. Asking children to complete patterned artwork or to copy adult models of art undermines children's sense of psychological safety and demonstrates disrespect for children including their ideas, abilities, and creativity. Children who are frequently given patterns to cut out or outlines to color in are in fact being told that they, and their art, are inadequate. Seefeldt gives the example of giving children egg cartons to paint and paste eyes to make caterpillars, an activity that she sees as ridiculous when compared to the artwork of children in Reggio.

An opposite approach is to be unstructured and completely **child-centered.** A teacher may distribute, pieces of paper and encourage children to make what-

Figure 10-2 Teacher has prepared the table with watercolors.

ever they want or encourage them to visit the easel or art center. In this approach, children have much input and choice. There is very little structure. For example, in Figure 10–2, the teacher has merely set the stage at the table. Some children do very well with this approach. They may have a bank of ideas to represent through art. They may also see endless artistic possibilities at the easel or art center. Many children, however, are uncomfortable with this approach. It may be too loosely structured. Some children quickly tire of inventing their own daily art program. They look to the teacher for some structure, guidance, or possibilities.

According to Wright (2003), unsupported arts learning in the classroom sometimes can lead to a laissez-faire or "anything goes" type of practice. In this noninterventionist approach, the underlying belief is that whatever children do in the arts is valuable. For a teacher to interfere would stifle a child's creativity. This hands-off approach restricts the teacher's role to one of organizing the environment only and discourages one from suggesting ideas or processes that could mediate and scaffold children's learning. With no input from others, children can sometimes become bored and even frustrated with experiences that invite only independent experimentation. Children cannot create from nothing. They need background ideas and suggestions. Teacher-directed and child-centered approaches are extremes. Teachers can elect for a compromise using support and guidance by adopting the role of facilitator within a guided approach.

Teacher As Facilitator

A **teacher-guided** approach offers the best of the two former approaches: subtle structure with much child direction and input (see Figure 10–3). For example:

NAEYC
- A teacher supplies the theme.
  "Children, it's getting very close to summer. Today, we will make a picture that reminds us of this season." Although the theme is given, there is no specified product. Children are free to use paint, crayons, markers, or clay to make their own versions of what summer means to them.

NAEYC
- A teacher introduces new materials at the art center.
  "Today I put some spools and buttons near the easels and art table. I want you to look at them and think of how they might be used in art. Try out different ways of using them." Children are free to use them as brushes, make a stamped impression, or paste them to a collage, as long as the rules for the art center are upheld.

NAEYC
- A teacher extends or builds upon an existing activity or suggests a new technique.
  "I've noticed how much we enjoy easel painting with our long-handled brushes. I found these small tree branches outside and am leaving them at the easels. Let's see if we could use them to paint with." Or, "Let me show you another way of doing watercolor by first wetting your paper." Or, "I see how much you enjoy your paper-bag puppet. If you like, I could show you how to sew one out of cloth." Or, "Did you enjoy your paper weaving? Would you like to learn how to weave on a loom with yarn?"

NAEYC
- A teacher poses a problem.
  "Let's see how many different shapes we can cut out of paper for pasting." Or, "How could we use these empty boxes and ribbon?" Or, "What will happen if we try painting on newspaper or the colored pages in this magazine?"

NAEYC
- A teacher extends art into other curricular areas. "There seems to be a lot of excitement in your picture. Would you like to share it by telling me a story?" Or, "The dog you painted looks so happy, let's work together and write a poem about it." Or, "Perhaps you would like to plan a play for your ferocious dinosaur."

Different approaches may work for certain activities and certain children. Young children will not automatically discover how to use a watercolor set. They will need some direction and instruction in its use and

Figure 10-4

Figure 10-5

Figure 10-3 A facilitator or guide gives help when needed.

Figure 10-6

care. They need not, however, be told what to make or what it should look like. For example, Emily is having difficulty deciding what to include in her summer picture. Her teacher senses her frustration and asks her to name things that remind her of summer. Emily answers, "Sun and swimming." Her teacher further structures the task by asking Emily to choose one. With the teacher's subtle guidance, Emily chooses the sun and now must decide if she should use paints, watercolor, crayons, markers, or clay to represent it.

Figure 10-7

Carefully examine Figures 10–4, 10–5, 10–6, and 10–7. Using the continuum of approaches to teaching art (see Figure 10–1), do two things. First, decide where along the continuum each picture best fits. Second, provide a rationale for each answer. Your instructor may use this in a small group activity and discussion (see Children's Drawing box on p. 224).

HOW TO CHOOSE ART ACTIVITIES

What should be included in an early childhood art program? Mr. Mills has baked cookies, and his toddlers will soon spread frosting on them for an art activity. Across the hall, kindergartners are neatly coloring in a butterfly photocopy as part of their unit on spring. Their teacher reminds them that they have only a few minutes left for art. What can one say about these activities? Which have artistic merit? Do they represent the essence of what early childhood art should be? The author would respond negatively to these questions. Although spreading frosting may be an enjoyable tactile, perceptual-motor, and edible activity, it is not art. Simply coloring in a butterfly photocopy may strengthen eye-hand coordination and figure-ground relations, but it offers little or no opportunity for creativity. A more creative version would be to let the children draw their own butterflies with little concern for realistic rendering.

Child-Centered Art or Teacher-Directed Projects

Arts and crafts are terms that are often viewed as opposite. Hirsch (2004) provides a distinction. The motivation for art comes from within the child. Young children are dealing with autonomy and initiative. They are often not responsive or interested in teacher-directed experiences. This is especially true with art. When art is forced or extrinsically motivated, it may lack meaning, expressiveness, or detail. The art may reflect external expectations, or the autonomous child may purposefully create anything but what was asked for. The approach is reproductive in that the child merely reproduces the teacher's product. By contrast, when the motivation and purpose for art come from within the child, the artwork reflects personal meaning and purpose. When children have free access to materials in an art center, they have the opportunity to create meaning and purpose. The approach is productive, not reproductive. In terms of approach, art activities are viewed as developmentally

Children's Drawing: Free Expression or Skill to Be Taught?

Controversy surrounds the issue of how children learn to draw. Can young children be taught to draw? Some people believe they can. A more important question is, Should they be?

Emberley (1991) views drawing as a skill that can be taught. His series of drawing books, developed for the K-3 population, consists of simple, step-by-step instructions using a collection of shapes to draw imaginary creatures, faces, and buildings. Brookes (1986), author of *Drawing with Children*, claims to be able to teach three-year-olds to go beyond stick figure drawing to make representational and realistic drawings. Her method is based on teaching five basic elements of shape: the dot, circle, straight line, curved line, and angle line. These five groups of form constitute basic visual building blocks that lie at the heart of all other shapes. She encourages children to notice these elements in everyday life and to use them to build their own artistic creations. Students begin by copying simple illustrations, moving on to more complex pictures, and finally drawing from real life.

Johnson's (1990) *Teach Your Child to Draw* is aimed at parents. Her method features learning from what real artists have done. At the heart of each lesson are examples drawn from both old and new masters. Johnson believes that over time readers will begin to see their surroundings with an artist's eye and will be able to break down objects and scenery into the following components: line, pattern, texture, light and dark, shading, negative and positive shapes, proportion, point of view, movement, and distance.

These three authors advocate an approach that is teacher-directed, according to Figure 10-1. A set of artistic elements is at the heart of each of these approaches. The author believes that although artistic elements are

the building blocks of art, there is no need to teach young children directly how to make them just to get them to draw realistically. The artistic elements can be used for analyzing art (Chapter 6) and in responding to children about what they have created (Chapter 15).

How do you feel about Emberley's, Brookes's, and Johnson's approaches to teaching young children to draw? Lowenfeld and Brittain (1987) and most early childhood educators, including the author, advocate an opposing position that views drawing as free expression. This child-centered position would lie at the opposite end of the continuum depicted in Figure 10-1. If children must be taught to draw something, they are not developmentally ready. Teaching them how to draw will not enhance their drawing ability. Teaching young children to draw emphasizes the product over the process.

Edwards's (1979) *Drawing on the Right Side of the Brain* assumes a middle position and compromise. Although she believes that older children need to be taught how to draw, she does not believe that they need a visual symbol system or group of shapes to help them to draw more effectively. She does not advocate that young children be taught to draw but instead believes that age ten is a good time to start. By age ten, many preadolescents are frustrated with their own crude attempts and are motivated to learn how to draw realistically. Her visual exercises include copying upside-down pictures, drawing a common object such as a stuffed animal without taking one's eyes off it, and paying attention to empty or negative space. The author has noted the popularity of Edwards's methods in elementary and secondary art education programs. Her approach has also been successfully used with adults who claim they could never draw.

---

appropriate while crafts are often teacher-directed, product-oriented, and lacking artistic merit. The term *project* is presently used in place of *craft*. Although some would refer to teacher-directed activities as crafts, the terms are not interchangeable. Crafts have artistic merit, and craftspeople work long and hard to produce products, many of which reflect their culture. Crafts may also be functional as with candles, jewelry, clothing, or windchimes. Therefore, it would not be fair to use crafts in the same sense of teacher-directed art projects. Instead, teacher-directed projects, rather than crafts, are the opposite of child-centered art. Substituting teacher projects for art does children a disservice for it robs them of the opportunity to make self-expressive, self-initiated art. See Table 10–1 for a comparison and contrast of these two approaches.

Is There a Place for Teacher Projects?

Although teacher projects should not dominate your art program, they do have a place and are to your art program as spices are to cooking. Some people avoid spices while others use them sparingly to enhance but not overpower or dominate the taste of food. When should teacher projects be used? They can be used occasionally

- with older children who have a solid foundation in processing and are interested in learning how to make art products.
- when children tire of visiting the art center and appear to run out of ideas for processing. They appear stuck or out of ideas. It appears the art center is not being used.
- to introduce children to new cultures by directly experiencing representative crafts. The process

Table 10–1 Child-Centered Art Activities or Teacher-Directed Projects

ART ACTIVITIES	TEACHER-DIRECTED PROJECTS
are creative, unique, original	are uncreative and resemble each other, appear mass-produced and very similar if not identical to each other
are diverse and individual like the children who create them	are uniform and resemble each other or the teacher standard or model
are open-ended and unstructured	are closed-ended and structured
are child-centered and child-directed	are teacher-centered and teacher-directed
come from within the child	are imposed from without by the teacher
involve much child input	involve much teacher input
empower children who say, "Look what I made by myself."	empower teachers who think, "Look what I got the all children to do. Won't the parents be pleased?"
involve self-expression	involve copying and imitating
foster autonomy	foster compliance and following directions
are process-oriented	are product-oriented
may not be recognizable	are recognizable
may not appeal to adults because the finished product may not be recognizable	usually appeal to adults because the finished product is recognizable
may not be useful or practical	may be useful and practical
are success-oriented, no fear of failure	may be unsuccessful if the child is unable to approximate the teacher's model or standard
empower children to decide on content	are decided by the teacher and related to holiday, season, theme, unit of study
please the child	please adults
need open blocks of time	may involve time constraints in giving everyone a chance to make one; the child may be rushed to complete
involve legitimate artistic media	may involve consumable and expensive supplies like glitter, feathers, wiggly eyes, and fur

involved in making crafts must be tailored to meet the developmental needs of your group.

• while allowing for individual expression, as in the choice of color or type of decoration added. For example, children can be taught how to make a piñata without specifying what it should look like when finished.

WHAT EARLY CHILDHOOD ART SHOULD BE

Often it is easy to recognize negative examples or instances of uncreative art. Just what should one look for in planning an early childhood art activity? Early childhood art should

1. allow children to be personally expressive.
2. subtly balance artistic process and product.
3. be open-ended, allowing children to be creative.
4. allow for discovery and experimentation.
5. allow for active engagement and sustained involvement.
6. be intrinsically motivating.
7. be success-oriented.
8. be developmentally appropriate.
9. involve legitimate artistic media.
10. be available to all children.

1. Allow Children to Be Personally Expressive

Young children need to express themselves personally with a variety of artistic media. The expression should be personal because individual children will approach art in unique ways. After visiting the zoo, several three-year-olds were encouraged to make or do something related to what they had just experienced. At the easel, Jean painted a caged black bear. Three children headed for the clay table. Jim squeezed a ball of clay and called it a seal. Tam rolled tiny clay snakes to make the rays of the hot shining sun. Kaley cut an outline of an elephant into a slab of clay using an ice-cream stick. Personal choice was reflected in the use of paint or clay. Furthermore, the children at the clay table found three different ways to express what was personally meaningful to them.

2. Subtly Balance Artistic Process and Product

The art activities provided should subtly balance artistic processing and the making of art products. A good

art program understands and accepts the fact that individual children can be oriented toward process, product, or both in their approach to art. Art processing includes the skills involved in a given art activity. For example, paper work involves tearing, cutting, folding, pasting, stapling, braiding, and weaving. The product refers to the result. For example, processing with paper may result in a paper collage, paper weaving, or paper sculpture. Young children are process-oriented (see Figure 10–8). They enjoy art for the sake of doing and making, often with little concern for how it turns out. Perhaps this is why some children fail to claim their finished art products. They forget which one they did or merely toss it into the wastebasket as they depart. One carpool mother complained about how the backseat of her van was strewn with children's art. For these children, the joy was in the actual doing or process rather than in what resulted, the finished product. Older children, however, become product-oriented. They are very concerned about size, shape, color, placement, detail, and realism. They are quick to put their name on their art and may become upset when papers tear or curl or when paint smears. It may be important for these children to take one or several art products home each day.

The author once observed a boy in a transitional kindergarten diligently working on a clay dinosaur. When the teacher announced, "Cleanup time; every-

Figure 10-8 Processing with art media is as important as making a finished product.

body clean up," he was devastated. He pleaded to take it home or at least keep it out for display. He was near tears when he was directed to roll it back into a ball and return it to the clay tub. Clearly, he was product-oriented in his approach to art. Art is dependent on both process and product. Artistic processing is necessary to arrive at a finished product. Elaborating or refining a product involves processing.

3. Be Open-Ended, Allowing Children to Be Creative

Early childhood art programs should also encourage young children to be creative. They can encourage children to represent their world creatively by allowing them to choose

- what they want to make (content).
- how to go about making it (process).
- what it will end up looking like (product).

In general, planned activities that are loosely structured set the stage for creative expression. For example, paints, brushes, and paper at the easel may be enough for some children. All they need is to invest time and pursue an idea. Others may need a teacher's subtle guidance. "Try to think of something that happened over the weekend, maybe involving someplace or someone special. This could give you something to paint." We rob children of the opportunity for creative artistic expression when we specify what the finished product should be or look like and exactly how to do it. For example, coloring, cutting out, and correctly pasting together a train do not involve much creativity.

Still, creative expression must abide by general rules, guidelines, and limits. Pretend-fighting with scissors is dangerous and not creative. Children need to be taught the proper way to handle scissors and all other artistic media, equipment, and supplies. Rules need to be discussed and posted. "Chris, bring me your scissors. They are only for cutting paper."

4. Allow for Discovery and Experimentation

NAEYC

Children can arrive at artistic products through discovery and experimentation. For example, teaching sponge painting or printing directly may not be necessary. It is possible to provide paints and an array of sponges, cookie cutters, and Styrofoam® shapes, and encourage children to see what they can do with these "painters" and the paint (see Figure 10–9). They may experiment by spreading paint with sponges or using the sponges in a stamping motion. Either way, they have discovered for themselves a new artistic tech-

Figure 10-9 Different brushes help children discover and experiment.

nique through their own active experimentation. Planning each art activity with a predetermined product and step-by-step procedure robs children of the opportunity to explore, discover, invent, and creatively experiment on their own.

5. Allow for Active Engagement and Sustained Involvement

Art should actively engage your children. They are active physical beings, and their artistic expression should reflect this. They need upright easels to encourage sweeping whole-arm movements while standing. Clay needs to be torn, punched, pulled, rolled, flattened, pinched, and pounded. Recommended early childhood art activities will encourage and capitalize on the young child's need for sensory-motor exploration and movement. Ample blocks of time are needed to foster sustained involvement. Not all children are able to complete an art activity in a predetermined block of time. Some will want to continue working later or even the following day. Other children will impulsively finish their art in a matter of minutes. "Look, teacher, I'm done! What can I do now?" Teachers may want to encourage such children to continue their involvement. Obviously, few young children will work for hours at the same art activity.

Still, they can be encouraged to examine and extend their art. "Tara, I see you finished your painting. Is there anything else you want to add?" "Yes, I see. It is a turtle. Have you thought about where it lives or what it might like to eat? You have a lot of time and more paper, so keep working on your turtle." The teacher did not tell Tara her turtle was wrong or bad. She encouraged Tara to refine her art and continue her involvement. In this case, Tara chose to ignore the teacher's suggestions and announced that her turtle picture was finished. Over time, Tara may begin to see that additional time and effort spent working usually produce a more elaborate and detailed picture.

6. Be Intrinsically Motivating

Art—like music, movement, and play—is an activity with **intrinsic motivation.** Children will engage in art for the sheer pleasure and reward inherent in painting, coloring, working with clay, or making a collage. The author believes that one of the major joys of being an early childhood educator is working with young children who are so internally motivated to learn and to make sense out of their world. They manipulate, explore with all their senses, and ask endless questions. Although praise and rewards are effective, they are not always needed in art. The author observed a teacher praising a child's finished art product. "Oh, look how pretty Marla's painting of a house turned out!" Later, several children copied Marla's idea and style to win this teacher's praise. Their motivation for doing art had moved from internal to external. Instead, Marla's teacher could have praised her efforts and involvement. "Maria, you are working so long and hard" or "I see a lot of action at the clay table. Sam will keep working until he gets it just the way he wants." Research by Lepper and Greene (1975) has shown that external motivation and techniques of behavior modification actually decrease a child's intrinsic motivation. Praising preschoolers' use of felt-tip markers actually decreased their interest in using them. Anderson, Manoogian, and Reznick (1976) studied the effects of different rewards on four- and five-year-olds' intrinsic interest in drawing. They found that monetary and symbolic rewards—for example, money and stickers—decreased children's interest in drawing. A teacher's verbal praise, however, actually increased it. Still, it is recommended that the praise be aimed at the process and involvement rather than at the outcome.

7. Be Success-Oriented

Early childhood art activities should be planned to be success-oriented. Choosing art activities that are devel-

opmentally appropriate and moderately challenging will ensure a child's success. In turn, feelings of success and mastery foster a child's positive self-concept. A major goal of early childhood education is to help children become competent and feel good about themselves. Activities that are too difficult or detailed may frustrate children and lead to failure. The danger is that young children may generalize their failure at a task to failure as a person. For example, a group of four-year-olds at summer day camp was given a group of cardboard insects to trace, cut, and paste. The objects were small, with many details, including thin legs and feelers. The cardboard was flimsy, and the scissors were dull. Papers were torn, and insect heads and tails were missing. Few, if any, of the children could match the teacher's standard, which was hanging overhead. The children became restless and frustrated. The camp counselor meant well but did not translate the developmental abilities of four-year-olds into a success-oriented art activity.

8. Be Developmentally Appropriate

What could be an alternative to the activity described earlier? A good art activity can foster success by taking into account a child's developmental abilities. For example, the camp counselor, after reading a book on insects and taking a nature walk to collect specimens, could have encouraged the children to draw a favorite bug or create a new one. What might a "butter-quito" or "spider-hopper" look like? There is no one right answer; there are many possibilities. Art activities that require excessive cutting, fine detailing, pasting of small pieces, or precise folding are not developmentally appropriate for young children with limited fine motor control and coordination. The author recalls a first attempt at origami, a precise Japanese paper-folding activity. Although the teacher produced an intricate, correctly folded swan, the author's looked like a lop-sided beast. Anyone who has felt discouraged and unsuccessful can easily empathize with young children who do not experience success through art.

The National Association for the Education of Young Children (NAEYC) has drafted a position statement on **developmentally appropriate** practice in early childhood programs serving children from birth through age eight (Bredekamp, 1987) (see inside front cover). A major determinant of program quality is the extent to which knowledge of child development is applied in educational practice.

9. Involve Legitimate Artistic Media

A variety of art media, such as easels, finger paints, and clay, should be available for creative expression.

Developmental Appropriateness

NAEYC published and revised a widely used position statement advocating developmentally appropriate practices for programs serving young children from birth to age eight (Bredekamp, 1987; Bredekamp and Copple, 1997).

The concept of developmental appropriateness has the following three dimensions:

1. Age/Developmental

According to child development knowledge and research, all children grow and develop in a universal, predictable sequence during the early childhood years. An activity must be within a child's developmental ability. Knowledge of the typical development of children within the age span served by one's program provides a framework from which teachers prepare the learning environment and plan activities deemed age appropriate. However, chronological age can be very misleading. For example, one may have reached their fourth birthday yet exhibit developmental characteristics shared by most three-year-olds. A child's developmental age would be a more useful construct.

2. Individual

Children are unique individuals. Each child has his or her own unique patterns of growth, strengths, interests, experiences, temperament, and personality. What interests one child may bore another. Because each child is unique, materials and activities must also be individually appropriate and responsive to individual differences. An activity may be developmentally appropriate for a particular age group yet irrelevant, meaningless, boring, and inappropriate for a particular child. For example, cutting with scissors may be

age appropriate for older four-year-olds but individually inappropriate for Lashonda, who is in your group but lacks fine motor skills and is more interested in tearing paper. Cutting with scissors may be a developmentally appropriate activity for most of your older fours but would not be a good instructional match, given what we know about Lashonda.

3. Family/Culture

Children grow, learn, and develop within the context of their family in which they learn values, beliefs, and ways of behaving. Teachers must recognize and respect each child's social and cultural context. A cultural group may disapprove of an activity that is appropriate in other ways. For example, finger painting may be developmentally and individually appropriate for Xu but disturbing for her parents who value neatness and cleanliness and warn their child to stay clean at school. Imagine the look on their faces when they come to pick up their daughter and her hands are stained and her clothes splashed with paint.

How do the NAEYC guidelines for developmentally appropriate practice apply to early childhood art education? In a National Art Education Association briefing paper, Colbert and Taunton (1992) suggest three major themes evident in high-quality, developmentally appropriate early art education. These include the following:

1. Children need many opportunities to create art.
2. Children need many opportunities to look at and talk about art.
3. Children need to become aware of art in their everyday lives.

Toddlers are able to explore and manipulate art materials, but they cannot be expected to produce finished art. Although older children's scribbles are more controlled than those of toddlers, and three-year-olds will create and even give names to designs with horizontal and vertical strokes, adults should not expect representational products from this age group.

The NAEYC guidelines suggest that children be given developmentally appropriate art materials. This means that toddlers should be given such art materials as large crayons, watercolor markers, and large sheets of paper. It also means that four- and five-year-olds should have daily opportunities for aesthetic expression and appreciation of art and music. In the primary grades, art and other expressive activities

NAEYC Guidelines for Developmentally Appropriate Art Practice

Curriculum planning emphasizes learning as an interactive process. Teachers prepare the environment for children to learn through active exploration and interaction with adults, other children, and materials. Workbooks, worksheets, coloring books, and adult-made models of art products for children to copy are not appropriate for young children, especially those younger than six. Basic learning materials and activities for an appropriate curriculum include (among others) supplies of paper, water-based paint and markers, and other materials for creative expression.

Adults provide opportunities for children to choose from among a variety of activities, materials, and equipment; and time to explore through active involvement. Adults facilitate children's engagement with materials and activities and extend the child's learning by asking questions or making suggestions that stimulate children's thinking.

Children of all ages need uninterrupted periods of time to become involved, investigate, select, and persist at activities. The teacher's role in child-chosen activity is to prepare the environment with stimulating, challenging activity choices and then to facilitate children's engagement.

Once we understand that young children learn by active involvement with people and by manipulating objects, it becomes clear that such activities as coloring books, worksheets, and models made of clay or other materials that children are expected to imitate are inappropriate.

What do we know about toddlers? We know that toddlers are very active. They are better at moving about and chattering than sitting still and listening. They have very short attention spans and like quickly to move from activity to activity. Their large muscle and gross motor skills are better developed than their small muscle, fine motor, and eye-hand coordination. They can be very egocentric and are just being introduced to social skills. They are very oral and like to put things in their mouths. How can we use this information to plan art experiences? The following is a set of guidelines useful in deciding whether an art activity is appropriate or inappropriate.

Appropriate for toddlers:

- Toddlers are given appropriate art media such as large crayons, watercolor markers, and large paper.
- Adults expect toddlers to explore and manipulate art materials and do not expect them to produce a finished art product.
- Adults never use food for art because toddlers are developing self-regulatory skills and must learn to distinguish between food and other objects that are not to be eaten. Toddlers need very close supervision.

Inappropriate for toddlers:

- Toddlers are "helped" by teachers to produce a product, follow the adult-made model, or color a coloring book or ditto sheet.
- Tactilely sensitive toddlers are required to finger paint or are given edible finger paint or play dough because they will probably put it in their mouths.

What do we know about three-year-olds? Threes are less oral than toddlers and are beginning to develop basic social skills. They will spend more time working at a task. They are less impulsive and more self-controlled than toddlers. They have developed some basic fine motor skills, though they have difficulty manipulating very small pieces. How can we use this information to plan art experiences? The following is a set of guidelines useful in deciding whether an art activity is appropriate or inappropriate.

Appropriate for threes:

- Adults provide many materials and opportunities for three-year-olds to develop fine motor skills, such as crayons, brushes, paints, markers, play dough, and blunt scissors.
- Although the scribbles of three-year-olds are more controlled than those of toddlers, and they will create designs with horizontal and vertical strokes, and will sometimes name their drawings and paintings; adults do not expect a representational product.
- Art is viewed as creative expression and exploration of materials.

NAEYC Guidelines for Developmentally Appropriate Art Practice (continued)

Inappropriate for threes:

- Adults expect children to demonstrate fine motor skills by cutting out figures or shapes, by coloring within the lines in coloring books or on ditto sheets, or by following the teacher's directions and models to create identical art products.
- When children draw or paint pictures, teachers ask, "What is it?" and lead children to believe that only a representational picture is valued.

What do we know about four- and five-year-olds? They have better self-control and basic social skills. They enjoy working with others on group projects. Improved eye-hand coordination and fine motor skills enhance their success using art tools. They are fairly fluent in oral expression and enjoy dictating words or stories to accompany their art work. They also use invented spelling as they attempt to write down their own words. How can we use this information to plan art experiences? The following is a set of guidelines useful in deciding if an art activity is appropriate or inappropriate.

Appropriate for fours and fives:

- Children have daily opportunities for aesthetic expression and appreciation through art and music.
- Children experiment and enjoy various forms of art and music.
- A variety of art media is available for creative expression such as easel and finger painting and clay.

Inappropriate for fours and fives:

- Art and music are provided only when time permits.
- Art consists of coloring predrawn forms, copying an adult-made model of a product, or following other adult-prescribed directions.

What do we know about school-age children? Older children have longer attention spans and can work fairly independent of direct supervision. They are very social and easily make, break up, and reunite with friends. They are successful with ongoing projects that involve cooperation and joint effort. They read and write their own stories. Developmentally, they are able to handle more complex art media. How can we use this information to plan art activities? The following is a set of guidelines useful in deciding whether an art activity is developmentally appropriate or inappropriate.

Appropriate for school-age children:

- Art, music, movement, woodworking, drama, and dance (and opportunities for other physical activity) are integrated throughout each day as relevant to the curriculum and as needed for children to express themselves, aesthetically and physically, and to express ideas and feelings.
- Specialists work with classroom teachers and children.
- Children explore and experiment with various art media and forms of music.

Inappropriate for school-age children:

- Art, music, and physical education are taught as separate subjects only once a week.
- Specialists do not coordinate closely with classroom teachers.
- Representational art, evaluated for approximation to reality, is emphasized.
- Children are expected to follow specific directions resulting in identical projects
- So-called crafts substitute for artistic expression.

should be integrated as relevant to the curriculum and as needed for children to express themselves aesthetically and physically. Children can also use art to express ideas and feelings. It is sometimes appropriate to call in specialists to work with classroom teachers and children.

A recommended early childhood art program will involve legitimate artistic media. Children work with paint, watercolor, collage, paper, clay, printing, design, resist, and sculpture—the same media that adult artists use. Providing legitimate artistic media tells children, "You are creative artists, and you can be trusted with the appropriate tools and media." The materials, equipment, and supplies related to these media are basic, moderately expensive, and good investments. Paintbrushes, easels, and watercolor sets of good quality will last if given proper care. Generally, buying in advance and in bulk gets the major art expense for the year out of the way. Expense, however, does not guarantee creative art. For example, one teacher distributed a precut doll shape to a small group of three-, four-, and five-year-old children. The children were instructed to glue on button eyes and precut fur for hair, sprinkle glitter, and to attach an ice-cream stick base. The activity was costly and short-lived, and it involved little artistic processing. The doll puppets all looked identical. Creative input from the children was absent. Many parents and local businesses would be willing to donate extra fabric, trim, magazines, and papers to supplement the basic artistic media and hold down expenses. See Appendices A and B for a list and sources of artistic junk.

10. Be Available to All Children

Art should be available to all children. Older infants who can hold a nontoxic marker or crayon can be subtly guided to make marks on paper. They can scribble while seated in a high chair or sprawled atop a long roll of paper. Toddlers enjoy painting and using markers, crayons, and clay. The preschooler can be provided with an even wider array of legitimate artistic media. Art is neither masculine nor feminine; both boys and girls should be encouraged to engage in art. If the easels or art center become monopolized by one sex, a teacher may need to do some social engineering. For example, girls in one kindergarten were drawing pictures of food to take to the housekeeping center. The boys avoided both the art and housekeeping centers and concentrated in the block area. After two days of this sex-segregated play, the teacher took action. She suggested that the boys work together with the girls in building a restaurant. One boy designed his own play money from scrap construction paper. Another painted a store sign.

All children should have access to art. Because art can foster a child's feelings of esteem and success, it is vital for children who have special needs, exceptionalities, or multicultural backgrounds. Art gives them the vehicle to validate themselves by making a personal statement: "I am unique, and my art proves it!"

Some teachers report that they use art as a reward for work completed. The good students get to visit the art center or engage in art. Others may be denied art. Although misbehavior and incomplete work cannot be tolerated, the punishment does not fit the crime. The children in question may be those who need art

the most. Academic deficiencies or behavior problems leave them with few routes for success in school. Success in art may generalize to success in academics. Art can also be used as a springboard to academics. For example, eight-year-old Dusty is a poor reader who draws detailed hot rods. Perhaps his hot rod drawings could be used as a way to help him talk, read, and write about his interests.

ACTIVITIES MASQUERADING AS CREATIVE ART

Merely labeling an activity *art* is no guarantee that the activity will have artistic merit. Likewise, uncreative activities are often mistakenly called *creative*. Too many activities masquerade as creative art. Some of these include the following:

- photocopied or mimeographed sheets
- cut-and-paste activities
- tracing patterns
- coloring book pages
- dot-to-dot sheets
- crafts
- holiday gifts
- seatwork or busywork

Although these activities may have some merit for developing fine motor control or eye-hand coordination, they lack artistic and creative merit. Activities that masquerade as creative art share the following three criteria:

1. an emphasis on teacher input and direction
2. a high degree of structure
3. a specified product

Workbooks, worksheets, coloring books, and teacher-made models of art products for children to copy are not appropriate for young children, especially those younger than six (Bredekamp, 1987).

Cherry and Nielsen (1999) also recommend avoiding the use of models and patterns. They believe that if art is to be used as a means for creative expression and for the development of aesthetic values, then children should be allowed to use art materials in their own way, without being required to follow a model or pattern that a teacher has created for them. A common misconception is that children need to have a new type of art project or different art materials each day. In desperation, teachers resort to patterns and cutouts in the quest for presenting something new and different. Cherry and Nielsen (1999) disagree. They believe that, in actuality, young children like repetition. This is evident in their request for hearing a favorite story told over and over or a favorite book read again and again. The same holds true for music, finger plays, as well as dramatic play and block play scenarios. Children enjoy repeatedly processing with the basic art media as well as a teacher's addition of new and different materials which extend the basic activity. For example, children enjoy painting at the easel on a daily basis. They also appreciate the introduction of new and different colors, paper shapes, and painting tools. This provides repetition and eventual mastery with the basic media but without it becoming too boring or monotonous. The keys are repetition and variety. Teachers who work with young children with special needs find that these children not only need and enjoy repetition to enhance learning but also welcome elements of novelty and variety.

Lowenfeld and Brittain (1987) warn against the use of photocopies, coloring books, and patterns by citing the research of Russell and Waugaman (1952), who found that children who had originally been interested in spontaneously drawing birds lost their creativity when exposed to workbook drawings. They quickly changed their once-creative pictures to resemble the common stereotype. Photocopies, cut-and-paste activities, and tracing patterns (see Figure 10–10) have a high degree of teacher input and direction, with the responsibility for making art shifted from child to teacher. For example, Miss Sally drew a teddy bear and ran off copies for the children to color. They were encouraged to take their time, color neatly, and stay within the lines. The teacher imposed her concept of what a teddy bear should look like. A photocopy can easily become a cut-and-paste activity. Miss Sally could have asked the children to cut out their teddy bears

along with a predrawn hat and cane and paste them on construction paper. Or she could have provided cardboard patterns for the children to trace. These activities, however, lack artistic merit because the focus is on the teacher's concept of a teddy bear, not the child's. Instead, Miss Sally could have encouraged each child to represent a personally meaningful symbol of a teddy bear without concern for realistic use of color, shape, size, body parts, placement, or detail.

Teacher-directed art activities usually entail a high degree of structure, reflected in specific directions and step-by-step progression. The teddy bears in Miss Sally's room looked alike and appeared mass-produced.

Other examples of highly structured activities include coloring book pages and dot-to-dot sheets. Pages from coloring books reflect the artist's concept and representation of an object. A steady provision of coloring books frustrates young artists and leads them to question their own creative ability. Further, it denies them practice in making personally meaningful art. Instead, they merely complete someone else's art. This may be why some older children are at a loss when asked to draw anything they want. They have become too dependent upon coloring books and cannot create for themselves.

An anticipated response in defense of coloring books is that children like them. Children, however, are not the best judges of what is good or bad for them. For example, children like candy and some would eat it to the exclusion of vegetables, but adults would not allow this to happen. The same holds true for coloring books and creativity. A steady diet of coloring books inhibits a child's creative expression.

Dot-to-dot pages add an element of math to the coloring book page. Connecting the dots in proper numerical sequence results in closure by completing the picture.

Highly structured, teacher-directed art activities often focus on making a finished product, like Miss Sally's teddy bears. Sometimes teachers display their own finished products as standards or models. Although well-intended, this practice will frustrate young artists who cannot trace, color, cut, or paste as well. Although a teacher quickly adds, "Do your best," children know that their products will never come close to looking like their teacher's.

So-called crafts and holiday gifts are examples of finished products that masquerade as creative art. Two small stones glued to a larger stone can be painted to resemble a frog. It looks like something, and it is useful in that it can be used as a paperweight. However, creative art may not look like anything and may not have any use beyond the initial joy of self-expression.

Figure 10-10 This activity is masquerading as art.

Figure 10-11 The perfect gift for a child to give.

Figure 10-13 What can I make the paint brush do?

Moyer (1990) has identified practices that do not challenge children to grow artistically. These include providing children with premarked papers to fill with specific colors, giving them patterns to produce an identifiable product and expecting them to replicate the teacher's model step by step. Children become dependent on patterns; they learn very early that their ideas and artistic expressions are not valued by the teacher and therefore are unacceptable. When the emphasis is on the end product rather than on the process, undesirable competition results. Displaying only the "best" artwork, or the products that most nearly meet the teacher's example, discourages individual expression. Moreover, it is difficult, if not impossible, to discuss individual art if all the children have produced identical work.

"Crafts" are often given as holiday gifts. Most parents would be delighted to receive a paperweight or pencil holder constructed by their child. Although it is important to please parents, it is equally important to

meet the creative needs of children. Providing for child input, planning, decision making, and creative processing guarantees that each finished product will be as unique and individual as the child who produced it. Gifts need not involve time or expense. A completed finger painting could also be ironed flat, framed, wrapped, and presented to parents as a gift (see Figure 10–11). Taking the time to talk with parents about the nature of children's art will help them appreciate the finger painting for the unique gift it is. See Figure 10–12 for a Christmas card Mandy made for her family.

Alternatives to activities that masquerade as art take a commitment of time and planning. Art should not be used merely to fill in extra time before lunch or dismissal. Coloring in the figures on a math, phonics, or reading-readiness workbook sheet is not art. Generally, the figures are small, blurred, and drawn by someone other than the child. This is seatwork or busywork, not art. Art is more like turning your finished work over and drawing whatever you want.

In Figure 10–13, Samantha is totally involved and caught up in making art her way.

See boxes on pages 236–237 for various approaches to teaching art activities.

 **PAPER ART**

Children have many experiences with paper long before they enter school. Some papers are scrap, whereas the pages in books are not to be written on, cut, or torn. Children see their parents handle paper money and write checks. Greeting cards and mail are made out of paper. Paper serves many purposes. Art activities dealing with paper will be introduced in

Figure 10-12 The artist has been personally expressive.

this section. Instructions for making paper are also provided.

Processing with Paper

What can an artist do with paper? Many different things can be done to and with paper. As children experiment and explore with paper, they find that it can be any of the following:

- torn
- cut
- glued or pasted
- taped
- stapled
- folded
- slit
- curled
- pleated
- twisted
- braided
- fringed
- looped
- scored (made to curl by pulling it against the blade of scissors)
- chained (rings or loops made into a continuous chain)
- punched with a hole punch
- pricked with a toothpick (and placed against a contrasting-color background)
- made into a cone or cylinder
- ringed (a strip made into a crown, headband, or bracelet)

Cones and Cylinders

Children will discover that paper can be folded into three-dimensional forms, including cubes, cones, and cylinders. Cones and cylinders are easy to make. Rolling paper into a tube shape makes a cylinder. Cylinders can be creatively combined to make people, animals, buildings, castles, towers, tunnels, spyglasses, and vehicles. A round piece of paper can be cut to its center and gently turned to form a cone. Cones suggest heads, bodies, animal beaks, hats, ice-cream cones, horns, teepees, and mountains.

Monofold Creation

Fold a piece of paper in half once (monofold). Keep the creased edge at the top. Children can draw an object and carefully cut through both thicknesses of paper. The object, however, must remain joined at the top. When the paper is opened, the vehicle, animal, or object will be joined at the top and able to stand up. It will be symmetrical.

Stars and Snowflakes

Round or square paper of thin weight, such as tissue paper or origami paper, can be used. Construction pa-

per is too thick to fold and cut through. Coffee filters are an ideal size, shape, and thickness. Encourage children to fold their paper into quarters (in half and half again). Older children with good scissoring skills can continue folding. The more folds there are, the thicker the paper will be to cut through but the more intricate the design. Encourage children to cut out small snips or to make angular cuts into the folded paper without cutting through or cutting any off. Carefully open. Refold and continue cutting if not satisfied with the star or snowflake. Finished products can be taped over windows for the light to shine through. Or an adult can seal them between two pieces of wax paper using a warm iron.

Paper Weaving

The teacher may need to provide most if not all of the paper for this activity. Fold a 9 × 12 sheet of construction paper in half either way. Cut slits from the folded edge out, stopping about 1 inch from the opposite end. The slits can be even or randomly spaced. They can be cut straight, curved, or jagged. Open the paper. Measure how long a strip of paper must be to be woven through the slits from one end to the other. Make several strips. Again, the paper strips can be cut straight, curved, or jagged. Children can weave with the paper strips, using an over-under motion. The next row will necessitate an opposite under-over motion. The ends of the woven paper strips can be secured with a dab of paste or glue. Trim paper strips that extend beyond the edge of the paper.

Cutting the paper and strips straight produces a neat, uniform checkerboard effect. Cutting strips of different widths or angles produces an optical illusion-type design. Try to provide a variety of papers to weave with. Adding strips of wallpaper provides a dramatic touch. Paper weaving is like finger painting, a basic early childhood art activity with many possibilities. Try adding ribbon, lace, yarn, and pipe cleaners along with your paper strips.

Magazine Picture Weaving

Children can find a large picture in a magazine that they find interesting. National Geographic, with its vivid animal pictures, is highly recommended. Carefully remove the page or cut the picture into a large square or rectangle. Cut the picture into strips. Use the guidelines given in the paper-weaving activity to make a larger slit frame. Weave the magazine picture strips. The result will be a slightly distorted but visually pleasing rearrangement of the selected picture. Or weave the strips in incorrect order for a visually

Teaching Art to Children: Different Viewpoints

The author views art developmentally as a child-centered, open-ended, creative, self-expressive emergent activity that is discovered by the child. The teacher takes a hands-off approach being more stage setter and facilitator than instructor. In turn, the author does not directly endorse teaching art to young children in the early years through the K–3 primary grades. Yet it is important to teach skills such as how to hold scissors or how to use a glue bottle. Our goal is to teach children how to have enough control over the media to be able to use them creatively. But this is very different from teaching children how to draw a tree with branches. Edwards and Nabors (1993) insist that the focus of early childhood art be on the process. They believe it is wonderful when children produce something that is theirs, that they have created and own, but that product must not be the ultimate goal. They go on to add that older children may need specific procedures for completing a project, but for young children these techniques should remain closely guarded secrets and revealed only if a child asks. According to Seefeldt (1995), children can be taught to draw in ways that are more mature and complex than is typical for their age. But when they do so to please a teacher, then their drawing is no more an expression of their experiences or ideas than is coloring in a worksheet or cutting out a pattern.

Older children need instruction in art to advance artistically. Gardner (1980) sees the years of middle childhood as a time when older children develop particular technical skills and become susceptible, if not eager, for specific training. They will not magically discover all there is to know through trial and error processing. Wright (1997) believes it is inappropriate to believe that children should be left to their own learning devices in arts education. She believes that children's knowledge of, skill in, and attitudes toward the arts can be enhanced with sensitive guidance. Adults must be present without being intrusive. The teacher must encourage children's response to aesthetic qualities and model interactive dialogue through hands-on and "words-on" approaches.

There are different opinions regarding the teaching of art and the role of the early childhood art educator. For example, teachers in the Reggio Emilia tradition do provide opportunities for children to draw from life. According to Seefeldt, teachers in Reggio think of children's art as very serious work and take a very active role in children's art making, probably more direct when compared with art education in the United States. Strategies used in Reggio include modeling, praising, and showing children how to draw. Based on her visit to Reggio, Hendrick (1997) observed that children are often asked to first draw their ideas, e.g., cherry blossoms, and are then taken to visit real cherry blossoms in the garden. There they are encouraged to observe the flowers closely, draw them on the spot, and compare their first drawing with those done after the visit. The process greatly enhances the children's powers of observation. It is not intended to promote copying. Edwards, Gandini, et al. (1993) believe that Reggio children's extensive experience of drawing from observation does not appear to inhibit their desire or ability to draw or paint imaginatively. Contrary to fears, the work of the Reggio Emilia children suggests that they appear to be competent in both representational and non-representational art; realistic and abstract visual expression. They add that the visual arts are integrated into the work simply as additional languages available to young children not yet very competent in conventional writing and reading. The key is taking one's cues from the children. For example, if a child asks a teacher's assistance in how to draw a cherry blossom one would not ignore the request. Nor would a teacher simply do the work for the child. One would use the Vygotskian (1986, 1987) strategy of scaffolding. Observe what the child can do and match it with an instructional strategy that is optimally challenging. For example, if the child is capable of drawing lines, help her see how branches can be represented with different types of lines. Carefully examine the bud; break down the whole into its smaller shapes.

How Would You Approach This Art Activity?

It's spring and the flowers are blooming. Cherry blossoms in shades of pink, red, and white are everywhere. For many children, cherry blossoms are strongly embedded in their culture. There are cherry blossom festivals and the flowers find their way into many households. Two teachers are planning their upcoming weekly art activities. Both have decided to have the children make cherry blossoms. One teacher provided white sheets of paper upon which were drawn brown branches (see Figure 10-14). Children were given small squares of tissue paper and shown how to twist them into shapes resembling cherry blossoms. They were instructed to glue them on to their branches. Each white paper was mounted onto a black sheet of construction paper and displayed. There appears to be some variation among the different art samples.

The second teacher took a different approach. She brought in a vase of cherry blossoms on branches. Children were encouraged to use their senses to look at, gently touch, and smell the flowers. The vase was displayed in the middle of the art table and children were given the opportunity to make their own cherry blossom picture if they wanted. Paint and papers were provided along with other supplies, including glue, usually kept at the art center. Figures 10-15, and 10-16 capture the children hard at work. When completed, the art work was displayed (see Figure 10-17).

What can you say about either or both of these approaches to art? Compare and contrast the two displays depicted in Figures 10-14 and 10-17. How does each relate to the discussion in this chapter regarding teacher- vs. child-centered art?

Figure 10-14

Figure 10-15

unexpected effect. Or interchange strips from different pictures—for example, an animal head with a child's body.

Stuffed Paper Pillow

Each child will need one large grocery bag for this activity. Cut through the three joined edges until only the flat front and back remains. Encourage children to draw a simple but large object that fills up most of the paper bag. Animals, vehicles, or shapes with a minimum of fine detailing are recommended. Carefully cut

through all layers. Separate the layers into a top and a bottom. Children can decorate the front and back sides with crayons, markers, or paint. Later, they can use a stapler to carefully staple the outer edge shut while slowly stuffing the bag with small pieces of wadded newspaper. Continue to staple and stuff.

Figure 10-16

I'm Stuffed

Children will need a length of mural or butcher paper that is slightly more than twice their length. Fold the paper in half for double layers and have the child lie on top. Trace around the child with a thick pencil, crayon, or marker. Cut out the outline. Encourage children to decorate with crayons, markers, or paint. Provide a mirror for them to note the color and placement of facial features and clothing. Use a stapler to carefully staple shut the outer edge while slowly stuffing with small pieces of wadded newspaper. Continue to staple and stuff. Children will enjoy taking their "twin" home.

Paper Strip Critters

Strips of paper ½-inch and wider can be formed into three-dimensional characters or animals. Three strips on top of one another form a snowman. An accordion-pleated strip of paper becomes a snake. The possibilities are endless. Try to suggest possibilities without telling children what to make. Encourage them to play around with the paper and see what results.

Paper Mosaic

A mosaic is a design made by placing pieces of tile, stone, glass, or other material very close together. Children can do a mosaic using paper. Begin by drawing a fairly simple large picture on a piece of drawing paper. Cut out small squares of colored paper. Here is where scrap pieces of construction paper that have been saved come in handy. Squares can range from ½ to 1 inch square, depending on the age of the child. A teacher may decide to use the paper cutter to cut up squares for young children. Squares can be sorted by color and placed in an egg carton for easy access. Encourage children to paste them inside their sketched picture. Mosaic squares should be close but not touch-

Figure 10-17

ing. A paper mosaic takes much time, planning, and patience. It need not be completed in one sitting and is recommended for older children.

Paper Relief

Relief refers to a raised or three-dimensional effect. One way to get this is to build up layers of paper. Begin with a cardboard base. Use additional cardboard or thick paper to cut out designs or pieces of a picture. Continue building up layers. Cut additional shapes, but make them smaller than the previous ones. Continue to cut and glue smaller pieces until a design or picture with different levels results. This activity takes much time and patience and is recommended for older children.

Grocery Bag Top Hat

Children enjoy decorating and wearing their grocery bag top hats. Each child will need a large grocery bag. Open bag and stand on its open side. Help the child gather one side and begin rolling up. This forms the brim. To make it child-sized, gather the paper as you roll. Rotate bag and roll up all four sides until you get a top hat shape that fits the child's head. Remove and let child decorate with paint or trims.

Paper Making

This activity involves making decorative papers from recycled papers. There are many variations. It is a multistep process but not difficult. It does take much advanced preparation and one-on-one assistance. Try the process out yourself first before doing it with children.

Preparation:

1. Collect the following:
   - any nonplastic and nonmetallic papers that will easily break down when soaked in water: toilet paper, facial tissue, grocery bags, paper towels, paper napkins, bond paper, newspaper, construction paper, junk mail, computer paper, tissue paper, egg cartons, gift wrap, glossy magazines, old yellow- and white-page phone books
   - one or more kitchen blenders
   - measuring cup
   - sponges
   - flat tool such as a blunt plastic knife (use with adult supervision)
   - old cloth towels for blotting
   - embroidery hoops (can be shared)
   - mesh window screen (fine), one piece per child
   - tubs or dish pans (at least two)
   - additions to the paper: dryer lint, rose petals, metallic confetti, potpourri, dried flowers, scents, spices like cinnamon, perfume, Easter grass, glitter, coffee grounds, tea leaves, small seeds, thread

2. Fill tubs about 6 inches full with water. Cover tables with layers of newspaper. Place tubs on newspaper.

3. Make screen frames by placing the mesh screen inside the two pieces of the embroidery hoop and tighten the screw. Hoops can be shared, but children each need their own piece of mesh screen. Measure size of the hoop and allow extra screen to extend beyond the edge for a tight fit.

Process:

1. Choose your paper and tear into approximately twenty 1- or 2-inch squares. Place in kitchen blender and add 4 cups of water. Put on lid and grind at lowest speed for a few seconds or until paper has turned into pulp. Add more water and repeat at high speed. Paper makers call this pulp a *slurry.*

2. Pour pulp into another tub filled half full with water. Mix pulp with hand. Add any of the desired additions listed earlier. Use sparingly, for example, a spoonful of scent.

3. Put screen frame into tub vertically. Slide screen frame on bottom of tub to reach pulp and additions that have sunk to the bottom.

4. Gently stir pulp with one hand while lifting screen to catch pulp and any additions. You want pulp and any additions to float and evenly settle on top of screen. Use both hands to lift screen out, allowing excess water to drain through screen. Gently blot with sponge. You should have a thin layer of pulp with no holes or thin spots. If not, turn screen upside down and lightly tap it in water to remove pulp. Repeat steps.

5. When satisfied with layer of pulp, remove screen from the frame (hoop) without disturbing the pulp on top. Lay pulp-covered screen on a flat surface and use cloth towels to gently blot. Let thoroughly air dry by placing the screen out in the sun.

6. When dry, run finger around bottom edge to lightly lift edge of paper from screen. If necessary, use a flat tool to separate the dried paper from the screen and carefully peel.

Hint: The color of your homemade paper depends on the color of your original paper. Newspaper ink runs and muddies the pulp. Sort and use similar colors with construction or tissue paper.

Hint: Add a small amount of food coloring or liquid watercolor to your pulp while it is in the blender, if color is desired.

Hint: Coarse paper such as grocery bags may need to soak overnight to break down.

Hint: Coarse additives such as flower petals and seeds can be added to the ground pulp in the blender and blended for a few seconds if you want them to blend in rather than stand out. Dryer lint must be blended or it will produce large lumps.

Hint: If there is no blender available, children can use rotary egg beaters. Or put pulp in a jar with a lid and shake.

Hint: Although young children need the sturdy hoop frame, school-age children can use berry baskets for retrieving pulp. Follow the above steps. You can also use old coffee cans.

Use a can opener to remove the top and bottom lids. Hold screen over one end of can and use as you would the hoop in above steps.

Hint: This variation uses a kitchen whisk and adds cornstarch for a creamy consistency. Let watery paper mixture sit overnight. Use a wire whisk and beat the watery paper mixture into a pulp in tub. Dissolve 3 tablespoons of cornstarch in one cup of water. Add the dissolved cornstarch to the pulp in tub and stir thoroughly. Submerge the screen into the creamy mixture and remove the pulp following the above steps.

Molded Paper

Follow the above steps but mold pulp into fancy ice-cube trays or candy molds rather than drying flat. Make sure excess water is completely drained. Molded paper can be carefully removed by gently tapping the tray. Given their thickness, allow ample time to dry thoroughly. Molded paper can be used as beads on a necklace or for holiday decorations. It can also be used in collage or glued onto folded paper for a greeting card.

Hint: Lightly spraying the mold with cooking oil makes the molded paper easy to remove.

SUMMARY

Sometimes activities that lack artistic or creative merit masquerade as art. Perhaps teachers merely forget to examine critically what they do with children. This unit provided some criteria or guidelines to help determine what early childhood art should be. Art activities that allow all children to be actively engaged, personally expressive, and creative were recommended. Art should also be success-oriented and intrinsically motivating. It should allow for both process and product, be developmentally appropriate, allow for experimentation and discovery, and involve legitimate artistic media. Not all those criteria apply to any one activity. They can, however, be used as guidelines for planning appropriate art experiences.

Key Terms

child-centered   intrinsic motivation   teacher-guided
developmentally appropriate   teacher-directed

Suggested Activities

1. Observe a teacher involved in an art activity. Use the continuum of teaching approaches to decide whether the activity was teacher-directed, teacher-guided, or child-centered.
2. Use the continuum of teaching approaches to plan a single art activity in three different ways:
   • structured and teacher-directed
   • unstructured and child-centered
   • teacher-guided
3. Recall your earliest experiences with art. What did you do? Did you enjoy art? Why? How did your parents or teachers respond to your art? How do you feel at present about your artistic development? What, if anything, has happened since your childhood to influence your feelings and abilities in art? Write your impressions, feelings, and thoughts in a brief one-page diary entry.

4. Observe an experienced teacher conducting an art activity with a group of young children. Does the activity require the children to be creative? List specific suggestions for making the activity more creative.
5. Visit an early childhood center during art time. Critique the ongoing art activity using our ten-point criteria or guidelines for recommended art activities. Does the activity masquerade as art?
6. Ms. Wilton, a kindergarten teacher, has made sturdy cardboard stencils of a cornucopia and harvest food as a tracing and coloring activity for her unit on fall. Critique this art activity. Suggest an alternative if necessary.
7. Facilitate paper art activities with children.

Review

1. What are the indicated three points along a continuum of approaches to teaching?

   X _____ X _____ X _____

   1. _____ 2. _____ 3. _____

2. What is the correct approach to teaching for each corresponding activity?

   a. The children are free to explore at the art tables or easels.

   b. The teacher encourages children to design their own Valentine's Day cards for their parents. She provides paint and paper.

   c. Children cut out the outline of a heart traced by their teacher. The teacher writes, "I Love You Mom and Dad" across the front.

3. Determine whether each of the following is true or false.

   a. Art should allow children to be creative.

   b. Art should always result in something to take home.

   c. Children should be externally motivated to do art.

   d. Art activities should be planned according to a child's development.

   e. Discovering and experimenting through art are a waste of precious time.

   f. Art activities for young children should take no longer than eight to ten minutes to complete.

   g. Art activities should be planned to ensure a child's success.

   h. The finished art product is more important than the steps leading up to it.

   i. Art is best used as a reward for children who do their work or behave.

   j. It is important for children's art to resemble very closely what the teacher had in mind when developing the activity.

4. A teacher has photocopied a bunny pattern for a unit on spring. Children will color, cut, and paste bunnies on egg-shaped pieces of purple construction paper. Critique the creative merits of this activity. Is this an example of child-centered art or a teacher-directed project? Justify your position. Offer specific suggestions for making it more creative. How might you plan a spring art activity without using any patterns?

5. Which of the following activities are masquerading as creative art?

   a. Staying within the lines and neatly coloring in the pages in a holiday coloring book.

   b. Cutting and pasting a picture of a seal carefully drawn by the teacher.

   c. Using watercolors to paint a picture that shows what each child liked best about a recent field trip.

   d. Coloring in a picture of a rocket ship, using red for all the areas marked 1, yellow for 2, and blue for 3.

6. Choose the correct term within each statement. Recommended early childhood art activities should have

   a. an emphasis on (teacher/child) input and direction.

   b. a (high/low) degree of structure.

   c. a(n) (specified/unspecified) product.

For additional art and creative development resources, visit our Web site at
www.EarlyChildEd.delmar.com

Chapter 11

Planning, Implementing, and Evaluating Art

A saying goes something like this: Fail to plan; plan to fail. This certainly applies to curriculum development in early childhood education. Although advanced planning does not guarantee success, it does increase the probability. Even the best-planned activities may not be well received for any number of reasons. For example, a teacher may plan an activity that appeals to her rather than one that matches the needs, interests, and abilities of her group. Examine the opening picture. What do you see? How do you think the teacher could have planned out this activity? What did she provide? The teacher has provided an array of tools to supplement the children's use of their hands. Some children sculpt vertically building up from a base like a snowman; others start with a base such as a body and then add appendages like legs that reach to the base. What can you say about this our featured sculptor?

Objectives

After reading this chapter, you should be able to:

- Describe the *PIE* cycle in curriculum development.
- Identify the major developmental goals in early childhood education.
- Compare and contrast strategies for integrating art into the early childhood curriculum.
- Compare and contrast the following curricular approaches: *planned, emergent,* and *Project Approach.*
- Provide a definition and rationale for capitalizing on teachable moments.
- Make and use *clay* and *play dough* with children.

INTRODUCTION

It is time to move beyond our knowledge of child development and translate it into curriculum. Actually, it is as easy as **PIE**—Plan, Implement, and Evaluate. Goals will give direction to our long-range planning; objectives are useful for our daily work with children. Our values and beliefs will influence our goals and the experiences chosen to meet these goals. Our holistic model of child development will serve as a framework to ensure that our program is child-centered and developmentally focused. Taking into account management concerns and devising effective procedures will help us implement our activity. Evaluation helps us check on our effectiveness as teachers and providers. Different teachers use different strategies in teaching. Four strategies for planning and providing art experiences will be portrayed.

TEACHER AS PLANNER AND CURRICULUM DEVELOPER

All teachers are planners and curriculum developers. Some build their own curriculum; others follow a prescribed one. **Curriculum development** involves planning what to teach and how to teach it. A unit on dinosaurs may send the beginning teacher to the library to do some research. Learning activities must be organized. Centers must be stocked with materials, equipment, and supplies that are relevant to the curricular theme. Teaching without a curriculum or plan is like traveling cross-country without a map. It does a disservice to the children and hinders professional development. Without a curriculum, the teacher operates in a random, disorganized way. Quality teaching requires planning and curriculum development.

One way of planning and developing a curriculum is to ask oneself a series of questions. These could include the following:

- WHO?
  Who am I as a teacher? What types of things do I know about and do well? What special interests or skills do I have? What do I value and believe about early childhood? Who are my children—ages, needs, interests, abilities, likes, dislikes, family, culture, background?
- WHAT?
  What do I want my children to learn, know, or be able to do?
- WHY?
  Why am I planning this activity? Why should my children know, learn, or be able to do it? Why is this important or relevant?
- HOW?
  How will I carry out this activity? How will I present it? How will I motivate the children or capture their interest? How will I know if I have been successful? How will I know if the children have learned anything? How many children can do this activity at one time? How will it be done—individually or in small groups on a rotating basis?

Types of Learning

How do young children learn? Katz (1987) identified four types of learning: knowledge, skills, dispositions, and feelings. Knowledge is information children construct through hands-on, multisensory experiences and exploration. Skills are abilities or techniques that build on and apply knowledge. Skills are developed through repetition and practice. Dispositions are inclinations or habits of the mind such as curiosity or flexibility. A disposition is an orientation to the world one has learned from working with enthusiastic role models. Feelings are the emotions associated with a learning experience.

How may the types apply to learning in the arts? Jalongo and Stamp (1997) address this question. Children construct knowledge about clay and its properties when they are given ample opportunity to process with it (see Figure 11-1). They discover that clay is solid yet malleable and can be shaped with hands or tools. They can also learn about sculptors as well as types of clay art. In turn, they build up a set of skills, including kneading and rolling along with painting and drawing. Dispositions are a major goal of aesthetic education and experience in the arts. Children interact with their peers and a more competent artist-teacher. They learn that it is safe to take risks and trust their creative impulses, to value their own work and that of others, and to persist at a task. Feelings of success should accompany a young child's artistic endeavor. Art should make children feel good, special, and unique rather than inadequate or unhappy.

Figure 11-1 What could this child be learning?

- WHERE?
  Where will this activity take place?
- WHEN?
  When will this activity take place? How long will it take?

We need to act on what we know about children and their development in developing curriculum and planning activities. We need to translate theory into practice. How do we begin? Basically, planning is as easy as PIE. The three key components of early childhood curriculum development are

- P lanning.
- I mplementing.
- E valuating.

Developing an early childhood curriculum is a lot like taking a trip. **Planning** helps us decide where we want to go. Do we want to take the fastest or the scenic route? What do we need to take along? All these concerns are taken into account during our planning. **Implementing** is similar to actually taking the trip. We think we have done a good job of planning and now are ready to depart. Implementing our trip involves reading the map, stopping as planned, and allowing for unexpected diversions. Was the trip worth it? Did it cost too much or take too long? Were the benefits appropriate to the expense? Would you do it again? How could you improve on the trip? All of these questions attempt to evaluate the trip.

Teachers follow the same steps in developing curriculum. Planning involves deciding what we want children to learn and be able to do. Planning is a continuous, ongoing process. It involves acting on what we know about children and their development in setting appropriate goals and objectives. All planning is influenced by the values and beliefs one holds about children and education.

Implementing involves two major processes. First, management concerns must be considered. Second, effective procedures for carrying out one's activity must be established.

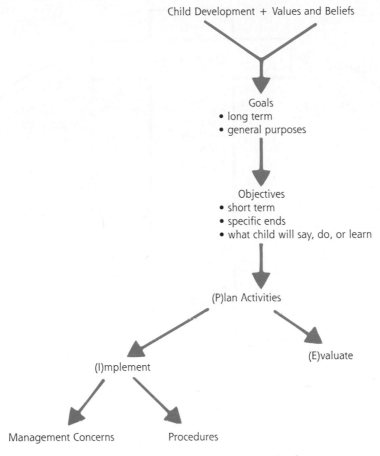

Figure 11-2 PIE model for planning and curriculum.

When **evaluating** art we attempt to assess the effectiveness of what was done by answering the following question: How do I know if what I set out to do was ever accomplished?

The three PIE components can be illustrated with the following example. A teacher could devise an art activity that would help children discover that different types of brushes can be used in painting (planning). Different brushes are located, identified, introduced, labeled, and displayed at the art center (implementing). Evaluation could entail observing the different ways children use the brushes and their ability to use many different brushes for painting. The PIE model for planning and curriculum development is depicted in Figure 11–2.

GOALS

A **goal** is something to strive for. For example, being creative is a lifelong pursuit and goal. Few reach their creative potential. A goal is like the brass ring on the merry-go-round. We reach out for it but rarely capture

it. Still, goals give direction or focus to what we do with children on a monthly or yearly basis. Translating goals into more manageable objectives helps us plan for the week, day, and hour. Try as one may, however, one can never plan completely. At times, plans will change because of unexpected or unforeseen events. The relationship between long-term and short-term planning and between goals and objectives is depicted in Figure 11–3.

The Goals of Early Childhood Education

What are some of the goals of early childhood education? Our holistic model of child development can help us further identify goals for early childhood. These may include the following:

1. PHYSICALLY (to develop):
   * large muscle or gross motor coordination
   * small muscle or fine motor coordination
   * perceptual-motor or eye-hand coordination
   * sensory awareness
   * self-care

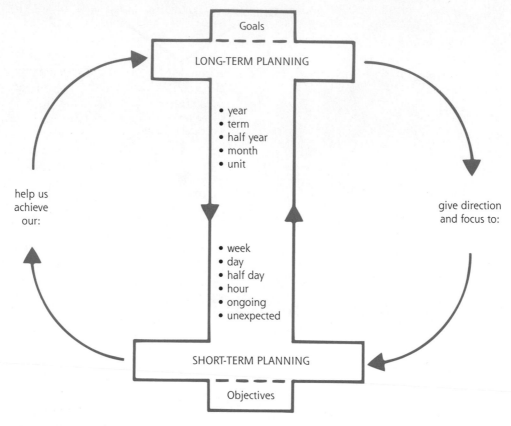

Figure 11-3 Planning cycle.

2. SOCIALLY (to develop):
   - self-understanding and acceptance
   - positive relations with others
   - positive self-concept
3. EMOTIONALLY (to develop):
   - a positive self-concept
   - positive and appropriate emotional expression
   - self-control
4. COGNITIVELY (to develop):
   - a wide range of thinking skills, including problem solving and discovery
   - concepts, skills, and learning in the curricular areas
   - language
5. CREATIVELY (to develop):
   - original thinking
   - imagination
   - verbal and nonverbal expression

If these are important developmental indicators, and if our program is child-centered, it follows that these can serve as goals or aims that can influence what we do with the children in our care. For example, creative expression, both verbal and nonverbal, is an important aspect of creative development. Art is one way

to express one's creativity nonverbally. Art activities help us reach our goals for creative development.

VALUES AND BELIEFS

Goals also reflect our **values** and **beliefs** about children—how they develop and learn, what they should know, and the purpose of schooling and life. Teachers who value early academic performance and competition may view early childhood as a time to push children ahead by filling their heads with facts. They will set goals that stress competition and early academic accomplishment and will select activities in reading, writing, and counting to meet those goals. Teachers who view early childhood as a time for discovery and social interaction will set goals for developing curiosity and will provide socializing experiences in play to meet those goals. Different values and beliefs lead us to set different goals and activities. There are no right or wrong, good or bad beliefs. Some values and beliefs may, however, suggest educational practices that are not in line with what we know about young children. The key is to consistently match what we value and believe about children and schooling with an appropriate curriculum, one that is firmly grounded in child development. Although one may value and believe in the formal teaching of reading in the early years, our working knowledge of child development suggests that this practice is developmentally inappropriate.

OBJECTIVES

Objectives are the bridge between goals and activities. They are specific and short-term intended outcomes. As a result of a given activity, we expect children to be able to say, do, or demonstrate what they have learned. Objectives can be worded loosely or in precise behavioral terms. Regardless of the wording, teachers need to be able to set objectives and develop activities to meet them. For example, Karen Thomas wants her four-year-olds to interact with others, to be creative, to be successful at what they do, and to develop fine motor control. These are some of her goals. Her objective is for children to creatively experiment with different ways of painting. She plans to bring in an old toothbrush and shaving brush for her proposed art activity.

Referring to Figure 11–2, Ms. Thomas must still address how she will implement and evaluate this proposed activity. She must consider some concerns related to classroom management.

- Where should this activity take place—indoors, outdoors, at the easel, on the floor, or at a table? These are space considerations.
- When will this activity take place—before or after snack, in the morning or afternoon? Will it be offered as an additional free-choice activity, or will it be added to the ongoing art center? How much time will be allotted? These are time considerations.
- What is needed? Ms. Thomas has already found two different types of brushes. She will also need to think about paints, paper, and smocks.
- How many children can do this activity at one time? Will everyone get a chance in one session, or will it continue throughout the week? Will children self-select to do this activity, or will she need to systematically rotate them through? These are considerations related to grouping.
- How will this activity be supervised? Will it need the constant supervision of an adult? Probably not.

Ms. Thomas will also need to think through her procedures.

How will she introduce the activity? Would a story, book, or picture be appropriate? How can she capture the children's interest and get them motivated? She chooses to introduce her activity with questions during morning circle time. "Children, today I brought in two things to show you" (holding up a toothbrush and a shaving brush). "Yes, they are both brushes. Each has a special name and use." "Yes, this one is a toothbrush. How many of you have one and use it? Good. What about the other one?" Jamie says his grandfather has one, but he does not know its name. "Jamie, what does he use it for?" "Yes, for shaving. It's called a shaving brush. You use it to mix shaving soap and water and put it over your whiskers and beard before you shave." The children giggle. "Well, I have a different idea. I wonder if we could use them in our art center?" Children gasp and groan. "Let's quietly think of how we could use these new brushes to paint." Stephanie says, "You could use the toothbrush to paint up and down just like when brushing your teeth." Lacey says, "You could just make touches of paint on your paper." "That's very good thinking. I bet there are many, many different ways to use them as we paint. Remember to try out some different ways when you get your turn."

Actually, there is no definite teacher-directed procedure, because this is a creative discovery lesson. Ms. Thomas also reminded them to explore creatively while upholding the rules.

Evaluation was ongoing. Ms. Thomas checked to see whether the brushes were being used in different ways. They were. Some children used a pulling, pushing, swirling, dabbing, dotting, stamping, or circular motion. The finished products also revealed differences. From this she concluded that her activity was a success. She had met her objective. This activity helped children become more creative and versatile in their painting. As a follow-up activity she planned to bring in two additional types of brushes from home to increase the possibilities. As a recommendation, she noted that she should bring in two of each, because it was very difficult for the children to wait their turn. Also, the child with the brushes was very engrossed and spent more time than she had planned. Even though her activity was successful as planned, she knew it could be improved upon.

Karen Thomas is an experienced preschool teacher for whom planning and curriculum development now come easily. She relies on brief plans that work for her. That was not always the case. She began teaching by

A Time and a Place for Teaching Art

There is a time and place for teaching art. Use direct instruction sparingly. The criterion is whether children could better discover a process on their own. For example, collage need not be taught. Simply laying out an array of collage items along with paper and glue is all that most children need. They will take it from there. Other activities introduced throughout the text, however, may never be discovered and therefore should be introduced in unobtrusive ways that still allow room for individual creativity. For example, some children may never discover the artistic process called resist, as discussed in Chapter 8. Introducing children to the process and how to do a resist is very different from specifying what they should make or what their finished product should look like. Art activities can also be informally introduced at times when children appear restless with processing on their own. They appear ready and motivated to move on and learn something new. The following guidelines will help you decide when and how to teach art.

1. Practice the activity by yourself. Make sure you have mastered it and it works. Think of the interests and abilities of the children in your group. How could you adapt the activity for a child with special needs or one who does not speak any English?

2. Plan and be prepared in advance. Have all the materials at hand. Waiting is stressful to children, as is having to share one art tool with several children.

3. Limit the number of children. The smaller the group, the easier to supervise and give individual assistance. Adjust the number according to their age level, complexity of the activity, and amount of art supplies available.

4. Cover table with newspapers and drape smocks over chairs. Locate a space for messy art activities to dry as well as to display.

5. Decide on a system—either group or individualized. If group, arrange materials in baskets, trays, or clear containers in center of table along with items to be shared, including tape or glue. If individualized, arrange individual setups with each child receiving a tray holding portions of all the materials needed to complete the activity. This avoids problems with sharing, waiting, and taking turns. It allows children to work at their own pace. When a child is finished, his or her tray is restocked for the next child. Involve children in the cleanup.

6. Build in choices and options by providing construction paper and paper plates, masking tape and glue, crayons and markers.

7. Reassure children waiting for a turn that they will get one. Neatly print their names and cross them off as children get their turns. This helps anxious children who fear you will forget that they were next to have a turn. It also becomes a literacy event as children read names.

8. Briefly introduce your activity. Model the process without making and displaying a finished product. Again, your aim is to help children learn a new way of doing art, rather than making art that resembles yours.

9. Allow children to go about the activity in their own ways, as long as health and safety safeguards are upheld. If they choose to ignore your invitation to do resist and want to simply color, that's OK. It does not mean you failed; it means they are simply not interested in doing it at this time. Allow them to pursue their own creative route or even leave without finishing. Serve as a resource or consultant offering minimal help and only when needed.

10. Talk with children. Focus on what they are doing. Describe colors and effort while avoiding remarks that judge their products as wonderful or beautiful.

writing extremely detailed plans. She was afraid of leaving something out. She believes that her prior experience in writing out lesson plans, although it was time-consuming at the time, has helped her become the professional early childhood educator she is today.

A lesson plan format that closely follows our model for planning and curriculum development is given here.

STRATEGIES FOR INCLUDING ART IN THE EARLY CHILDHOOD CURRICULUM

Although we have introduced goals, values, and beliefs, we have yet to systematically deal with the nuts and bolts of daily planning and curriculum development. Let us continue by studying general ways to include art in the early childhood curriculum. The examples that follow illustrate the following five strategies:

1. art as a separate activity
2. art used to extend or reinforce learning in another curricular area
3. art as a superactivity integrating several curricular areas
4. art as an integrated part of an extended unit of study
5. art as a child-directed pursuit

1. Art As a Separate Activity

A teacher may find, hear about, or read about something that sounds like a good art activity that the children would enjoy. For example, Mr. Kent was glancing through a magazine in the director's office when he got the idea for painting or printing with sponges of different geometric shapes. The children had not done this activity before. He felt it would encourage creative processing with different shapes to make new forms. The activity would also help his four-year-olds and young five-year-olds with their fine motor skills. The activity was developmentally appropriate and sounded enjoyable. He planned to do the activity the following morning, because he had not yet planned an art activity. Further, he planned separate activities for the morning, but did not try to integrate or relate them. His daily lesson plan is found below.

DAILY LESSON
TEACHER: Mr. Kent
CLASS: four- and five-year-olds
DATE: Monday
Areas/Activities:
Art—painting and printing with sponges cut into different geometric shapes

Music—sing a "silly song"
  I know an old man who had a black dog . . .
Movement—alphabet march in a circle
Concept—science (for Monday)
  Sort and discuss attributes of nature specimens.
Bring in pinecones, leaves, grass, twigs, stones, acorns, and so on.
Group—discuss weekend activities
  Encourage Ariel to discuss her hospital stay.
Snack—vegetable slices and cottage cheese dip
  Double-check for allergies to milk products.
Play—continue work on airport (block corner); restock shelves in grocery store (housekeeping)

Mr. Kent wished he had discovered this art activity last week, when they were studying geometric shapes in concept time. He did not think to find a song or movement activity that would tie in. Mr. Kent's approach is not bad or wrong. It is fragmented, with the different learning experiences left without integration or relation to each other.

2. Art Used to Extend or Reinforce Learning in Another Curricular Area

Mrs. Gomez's four-year-old pre-K group had also been studying geometric shapes during math concept time. She tried to find an art activity that would tie in. She cut sponges into geometric shapes and encouraged the children to print with them. During group or circle time, the children had a show-and-tell session during which they discussed the different shapes they invented and also named the shapes used. Art extended and reinforced what the children were learning in math. Her lesson plan for the day is found below. The arrows indicate integration between the different activities. Group time and art extended or reinforced the concept of geometric shapes discussed during math concept time.

DAILY LESSON
Mrs. Gomez
four-year-olds
Monday

Welcome:	• do calendar
	• sing good morning song
	• read Little Red Hen
Blocks:	• take large hollow blocks outside (with Mrs. Raines) if nice day
Dramatic Play:	• introduce doctors and nurses, tools, careers
	• encourage hospital play
Table Toys:	• put out Legos®, new puzzles, flannel boards

Concept Time: • math (Monday)—discuss geometric shapes
↕
Creative Arts: • sponge painting with geometric shapes
↕
Group Time: • show-and-tell with geometric shape pictures

3. Art As a Superactivity Integrating Several Curricular Areas

Ms. Lansky's kindergartners were reviewing geometric shapes. She planned to devote Monday to this review. She included the following activities in her superactiv-

---

Lesson Plan

Activity:

PLANNING

   Goals:

   Objectives:

IMPLEMENTATION

   Management concerns:

   Procedures:

EVALUATION/REFLECTION

EXTENSION/VARIATION

ity. Note the curricular areas in parentheses, indicating integration.

- Children counted and classified the different sponge shapes on the basis of color, shape, and size (math).
- They observed a dry sponge being submerged in water. They noted differences between wet and dry sponges. They put the wet sponge in the sun and predicted and observed what would happen (science).
- They took a field trip outdoors to identify geometric shapes in nature (science).
- They played shape bingo (visual discrimination, pre-reading).
- They discussed things that are hard and soft and the many uses of sponges (speaking, creative thinking).
- They listened to a story on shapes (listening).
- They printed their name or initials with rectangular shapes dipped in paint (pre-writing).
- They created their own geometric shape pictures (art).
- They listened to a march and participated in a shapes dance (music and movement).
- They moved like dry stiff sponges, sponges in a bubble bath, sponges being squeezed dry, wet sponges lying in the sun on a beach (movement).
- They discussed diving for sponges and people who dive for a living (social studies).

Ms. Lansky's approach to planning helped children integrate and coordinate all experiences related to learning about geometric shapes, as well as incidental learning about sponges (see Figure 11–4). Ms. Lansky's only objection was that she felt the children's enthusiasm for and interest in studying shapes and sponges were more than she had expected and planned for in one day's flow of activities. Chapter 12 continues our discussion of integrating art across the early childhood curriculum.

4. Art As an Integrated Part of an Extended Unit of Study

Miss Susan enjoys teaching four-year-olds through the use of units. Her units are organized around a theme, such as geometric shapes. Her units are planned for days and even weeks at a time, depending on the level of interest and involvement of her particular group. She believes that a unit approach provides a focus for all of her planning. Each activity relates to her theme. In turn, everything children experience

during the unit is somehow related to the theme under study.

Miss Susan begins by sketching out a flowchart (see Figure 11–5). She writes her theme of shapes in the center and merely writes in anything and everything related. At this point she is more concerned with terms, concepts, and understandings than with actual activities. Items on her flowchart will suggest activities. Miss Susan brainstorms with her fellow teachers sometimes, using a blackboard in working and reworking her flowchart. She may have more on her flowchart than will appear on her plan. Some concepts may be too difficult or may not translate into a specific early childhood activity.

The second step is moving from a flowchart to a general plan of activities. Miss Susan decides to allow one week for the study of shapes. She bases this decision on the interests of her particular group and her experience with teaching this theme in the past. Although she does not teach shapes exactly the same way every year, she does use her flowchart and plans as a general guide. Slowly, she is accumulating a wealth of flowcharts and thematic plans. Her weekly plan for shapes is found in Figure 11–6.

Let us compare the four strategies. Mr. Kent taught art and all other areas as separate activities. There was no integration or tie-in. Mrs. Gomez used art and group time to extend and reinforce what children were learning during math concept time. Ms. Lansky planned a superactivity, focusing on geometric shapes and sponges that integrated the day's activities. Miss Susan planned for a week around the theme of shapes. Separate activities throughout her day were all related to a study of shapes.

▶▶
N
A
E
Y
C

The first four strategies place the responsibility for curriculum development with the teacher. The problem is that the curriculum can become overly teacher-directed. What he or she plans may not be what the children want to do. There may be a mismatch between planned activities and children's interests. A well-planned unit on whales may not work for a group of children who have little interest or a pressing need to learn about whales. A good curriculum aims for a balance between the teacher-planned and the spontaneous. This should not be equated with abdicating one's role as planner and curriculum developer. Children cannot plan curriculum. This is not about replacing all organization with unplanned chaos. Children do, however, provide cues as to what interests them. A skilled observer who watches and listens as children play is privy to a host of cues. Rather than dismissing them as unimportant, seize them as indicators of what children are about. Use them as avenues for high-interest learning. In turn, the curriculum organically

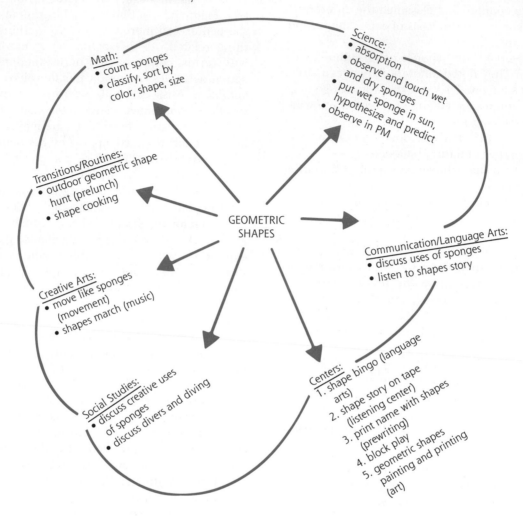

Activity: Geometric Shapes (integrated curriculum)
Grade: Kindergarten
Teacher: Lansky

Math:
• count sponges
• classify, sort by color, shape, size

Science:
• absorption
• observe and touch wet and dry sponges
• put wet sponge in sun, hypothesize and predict
• observe in PM

Transitions/Routines:
• outdoor geometric shape hunt (prelunch)
• shape cooking

GEOMETRIC SHAPES

Communication/Language Arts:
• discuss uses of sponges
• listen to shapes story

Creative Arts:
• move like sponges (movement)
• shapes march (music)

Social Studies:
• discuss creative uses of sponges
• discuss divers and diving

Centers:
1. shape bingo (language arts)
2. shape story on tape (listening center)
3. print name with shapes (prewriting)
4. block play
5. geometric shapes painting and printing (art)

Figure 11-4 Geometric shapes activity.

emerges. Based on Kristeller (1994), the comparison and contrast between a planned versus a spontaneous or emergent curriculum is depicted in Table 11–1.

5. Art As a Child-Centered Pursuit

There is a fifth strategy. Child-centered art is the type that children discover, invent, construct, and create on their own. It empowers them to be autonomous and in control. It may not look like something but children take great pride in their individual accomplishments. Child-centered art is deceivingly simple but it does not just happen. It occurs when teachers plan and subtly set the stage. Herein lies the delicate balance between teacher-directed art

and child-centered art. Let us try a food analogy. You may appreciate the opportunity to build your own salad because only you know your food preferences. You are grateful for a well-stocked salad bar that offers many items from which to choose. And so it is with art and young children. Provide easy access to a wide variety of art supplies and let children create on their own. Children are motivated indefinitely to pursue this type of art. When they temporarily run out of interest or ideas, supplement by teaching one of the activities listed throughout this book. As always, model the process without specifying the finished product. Chapter 13 continues the discussion of viewing art as a child-directed pursuit by offering guidelines for setting up and maintaining an art center.

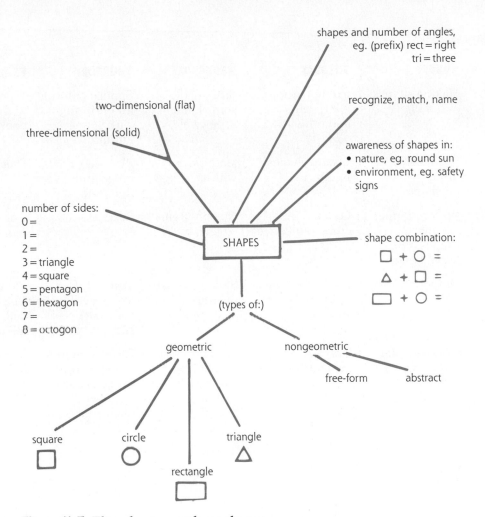

Figure 11-5 Flowchart or web on shapes.

| able 11-1 | Planned vs. Spontaneous or Emergent Curriculum |

PLANNED CURRICULUM	SPONTANEOUS OR EMERGENT CURRICULUM
is teacher-centered	is child-centered
focuses on the teacher's product	focuses on the child's processing
stresses program goals and objectives	stresses children's interests and choices
provides security and familiarity	offers challenge and risks
meets needs of the group	meets individual needs
is predictable and routine	is flexible and open
may not match children's needs and interests	matches children's needs and interests
is a solitary venture	is a joint venture between teacher and child
empowers the teacher	empowers the child

Theme: Shapes

	MONDAY	TUESDAY	WEDNESDAY	THURSDAY	FRIDAY
EXPRESSIVE ARTS	Making shapes out of clay	Making shapes using self and others	Sing shapes song: I'm a little circle . . .	Sponge painting and printing with sponges cut into shapes	Make, bake, and frost shape cookies
LANGUAGE ARTS	Read and discuss story on shapes	Locate shapes in our *ABCs*	Match word with its shape	Play shape bingo and dominoes	Dictate story: "If I were a ○, □, △, ▢ I would . . ."
MATH	Count number of square shapes on flannel board	One-to-one correspondence with: ○, □, △, ▢	Classify items by shape	Seriate circles	Conservation game: more, less, same ○, □, △, ▢ shapes
SCIENCE	Outdoor shapes hunt shapes in nature	Indoor shapes hunt: I spy . . .	Sink and float: does an item's shape make a difference?	Test out: Can all shapes roll? fall? slide?	Blow up balloon: Discuss shape deflated and inflated
SOCIAL STUDIES	Discuss facial features as shapes	Draw self using geometric shapes	Show filmstrip on housing. Discuss shapes of igloos, pyramids, teepees	Discuss shapes in foods: round pizza, square sandwich, triangular half-sandwich	Identify shapes in safety signs

Figure 11-6 Weekly Plan.

CLAY AND PLAY DOUGH

Many children will have had experience at home with commercially available Play-Doh® or the home-made type. They will find the look, smell, and feel very pleasurable. It may remind them of cookie dough.

They will approach **clay** with active processing in mind: "What can I do with clay?" By manipulating and handling it they will discover that clay can be pulled, torn, cut, rolled, and so forth. Older children may have a product in mind when they approach the clay table: "What can I make out of my lump of clay?" Three seriated balls of clay on top of each other will make a snowman. Often, there is much verbalizing

Teachable Moments

Teachable moments are those unplanned events that open the door to high-interest activity and a burst of learning. Seize those teachable moments and capitalize on their potential for learning. Two examples illustrate the concept of teachable moments. A group of three-, four- and five-year-olds found spiders out on the playground. They informally organized a spider hunt. They requested bug houses to catch them. The teacher provided plastic cups with clear

plastic wrap for lids. She offered magnifying glasses for good measure. One child wanted to kill his spider, which led to a discussion on the value of life. Another child said, "Don't hurt it; it might be somebody's mama." The children compared their spiders while focusing on size, shape, color, and markings. Legs were counted. One child expressed dismay at the "poor trapped spiders." The group voted to release the spiders to their natural habitat before coming

Teachable Moments (continued)

indoors. The teacher decided to forego her book on colors to continue the discussion on spiders. She was sure that writing spider stories and making books would dominate the afternoon. Her flexible approach to planning allowed her to capitalize on this teachable moment.

A week later, Mindy's mother brought her baby sister to school. The teacher asked if she could visit with the children. The children were told to look with their eyes and to touch by gently stroking the baby's arms and legs. They talked about size and age differences. One child asked if the newborn could stay and play. This fostered a discussion of infant capabilities and helped the children see how much they had grown and developed in only a few

short years. Mindy wanted the children to see the baby's funny belly button. This prompted an informal discussion of reproduction and the origins of maternal attachment. The interest in babies continued in the dramatic play area long after the baby left. The teacher used a small group time to graph names of children who had a baby sister or brother versus those who did not. The teacher was amazed at how much the children learned from these unplanned activities or teachable moments. She wished more of her planned activities generated this level of excitement. Be responsive to possible teacher moments and capitalize on their learning potential.

Emergent Curriculum and Project Approach

Emergent curriculum is an approach that is not new. There have always been early childhood programs with curricula that slowly developed or emerged day by day and week by week. Rather than planning out everything months in advance, informed teachers loosely planned curriculum that emerged from the children's interests and activities. Jones (1999) is given credit for introducing the term *emergent curriculum* back in the 1970s. Admittedly, the approach may be *scary* for some teachers, those who have not yet learned how to plan well. For those with some practice in observing and reflecting on child behavior, it can be a challenge to take children's interests seriously and become coplayer with them.

There are many ways to develop curriculum. Jones identifies the following: canned, embalmed, accidental/unidentified, and emergent. *Canned curriculum* comes from the district, state, textbooks, workbooks, and tests. Supposedly, it contains everything children are supposed to know. An added benefit is the claim to be "teacher-proof." Even the novice teacher will experience success. The canned curriculum will always "fit" some children but not others. It is not intended to be changed to meet the needs of individual children or teachers.

The *embalmed curriculum* is the product of a teacher who has taught for many years. The result is a stack of themes, units, and activities that appear to have worked for many years. For example, every January the children study sea life and engage in a storehouse of sea life activities. The teacher believes she has been fairly successful with this approach based on the feedback from parents, who rave about the wonderful things children bring home.

The *accidental/unidentified curriculum* just happens. It is full of starting points for an emergent curriculum but these teachable moments remain missed opportunities, for there is no follow-up by the staff. For example, in group time one child announces, "I have a new puppy dog," and another follows with, "Well, my Mom's gonna have a baby." The teacher replies, "That's nice," and the potential for extending these comments and translating them into a learning experience is lost. Perhaps the teacher perceives that it would take too much work in the form of individualizing the curriculum and departing from her preset curriculum. In critiquing the first three curriculum approaches, Jones concludes that a preplanned, rational curriculum routinizes teaching and cannot work because there are too many variables involved.

(Continued)

Emergent Curriculum and Project Approach (continued)

What about the use of themes and units? The *emergent curriculum* is different from the typical thematic approach, which is often predetermined and laid out by the teacher months in advance. For example, in February the children will learn about the color red, friendship, hearts, and love. The teacher prides herself on her planning for her activities will also tie in with Valentine's Day. By contrast, the emergent curriculum has no time constraints. The projects evolve on their own organic timetable. In theme or unit work children are rarely involved in posing questions or taking initiative for investigating the topic.

Do not think of emergent curriculum as an *anything goes* approach. On the contrary, this approach results from negotiating an intricate balance between children's interests and a teacher's understanding of what knowledge, skills, and dispositions children are ready to learn. The emergent curriculum is based on the belief that curriculum planning needs to emerge from the daily life of the children and teachers working collaboratively in a learning community.

What are the sources of emergent curriculum? Jones identifies the following nine.

1. Children's interests

   Children whose own interests are acknowledged and supported do not need to be motivated to learn; their own excitement will keep them engaged. For example, the children who were excited about the new puppy and baby.

2. Teacher's interests

   Teachers have interests of their own that are worth sharing with children.

3. Developmental tasks

   At each developmental stage there are tasks and skills to be mastered such as walking, skipping, cutting with scissors, and making friends.

4. Things in the physical environment

   Children need experience with both manufactured things and natural things such as plants and animals.

5. People in the social environment

   Children are interested in all sorts of people, who they are and what they do. Family members and community helpers have roles and experiences to share.

6. Curriculum resource materials

   Libraries and teacher resource centers are full of curriculum ideas. Modify and adapt them to fit your own setting, teaching style, and children's interests.

7. Serendipity: unexpected events

   Become skilled in on-the-spot decision making. Think of how attentive children become at the sight and sound of a fire truck racing by their playground. What about the unpredicted hailstorm?

8. Living together: conflict resolution, caregiving, and routines

   Cooperation, expressing feelings, problem solving, and conflict resolution are the daily tasks of living together that are potential sources of curriculum.

9. Values held in the school and community, family, and culture

   If peace is valued, then a learning opportunity arises when children engage in war play. If anti-bias is valued, then a learning opportunity presents itself when children exclude a peer on the basis of skin color or make fun of a child because of his or her special needs.

Are all topics equally valuable? Jones (1999) answers *No*. Adult judgment must enter in. A good topic is one of interest to the adult as well as to the children. The adult must know enough about the topic or be willing to learn. The teacher facilitates learning by introducing more ideas and confronting children's misconceptions. A good topic does not promote bias, violence, or commercial exploitation.

Although themes and units have a place in the early childhood and elementary curriculum, Katz (1994) believes

(Continued)

Emergent Curriculum and Project Approach (continued)

they are no substitutes for Projects. The Project Approach children ask questions that guide their investigation and make decisions about the activities to be undertaken. Project topics draw children's attention to questions such as: How do things work? and What do people do? According to Katz and Chard (1989) projects are one of the most child-appropriate teaching strategies. They claim the appropriateness of the project approach stems from the opportunities it provides for children to engage in learning which is both personal and meaningful by emphasizing through active participation in their own studies. Open to children's ideas and questions, projects serve to build a flexible curriculum based on children's experiences with the real world. Projects respond to the interests of all children. Activities can engage a whole group, small group, or individual children. Chard (1997) sees no time constraints with projects. They can range from several days to several weeks. Projects are at the core of Reggio Emilia, which is discussed in Chapter 7.

Katz and Chard (1989) see projects developed in three phases. Planning and getting started comprise the initial phase. Teachers do their preliminary planning and set the rationale for the upcoming project. Some teachers engage in webbing and build a curriculum web during this first phase. A webbing structure records children's ideas, interests, and questions about a topic. Webbing is the creating and recording of the ideas suggested by children during brainstorming sessions. The webbing process visually graphs ideas for activities that emerge from the children's knowledge and interests with guidance and input from the teacher. The projects develop during phase two. Here children are introduced to the topic and engage in project work. Reflections and conclusions characterize the last phase. The objective is to bring closure to the project. According to Katz and Chard for younger children through age five, culminating experiences include project constructions and role-playing. For example, children may conclude a project work on veterinarians by constructing their own classroom animal hospital and acting out the different roles involved (see Figures 11-7, 11-8, 11-9).

In summary, there are many approaches to curriculum development. The canned, embalmed, and accidental/unidentified are teacher-directed. The same holds true for the use of units and themes. Children have no input into their development. The emergent curriculum and project approach do involve children in the process of curriculum development.

Figure 11-7

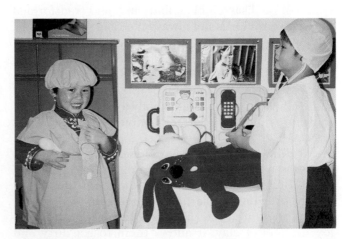

Figure 11-8

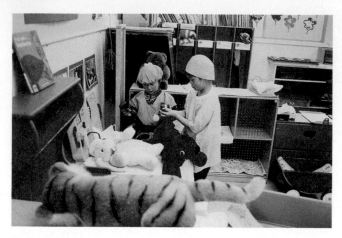

Figure 11-9

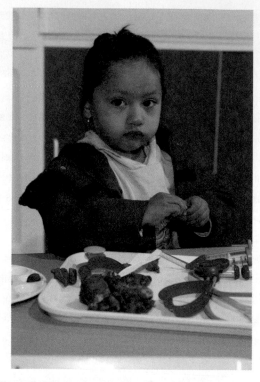

Figure 11-10 Older toddlers discover what they can do to and with play dough.

and socializing at the clay table. "My clay is so hard." "Keep rollin' it till it gets soft." "Can I use the roller when you're done?" Verbal exchange and social skills are demonstrated at the clay table. Children make direct physical contact with clay. There is no brush, scissors, or marker between them and the medium.

Working with clay fosters large muscle and fine motor control. Clay is fairly resistant and will need to be kneaded and worked to make it pliable. Children can stand or sit while using clay. Standing provides the advantage of a whole body muscular reaction to the clay. Hard clay provides a solid resistance that the child must overcome. This will involve using muscles in the shoulders, arms, hands, and fingers if the child is seated. Slowly, the child gains control over the medium, making it do or become what he or she wants it to (see Figure 11–10).

Children enjoy working with clay for many reasons. For one, it is a natural material and has the same appeal that water, sand, and wood hold for young children. As a preferred art form, it allows them to change or undo what they have begun. For example, a snowman can be disassembled, flattened, and transformed into a pizza. This is not always possible with crayons, markers, or paint. It also gives them control over a medium. The snowman's head will stay on top of the body if the two are joined together. The painted outline of a snowman might run or mix with other colors. If the clay head falls off, it can always be put back on. It is more difficult to correct a painting, especially if it has dried.

Working with clay is a multisensory experience. Clay has a distinct texture, temperature, color, and smell. Involving children in making homemade play dough provides a learning opportunity to read a recipe, measure, and mix ingredients. Children enjoy the feel of clay. It allows them to get dirty and messy. It may remind them of infantile pleasures at-

tained during earlier, toilet training days. Because of this, some children will find clay appealing, while others may find it repulsive. Playing with clay should be an option. Over time and with subtle encouragement, the reluctant child may become an active participant at the clay table. Seeing that clay can be washed off hands and from under fingernails may also add reassurance.

Using real mud provides an earthy experience in which children are brought in close touch with nature. Check local soil conditions for levels of bacteria found in mud. Working with clay provides an opportunity to release feelings in a socially acceptable way. A child may not display aggression against a peer but is free to pound on a clay person. Clay has a therapeutic effect. It allows the working through of emotions and creating of model situations. A child who is upset by a recent divorce may be unable to express how he or she feels verbally. Clay, however, provides this child with the opportunity to work through his or her feelings by talking to and dramatizing with a family made out of clay.

Children need lots and lots of clay. A grapefruit-sized ball for each sculptor is recommended. Play dough and clay, in particular, will require a lot of kneading to become pliable. Clay must be kept in a sealed container, such as a plastic tub with a snap-on lid. Over time, certain types of clay (earth) washed from hands will clog up the sink. Some teachers prefer that children rinse their hands in a bucket and flush the muddy water down the toilet.

Types of Clay

Different types of clay let children process in different ways. Below, three major types are described.

Real Clay. Different parts of the country have their own characteristic clays. Many types can be used in the classroom. Soak the clay in a bucket and pour it through a screen to remove sticks and stones. This treatment will help make the clay more pliable. Real clay is dug up from the earth and can be purchased in art supply stores. Water-based or potters clay products can be fired and preserved. It is the type of clay that adult sculptors work with. Make sure the brand is nontoxic. It can be bought in a ready-to-mix powder or premixed form. Premixed is more expensive. However, extra time will be needed if you are using a ready-to-mix powder that also needs to set. Real clay is less expensive, messier, but more pliable than plasticene. Its dull gray or brown color may not be visually appealing, but its cool feel and inviting texture will attract participation. Because it is water-based, it will dry out when exposed to air.

Provide a small pan of water and encourage children to wet their fingers and moisten real clay to keep it pliable. This clay will also dry unfired or can be reused by forming it into 4-inch balls and putting it back in the storage container wrapped in a wet paper towel. Poke a hole in each clay ball and fill it with water to further preserve pliability. Check your clay from time to time. If it is too wet, it will get moldy and smell. If it is too dry, it will harden. Add or remove moisture as needed. Real clay is messy and is best suited for outdoor use. Simply hose down the area when you are finished. Products made from real clay can be glazed and fired in a kiln for the beautiful shiny finish that you see on ceramic pieces. Most centers and schools for young children will not have access to a kiln. This is no problem. Finished pieces can also be left to dry on their own; this will take several days. Of course, most young sculptors will be happy returning their mass of clay to its original ball shape for the next clay session.

Koster (1999) discusses the potential for cultural awareness through the use of clay. She recommends bringing in beautiful earthenware serving pieces. Explain that for many years people have used clay to make eating utensils. On occasion one could serve the children's daily snack in this handmade pottery. Visit the local thrift store and purchase the real dishes for the dramatic play area. Collect and display examples of pottery and clay sculptures from various places

and cultures. Examples include Mexican earthenware, Chinese porcelains, Japanese teacups, and Peruvian clay figurines.

Books about clay or people's relation to clay can be shared with young children including the following:
Aarrestad, T. *The potter Giselle.*
Baylor, B. *When clay sings.*
Cohen, C. *The mud pony.*
Dixon, A. *Clay.*
Engel, D. *The little lump of clay.*
Gibbons, G. *The pottery place.*
Ginsburg, M. *Clay boy.*
James, B. *The mud family.*
Podwal, M. *Golem—a giant made of mud.*
Ray, M. L. *Mud.*
Winter, J. *Josefina.*
Teachers and children also may make their own original big books about clay, illustrated with photographs of the children's clay works along with their dictated captions.

Plasticene. Plasticene is a type of clay with an oil base. It is fairly inexpensive, does not stick to surfaces, and will not dry out if kept covered when not in use. It is fairly solid and requires a good deal of kneading and heat from the hands to become pliable. It is reusable and cannot be fired or painted. It may frustrate the toddler or young preschooler who lacks muscular strength in the fingers and hands. Not all children like the smell of plasticene.

Play Dough. Play-Doh® is commercially available. It comes in bright colors and is fairly inexpensive. It is also very fragrant and may tempt the young sculptor into tasting it. Its major disadvantage is that it tends to crumble and flake, with tiny pieces spreading all over the table and floor. Even in its lidded can, Play-Doh® will dry up, harden, or mold over time. Try placing the Play-Doh® in a sandwich bag sealed with a twist tie before storing it in the container to make it last longer.

Play dough can also be homemade. Children enjoy making and using play dough because it is soft and pliable. It also combines cooking with art. One major ingredient is flour, making this type of clay fairly inexpensive and able to be baked and preserved. Place it in a covered container and store it in the refrigerator. Recipes are provided later in this chapter. Different recipes provide different textures. Be sure to vary the color and scent added.

Very young children will find play dough more appealing and easier to work with than plasticene. Inhibited children may prefer play dough or plasticene to real clay. Still, young children should be exposed to a wide variety of clays and play doughs.

Processing with Clay

Young children can discover that there are many, many different ways to work with clay. Processing with clay may, but need not, result in a finished clay product. Some ways to process with clay include:

- fingering and squeezing clay.
- rolling clay into round balls, eggs, eyeballs, marbles, peas, or meatballs.
- coiling, stretching, and lengthening clay into long snakes, worms, rope, hot dogs, spaghetti, noodles, or sausage; smaller coils often become a ring, bracelet, or necklace.
- patting, flattening, hammering, squashing, or pounding clay into a pancake, pie, hamburger, cookie, pizza, or face.
- pinching off pieces of clay to make facial features, bugs, or bits of candy.
- cutting clay with blunt scissors to make french fries.
- poking holes or openings into clay to make a donut or facial features in a face or head.
- tearing or pulling apart as well as joining pieces of clay.
- stamping or imprinting clay with cookie cutters, bottle caps, buttons, pinecones, seashells, and so forth.
- twisting or braiding lengths of clay.
- forming or molding clay into nests, bowls, or birthday cakes.
- squeezing or sculpting clay into a solid three-dimensional, self-standing form, such as a snowman, animal, or human figure.
- incising or cutting into clay with a plastic knife, fork, Popsicle® stick, toothpick, fingernails, and so forth.
- processing with clay and a variety of clay tools and accessories (see Figure 11–11).
- folding or bending clay into a taco, flower, or boat.

Stages of Working with Clay

More has been written about stages of children's drawing and painting than about working with clay. The author has synthesized the research on the child's developmental progression in the use of clay (Brittain, 1979; Golomb, 1974; and Hartley, Frank, & Goldenson, 1952) in proposing the following stages:

Stage 1: What is Clay? In this first stage, two-year-olds experiment with and explore the properties of clay. They use their senses to visually explore, touch, smell (and often stick up their noses), lick and taste, and lis-

Figure 11-11 Processing with play dough, tools, and accessories.

ten to clay being worked with their hands. They will drop it, step on it, throw or try to bounce it, and stick it to their skin. They are not interested in making something out of clay. Their talk will be limited to words related to their sensory experiences with clay, for example, "yucky," "gooey," "mushy," or "mmmmmm."

Stage 2: What Can I Do with Clay? The first stage quickly builds into the second. Three-year-olds are more systematic in their attempts at processing with the clay. As scientists, they put clay to a series of tests by rolling, pinching, tearing, pulling, and poking it. By physically acting on clay they discover its properties. Clay can roll, but it cannot bounce or pour. The child does not deliberately set out to make something at this stage. By chance and through active manipulation, simple forms such as small balls, patted cakes, or snakes may result. These actions will be repeated, with the child making several products.

Stage 3: Look What I Made! Four-year-olds will creatively combine clay forms and actions performed on them. One clay ball is put on top of another. Flattening and rolling a piece of clay produces a new shape. Openings will be pushed into the mass of clay, and pieces will be pulled out. There is more labeling and talking about what they are making. For example, while a stage-2 child may simply poke a hole through a thin sheet of clay, the older stage-3 sculptor may make a total of three pokes and call it a face. The finished product may be crude and simple. Balls of clay can be added to a coiled snake, with the child saying, "My snake can see you." Children in this stage often dramatize with their clay products. The clay snake slithers around the table, hissing and biting the children. Clay products are becoming more complex at this stage. Still, many clay creations are more the accidental result of processing than the result of systematic planning in advance or intention. Clay creations are idiosyncratic and personal, and others may not recognize the finished product.

Stage 4: I Know What I'm Going to Make out of My Clay!

Five-year-olds approach the clay table knowing what they want to make out of clay and announce this in advance. They have an idea, a name, and a finished product in mind. They need to find a process or technique that is suitable. There is more discussion while processing and about the finished clay product. Products evidence fairly realistic representation and can be recognized by others. Children in this stage know that their clay food or snake is only a symbol or model and not the actual object itself. They will not try to eat the food as a younger child in stage 3 might. Five-year-olds enjoy adding details using clay tools and accessories, as well as artistic junk such as buttons and toothpicks

The stages of clay appear to parallel stages of the child's artistic development in painting or mark making. Scribbles come to be named just as children give names to their clay creations. Still, clay is a three-dimensional art form, whereas painting and mark making are two-dimensional. Since children live in a three-dimensional world, it may be easier for them to use clay to represent their world. Putting the three-dimensional world on a flat two-dimensional surface with paint, crayons, or markers involves abstraction and may be more difficult. Does this mean that children should be given clay before other art media? Brittain (1979) conducted a study to determine whether clay would facilitate a more advanced type of representation than drawing. In carefully examining the artwork of 17 preschoolers, he found no superiority of clay over drawing when judging the accuracy of representation. A child who is having difficulty drawing a person would have similar difficulties making one out of clay. Young children need experience with a wide variety of artistic media, and no strict order of presentation is supported by the research. Still, our working knowledge of children and their development tells us that batik is inappropriate for most two- and three-year-olds, whereas play dough is recommended.

Clay Techniques

Above and beyond processing with clay, there are specific techniques for making clay products that the older child might enjoy learning. Often, they are discovered. Here are some of those techniques.

Pinch. Using the pinch method will result in a clay bowl or pot. Begin with a clay ball. Stick both thumbs into the center of the clay ball with the fingers holding the outside. Gently press the thumbs against the sides while pinching and rotating the clay ball. Continue pinching and pulling the sides upward and out into a pot or bowl.

Coil. The coil method builds on the child's experiences with rolling long clay snakes. A pot or bowl can also be formed with this method. Native Americans made pottery using the coil method over a pinch pot. Begin by wrapping coils of clay over the basic pinch pot or into any shape or form desired.

Slab. Begin with a slab of clay. Roll it flat with a rolling pin until it is about ½-inch thick. Use a plastic knife or other clay tool to cut out the outline of the desired object. Smooth out the cut edges.

Adding Clay. Start with a ball or lump of clay and slowly add parts and details. For example, one child made a horse from a solid mass of clay. A head, legs, and a tail were carefully added. Clay pieces made this way tend to be fragile, and the added parts do not always stay attached. The child was very frustrated because her horse's legs kept breaking under the weight of its heavy body.

Pulling out Clay. This method will avoid the problems associated with adding clay. Start with a fairly large mass of clay. Think of the total object as a solid piece rather than as made up of connected parts. Slowly pull out the parts you need. For example, by molding and carefully pulling out legs, arms, and a head, one child made a person out of clay. It was fairly sturdy and stable, because it was an intact mass without added-on parts and pieces.

Taking Clay Away. Start with a fairly large mass of clay. Take away the excess or unwanted pieces of clay, using fingers or clay tools and accessories. For example, one child used a plastic knife to carve her irregularly shaped clay ball into a round jack-o'-lantern. Facial features were cut out.

Outlining with Clay. Some children use strips of flattened clay as if they were strokes of paint or lines drawn with pencil, crayons, or markers. They approach clay as if it were a two-dimensional medium and overlook its three-dimensional possibilities. This is to be expected, and for most it will be a temporary stage. Objects can be outlined in clay rather than represented with a solid mass of clay. Because the object is outlined flat and stationary on the clay board, there is no need to worry about it moving, falling over, or coming apart. This technique allows children to add small details.

Clay and Accessories

alphabet clay cutters—commercial set makes miniature *ABC*s
apple divider—for slicing clay
cheese slicer—for slicing clay
clay board—with nonstick surface
clay cutters—plastic knives and spoons
clay hammers—for pounding and flattening clay
cookie cutters—for making shapes out of clay
dough press—for making decorations out of clay
dowel rods—for rolling, poking, and designing clay
egg slicer—for slicing clay balls
Formica®—for clay boards
funnels—for making circular impressions in clay
linoleum—for clay boards
meat baller—for scooping and making clay balls
meat tenderizer mallet—for flattening and making impressions in clay
melon baller—for scooping and making clay balls
modeling clay
natural or real clay
pastry blender—for kneading and working clay
pastry tube—for making decorations out of clay
pie crimper—for incising clay
pizza cutter—for cutting through clay
plasticene
Play-Doh®
play dough
potato masher—for mashing clay
rolling pins—for rolling clay
scoop—for scooping and making clay balls
self-hardening clay
storage container with tight lid to keep clay from drying out
tortilla press

Hint: Remember that clay tools are mere accessories and are not intended to replace manipulative processing with the fingers and hands. Do not begin with the tools, but slowly add them as a variation to working clay with the hands (see Figure 11–12).

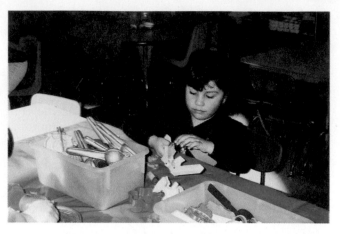

Figure 11-12 Fingers and hands first; tools later.

Hint: Floor tiles, Formica®, and linoleum make good individual clay boards. Some have interesting colors, lines, and designs. Cut into 1-foot squares if they come in a large sheet or roll.

Hint: Add a few drops of perfume, bath oil, or peppermint oil to homemade play dough to keep it sweet-smelling and to prevent spoiling.

Hint: Add a few tablespoons of vegetable oil to play dough to make it easier to sculpt.

Hint: Add a tablespoon of powdered alum when making homemade play dough to keep it from getting moldy.

Clay Activities

Clay Creations

Children may enjoy decorating their clay creations with recycled junk materials. Some items that go well with clay include the following:

- toothpicks
- pipe cleaners
- nuts and bolts
- screws and nails
- keys
- buttons
- straws
- Popsicle® sticks
- paper clips
- acorns
- seashells
- small sticks and twigs
- golf tees
- short pencils

Baked Ornaments

Check the recipe section in this chapter for play dough recipes that allow you to paint, bake, and preserve the finished product. Remember to poke a hole in the product before baking if you want it to hang.

Plasticene Print

Children can use clay tools and accessories, such as a plastic knife, to carve designs into a thin slab of plasticene. Carefully dip the carved piece of plasticene in paint or press it on a stamp pad. Press on a piece of paper. Repeat the impression to make a pattern.

Clay Numbers and Letters

Young children who are interested in the world of letters and numbers may enjoy using magnetic letters and numbers to make clay impressions. Remove the small magnet piece from each. Children can also use plastic knives, Popsicle® sticks, or toothpicks to carve their name, their initials, the alphabet, words, their address, or their phone number out of clay. These could also be formed by combining small coils of clay.

Clay Overs

Children may enjoy sculpting clay pieces or parts and attaching them to a larger base. For example, a small juice can or box can be decorated with coils and balls of clay.

Clay and Play Dough Recipes

Bread-Dough Clay (inedible)

4 slices bread
3 tablespoons white glue
2 drops lemon juice
plastic bag

Remove crusts from bread. Tear bread into small pieces. Mix pieces of bread with glue and lemon juice. Knead. Do not eat. Sculpt. Allow to dry for a couple of days before decorating. Place unused bread-dough clay in a plastic bag and store in the refrigerator.

Edible Candy Clay

⅓ cup margarine
⅓ cup light corn syrup
¼ teaspoon salt
1 teaspoon vanilla or peppermint extract
1-pound box powdered sugar
food coloring

Mix all other ingredients, then add powdered sugar. Knead until smooth. Add more powdered sugar if necessary to make nonstick, pliable clay. Sculpt and eat.

Edible Dough Clay

1 package of dry yeast
1½ cups very warm water
1 egg
¼ cup honey
¼ cup shortening
1 teaspoon salt
5 cups flour

Mix yeast with water. Add egg, honey, shortening, and salt. Slowly add flour until a ball of dough forms. Add more flour if too sticky. Knead dough. Sculpt. Make only flat figures, because dough will rise. Cover the sculptures with a towel. Let rise in a warm place for about a half hour. Let it rise longer if you want it fatter. Bake at 350° F for 20 minutes or until golden brown. Sculptures can be eaten or painted and coated with shellac to preserve.

Decorating Dough

4 cups self-rising flour
1 cup salt
1½ cups water
food coloring or powdered tempera (optional)

Mix flour and salt in large bowl. Slowly add water. Mix thoroughly. Add food coloring. Knead for 5 to 10 minutes. Add more water if dough is too stiff, more flour if too sticky. Food coloring is optional. Sculpt or cut with cookie cutters. Sprinkle board with flour to keep from sticking. Press in hairpin holder if hanging is desired. Dry at room temperature for several days, or bake at 300° F for 1½ hours. Refrigerated dough will last for 5 days.

Goop

2 cups salt
water
1 cup cornstarch

Mix salt and ⅔ cup water. Heat in pot for 3 to 4 minutes. Remove from heat and quickly add a mixture of the following:
1 cup cornstarch
½ cup cold water
Stir quickly. Return to the heat if too "goopy."

Play Dough (cooked)

2 cups flour
1 cup salt
2 cups water
2 tablespoons cooking oil
4 teaspoons cream of tartar
food coloring (optional)

Mix the flour, salt, and cream of tartar together. Add the water, oil, and food coloring (if desired). Cook the mixture over low to medium heat for 3 to 5 minutes. Keep stirring until the mixture forms a solid ball. Cool. Items made can be baked at low heat for 20 to 25 minutes, depending on their thickness.

Play Dough (uncooked)

2½ cups flour
½ cup salt
1 tablespoon alum
3 tablespoons cooking oil
1½ cups hot water
food coloring

Combine oil, water, and food coloring. Combine dry ingredients. Pour liquid into dry ingredients. Mix thoroughly. Knead.

Soap and Sawdust Clay

1½ cups soap flakes
1½ cups sawdust
water

Slowly add water to soap flakes. Make a thick, creamy mixture. Whip soap until it is stiff and fluffy. Slowly mix in sawdust. Sculpt. Let figures dry for several days.

Soda and Cornstarch Clay

1 cup cornstarch
2 cups baking soda
1¼ cups water
food coloring

Combine cornstarch, baking soda, and water in pan. Cook over medium heat. Stir constantly. Stop when mixture thickens like dough. Knead and add food coloring when cool.

Mud Dough

2 cups mud
2 cups sand
½ cup salt
water

Slowly add water until pliable. Children enjoy the texture.

Peanut Butter Clay (edible)

4 tablespoons peanut butter
1 tablespoon honey
1 tablespoon wheat germ
2½ tablespoons powdered milk
Mix. Sculpt. Eat!

Peanut Butter Play Dough (edible)

1 cup peanut butter
1 cup honey
1 cup powdered milk

1 cup oatmeal
food coloring (optional)
Mix thoroughly. Adding food coloring is optional. Sculpt as if it were clay. Eat!

Pretzel Clay I (edible)

1 package dry yeast, dissolved in cold water
3 cups flour
1 teaspoon sugar
1 teaspoon salt
water

Mix yeast mixture and flour. Slowly add about 1 more cup of flour until the mixture can be kneaded. Let children take turns kneading it on a floured countertop. Sculpt as clay. Sprinkle with kosher salt. Bake at 350° F for about 20 minutes. Makes approximately 20 small pretzels.

Pretzel Clay II (edible)

1 cup warm water
1 package yeast
1 tablespoon salt
2½ cups whole wheat pastry flour

Mix water and yeast. Let sit for a few minutes. Add salt and flour. Mix and knead. Roll into shapes. Place on lightly greased cookie sheet. Bake in preheated oven at 425° F for 12 minutes or until brown. Beat an egg and brush on your creations if want a glazed look.

Silly Putty

white liquid glue
liquid starch
food coloring

Mix equal parts of white liquid glue and liquid starch. Stir immediately. Add a few drops of food coloring. Knead until silly putty is soft and smooth. Store in container with lid.

Frosting Dough (edible)

1 can frosting mix
1½ half cup of powdered sugar
1 cup peanut butter

Use a large spoon to mix all ingredients in a bowl. Knead into workable mixture. Provide a small ball for each child. Model as with any dough. Eat if desired.

Kool-Aid® Play Dough

2½ cups flour
½ cup salt
2 13-oz packages of Kool-Aid®
3 tablespoons vegetable oil
2 cups boiling water

Mix flour, salt, and Kool-Aid®. Add vegetable oil and boiling water in a large bowl. Knead until a good consistency is attained. Store in an airtight container or in locking plastic bags. Play dough smells good but should not be eaten.

Soft Cloud-Like Play Dough

6 cups flour
1½ cups vegetable oil
1 cup water
If color is desired, add food coloring or tempera to large bowl with flour. Add oil and water to flour and knead well. If needed, add small amounts of water until dough is soft and fluffy. Add more flour if dough is too sticky. Store dough in a covered container and refrigerate.

Vinegar Dough

3 cups flour
1 cup salt
1 cup water
¼ cup vegetable oil
2 tablespoons vinegar
Mix all ingredients together in a large bowl. Add more water if too dry. Knead. This soft play dough keeps well when stored in a plastic bag and refrigerated. Knead water into dough to refresh.

Ooey-Gooey: Cornstarch and Water

1-pound box cornstarch
1½ cups water
food coloring or liquid watercolor (optional)
Mix all ingredients together into large container like a shallow dishpan where children can experiment to-

Figure 11-13 Ooey-gooey.

gether. Or mix individual portions of ooey-gooey in small plastic food savers. Adding more water or cornstarch changes the consistency. Encourage children to discover what happens when they handle the ooey-gooey by grasping, squeezing, and pouring (see Figure 11–13).

Borax® Putty

1 cup water
1 cup white glue
food coloring or liquid watercolor (optional)
Mix water and glue together, color if desired. Set aside.
1 teaspoon Borax® powdered laundry detergent
hot water
Dissolve Borax® in 2 tablespoons of hot water. Add Borax® mixture by stirring it into the glue mixture. Pull out gooey mixture. Knead. Repeat pulling-out step. May need to add more glue or Borax® depending on consistency of putty. Store in plastic bag and refrigerate.

Rainbow Stew

1 cup cornstarch
¾ cup sugar
4 cups water
2 different primary colors (food colors or liquid watercolors)
Zip-lock® freezer bags
sturdy tape, e.g., duct
Mix first three ingredients in a pot. Place on medium heat, stirring constantly, until thickened. Remove from heat and let cool. Divide into two bowls and add one color to each bowl. Place one or two heaping tablespoons full of each colored mixture into each child's freezer bag. Use sturdy tape for extra security. Encourage the children to mash and mix the colors together and discuss what they see happening. Repeat on another day using two different primary colors and note resulting combinations. Hold bags up to light, or tape them on window.

Fake Snow Dough

3 bars of Ivory® soap
1 to 2 rolls of toilet paper
hot water
Grate 3 bars of Ivory® soap. Tear individual sheets of toilet paper. In a big bowl mix the grated soap with the torn toilet paper. Slowly add a few tablespoons of hot water. Mix with your hands until it reaches the consistency of whipped dessert topping. Add more hot water if needed.

SUMMARY

This chapter focused on curriculum development by presenting a PIE model for planning, implementing, and evaluating. A theme can be woven into many art activities. Goals, based on what we know about children and their development as well as our values, give direction to our planning. Breaking goals down into short-term objectives assists in daily planning. Implementing raises management and procedural concerns about carrying out activities. Evaluation addresses the match between what we set out to do and what actually happened. The chapter also compared and contrasted different strategies for integrating art into the early childhood curriculum.

Key Terms

beliefs	goal	play dough
clay	implementing	Project Approach
curriculum development	knowledge	skills
dispositions	objectives	teachable moments
emergent curriculum	PIE	types of learning
evaluating	planning	values
feelings		

Suggested Activities

1. As a group, brainstorm your goals for early childhood education. Are they developmental in focus? Do you agree? How do they reflect different values and beliefs? Can you reach consensus? What could this indicate about the state of early childhood education?
2. Observe how different teachers use planning, implementing, and evaluating in their programs.
3. Use the lesson plan format to write and implement an art activity.
4. Divide the class into four groups. Each group is responsible for very general daily planning for teaching the concept of primary colors, using one of the five strategies discussed in this chapter.

5. Capture a teachable moment during one of your classroom observations. Record the stimulus and how the event transpired. Did you see any learning take place? Were the children involved? What could this tell you about teachable moments?
6. Observe in a classroom where your instructor verifies that one of the following curricular approaches is in place: emergent, Reggio Emilia, or project approach. Write up what you observed and your reactions. Compare this observation with others where approaches such as thematic, academic, or completely teacher-directed were evidenced.
7. Facilitate an activity with play dough or clay.

Review

1. Complete the cycle of curriculum and development.

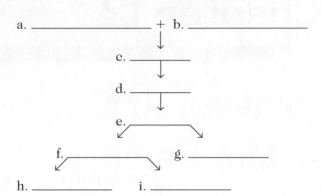

a. _____ + b. _____

c. _____

d. _____

e.

f. _____   g. _____

h. _____   i. _____

2. Identify the components of the PIE approach to curriculum development.

   P =

   I =

   E =

3. List strategies for including art in the early childhood curriculum.

4. Identify and briefly explain the four types of learning.

5. Compare and contrast a completely teacher-planned early childhood curriculum with the following: teachable moments, emergent curriculum, and project approach.

For additional art and creative development resources, visit our Web site at
www.EarlyChildEd.delmar.com

Chapter 12

Integrating Art across the Early Childhood Curriculum

What do you see happening in this picture? Notice the intent look on this boy's face. He is working on a three-dimensional sculpture or construction. The group work is done outdoors and belongs to everyone. Children are free to add to the sculpture during outdoor play time. Although the boy speaks little English, it does not keep him from making a creative contribution. Artists speak the universal language of creative expression. And the activity was easy to plan—lots of newspaper, glue, and wooden scraps, along with ample time and space. Although the teachers are nearby and subtly supervising, there is no need for teacher intervention. The materials speak for themselves. A child can easily figure out how to adhere objects. If a child were to misuse materials, a teacher would gently intervene and offer guidance. Chapter 12 introduces the reader to an array of three-dimensional activities often referred to as *sculpture* or *assemblage*. Just as collage was two-dimensional or *flat* art, assemblage provides children with a new dimension—depth. Remember to provide a range of art activities that encourage children to create in both two and three dimensions.

Objectives

After reading this chapter, you should be able to:

- Compare and contrast two different ways of viewing the early childhood curriculum.
- Identify the major early childhood curricular areas.
- Provide reasons for integrating art across the early childhood curriculum.
- Discuss how art fosters learning in the following early childhood curricular areas: math, science, language arts/communication arts/literacy, social studies, and the expressive arts.
- Describe the outcomes of implementing anti-bias curriculum in an early childhood classroom.
- Provide three-dimensional art activities.

INTRODUCTION

Curriculum means different things to different people. Two major ways of viewing the curriculum are as an overall program or as subject areas. Each view will be discussed in this chapter. Art is merely one of many curricular areas. How can art reinforce and extend learning in the other curricular areas? Integrating art throughout the early childhood curriculum will be the focus of this chapter.

Integrating Art across the Early Childhood Curriculum

Why integrate art into other areas of the early childhood curriculum? According to Dever and Jared (1996), integrating art activities into an ongoing unit of study benefits the learners in at least two ways. First, art gives children the opportunity to think about what they are learning as they create representations and products that reflect their new understandings. For example, when children make their own farm animals out of clay they are learning about the animals under study. Second, as children manipulate the art materials, they learn about the characteristics of the art materials as well as what can be done with them. For example, when trying to fashion an animal with head, body, and legs, children are learning about the properties of clay and how they need to work with it to get a creation that somehow represents the animal under study. For those who have yet to try, getting a clay animal to stand on four legs is quite a technical accomplishment.

Let us try another example. A group of older preschoolers has been studying dental health. This unit was a follow-up to learning about eating healthy. It was based on a teacher's observation of children's eating habits and dental hygiene. Her informal talks with parents also helped her decide on this topic for study. Because some children had older siblings with missing teeth, it was decided that a unit on dental health would be warranted. If you were the teacher, how could you approach a unit on dental health? What experiences and activities could you provide? The teacher in question provided an array of activities

Figure 12-1 What could this child be learning?

including books, songs, flannel board stories, media, food activities, a class visit by a parent who was a dental hygienist, a field trip to a dentist's office, and an array of art activities, all of which reinforced learning about eating healthy foods and proper care of one's teeth. In one integrated art activity, the teacher encouraged the children to think about good health/dentition and paint a "healthy" picture (see Figure 12–1). It appears some children painted themselves smiling, hopefully the result of what they had learned and would practice.

ART AND THE EARLY CHILDHOOD CURRICULUM

The word **curriculum** is used to refer to an educational program, activity, or set of activities, and to guidelines set by a school district office, state, corporation, or professional organization. In its widest sense, curriculum refers to what happens in schools or centers. Two major ways of viewing the early childhood curriculum are

- curriculum as program.
- curriculum as subject matter, content, or academic area.

Curriculum as Program

To some, curriculum means the total program, such as an infant, toddler, preschool, Montessori, Head Start, or kindergarten program. In this view, curriculum refers to all the things children learn in school or center. This is a very broad view of curriculum. It would include learning how to wait one's turn, sit in a circle for group time, and share toys, as well as learning

about colors and shapes. In this view, children learn through specifically planned learning experiences as well as through incidental learnings. For example, Mel's parents are pleased that he enjoys his child-care program and is making friends. However, they are concerned that he has become more verbally and socially aggressive, behaviors that they had never observed before he attended child care. Children who are in groups for long periods of time learn these behaviors as ways to cope and protect themselves. Children learn much more than is planned and intended in any curriculum or program.

Curriculum as Subject Matter, Content, or Academic Area

A second way to look at curriculum is to view it as a separate subject, content, or academic area of study. The present text focuses on art in the early childhood curriculum. Traditionally, the school curriculum has centered around the following curricular areas.

1. math
2. science
3. language arts/communication arts/literacy
   - speaking
   - listening
   - reading
   - writing
4. social studies
5. expressive arts
   - art
   - music
   - movement

See Figure 12–2 for a visual portrayal of this model of the early childhood curriculum.

▶▶ **N A E Y C**

Just as child development cannot be dissected into neat divisions, the curricular areas are not separate entities. The model indicates that the curricular areas interact and influence each other. Children do not simply *switch channels* or *change gears* to move from mathematical to scientific thinking. Knowledge and skills are not neatly compartmentalized according to subject area. This is why math and science, communication and language arts, and the expressive arts are depicted with overlapping circles. Experiences such as cooking and play are highly recommended because they cut across and involve learning in many, if not all, of the curricular areas. Although the separation will work for our present analysis, children are holistic individuals who learn in holistic ways. For example, they engage in creative thinking and problem solving that may cut across the areas of math and science, art, and social studies.

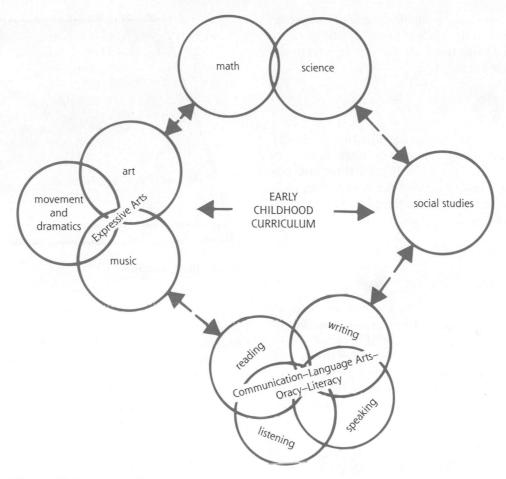

Figure 12-2 Model of integrated early childhood curriculum development.

ART AND MATH

Children naturally quantify art materials, equipment, and supplies. "There are four jars of paint out, but only three brushes. There are more jars than brushes." The teacher asks, "How many more brushes do we need to make them equal?" Some paintbrushes have longer handles and wider bristles than others. "My red crayon is longer than your blue one." "Yes, but mine is fatter and wider than yours." "This paste cup has less than the others," states Evie. Her teacher asks, "What can you do to make them the same?" Evie gets the large paste container and adds more.

Children quantify as they create. "There, now my bug has six legs, just enough," announces Ty as he coils a final leg out of clay. Marcy adds a second eye to her self-portrait. She carefully counts fingers and toes as she paints them on one by one. Some children use geometric shapes in composing their picture. "A tall brown rectangle with a green circle on top. Now, I'll color in my tree," announces Tess.

Some activities that incorporate art with math follow.

Geometric Shape Picture

Older children can cut an array of circles, squares, triangles, and rectangles of different sizes. These can be creatively arranged and pasted to form a picture. Teachers may want to cut out the geometric shapes for younger children. Precutting for children is warranted in this activity. Children see how common objects, people, vehicles, and animals are made up of geometric shapes and can be constructed from them.

There are two ways to vary this activity. Teachers can cut shapes out of flannel, including circles, squares, triangles, and rectangles that vary in color and size. Children can creatively arrange these shapes on a larger piece of flannel that forms the background. Some teachers pin or tape pieces of flannel to a bulletin board or chalkboard. Others cover a large piece of cardboard with flannel. A second variation is to use magnetic tape. Wide strips of magnetic tape can be cut into geometric shapes, or small pieces of magnetic tape can be glued to the back of poster board or cardboard shapes. In turn, these shapes can be creatively arranged on a cookie sheet.

Cube Art

Older children may enjoy making a picture or design using graph paper. Graph paper with large squares is recommended. This activity will take time and patience and is not recommended for very young children. The paper may need to be cut in half or quarters if children become overwhelmed by all the squares on the paper.

Lines, Arcs, and Circles

Young children enjoy using the tools of the mathematician: ruler, compass, and protractor. Specific instruction in the proper care and use of these instruments should be given. Model different ways of using a ruler, compass, protractor, and pencil to produce interesting designs and patterns. Children may want to color in the spaces between or connect forms with thin markers.

Variety of Paper Shapes

Art can be done on round, square, triangular, diagonal, rectangular, and odd-shaped pieces of paper. Each unique shape poses a new challenge to the child artist. Wide, sweeping strokes are appropriate on a big rectangular sheet of paper. A smaller, detailed picture may fit better on a smaller six-sided sheet.

Teachers can point out and discuss the different shapes of the paper provided. For example, "I put out some different paper today. What shape could we call it?" (holding up a piece of round paper). Because it is round with a hole cut out of the center, the children decide that circle, wheel, and doughnut are appropriate terms.

Teachers can also discuss how a large square sheet can be cut into smaller square pieces of paper. Four small squares make one larger square. Cutting the large diamond-shaped sheet of paper in half makes two triangular pieces of paper. In this way, children are slowly introduced to fractions through an integrated art activity.

Geoboard

Children can practice making geometric shapes with rubber bands on a geoboard (see Figure 12–3 for a

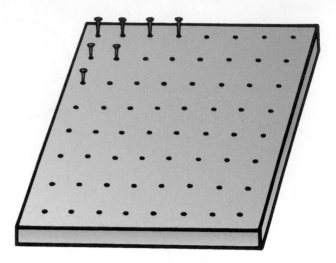

Figure 12-3 Geoboard.

geoboard pattern). Find a piece of wood. Carefully hammer in rows of evenly spaced nails.

Use short nails with wide heads or upholstery tacks. A 1-inch space between rows and columns of nails is recommended. The total number of rows and columns will depend on the size of the board. Eight rows and eight columns are recommended.

Encourage the children to answer:

- How many nails can you fit under just one rubber band?
- How many nails do you need to include to make a circle (square, rectangle, diamond, triangle, and so on)?
- Does it take more or fewer nails to make a square, triangle, circle, or rectangle?
- How many different shapes can you make using 10 nails?

String Design

Children can make abstract linear designs with string on a wooden frame. Find an old picture frame. Lay the frame down flat and hammer in a row of nails on each of the four upright sides. Encourage children to connect the nails using string, rope, or yarn. The result will be a creative linear design. Children can note the designs, patterns, shapes, and angles produced.

Tangram

The tangram is an old Chinese puzzle consisting of seven angular shapes that can fit together to make a square (see Figure 12–4 for a tangram pattern). The shapes can also be creatively combined to make pictures and designs. You may want to reproduce, cut

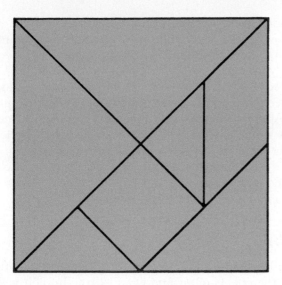

Figure 12-4 Tangram.

out, mount on poster board, and laminate the individual pieces to ensure durability. Time invested in protecting the pieces will pay off in the long run. When laminating, remember to cut out the individual pieces first, then laminate them to avoid frayed ends. Covering the pieces with clear contact paper is also recommended.

Crayon Patterns

Empty several boxes of crayons onto a table. Allow children to create patterns, for example, red-blue-red-blue, etc. They may enjoy making patterns for their friends to copy. Start a pattern, for example, one red-two blue-three yellow-one red-two blue-? and have the child complete the pattern.

Numerals Rubbing

Find a puzzle with numerals. Lay a thin sheet of paper like onionskin (rather than thick construction paper) over the puzzle. Unwrap some crayons and also provide chalk. Encourage the child to rub with the side of the crayon or chalk on the paper. The numerals will appear. Read the numerals together. Children may want to try making their own numerals or finding sets of objects that correspond with the numerals. You can also provide old license plates and wooden blocks with numerals.

Dominoes Rubbing

Lay a thin sheet of paper over a domino. Encourage children to rub with the side of the crayon or chalk on

the paper. The numerals will appear. Resulting dots can be counted, matched with numeral, added together, or used in subtraction.

Numeral Sponges

Do sponge painting with sponges in numeral shapes. Fill low plates with liquid paint. Provide brushes so child can paint on bottom side of numeral. Gently press onto paper. Children can print their age, address, phone number, numerals in sequence or just make a collage by combining and overlapping numeral shapes. Numeral sponges can also be used at the water table.

Seriation Art

Provide corks in a variety of widths. Children can seriate them from smallest to largest. Provide ink pads and paper for them to print their own designs made up of different-sized circular shapes. Encourage children to use comparative words when talking about their picture. For example, "Let's find the biggest shape." A variation of this activity is to provide round lids in a variety of sizes. Children can trace around the lids creating their own circular designs.

Addition Prints

Children can use their hands and/or feet to make prints. Think of the number of possibilities. One hand, five fingers; two hands, ten fingers; etc. Hands, feet, fingers, and toes can be added. Hand prints can be made indoors, whereas foot printing is best done outdoors on a warm day. Children can also compare their prints, noting size differences.

Math Cards

Children can use markers, crayons, or colored pencils to draw sets of objects which match numerals or number words. Separate pages or individual math cards can be bound into group books.

ART AND SCIENCE

Art activities help children discover scientific principles. Adding water to watercolor cakes produces a liquid. Over time, wet paint dries. Placing wet paintings in the sun will hasten the drying process. Clay remains moist if it is kept wrapped. On Monday morning Ms. Carlson announces, "Someone left their clay work out on the table over the weekend. What has happened to it?" "It turned hard," answers Juan. "Yes, it got hard and brittle when exposed to the air for three days," explains his teacher. "Also, someone left a wax crayon on the radiator. What has happened to it?" "Yes, it melted. Why?" "Yes, the heat from the radiator melted the wax. What would happen if we left our crayons out in the sun on a hot summer day?" The possibilities of scientific thinking, hypothesizing, predicting, observing, questioning, discussing, and explaining are endless.

Too much water makes paint runny and uncontrollable. Little or no water produces a thicker, intense stroke. Pressing hard or lightly produces different effects. Children are learning about force. Children learn about resistance when they discover that they can cut paper but not cardboard with their scissors.

Some activities that incorporate art with science follow.

Food Groups Collage

After studying the major food groups, children can be encouraged to find pictures of foods in magazines. These can be cut and pasted onto poster board sheets, one for each of the major food groups.

Nature Art

Young children and nature go hand in hand. Children enjoy taking short nature walks and collecting nature specimens. These can be creatively arranged and glued onto a paper plate, cardboard, or construction paper.

Children also enjoy making nature rubbings. Thin white paper can be placed over leaves, flowers, bark, stones, or other objects. Children can gently rub one side of an unwrapped crayon over the specimen. The texture and outline of the item will leave an impression. Children can also take their crayon and paper outdoors and make rubbings as they find them. Overlapping produces a different, more complex impression.

Children can also make nature prints. Paint can be brushed on a leaf, or an acorn can be lightly dipped in paint. The items can then be carefully pressed onto white paper. Gently lifting the item results in a print. Repeated prints result in a pattern. Separate prints can be creatively combined into a new design.

Color Mixing

Children can discover the principles and joys of color mixing. Provide paint and a separate brush and con-

tainer for each of the primary colors: red, blue, and yellow. Encourage children to mix any two colors in equal parts or dabs and see what happens. What color did you make? What happens if three colors are mixed together? This activity can also be done using food coloring, a plastic egg carton, and an eye dropper.

After this tempera paint activity has been successfully completed, white paint can also be provided. What happens if white is mixed with red, blue, or yellow? What happens if white is added to your mixture of red and yellow, red and blue, or blue and yellow? Let's find out.

Mobile

Mobiles help children learn about balance, motion, and the effects of air and wind. A tree branch makes an excellent support or base for a mobile (see Figure 12–5). Acceptable nature items include shells, pinecones, feathers, leaves, and anything else that can be hung with thread, string, or fishing line. Items for a mobile can also be suspended from a coat hanger, yardstick, dowel rod, or broom handle.

Advanced mobile makers can experiment with different levels or planes. This provides an opportunity to experiment with weight, placement, space, and balance. A coat hanger mobile with several levels is shown in Figure 12–6.

Figure 12-5 Mobile.

Figure 12-6 Coat hanger mobile.

Ecology Construction

Children can assist in the cleanup of litter, both indoors and outdoors. Recycled items can also be brought from home. Children can discuss the importance of avoiding needless waste, not littering, and recycling. Such items as scrap paper, boxes, containers, and plastic packaging can be recycled into a construction activity. For example, boxes and bottle tops inspired one preschooler to construct a robot.

Color Magic

Provide three clear cups or containers and three brushes or plastic spoons per child. Tear red, yellow, and blue tissue paper into 1-inch squares. Have the child dip several like-colored papers into the container and use brush or spoon to mix. Observe what results. The primary colors can also be mixed to produce orange, purple, and green. What happens when three of the primary colors are mixed together? How can we make our colors light or intense? Does it matter how much water is used or the amount of tissue paper in a container? Experiment and find out. Provide eyedroppers and coffee filters or paper towels for dripping and further color mixing.

Color Overlays

Children can also mix colors using cellophane or acetate book-report covers. Each child will need small squares of cellophane in each of the three primary colors. Distribute one color, such as red, and have children look through it and discuss its transparent quality. Hold up to natural light and place on skin and clothing. Tape an extra piece to the window. Discuss how you can see through it but it makes everything look red. Distribute the yellow pieces. Repeat the above step. Have children place their two pieces together. They can discuss their observations. What happened when we put red and yellow together? Repeat with the combinations of red and blue and yellow and blue. Children can save their pieces in a bag to take home or have the option of making a picture or collage with them.

Colors in a Bag

This no-mess activity helps children discover that two colors can produce a third. Give each child a zip-lock bag. Write child's name on masking tape and place on bag. Provide liquid paint in red, blue, and yellow. Ask them to pick any two colors and put a spoonful of each into their bags. Securely seal. Encourage the child to gently squeeze and mix the colors. Discuss what is

happening and what results. The child can make a second bag using two different colors or the activity can continue on another day. Bags can be taped to a window.

Pet Rock

Take a nature walk and allow children to find a rock or stone that appeals to them. It should be large enough to paint or decorate but small and light enough to fit in a child's hand. The teacher may want to collect a few extras. Upon returning, talk about how the stones and rocks look and feel. Use descriptive words and open-ended prompts like, "Use words to tell me all about your special rock." Provide paint, brushes, and collage trims. Let children personalize their own rocks.

Dental Art

To incorporate art into your health program, use toothbrushes to paint with. Use dental floss for stringing or in string art activities. Coordinate with dental health week.

Erupting Colors

Pour milk into a cake pan until the bottom is covered. Sprinkle several large drops of food coloring on the milk. Add a few drops of liquid dishwashing detergent into the rings of color. Observe what happens. Colors will erupt. If erupting stops, add more food coloring and then more detergent. If no results, begin again with new ingredients.

ART AND THE LANGUAGE/ COMMUNICATION ARTS AND LITERACY

Art gives children the opportunity to represent what they know nonverbally or graphically. With encouragement, they may also choose to talk about what they have created (see Figure 12–7). Children read their artwork just as adults read words from a book. At times children enjoy having their titles or story lines printed on their pictures. They can be encouraged to read along with the teacher. Older children may attempt to print their own words as a story line. They may invent letters and misspell. This is to be expected; it is an important step that children go through as they become writers and readers. Scribbling, mark making, and painting strokes are important steps in the development of printing and writing.

Figure 12-7 Neo's story.

Because art is a form of nonverbal expression, there is no language prerequisite and no need to understand verbal directions. Children can discover on their own or observe each other. Art time is a good opportunity for children who do not speak it to hear and informally practice standard English. The setting for art is usually relaxed, and the child may feel less inhibited about speaking. Art time is also a god time for children who speak standard English to hear and practice other languages.

Art gives children an opportunity to include art vocabulary in their discussions with peers and adults. Teachers can introduce and model the use of these terms as they talk with children about their art. Children recognize colors, shapes, textures, lines, and movement in their own art and that of others. Lines can be thick, intersecting, criss-crossed, wavy, horizontal, vertical, diagonal, curved, or broken. Paint can be dry, wet, dripping, sticky, tacky, runny, slick, or crackled.

Anne Haas Dyson (1982, 1985, 1986, 1988, 1989, 1990) has studied the link between children's play, pictures, and print. She emphasizes the critical role of art and play in children's growth as symbol makers, particularly as makers of written symbols. Drawing is viewed as a literacy activity, because both drawing and language provide children with opportunities to reflect upon, organize, and share their experiences. When children draw, they are not simply communicating about their experiences; they are also solving visual problems. The problems they solve influence the nature of the texts they create. Although children need opportunities to give dictation and have their words written down for them, they also should engage in their own writing. They need to take marker or pencil in hand and explore the connection between meaning and print.

Some activities that incorporate art with the language/communication arts or literacy follow.

Art Talk

Encourage children to talk about their art, but do not require that art be followed by verbalization: "What would you like to tell me about your picture?" or, "Your colors and shapes make an interesting design; what words could you use to tell about it?" Labels, titles, and story lines can be recorded. For example, Marie asks a parent volunteer, "Can I tell you about my bunny picture?" Marie's words are carefully printed across the top of her paper. The parent points to each word as she reads the story back to Marie. She encourages Marie to read along. Marie says she's done for now but will trace over the letters with a pencil tomorrow. Ned prefers to talk his story into the tape recorder. His teacher will listen to it, transcribe it, and read it back to him.

Puppets

Making a puppet is an art activity that can evolve into a speaking activity. For example, Tami, a shy four-year-old, makes an animal puppet out of a folded paper plate. She hides behind a bookshelf and lets her animal speak to and answer questions from two other children. Tami's puppet is a prop that gives her the psychological boost to speak in a group. After all, it is the puppet, not Tami, who is speaking.

Consonant Collage

One kindergarten class had been studying words that begin with the letter sounds. They practiced these sounds at concept time. They hunted through magazines for pictures of things that start with these sounds. The *b* page had pictures of a book, bicycle, bird, boy, Big Bird®, bag, and Band-Aid®. Pictures of a dog, duck, doll, doughnut, dishes, and dancers were pasted on the *d* page. By the end of the year, the children hoped to complete a collage page for each of their sounds.

Art Words

Children at the clay table were trying to think of something new to make. Their teacher suggested that they form the letters in their names. Some also made their initials, *ABC*s, and simple words out of rolled clay.

As a variation, children could finger paint their names or letters of the alphabet. Getting the actual feel and direction of making a *b* and *d* may help some older children who are learning to print and who tend to reverse these letters.

Children also enjoy using squirt bottles to paint their names, letters, or words. Find a bottle with a pointed tip and a fairly small opening so that the paint will not merely run out. Bottles that hold white glue are a recommended size and shape for young hands.

Listen and Draw

Mrs. Banks enjoys reading books to children. She wants children to listen attentively, appreciate literature, and get the main idea. She knows how important these skills will be when they learn to read. She often asks her children to draw a picture about the story she has just read. Sometimes she stops short of the ending and asks them to draw how they think the story will end. The pictures clearly reveal which children were listening and which may need additional practice in this area.

The creative teacher will invent many variations on this activity. For example, children can be encouraged to listen and then draw what the teacher requests. For example, "Please draw three cats of any color with long tails sitting by a tree." Children need to listen, remember, and represent. The details requested must be minimal and within the memory range and drawing ability of young children. Details such as "inside," "behind," "checkered," or "star-shaped" may be too difficult to represent.

Alphabet Letter Collage

Use stencils or die-cut press to create precut lowercase letters of the alphabet. Children can find and name letters they recognize. Some may want to make their names or simple words; others may want to make creative designs by combining and overlapping letters.

Alphabet Letter Rubbing

Find a puzzle with the alphabet. Lay a thin sheet of paper (e.g., onionskin) over the puzzle. Encourage the child to rub with the side of unwrapped crayon or chalk on the paper. The alphabet will appear. Read the letters together. Children may want to try making their own letters.

Alphabet Letter Print

Provide alphabet sponges, wooden alphabet blocks, and alphabet magnetic letters which can be painted

and pressed on paper for a print. Children can make their names or familiar words. Smaller items, such as the magnetic letters, can be pressed into ink pads and stamped on paper. Rubber stamps featuring the alphabet are also commercially available.

I Can Make My Name

Provide finger paint and encourage children to make their names and other familiar words on glossy paper. You may want to keep their name tags close for reference. Provide craft sticks and have children scrape out their names in paint or shaving cream. Children can also form their names out of play dough.

Personalized Placemat

Provide each child with a large sheet of white paper. Ask where they would like you to put their names. Print them neatly in large letters, capitalizing the first letter of their names. Provide crayons and markers and encourage children to decorate the space around their name. For each mat, cut two sheets of contact paper about an inch or two larger than the placemat. Peel off backings and cover both sides of the mat. Trim edges and round off corners. Use at snack or small group time.

ART AND SOCIAL STUDIES

Art helps children get in touch with themselves and others. Representing oneself through self-portraits and human figure drawings increases one's awareness of self, body parts, and others. Through art, one takes on and identifies with the role of artist. A study of artists can be part of a lesson on community helpers. Children can visit a museum or gallery. An artist can come in and model artistic processing and work with the children. This can also be a brief introduction to history and culture, because artists and their different styles have been around since prehistoric times. Different cultural groups have their own art forms.

Making art is an element of culture. According to McFee (1993), art, as a form of cultural communication, is one of the basic language skills children need to participate in a multicultural democracy. All cultures have their respective art forms. Experiences in making and appreciating art forms from other cultures help children to understand similarities and differences across cultures.

Some activities that incorporate art and social studies follow.

Multicultural Arts and Crafts

Including *multicultural arts and crafts* in the early childhood curriculum is an issue that divides educators. Many believe that a commitment to cultural diversity includes exposing children to the arts and crafts of various cultures. Since the beginning of time, all people everywhere have participated in making arts and crafts characteristic of their group. For those educators who include crafts and adult-directed activities in their art program, this box will merely provide additional resources. People who have grown up in countries where crafts were taught to them as children may also be comfortable with teaching crafts to children at an early age. Others would disagree. Exposing children to cultural artifacts and crafts is one thing; teaching children how to make them raises several issues. First, most crafts are made by adults and attempts to teach children result in a teacher-directed approach, which is more product than process-oriented. This raises the issues of developmental appropriateness and creativity. One's intentions may be good in teaching children how to do a craft, but what has been gained if children become frustrated and unsuccessful when asked merely to copy or use skills that are beyond their developmental level? Second, some crafts such as tie-dye or batik are not only difficult but also dangerous for children. Third, there is a risk that the craft may not reflect the total cultural group. This would lead to a stereotype and negate efforts to portray all cultures accurately. Fourth, the study of a group of people and their representative crafts must be done in a way that is holistic and integrated, as opposed to being randomly addressed. Our intent should be to help children construct a view of cultural similarities, including the making of arts and crafts, which includes a recognition and valuing of differences.

"Me" Book

Children can illustrate pages of their "All about Me" book. Sample activities include drawing one's face, body, senses, likes, dislikes, house, family, and friends.

My Twin

After learning about "me," children can lie down on a long sheet of butcher paper. Encourage children to spread out their arms and legs slightly. The teacher can carefully trace around the outline of each child. Children can cut and color their twin, paying attention to color of hair, eyes, and clothing. A full-length mirror should be handy. Do not, however, expect a mirror image or realistic likeness.

My Three-Dimensional Twin

Using two sheets of butcher paper, follow the directions for the previous activity. Children can color or paint in the front and back. Slowly staple both sides together while gently stuffing with crumpled newspaper. As with the previous activity, expect children to take creative liberty. Because this tends to be a long activity, you may want to split it into several sequences. For example, separate sessions to trace, cut, color, stuff, and staple may be warranted. Art projects or activities need not be hurriedly completed in one session.

Family Flag

Briefly discuss how flags are symbols for countries. In our country, the United States, we use stars and stripes and the colors red, white, and blue. Let children carefully examine the flag. Encourage them to make their own flag for their family. "What can you put on your flag that tells us about you and your family?" Family members and things that remind them of their families can be included.

Murals

Making a mural is a good activity to wrap up or synthesize something. It is an activity that can be repeated with different areas or concepts being studied. For example, after a field trip to the bakery, children can draw a mural to represent what they experienced—people baking, decorating baked goods, rolling and kneading dough, selling bakery products, stocking shelves, and so on. After studying a unit on the farm, children can represent what they have learned about the farm in a mural. If a farm mural does not contain animals, vehicles, and buildings related to the farm theme, the teacher may conclude that perhaps the children did not learn much about the farm. The teacher may want to review key concepts in discussing the farm mural. Or it may simply be that the bus ride over and the picnic lunch were more meaningful.

Feelings Puppet

Use group time to discuss different feelings. Label feelings and discuss events that make us feel this way. Make a face and pass around a hand mirror so children can see how a certain feeling makes them look. Discuss how feelings are always good although the behavior that accompanies them may not be acceptable. For example, it is OK to feel angry and everyone does; it is not OK, however, to hit someone because you are angry. Make a two-sided puppet. Begin a feelings discussion by introducing and comparing feeling happy and sad. A child can make a happy face on one side of the plate and a sad face on another. Discuss what makes each child feel happy or sad. Attach a craft stick for a handle. Children can turn their puppet to either happy or sad as you discuss specific situations, such as not having a friend to play with.

Group Mobile

This activity provides a sense of group belonging and is recommended for the beginning of the year. Some teachers use photographs while others ask children to draw their own pictures. Names can be added. Provide a forked tree branch or dowel rods and let each child hang his or her own picture. Mobiles are versatile and children can make their own. Pictures cut from magazines symbolizing children's feelings, interests, and so forth can also be hung from a smaller base, such as a pencil or single branch.

"Me" Prints

Children can use their fingers, hands, or feet to leave marks that represent who they are. Fingers can be pressed on water-soluble ink pads and printed onto paper. Hands and/or feet can be painted and printed onto paper. The shapes suggest possible designs and children may want to combine and customize their body prints.

Holiday Art

Before Thanksgiving, use group time to engage children in a discussion of things they are thankful for

and ways to give thanks. Lay out a long piece of butcher or mural paper. Provide markers and crayons and let children represent the people, events, and things in their lives for which they give thanks. In the spring, around Easter time, make a collage using eggshells. Make hard-boiled eggs for snack and save the shells to make a collage. Place large shell pieces in bag and carefully crush. Provide colored construction paper and encourage children to glue pieces into a design. Dying or decorating eggs before eating them is another option.

Holiday Sentiments

Art, child-centered and initiated, is the perfect gift for a child to give. It may be nonverbal, but it conveys personal meaning and love. After studying any of the major holidays, children can be encouraged to plan and implement an artistic representation of the joy, hope, love, and fellowship associated with that particular holiday. A simple but personalized greeting card or collage may result.

ART AND THE EXPRESSIVE ARTS

Art is merely one mode of creative expression. Music and movement are two other **expressive arts** that are vital to early childhood. Both art and movement involve nonverbal expression. What children represent in art can also be represented through movement. Tracy is fascinated with unicorns and attempted to make one out of clay. Its long horn was prominent. During a "Guess what I am" movement session, Tracy pretended to be a unicorn, moving on all fours while indicating something sticking out of her forehead. Just as music can foster artistic expression through a certain mood, tone, tempo, or beat, it can also trigger spontaneous movement.

Some activities that incorporate art with the other expressive arts follow.

Musical Painting

Encourage children to hand paint or color to different types of music. These may include slower classical, pop show tunes, and rock music. Discuss how paint strokes, movement, and design are related to the tempo of the music.

Costumes and Props

Children can design, paint, or color masks, costumes, scenery, and props related to a play or movement

Anti-Bias Curriculum

What do we mean by the terms *bias* and *anti-bias*? According to Derman-Sparks (1989), *bias* is any attitude, belief, or feeling that results in and helps to justify unfair treatment of one's identity. *Anti-bias* refers to an active approach to challenging prejudice, stereotyping, bias, and the "isms," including sexism, racism, and handicappism. It is necessary for each individual to intervene, challenge, and counter behaviors that perpetuate bias and oppression. The activist approach characterizes empowerment, knowing what is morally right and acting on one's convictions. To do nothing to counteract bias amounts to supporting bias (Derman-Sparks, Gutierrez, and Phillips, n.d.).

Because bias undermines the optimal development of children as unique individuals, antibias attitudes must be fostered early. According to Derman-Sparks (1989), pre-prejudice, the beginning ideas and feelings in very young children, may develop into real prejudice. Pre-prejudice takes many forms. It may be misconceptions based on young children's limited experience and developmental level, or it may consist of imitation of adults at home or in the media. More serious forms are behaviors that indicate discomfort, fear, or rejection of differences.

Derman-Sparks' (1989) notion of empowerment advocates implementing an anti-bias curriculum that incorporates the best of multicultural education, but it is broader in scope. An anti-bias curriculum provides a more inclusive education in three ways. First, it addresses more than cultural diversity by including gender and differences in physical abilities. Second, it is based on children's developmental tasks as they construct identity and attitudes. Third, it directly addresses the impact of stereotyping, bias, and discriminatory behavior in young children's development and interactions.

Derman-Sparks and the ABC Task Force (1989) identified four goals for children in an anti-bias curriculum. Through class activities and interactions with peers and adults, each child should:

1. construct a knowledgeable and confident self-identity.
2. develop comfortable, empathetic and fair ways of interacting with others.
3. develop critical thinking about bias and stereotypes.
4. learn the skills for standing up for self and others in the face of injustice.

Early childhood teachers help children move toward those goals by providing materials that depict individuals of differing cultures, races and genders engaged in a variety of positive activities, and by actively teaching children to recognize and address bias and prejudice in their environments. Appendix I provides a list of tradebooks that teachers may use in an anti-bias curriculum.

---

activity. For example, children can design paper-plate masks for the different characters in "The Gingerbread Boy." A mural can be decorated and used as scenery.

Musical Instruments

Children can make and play their own homemade musical instruments. There are many possibilities. We will focus on making a guitar. Children will need their own shoe box, which can be decorated with paint, crayons, markers, and stickers. The teacher needs to cut a large oval hole in the lid. Cover box and tape the edges of the

lid to the box. Wrap four strong rubber bands around the box lengthwise. Children can strum their guitars.

Streamers

Children can make their own streamers to accompany their creative movement and dance activities. Provide small paper plates which the children can decorate. Assist them in attaching lengths of crepe paper. These can be stapled on or threaded through punched holes and knotted. Turn on the music and watch children run outdoors or move creatively indoors while holding their streamers. Variations for streamer holders include wooden paint-mixing sticks and cardboard tubes from toilet paper or paper towels.

 THREE-DIMENSIONAL ART

Assemblage refers to a three-dimensional collage in which children creatively assemble an array of objects. *Construction* and *sculpture* are similar terms referring to **three-dimensional art** that may or may not resemble anything. Technically, children can also sculpt with clay; this was discussed in Chapter 11. Our present discussion of sculpture will address forms other than clay. Even young children are aware that objects are composed of parts and pieces. A table needs a top supported by legs. People have a trunk that supports their head and rests on limbs. Cars have a body supported by a frame on wheels. "How can I make my own three-dimensional model of the things that are important to me?" asks the young sculptor.

Fixatives and Fasteners

Most three-dimensional creations will require some sort of fixative or fastener. Some common types include the following:

brads
clothespins—pinch type
glue sticks
metal fasteners
paper clips
paper fasteners
pipe cleaners
rubber bands
stapler—small, but not miniature, and staples
string
tape—cellophane, masking, and colored
twist ties
white glue
wire
yarn

Here are some three-dimensional art activities recommended for young children.

Container Creations

The shapes of containers suggest the shapes of people, animals, vehicles, buildings, machines, and objects. Children enjoy using tape, glue, and staples to hold together an array of boxes, bottles, and cartons. Encourage children to think of something—an animal, a vehicle, or an object—that the containers suggest. For example, square boxes stacked together might suggest a robot. A row or strip of egg cups from an egg carton may suggest a caterpillar, snake, or train. A plastic milk container could suggest a head if yarn is added for hair. Look for boxes, bottles, and cartons that have an unusual shape. As always, container creations need not resemble anything at all. Some recommended containers include the following:

- oatmeal boxes
- salt boxes
- small gift boxes
- cereal boxes
- pill bottles
- milk cartons, cardboard and plastic
- coffee tins
- detergent bottles
- toilet tissue rolls and cardboard tubes
- egg cartons
- film containers
- food containers
- berry baskets
- cigar boxes
- round pizza plates
- deli containers

Containers can be glued or taped together. Decorate them with bottle caps, lids, ribbon, paper cups, paper scraps, straws, and other small pieces. Creations can be painted, with detergent added to paint to help it adhere.

Egg Carton Art

Individual egg cups from egg cartons or groups of cups can be creatively combined on a piece of cardboard. Children will enjoy varying the color, placement, shapes, and sizes. The raised, patterned three-dimensional effect is visually pleasing.

Wooden Wonders

Children can use liquid white glue to affix small wooden scraps together. A hammer and nails can also be used. The resulting construction may represent something or merely be an assemblage of wood pieces. Check with local lumberyards, carpenters, or high school shop teachers for small wood scraps. Request wood scraps with interesting shapes and angles. Creations can also be decorated with trim or nature specimens and painted if the child decides it is necessary. One teacher suggested that children think up their very own machines and then try to make them out of wood scraps. Some children decided to make candy, toy, and fun machines. Pieces of string (for fan belts), wire, nuts and bolts, and small machinery parts were added for decoration. Others decided to merely glue together their wooden scraps. All products were accepted and valued (see Figure 12–8).

Tinfoil Treasures

Children can glue an array of small objects onto a piece of sturdy cardboard. Recommended three-dimensional items include the following:

- golf tees
- rubber bands
- paper clips
- buttons
- nuts, bolts, washers, and screws
- small nature specimens
- beads
- cotton swabs
- pieces of yarn, string, or cord

Use an old brush to paint white liquid glue over the entire surface. Arrange the items on the gluey cardboard. Carefully place a larger sheet of tinfoil over the raised surface. Very carefully, press, wrinkle, and mold the tinfoil around the raised objects to reveal their characteristic shape. Be careful that the embedded objects do not tear through the tinfoil. Fold the excess tinfoil under the cardboard and secure it with tape or glue. The result will be an interesting raised effect or relief, done in silver. Thoroughly wash the glue out of the paintbrush before it gets a chance to harden.

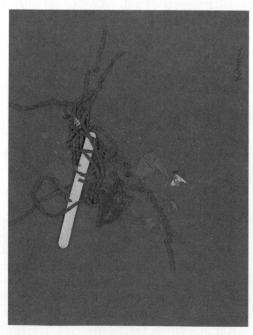

Figure 12-8 Using wooden craft sticks to make art.

Tinfoil Sculpture

Children will enjoy working with tinfoil as the medium for sculpture. For example, tinfoil can be rolled to form an elephant's trunk and wadded to form its head. Individual parts can be taped together or stuck together with straight pins. Or children can form their sculpture out of one piece of tinfoil. For example, the elephant's legs can be carefully pulled, pinched, molded, and rolled out from the body. Remember to start with a fairly large piece of tinfoil—about 12 inches × 16 inches. Remind children that since they are starting with a large, flat sheet, they can expect their finished three-dimensional product to be much smaller.

Plastic Foam and Toothpick Sculpture

Children enjoy sticking toothpicks into plastic foam. An upside-down foam tray or thicker solid piece can form the base. Smaller pieces of plastic foam—chips, squiggles, or egg carton sections—can be stuck on toothpicks and inserted into the base. Individual plastic foam pieces can also be connected with toothpicks to add height and a three-dimensional effect. The sculpture can also be decorated with paper, ribbon, lace, and other scraps. These sculptures will be very fragile and may not make it home intact. They can be proudly displayed in the classroom art gallery.

Hanger Head

You will need old stockings or pantyhose and coat hangers for this activity. Stretch the hanger out into a fairly round face shape. Cover it with pantyhose or a stocking and tie to secure. This will form the head. Encourage children to complete the face by adding yarn, felt, fabric scraps, or paper. Leaving the hook on top will allow it to hang. Keeping the hook on the bottom allows it to be held and used as a mask.

Spool Sculpture

Some craft supply stores sell wooden spools. Children love to stack them and glue them together. Spools can be added to a basic wood construction. Spool shapes may suggest people, animals, or vehicle forms.

Paper Sculpture

As discussed in Chapter 10, paper can be rolled, folded, coiled, and made into three-dimensional cones, cubes, and tubes. These may suggest legs or body forms and the base for further paper sculpting.

Paper Strip Sculpture

Strips of construction paper are ideal for making sculpture. Start with a plastic foam tray for a base. Children can secure one end of a paper strip to the base. The balance of the strip can be pleated, folded, or connected to other strips. Continue processing with paper in sculpting a three-dimensional form. Remind children that the result can be an interesting intersection of paper strips and need not look like anything.

Stuffed Newspaper Sculpture

This activity is similar to "My Three-Dimensional Twin," presented earlier in this chapter. The present activity extends beyond a self-portrait. Each child will need four large sheets of newspaper. Older children may want to draw their outlines first and then cut them out. For example, a large dinosaur can be sketched. Avoid adding fine details and small parts. Carefully cut out the outline through all four layers of newspaper. Two layers will form the front and two the back. Slowly, stuff with small wads of crumpled newspaper while stapling shut. Use paint, crayons, or markers to decorate.

Totem Pole Sculpture

Ice-cream parlors may save round gallon-size ice-cream cartons for you. The shape and size are ideal for making masks. Individual cartons can be decorated and stacked on top of each other like a totem pole. Secure with tape between cartons.

Soap Sculpture

Older children who know how to use a knife properly can be trusted to do this activity with supervision. They will need their own bar of soap and a small but fairly sharp knife for carving. Encourage them to draw the outline of an object on their bar of soap and to use their knife to sculpt. Advise them to select a fairly simple shape, without intricate parts or details. Rough edges or cut sides can be smoothed by rubbing with a wet finger.

Soap Suds Sculpture

Children enjoy sculpting and molding this white clay substance. To make, pour 1 cup of soap powder and 1

tablespoon of warm water into a mixing bowl. Beat with electric beater to clay-like consistency. This will make about 1 cup. Have children sculpt and mold as they would clay or play dough. Items can be decorated with trims. Allow to harden. The clay dries with a permanently hard finish.

Ice Sculpture

Making an ice sculpture is a good outdoor activity on a hot day. Freeze water in a large container, such as a plastic mixing bowl, the day before. You can also use a balloon that has been filled with water and left in the freezer for two days. Tear and pull away the balloon. Place the ice chunk in a dish tub or large baking pan. Provide plastic spray bottles. Fill some with clear water and others with water to which you have added liquid watercolor. Provide colors that mix and complement rather than turn muddy when mixed. Also provide shakers of salt and glitter. Set the bottles for *stream*, not *spray*. Encourage children to "mist" the ice with water and observe. What happens when salt is sprinkled on the ice? Shaved ice and ice cubes can also be added and compared. Do some melt faster than others? You can also provide eyedroppers or plastic meat basters, along with containers of warm water. Does water temperature make a difference in the time it takes for the ice to melt?

Wire Wonders

Use a fairly sturdy but flexible grade of wire for sculpting. Types of thin wire that are recommended include copper, brass, steel, florist, aluminum, baling, insulated telephone (in a rainbow of colors), and no. 19 stovepipe wire. Look for wire in various gauges ranging from 14 to 28. One foot is a good length. Children will enjoy twisting and turning the wire into unusual shapes. They may also try to represent something. The wire sculpture can be glued or nailed to a small piece of wood for a sturdy, supportive base.

Scene in a Box

Children will need their own shoe box for this activity, which is also called a diorama. This activity takes much time, planning, and patience in positioning smaller items and is recommended for older children. The shoe box becomes the overall three-dimensional frame or stage. Children can choose a theme—for example, family or a favorite story. The inside of the box can be decorated like one's house, with family members added. Remember, the internal space is deep, allowing for three-dimensional placement. Objects can be placed in several rows to suggest depth. Items such as fish could be suspended from the inside top with string for an underwater scene. One young girl did just that, basing her Scene in a Box on the book *Swimmy* by Leo Lionni. (See Appendix E for a list of art-related books.)

Salt Sculpture

Children will need their own clear glass bottles or jars with lids. You will need several different colors of salt. Salt can be colored by rubbing it with colored chalk. Place one color in each section of a muffin tin or in a paper cup. Gently pour one color into the bottle or jar. Use a small spoon or paper cup, or let it slide in from the fold of a creased paper. Make the layer any height. Add a second color by carefully directing the flow and position as you pour. There is no need to shake or tip the bottle or jar. Each layer will form its own uneven shape. Use a pencil to carefully poke along the sides and through layers for an interesting effect. Add different-colored layers until the jar is full. Let it sit overnight to settle. You may need to add an additional color the next day to get it completely full. Cover the jar tightly with the lid. This makes an excellent gift, especially if the children did most of the work by themselves. Very young children may need to use a fairly small container with a wide top.

Glue Overs

Each child will need a piece of plastic foam cut from a meat tray. Encourage them to use markers to make a picture or design. Use a wide variety of colors, and leave little empty space. Let dry. Use an old paintbrush to paint liquid white glue over the entire surface. Let dry thoroughly. This will produce a sealed, slick surface that enhances the colors underneath. These make attractive ornaments or items to hang from a mobile.

Three-Dimensional Junk Collage

A collection of three-dimensional items can be glued to sturdy cardboard. The result is a series of three-dimensional collage using recycled or *junk* items including but not limited to corks, craft sticks, Easter grass, and plastic bottle tops from milk, soft drink, and other containers. Notice how some artists used items to extend their art outside the cardboard base. This reflects creativity, because children selected their own materials and arranged them into their own plan for a collage.

Papier-Mâché

Papier-mâché means "chewed paper" in French and refers to the process of building up layers of paper that has been torn, wadded, and molded (although not chewed) to make a three-dimensional form. The paper is dipped in an adhesive mixture. Newspaper that has been torn in strips and soaked overnight will be more pliable. Squeeze excess water. Some of the many ways to do papier-mâché that are appropriate for young children are described below.

Paper Strip Method. Strips of newspaper or paper towels, about ½ to 1 inch wide, are dipped in a mixture of white glue and water or other papier-mâché medium (see recipe). Strips cut from paper bags are also recommended because of their thickness and texture. Carefully squeeze out the excess liquid between your fingers. Layers that are too thick with glue or paste will mold when drying. Begin to form your object. The strips should be smooth and overlapping. The layers should go in different directions to provide strength. Remove wrinkles or bubbles by smoothing with the hand. Apply only two or three layers at a time. Let dry. Details can be added to transform the basic shape. Or add additional layers. For example, a wadded ball of newspaper can be added to the top of a jar or bottle to form a head. Secure with masking tape. Let dry thoroughly before adding additional layers. Add a final layer of paper towels to give a clean top surface for painting or final decorating. Set on wax paper to dry thoroughly before painting. An adult can seal tempera paint by spraying with a fixative or cheap hair spray. This activity should be conducted over a series of days. It may prove frustrating for the very young child who wants the project completed in one short session.

It is recommended that young children do their papier-mâché over some solid base or form such as a

- blown-up balloon: carefully cut finished product in half to get two bowls or two face masks.
- bottle or jar.
- gift box.
- tissue roll.
- container.
- crushed or rolled newspaper.
- plastic milk or detergent bottle.
- light bulb: to make a sound shaker or music maker similar to a maraca. When it is decorated and dry, gently hit it on the floor to break the inside bulb without damaging the exterior papier-mâché shell. Patch if necessary.

Papier-Mâché Paste (cooked)
3 cups water
1½ cups flour
oil of peppermint

Stir flour into cold water. Cook over low heat until mixture thickens and resembles creamy paste. Add more water if too thick. Cool. Add a few drops of peppermint oil. Use this paste to coat strips of paper.

Hanger Objects

The "Hanger Head" activity can also be used with papier-mâché. Stretch a coat hanger into a desired shape or form. Add long strips of newspaper dipped in papier-mâché mixture to form a solid base. Decorate as a face or whatever the shape suggests. For a self-portrait, add yarn for hair and buttons for eyes.

Stuffed Bag

A paper bag can be filled with wads of newspaper and shaped into a general form. This can be the base. Strips of newspaper dipped into a papier-mâché mixture can be wrapped around the base and used to form details, such as arms, legs, head, tail, and so forth.

Papier-Mâché Relief

The older child who is experienced in papier-mâché may like this variation. A piece of cardboard is needed for the base. A simple picture or design should be sketched in pencil. The picture or design will be continued in relief by building it up with strips or small pieces of paper that have been dipped in a papier-mâché mixture. The paper can be twisted, rolled, coiled, or formed into the needed shape. For example, a round, flat mass could be used for the sun, and thin, rolled paper snakes could be the rays. Keep building up additional layers to give the three-dimensional or relief effect.

Piñata

A blown-up balloon can be used as the base for a Mexican piñata. Wrap papier-mâché over the balloon. Follow the directions for papier-mâché. Poke the balloon with a needle when you are finished. Cut open a small hole and fill the piñata with stickers, candy, tokens, or small treats. Cover the hole with additional strips of papier-mâché. Hang it overhead or from a tree limb outdoors. Blindfolded children will enjoy swinging a stick at the piñata. Breaking the piñata will result in a shower of goodies and shrieks of excitement.

Casting Capers

See the recipe for making plaster. You will also need some damp sand to form the mold for casting with plaster. Line a box, grocery bag, or old dishpan with a plastic trash bag or tinfoil and fill it with 4 inches of sand. Make an impression by carefully scooping out the sand. Wiggle your fingers for an interesting effect. Do not scoop down to the bottom of the container. Add nature specimens and small pieces of artistic junk. This will form the front of your cast sculpture and will become your mold. Remember, the casting will be the opposite of the impression you make. For example, holes dug into the sand will be cast as bumps protruding out of your sculpture.

Always add water to powder and mix plaster to a milkshake consistency. Keep stirring and work quickly. Carefully pour plaster into the mold. Add food coloring or tempera if coloring is desired. Gently shake or tap the container to help settle the mixture. Insert a hairpin, paper clip, or bent wire at the surface (which will really be the back side) if you want the sculpture to hang. Or simply insert both hands to cast a hand print. The top will now be your front side. Let the plaster set, and when it is thoroughly dry, gently brush away the sand. Casting is a time-consuming activity that only one child can do at a time, given this setup. It may be easier to do this outside in the sandbox, or ideally at the beach!

Plaster (for molds)

8 cups patch plaster
5 cups water
Mix thoroughly. The recipe will make enough for four molds. This recipe can be used in place of plaster of paris, which dries very fast. Patch plaster is inexpensive and takes at least 30 minutes to dry.

Squeeze a Sculpture

For this activity, simply pour plaster into a small, sturdy, zip-lock, plastic bag. Fill it 3 inches full, squeeze out excess air, and add nature specimens, artistic junk, or coloring. Seal bag securely. Wait several minutes for the plaster to thicken. Encourage children to squeeze and manipulate the filled bag into an interesting shape. Hold it in place for a few minutes until it feels warm and it begins to harden. Let the plaster dry overnight. Tear away the plastic bag and paint or decorate the sculpture with markers. The result will be a piece of sculpture with an interesting shape that would also make a good paperweight or gift for parents.

Balloon Creatures

Using an old bowl, an adult stirs and mixes plaster of paris until creamy. Pour into an empty balloon using a funnel with a large opening. This takes teamwork involving at least two. Set the plaster-filled balloon on table, gently molding until it starts to harden. This will take several minutes and may exceed the patience of the very young. Stop handling. Let go and allow to completely dry for at least 30 minutes. Gently tear off balloon. Decorate and paint if desired. Disposable kitchen gloves can also be used as the mold. Remember to work quickly, for once mixed the plaster begins to harden. Do not pour excess plaster down the drain for it may harden in the pipes, causing a plumbing problem.

SUMMARY

Curriculum means different things to different people; it can mean the overall program or a particular subject area. In this second view, art is merely one curricular area. A discussion and suggested activities emphasized the relationship between art and math, science, communication/language arts or literacy, social studies, and the other expressive arts.

Key Terms

assemblage

curriculum

expressive arts

papier-mâché

three-dimensional art

Suggested Activities

1. Interview two teachers regarding their views and definitions of curriculum. Do they agree or disagree? Do their views match those in this chapter?
2. Devise an activity that integrates art with one or more of the early childhood curricular areas.
3. Implement one of the integrated art activities with an individual or small group.
4. Your instructor can recommend a site where an experienced teacher skillfully merges art with other activities. Examine the lesson plan and get a feel for how an integrated curriculum is planned and carried out.

5. Consider carefully the views outlined in this chapter about including multicultural arts and crafts in early childhood curriculum. What are your views on this issue? Discuss your position with a friend.
6. Facilitate a three-dimensional art activity with children.

Review

1. Identify the two major ways of viewing the early childhood curriculum.

2. List the major early childhood curricular areas.

3. Match each art-related activity with a curricular area that it attempts to incorporate or integrate.

   a. counting the number of children at the art center to see if there are too many

   b. explaining to another child the steps involved in making a print of one's finger painting

   c. doing a Thanksgiving collage of people and things we are thankful for

   d. Zak painting XZo across his picture for his name

   e. Larry finding that quickly stirring water into powder tempera makes colorful bubbles

   1. speaking

   2. writing

   3. science

   4. social studies

   5. math

4. Discuss the benefits of an integrated early childhood curriculum.

5. Develop a plan to integrate anti-bias curriculum in your early childhood curriculum.

For additional art and creative development resources, visit our Web site at www.EarlyChildEd.delmar.com

Chapter 13

The Art Center

Think of a young child faced with the opportunity to engage in art. There are many decisions to make. The child asks, "What should I make?" and "What should I use to make it?" What message does this art center convey to the child? Would you like to have this art center in your classroom? Why or why not?

The materials appear to be arranged, organized, and grouped together. For example, all the pipe cleaners go together in one tub. The tubs are constructed of clear plastic so that the contents are visible. Clear containers help not only in locating materials but also in cleanup. There are several, but not too many, choices. Materials are rotated weekly to sustain children's interest in returning to the art center.

Objectives

After reading this chapter, you should be able to:

- List and discuss the five criteria for setting up an early childhood art center.
- Compare and contrast two- and three-dimensional art media.
- Describe ways to make the art center accessible to *all* children in the classroom.
- Identify potential rules and limits for successfully operating an early childhood art center.
- Evaluate the effectiveness of an art center/program.
- Make puppets and masks.

INTRODUCTION

Have you ever attended a buffet dinner? Salads were grouped together. Dishes, silverware, and napkins were arranged at the ends of the table. Desserts were clustered near the end of the table. Special arrangements were made for keeping certain dishes warm. This logic and organization can be applied to setting up an art center.

In many classrooms, similar materials are grouped together. Opaque containers are labeled with a piece of their contents glued to the outside. An outline and drawing of the contents of each container appear on a label adhered to the shelf on which the container rests. Art centers will vary depending on available space, resources, and individual teacher's style.

The art center will take care of itself most of the time. Many children will be able to make choices, decisions, and see connections between media and materials. Others will process until they tire or until they create a product that pleases them. Some will have an idea of what they want to make beforehand. Rotating materials will keep the children returning. Offering new activities will also extend the array of possibilities.

The rationale for setting up the art program around a center format is that this allows for discovery, choice, responsibility, and independent activity. The early childhood art center should be an artist's studio, conveniently located and easily accessible, well stocked, orderly and organized, with rules and limits. These criteria or guidelines will be explained in this chapter.

THE ART CENTER

The classroom **art center** is an area where children can go to do art. Most programs already have centers set up for manipulatives, table toys, blocks, books, and dramatic play. Others have centers for science, water play, and sand play. Although space is always at a premium, an early childhood art center is warranted. Just what is an art center, and how does one go about starting it and maintaining it? The criteria for an art center would include the following. An art center is

1. an artist's studio.
2. conveniently located and easily accessible.
3. well stocked with developmentally appropriate materials.
4. orderly and organized.
5. a place with rules and limits.

Each of these five points will be examined in detail.

▶▶ 1. An Artist's Studio

N
A
E
Y
C

An artist's studio should be visually appealing and inviting. By its appearance it conveys a message that this is a place where creative art happens. Children need a well-thought-out space where they can explore, not just a table from which the teacher conducts adult-directed projects. An artist's studio is a place to make connections and choices from an array of materials conducive to making two- and three-dimensional art. An artist's studio is an inviting spot that reflects creative clutter and often some noise rather than an emphasis on excessive quiet and neatness. It is a place to go and discover, process, experiment, and explore. The art center resembles a workshop where participants engage in maximum effort with some mess. Artists enjoy visual stimulation and like to see the work of artists depicted in posters, prints, or calendars, as well as their own work, displayed at their eye level. Reserve adjacent wall and counter space for displaying children's creations. Be sure to include books about art and artists, thereby connecting your art and literacy program.

The child should be exposed to a variety of stimulating activities and experiences with legitimate artistic media. These will complement, broaden, and balance self-directed free expression. They will depend, in part, upon the individual child's developmental level, coordination, ability, and interest level. A balance between process and product can be built into one's art center. The creative process of painting and exploring visual symbols is as important as the finished product, perhaps a painted picture. Pounding, rolling, pinching, and stretching clay are as important as the aesthetic quality of the finished clay piece.

Art Activities As Suggestions, Not Prescriptions.

There is danger in merely listing or prescribing a set of art activities. These are included merely as suggestions or possibilities, not as a set of activities to fill the pages of one's lesson plans on a day-to-day basis. Teaching them directly as specific activities would negate everything we have discussed about art as a creative discovery process. Instead, encourage children to discover many of these extensions or possibilities on their own. The activities are based on a few media (see Figure 13–1).

▶▶ Mixing Media.
N A E Y C

Mixing media results in the discovery of new artistic possibilities. For example, let us assume that children have worked with crayons at

Figure 13-1 Mixed media: paper art and coloring.

the table and paints at the easel. Ask children, "What would happen if we used them together? Can you paint over your coloring? Or can you use markers along with colored pencils? Have you ever tried to do a collage over your dried hand painting?" The possibilities for creative mixing are endless. One need not suggest specific combinations but merely reinforce experimenting with and joining different artistic media.

▶▶ Varying the Tool, Method, and Media.
N A E Y C

Varying the tool will help children discover new artistic possibilities. For example, they have painted with an array of paintbrushes, flat and round. Ask them, "Can we paint with a toothbrush? Is there a brush in your house or garage that could be used for painting? Let's think of things other than brushes that we could use for painting."

Varying the method will also lead to new possibilities. Paint can be spread with a brush to make long, sweeping lines. There are also many other ways to apply paint. It can be dabbed, swirled, sprayed, dripped, and dribbled.

Varying the medium also increases the range of possibilities. Children can paint with water, colored water, transparent watercolors, thick opaque tempera, or tempera to which sand, salt, or sugar has been added.

Incorporate Both Two- and Three-Dimensional Art Media.

Similarly, there should be a balance between two-dimensional and three-dimensional art media. Two-dimensional activities involve a relatively flat artistic surface with height and width portrayed. Three-dimensional art activities also portray depth. Some activities, including work with paper, allow for both two- and three-dimensional expression.

2. Conveniently Located and Easily Accessible

An art center should be conveniently located and easily accessible, not cramped into a crowded corner. It should be located near a sink and removed from the main stream of classroom traffic. The location of the sink and of neighboring centers will determine where the art area is placed. For example, an art center should not be placed in the middle of the room, where children will walk through it while visiting other centers. Because different activities or centers have their own noise levels, it would be wise to locate the art center near other noisy activities. For example, the art center could be located near the block area, since both centers encourage children to move, talk, socialize, and be active. It is not recommended that the art center be located adjacent to the book corner or quiet area. If your room does not have a sink, pails of water can be stored in the art area. Paper towels should also be provided.

An art center need not be restricted to the indoors. Art can be offered as an activity during outdoor free play. An easel or art cart on wheels can be easily rolled in and out as needed. When identifying the best spot for your art center, try to select a spot that is easy to view and supervise, both up close and from a distance. The tabletops should be easy to clean. A plastic-laminated tabletop can be easily wiped clean with a damp sponge. Try to avoid placing the art center in a carpeted area. If necessary, cover the flooring under the easel and art table with newspaper or an old shower curtain. An old washable throw rug placed under the easel would be both practical and attractive. Ideally, children will clean up after themselves. Good lighting is also important in the art center, particularly for children with marginal vision. If possible, locate the art center close to a window for natural lighting. If not, make sure that adequate artificial lighting is available. Try to reserve adjacent wall space to display children's artwork. Samples of artists' work reflecting different artistic styles can also be displayed. The intent is not to encourage children to copy but to expose and educate them to the different ways in which people have done and continue to do art. If space permits, art books, laminated prints, and art postcards can also be kept close, but at a sufficient distance from water, paint, and other media that might soil them. Adjacent counter space can be reserved for displaying three-dimensional artwork, including clay, sculpture, construction, assemblage, and papier-mâché. Adjacent floor space can be reserved for drying paintings, or a commercial drying rack can be used.

3. Well Stocked with Developmentally Appropriate Materials

The art center should be well stocked with developmentally appropriate basic art media, tools, equipment, accessories, and artistic junk (see Figure 13–2). An art center need not entail great expense and can operate on a modest budget if planning and economical purchasing are involved. Plan with other teachers to order in bulk.

Buy high-quality nonconsumable items such as brushes, which will last. Much of your art budget will go for purchasing consumable items such as paint and paper, which will be used up in time and will need to be reordered. Frills like glitter, fur, feathers, sequins, and wiggly eyes are not necessary. They are expensive and can be quickly used up. Supplement purchased

Figure 13-2 A well-displayed art center.

items with things you can recycle. Thrift shops, garage or yard sales, and rummage sales are good sources of inexpensive items that can be recycled into art activities. Families are an excellent source of contributions. Send home a list that specifically lists what you need. Mom may be able to bring computer paper or outdated office forms from work. Grandma may respond to your request for buttons and fabric by donating the contents of her old sewing box. Donating benefits everyone. The family feels involved and your art center becomes well stocked.

What should be on the shelves of your art center? There are at least six basic categories of art materials, including:

- tools for mark making, e.g., crayons, pencils, markers, chalk.
- papers in a variety of shapes, sizes, and textures (specific examples to follow).
- modeling and molding materials, e.g., clay and play dough, and tools.
- items for cutting, fastening, and attaching, e.g., scissors, glue, paste, tape, hole punches, staplers and staples, string, pipe cleaners.
- items for painting and making prints, e.g., paint, brushes, and related tools.
- collage items, e.g., nature specimens, fabric, old jewelry, wallpaper, yarn, gift wrap.

Remember to include materials to provide meaningful experiences for all the children in your classroom, including those children with special needs. For example, children with low vision and/or poor hearing will enjoy

- tactile and multisensory experiences with textured and scented paint and play dough.
- brightly colored or fluorescent paint that contrasts with the background paper and table top.
- reflective safety tape for sticking.

- rebus charts with pictures illustrating steps or directions.

Papers

The number of different types of paper that children can use in their artwork is practically infinite; for example, they can use the following:

adding machine tape—for paper sculpture and paper chains

adhesive-backed—solicit scraps for paper art activities

blotter—for soaking up excess water with watercolors

boxes—for painting and marking on

brown wrapping paper—for murals, puppets, papier-mâché, paper sculpture, and paper art activities requiring sturdy paper

butcher paper—a long roll for making murals; good for finger painting

calendars

carbon paper—for transferring designs

cardboard—flat, corrugated, tubes for a variety of art activities

catalogues—for paper tearing, cutting, pasting, and collage

cellophane—for color paddles, collage, and paper art activities

colored plastic wrap

coffee filters—for use with mark making, melted crayons, or dip and dye with food coloring

computer paper scraps—use the clean side for paper art activities

construction paper—good for crayons, chalk, and paint but not watercolor; difficult to fold in different directions; will fade over time; buy large sheets in assorted colors and cut down

contact paper

crepe paper—optional; buy other basic art papers first

doilies—for collage and other paper activities

egg cartons—cardboard and plastic

envelopes—good for mark making and artistically addressing

fadeless art paper—easier to fold and cut than construction paper but more expensive; only one side is colored and will not fade

finger paint paper—glazed surface; buy the largest size!

gift wrap or wrapping paper—for collage and other paper activities

Make Your Art Program Culturally Responsive

- Avoid presenting only white and black art media for people making. Few people have pale white skin, and not all dark-skinned people identify with the color black.

- Include multicultural art products (paint, crayons, markers, fabric, felt and paper) available from Crayola, Lakeshore, and other art suppliers.

- Help children mix paint that matches their skin colors. Keep a mirror handy for close examination. Comment on the beauty of the color.

- Mix play dough in shades of light, medium, and dark brown, as well as beige, tan, pink, and black. Add cocoa to your basic play dough recipe to make shades of skin color.

- Include fabric scraps representative of different culture and add it to your collage box.

- Provide diverse magazines such as *Ebony* and *National Geographic* for children to use in making a collage or a mural about people.

- Include cultural artifacts such as a garlic or tortilla press with your clay and play dough tools.

- Provide thick and thin lengths of yarn in shades of yellow, red-orange, brown, black, and gray for making hair.

- Display art posters depicting children and adults from around the world. Make sure the depiction of people is authentic rather than exotic. Include pictures of people engaged in art activities.

- Avoid commercial displays and patterns that are stereotypic or inaccurate and will give children the mistaken impression that all Hawaiians wear hula skirts or all Africans wear dashikis.

- Look for similarities. Hunt (1995) used the theme of light when planning for December holidays. She realized that Christmas, Hanukkah, and Kwanza all have light as a focus of their celebration. Each one has a candle-lighting ceremony. Christians light Advent candles, Jews light the menorah, and African-Americans light Kwanza candles. Art activities that flow from the theme of light including making Stars of David (six-pointed) and stars of Bethlehem (five-pointed) and making holiday cards for Hanukkah, Kwanza, or Christmas.

graph paper—large squares; you can easily make your own

greeting cards—recycled, for cutting, pasting, mobiles, and collage

grocery bags—all sizes and colors, heavy weight for painting and paper work activities

gummed stars, stickers, and labels—for licking and sticking on paper

kraft paper—3 feet wide to make murals, trace around children, and use for bulletin boards

magazines—for collage and montage

manila paper—a better grade than newsprint: rough surface, cream color, heavier weight; more expensive than newsprint but less expensive than white drawing paper. Manila paper is good for collage, gluing, coloring, painting, and pasting activities. Buy big and cut down.

manila file folders—old, used, sturdy

matboard—for making mats in picture frames; expensive

metallic paper—too expensive to put out on a daily basis

newspaper—for painting, stuffing, and cleanup

newsprint—least expensive paper for marking, scribbling, drawing, and coloring. Thick or heavy paint will bleed and soak through. Easy to fold, but tears with pressure. Comes in a variety of sizes. Buy big and cut down.

oak tag—comparable to manila paper in use and cost

oatmeal paper—textured paper for crayons, chalk, and prints

onionskin paper—nice texture for watercolor

origami paper—special paper for Japanese art form of paper folding

paper bags—in all sizes, for puppets, masks, and so forth

paper plates—plain white for masks and a round art surface

paper reinforcements—for stringing and making eyes, Os, and buttons

paper scrap saver—empty box or container

paper towels—for painting, dyeing, papier-mâché, and cleanup

picture story—to draw a picture and dictate a story

place mats—a good background for paper and other art activities

poster board—cheaper than matboard for making mats and frames

rice paper—fairly expensive; good surface for ink and watercolor

sandpaper—for resist, collage, and melted crayon wax

shelf paper—for making murals; good for hand painting if surface is glazed

shopping bags—cut open and lay flat for painting

tinfoil—for sculpture and special paper activities

tissue paper—comes in a variety of colors. Buy big and cut down.

tracing paper

typing paper—good for ink and watercolor

velour paper—nice velvety texture but expensive; use sparingly

wallpaper scraps, samples, and books—for matting, framing, collage. Also, most wallpaper will hold up to painting.

watercolor paper—expensive if bought by the sheet; also comes in tablet form

wax paper—for sealing paper shapes, resist activities

white drawing paper—a very good grade, heavy and fairly expensive. Good for all art projects, including painting. It looks clean and stands up to erasing; 60-pound weight is recommended. Buy big and cut down.

wrappers—from gum and candy, for pasting and collage

Hint: The larger the paper, the more expensive it will be. Still, large sheets can be used sparingly in their entirety and creatively cut down into smaller sizes and shapes. This will avoid boredom and needless waste and will be more economical in the long run.

Hint: Try butchers, carpet stores, print shops, and newspaper plants for newsprint, end rolls of paper, and brown wrap. These are good for making murals.

Hint: Use different types of paper, and be sure to include newspaper, grocery bags, and cardboard. The want ads make a good backdrop for a painting or collage. The colored comics section makes a good background for linear designs in black. Different surfaces pose a new problem and challenge for the painter. A torn-paper collage would work on the colored advertisement section. Grocery bags are heavy and can stand up to the repeated strokes of heavy paint from the very young painter.

Hint: Provide papers that pose a challenge. For example, cut papers into flag, diamond, rhombus, or amorphic shapes. Cut circles, squares, rectangles, and triangles from the inside of papers. This will force the artist to modify or adapt his or her processing to fit the paper. For example, one cannot merely sweep paint, crayons, or markers across a figure-eight-shaped paper. The curves will suggest a different swirling or circular type of arm movement and stroke.

Hint: For children with special physical needs, try using contact paper sticky side up for collage activities. This will eliminate the need for glue.

Tools/Accessories/Miscellaneous

Accessories for children to use in their artwork are limited only by the imagination. Some items the author has used with success include the following:

brayer—for painting and making prints

cookie sheets—as an art surface

cutting board—acrylic, undecorated for monoprints and clay

eggbeater, rotary—for art recipes, water play

Formica®—as an art surface

hangers—for making mobiles, weaving, puppets, and so forth

hot plate—for melting crayons

kitchen tools—for mixing ingredients, painting, and printing

linoleum—as an art surface

measuring cups and spoons—for recipes

mixing bowls—for mixing ingredients in recipes

paper punch—for mark making

pencil compass—for mark making

protractor—for mark making

rolling pin—for clay, painting, and printing

rubber stamps—for printing

ruler—for making marks with a pencil

screen—for spatter screen prints

spatula—for mixing paint and ingredients, work with clay, and printing

sponges—for painting and printing

spray bottle—for adding water to paint, as during hand painting and for wet watercolor

stamp pad—for printing

trays—for art surfaces

wax—for resist

wire—florist's, telephone, electronics—for construction, assemblage, weaving, sculpture, mobiles, and stabiles

To ensure full participation in the art center for children with differing physical abilities, be sure to include the following:

- Adaptive art tools such as fat bingo markers, chunky crayons, large markers, and large items

for printmaking and collage. Markers are easier to mark with than crayons.
- Double-handed ambidextrous scissors or spring scissors activated with a squeezing motion
- A cutting wheel and mat to use instead of scissors
- Glue sticks rather than bottles of glue
- Thickened paint in no-spill paint cups attached to the table with Velcro®
- Old knobbed shaving brushes, sponges, foam brushes, or short-handled brushes for easier painting
- Foam hair rollers into which paint brushes, markers or crayons can be inserted for a more secure grip
- A small wall-paint roller to paint on paper taped to a wall or easel

Hint: Formica® and linoleum make good art surfaces for painting with brushes, hand painting, sculpting with clay, or monoprinting. They define the individual artist's space, are easy to obtain, and are easy to clean. Old trays or cookie sheets are also recommended.

4. Orderly and Organized

The art center is orderly and organized to maximize efficiency. Although surplus junk may have creative potential, it remains useless junk unless it is somehow organized and attractively displayed. Children do not know where to begin with a box of fabric, ribbon, yarn, and gift wrap all thrown together. Too many items, fostering too many possibilities, overwhelm young children. Materials that are similar should be grouped together on low, open shelves. Therefore, basic tools like crayons, markers, and pencils should be placed next to each other. A second shelf can hold an array of papers grouped by size and shape. Ideally, containers should be clear so the contents are clearly visible. If not, add labels. Use a glue gun to affix an actual sample of the contents to the front of the container. For example, glue a twig and pinecone to the front of the box housing nature items. These tactile labels are especially important for children with low vision. You may also want to neatly print the words *nature items*. Labeling surrounds children with functional print that enhances their emerging literacy. Some teachers prefer to stock their shelves with activities set up on individual trays. For example, the tray for doing watercolor holds all the equipment one needs, including watercolor set, brush, sponge, and water container. Teach children the find-use-return cycle. Every item has a special place where it can be found. Use it safely and remember to return it when finished. This teaches personal responsibility and frees the teacher from total responsibility for maintaining the art center.

>> **N A E Y C** Shelves that are well stocked with materials, equipment, and supplies provide options from which to select. Start by putting out a limited number from which to choose. If you feel compelled to put out everything, children will feel obligated to use it all. Remember the three *R*s: replenish, rotate, and renew. Some items such as markers and crayons will stay out all the time. Other items such as collage materials will be rotated over time. For example, replace the nature specimens with fabric scraps. Initially, take children on a walking tour of the art center explaining the items, what they are called, how they are used, and where to find and return them. Continue to add items and enrich your art center over time as children display their ability to handle additional options. New items should be introduced during group time. For example, when placing sponges or twigs at the easel say, "Today I replaced the brushes at our two easels with twigs. Think of how you might use a twig to paint and see what happens." Aim for a balance between new and old. Replenish materials when children become bored but do not feel compelled to present new materials on a daily basis. According to Dighe, Calormiri, and Van Zutpen (1998) constantly introducing or changing art materials may actually stand in the way of a child's mastering the material enough to adequately and thoroughly express one's ideas or feelings.

Encourage children to keep their work spaces in the art center organized and orderly as well. This is especially important for children with special needs. Providing a tray will define a specific work space for a child unable actually to see when others are working and will set boundaries for a child who has not yet learned to share space with peers.

Through this subtle structuring, regularity, and predictability, the ordered environment of the art center serves as a model for children, who are often confused by disorder in their life and surroundings. In the art center, everything has its rightful place, and the child artists are responsible for daily maintenance and operation.

Storage and Containers

art carryall—plastic divided carrier with handle. Good for storing art supplies. Available at discount stores in housewares. Recommended for artist at home.

art cart—a two- and three-tiered cart on wheels. Lets you take your art program around the room and outdoors.

baskets—for storing ribbons, lace, trims, crayons

beverage carriers—cardboard with individual compartments to hold jars of paint

bookcase—with deep shelves for storage

boxes—to organize art supplies

bureau—old, for storing art supplies

cabinet—with doors removed and shelves for storage

cake pans

cardboard cartons

cigar boxes—for crayons, markers, lace, ribbon, and trims

classroom materials organizer—good for cubbies or for organizing different types of paper

coffee cans—with lids, to store clay

commercial ice-cream containers—fasten together and stack pyramid-style with open end visible; use for storage or art cubbies

corrugated cardboard cartons—sturdy, for storage

crates—stackable, for storage

cutlery tray—plastic, with compartments for organizing art supplies that go together, such as brushes

desk organizer—with compartments for small art supplies

dishpans—to hold papers, paste, glue, jars of paint, and brushes

easel and art storage—expensive but ideal! A large easel allows two painters at each side. Below are shelves for ample storage. Commercially available.

egg cartons—cardboard or plastic foam for storing small art supplies, such as buttons and beads

file cabinet—metal or cardboard; can hold art supplies. The problem is that the contents are not visible.

food keepers—see-through, good for storage

frozen dinner tray—with dividers, for holding small items

fruit basket—plastic, for holding ribbon, lace, spools, and so forth

hardware organizer—small plastic drawers for holding nails; good for organizing very small art items like buttons and jewelry pieces

ice-cream tubs—commercial, to hold paper and fabric scraps

juice cans—large, for storing paint, pencils, rulers, brushes, and other tall items

lazy Susan—good for organizing small items; rotate to bring close the items you need

loaf pans

margarine tubs—for storing paint, clay, and small art supplies

mini bins—stackable; good for storing art supplies

muffin tins—for melting crayons and sorting small art supplies like buttons and beads for collage

pie tins—to hold paint when making prints

pizza pans

plastic—pail, tubs, containers, squeeze bottles, pump sprayers, lidded food savers, cups, housewares

plastic foam—produce, meat, and fruit trays

shelving—sturdy, wood planks stacked on cinder blocks

shoe boxes—several the same size could be uniformly stacked and labeled with the word and picture of contents

shoe file—cardboard organizer with individual compartments, good for cubbies; available at discount stores

shoe organizers—with pockets to hang on wall; can hold rolled paper and other art supplies

storage bins—stackable in different sizes and colors

storage boxes—large plastic boxes with lids. Select clear so that you can see at a glance what is inside.

storage crates or cubes—plastic milk-type crates to stack; great for storing; found at discount stores; some can bolt together for stability

storage pails or buckets—with lid and handle; good for clay

storage unit—with shelves

sweater boxes—plastic with lids for storage

tin boxes—for holding crayons, chalk, and markers

trays—to define individual art space, hold paper, and so forth

utility cart—plastic pullout drawers in stand with wheels. Carts with solid frames are durable and stand up to constant pushing and pulling. Available in housewares at discount stores.

utility pans

Hint: Shelving can be made using sturdy lumber, thick and wide, stacked on cement blocks. Boards should be sanded free of splinters or covered with fabric or adhesive-backed paper. Position the blocks in a safe way so that young walkers will not bump into or trip over them.

Hint: A peg board with hooks by the art center is very useful. Smocks can be hung up on hooks. A sign system to indicate the number of people allowed at the art center at any one time can be displayed—for example, four palettes, one per hook, in the top row. Some art accessories can be hung from the hooks. For example, clear plastic or vinyl bags containing ribbon, fabric, and trims can be hung.

Hint: Regardless of the storage facility, make sure all containers are clearly labeled in print as well as with a picture. For example, a cigar box filled with markers would have the word *markers* and a sketch or picture of markers on the side facing the room.

Hint: Display paper on flat shelves. Put paint and brushes on a plastic-lined shelf. This will stand up to water and drops of wet paint.

5. A Place with Rules and Limits

Why rules and limits? Do not rules and limits stifle creativity? According to Cherry and Nielsen (1999), by carefully setting limits, teachers can be free to help children make the fullest use, according to their needs and interests, of the art materials provided. Creativity happens within the confines of safety. With a few, reasonable and appropriate limits, children have greater freedom for creative self-direction and for self-pacing than if there are no guidelines at all or if the limits are too many and too restricting.

Rules and limits should be fairly and equally applied to all children in the class. Young children with special needs may require special assistance and/or additional teacher monitoring. They may need to have directions repeated or broken down into smaller steps. In turn, special needs are accommodated. Still, children are children, and all need to follow classroom rules, although different incentives and strategies may be needed by some children to foster compliance. All children want to belong.

An art center provides the child with unlimited opportunities for attaining self-responsibility. Children abide by reasonable rules and limits. These rules and limits should be verbally discussed in advance, with the reasons for each rule clearly explained. Children need to know both the rules and the reasons behind them. For example, children discuss the proper use of materials. Paintbrushes are for painting. Waving paintbrushes in the air could either splash paint or hurt someone. Rules can also be posted in writing and pictures near the art center for easy reference. Rules and limits need to be discussed, posted, and enforced. Children who break a rule can be removed from the art center. When they have had time to reflect and believe that they are ready to abide by the rule, they can return.

Rules and limits will vary from teacher to teacher, center to center, classroom to classroom, program to program, and age group to age group. Children's health and safety always come first. Encourage children to wash their hands after working with arts and crafts materials. Children should not eat or drink while engaged in art. Carefully supervise and remind the very young and oral child that paste, paint, glue, chalk, or any other art material is for making art, not eating, tasting, or drinking. Provide age-appropriate materials. The following is a comprehensive list of guidelines from which you can select those that work best for you and your group.

Limit on the Number of Children at the Center at Any One Time.
This number will depend on the number and size of tables, floor space, and easels. For example, Mrs. Tull displays four *Art* signs on clothespins at her art center. When all have been removed, children know the art center is full. Ms. Valdez allows eight children in her larger art center. Four children can work at the tables, two at the easel, and two on the floor. When children ask if they can do art, she asks them to count the number of children or see if there is an open or vacant spot for them.

Use a Smock during Art Activities.
Children whose parents warn them about staying clean and avoiding messy activities may be apprehensive about doing art. Teachers can strongly recommend that parents provide "work" or "play" clothes rather than party attire. Young children need to dress appropriately for an active day at school, and art activities will involve getting dirty. Adding liquid detergent to paint will also make the paint easier to wash out when doing the laundry. Children should be reminded to let their paintings dry thoroughly before moving them or attempting to take them home. This will minimize smudging and smearing of paint onto clothing.

Slightly oversized children's shirts make good smocks. Cut off the sleeves, put them on backwards, and have someone button up the back. Daddy's old shirts are often too long, bulky, and awkward. The sleeves constantly need to be rolled up and often dangle in the paint. Smocks are vital during painting. They also protect clothing when children are using glue, paste, and markers. It is a good idea to wear a smock for any and all art activities. Shirt sleeves should be rolled or pushed up above the elbows. Removing sweaters is a good idea, because this will allow greater freedom of movement and eliminates the possibility of their getting stained with paint. Attractive smocks can also be made from oilcloth or vinyl cut into a large square with a head opening and worn as a poncho. Velcro® or elastic can hold the sides (see Figure 13–3). Or, a child-sized apron can be made, with elastic at the waist and neck. Allow about 18 inches for the neck and about 20 inches for the waist. Adjust according to specific needs and sizes within your group (see Figure 13–4).

A painting smock could be made out of an old large bath towel. Fold it in half and cut a large opening for the head. Sew up the sides, leaving ample room for the arms. Young children do not like clothing that fits snugly over their heads, so make sure you use a large towel and leave plenty of extra room for it to slide on easily.

The author saw one teacher effectively use a plastic trash bag as a makeshift smock. Holes for the head and arms were quickly cut at the closed end. The children enjoyed wearing their artist's costume.

Use Art Tools Properly.
This is not to suggest that there is only one way to paint or draw. It does mean that brushes are for painting and scissors are for cutting paper. Teachers should discuss and model the proper care and use of all art media in advance.

Use Only What You Need.
Discuss the economical use of paper, glue, paste, and so forth, and the avoidance of needless waste. Have a variety of paper sizes available. Not all children need or want to work on a large sheet of paper. Some children have a small idea that fits nicely onto a smaller paper square. Avoid putting too much paper out at any one time. Children may feel obligated to deplete the pile or believe that there is an endless supply.

Figure 13-3 Art smock.

Figure 13-4 Art apron.

Complete Your Art Activity. The writer has seen children go through a pile of papers by making a series of aimless, quick marks. Quality rather than sheer quantity should be the goal. Teachers can encourage children to take their time and finish each picture. "Jill, you have started a picture that has a lot of action and movement. But there is so much more room on your paper. Maybe you would like to keep working on it." Jill is free to accept or reject her teacher's suggestion.

Share Supplies. Items at the art center need to be shared. There may not be enough glue or staplers to go around. Children learn that the items belong to the school or center and are available for all children to use. Some children will have difficulty following this rule. They may become possessive and clutch the newest pair of scissors or the prettiest roll of ribbon.

Respect Others. Children learn to respect and value the ideas, styles, and work of others, just as they have come to value their own. Children cannot ridicule or criticize the ideas and work of others: "That's a dumb picture," or "That's no good; it don't look like no train!" Children's statements may be well intended, but the message hurts. It also hampers creative expression. Teachers can discuss how children can draw, color, or paint anything in any way they want. It is their decision and their rendering, not someone else's, that matters. "I'm sure James knows the sun is yellow, but he chose to paint it purple. It's his picture, and he can paint it any way he wants." Perhaps children who receive criticism or correction for their own artwork also become overly critical of others.

Children may also get possessive of available space. They may try to occupy the majority of the table. Young children who are used to having their own way and having one of everything at home will need guidance. Young children who have little space and no toys may also squander and require intervention. "The art center is for everyone, but only four at a time. This means we each have this much space [marking off with fingers] and we must share our things. Anyone who cannot share will have to leave the art center."

Return Everything to Its Place when Finished. Small paper scraps are thrown in the wastebasket. Larger scraps of construction paper can be saved in a scrap paper box for collage. Smocks are hung up on a hook.

Clean Up When Done. Brushes need to be washed. Spilled glue needs to be wiped up with a wet sponge.

Remind children to leave their space clean for the next artist to use. Children know that they need to wash their hands and clean up the space they occupied. They should also check the floor before they leave. In short, children learn that the art center is primarily their responsibility, with the teacher playing only a minor role in its subtle guidance, maintenance, and supervision. To combine art with a literacy experience post directions cards in your art center. For example, the directions cards for easel painting in Figure 13–5 depict the series or sequence involved in painting a picture. Words and pictures are used to help children learn the following set of direc-

1. Put on smock

2. Paint picture

3. Hang picture to dry

4. Wash hands

5. Hang up smock

Figure 13-5 Direction cards for easel painting.

tions for easel painting: put on your smock, paint a picture, hang your picture to dry, wash your hands, and hang up your smock.

Some important cleanup supplies include the following:

brooms—child-sized and whisk
dustpan with rubber edge and small broom
liquid dishwashing soap
mop
paper towels
plastic pail, bucket, dishpan; utility organizer with compartments and handle for cleanup supplies
rags
scrub brush
shower curtain—to protect floor or carpeting
smocks
soap
sponges
table covering, e.g., newspaper, oilcloth, vinyl, plastic
throw rug—old, washable, to put under easel
wastebasket

EVALUATING AN ART CENTER/PROGRAM

You can evaluate the effectiveness of your art center/program by asking yourself the following questions.

1. Is your art program comprehensive? Does it include provisions for sensory experiences; time, space and materials for making art; aesthetics; and introducing children to the world of art, artists, and a variety of art forms and styles?
2. When providing art experiences is your approach more child-centered than teacher-directed? Do you let children discover, invent, and process with the media as opposed to *teaching* art?
3. Do you engage children in creative experiences that extend beyond art? Do children's thinking, language, music, movement, and play activities reflect creativity?
4. Do you integrate art across your curriculum?
5. Do you capitalize on the language/literacy potential in art by providing labeled supplies, taking dictation, and viewing scribbling and mark making as beginning attempts at writing?
6. Do children have ample time and equal access to an art center on a daily basis?
7. Do you follow the three *R*s—replenishing, rotating, and renewing the items in your art center?
8. Do you provide art experiences outdoors on a regular basis?
9. Do you include multicultural arts as a way to help children learn about their similarities to other cultures?
10. Do you encourage children by commenting on the artistic elements found in their art as opposed to simply praising them?
11. Do you facilitate children's artistic development by supervising and offering yourself as a resource? Are you careful not to impose your suggestions and solutions?
12. Do you value developmental appropriateness in art and thereby provide multisensory, messy activities which involve more processing than the making of a predetermined product? Do you supplement by occasionally teaching children a new art technique?

The ideal would be to answer affirmatively to all these questions. This may not always be possible or practical, given individual situations and constraints. The purpose of answering the questions is to assess where you stand in terms of your art program and to suggest some next steps to take to make your program comprehensive, developmentally appropriate, integrated, and child-centered. It is a process that takes time, commitment, and faith in children's innate capacity to be creative and make art.

PUPPETS AND MASKS

Puppets and **masks** serve many developmental ends. They are psychological props. They give young children something to hold and hide behind when speaking. After all, if a child makes a mistake or speaks incorrectly, it is the puppet or mask rather than the child who is to blame. Puppets and masks allow children to hide their identity and become someone or something else for a period of time. Children also have a way of telling us emotionally important events through their play with puppets and masks, often things they would never say or do without the props.

Young children enjoy making puppets and masks as much as they enjoy dramatizing and verbalizing with them. They also provide the opportunity for problem solving. Puppets can help children decide how disagreements can be resolved. A teacher can use a puppet to play the part of an imaginary young child who refuses to share. Children can use other puppets to discuss and act out this scenario and possible solutions.

There is an infinite number of ways to make puppets and masks. Here are some that are recommended for use with young children.

Puppets from Paper

Papier-Mâché Puppet

A puppet head can be slowly built up by draping gluey paper over a crushed ball of newspaper and a tissue paper roll. Refer to the section on papier-mâché in Chapter 12. Begin winding paper around the roll to form a neck and continue to build up a head over the crushed newspaper ball. Paint with tempera when thoroughly dry. Attach a piece of fabric for a body.

Or the papier-mâché can be made over a clay base. Children can use clay to make their puppet head. Next, wind strips of papier-mâché over the form. Make the layers go in different directions for strength. Let dry thoroughly. Carefully cut the head in half with a sharp knife and remove the clay. Use additional papier-mâché to seal the two halves together. Reinforce the neck with additional strips. Carefully smooth rough spots with sandpaper. Paint or decorate with trims. Seal with cheap hair spray if it is painted with tempera. Add a puppet body following the directions given here.

Puppet Body. A very simple puppet body or clothing can be made from a 12-inch-square piece of scrap fabric. Fold it in half and cut three small openings along the center fold. The middle opening will be for the index finger, which also supports the puppet head. The two side openings are for the thumb and middle fingers, which serve as hands. Measure the children's hand span before cutting to ensure that the openings are neither too close nor too far apart.

Paper Bag Puppet

Provide each child with a lunch-size paper bag, neither too big nor too small for their hand to fit in and grasp. Paper bags are recommended because their construction provides a built-in movable mouth. Children will enjoy using paint, crayons, markers, and trims to decorate their puppet. Clear, undecorated sandwich bags provide a small, snug-fitting, see-through puppet that can be used as a last resort.

Stuffed Paper Bag Puppet

Stuff a large paper bag with crumpled newspaper. Insert a stick, ruler, or dowel. Make sure the end of the handle is sticking out for a handle. Continue stuffing. Gather the bag and tie it securely at the handle with string to form a neck. Decorate the stuffed paper bag head with paint, crayons, or markers. Add paper scraps, yarn, and trims.

Paper Plate Puppet

An easy puppet can be made by decorating a paper plate and attaching it to a handle, such as a stick or ruler. Or, paper plates can be folded to make a talking puppet. Each child will need two paper plates. Fold one in half. Cut the other in half. Staple one half to the top and the other half to the under side of the folded paper plate. This will allow four fingers to be inserted into the top jaw and the thumb in the lower jaw. This will help the child move his or her fingers and get the puppet to talk. Although a frog readily comes to mind, a folded paper plate puppet can be used to make a variety of animals, people, and objects. Decorate with crayons, markers, paper scraps, and trims. A cloth sleeve can be placed on the child's arm for an added effect. For example, one child wore a sleeve made out of green printed fabric, which worked well with his dragon puppet made from a paper plate.

Cardboard Tissue Tube Puppet

Children will enjoy using paint, crayons, or markers to decorate their cylindrical puppet. A roll or tube is an ideal size for small hands. Nothing else is needed. A smaller section can also be used as the head with a puppet body made from fabric. Place the puppet's cloth body over the fingers and insert the puppet head over the index and middle fingers.

Me Puppet

Children will thoroughly enjoy making and using their life-sized puppet. An added touch is that it can be decorated to look like them. Each child will need two sheets of sturdy butcher paper that matches their height along with 1½ paper plates. Buy the heavy-weight cardboard type. Each child will need one for the face and the other half for the back. This is where they will insert their hand to walk, dance, and move with their Me Puppet. This activity is best done in shifts over a period of time. You may want to set up the activity at different stations so long as adults are present to supervise and offer assistance when needed. On the floor, one adult can trace each child's body onto the double sheets of paper. Children can use crayons, markers, or paint to add clothing and details. Another adult can provide a mirror and have children carefully note their face and then make it on the paper plate. You may want to provide yarn for hair as well as buttons and trims. Think multiculturally and provide paint, markers, and crayons in a variety of skin tones. It may also be possible to buy paper plates in beige and brown tones. You may need to assist the children in stapling their two body outlines together. As you staple be sure to stuff with crumpled newspaper to give a full, three-dimensional effect. An adult can staple the paper plate half onto the back of the puppet's head. Children can slip their hand into the half paper plate. The last step is to attach the head to the body. An adult can use strong glue or a hot glue gun to make sure the head is securely attached to the body.

Puppets from Wood

Wooden Stick Puppet

Tongue depressors and Popsicle® sticks can be used and decorated as the puppet itself. They can also be used as the base or handle to which a paper plate, magazine picture, cardboard, poster board, or other type of puppet is attached. Dowel rods or straws can also be used as handles for puppets.

Wooden Block Puppet

A small rectangular piece of scrap wood that can be held in a young child's hand can be fashioned into a puppet. Features can be added with paints, crayons, markers, small wood scraps, or trims. Make sure the edges are sanded smooth and free of splinters.

Wooden Spoon Puppet

An old, large wooden cooking spoon can be turned into a puppet. Decorate with fine markers. A piece of scrap material can be tied at the neck of the spoon to add the element of clothing and conceal the stickhandle. Add yarn for hair. Children can hold on to the stick handle while working their puppets.

Puppets from Fabric

Sock Puppet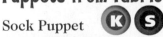

Find an old sock. Cut a slit across the toe, halfway to the heel, for the puppet's mouth. Cut a piece of felt or material to fit inside the mouth. Fold it in half, position it in place, and sew it on (see Figure 13–6). Four

fingers will fit into the upper jaw. Glue a piece of cardboard under the lower jaw. This will help the thumb. Add trims: buttons and beads for eyes, yarn for hair, and so forth.

Glove Puppet

Old garden, work, utility, driving, dress, or plastic gloves can be made into puppets. Encourage the child to put on the glove and think of decorative possibilities. Small trims—buttons, yarn, and so forth—can be sewn or glued on. Or single fingers can be cut off to make one puppet, which will nicely fit on one or two child-sized fingers.

Puppets from Containers

Plastic Foam Cup Puppet

Cut one hole into a plastic foam cup. Encourage the child to put one finger through. Does it remind you of anything? It could be an elephant with the finger for a trunk. Or could it be a head, tail, leg, or tongue? Try cutting two holes at opposite sides. Encourage children to put one finger into each hole. What does it remind you of? Could these be arms or legs? Do four holes allow fingers to represent arms and legs or wheels on a vehicle? Or the cup could be decorated with markers without cutting holes and snugly positioned on a toddler's clenched fist or raised fingers.

Tin Can Puppet

A juice can that is tall and slim can be transformed into a puppet. Discard any with rough or sharp inner rims and edges. Cans can be covered with paper and decorated. Add yarn, pipe cleaners, buttons, and other trims.

Container Puppet

Plastic and cardboard containers for holding milk, detergent, shampoo, toothpaste, or bleach have their own characteristic shapes and will suggest vehicle, person, or animal puppets to make. Skinny necks on

Figure 13-6 Sock puppet.

containers make good handles to hold when using the puppet. Other containers come with built-in handles. Decorate the containers with paper and other trims.

Box Puppet

Boxes with interesting shapes, including toothpaste and fast-food boxes, may suggest puppet possibilities. Decorate them with paper and other trims. Add dishwashing detergent to tempera paint to make it stick if the surface is slick. A small milk carton is an ideal size for a fist puppet.

Coat Hanger Puppet

Bend a wire coat hanger into a geometric or abstract shape of a puppet. Keep the hook at the bottom for a handle. Place a nylon stocking or pantyhose over the coat hanger and fasten it with string or a rubber band. Decorate the puppet with fabric scraps, yarn, ribbon, trims, and paper.

Puppet Stage

There is no need to spend a lot of money on a commercially made puppet stage. Children will enjoy making, painting, and decorating their own. Find a very large appliance box, such as a refrigerator carton. Carefully remove the back side and cut a window opening in the front panel for the puppets. The opening or window should be placed such that when the children are sitting or kneeling behind the screen it is above their heads, but within arm's length. Children may enjoy a window in their puppet stage that opens and closes by folding the cardboard back. Curtains can also be hung. To provide a backdrop, hang scenery that the children create from a dowel rod, curtain rod, or broomstick. Make sure that the pole fits across the top. Make a small notch in each side panel of the carton in which the scenery hanger can securely rest. Allow ample room for the puppets to move about freely in front of the scenery. One foot from the front is recommended. The puppet stage can be painted and decorated as the children see fit. It should be a project inviting group participation and planning. The result may not be as pretty as a commercially available puppet stage, but the children will be proud of their accomplishment and will likely use it as a result.

Masks

Making masks is an ancient art form that is presently practiced in many cultures. Often, the masks also have utilitarian value in religious and cultural celebra-

tions. Presently, masks are used in the celebration of Halloween. Many children are frightened by masks. Some will refuse to put something over their heads or against their faces. They may fear suffocation or loss of identity. Their wishes should be respected. Others enjoy losing their identity, at least for the time being, by putting on a mask and becoming someone or something else.

There are many different ways to make a mask. Basically, there are two ways to wear a mask: by putting it over the head or by attaching it to the face. Figure 13–7 shows a mask that a child has painted on

Figure 13-7 Display of masks.

construction paper. It will be displayed on a wall in a common eating area of a preschool. Commercially designed masks from other cultures will be included in the display. Here are some examples of masks that are appropriate for use with young children.

Over-the-Head Masks

Grocery Bag Mask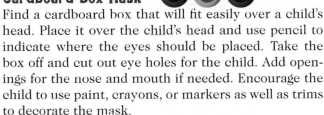

Find a grocery bag that will easily slip over the child's head. Place it over the child's head and use pencil to indicate where the eyes should be placed. Take the bag off and cut out eye holes for the child. Cutting additional openings for the nose and mouth will help the child breathe better. Slit the four sides so that the bag easily slips over the child's shoulders and stays in place. Encourage the child to use paint, crayons, or markers as well as trims to decorate the mask.

Cardboard Box Mask

Find a cardboard box that will fit easily over a child's head. Place it over the child's head and use pencil to indicate where the eyes should be placed. Take the box off and cut out eye holes for the child. Add openings for the nose and mouth if needed. Encourage the child to use paint, crayons, or markers as well as trims to decorate the mask.

Ice-Cream Carton Mask

Ask ice-cream parlors to save the drum-shaped commercial ice-cream tubs for you. They are good for making a stacked totem pole as well as individual masks. Place the tub over the child's head and use a pencil to indicate where the eyes should be placed. Take the carton off and cut out eye holes for the child. Encourage the child to use paint, crayons, or markers, as well as trims, to decorate the mask.

Face Masks

Paper Plate Mask

Hold a paper plate over the child's face and indicate where the eyes should be placed. Cut out eye holes for the child. Encourage the child to use paint, crayons, or markers, as well as trims, to decorate the mask.

Figure 13-8 Paper plate mask.

When the mask is completed, attach a string to each side and tie in back (see Figure 13–8).

Pie Plate Mask

Hold a pie plate over the child's face and indicate where the eyes should be placed. Cut out eye holes for the child. Make sure the cut metal leaves no sharp edges. The mask can be painted with paint to which dishwashing detergent has been added. Trims can also be glued on. When the mask is completed, attach a string to each side and tie in back. Children like the slick, shiny metal surface, which often suggests robots or superheroes.

SUMMARY

This unit focused on setting up an art program around a center format. By definition, an art center is an artist's studio, conveniently located and easily accessible, well stocked, orderly and organized, with rules and limits. It was recommended that the art center provide for an array of two- and three-dimensional art media and that children be encouraged to creatively mix media and invent their own activities.

Key Terms

art center	masks	puppets
mixing media		

Suggested Activities

1. Observe a successfully run art center. Note the teacher's role.
2. Use the criteria for an art center informally to evaluate an early childhood art center.
3. Set up an informal art center. Observe its operation for a period of several days. Play an indirect role as guide or facilitator. Document your findings in a journal or diary.
4. Evaluate an early childhood art center program. Make recommendations if necessary.

5. Facilitate a puppet- or mask-making activity with children. Integrate it with another curricular area. For example, a puppet- or mask-making activity may extend or grow from the reading of a book or a storytelling session. Refer to Chapter 12 for a discussion of integrating art across the early childhood curriculum.

Review

1. List the criteria or guidelines for an early childhood art center.

2. List five major rules for successfully operating an early childhood art center.

3. List any five questions that address the effectiveness of an early childhood art center/program.

4. A recommendation from this chapter is to aim for a balance between old and new. Use a nontext example to explain this quote.

For additional art and creative development resources, visit our Web site at
www.EarlyChildEd.delmar.com

Section Five

Roles and Strategies

What do you see in this picture? Denise is in a K-1 combination class. She is fortunate to have a teacher who works hard to individualize the program and be *present*. What do you think it means to be *present* for the children? Denise knows that her teacher is accessible, approachable, and there for her. For example, after she drew her self-portrait, Denise knew her teacher would want her to share it. She asked Denise to tell her all about it. Denise also read the words that she had neatly printed. She asked Denise to share it with the others during group time and if she wanted to find a special place on the wall to hang it up. Denise declined the invitation stating that she was spending the weekend with her dad and really wanted him to see it.

Planning is but one of the many things a teacher will do in providing art experiences. Chapter 14, Art

Experiences through Technology, discusses the impact of technology on children's teacher's role in selecting hardware and software to provide appropriate, supportive art experiences for young children.

Chapter 15, Roles, Responses, and Strategies to Support Children's Art, focuses on the teacher's interactions with children during the artistic process. It also provides ideas for sparking the production of children's art and ways to celebrate it.

How do you know how children are doing in art or whether they are progressing? Chapter 16, Art Assessment, focuses on children's artistic development and stresses the importance of observation coupled with art samples as a way of gathering valuable developmental information. The instrument for artistic evaluation, based on the whole child, informally attempts to evaluate children's artistic development.

Chapter 14

Art Experiences through Technology

The photograph at left depicts a computer center in a kindergarten classroom. Children visit this center singly and in small groups to play games with numbers and letters, to write stories, and to explore far away places on the Internet. Children also visit this center to participate in art appreciation and art production activities.

The computer can provide an exciting extension to the art center in an early childhood classroom. Creating art on the computer requires children to use many of the same skills and thinking processes used in more traditional art activities, as well as abilities that are unique to the computer as an art medium. The teacher sets the stage for computer use in both art appreciation and production activities. It is up to the teacher to provide the resources and the opportunities for young children to engage in art activities in the computer center.

Objectives

After reading this chapter, you should be able to:

- Discuss relevant research on the impact of computer use on young children's learning and development.
- Critique the use of computers with young children, including both advantages and disadvantages.
- Discuss and critique the concept of computer art, including both advantages and disadvantages as they pertain to young children.
- Identify four keys to successful integration of computers into the early childhood curriculum.
- Identify ways in which technology may be used to communicate with the families of young children.
- Help school-age children make mobiles and/or stabiles.

INTRODUCTION

Computers have become commonplace in homes, businesses, and classrooms. We have come to expect the efficiency and convenience that technology contributes to our daily activities in most settings. As we consider the use of computers in early childhood classrooms, however, teachers need to consider issues beyond efficiency and convenience. For example, are computer activities developmentally appropriate for young children? What can computers and technology contribute to an early childhood art curriculum? How

NAEYC Position Statement: Technology and Young Children—Ages Three through Eight

The National Association for the Education of Young Children (NAEYC) (1996), in evaluating the appropriate use of technology believes:

1. In any given situation, a professional judgment by the teacher is required to determine if a specific use of technology is age appropriate, individually appropriate, and culturally appropriate.

2. Used appropriately, technology can enhance children's cognitive and social abilities (see Figure 14–1).

3. Appropriate technology is integrated into the regular learning environment and used as one of many options to support children's learning.

4. Early childhood educators should promote equitable access to technology for all children and their fami-

lies. Children with special needs should have increased access when this is helpful. Educators using technology need to be especially sensitive to issues of equity. Efforts should be made to ensure access to appropriate technology for children with special needs, for whom assistive technologies may be essential for successful inclusion.

5. The power of technology to influence children's learning and development requires that attention be paid to eliminating stereotyping of any group and culminating exposure to violence, especially as a problem-solving strategy. Technology can be used to affirm children's diversity. Teachers should actively select software that promotes social values.

NAEYC Position Statement: Technology and Young Children—Ages Three through Eight (continued)

6. Teachers, in collaboration with parents, should advocate for more appropriate technology applications for all children.

7. The appropriate use of technology has many implications for early childhood professional development. As early childhood educators become active participants in a technological world, they need in-depth training and ongoing support to be adequately prepared to make decisions about technology and to support its effective use in learning environments for children. Early childhood educators should use technology as a tool for communication and collaboration among professionals as well as a tool for teaching children.

Figure 14-1 Working together on the computer.

Figure 14-2 Computers can individualize learning.

can teachers best support children's interactions with technology? This chapter will provide an overview of the role of computers and other technology in an early childhood art curriculum. A discussion of the impact of computers on child development will be presented, along with suggestions and strategies for effective computer use in the classroom.

COMPUTERS IN EARLY CHILDHOOD EDUCATION

The dramatic increase in home computers has resulted in introducing young children to technology at a very early age. Computers empower young children and totally immerse them in the joys of learning (see Figure 14–2). Computer technology has the potential to engage children in exploration, experimentation, problem solving, and creative thinking with the appropriate software. Computer use can be a social activity

with children speaking, working, and learning together. Computers provide avenues for children to use their multiple intelligences. Computers are both patient and forgiving in that they allow for children to correct or change their response.

Papert (1980) is a pioneer in the area of children and computers. A student of Piaget, Papert applied Piaget's developmental theory and a constructivist point view to children's use of computers. He created a graphics program named **LOGO**®, which is programmable rather than direct-manipulation software. Rather than manipulating a program designed by someone else, the child assumes full control. Through LOGO®, young children can discover fundamental principles of math while learning to write simple computer programs. How does this work? With LOGO®, students develop their own learning by exploring and programming a computer. Also called "turtle geometry," LOGO® invites the child programmer to input commands to a small turtle icon on the screen, which then walks a certain number of steps drawing a line as it goes. The "turtle" is actually a futuristic-looking object that beeps, walks, and turns on typed commands from the child at the keyboard, thus making the experience appropriate for young programmers. For example, in programming the turtle to draw a square, the child will develop his or her own process of walking a straight line, turning 90 degrees, then repeating the movement three more times to complete the shape. Papert views computers as the way to revolutionize the future of education. Specifically, he believes that discovery-oriented interactions with computers enhance learning by encouraging children to explore interests in art, music, or engineering through technology and mathematics. Terrapin LOGO® and MicroWorlds Jr. are two of the latest versions of LOGO® appropriate for young children.

Terrapin LOGO® is a collection of tools designed to encourage children to explore their ideas, questions, and strategies for problem-solving. Using the programming skills associated with earlier versions of LOGO®, children engage in science simulations, mathematical and artistic explorations, and interactive multimedia stories. Terrapin LOGO® can provide creative experiences for children in the primary grades, as well as for older children and adults.

MicroWorlds Jr.® combines the creative aspects of an art program with the acquisition of basic programming skills. Children program the LOGO® turtle to experiment with lines, shapes, spaces, and colors. Sounds and text can be added to their creations.

These two new versions of LOGO® provide children with early computer experiences consistent with how children learn and developmentally appropriate practices.

Computers are merely one of many tools in a developmentally appropriate program. A computer should neither be a substitute for concrete learning nor replace the human factor, the teacher (see Figure 14–3). Therefore, the appropriate question for early childhood educators is no longer whether computers

should be used in a classroom setting, but how to use them effectively to support learning and the development of the whole child. As computers are connected with young children and integrated into their curriculum, the benefits to children become clear. However, if computer experiences are not developmentally appropriate, children would be better off without them. When should young children be introduced to computers? Haughland (1999) recommends introducing computers when children are about three years of age.

Still not convinced? Let us see what the experts have to say about the benefits of computers. The positive impact that computers have on young children is really dependent on the types of experiences that children have with the computer. Seymour Papert (1998), the creator of LOGO®, stresses that computers in the classroom should provide concrete experiences for children and that children should have free access to the computer. While working at the computer, children should have control of their learning experiences, making decisions about the purposes of their work and the software they will use, and making choices about how to proceed through a specific piece of software. Papert recommends that teachers facilitate peer tutoring at the computer, rather than engaging in adult problem-solving and that teachers take advantage of the computer's capabilities to teach powerful ideas.

When computers are used under these general guidelines, research indicates that the positive impact of computers on young children's learning and development is significant across several developmental domains. Young children's socioemotional development has always been an important focus in early childhood curriculum and classrooms. Appropriate use of computers has been found to be a positive factor in socioemotional development. Anderson (2000) found that children will engage in cooperative play in the computer center and the block center for similar amounts of time. This research suggests that both the computer and the block center provide a context for beginning and prolonging social interaction among young children. Clements (1994) believes that computers can be catalysts for social interactions. His research on children's social interactions at the computer showed that children prefer to work with friends, rather than alone, and that they displayed more positive emotions and interest in the activity when working together. While working at the computer, the children in Clements' study spontaneously provided help and instruction for their peers and they talked about and built on each other's ideas. Research on young children with special needs also supports the idea that computers have a positive impact on socioemotional development. When young children with special needs work on the classroom computer, they

Figure 14-3 Teacher as facilitator.

have more social interaction with their typical peers (Spiegel-McGill, et al, 1989) and show greater gains in their overall socioemotional development. Again, however, the types of experiences children have on the computer will affect the nature of their interactions. Open-ended software, such as draw-and-paint programs, encourages children to collaborate. Drill-and-practice programs, however, foster turn-taking and competition among the children.

In terms of cognitive development, **drill-and-practice software** has been shown to help children's with certain memorized skills, like counting and sorting (Clements & Nastasi, 1995). **Open-ended software** that encourages children to solve problems, however, can enhance children's creativity, logico-mathematical thinking, and critical thinking. For example, Wright (1994) found that software allowing the creation of pictures with geometric shapes helped children come to understand concepts such as symmetry, patterning, and spatial order. Software that allows children to manipulate objects and shapes can have other benefits to cognitive development, as well. Such programs allow children to save their work and come back to it for long-term projects. Shapes and objects can be resized or cut and children's awareness of mathematical operations is raised as they rotate, flip, and rearrange the manipulatives (Clements & Sarama, 1998).

Despite the computer's positive impact on children's learning and development, however, teachers must consider carefully how they will integrate the computer into the classroom. Lemerise (1993) believes children's free exploration of software is essential, but cautions that too much free exploration can lead to boredom. Open-ended projects with the software encourage children's purposeful engagement and problem-solving with the computer. Computer activities need to be accompanied by "off-computer" activities in the classroom. Haugland (1992) found that children exposed to appropriate software showed gains in intelligence, nonverbal skills, long-term memory, and manual dexterity. However, children who also engaged in related off-computer activities had similar scores in all these areas as well as higher scores in verbal problem solving and conceptual skills. The research supporting the use of computers with young children is powerful. Success, however, is dependent on the teacher's decisions about how the computer will be used in the classroom and the software that will be provided.

Are there any critics? Is work on the computer nothing more than an animated workbook? Some question the sedentary nature of two-dimensional computer work with mobility confined to fine motor movements. This view contrasts with our belief that young children learn best through concrete, hands-on manipulative activity with real objects. Perhaps

graphic images on the screen, such as animals, are real to the child; as real as the pictures of animals in books or toy stuffed animals.

Elkind (1996) believes the danger is that the young child's proficiency with the computer may tempt us to ignore what we know about cognitive development. Despite their skill with computers, many kindergarten children have yet to attain the concrete operations described by Piaget. Concrete operations enable children to follow rules, for example. Elkind warns that if we forget how time consuming and effortful the path to these attainments is, and if we rate a child's intellectual competence by his or her performance on a computer, then we have lost what we have been working so hard to attain: a broad appreciation of developmentally appropriate practice. Morgan and Shade (1994) offer a different view on this criticism. They believe that although Piaget did assert that young children construct much of their knowledge through active manipulation of the environment, this interpretation of his theory is too narrowly literal in two major ways. First, the meaning of active construction and concrete operations may be taken verbatim. For the child, concrete may refer to what is meaningful and manipulable to the child. Active mental processing and reflection may be equally important. Children can be active learners with symbols such as a toy stuffed bear or computer images of dancing teddy bears. Second, descriptions of Piaget's stages represent milestones along the developmental pathway rather than rigid age-based norms. Perhaps in the last few decades children have become more capable and technologically ready than once thought.

Young Children with Special Needs

For most children, working on a computer is one of many activity choices available in an early childhood classroom. For other children, however, working on a computer may be the key activity that makes learning and social interaction possible. Children with special physical needs (including blindness and deafness) may use computers as assistive or communication devices to support their learning (Thouvenelle & Bewick, 2003). Voice-to-text software allows children to both receive and produce written communication, either with words or symbols, that would not be possible without the computer. Children with special intellectual or learning needs are able to practice concept mastery by repeating material and activities on the computer. The frequent and consistent positive reinforcement that occurs in developmentally appropriate software helps to sustain their attention and participation (Parette, et al, 2000). Some children with special physical and learning needs are challenged to write manually; providing kinesthetic sensory stimulation that supports their learning (Thouvenelle & Bewick,

2003). Adaptive peripherals, usually special switches or hardware that plug into the computer, provide alternatives for children unable to use a mouse or a keyboard. Particularly useful are touchscreens that allow children to point and touch with their fingers items on the monitor's screen. Touch screen technology is helpful for three- and four-year-old children who may have difficulty with the indirect cause-and-effect of using a mouse to change things on the screen or with children of any age who have physical difficulties using a mouse or keyboard.

High-Tech Tots?

Despite the existing research on the benefits for typically developing children and children with special needs, the use of computers in schools has come under fire from some quarters. Clements and Sarama (2003) believe that concerns centered on the negative effects of children's computer use are unwarranted. In reviewing the research, they cite the benefits of computers to children in the areas of social and emotional development, cognitive development and learning, creativity, and language and reading. The issue becomes how best to use computers in the early childhood classroom. These authors believe that, used well, computers can make a unique and substantial contribution to the education of young children. A national group of educators, doctors, and children's advocates believe that the billions spent on equipping and wiring classrooms is fueled more by parent fears and corporate sales pitches than any real evidence of computers helping children learn (Alliance for Childhood, 2000). See <http://www.allianceforchildhood.net>. Alliance for Childhood, a group of child development experts, claims that computers pose hazards to young children including eyestrain and obesity from being "mouse potatoes," while robbing them of the creativity, human relationships, and hands-on learning key to their development. According to the report, existing research shows that computers have little effect on academic achievement and early childhood development. The report calls for a moratorium on computers in elementary education and recommends that it return its focus to hands-on, real-world learning. The recommendation for older students is that they learn not only how to use a computer, but how it works and the ethical and social implications of technology. The Alliance asks the Surgeon General to study this issue.

Age-Appropriate Computer Use and the Teacher's Role

Some general guidelines for computer use in early childhood classrooms can be established from the ex-

isting literature. These guidelines can assist teachers in creating a structure for computer use in the classroom and in developing computer activities that support young children's learning and development. Guidelines can also outline the role that teachers should play as children at each age interact with classroom computers.

Most experts agree that children younger than age three years should not use computers. During this period, motor skills are being developed, but more importantly, networks supporting emotional, social, and cognitive capabilities are being established, primarily through emotional and language interaction with caregivers (Healy, 1998). Between the ages of three and five years, however, computers should be one of many experiences available to children in their classroom. Ideally, children should be working at the computer for short periods of time, about the length of time they would spend working a puzzle or building with blocks, and with a partner or in a small, teacher-led group. Open-ended software, such as drawing and music-making programs, are most appropriate at this age and will allow children to explore and develop awareness of the computer's capabilities. The teacher's role for children ages three to five years is to introduce new software by modeling in small groups. As the children begin to explore the software independently, the teacher stays near to provide prompts or scaffolding as needed.

In kindergarten and the primary grades (five to eight years of age), children can continue working at the computer with a partner, but they should also begin to work independently. Simple word-processing software should be added to the drawing and music-making programs previously available. Word-processing software will encourage young children to use and expand the written language skills they are acquiring in other curriculum activities. It will also provide an avenue for children to express themselves in written language when their developing fine motor skills limit expression with traditional paper and pencil. The teacher's role for children in kindergarten and the primary grades is to furnish the computer center with appropriate software that complements the curriculum and grade level objectives. The teacher monitors the children's activities and intervenes when needed to pose questions and provide support.

COMPUTERS AND ART

How do you feel about the use of computers to make art? Do you see it as uncreative and threatening to the nature of creative art? Do you believe children's time would be better spent messing about with real art materials? Try viewing computer art as one component of your art program rather than as a replacement of all hands-on art experiences in your classroom. The computer becomes another art medium, not a rejection of all other media. A computer loaded with a simple graphic painting program is another way to create lines and shapes (see Figure 14–4). The screen is the canvas or paper and the mouse is the tool for applying the lines, shapes, and colors. Although the child manipulates colored light rather than the actual media, the artistic decisions and choices are the same.

What are the advantages? In most schools, public and private, funding for art in the curriculum is not a priority. Even including time in the school day for art production and appreciation activities is frowned upon in some settings. Engaging children in activities that promote computer training and literacy, as well as creative thinking and expression, may provide them with opportunities that would otherwise be denied (Sabbeth, 1998). Because of experiences with computers at home, many young children enter early childhood programs already familiar with computers and excited about their abilities to use them. Including computer art activities and opportunities in the curriculum may very well attract children who would have little interest in traditional art activities (Matthews, 1997). Computer centers are set up to foster peer interaction and communication. A computer artist can easily reverse his or her actions and *unpaint* or remove color if needed. Good painting software provides an unlimited number of colors and trims for embellishing your computer art. The computer fosters an art-language connection. It is easy for a child to type words to accompany what he or she has painted.

What are the disadvantages? For some children, using a mouse may be more difficult than using a paintbrush, marker, or crayon. The sensory qualities of the media, including the touch and smell, are missing. Moving colored lines on the computer screen is quite different from smelling and smearing cold paint. Young children can be impulsive and may lack the patience needed to print out their computer art. Is the drawing in Figure 14–5 just mechanized lines and designs or is it art? Philosophers have debated the nature of art for centuries. What do you think?

Draw and Paint Programs

Children can create images on a computer in two ways: **painting programs** and **drawing programs.** Although these two types of software are often discussed interchangeably, there are some basic differences that teachers should be aware of before introducing them to the classroom.

Painting programs use **bitmapping** as created images are displayed on the computer screen (see Figure 14–6). Children working in a bitmapping program will be able to draw shapes and lines on the screen and then use the eraser tool to remove any part of their drawing. Erasing a shape or line drawn on top of something else leaves an empty space in the drawing. Adding text to a drawing in a painting program is much different from word processing. The cursor cannot be inserted for editing or making corrections. If a typing error is made, all of the text must be erased and started again (Sabbeth, 1998).

Text is much easier to work with in a drawing program; it can be edited at any time by inserting the cursor where it is needed. Revising their drawings, however, may be more challenging for young children working in a drawing program. Drawing pro-

Figure 14-4 Simple graphic computer art.

Figure 14-5 A child's perspective through computer art.

Figure 14-6 Computer art created from a painting program.

grams are object-oriented. There is no eraser tool for changing parts of lines or shapes. Instead, the entire object (shape or line) is clicked on, highlighted and deleted so that the artist must begin again (Sabbeth, 1998).

Before purchasing a drawing or painting program for your classroom, consider how the children are likely to use it. Although a painting program with its bitmapped images is likely to be easier for young artists to use, if your program goals include engaging students in the writing process you may want to invest in a drawing program.

Art Appreciation

Computers in an early childhood classroom can also be used to provide children with unique experiences in art appreciation. **Simulation software** may be used to take children on a virtual museum tour. Although most of this software is designed for adults or older children, a teacher-directed activity can effectively be used to prepare children for an upcoming field trip or even in place of a field trip if an art museum is not located nearby. The software packages listed below can provide such experiences, as well as narratives to give teachers background information:

- Great Museums of the World® published by Countertop
- Art for the Ages® published by Topics
- Virtual Art Museum® published by Fogware

Most of the major art museums in this country and abroad have Web sites that offer art appreciation experiences. The Louvre in Paris provides a virtual tour of its holding, while the Art Institute of Chicago and the Museum of Fine Arts in Boston allow visitors to their Web sites to view their collections on-line. The Web site of the Museum of Fine Arts in Boston also has a *My Gallery* function that enables visitors to select pieces from the on-line collections to save in their own minigallery for later viewing. Although most museums have on-line resources for teachers and parents, some also offer special activities for children related to their collections. The Museum of Modern Art in Queens, for example, features the children's Web site *Destination Modern Art* through which children can view artwork by painters Van Gogh and Kahlo and sculptor Boccioni. Age-appropriate activities related to the artwork and the artists encourage children to examine details, look for meaning and describe what they see. Likewise, the National Gallery of Art in Washington, DC, includes the *NGAKids* Web site with activities similar to those of the Museum of Modern Art in Queens, as well as the animated musical story *Lizzy and Gordon in the Sculpture Garden*. The Web sites for these museums are listed below:

- Museum of Fine Arts in Boston
  http://www.mfa.org
- Art Institute of Chicago http://www.artic.edu
- The Louvre in Paris http://www.Louvre.fr.
- Museum of Modern Art in Queens
  http://www.moma.org
- National Gallery of Art in Washington, DC
  http://www.nga.gov

What are the keys to integrating computers successfully into the early childhood curriculum and to maximizing children's learning? According to Haugland (1992), the following four steps are critical:

1. Select developmentally appropriate software
   Software is the set of coded instructions that tells the computer what to do. Software can be installed or accessed by the computer in a variety of ways including: diskette or CD-ROM drives, the hard drive, or through a modem from the Internet. While most software is hybrid and can run on either a MacIntosh or a Pentium, so will run on only one type of computer. Because many educators and parents prefer not to evaluate software themselves, there are resources that offer suggestions for good age-appropriate software.
   Children's Software Review
   44 Main Street
   Flemington, NJ 08822
   908-284-0404

Family PC
P.O. Box 40045
Des Moines, IA 50340-0454

High/Scope Buyer's Guide to Software for Young
Children
High/Scope Press
600 N. River Street
Ypsilanti, MI 48198-2898
313-485-2000

Software Review and Catalog
Peak Learning, Inc.
4252 SW Luana Beach
Vashon Island, WA 98070
206-463-6787

Broderbund Software, Inc.
P.O. Box 6121
Novato, CA 94948-6121
800-521-6263
http://www.broderbund.com

Compu-Teach, Inc.
P.O. Box 9515
New Haven, CT 06534
800-44-Teach
http://www.compu-teach.com

Corel Corporation
1600 Carling Avenue
Ottawa, Ontario, Canada K1Z 8R7
800-772-6735
http://www.corel.com

Creative Wonders (formerly EA Kids)
1450 Fashion Island Blvd.
San Mateo, CA 94404
800-543-9778

The Discovery Channel, Inc.
7700 Wisconsin Avenue
Bethesda, MD 20814-3579
800-762-2189
http://school.discovery.com

Disney Interactive, Inc.
500 South Buena Vista Street
Burbank, CA 91521
800-228-0988
http://disney.store.go.com

Don Johnson, Inc.
1000 North Rand Road
Bldg. 115
Wauconda, IL 60084
http://www.donjohnson.com

Edmark Corporation
P.O. Box 3218
Redmond, WA 98073
800-426-0856
http://www.riverdeep.net

Ehrlich Multimedia
One Maynard Drive
Park Ridge, NJ 07656
http://susanprager.com

IBM Multimedia Studio
1500 Riveredge Drive
Atlanta, GA 30328
404-897-2300 x327
http://www.ibm.com

Josten's Home Learning (Compass Learning)
9920 Pacific Heights Blvd.
Suite 100
San Diego, CA 92121-4330
800-238-3224
http://www.compasslearning.com

Mattel, Inc.
333 Continental Blvd.
El Segundo, CA 90245–5012
http://www.service.mattel.com
http://www.mattel.com

Micrografx, Inc.
1301 Arapaho
Richardson, TX 75081
800-417-8312
http://www.micrografx.com

Microsoft Corporation
1 Microsoft Way
Redmond, WA 98052–6299
800-376-5125
http://www.microsoft.com

Mindscape, Inc.
60 Leveroni Court
Novato, CA 94949
800-234-3088
http://www.mindscape.com (British version of
the United States Company)

Mobius Corporation
405 North Henry Street
Alexandria, VA 22134
703-684-2911
http://www.kidware.com (owned by Mobius)

O'Connor House Software
2207 South Gladys Avenue
Appleton, WI 54915
414-734-0250

Optimum Resource, Inc.
12 Laurel Way
Norfolk, CT 06434
800-327-1473
http://www.stickybear.com

Queue
338 Commerce Drive
Fairfield, CT 06434
800-232-2224
http://www.queueinc.com

Scholastic New Media
708 Broadway
New York, NY 10003
800-541-5513
http://www.scholastic.com

Sunburst Communications
101 Castleton Street
Pleasantville, NY 10570-9961
800-321-7511
http://www.sunburst.com

Teacher Support Software
1035 NW 57th Street
Gainesville, FL 32605-4486
800-228-2871
http://www.gameco.com

Information on how to buy educational software can be found at the following Web sites:
- *http://www.superkids.com*
- *http://www.reviewcorner.com*

If you evaluate your own software, Shade (1996) recommends three criteria. First, child features should include provisions for active learning, child-controlled interaction, potential for discovery, experimentation, and ability of the child to use the software independently. Second, teacher features should include the ability to individualize and integrate across the curriculum, anti-bias, diversity, and emphasis on child exploration rather than drill and rote learning. Third, technical features include degree of user friendliness, clarity of sound and graphics, level of simplicity/complexity, and aesthetic quality. See Haugland and Shade (1994) for a software evaluation checklist. Specifically, in selecting art software, look for the following:
- a program that is mouse-driven, not key-driven
- a large open workspace of white or black as the canvas on which to draw or paint

- menu boxes that are large and contain a limited number of options. Symbols for different types of lines, shapes, and colors should be easy for children to "read."
- color, shape, and line options clearly visible and easy for children to "read"
- a program that is open-ended and conducive to creativity. This is opposed to merely filling in colors on a coloring book page or moving shapes and images around on an already drawn background. Art software can be labeled *draw, paint,* or *color* yet still stifle creativity.
- the ability to save and print artwork.

In applying the foregoing criteria, the following art software programs for young children are recommended:
- Crayola Make a Masterpiece® available from IBM
- Create & Draw in Elmo's World® available from Mattel
- Magic Artist Studio® available from Disney
- Kid Pix Studio® available from Broderbund
- Orly's Draw-A-Story® available from Broderbund
- Sesame Street Create & Draw in Elmo's World® available from Mattel
- Sketchboard Studio® available from KB Gear Interactive

2. Select developmentally appropriate Web sites
Many rich educational opportunities await children on the Internet. Some have great educational value; others may not. There are four types of children's Web sites, including information, communication, interaction, and publication. Go to the Online Companion™ for a list of Web sites that would be appropriate for use in an early childhood classroom.

3. Connect software and Web sites to the curriculum
For computers to have an impact on children's learning and for teachers to tap into their learning potential, computer activities need to mesh with children's educational goals. According to Haugland (1992), only when computers are integrated into the curriculum do children demonstrate gains in conceptual understanding, develop abstract thinking, increase verbal skills, and have gains in problem solving.

4. Select a computer wisely
What kind of computer should be purchased for an early childhood classroom? Three factors are helpful in answering this question: software compatibility, access to maintenance and repair, and promotional sales events.

Computer Learning Center

Some believe that young children can get by with outdated, less powerful computers that have been previously owned and/or donated. This is not true. The quality of graphics, sound, animation, and visuals that children need demands the most powerful technology. Outmoded hardware cannot support the newer, more challenging and interesting software programs. New, high-quality software often cannot run on older machines. When selecting a computer, try to anticipate your computer needs for the next three years. Generally, a computer setup with printer will last about three years. By then, the advances in operating features and software capabilities to use these features will render today's computers obsolete. With this in mind, select computers that have the ability to be upgraded. Ideally, your Web-connected computer should be a Pentium-class system. Processors come in a variety of speeds: the faster, the better. The term megahertz (MHz) denotes speed, and Pentium refers to the speed of an internal processor.

Most public school systems have technicians responsible for maintaining classroom computers. Teachers should consult these technicians when computers malfunction or if questions arise about software compatibility, Internet connectivity, or general classroom use. The purchase of a new computer may also be accompanied by the purchase of a service warranty through which repairs and replacement parts may be obtained at no additional cost. A service warranty is well worth the additional investment if technology support is not available to the teacher through the school or school system. Schools should purchase computers only from reputable vendors who will provide maintenance as needed and can make informed recommendations about operating systems and software packages that are compatible with the classroom environment and objectives.

What is needed to equip a computer learning center for young children? A basic computer setup requires a **central processing unit (CPU),** monitor, mouse, speakers, keyboard, developmentally appropriate software, CD and diskette drives, input devices, printer, and an appropriate desk or work station. The CPU is the "guts of your system." The internal parts of the CPU can include the modem, motherboard, fan, electric components, cards, and CD–Rom and disk drive. With CD–ROM encyclopedias, information is presented incorporating visual and auditory as well as text formats. This feature accommodates a wide range of learning styles. A standard mouse is a must, although you may want to consider a large, trackball-type mouse such as Microsoft Easy® ball or KitTrac®.

Most developmentally appropriate children's software does not require a keyboard to access the program, but older children may be ready to use the keyboard. For young children, using a mouse is the best way to draw. There are alphabetical keyboards made for children although it makes sense to start older children on the standard keyboard. Put away or cover your keyboard when younger children are using the mouse. A color printer or touch screen monitor is not absolutely necessary but can add additional dimensions to children's computer experience, especially when making art. Children can use the printer to print out their stories and art creations. A touch screen allows children to manipulate software with a simple touch on the screen instead of using a mouse or keyboard. It is advisable for an adult to load the software onto the computer hard drive. It is too easy for children to accidentally damage the magnetic medium on the software while attempting to load and unload the CD.

Technology Tools

Technology tools are computer hardware or software that are used to create original work. According to Blanckensee (1999), open-ended tools can support learning and development when used appropriately. Today, there is a wide range of technology tools available for use with young children including the following:

- *Cameras:* Polaroid, video, and digital. Polaroid cameras allow teachers to record and immediately document children's art activities and help children recall art processes. Photographs can be enlarged by scanning and digitizing the pictures. A digital camera allows photographs to be printed immediately and without chemical processing. Photo Kit Jr.®, a software package published by ATPE, allows children ages three and up to "play" with their digital photos using editing tools and a variety of games.
- *Printers and scanners:* allow for customizing of image size and type font. Because children enjoy taking their original work home, a scanned copy of their art work can remain in their portfolio.
- *Photocopier:* useful for documentation. Enlargements of photographs of children engaged in art activities can be hung in the art center along with any written dialogue.
- *Drawing tablets:* Tablets such as Sketchboard Studio® from KB Interactive allow children to draw on a natural, flat surface that can be transferred to the computer screen (see Figure 14–7).

Figure 14-7 Creative computer art.

- *Multimedia or hypermedia authoring tools:* combine text, sound, animation, and graphics to create teaching aids, reports or projects. Even young children can write a story and use computerized drawing tools. The use of multimedia empowers learners by putting them in charge of developing a project and constructing knowledge using digital photos, videotaping, and recorded sound to create powerful and personally meaningful work.
- *Scanner:* for digitizing artwork and photographs. A scanner converts a paper image such as children's drawing into a digital image that can be stored as a computer file. A scanner looks and functions like a small photocopier but attaches directly to the computer where the image is stored.
- *Electronic mail or e-mail:* This is used for writing and receiving communication from families of students or expert sources of information from around the world.
- *Internet and access to the World Wide Web:* for finding information, publishing and visits to community sites by taking a virtual field trip. You will need an Internet service provider and a modem. Children can also publish their own work on the Internet and see other children's work. Precautions must be taken. Because the World Wide Web is unregulated, anyone can place anything on the Internet. Use an Internet filtering software or desktop management program such as Kid Desk: Internet Safe®, Net Nanny® (http://www.netnanny.com), or Cyber Patrol® (http://www.cyberpatrol.com) to block children's access to inappropriate websites. Although filtering devices are essential in

early childhood classrooms, they are not by themselves sufficient to keep children safe on the Internet. Information, although age-appropriate, may be inaccurate, biased, sexist, or racist. Regular monitoring by the classroom teacher is needed.
- *Videotapes:* These are useful for documentation of how individual children process with art materials.
- *Kids Works Deluxe®:* This talking word processor is available from Great Wave Software.

How Should the Computer Center Be Arranged and Set Up?

The table or work station should be large enough to hold all the computer equipment and accommodate four children. Place two child seats in front of the computer and one or two at the side which the teacher will often use. Ideally, each computer learning center should house two computers and one printer. Strive for a 10:1 ratio (or better) of children to computers to encourage ample time on the computer, social and language interaction, and equal access for all children. Partner children at the computer, and encourage turn taking and shared problem solving rather than competition. Include curriculum integration activities that incorporative learning strategies.

Children in the K–3 grades who are beginning to use the word processor more extensively as well as researching with CD-ROM encyclopedias can benefit from three or four computers available. Adjustable work stations are highly recommended to avoid the strain from a monitor and keyboard or mouse that is either too high or too low. The table should be low enough for children to sit comfortably in chairs with the keyboard at waist level and the monitor at eye level. Provide an adult-sized teacher chair where you can facilitate, engage children in problem-solving, monitor progress, and supervise use of the Internet. The computer table or work station should be placed against a wall with direct access to a power source and surge protector to guard against electrical damage to the computer. The computer should be located away from direct sunlight, traffic, as well as any source of water, such as a water table, magnets, paint, chalk dust, and windows that could cause a direct glare on the computer screen. Heat is another potential hazard both to the disks and the CPU itself. To enhance learning in curricular areas, some teachers place their computer center in the close proximity to other centers such as near math manipulatives, a book area, or writing center. Use a sign-up book or clipboard along with kitchen timer to manage turn taking.

Computer Center Rules and Limits

1. The computer stays on.
2. Keep food and drink away from the computer center.
3. Use only the controls found on the keyboard or mouse.
4. If you need help, ask a friend or teacher.
5. Wash hands before using the computer and handling disks.
6. Use gentle hands and soft touches with the mouse or keyboard.
7. Only the computer operator uses the mouse or keyboard. Help only if you are asked.

How to Best Use Computers in the Classroom

The issue is not whether or not technology should be used with young children. Computers are here to stay and are housed in many, if not most, classrooms. The real issue is how they are used. One concern is the issue of software, which is like food for the computer. The analogy between eating nutritious foods to optimize health makes the point. Junk food is analogous to junk software. Different types of software have different effects. Inferior or developmentally inappropriate software cannot foster a positive computer experience for young children. Open-ended programs foster collaboration and creativity, whereas drill-and-practice programs support competition.

How to best choose developmentally appropriate software? Thouvenelle and Bewick (1999) offer advice. Identify your educational goals, what you want children to learn, and specifically how this particular software will get you there. Read reviews of the software you are considering and preview it yourself. Be wary of boastful advertised claims. Evaluate the software for bias and hurtful messages related to gender, race, abilities, violence, and family composition. Healy (1998) recommends looking for programs with varying levels of difficulty, and clear and understandable graphics enabling children to easily navigate through the program's features. Graphics should have aesthetic merit. Software should be multisensory and interactive, and it should allow children to express their creativity. Choosing open-ended software encourages discovery, experimentation, problem solving, original thinking, and children's personal construction of knowledge.

Teachers should consider how the computer will interface and connect with their curriculum. There are many ways to use computers depending on one's intended purpose. In some classrooms, computers are used mostly for educational games or as a reward for work completed. The purpose is more entertainment and "time filling." Computers are treated as video arcade games. In other classrooms, computer activities resemble electronic workbooks teaching and reinforcing what has been taught with skill-oriented drill and practice tasks such as matching shapes, letters, or numbers. This approach is tutorial in nature. Software provides ways for children to work on skills that need to be practiced to be mastered. Children are given a certain number of problems, feedback on whether their answer is right or wrong, and a reward for the correct answer. Healy (1998) characterizes this type of software as "edutainment." Some software programs help children progress independently through levels of ability while others focus on problem solving and concept building skills. This approach should be used after children have learned a concept, for example, with manipulatives and need additional practice for mastery. Both these approaches free the teacher to work with other children, but the valuable teacher-child interactive feature is missing. Opportunities for mediating and scaffolding are lacking because the teacher is busy doing something else. However, adult participation, support, and guidance are critical to children's successful computer experiences. Along with questioning the developmental appropriateness of these two approaches, the issue of creativity can be raised. Software can be either closed-ended or open-ended, as with some writing and drawing software. Computers can reduce creativity if children's use is restricted to drill and practice with closed-ended software in which they merely provide correct answers. The availability of interactive books, generally on CD-ROMs, is another popular form of tutorial software that features instantaneous animation, sounds, and voice output when the child selects any item on the screen. CD-ROM storybooks foster an interactive literacy experience by allowing children to read at their own pace, repeating lines of text when desired, having the computer speak words they do not know, and manipulating characters within a story. A high-quality interactive book begins with a good story that motivates children to read it again and again. Children control the story by clicking on objects to begin animations, hear the story in different languages, turn off the "reader" altogether, and/or choose alternative events and endings. There are other approaches. Teachers do successfully integrate children's use of computers with what is being taught. Chosen software supports, interfaces with, enhances, extends, and enriches the curriculum. In the primary grades, teachers are asking children to find Internet resources for their work. Some help children use technology to create multimedia themselves. According to Blanckensee (1999), technology tools are most valuable when teachers scaffold and design projects that encourage children to push the limits of their current knowledge. The teacher acts as a facilitator to young students who construct ideas and develop skills as they work on personally meaningful real-world tasks.

What is the role of the teacher? Because the computer is meant to supplement rather than replace the teacher, there are many roles for teachers to play. Once purchased and set up, the teacher needs to develop expertise with this particular computer and the software that will be available in the classroom. Operating systems have varied capabilities and avenues for problem solving. Because troubleshooting problems while a group of children are waiting can be frustrating for teacher and students alike, teachers should acquaint themselves thoroughly with the operating system before introducing a new computer into the classroom. Likewise, teachers should familiarize themselves with the software that will be available to children in the computer center. Checking out the activities available to children on a particular piece of software not only can help teachers decide how to use the software as a part of the curriculum, but also will equip the teacher to help children solve problems during computer activities. Second, teachers need to find out about children's computer experience: what they already know and can do on a computer. Computers and software should be introduced to young children in the same way that any other new material or activity would be introduced: individually or in small groups. With a small group approach, gather several children at a time around the center while two children sit in chairs. Name and point to the parts of the computer the children will need to know. These include the keyboard, monitor, mouse, and printer. Show the seated children how to turn on the computer. Start with a simple program and encourage the children to figure out how it works. Some teachers prefer to use only one program at a time until everyone in the group understands how to use it. Let this first small group use the computer as soon as it has been introduced. Children need to apply what they have learned immediately. This approach ensures that all the children use the computer, including those who are hesitant or reluctant to try new things. Otherwise, children using computers may be only those who are confident, experienced, or used to using a computer at home. Once computers have been introduced, teachers need to monitor and facilitate children's computer's use.

How can teachers match computer to curriculum? Thouvenelle and Bewick (2003) suggest consulting national, state, or district-level curriculum standards for your grade level to identify educational goals for your group. Review assessment and reporting require-

Figure 14-8 Three children collaborated together to create computer art.

ments. Then use curriculum strategies such as webs, themes, or projects to create a meaningful framework that connects computer experiences with other hands-on classroom activities. Determine how computers can assist in the assessment process.

Can computers assist teachers in assessment? According to Thouvenelle and Bewick (2003), one additional benefit of technology is that it can support documenting student progress in meeting curricular goals. Teachers can carefully observe children's computer use and collaboration with others, as well as thinking processes and computer-generated products, such as stories. In order to successfully use the computer as an assessment tool teachers must focus on children's processes as well as on their products. Consideration of the computer-generated artwork in Figure 14–8 yields little information of the artist's knowledge or skills. Teacher observation of the children in the process of creating the picture, however, revealed the children's detailed knowledge of story structure, and their willingness to explore the capabilities of the draw and paint software.

Communicating with Technology

Technology also provides useful tools for teachers in communicating with the families of the children in their classroom. In the past, teachers relied on telephone calls, notes, and letters to inform families of classroom events and children's achievements and difficulties. Because almost 50% of families in the United States have Internet access in their homes, many teachers can now use e-mail and classroom Web sites to keep families up to date.

Although the telephone may be a preferred mode of communication because it allows for direct interaction between teacher and parent, it is often difficult for teachers to take advantage of. Many teachers do not have telephones in their classrooms and so have difficulty placing calls to family members. Family members who work during the day may not be able to receive personal calls, thus requiring teachers to attempt communication during the evenings, and thus interrupting the teachers' personal time. E-mail communications allow teachers to send communications to families at times convenient to their instructional schedules and allow families to respond at their own convenience.

E-mail communications sent from teachers to families should follow much the same format as traditional notes and letters. Although the convenience of communicating by e-mail may lead users to abbreviate spelling and take grammatical short-cuts, it is important for teachers to recognize that e-mails are still professional communications with the families of students and should follow a professional format. For example, the following outline may be used to contact a parent about a problem or concern for a child:

- Begin with something positive.
- State the problem/issue with tact, but do not minimize its seriousness.
- Describe what has been done thus far to address the issue.
- Invite parents to meet for a discussion of the situation.
- Always leave the door open for discussion.
- Always invite parent input before implementing a program to address the problem.

Classroom Web sites provide a simple way for busy classroom teachers to keep families abreast of routine information and events in the classroom. Although professional website designers may easily be accessed by teachers, these are often quite expensive. Instead, teachers may use a program such as Microsoft Publisher® to design their own Web pages to be posted on school Web sites, or they may take advantage of an on-line company that has designed Web pages for teachers simply to fill in information pertaining to their own classrooms. Such companies usually charge a small monthly fee for posting and maintaining a single teacher's Web sites, or schools may pay a larger fee for an entire Web site on which teachers may post individual Web pages. Following is a list of on-line companies through which teachers may design and post classroom Web sites or pages for parent access:

ClassWebs. Net
http://www.classwebs.net/
30-Minutes Websites for Teachers
http://www.classroomwebsites.com/
MyTeacherPages
http://www.myteacherpages.com/
Homestead for Classrooms
http://classrooms.homestead.com/

A variety of information may be included on classroom Web sites. To begin, the Web site should obviously include the teacher's name and an e-mail link through which families can communicate. The grade or age level of the teacher's students and a room number, as well as the school address and phone number, may also be helpful for families attempting to contact the teacher by mail or telephone. Including the class's daily and weekly schedules will assist family members planning to visit or volunteer in the classroom. Dates and times for which special events such as field trips, guest speakers, parent-teacher conferences, parent meetings, school pictures, and health screenings are scheduled can also assist parents in planning and preparing their children for school each day. Primary grade teachers may also include information on homework assignments, upcoming test dates, and the list of spelling or vocabulary words the children will be studying during the current week.

Many teachers also use Web sites to provide families with information on the children's activities and interactions during the school day. A description of learning centers and curriculum topics, illustrated by digital photographs of the children actively engaged, can help families to understand the nature of learning in an early childhood classroom. A classroom Web site can also be used as an on-line museum for children's artwork. Digital photographs displaying children's drawings, paintings, sculptures, and designs may be posted on the Web site, along with the child's dictated description or explanation of his or her creation. An on-line museum can be valuable in helping the children to see that their creative work is enjoyed by others and by helping families to see the development in children's artwork as the school year progresses.

Whatever is included on the classroom Web site, it is critical that the teacher makes the commitment to update the Web site regularly. A Web site is useful to families only if the information is current and accurate. Teachers should also keep in mind that although 50% of families have Internet access at home, 50% do not. A careful survey of families at the beginning of the school year will tell teachers whether more traditional routes of communication will be more appropriate.

 **MOBILES AND STABILES**

Mobiles and *stabiles* are three-dimensional works of art consisting of separate parts joined together by thin connectors, usually wire or string.

Mobile

A **mobile** is a hanging sculpture that moves. Generally, it has pieces that are suspended and are free to move about. Wind or movement will activate a mobile. Wind chimes and hanging infant toys suspended over the crib are good examples of mobiles. Mobiles contain at least one level from which items are suspended. A mobile can be suspended from a ceiling or doorway using string and a thumbtack. Advanced mobile makers are faced with the problem of balance when they work with more than one level. To start, one must find a sturdy overhead base from which the items will be suspended, using string, rope, yarn, thread, or fishing line. Some recommended supports from which heavy items can be suspended include the following:

- driftwood
- dowel rod
- broom handle
- thick tree branch
- pencil
- stick
- yardstick
- coat hanger
- three coat hangers wired together at their hooks
- wood ruler

Supports from which light objects can be suspended include these:

- straws
- tongue depressors
- ice-cream sticks

These smaller supports can be creatively combined with the items previously listed. Here are some mobile activities recommended for use with young children.

Group Nature Mobile

You will need a fairly sturdy tree branch. Look for one that has an interesting branched-out shape. This will provide a number of different levels from which items can be suspended. Rest or prop up the branch as it will later be hung, but closer to the children's level. They need to be able to reach the branches to attach nature items. Nature items can be collected on a nature walk or brought from home. Encourage children to look for nature specimens that have

fallen to the ground. Not all items will be able to be tied or secured. Seashells, feathers, acorns, mushrooms, twigs, leaves, and pinecones are well suited. Attach them with string or yarn and suspend them from a branch. Nature specimens should be suspended at different lengths rather than in a neat row. Lengths of string can have more than one item suspended from them. When the mobile is completed, place it near a window or doorway where a breeze will activate it. This is a good multisession activity. Items on the mobile can be continually added to or changed.

Group mobile projects need not be restricted to the use of nature items. Include any of the recycled junk items listed in Appendix A, as well as

- paper scraps, cut and torn pieces.
- pictures from magazines.
- tissue paper shapes sealed in wax paper.
- plastic tops and caps.
- anything interesting that can be suspended; be creative!

Remember to decorate the front and back of items, since both sides will be visible. Mobiles can be made around the above-mentioned nature theme or

- main characters in a favorite story, book, or song.
- weather and seasons.
- holidays.
- animals.
- community helpers.
- traffic signs and safety.
- food groups.
- transportation.

Yarn Shapes Mobile

Begin with a papier-mâché mixture (see recipes in Chapter 12). Children will each need their own piece of wax paper to work on. Take lengths of rug yarn and dip them into the papier-mâché mixture. Squeeze out the excess between your fingers. Arrange the yarn lengths into a shape or object. Be sure to crisscross and overlap the yarn. Let dry thoroughly. Carefully peel off the wax paper. Hang the yarn shape from a mobile.

Multilevel Mobile

Advanced mobile makers can make a mobile that has more than one level. For example, begin with a dowel rod and suspend pencils attached to string of different lengths. Do not worry if the mobile does not balance at this point. Start to suspend items and glue string or yarn in place. Slowly work toward balance. One object on a very short line may balance a much lighter object suspended from a long line. More than one object can be placed on any one line, which will also influence balance. Older children may enjoy the challenge presented by this activity.

Baked Clay Mobile

Check Chapter 11 for a clay recipe that involves baking the finished product. This will provide a nice tinkling sound when the items rustle in the wind. Children can use cookie cutters or clay tools when making their items. Remember to make a hole through each item to allow for hanging.

Picture Parts Mobile

Discuss with children how objects can be cut up into parts. For example, a person could be divided into a head, a body, and legs. Each could be connected separately on a line, with a small space left in between. This will provide a comical effect when the wind moves the cut-up parts about. This same process can be done with animals, vehicles, or whatever. Magazine pictures are a good source, or children may want to draw their own pictures. A clown, a rocket ship blasting off, and a Christmas tree are just a few that the author has seen.

Stabile

A **stabile** is nothing more than a self-standing, stationary mobile. Whereas a mobile is suspended, a stabile, with one or more arched wire arms, rests on a fixed base. Although it is fairly similar to a mobile, a stabile is more difficult to make. You will need at least one length of fairly sturdy wire attached to a wood base. The base must be large and heavy enough to support the wires

and suspended items without tipping over. Basically, any of the activities recommended for the mobile apply to the stabile. Suspended items that are too big or heavy will pull down the wire. Also, it will be much more difficult to get several layers hanging from a wire that is bent close toward its base than from a mobile hanging overhead.

Simple Stabile

Provide each child with a drinking-cup lid, pipe cleaners, and play dough or plasticene, as well as an array of greeting cards, postcards, or magazine pictures. Children can glue or tape their cutout pictures onto one end of a pipe cleaner. A piece of play dough is molded either inside or on top of the cup lid. Children gently push their pipe cleaners into the play dough. Pipe cleaners can be creatively twisted and arranged at different heights and positions. Stabiles can complement a holiday theme by using relevant pictures. Children may also enjoy making a stabile titled "me" or "my family."

SUMMARY

This chapter focused on the children's use of technology in art production and appreciation activities. Although young children's use of computers is questioned by some adults, current research supports the benefits of computer use for children's cognitive and socioemotional development. It is important that teachers make careful choices in setting up the classroom computer center and in providing software for young children. The most appropriate software for young children allows for open-ended interaction with the computer. Drawing software and painting software encourage such interaction as children engage in art production activities.

Key Terms

bitmapping	drill-and-practice software	open-ended software
central processing unit	LOGO®	painting programs
drawing programs	mobile	simulation software
drawing tablet	multimedia authoring tools	stabile

Suggested Activities

1. Your instructor will know teachers who have successfully integrated computers into their program. Arrange to observe and focus on management concerns. Who gets a turn and for how long? What software is being used? How was it selected? Record your observations.
2. In a separate observation of the classroom computer center, observe the children. What are they learning? How are they interacting with each other? Record your observations.
3. Preview some of the software suggested in this chapter. Consider how it could relate to curriculum objectives in an early childhood classroom. Think of ways you could use this software in your own classroom.
4. Visit the art museum Web sites listed in this chapter. Complete some of the activities the Web sites provide for children. Consider the age-appropriateness of these activities for children in your classroom. How could you integrate these activities into your curriculum?
5. Facilitate a mobile or stabile activity with school-age children.

Review

1. Discuss research findings on the impact of computer use on young children's cognitive development.

2. What are the differences between drawing software and painting software?

3. List the three criteria teachers should use when evaluating software for classroom use.

4. List the rules for children's participation in the classroom computer center.

5. Describe three technology avenues for communicating with the families of the children in your classroom.

For additional art and creative development resources, visit our Web site at
www.EarlyChildEd.delmar.com

Chapter 15

Roles, Responses, and Strategies to Support Children's Art

Most of us enter the field of early childhood education for the joy of working with young children. The teacher in the photo clearly enjoys what she is doing. She has just joined a boy working with play dough. She had been observing him from a distance and decided to sit down and talk with him. He was quite proud that he had mastered using the tool to cut up the play dough. The teacher is sharing in his delight. She responds both nonverbally and verbally. What could she be saying? What would you say to acknowledge the boy's accomplishment and share in his delight at working with play dough?

Objectives

After reading this chapter, you should be able to:

- Discuss the teacher's role as a model and participator in early childhood art.
- Identify ways in which a teacher can be a creative individual and art specialist in the center or classroom.
- Identify specific strategies for enhancing children's artistic expression.
- Compare and contrast art group time with traditional show-and-tell.
- Help school-age children make mobiles and/or stabiles.
- Critique different approaches to talking with children about their art.
- Apply the six questions posed by Engle (1995) to help one really look at children's art.
- Discuss the value of art dictation.
- Use the artistic elements to analyze and discuss children's art.
- Discuss how a family's culture could influence their child's artistic expression.

INTRODUCTION

There are many different ways to approach the teaching of art. What is the teacher's role in children's art? Adults can stimulate children to make art by being a model and participant. Adults can model creativity in their daily lives and actively participate in art activities themselves. Although it is important to be an art specialist and to know about art, an adult does not need to be a talented artist to provide creative art experiences for children.

Teacher as Model

Children learn in different ways. Some profit best by listening to a teacher. Others may learn by simply observing what a teacher does. For example, it would be more beneficial for a teacher to simply demonstrate how to sew or weave than verbally to tell children all the steps involved. Rather than telling children to "walk quietly," showing them how to walk quietly is more effective. In these cases, the teacher serves as a **model** or demonstrator. Simply modeling or demonstrating a new activity will draw a small group of curious observers who can be eased into participating. For example, a teacher who models different ways to work with clay and clay tools will soon find the clay table filled with willing sculptors. One way of learning how to be a good teacher is to observe others modeling good teaching.

Teacher as Participator

Children enjoy playing, both by themselves and with other children. They also enjoy an adult's participation in their activities. There are times when a teacher would be most welcome as a **participator** or player in one of the centers.

▶▶ N A E Y C

Do art with children but be careful not to do art for them. Doing art for children sets them up for disappointment. Inevitably they will try to copy you and end up frustrated and discouraged. Announce that sometimes you do not like what you do on the first try and you simply try again. Share your frustration with trying to get it just the way you want when the paint runs and colors bleed in ways you do not like. Children will welcome your participation, especially if they appear stuck or frustrated. Work along with them but focus on just doing, rather than overwhelming them with your adult products. For example, the play dough table is one of the author's favorite spots. Sit with the children and observe what is or is not happening. If children appear stuck, participate by modeling options. Say, "I think I'll try squeezing and flattening my play dough. Let's see what happens." Children may join in by squeezing and flattening their play dough which provides them with a new option and opens the door to discussion. Children may begin talking about their "pancake" shapes. They can also choose not to follow your suggestions.

In Figure 15–1, a parent engages in art alongside a child. At other times, children will not welcome a

Figure 15-1 Enabling children to engage in art.

teacher's presence and may even ask him or her to leave. "No big people, just kids!" states a group of block builders. Their wishes should be respected. It is important that all children sometimes have a teacher's participation in their activity. The close contact is valuable, especially since the children are being met on their terms. This stands in opposition to a teacher-directed activity, where children are simply assimilated into the existing activity.

Although the author recommends taking on the role of participator, some may feel that it is intrusive and robs children of the opportunity to discover techniques on their own, for example, squeezing and flattening play dough. Where do you stand on the adult's role as participator in children's art activities?

Teacher as Creative Individual

A teacher must also be a creative, unique individual. Creative teachers encourage creativity in their children. They model creativity. "I don't have a paper cutter. What else can I use to make paper strips for our weaving?" "We don't have an easel to take outdoors. How else can we have art outside?" Children come to see that problem solving and creative solutions are necessary and vital parts of daily living.

The creative teacher develops:

FROM	TO
1. viewing children in terms of groups on the basis of sex, age, or ability	1. viewing children as unique individuals
2. viewing highly creative children as a threat, nuisance, or menace	2. seeing creativity as an asset
3. stressing conformity in thinking and behavior	3. encouraging creative thinking and different ways to do things
4. looking for children to give the one right answer or best idea	4. considering many possible solutions and ideas
5. viewing self as uncreative	5. seeing how all people have the potential to be creative
6. providing a teacher-centered program	6. providing a child-centered program that values child input and decision making
7. providing a structured program, planned in detail	7. offering subtle planning that allows for diversion and sudden twists and turns
8. equating creativity with art, music, and movement	8. seeing creativity as a skill that cuts across the program
9. adding creative activities here and there	9. weaving creativity throughout the entire program
10. confining creativity to a certain day, time, slot	10. including creativity throughout the entire or day

Creativity is something we strive for. We may not be very creative during our internship, student teaching, or first year of actual teaching. We hope, however, to be successful and slowly move toward our lofty goal of becoming creative early childhood educators.

TEACHER AS ART SPECIALIST

It is also important for us to be **art specialists.** We need to know about art, artists, artistic elements, and developmentally appropriate art activities. Just as one need not be a hockey player to enjoy viewing a game or be a musician to appreciate a concert, one need not be a gifted or talented artist to provide art experiences for children. It is more important that teachers display artistic sensitivity, awareness, and discovery, than that they develop an endless list of art activities. Encouraging children to use all their senses, to experiment, to explore, and to represent what they know about the world does make one an art specialist.

Atelierista is the name given to the art specialist working in Reggio Emilia classrooms. The relationship between student and art specialist is similar to that between apprentice and master. Young children profit from observing, talking with, and working beside highly educated and more experienced peers and adults. When young children *intern* with a teacher of art, they are able to directly learn necessary skills and processes associated with the various artistic media. Although it is not important, as an atelierista, to excel in any one of the arts, it is important to think in artistic ways.

TEACHER AS RESPONDER

Adults can respond both verbally and nonverbally to children's art. What should one say to a child artist? Should a teacher praise, judge, question, or correct? This chapter will overview and critique different strategies. **Art dialogue,** a strategy using the artistic elements, will be presented as a preferred approach. Although the art program will run smoothly most of the time, individual children may have difficulty on occasion and will need direct intervention. The role of the teacher as troubleshooter will be portrayed.

Teachers can respond and react to children's art both nonverbally and verbally. Often, we are unaware of our nonverbal communication. A smile conveys approval, while a frown or puzzled look conveys disapproval. For example, a teacher may verbally say that she likes a child's abstract artwork, but her wrinkled forehead and squint convey quite the opposite. Posture and overall body language also communicate a message. Giving a cold stare to a child who is making a creative mess communicates one's preference for order and neatness. Hands on hips or crossed arms while staring down at a child conveys a cold, aloof message. Stooping down to eye level or sitting close to a child conveys warmth, respect, and acceptance. Young children are physical beings who use their bodies to express what they feel. In turn, they are sensitive to the nonverbal messages conveyed by adults. One goal for early childhood educators is to develop positive nonverbal communication and establish congruence between our nonverbal and verbal messages to children. Research indicates that between ages two and five, children become aware of gender, race, ethnicity, and disabilities. Because some of the most ba-

sic elements of ethnic identity are established before age three, very young children thrive in a setting that is culturally diverse and culturally respectful. Caregivers and teachers must recognize and support what is unique, and possibly culturally inspired about individual children (Bredekamp, 1987) and their artwork.

According to Engel (1996), when talking with children about their art, well-disposed adults usually resort to positive, appreciative comments including:

- "What a nice painting! Let's hang it up where we can enjoy it."
- "How interesting. How long did it take you to paint that?"
- "I really like your painting. Would you like to have another turn at the easel tomorrow?"
- "You're painting much better now. I can see you wiped off your brush so the paint didn't run down."
- "All done? Do you want to tell me about it?"
- "Let's put it up on the refrigerator where Mommy can see it when she comes home."

Remarks such as these are supportive and encouraging. They are also appropriate at some times for some children. On the positive side, we have learned not to criticize or correct the creative work of young children. We can also learn how to discuss children's artwork with them in more serious, constructive ways.

ART DIALOGUE*

Verbal comments that teachers traditionally make concerning children's art take the following six approaches:

- complimentary
- questioning
- judgmental
- probing
- valuing
- correcting

The impact of each of these on the child artist will be analyzed, and an alternative to the six traditional approaches will be presented.

With the **complimentary approach,** teachers tell children that their art is nice, pretty, lovely, super, or beautiful. Specific comments include, "That's a beautiful painting," "Oh, how lovely," "Pretty, a very pretty picture," or "Yes, very nice." In turn, the child will often smile, say "thank you," and walk away. The opportunities for rich verbal dialogue are limited. A second limitation is that these terms become vague and overworked platitudes. For example, the term

* This section has been adapted from the original work by Schirrmacher, R. (1986). Talking with young children about their art. *Young Children, 41,* 3–7.

Learning How to Really Look at Children's Art

Engel (1995) feels it is important that each child's art be understood, commented on, appreciated—and taken as serious work. Why? Because a close observation of children's art reveals something about them—what they see as important, how they view their surrounding world and are connected to it. How is this accomplished? By learning to look. Engel (1996) stresses the importance of closely observing the visual art of young children and, as a result, see more in it, have more questions to ask, and more to say about it. Her questions are useful in considering a child's artwork as well as having a conversation with artists about their artwork. Observers can ponder the following questions or pose them to the child artist.

1. **What is it made of?**

   This refers to materials used including size, tools, and media.

2. **What does the observer see?**

   This refers to artistic elements including lines, angles, shapes, colors, etc. Please refer to Chapter 6 for a more detailed discussion of artistic elements.

3. **What does it represent?**

   This refers to design, story, scene, or symbol depicted.

4. **How is it organized?**

   Aspects of meaning include perspective, composition, action, point of view, and completion.

5. **What is it about, what is the nature of involvement?**

   This refers to the function or intent that might include providing information, explaining, expressing feelings, experimenting, exploring ideas, etc.

6. **Where does the idea come from?**

   Source or origin could include the child's imagination, observation, literature, imitation, media, conversation, as well as "messing about."

Ask yourself the above six questions while studying the sample of child art (left side of the easel) seen in Figure 15-2. Possible answers include:

1. The boy has been using tempera paint and a brush while painting at the easel on a large sheet of white paper.

2. He uses vertical and large circular brush strokes resulting from colors mixing together. He has used different shades of blue and has mixed them to create different colors.

3. A design composed of blue brush strokes and circular shapes is seen. The observer refrains from trying to guess what it is. Talking with the child may provide verbal cues as to what it's supposed to be. It may be a design composed of blue lines and shapes.

4. The painting is set in the center of the paper. Top corners remain unpainted. Most of the paper is filled with painted lines and shapes.

5. While observing the child it appears he is interested in experimenting and exploring with the paint and watching colors mix. He also enjoyed watching his vertical strokes of thick blue paint run to the bottom of the paper.

6. The observer would guess that the boy is "messing about" with the media to see what he can make his wet brush do on paper.

Analyzing his art in this way will help the teacher engage in a meaningful dialogue with the boy.

nice is used so freely, as in "Have a nice day!" that it conveys very little meaning or sincerity. What are the criteria for a *nice* picture? Is an abstract picture *not nice*? The term *pretty* is another example. Not all children's art is pretty. A solid mass of black paint may be dark, massive, thick, layered, or rectangular, but it is not pretty. The terms *nice* and *pretty* are empty ones

and should be replaced with terms that provide specific feedback to the child.

With the **judgmental approach,** the teacher tells children that their art is good or great. Specific comments include, "Very good" and "That's great work." Because most teachers do not want to judge and rank children's art as good, better, or best, they may simply

Figure 15-2 "Look, teacher."

tell all children that any and all of their art is good. In turn, these judgmental terms become overworked and meaningless. A teacher may lose credibility with the judgmental approach. How can one child's impulsive scribble and another's detailed portrait both be good? Is the teacher not telling the truth? Or could it be that the teacher is not really looking, but merely rubber-stamping them in production-line fashion with the same empty judgment?

With the **valuing approach,** the teacher tells children that she likes or even loves their art. Specific comments include, "I like that a lot" and "Oh, I just love it." Obviously, it is important to tell children that you recognize all the time and effort they have spent processing with the medium. You can appreciate how hard a child worked to get a clay dinosaur to stand up. Rewarding and encouraging the child for processing, however, is different from putting the teacher's seal of approval on the finished product. Children create to express themselves. They should not make art to please a teacher. Unfortunately, many children create art that is personal and therefore devalued by adults. Stereotypic, impersonal art is often the type valued by adults. A classic example is the square house flanked by trees with a triangle roof and a smoking chimney. Often there are two windows with parted curtains and a smiling sun in the sky. Adults understand and may even encourage the making of stereotypic art. This type of picture gets praised and displayed at home on the door of the refrigerator. The stereotypic symbols or schema convey public meaning. Although they may reflect a developmental landmark in attaining realism, they are not better than children's abstract art.

With the **questioning approach,** a teacher directly and bluntly asks children, "What is it?" or "What is that supposed to be?" An older or very verbal child may answer. Some children may not be able to verbalize what they have represented on a very personal level. It may be difficult for a child to respond, "I

just painted how I feel inside when I'm mad." Young children may not know why or what they have painted. In response, they may shrug their shoulders, cast their eyes downward, say, "I don't know," or walk away. Some teachers continue their questioning. "Well, is it a _____ or is it a _____?" A child may verbally play along just to end the interrogation.

Much of young children's art is private, egocentric, and not intended to look like something. According to Smith (1983), it is unwise and even harmful to ask, "What is it?" of a child who is making nonrepresentational art. According to Kamii and DeVries (1978), for young children who engage in nonrepresentational art, art may have primary value as a physical knowledge activity. Motoric hand and arm movements result in brushing, dabbing, swirling, and smearing paint. The finished product or end result is of no consequence. Other children may be hurt or insulted that their teacher did not immediately recognize their splash of thick blue paint as the ocean.

With the **probing approach,** the teacher attempts to draw from children some hint, title, or verbal statement about their art. Typical comments include, "Please tell me all about it" or "What can you say about this?" This approach is less forward and abrasive than the previous one. It is supported by an integrated approach to curriculum development (Chapter 12) in which children's art is used as a lead-in to other curricular areas. This probing approach has merit, but it should be used sparingly. Children cannot and need not always verbalize, dictate a story, or write about their art. Also, there is a tendency for this approach to grow stale with repeated use. A young boy once told his peers not to show their artwork to the new student teacher because "she will make you tell a real long story about it and then you have to wait while she writes it across your picture." Encouraging but not mandating that children talk about their art is sound practice (see Figure 15–3).

The **correcting approach** attempts to provide children with specific feedback that will enable them to improve their art or make it *better* by more closely approximating reality. For example, a child shows her teacher a drawing of a green spider. The teacher replies, "Very good, but remember to draw legs on your spider. Spiders have many legs. And remember when you color that most spiders are black." This teacher's intentions were good but misdirected. Art, and child art in particular, is not a copy of the real world. Photography, not art, copies reality. Instead, the child artist freely chooses to creatively improvise. For example, children know what their faces look like. Still, their self-portraits may reflect faces that lack ears or eyebrows. Lowenfeld (1968) warns that a teacher's corrections or criticism only discourage children and do not foster their artistic growth.

Figure 15-3 Children enjoy inventing their own spelling. Teachers can also record children's talk about their work.

So what is a teacher to say or do? Nothing? Smile or nod approvingly? Eisner (1976, 1982) recommends that teachers shift from searching for representation in child art and focus on the abstract, design qualities or *syntax,* such as shape and form. Children's art is related to the work of adult artists in the use of these artistic fundamentals. Discussing the formal elements of the visual arts is vital to the development of aesthetic awareness and aesthetic potential. Even very young children can understand artistic terms such as shape, pattern, line, design, and color.

Merely knowing about the artistic elements will not suffice. Teachers can use the aesthetic elements of art as a framework for verbally responding to children's art. One need not be an artist to understand and implement this approach. There are different ways of identifying and organizing the artistic elements. Consensus is lacking on the one best list or approach. Hardiman and Zernich (1981) emphasize the following seven artistic elements.

- color
- line
- mass or volume
- pattern
- shape
- space
- texture

Balance, overall design or composition, and time and effort can be added to the above list.

This expanded list is both manageable and developmentally appropriate for talking with young children about their art. It will serve as the framework for the alternative approach advocated in this section.

Keep three principles in mind when talking with young children about their art. First, consider children's developmental levels. For toddlers and young preschoolers, keep your comments short and to the point. Talk about physical movement, saying, "Look how fast your arm is moving the crayon." Or, "I see thick dots where you pressed hard." Second, relate comments to the artistic elements the child has used in picture making. Say, "Look at all the colors; let's name them—red, blue, and purple." Or, "Big squares that make rectangles are up at the top of your paper." Third, use encouragement rather than praise. Say, "I know you feel proud when you get the scissors to cut all by yourself." This conveys a very different message than saying, "Good girl" or "Great job." Saying, "The smiling sun in the sky matches your happy face" conveys your interest and appreciation. Words of encouragement help children feel good about their art. Children can easily get addicted to praise and end up doing art to please adults and get the verbal rewards.

When talking to children engaged in art activities, Dodge and Colker (1996) recommend the following strategies.
Describe what you see—
"I see you used all the colors at the easel today."
"I see three round white balls painted on top of each other."
Talk about children's actions—
"You like to roll and pound the play dough."
"You used tape over your glued-down button to make sure it would stick."
Ask children about the process—
"How did you make that new color?"
"Would you like to tell the children in group how you got your wood pieces to stay glued together?"
Ask open-ended questions that encourage children to think and respond—
"What might happen if you tried mixing different colors?"
"What might you paint that would be new and different today?"
Use words to encourage and support children's efforts—
"You painted two paintings today. You decide which one we should hang up."
"You have been busy at the play dough table. I see three different things you have made."

Develop an Art Vocabulary Based on the Artistic Elements

Let us match specific comments to each of the 10 artistic elements listed previously.
color—
"I see bright colors. Here (pointing) are the three primary colors—red, blue, and yellow."

"You made purple on your paper. Do you know how you did that? Yes, you mixed red and blue together."

line—

"So many lines are on your paper. Some are straight up and down; others are curvy. These two lines formed a cross and here you made an *X*."

mass or volume—

"Your clay animal is heavy and solid."

"Let me see what you have put on your Styrofoam®. You used toothpicks, yarn, and sticks deep in the back. What a massive piece of art."

pattern—

"I see a pattern of painted shapes. It goes: tree, then a house, and then another tree."

shape—

"Look at all the different shapes you made. Help me name them. Yes, there's a circle and here's a rectangle. And over here? Yes, your square house has a triangle roof."

space—

"Your hand painting fills up all of your paper. There is no empty space left."

texture—

"Thank-you for showing me your collage. The shiny metallic paper feels so smooth. But over here the dried glue with sand feels bumpy and rough. You have two different textures."

balance—

"Do you know your picture is balanced? What do you think that means? On the left side (pointing) you drew yourself and over here on the right (pointing) you drew your bunny."

overall design or composition—

"You used many different lines and shapes to make your picture. Here they fit into each other like puzzle pieces. You placed them all over your paper. It makes a very interesting design."

time and effort—

"I can tell you worked very long and hard at this picture. You must be very proud of yourself" (encouraging remark).

"I bet you're glad you didn't give up. You finally got the play dough to work so your animal can stand up."

Teachers can also say, "I like the way you . . .

- are working so hard."
- are being so creative."
- are trying to come up with your very own idea."
- are not giving up."
- are trying new ways."
- are putting things away."
- are sharing at the art center."

Teachers can also verbally reflect the way a piece of art makes them feel. For example, "Robbie, your bright colors make me feel so happy." Or, "The big, bright yellow sun makes me feel so warm all over." Or, "All those lines racing around your paper make me feel like moving around."

Teachers are being responsive when they carefully examine children's art and provide a rich dialogue in which the artistic elements are pointed out and discussed. No one piece of children's art will contain all of the artistic elements. Texture is useful in describing collage or painting, where surfaces are

Art Dictation

Many children will want to talk about their art. Some will provide a title, labels, or sentence to accompany it (see Figure 15-4). Some teachers elect to very neatly print these words across the picture. The author, however, recommends using a separate piece of paper for two reasons. First, adult artists rarely have words written across their canvas. Second, often there is little blank space, and the words have to be written too small or squeezed in. Using a separate piece of paper has a few advantages. It allows a separate story to be stapled or taped to the bottom. A blank sheet allows you to print in fairly large letters. Therefore, it will be easier for the child to see and read back. Last, it allows room for the child to trace over the letters and words. Leaving blank space between lines provides room for the child to attempt to copy the letters, words, and sentences.

Why take art dictation? According to Greenburg (1999), there are at least five different reasons. First, it deepens your understanding of each child. Second, it furthers your relationship with each child. Third, each child receives your undivided attention. Fourth, it shows each child that you respect their work and ideas. Fifth, it teaches literacy as children learn the connection between spoken and written word.

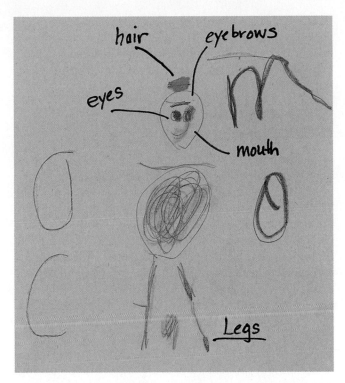

Figure 15-4 A teacher can label as a child dictates.

rough, smooth, nubby, or layered. Mass or volume in three-dimensional art is a useful term in describing a child's clay work, sculpture, construction, or assemblage.

A teacher may want to comment on other qualities that are not formally considered artistic elements. It is also important to comment on the handling of the materials and media. A child's unsuccessful attempts or disappointments with the media should be discussed. For example, a child tries to paint a rainbow with watercolors, but the colors run together. A teacher could say, "I know you worked hard at trying to keep your colors separate. Watercolors get very wet, and colors sometimes run. What could you do differently next time?" Or, "Try using less water next time."

A teacher may want to relate art to life. "You have drawn so many colorful flowers they remind me of my backyard flower garden." Or, "I see so many squares and rectangles in your picture. Remember when we went on our field trip downtown and saw all those tall buildings that looked like squares and rectangles." Or, "How is your robot like the ones you see on TV?"

At times it may be wise to wait and say nothing. This serves two purposes. First, it gives the teacher time to study the child's art and reflect on the artistic elements evidenced before speaking. This will eliminate an impulsive, curt response like, "That's nice." Second, it will give the child an opportunity to talk first if he or she so chooses. This provides a lead-in

and agenda for a teacher's comments. It may be difficult to break the habit of immediately responding with words like good, great, nice, wonderful, or beautiful when children share their art with you. Learn the 10 elements and practice using them as you would in learning a second language. Add them to your art vocabulary. Do not feel compelled to give an immediate response. Saying, "That's interesting," or "Let me look for a minute" allows you to buy time, think, and structure a meaningful comment.

It is also important to help parents respect and encourage their children's artistic processing and production. Perhaps a letter similar to the one below will help.

Dear Parents,

This is one of many pieces of artwork your child will be bringing home this year. Please consider it a personal gift from your child and thank him/her. Use magnets to proudly display it on the refrigerator door where all can see it.

Do not worry if you cannot figure it out. Its beauty may reside in your child's use of colors, lines, and shapes. Do not ask, "What is it?" Consider it a design. Encourage your child to discuss it if he or she chooses.

Your child would probably enjoy doing art at home. Art supplies make good gifts. Keep a small box filled with the following: scissors, glue, paste, tape, crayons, markers, ruler, stapler, watercolor set, clay or Play-Doh, and paper in a variety of sizes, shapes, colors, and textures.

Your child will also enjoy doing art with you. Enjoy art together!

Your Child's Teacher

TEACHER AS TROUBLESHOOTER

Not all young artists will trust their own creative urges and impulses. Some have learned to doubt their own ability or personal worth. Others are frustrated by their inability to meet a standard of realism held by others. From time to time, all children will need a teacher's subtle guidance and direction in making art. They may need verbal and nonverbal encouragement to accept, trust, and act on their creative impulses. Dodge and Colker (1996) offer advice for handling the following specific suggestions for when a child:

needs encouragement—

Try saying, "What do you think you could do with these brushes?"

is reluctant to join in—

Try saying, "You can put on a smock if you are worried about getting paint on your clothes."

ends an activity abruptly—

> Try saying, "Is there anything else you would like to add to your collage?"

is unsure about the next step—

> Try saying, "Here is some colored chalk. What do you think will happen if you dip it in water before drawing?"

wants you to make a drawing for her—

> Try saying, "Let's think about what you want to make. What's the biggest part of your animal? Try drawing that first."

A teacher can act as a **troubleshooter,** identifying children who are artistically or creatively *blocked* and use an appropriate intervention strategy. Below are some examples of how to recognize blocked children and intervention strategies.

Children Who Criticize Another's Art

One child at an easel tells another at the other side, "Your picture is dumb; it doesn't look like nothing!" The second child gets upset and begins to cry. Children need to know that they cannot criticize another's art idea or work. "Tyrone has worked very hard at painting his colorful picture. Remember, pictures can be made up of bright colors without looking like anything." Or, "It is Tyrone's picture, and he can paint anything he wants. If he doesn't want it to look like something, that's okay too."

Children Who Copy and Imitate

Although imitation and copying are forms of flattery, children do not see it that way. "Teddy has spent a lot of time making his picture. Let's all come up with our own ideas." "Remember, it's yours—your idea, your way, and your very own picture."

Children Who Are Not Progressing Artistically

Artists, whether young or old, sometimes get stuck in a rut. They continue to make the same things in the same way. A teacher can help by suggesting a new activity. "Les, try watercolor today. You have been painting at the easel for days, and it is time for a change." Or, "Les, I see how much you enjoy painting houses at the easel. What other kinds of buildings could you paint? Let's try to paint something different today."

Children Who Refuse to Try

Some children will totally avoid involvement in art. They will stand close by but refuse to try. They may need a teacher's subtle prompting, guidance, and guarantee of success. "Here, Susan, I'll stay with you and get you started. I'll dip the brush in the paint. Now you take over. I know you can finish on your own."

Children Who Do Not Like to Get Dirty or Messy

For some young children, staying neat, clean, poised, compliant, quiet, and obedient reflects cultural values. In turn, they will avoid messy art activities. There is a cultural difference because the school may operate valuing messy art activities. The issue is not who is right or wrong but how to resolve the issue diplomatically. Other children grow up in homes where they are discouraged from getting messy or dirty. They may have been punished for playing with their food, soiling their clothes, or walking in mud. Others will come to school inappropriately dressed in expensive outfits with a warning to "stay clean." Young children do get messy and dirty. This is a fact of childhood. Smocks, however, can protect clothing, and hands can be washed. Children need to be reassured that they will not get in trouble for getting dirty or messy. "Your parents know we paint at school and want you to enjoy it. You can wear a smock and clean up afterwards." It is also important to inform parents of the importance of art and that making a mess and getting dirty are part of the process. Encourage parents to send their children appropriately dressed for dirty, messy work.

A child may be repulsed by messy art activities. Allow time for the child to see that others enjoy the activity and the paint does wash off. Offer activities that use brushes rather than hand painting, or perhaps plastic gloves may be acceptable to the child. Go slowly. Putting only one finger in the paint may be the first step. Keep paper towels nearby for a quick cleanup if the child appears uncomfortable.

Children Who Avoid Art

Some children will completely avoid the art area. Given the choice, they will choose other areas. It is like the child who, if given a choice, eats only meat and refuses any vegetables. Occasionally, this may be acceptable. However, the author believes that over time all children need to participate at all centers. One solution is to rotate children through the centers. "Joey, I know you like to go to blocks every day, but there are many other things to do at school. Today, I want you to spend some time at the art area and try at least one activity. Let me know when you are finished so we can talk."

Art, Children, and Culture

Be aware that children's culture may influence their artistic production. Families that value art and child art will encourage it. Families that value academics to the exclusion of the arts will not. Children who grow up in families where independence is valued will feel free to trust their creative impulses. They will do art their way and may have difficulty making a teacher-directed project. They are pleased with what they make and are not troubled if others do not appreciate it. They may be very process-oriented and have no need to take their finished product home to share with their family. They do not do art to please others. They may prefer working individually as opposed to a group project.

By contrast, children who grow up in families that value interdependence may avoid art for various reasons. They may fear getting their clothes and hands dirty. This may displease their family. They may ask an adult to do art for them or say they do not know how to draw. Rather than trust their creative individualism, they may prefer making and repeating stereotypic symbols that are both recognizable and rewarded by significant adults. "Oh, yes, I see pretty flowers and a beautiful sun. Good girl." This is especially true if their culture values realistic art. They may be sensitive to criticism from others and need much verbal praise and encouragement from their teacher. They may prefer group activities such as working together on a mural that values the contributions of many and for which no one individual takes credit.

Children Who Do Not Know What to Make

"Teacher, what should I make?" "I don't know what to paint." Some children say this hoping that someone else will give them an idea. Usually this is the case for a child who has been pampered, spoiled, or catered to at home. Try diverting the question back to the child. "Fay, that's a good question. What should you make? Since you are the artist, you need to think and come up with an idea. Try to get a picture in your head. Look around the room, outside, or in our books. There are many, many things just waiting for you to make in art." A list of books on color, shape, senses, and art, which may also be a stimulus for making art, is found in Appendix E.

Children Who Dislike Their Own Art

Some children are overly critical of their own artwork. They may tear up picture after picture because it does not turn out just right. Sometimes they are frustrated with their childlike results. Others have poor self-concepts and doubt their own ability. These children will need heavy doses of praise, support, and encouragement. "Oh, Todd, please let me have that picture. Don't throw it away. I would like to add it to my collection of children's art." Or, "I don't think it looks like a dumb giraffe. I see a tall yellow animal. You did a very good job of painting and worked very hard."

Children Who Set Unreasonable Expectations

Some children may set themselves up for disappointment. They expect photographic realism that they are developmentally incapable of producing. They may want perfect pictures without smudges, smears, runs, or tears. Perhaps their parents hold unreasonably high expectations and expect and will accept only the best. These children become their own worst critics. They need to be accepted for what they are—young artists. "Cammy, I enjoy seeing all the bright colors in your picture. It doesn't matter that the colors have run together; it helped mix new ones." Or, "Remember you are making your idea of a rainbow, not taking a picture with a camera. I think your rainbow is just as colorful as the ones I see in the sky."

Children Who Want an Adult to Do Art for Them

"Teacher, make one for me. I can't do it." Or, "Teacher, I can't draw a pig. Please make one for me." Adults should not do art for children, regardless of how much they plead. It makes them dependent on others and teaches them to distrust their own ability. "Sean, I have difficulty drawing animals, too. Just try and do your best." Or, "Sean, everyone has to do his own work. I make my own pictures, and you need to make your own, too. I can help you in many other ways, but I cannot make art for you. I know you are an artist, and artists just have to keep trying and practicing."

 SEWING AND WEAVING

Sewing, stitchery, appliqué, and weaving are activities that allow both creative expression and practice in eye-hand coordination and fine motor control. They are recommended for both boys and girls. Unfortunately, they are often overlooked when developing an art program for young children. Some simplified ways of approaching these activities are provided in the following experiences.

Sewing

Sewing involves little more than painting with needle and thread or yarn. Young children can invent their own simple in-and-out or over-and-under way to sew and need not learn fancy stitches like the French knot. Here are some simple sewing activities.

Yarn Picture

This is a presewing activity that is recommended for young children who are not able to use a needle and yarn. You will need a piece of wood. Sand the edges to remove sharp edges or splinters. Hammer nails in randomly. One-inch round-head brass brads are recommended. Nail them halfway in. Encourage children to take a length of yarn and wrap it around the nails to make a picture or design. Rug yarn is recommended because it is heavy and sturdy and will not tear easily if pulled tightly. It is also possible to make an outline of a specific object, such as a house, with nails, but that would severely restrict the range of artistic possibilities.

Sandpaper Designs

Each child needs a sheet of fine sandpaper. Cut pieces of colored yarn, lace, or embroidery floss. Arrange in a basket or clear container. Encourage children to arrange their yarn pieces onto the sandpaper. The yarn will stick to the sandpaper much like Velcro. The design is nonpermanent and children can repeat the process.

Simple Sewing

We can reduce some of the steps and frustration involved in sewing by providing a sewing surface that is already perforated with holes. Such a surface is similar to the commercially available sewing cards, al-

though we need not provide a specific outline to complete. Carefully poke or punch out smooth holes. All the child needs to do is guide a needle and yarn in and out of the holes. Select a fairly sturdy surface. Some recommended sewing surfaces include the following:

- plastic foam tray
- cardboard shape with holes punched out around the edges
- berry basket
- poster board
- mesh hardware cloth (¼-inch), cut into squares with tin snips
- plastic screen
- paper plate

Flimsy sewing surfaces, such as burlap and other open-weave fabrics or the mesh bags that onions or grapefruit come in, should be secured in an embroidery hoop. Beginning sewers have a tendency to sew over the hoop. This poses no problem, because the stitches can later be cut to provide a fringed effect. Provide a large, blunt plastic needle and yarn. Or use a bobby pin as a needle. Enclose the yarn and wrap the open ends shut with tape. There is no need to even use a needle. Merely dip the sewing end of the yarn into white glue. Form the yarn into a point and let it dry. The end can also be wrapped with clear tape and shaped into a point. Tie a knot at the opposite end. The older child with experience in sewing can move on to using a smaller needle with embroidery or sewing thread.

Paper Stitchery

The older child with experience in sewing might enjoy making stitches in heavy paper. This will be good preparation for sewing on fabric. Paper has the advantages of being easier to get and providing a sturdy surface. A large plastic needle with yarn will tear the paper. Provide a large metal needle and embroidery or sewing thread. A picture can also be drawn in advance. This same activity could also be done on a plastic foam meat tray.

Mixed Media. Why not encourage children to creatively combine art media that usually do not go together? For example, they could stitch a frame around their drawing. Or they could use needle and thread to highlight lines in their painting. Or they might enjoy stitching fabric to a paper collage. What are some other creative ways to combine art media?

Fabric Stitchery

The older child with experience in sewing would enjoy using cloth as the background for his or her stitchery. Any loosely woven fabric will do. A piece of old sheet can be secured in an embroidery hoop as a preparation for fabric stitchery.

Metal Cloth Stitchery

Metal or hardware cloth is a screen with ¼-inch holes. It is often used for the tops of cages for small animals and is available at hardware stores. An alternative is soffet screen, a more pliable screen which comes in a roll. Cut into 6-inch squares and remember to tape the edges with masking tape. Children will need their own square as well as a blunt, plastic yarn needle. A needle is not necessary if the end of the yarn is taped with masking tape to resemble a needle. String with yarn, string, or embroidery floss. An arm's length of yarn is a good length to use. Encourage children to stitch or sew by pushing the threaded needle in and out of the holes. Items such as buttons or beads can also be stitched into the design. Pieces of ribbon or lace can also be added. Stay close by to help children tie or tape the yarn to the back of the hardware cloth when finished. You can also help children change colors of yarn and rethread their needle.

Appliqué

Appliqué involves sewing pieces of fabric onto one another. The result might be a stitched fabric collage. Burlap, with its open weave, makes an excellent background. Try to find material scraps with interesting colors, patterns, sizes, shapes, and textures. Some recommended ones include these:

- gold lamé
- felt
- silver brocade
- fur
- velvet

Items other than fabric scraps to appliqué include these:

- lace
- beads
- buttons
- shells
- ribbon
- small straw sections
- rickrack
- jingle bells

Encourage children to glue their fabric scraps in place first before sewing. This will help them sew without the scraps moving around.

Stuffed Pillow

Children will need to draw the outline of an object, such as an animal, on a piece of folded fabric, perhaps an old white sheet. Carefully cut through both pieces of material. Begin to sew the two together while stuffing with small pieces of crushed newspaper, cotton, or stuffing. Continue to sew and stuff. Decorate the pillow with fabric markers when it is completed. Chil-

dren enjoy making stuffed people pillows by adding yarn for hair and buttons for eyes after the sewing and stuffing is completed.

Weaving

Weaving is another art activity that is often overlooked in early childhood programs. This may be so because weaving is a detailed activity, involving much patience, eye-hand coordination, and fine motor control. The paper weaving activities discussed in Chapter 10 provide a good introduction. Once children have mastered the alternating over-under and under-over movement with paper, they may want to continue by weaving with yarn or other items. Weavers use their own terminology.

- The *loom* is the structure you weave on.
- The *warp* is the lengthwise yarn or string that is strung on your loom.
- The *weft* is the yarn that is woven over-under and under-over the warp.

Here are some simplified weaving activities recommended for use with young children.

Twig Weaving

Provide each child with a Y-shaped or forked twig for a loom. Try to find one that has fallen to the ground or has been carefully removed from a dead tree. Wrap the twig with parallel rows of yarn stretching between the two branches. This will form the warp. Do not pull too tightly or the branches will snap. Weave lengths of yarn (weft) with an alternating over-under, under-over movement, starting from the notch and moving to the top of the Y shape. Encourage children to push their rows fairly close together. Alternate colors. Since no two twigs will be exactly the same, the finished products will be unique. Older children who are experienced weavers may enjoy weaving on a larger twig with three or more forked branches.

God's Eye Weaving

Ojo de Dios means "eye of God" in Spanish. Mexican tribes made these for good luck. They are visually attractive and culturally meaningful. You will need two crossed sticks for the base. Some recommended sticks include a pair of the following:

- pencils
- sticks
- dowel rods
- plastic stirrers
- plastic straws
- chopsticks
- ice-cream sticks
- pickup sticks
- cotton swabs
- Tinker Toys®

Form a cross with the two sticks and tie yarn in a knot around the sticks where they cross. Add a dab of glue to secure. Encourage the children to use their over-under and under-over motions. With a length of yarn, weave over one stick and under the next, back over and under again to where you started. Continue this pattern without crossing over previous rows. Each successive layer will build the diamond-shaped pattern, or God's eye. Change colors of yarn often if you want a multicolored effect. Also, vary the thickness of the yarn. Lengths of yarn can also be twisted before wrapping to provide a different visual effect.

Burlap Weaving

Burlap, with its loose, open weave, is recommended for sewing and weaving projects. Cut small, individual, square or rectangular pieces. Pull out 10 to 20 threads every few inches to allow open space for objects to be woven into the burlap. Objects to weave in include these:

- feathers
- yarn
- lace
- ribbon
- old jewelry
- paper strips
- tinfoil
- leaves, stems, twigs, and other nature specimens
- fabric strips
- plastic straws
- rickrack
- sewing tape
- bias tape

Nature specimens are especially attractive when woven into a natural fabric like tan-colored burlap.

Bag Weaving

Look for mesh bags the next time you go grocery shopping. Check the produce aisles for mesh bags that hold potatoes, onions, and other vegetables. These bags provide a good flat surface for weaving and the webbing has spaces that are large enough for young weavers to use an in-and-out motion. Each side of the bag results in at least one section. Provide strips of ribbon, yarn, fabric, or cord to weave into their mesh section. One foot is a recommended length. Encourage children to weave both horizontally and vertically.

Mixed Media

Sewing and weaving go well together. Experienced weavers may enjoy sewing or stitching onto their weaving. Individual lengths or widths of burlap can be gathered and tied with thread, ribbons, or lace to break the monotonous solid appearance.

Loom Weaving

Professionals use a large commercial loom to do their weaving. Child-sized looms are commercially available but costly. It is very easy to provide a child-sized substitute. Objects that make good improvised looms include the following:

- wooden picture frame
  Place the picture frame flat and hammer a row of evenly spaced nails across the top and bottom. Wrap string or yarn from the top nail to the matching bottom nail. Continue until the warp is completed. Children can weave from right to left and left to right using their alternating over-under, under-over motion. Weave with yarn, but feel free to add lace, ribbon, nature specimens, fabric, paper, and other recycled junk.

- berry basket
  Small plastic berry baskets come with the warp completed. Children will enjoy weaving yarn, fabric, or paper strips in and out of the openings. This is a good starting point for the young, inexperienced weaver.

- plastic foam tray, flat cardboard, or cardboard box
  Carefully cut ¼-inch slits into the top and bottom edges. Wind string or yarn from top to bottom. Your warp will cover the front and back. Children can weave with yarn with an over-and-under alternating motion. The raised edges of the tray and cardboard box will allow room for the child's hand when weaving under.

- wire coat hanger
  Carefully spread the hanger into a round, square, or diamond-shaped loom. Wrap string around one end and pull it to the other side. Continue until the open section is filled with parallel lines. The warp is then completed. Encourage children to use lengths of yarn to weave in and out of their loom.

- two hanging sticks
  You will need two sticks for this loom. Lay them out on a table, about 1 foot apart; one will be the top, and the second will be the bottom. Begin to fashion a warp by wrapping yarn around the top stick, down to the bottom, around the bottom, and then back up to the top. Continue this process until the warp is completed. Tie the yarn to the top stick and hang it on the wall where children can weave with yarn and other nature specimens. This loom is flimsy and is recommended for the more experienced weaver.

- big looms strung from tree branches
  These work well outdoors where children can weave in vines, sticks, long grasses, branches,

ferns, husks, stems, twine, and natural fabrics like lengths of burlap.

- paper plate or round cardboard or poster board
Cut an uneven number of slits, such as seven, on the outer edge. Make each slit ¼-inch deep. Cut a 1-inch circle out of the center. Your loom is ready. To prepare the warp, wrap yarn or string from the center hole over the notch, around the back, through the center hole, and up to the next notch. Continue until all spokes and notches are filled. Start at the center and weave in and out or over and under the spokes with a length of yarn. Tie a different color to the end and continue weaving. The back side can also be woven. When finished, cut through the yarn covering the notches. The result will be a colorful, round, woven, fringed plate or decorative piece.

 Or cut an uneven number of slits from the outer edge in. Stop about 1 inch from the center. Weave lengths of yarn over and under the wedges, starting from the center and working out. Change colors of yarn often.

- soda straws
You will need four or five plastic straws to make this loom. The straws become the warp and are held in place with the hand. Tape the ends together. You may want to start this weaving for the child. Hold the straws in a spread fan position. Begin with the ends that are held close together in your hand and slowly wrap them with yarn in an over-under motion. When they are fairly secure, let the child take over. Continue weaving to the top of the straws.

Fence Weaving

Think of your outdoor chain-link fence as a loom just waiting for children to weave. This is a good activity for working together and practicing social as well as creative skills. Provide strips of fabric, old scarves, crepe paper, as well as lengths of string, rope, ribbon, lace, or yarn. Children can best handle strips which are no longer than 2 to 3 feet in length. Encourage children to begin weaving materials in and out of the openings in the fence. They will find creative ways to wrap and intertwine the materials they weave.

Weaving a Six-Pack Ring

Children will need their own plastic six-pack ring which serves as a loom. Provide short strips of paper as well as short lengths of yarn, ribbon, and lace. Strips should be at least 12 inches long so they do not fall out of the holes when woven. Also provide pipe

cleaners, straws, and feathers. Expect creative weaving. Younger children will most likely weave a random design. Older children may be interested in learning the over-and-under then under-and-over pattern. Weavings can be hung from the ceiling. Use string or small twist ties to join individual six-pack weavings to form a larger group weaving.

Sewing and Weaving Accessories

Some common sewing and weaving accessories include the following:

Easy Weaver® loom—commercially available and suited for young weavers

plastic screen—for sewing, weaving

standard-weight yarn—double-weight rug yarn is too thick

string—for a variety of art activities

thin crochet yarn—for sewing, stitchery, weaving, and appliqué

thread—colored, for sewing, stitchery, weaving, and appliqué

yarn needles—large, plastic, blunt, with big eye for threading

Hint: Yarn cones can be purchased in special containers that keep the yarns from tangling or getting unwound. You could stand each yarn cone in a box slightly larger than the cone itself, for example, an oatmeal box. Cut a small hole in the lid, pull the yarn through, and use the box as a yarn dispenser.

SUMMARY

This chapter focused on the teacher's multifaceted role with respect to children's art. A teacher can model and participate in art activities. Knowing about art will help the teacher to become an art specialist and to provide creative experiences for children. The teacher's responses to children's art were discussed as a powerful influence on the creative process. Complimentary, judgmental, valuing, questioning, probing, and correcting response approaches were critiqued. Art dialogue, a strategy incorporating the artistic elements as provided as an alternative to saying "pretty," "nice," "good," or "What is it?" Art dictation was proposed for children who may want their art talk put into written form. The chapter recommended that teachers become troubleshooters when individual children have difficulty or appear to be artistically stuck.

Key Terms

art dialogue
art dictation
art group time
Art Idea Book
art kiosk
art specialists
complimentary approach
correcting approach

framing
independence
interdependence
judgmental approach
matting
mobile
model
participator

probing approach
questioning approach
sewing
stabile
troubleshooter
valuing approach
weaving

Suggested Activities

1. Practice being a model and participator as you interact with children making art. Record what transpired as well as your reactions.
2. Listen to a teacher talking with a child about his or her art. Which approach was used? If necessary, think of some alternatives that would be more effective.
3. Encourage one child to show you his or her artwork. Use the artistic elements as a framework for your Art dialogue. If possible, tape record your session. Did you use any of the traditional approaches or remarks? If so, suggest alternative responses.
4. Encourage, but do not demand, that a child talk about his or her art. Conduct art dictation.

5. Identify a child who is having difficulty or who is artistically stuck. Act as a troubleshooter.
6. Make an Art Idea Book for use with young children.
7. Ask a teacher's permission to conduct art group time at the end of an art session. Encourage children to talk about their art using the artistic elements. Model the process for them.
8. Ask children's permission to attractively mat, frame, and display their art. Help set up a classroom/center/school display of children's art. Ask permission to use wall space in the cafeteria or library for the display.

1. List five different strategies that foster a child's artistic expression.

2. For each comment choose the approach to talking with children about their art.

   _____ "I love it!"
   _____ "I think you left something out."
   _____ "That's just wonderful."
   _____ "What is it supposed to be?"
   _____ "Explain it to me, please."
   _____ "Yes, very, very good."

   a. Correcting
   b. Probing
   c. Questioning
   d. Valuing
   e. Judging
   f. Complimenting

3. What artistic element matches each comment?

   _____ "I see red, blue, yellow, and green all over your paper."
   _____ "Here your dry paint feels so smooth, but over here where they mixed, it feels rough."
   _____ "So many lines —straight, crossing and swirly."
   _____ "Your picture fills the entire sheet of paper."
   _____ "Your clay elephant is thick and solid and can stand on its own."
   _____ "I see rows of circles, squares, and triangles."
   _____ "You repeated these trees across the bottom of your paper. What an interesting effect."
   _____ "Just look at how all the animals fit into your big circle. Yes, I can see how they are all performing in the circus ring."
   _____ "You have spent most of the morning painting at the easel. I can see how hard you have worked to get your painting just the way you want it."
   _____ "You have drawn a house in the middle of your paper with two tall trees, one on each side."

4. Discuss the importance of art dictation as it relates to a young child's self-esteem and language/literacy development.

5. How could a child's culture influence his or her art production?

6. List guidelines for art group time.

7. Identify and give an example of four roles teacher can play in early childhood art.

For additional art and creative development resources, visit our Web site at www.EarlyChildEd.delmar.com

Chapter 16

Art Assessment

What are the two children in this picture doing? One appears actively engaged in painting while the other is preparing to paint, checking to make sure the paint is just the right color or consistency. How does the painter hold the brush? Can you see any signs of the two artists working together or speaking with each other?

Observing children as they engage in art activities provides opportunities to gather and record valuable information about them and their artistic development. Which of your children enjoys art? Who is reluctant to get dirty? Who is willing to take creative risks? Who is more comfortable watching and copying others? Over time, these recorded observations, supplemented with actual samples of children's work, provide a developmental record.

Objectives

After reading this chapter, you should be able to:

- Discuss the teacher's role as observer, recorder, and assessor and discuss how observational data assist in artistic assessment.
- Discuss the role of assessment in art.
- Identify strategies for collecting and storing children's art.
- Distinguish standardized testing from authentic assessment.
- Discuss portfolio assessment, including guidelines for assembling, maintaining, and reviewing portfolios.

INTRODUCTION

Terms like testing, evaluation, and assessment may elicit a negative reaction. Some parents, teachers, and administrators may be suspicious of attempts at evaluating young children at all, let alone in the areas of creativity and art. This chapter adds observer, recorder, and assessor to our list of teacher roles. Being a keen observer of children and an objective recorder of their behavior will help in assembling individual portfolios. Observational data is essential in assessing children's artistic development in authentic ways. Actual samples of children's work and performance can also be included in a portfolio to provide a comprehensive developmental portrayal. In turn, the portfolio serves as a basis for noting strengths and documenting progress, matching weaknesses with recommendations, individualizing curriculum and communicating with parents. The chapter outlines procedures for collecting and storing artwork so it can then be used as an instrument for assessing children's artistic progress.

TEACHER AS OBSERVER, RECORDER, AND ASSESSOR

N
A
E
Y
C

This chapter adds three new roles to our list of roles that teachers play. These include **observer, recorder,** and **assessor.** Observation allows us to witness development and learning in progress. Recording helps capture the moments by putting our observations down in writing. Recorded observations can be later analyzed and used to informally assess children. Assessment tells us how children are progressing and is useful in our work with parents and in curriculum development.

The Importance of Systematically Observing and Recording Children's Behavior

Why study children? Studying children and their development provides a working knowledge of children at different ages and stages. Studying individual children helps you apply what you have learned about how they grow, learn, and develop. Reasons for studying individual children include the following:

1. to understand children
2. to document a problem or concern
3. to develop a comprehensive assessment including strengths, weaknesses, and recommendations
4. to plan a program that is developmentally appropriate and individualized
5. to communicate with families

1. To Understand Children

It is enjoyable and often amusing to watch children at play. One cannot help but notice their zest for life and energy. Random watching, viewing, and looking, however, may provide enjoyment but do not enhance our understanding of children. A careful study of children does (see Figure 16–1). Observing a child provides

Consider This...

Mrs. Pati has returned to teaching after raising her own children. She has been assigned to a K-1 combination classroom in a progressive school district. She is eager yet anxious. She has spent the last few weeks of summer arranging her room and planning curriculum with her colleagues. As she prepares for a full-day workshop on authentic assessment, she begins to feel inadequate. She asks herself many questions. What is the role of testing and evaluation in a K-1 classroom? Are they developmentally appropriate? How are they conducted? How does one manage to do them given a full schedule? Her list of questions seems endless. By lunch, most of her questions were addressed, but she still felt overwhelmed. The afternoon session stressed how authentic assessment is an ongoing process that can be integrated into the curriculum. It is not an additional requirement requiring an extra period. It is also a process that empowers children, in that they are actively involved. She was also given helpful strategies for building, maintaining, and using children's individual portfolios. Upon returning home, Mrs. Pati began making individual file folders and storage boxes for her group. She was convinced that what she had learned would help her know her group better and enhance her ability to work with families.

Figure 16-1 Observing children.

valuable baseline data about what the child knows and can do. Ongoing observation can be documented and included in a child's file or portfolio. Strengths, weaknesses, and recommendations across developmental areas should be included.

Just as photographs of children tell us much about what children look like on the outside, their artwork reveals what they look like on the inside. Children use art to tell us many things about themselves. Learn to

read their pictures. Observing children engaged in art and collecting samples of their artwork over time provide a wealth of information. Collecting and analyzing children's art will help us understand:

Who They Are. Children include themselves, the most important person in the world, in their artwork. They begin drawing themselves resembling large Os or potatolike shapes, balanced on stick legs with arms protruding where ears are usually found. This is a normal stage in artistic development. Children are learning about themselves and their bodies. Although they can look in a mirror and know what body part goes where, they are physically and mentally unable to represent it in realistic fashion. It serves no purpose to correct children's artwork. It will only erode their self-confidence and destroy their creative spirit.

Who and What is Important to Them. Children live in a family context and they will introduce you to their family through art. Grandpa may automatically appear in a child's art, announcing that he has come to stay with the family. Dad may suddenly disappear after a separation or divorce. Pets will be included as valued family members. Children choose as subject matter those things that make them happy. If they have just learned to use in-line skates there is a good chance that they will depict themselves skating in their artwork.

What is Going on in Their Lives and What They Know about Their World.

Children will use art to communicate how they feel about themselves, others, and their world. If happy with themselves and their lives, they may paint themselves large and grinning from ear to ear. If feeling unimportant, they might make themselves small or even missing from a family portrait. The way children use color, shape, size, and placement to portray themselves and significant others are valuable cues to how that child feels about self and others. Look for patterns but do not jump to conclusions. Children may draw themselves without facial features for reasons other than low self-esteem. It's when children repeat an upsetting image that one becomes concerned and looks beyond the canvas for other cues. Children will share both pleasant and unpleasant experiences. Art helps them celebrate the pleasant and deal with the painful and unpleasant. The content of children's art reflects things they have strong feelings about. For example, if they love their pets then these animals will be depicted. If they are afraid of monsters they may use art as a way to express, work through, and eventually master that fear. Their art may also reflect feelings of anger, hate, rage, rejection, and despair. An intense scribbling of color may be all that the child artist can express. The result may be unrecognizable but the content and underlying emotion are very real. The content of children's art reflects what they know. If they watch TV, there is a good chance that they will include what they view in their art. A child who has not been to a circus will not draw or paint it. Children's art reflects what is important to them—what matters. Some children draw horses, princesses, castles, and butterflies; others draw superheroes, vehicles, and villains.

2. To Document a Problem or Concern

When a problem is suspected or a concern arises, it is wise to collect observational data to substantiate your educated guess. For example, when reporting suspected child abuse or neglect, you are required to back up your suspicions with written proof or evidence based on what you have seen and heard. This forms the basis for making a referral or requesting special services. Likewise, you may be concerned about a child who does art to the exclusion of all other activities or one who never approaches the art center. Your observational data helps you decide on a plan for helping the child in question.

3. To Develop a Comprehensive Assessment, Including Strengths, Weaknesses, and Recommendations

Since children grow, learn, and develop at a rapid rate, it is important to celebrate their achievements. The Instrument for Artistic Assessment at the end of this chapter serves as one framework for informally assessing artistic development. Children who can only scribble in September may be able to make recognizable shapes by summer. Collecting samples of children's art documents this developmental progression. Art samples can be dated and placed in the child's portfolio. When laid out chronologically and carefully examined, the child's progress becomes apparent. Artistic and creative achievement is not only documented but also shared with parents. A child's concept of the body is reflected in the inclusion and spatial arrangement of body parts. Weaknesses can also be noted through observation or collection of performance samples. For example, children's involvement at the play dough table can be photographed at regular intervals. The photos can be dated and arranged in chronological sequence. Over time, the child may move from random processing to making flat pancake shapes. Moving on to making detailed three-dimensional human figures signifies a developmental advancement in the child's perceptual and spatial awareness. The child has moved beyond working in a flat, two-dimensional plane.

⏩ NAEYC 4. To Plan a Program That Is Developmentally Appropriate and Individualized

Observing what interests children and what activities attract their sustained involvement should provide a basis for curriculum development. For example, observing that a theme of dinosaurs permeates the block area could lead you to provide small plastic dinosaurs for making feet prints, or to offer children an opportunity to make dinosaur masks. If children are frustrated using scissors, you can plan art activities that involve tearing paper. You may also want to plan activities involving fine motor and eye-hand control to help prepare children for using scissors. Or, it may simply be that children need your individualized instruction and guidance in how to hold and use scissors.

5. To Communicate with Families

The observational data you collect from studying individual children will help parents better understand their child. Information collected from various child study techniques will form the basis for your ongoing communication and conferencing with parents. It is widely accepted that children may act one way at home but act very differently in a school setting. Although parents need to see the bigger picture, do not be surprised if they deny information that runs counter to what they have experienced or choose to believe. They may say, "I just can't believe what you are saying" or "That doesn't sound like my child." You will need to provide evidence and documentation. This is meant to support your views and assessment rather than proving the parents wrong. For example, observational notes based on a child's frequent aggressive use of art tools might help parents see the need for family counseling or a parenting course. Remember that communication is an ongoing two-way process. Parents may be wary of your attempts to communicate if you only seek them out to report problems. Daily, ongoing communication builds a relationship in which parents feel comfortable talking about their child and receiving feedback which not only celebrates their child's strengths but addresses problem areas. Families can provide a wealth of information, including a child's play interests and creative pursuits. A child who has no exposure to art materials at home and has been advised to stay clean at school may not approach the art center. Ask parents open-ended questions or prompts like, "Tell me about your child at home." Listen actively, attentively, and without judgment. Reassure parents that some behaviors are typical of children at certain ages. For example, many children prefer painting their hands rather than applying paint to paper. Others enjoy mixing several colors together until a dark, unrecognizable, thick mass results. First-time parents in particular may not know what to expect of their child at a given age. Empower parents by helping them become part of the solution. Brainstorm how you could work together to help their child trust and act on his or her creative impulses, instead of always asking others to make him or her a picture. Solicit their input and offer specific suggestions. Verbalize and restate a mutually agreed-upon plan. Record what transpired after the conference and plan a follow-up meeting to review progress, or rework a plan, if warranted.

▸▸ Observing and Recording

N
A
E
Y
C

Knowing and understanding children involves two major strategies: observing and recording. Although you may have excellent vision, you may lack the ability to observe. Observation is a learned skill that improves with practice. Observation requires time, a focus, an objective attitude, and patience. One must commit time to carefully study one or more children. Observation must also have a focus, such as children's art. An adult observer is unlike a mechanical video camera and cannot objectively observe and write for endless periods of time. Observation alone will not suffice. Observation and recording are complementary processes. Recording guarantees that what you have observed will not be forgotten. Observations must be objectively recorded, with subjective impressions or an analysis kept separate. Be factual, using words that are specific and descriptive. Imitate a video camera and tape recorder, documenting what you observe and hear. Later, become a commentator, adding your analysis, interpretation, or inferences.

Guidelines for Observing and Recording

There are five guidelines for effective observing and recording.

1. Be Prepared to Observe and Record

Develop a system that works for you. Some teachers wear a pen or pencil around their necks and carry clipboards with blank, lined paper. Other observers prefer to use index cards. Punch a hole through a small stack of index cards and attach them to a large key ring or shower curtain ring. This can be carried around your thumb. File individual index cards into a file box with dividers for each child. Still other observers wear an apron with small note pads in the pockets. You may want to use the larger sticky notes or peel-off adhesive labels that can be posted on the child's folder and later transferred into a permanent record. A tape recorder is useful when recording children's conversation, especially if you write slowly or your children talk fast. It also helps capture rich descriptive language that is sometimes lost. A video camera can capture the words and actions of one child or of children in small groups. This provides the advantage of repeated playbacks at a later time. Set a realistic schedule for observing. It is humanly impossible to observe and record the behaviors of all the children in your care in one sitting. Supervision is always your first priority. One suggestion is to plan on observing four children per day, so that the entire group is observed on a weekly basis. The main point is to be ready to observe and record at all times.

2. Be Unobtrusive

Maintain a distance and do not become involved with the child or children you are trying to observe. Avoid talking or interacting with the child or children observed. If they approach you, redirect them back to what they are doing. Tell them you are just writing notes about what different children say and do at school. You want children to act natural, talking and behaving as they would without noticing your presence. When children know they are being observed and that someone is writing down what they say and do, their behavior changes and your data are contaminated. Children may end up performing. What you observe and record may not be indicative of what they normally say and do.

3. Get a Focus and Be Selective about What You Observe

Know what you are looking for and observe and record when it happens. If you are interested in a child's artistic development, then observe during art time and at the art center. If you are interested in creative expression, it makes good sense to select art time. Be flexible and spontaneous enough to capture through observation those unplanned moments that may hold a wealth of developmental data.

4. Be Objective, Impartial, and Nonbiased in Recording

Record what the child says and does. Include nonverbal cues such as facial expression, body posture, and gestures. Add child's name, date, time, and overall setting, such as at the art center, as well as who else is involved. Develop a shorthand system using abbreviations that work for you. For example *J*=Julia or *rgu*=argue. Observe frequently. Observe the same child in different settings and at different times. Avoid comments like good, bad, nice, or naughty, for two reasons. First, they cannot be directly observed. Second, they are evaluative rather than descriptive. What is labeled bad behavior by one observer may not be considered bad by another. Be sensitive about using words that stereotype children on the basis of gender, race, culture, ethnicity, social class, or special needs.

5. Separate Your Observation from Your Analysis and Interpretation

Observation is descriptive and based on fact; analysis and interpretation are based on inference. For example, hitting and kicking behaviors can be directly observed, whereas *being aggressive* is a global interpretation, not directly observable. What does it mean to be aggressive? Does it mean swearing, talking back, punching, or shouting? The term is unclear. Some observers choose to add their interpretations at the end of their observations or at a later point in time. This allows time for reflection through a careful rereading and insightful analysis, rather than jumping to a quick conclusion. Others record observations down the left half of the paper, leaving the

right column blank, where an analysis is later added. A one-time observation will provide little if any significant data from which to draw conclusions. Patterns will emerge over time with ongoing observation. Patterns provide support for your analysis and interpretations.

Fact or Inference? Good observation is based on what is heard and seen rather than what is inferred. Decide which of the following statements are based on descriptive observation and which rely on inference.

1. Child is out of sorts and in a bad mood today.
2. Child used her fists to flatten the play dough.
3. Obviously, this child woke up on the wrong side of the bed and is having a bad day.
4. Child quickly ate two halves of toast and asked for seconds.
5. This child finally got a taste of his own medicine.
6. Child carefully turned the pages of the book while retelling the story in her own words.
7. Child appears distracted or detached today.
8. Child successfully reached the pedals of the tricycle and rode for three minutes without asking for help.
9. Once again, child is fussing to get his own way.
10. Child asks friend to paint with her at the easel. Her friend says, "No," and child frowns while painting alone.

Which are fact and which are inference? The odd-numbered items are based on inference, while the even-numbered items are based on fact.

6. Match a Strategy to Your Purpose in Observing

There is an array of child study techniques from which to choose. Some are quick to administer; others take much time and writing. Some must be constructed; others require only paper and pencil. Individual techniques provide different pieces of information necessary to understand the whole child. The more time invested in child study and the more strategies employed, the more complete and thorough your understanding of the child. Strategies include narratives, time and event sampling, and checklists and rating scales.

Narratives. **Narratives** are records of what the observer sees children do and hears them say. Narratives are conducted in natural settings in which the observer tries to remain unobtrusive. Diaries and anecdotes are forms of narratives.

A **diary,** as its name implies, is a journal or ongoing account. One observes and records what a child says and does in wide blocks of time. The diary is made up of a series of entries over a period of time. Compare it to writing your diary on a daily basis. At the end of the week, you can reflect on the preceding events, analyze and evaluate your week, and make plans for next week. Diary accounts provide a wealth of valuable data but require an investment of time in observation. Over time, the diary shows patterns or trends which help the observer make interpretations. Students of child development often do a child study which reflects heavily on a diary.

An **anecdote** is a shortened and more focused version of the diary. Although the diary attempts to capture anything and everything happening, the anecdote attempts to capture a specific event or behavior, including how it begins, evolves, and concludes. An anecdote may be the child's use of language or how frustration is handled and expressed. Given its broader scope, a diary may house or frame several anecdotes and therefore provides a bigger picture. The observer begins recording an anecdote when the specified behavior begins and stops recording when the child stops engaging in the behavior under study. For example, Martika's teacher has decided to use an anecdote to better understand the child's attitude toward art. She plans to observe Martika's involvement at the art center carefully. On Tuesday afternoon, Martika, age four, enters the art area and the teacher records the following:

It's 2:15 and Martika is standing in the art area. She twists her hair with her fingers while silently watching one girl paint at the easel and one boy play with play dough at the table. The girl asks Martika if she would like to paint with her. Martika does not answer. The girl hands Martika a paint smock but Martika does not put it on. She sits next to the boy at the play dough table. There are several large pieces of play dough available but Martika sits with her hands in her pockets. She says something that resembles, "It's yucky," and leaves the art area. Ending time is 2:22.

What, if anything, does this descriptive anecdote tell you about Martika and her behavior in the art area? It is too soon to draw any conclusions based on this limited data, and further observation is clearly warranted.

Time and Event Sampling.
Sampling observations use time intervals or categories of behavior as their focus. **Time sampling** provides a way of measuring the frequency of a behavior within a given period of time. With time sampling, the observer specifies the behavior under study and then counts how often it occurs

within a stated block of time. For example, Martika's mother complains that Martika never brings any artwork home and questions her level of involvement throughout the day. She claims Martika has always been a watcher rather than a doer. Ultimately, she fears Martika will not be ready for kindergarten. At school, Martika does spend a lot of time by herself merely watching others. The teacher chooses to do a time sampling to study the extent of Martika's lack of engagement at school. The teacher will count the number of times Martika is engaged at a learning center for five consecutive days. She is sampling time by selecting the first 10 minutes on each hour to observe. An assumption is made that what Martika does within this 10 minute block of time is representative of her behavior throughout the hour. A tally indicates the number of minutes that Martika was engaged in play. The teacher's findings for one week are depicted in Table 16–1.

What does the data tell you? Are there days of the week or times of the day when Martika is more engaged and involved than others? Do you see a pattern emerging? What could account for this? It is difficult and dangerous to generalize from this limited data. Based on the limited information provided, however, one can see how Martika's involvement increases and decreases, although the pattern is fairly consistent across the days, except Monday. What could explain the low level of involvement on Monday? Her teacher notices how Martika needs much time to wake up and face the day. Do the data in Table 16–1 support this hypothesis? Why does her participation drop off before lunch and before going home? Are there any questions you could formulate to ask Martika's mother to help you better understand the pattern observed in this time sampling?

The next step is to act on the information in the anecdote and time sampling. The teacher plans to question the mother regarding Martika's sleeping and eating habits. Perhaps she is coming to school tired and without eating breakfast. She will also discuss how Martika spends her weekends to better understand her lower level of involvement on Mondays.

With **event sampling,** the observer specifies the behaviors under study and then notes when it happens. Its occurrence is indicated with a tally. Martika's teacher has been observing the activity choices of her four-year-olds. She is concerned that Martika spends much of her day being idle, rather than engaged, although she spends more time at the art area than elsewhere. By using event sampling, she hopes to learn which art activities engage Martika. The child's initial, M, appears under the art activity at a specified time. Times with no initial indicate lack of engagement (see Table 16–2).

Table 16-1 Time Sampling: Martika's Engagement in Play

	MONDAY	TUESDAY	WEDNESDAY	THURSDAY	FRIDAY
8:00–8:10					
9:00–9:10	/	//	//	//	//
10:00–10:10		//	//	///	
11:00–11:10					
12:00–12:10					
1:00–1:10					
2:00–2:10		///	///	////	//
3:00–3:10		/	/	/	
4:00–4:10		/	//	/	
5:00–5:10					

What does the event sampling indicate? It appears that Martika's engagement in art is limited to drawing and coloring. Could it be that drawing and coloring are less risky and less messy than the other art options? Do the three observational tools work together to advance our understanding of Martika? Her teacher wonders whether Martika is bringing her artwork home to share with her mother. Her teacher is also planning to slowly encourage Martika's participation in other art activities.

Checklists and Rating Scales. Although commercially available, many **checklists** or **rating scales** are created by teachers. They take some time to develop but less time to complete than a narrative. In a checklist, the items are identified, and the observer merely indicates which items are present or absent. For example, a checklist for art could include the following developmental indicators.

_____ scribbles and makes unrecognizable marks
_____ makes geometric shapes
_____ draws mandalas
_____ draws self as face
_____ draws human figure
_____ enjoys using finger paint
_____ creates two- and three-dimensional forms with play dough
_____ art is rich with details
_____ child relies on own creativity rather than copying

The observer could place a check mark or write *yes/no* in front of those items that apply. Checklists may

be administered more than once and some forms provide for multiple observations, documenting progress or change over time.

A rating scale is a second time-saving observational tool. In a rating scale, items are identified and the observer makes a judgment regarding the degree to which the item is observed in the child. For example, the items in the art checklist on the previous page could be rated along a continuum of high-medium-low, usually-sometimes-rarely or always-sometimes-never. The rating scale provides for more accurate judgment than a checklist. What the checklist and rating scale share in simplicity, however, they lose in terms of judgment. How would you rate the following observed anecdote using a checklist or rating scale?

> Kea (who is three) shares toys but not art supplies or food at the snack table. She easily shares with adults and younger children but not with those her age or older.

A judgment must be made. Do you indicate yes or no for sharing? Actually, it may be easier to use a rating scale and rate Kea as *sometimes* or a mid-mark indicating a moderate or some degree of sharing. While being observed, Kea did not ask to be included in the play of others. What does this mean? Does she lack social skills? Does she not know how to ask to be included? Or, did it simply not happen this month? To avoid this problem, many rating scales include a *not observed* column.

Table 16-2 Event Sampling: Martika's Art Choices

		EASEL PAINTING	COLLAGE	PLAY DOUGH	DRAWING & COLORING
8:30–8:40	art center closed				
9:30–9:40					M
10:30–10:40	outdoors				
11:30–11:40	lunch				
12:30–12:40	rest				
1:30–1:40	rest				
2:30–2:40					M
3:30–3:40	outdoors				
4:30–4:40					M
5:30–5:40					

CHILDREN'S ART FILES AND FOLDERS

Keeping samples of children's artwork is a good way to collect evaluative data. Ask the child's permission to enter his or her name and the date on the back of the piece. Try to collect a sample at least once a week. Tell children you are saving pieces for their **art files** or **art folders.** Encourage their participation in making artwork they want included. Honor their requests for pieces they prefer to take home. Encourage them to make both "take home" and "folder" pieces. Use a large colored file folder or folded piece of poster board to hold the artwork. Periodically lay the pieces out in chronological order. Look for development, progression, and mastery in the use of media and materials and in the expression of ideas, concepts, objects, and feelings. Match what is artistically rendered with a particular child's artistic and overall level of development. Use these data in reporting to parents and planning future art experiences (see Figure 16–2).

Formal Standardized Testing

Would it not be easier to simply test children? Find a test that is quick to administer and easy to score? Would it not provide the same information? According to Lessen-Firestone (1995) **standardized achievement testing** of young children is often inappropriate and may actually be detrimental to school success. Test re-sults are often unreliable and invalid, influenced more by children's test-taking skills, cultural backgrounds, and stress levels than by what they know. Also, as teachers tend to teach with the test in mind, curriculum narrows and isolated, low-level, testable concepts and skills are stressed. Further, testing situations can be artificial, contrived, stressful, and intrusive, because they do not take place during children's regular activities. Standardized tests provide a formal, less authentic way to assess what young children know and can do. Young children are not good test takers, but they are good at revealing what they know and can do through their play and daily activities. Children can and should be assessed in less formal and more authentic ways.

Informally Assess Young Children in Authentic Ways

NAEYC

Assessment for young children should not and need not take the form of testing. View assessment as an ongoing process of documenting and recording a child's development. According to the National Association for the Education of Young Children (NAEYC) (1991) guidelines for appropriate assessment, assessment serves the following purposes: to plan instruction and communicate with parents; to identify children with special needs; and to evaluate programs. Assessment should be informal and authentic. It should not disrupt the daily program, but should happen naturally as children are engaged in playful

Figure 16-2 A girl's concept and drawing of herself develops over time.

pursuits. Observing and recording children's behavior are key components of authentic assessment. Any assessment that is authentic involves the person being assessed in the process. The professional artist's mentor does not assemble the portfolio; nor does the professional model's agent. Involvement fosters responsibility and ownership. Children can analyze and assess their developmental progress and learning over time. Authentic assessment offers a much more natural, sensitive, and realistic look at development than any set of standardized tests. Authentic assessment of children relies on observation and recording, along with samples of a child's performance and work assembled in a portfolio.

Portfolio Approach to Authentic Assessment

NAEYC

You may associate the portfolio concept with professional artists and models. Artists assemble a collection of their artwork in a large folder or **portfolio.** It represents what they can do with different art media. Artists may supplement actual art samples with photos, slides, or videotape of their larger pieces. They may include pieces done at different times to demonstrate their versatility, style, or professional development. Models do the same. They pour through an array of photos and select those that best capture their look. These are assembled in a binder and shown to potential agents. The same process holds for young children. They are building a portfolio based on what they have learned at school. A portfolio is comprehensive and contains multiple sources of information, including:

- samples of children's work, such as art, stories, writing samples.
- writing drafts and revisions.
- observational data of physical, social, emotional, cognitive, and creative anecdotes.
- photographs of blocks or three-dimensional construction.
- audio recordings of language, storytelling, reading, dramatic play episodes.
- video recordings of child doing art, moving to music, social interactions, dramatic play themes.
- systematic records of children's activities.
- health records.
- parent input, such as completed questionnaires, conference notes.
- notes forwarded from former teachers.
- special items selected by the child.

A portfolio, however, is more than a mere collection of information. According to Martin (1994), it is an attitude and a process. As an attitude, it reflects an ongoing openness and commitment to learning more about each child. As a process, it involves using multiple sources, including teacher, child, and family to provide valuable developmental data.

Guidelines for Assembling, Maintaining, and Reviewing a Portfolio

There are five basic guidelines for portfolio assessment.

1. Devise a System

Use large colored folders or boxes. Locate a spot where the portfolios will be kept. Decide on how the content will be organized. Provide one container for each child that he or she can decorate. This begins the process of ownership. Portfolio contents must be respected and confidentiality is important.

2. Add Entries Regularly

Date each sample you include. Provide background information. Arrange the items chronologically. Earliest work samples will appear in the front followed by more recent entries. Adding to portfolios should be an ongoing process. You may be overwhelmed if you add only a few times a year. Develop a schedule so that samples are added on a daily or weekly basis.

3. Focus on the Whole Child

Portfolios should be comprehensive. Remember to address all developmental areas, including entries and observations that reflect a child's physical, social, emotional, cognitive, and creative accomplishments.

4. View the Portfolio as a Collaborative Effort

No one person is responsible for the portfolio. All adults who know and either presently work or have worked with the child can have their entries included. Resource people and specialists can also have their notes included. The same holds for the child. Empower the child to be an active participant in the portfolio process. Let them decide which samples to include and which to display or take home. This also promotes responsibility and gives them a feeling of control over their education. Include parent questionnaires and/or notes from parent conferences. Ideally, portfolios can follow children throughout their educational career. An end-of-the-year summary sheet with a dated record of the child's progress goes on to the

Art Portfolios

What is an art portfolio? According to Althouse, Johnson, and Mitchell (2003), it is a purposeful collection of children's art work. It may include completed work or works in progress. Transcriptions of the language used by the children in the form of dictation to discuss their art work may accompany it.

Genishi (1993) believes that children's artistic progress may be documented and saved in portfolios that contain not necessarily the best of children's art, but instead samples that indicate children's abilities and preferences at specific points in time. These signed and dated pieces comprise the child's personal art museum.

next year's teacher. All other samples are bound and sent home in the form of a memory book.

Genishi (1993) recommends involving the child in the art portfolio process by asking questions like the following:

- Do you like this piece of artwork? What do you like about it?
- Which is your favorite piece? Why do you like it best?
- What art media do you like the best and why?
- Why did you choose to include this particular piece?
- Explain how you got this special effect (pointing to textured area).

Or ask the child to complete the following sentences.

- This is my favorite piece because . . .
- I want this included in my portfolio because . . .
- What I remember most about doing this is . . .

Record the child's comment on an index card and attach it to the corresponding work.

5. Review Periodically

The aim is not to compare children or portfolios but to look for and document individual growth, development, and learning over time. Plan a schedule to periodically review each child's portfolio, for example, two per evening. This is especially important before progress reports are due or to prepare for parent conferences.

ART ASSESSMENT

For many early childhood educators, assessment is a difficult concept to embrace. According to Wright (1994) this is particularly true in the arts in which symbolism, aesthetics, and personal expression are involved. A liberal view of assessment must be developed in arts education to embrace the child-centered, process-oriented philosophy which reflects developmentally appropriate practices. The emphasis is on meaning making and expression through arts symbol systems. For young children, the processes which closely resemble the artistic interests and abilities of young children also apply to all arts domains: music, dance, play/ drama, and the visual arts. Based on the works of Gardner (1990) and others, Wright (1994) identifies the following general artistic processes with some exemplary characteristics:

PROCESS	CHARACTERISTICS
Discovery—	observing, exploring options with a range of materials, comparing, questioning, seeking possibilities, finding alternatives.
Pursuit—	engaging in arts activities, focusing on specific ideas, exploring in-depth, working hard, carrying out one's plans, being goal directed, and staying on task.
Perception—	showing sensory awareness, visualizing, showing care and attention to detail, evidencing sensitivity to a variety of genres, cultures, and historical periods.
Communication—	expressing ideas or feelings, using symbols to represent, creating words, labels, captions, or stories to accompany one's art products.
Self- and social awareness—	working independently, tapping into personal feelings, being involved in preparation and clean up, sharing discoveries, tolerating frustration, participation in group activities, cooperating, empathizing, appreciating the work of others.
Skill use—	manipulating materials, showing eye-hand coordination and fine motor control, controlling basic techniques, showing aesthetic sensitivity.
Creativity—	responding flexibly, seeing afresh, taking risks with a medium, using imagination, showing inventiveness, exploring ideas in a variety of ways, crossing artistic domains, combining media.
Analysis—	describing to others what is seen, heard, felt, thought, or imagined; articulating artistic goals; reflecting on process and product; showing an interest in using arts terminology.
Critique—	appreciating artistic products, talking about one's own artistry, the works of peers and published artists, describing, interpreting, and judging, using the work of others for ideas and inspiration.

The characteristics and processes can be used as a basis for assessment. According to Wright (1994), it can help teachers to understand art processes, to recognize how they are used by young children, to focus on processes which will assist children to learn about the arts, and to explain children's art development to parents and others. When used as the basis of assessment, observations made of each of the above processes provide qualitative data about the child that enables a teacher to judge the effectiveness of the arts program being offered.

Observations of each of the above processes must be specific and focus on

- the child's learning experience described through anecdotal information.
- artistic elements that the child could use during the process.
- visual arts principles that could be implemented by the child.

In turn, the data gathered lead to implications for further planning.

INSTRUMENT FOR ARTISTIC ASSESSMENT

Our holistic model of child development has served many purposes throughout the book: to understand child development, to plan appropriate experiences, to report to parents, and to justify our programs. We can also use it as a framework, or instrument, for assessing children's artistic development.

Physical

In using artistic tools, the child demonstrates:

1. _____ large muscle or gross motor control.
2. _____ small muscle or fine motor control.
3. Proper use of the following artistic tools:
   _____ scissors   _____ markers
   _____ glue   _____ clay tools
   _____ brushes   _____ watercolor set
   _____ crayons
4. Concentration and sustained involvement in art.
5. Completion of the art activity.

Social

1. Ability to work alone at art.
2. Demonstrating self-responsibility:
   _____ in getting and returning art materials.
   _____ in cleanup.
   _____ in following the rules of the art center.
3. Self-direction in using own ideas in art rather than copying others.
4. Ability to work cooperatively with others at the easel, art table, or art center (see Figure 16–3).
5. Tolerance of others' art ideas, styles, and products.

Emotional

1. Acceptance of own mistakes, errors, and unsuccessful attempts at art.

Figure 16-3 These children share an opportunity to use their matching skills.

2. Self-assurance and confidence in art rather than an inhibited, fearful, overly cautious attitude.
3. Expression of feelings, moods, emotions, and personality through artwork.
4. Enjoyment and pride in own art.
5. Addition, omission, distortion, and/or exaggeration of things that are emotionally significant.

Cognitive

1. Understands art and why people have made art in the past and continue to do so.
2. Is interested in talking about own art and dictating labels, titles, sentences, or stories.
3. Knows and uses art vocabulary.
4. Evidences:
   _____ very personal representation.
   _____ public representation with subject matter recognizable to others.
5. Demonstrates a knowledge of colors and color mixing.
6. Reflects a knowledge of shapes, including:
   _____ circle.
   _____ square.
   _____ triangle.
   _____ rectangle.
   _____ lines.
   _____ combinations of above.
   _____ other nongeometric.
7. Reflects a knowledge of people, places, objects, experiences, and events of personal importance in the environment.
8. Draws human figures.

Creative

1. Demonstrates a willingness to discover, experiment, and explore with a variety of media.

2. Demonstrates ways of creatively combining media, materials, and artistic junk.
3. Uses detail, decoration, and elaboration.
4. Reflects originality, imagination, and creativity.
5. Makes individual and personally unique artistic statements.

Aesthetic

1. Enjoys:
   _____ processing with the media.
   _____ making artistic products.
2. Uses a variety of:
   _____ two-dimensional artistic media.
   _____ three-dimensional artistic media.
3. Demonstrates awareness and sensitivity through:
   _____ looking.
   _____ touching.
   _____ listening.
   _____ smelling.
   _____ tasting.
4. Demonstrates awareness and sensitivity to immediate:
   _____ surroundings.
   _____ nature.
   _____ environment.
5. Sees similarities and differences in artistic styles.
6. Appreciates work of artists encompassing a wide range of styles.
7. Knows the following artistic elements:

   _____ color   _____ shape
   _____ line   _____ space
   _____ mass or volume   _____ texture
   _____ pattern

8. Uses artistic elements to discuss and appreciate:
   _____ nature.
   _____ immediate surroundings.
   _____ environment.
   _____ own artwork.
   _____ artwork of others.

Personal

Number the child's favorite choices 1, 2, and 3.

Two-dimensional	Three-dimensional
_____ mark making	_____ sculpture
_____ painting	_____ clay
_____ printing	_____ papier-mâché
_____ watercolor	_____ construction or
_____ resist	assemblage
_____ stencil	_____ mask making
_____ paperwork	_____ mobile
_____ collage	_____ stabile
	_____ weaving
	_____ stitchery

SUMMARY

The roles of observer, recorder, and assessor were added to our list of teacher roles. There are many tools for observation. Guidelines for objective observing and recording were discussed. The developmental hazards of testing young children were also examined. Ways of assessing children that are more authentic, performance-based, and natural were offered as alternatives to standardized testing. The portfolio was identified as a key feature in authentic assessment. Guidelines for assembling and using portfolio information were discussed.

Key Terms

anecdote	diary	rating scales
art files	evaluation	recorder
art folders	event sampling	standardized achievement
assessment	narratives	testing
assessor	observer	time sampling
checklists	portfolio	

Suggested Activities

1. Working in teams, interview teachers about their views on assessment in early childhood, how they evaluate young children, and what they use to evaluate children's artistic progress.
2. Collect samples of one child's art over an extended period of time. Lay the artwork out in chronological order. Use the instrument for artistic evaluation presented in this chapter to make some statements about this child's artistic development. Can you make any recommendations?
3. Ask a teacher's permission to review children's portfolios for the purpose of learning how to devise a portfolio system.

4. Devise your own early childhood-style portfolio documenting what you have learned and can do as a result of teacher education.
5. Your instructor may have access to examples of standardized tests used with young children. If so, work in small groups and critically examine the test format and content. How do you feel about the use of standardized tests with young children?

Review

1. Identify and briefly discuss three teacher roles identified in this chapter.

2. Provide five reasons for the importance of observing and recording the behavior of young children.

3. Identify a major strategy for collecting and storing children's art.

4. Critique the developmental appropriateness of standardized testing for use with young children.

5. Discuss portfolio assessment as an authentic way to informally assess young children.

6. Identify the five steps in portfolio assessment.

For additional art and creative development resources, visit our Web site at
www.EarlyChildEd.delmar.com

Appendix A

Artistic Junk

Dear Parents,
We need your help! In our daily art program we use all kinds of creative junk. Our slogan is, "Don't throw it away! Recycle it by sending it along with your child."

If you have any of the following objects, please send them along with your child. We also encourage donations of creative junk from your office, business, workplace, or other sources in the community.
Thank-you!

A   adhesive-backed paper
    apple divider
    appliances (small, broken—good for parts)
    artificial flowers

B   bakeware
    baking cups
    baskets (plastic)
    bath brush
    beads
    berry baskets
    blocks (wooden)
    bolts
    bottle caps and tops
    bottles—plastic pump-type, squeeze, and roll-on deodorant
    bowl brush (new)
    bowls (plastic mixing)
    boxes (gift)
    braiding
    brayer
    burlap
    butter tubs
    buttons

C   calendars
    canceled stamps
    candles
    carbon paper
    cardboard fabric bolts

    cardboard sheets and tubes
    cards (old greeting)
    catalogues
    cellophane (colored)
    checkers
    cheese slicer
    Christmas cards
    cigar boxes
    clock parts
    cloth
    clothespins
    coat hangers
    coffee filters
    combs (cleaned)
    computer paper
    confetti
    cookie baking tray
    cookie cutters
    cord
    corks
    corrugated cardboard
    cosmetic brushes, sponges, and applicators
    costume jewelry
    costumes
    cotton balls, puffs, and swabs
    crayons (old, broken)
    cupcake liners
    cupcake tins
    curtain rings
    cutting board

D   deodorant bottle (roll-on)
    detergent bottles (squeeze-type with lids)
    dice
    dominoes
    dowels

E   egg cartons: cardboard and plastic
    egg slicer

electronic parts
embroidery hoops and thread
envelopes
excelsior
eyedropper
F fabric scraps
feather duster
feathers
felt
film spools
flannel
floor-length mirror
florist's foil, foam, and Styrofoam®
foam rubber
foil
food grater
food savers (Rubbermaid®, Tupperware®)
fruit trays
funnels
fur
G game pieces
gears
gift boxes
gift wrap
glass beads
glass pane (small)
glitter
grater (metal, food)
greeting cards
grocery bags
gummed labels
gummed paper and stickers
H hair rollers (cleaned)
hairbrushes (cleaned)
hangers
hat boxes
hats (old)
holiday decorations
hot plate
housewares
I ice-cream cartons (large, commercial)
ice-cube trays
iron (electric, in working order)
J jar tops
jars
jewelry
junk (any and all!)
junk mail
K keys
kitchen gadgets and utensils
kitchen shakers and containers
L lace
leather
lids
linoleum tiles

M machine parts (small)
magazines
magnets
maps
marbles
margarine tubs
material remnants
measuring cups and spoons
meatballer
melon baller/scoop
mesh—potato, onion, grapefruit bags
milk carton plastic tops
mirror (handheld, full-length)
mosaic tile
muffin tins
muslin
N nail brush
nails
necklaces
needles and thread
netting
newspaper
newsprint rolls
nuts
nylons and pantyhose (old, clean)
P packing material
pails (plastic)
paint charts
pans (old)
pantyhose plastic egg containers
paper bags
paper doilies
paper plates
paper reinforcements
paper scraps and tubes
pastry blender/brush
pastry tube
picture frames
pie slice lifter
pie tins
pill bottles and vials
pipe cleaners
pizza cardboards
place mats
plastic containers
plastic foam trays
plastic fruit baskets
plastic pieces and parts
poker chips
polyfiberfill
pom-pom dish scrubber
Popsicle® sticks
pot scrubber with knobbed handle
pots
puzzle pieces

Q   quilts, quilt scraps
R   razors (empty, plastic)
    rhinestones, rhinestone jewelry
    ribbon
    ribbon rolls
    rickrack
    rolling pin
S   sandpaper
    scraper spatula
    screening—plastic and wire
    seals (holiday)
    sequins
    sheets (old white)
    shoe boxes
    shoelaces
    shoe-polish applicator
    shopping bags
    sieves
    socks
    spice bottles (empty)
    splatter screen (for catching cooking grease)
    sponges (household)
    spools
    spray paint can lids
    sprayers
    springs
    squeeze bottles
    stamps (canceled domestic and foreign)
    stationery
    stationery boxes
    stickers
    stockings (old)
    straws
    string
    Styrofoam® balls, bits, packing, and pieces
T   telephone wire
    thread
    tiles
    tinfoil
    tissue paper
    tongue depressors
    toothbrushes (old)
    toothpicks
    towels (old)
    tracing paper
    travel brochures and posters
    trays
    trinkets
    tubes—toilet paper, paper towel, mailing
    tubs (margarine with lids)
    twine

U   upholstery fabric and stuffing
    utensils (old, cooking)
V   vegetables (if donated)
    velvet
    vitamin bottles
W   wallpaper sample books and scraps
    wax paper
    weaving loom
    wire (thin)
    wire mesh
    wire screen
    wire whisk/whip (kitchen)
    wood scraps
    wooden beads
    wooden blocks
    wrapping paper
Y   yarn

Nature Specimens

acorns
bark
corn husks
cornstalks
dried flowers and plants
driftwood
feathers
fossils
gems
gourds
hives
leaves
minerals
moss
natural clay
nests
nuts
pebbles
pinecones
pods
pressed flowers
reeds
sand
sawdust
seed pods
seeds
shells
smooth stones
straw
twigs
wood shavings

Appendix B

Where to Go in Your Local Community for Artistic Junk

The following list is by no means complete. The number and variety of possible sources will vary depending on the size and location of your community. Feel free to add, delete, and personalize depending on where you live and work. Please request more than is listed below. Individual sources may have a vast supply of colorful parts and pieces just waiting to be claimed. Most sources will be very willing to save, as long as you provide a prompt pickup. Specifically stating your purpose and suggesting some sample activities may help them identify artistic junk that is not contained on the list. Happy hunting!

Architectural firm
    blueprint paper
    outdated tools
    surplus paper

Art supply store
    damaged supplies
    surplus stock
    used goods

Attic sale
    anything and everything reasonably priced!

Builder's supply and contractors
    carpeting
    Formica®
    linoleum
    tile
    wallpaper samples
    wood scraps, trim, and molding

Building site
    discarded hardware
    Styrofoam® packing
    wood scraps, shavings, trim, and molding

Carpentry and woodworking shop
    sawdust
    wood scraps, shavings, molding, and trim

Church sale
    anything and everything reasonably priced!

Computerized office
    outdated forms
    scrap computer papers and forms

Container and packaging companies
    boxes
    cardboard

Craft and hobby shop
    damaged goods
    packing
    small boxes

Dentist's office
    see Hospital/medical

Department store
    gift wrap scraps
    hosiery boxes
    outdated forms
    small boxes
    store displays
    Styrofoam® packing

Doctor's office
  see Hospital/medical

Dressmaking and alteration shop
  bobbins
  buttons
  fabric
  spools
  thread
  trims

Drugstore and pharmacy
  pill bottles
  plastic containers
  store displays
  vials

Electric power company
  packing materials
  wire

Electronics firm
  circuit boards
  components
  metal parts
  pieces
  plastic parts
  wire

Estate sale
  anything and everything reasonably priced!

Flea market or swap meet
  anything and everything reasonably priced!

Florist shop
  dried flowers
  ribbon
  scrap Styrofoam®
  surplus nature items

Frame shop
  frame scraps
  mat board scraps

Furniture showroom
  cartons
  packing materials

Garage sale
  anything and everything reasonably priced!

Garment manufacturer
  buttons
  empty spools
  fabric scraps
  trim

General office and small business
  envelopes
  general supplies
  old rubber stamps
  outdated business forms
  surplus or outdated business machines
  surplus paper

Gift shop
  boxes
  ribbon
  spools
  Styrofoam® packing
  tissue paper

Gift wrap service
  cardboard rolls
  damaged gift boxes
  ribbon
  scrap wrapping paper
  tissue paper

Hardware store
  linoleum
  spare parts and pieces
  tile

Hospital/medical
  boxes
  containers
  pill bottles
  plastic parts and pieces
  trays
  vials
  X-rays

Ice-cream shop
  cardboard packing
  commercial drum-shaped ice-cream cartons

Interior design studio
  boxes
  displays
  fabric packing
  sample books

Lumberyard
  dowels
  molding
  sandpaper
  sawdust
  wood scraps and shavings

Machine shop or small plant
　　small specialized pieces and parts

Moving and storage company
　　cardboard
　　cartons
　　wrapping paper

Nature and outdoors
　　nature specimens

Newspaper plant
　　newsprint
　　paper roll ends
　　scrap papers

Office supply
　　cardboard
　　damaged goods
　　packing
　　small boxes

Paint store
　　linoleum
　　paint charts
　　surplus water-based paint
　　tile

Photography shop
　　containers
　　scrap papers

Plastic company
　　parts
　　plastic pieces
　　Plexiglas®
　　tubing
　　wire

Plumbing supply
　　plastic pipes and pieces

Print shop
　　cardboard pieces and tubes
　　heavyweight papers
　　paper "seconds" and scraps
　　tickets

Rug store
　　rug scraps
　　samples

Rummage sale
　　anything and everything reasonably priced!

Stationery store
　　"as is" papers
　　paper scraps
　　small boxes

Supermarket and grocery store
　　baskets
　　cardboard lining and packing
　　old price stampers
　　small boxes
　　store displays
　　Styrofoam®
　　thin tissue paper

Tag sale
　　anything and everything reasonably priced!

Telephone company
　　large spools
　　thin colored wire

Textile and fabric shop
　　cardboard bolts
　　fabric scraps
　　material remnants
　　spools
　　yarn cones

Thrift shop
　　anything and everything reasonably priced!

Tile and ceramic shop
　　linoleum
　　tile

Travel agency
　　displays
　　old posters
　　outdated forms
　　surplus brochures
　　tickets

Upholstery shop
　　buttons
　　fabric
　　spools
　　trims

Wallpaper store
　　drapery samples
　　wallpaper books and scraps

White elephant sale
 anything and everything reasonably priced!

Wine and liquor store
 cartons
 displays
 fancy boxes

gift paper
ribbons
wooden boxes

Yard sale
 anything and everything reasonably priced!

Appendix C

Art Resources

The following is a partial list of art resources: postcards, prints, reproductions, slides, posters, books, films, and videotapes related to art. Remember to also check local bookstores, museums, and art galleries.

American Federation of Arts
http://www.afaweb.org

Art Extension Press
http://www.home-school.com

Art Institute of Chicago
The Museum Store
http://www.artic.edu

Guggenheim Museum
http://www.guggenheim.org

Internet Art Resources
http://www.artresources.com/

Metropolitan Museum of Art
http://www.metmuseum.org

Museam of Modern Art
http://www.moma.org

Nasco Arts & Crafts
http://www.nascofa.com

National Gallery of Art
http://www.nga.gov

New York Graphic Society
http://www.nygs.com

Smithsonian Institution
http://www.si.edu

Appendix D

Catalogues

The following is a partial list of companies that carry art-related toys and basic art supplies. Generally they will send catalogues upon request. If possible, use school letterhead stationery. Shop around and compare prices, handling and shipping charges, discounts, and return policies.

ABC School Supply Inc.
http://www.abcschoolsupply.com

Beckley-Cardy
http://www.beckleycardy.com

Childcraft Education Corp.
http://www.childcraft.com

Community Playthings
http://www.communityplaythings.com

Constructive Playthings
http://constplay.com

Crayola Educational Products
http://www.crayola.com

Creative Playthings
http://www.creativeplaythings.com

DIDAX Inc.
http://www.didax.com

Discount School Supply
http://www.earlychildhood.com

Fisher Price Toys
http://www.fisher-price.com

Galt Toys
http://www.galttoys.com

Kaplan
http://www.kaplan.com

Knowledge Unlimited
http://www.thekustore.com

Lakeshore Curriculum Materials Co.
http://www.lakeshorelearning.com

Nasco Arts & Crafts
http://www.nascofa.com

Playskool, Inc.
http://www.playskool.com

Appendix E

Art-Related Books

The following list contains books that focus on the artistic elements, including color, shape, and line, and the five senses, artists, and art in general.

Adams, A. (1976). *Easter egg artists.* New York: Charles Scribner's Sons.
A family of bunnies design and paint beautiful Easter eggs as well as their surroundings.

Bang, M. (1981). *Tye May and the magic brush.* New York: Greenwillow Books.
Tye May is a poor orphan who is mysteriously given a magical paintbrush. Whatever she paints comes alive. She gives what she paints as gifts to the poor. The greedy emperor discovers this and makes her paint only for him. Tye May, however, wins in the end when she sends him off sailing in the ocean on a painted ship.

Baylor, B. (1972). *When clay sings.* New York: Charles Scribner's Sons.
A book for older children on the use of clay in prehistoric and primitive art. The book relies on a long narrative and explores symbols on Indian pottery. Highly recommended for multicultural education.

Blizzard, G. S. (1991). *Come look with me, enjoying art with children.* Charlottesville, VA: Thomasson-Grant.
Presents color reproductions of paintings of children done by artists ranging from Holbein to Picasso. Background information on artists and their paintings as well as questions are included to stimulate discussion. Recommended for older children.

Brandenberg, A. (1962). *My five senses.* New York: Thomas Y. Crowell Company.
Overviews the five senses. The choice of colors is limited and restricted to black, white, green, and blue.

Brandenberg, F. (1977). *What can you make of it?* New York: Greenwillow Books.
Fieldmouse family moves to a new home. They collect all sorts of junk, including milk cartons, toilet paper tubes, yarn, spools, egg cartons, and old magazines. In their new home they find wonderful uses for all this valuable junk.

Brenner, B. (1970). *Faces.* New York: E. P. Dutton & Co.
Tells how we learn about the world through our senses. Four of the standard five senses are covered, with touch left out. The book is illustrated with black-and-white photographs.

Carle, E. (1973). *I see a song.* New York: Thomas Y. Crowell Company.
A collage of colors and shapes without words. A violin player plays colorful music that forms designs and suggests realistic objects. The book will help children visualize, imagine, and come up with creative possibilities.

Chase, A. E. (1962). *Famous paintings—An introduction to art.* New York: Platt & Monk.
The author presents approximately 200 large pictures of famous artworks. The pictures are organized around themes, for example, children and their pets, playing games, and mother and child.

Cohen, M. (1980). *No good in art.* New York: Greenwillow Books.
Jim's art teacher in kindergarten did not approve of his work. Jim did not feel very creative during that year. Now, in first grade, he has a teacher who helps him see how creative and artistic he can be. Recommended for children who do not see themselves as skilled or creative in art.

Crews, D. (1978). *Freight train.* New York: Greenwillow Books.
The story of the journey of a colorful train as it goes through tunnels, by cities, and over trestles. The book is very well illustrated. The bright, colorful cars of the train bear their color name. The colors of the cars blend to suggest speed and movement and also depict color mixing.

Crews, D. (1982). *Carousel.* New York: Greenwillow Books.
Children climb atop a carousel animal. The music begins and the animals circle round and round, faster and faster. What results is a blur of color. The music stops, and the horses slow down. The original colors return. Illustrated with full-color collages and special photographic techniques.

Cumming, R. (1979). *Just look . . . A book about paintings.* New York: Charles Scribner's Sons.
Contains over fifty full-color reproductions of famous paintings. Discusses how artists have used the artistic elements, including line, shape, and color, in their work. Contains some difficult vocabulary and may be most appropriate at the kindergarten or primary level.

Davol, M. W. (1997). *The paper dragon.* New York: Atheneum.
Cut tissue paper art elegantly unfolds across triple page spreads in the dramatic story of a Chinese artist who saves his villages from a ferocious dragon.

de Paola, T. (1991). *Bonjour, Mr. Satie.* New York: Putnam Publishers.
Two talented Parisian artists end their feud with the help of Uncle Satie.

Diakité, B. W. (1997). *The hunterman and the crocodile: A West African folktale.* New York: Scholastic.
This traditional West African tale is beautifully illustrated with hand-painted ceramic tiles. The book is about a cautious hunter who helps some clever crocodiles and in the process learns a lesson about the relationship between man and nature.

Emberley, E. (1961). *Wing on a flea: A book about shapes.* Boston: Little, Brown and Company.
The author uses rhymes and lively drawings to help children recognize rectangles, circles, and triangles in everyday objects.

Emberley, E. (1968). *Green says go.* Boston: Little, Brown and Company.
A story about colors and color mixing. The author suggests that colors remind us of many different things, like holidays. Unfortunately, he stereotypically equates pink with girls and blue with boys.

Engel, D. (1989). *The little lump of clay.* New York: Morrow Jr. Books.
A little lump of clay that desperately wants to become something has its wish granted.

Fisher, L. E. (1984). *Boxes! Boxes!* New York: The Viking Press.
As the name implies, the book shows many possible uses for a box. The book has beautiful color illustrations. The words in the simplified text are set to rhyme. The book focuses on squares and rectangles.

Freeman, D. (1976). *Chalk box story.* New York: Lippincott.
When the lid of a chalk box opens, each colored stick helps tell the story of a little boy stranded on a deserted island and the little turtle who comes to his rescue.

Friskey, M. (1973). *What is the color of the wide, wide world?* Chicago: Children's Press.
Different animals each claim that the world is their color. Each appears on a separate page telling about things that are their color. A beautiful white bird corrects them by saying that colors change with light and seasons. The world is full of many beautiful colors. A good book for older children.

Hawkinson, J. (1978). *Pat, swish, twist and the story of Patty Swish.* Chicago: Albert Whitman & Co.
The book has beautiful watercolor illustrations and is divided into two major parts. First, there is a wordless picture story of Patty Swish, a horselike animal. Second, there is a discussion of tools and techniques for watercolor.

Ho, M. (1996). *Hush! A Thai lullaby.* New York: Orchard Books.
Cut paper collage art beautifully complements the story of a mother who asks nocturnal animals of the Thai countryside to "hush" so baby can sleep.

Hoban, T. (1970). *Shapes and things.* New York: Macmillan.
There are no words, but beautiful photograph-type white impressions of common objects appear against a black background. This book will help children see the beauty in shape, outline, and form.

Hoban, T. (1971). *Look again.* New York: Macmillan.
Excellent black-and-white photography. The sequence begins with a square cutout of a page with a photograph underneath. Guess what it is? Turn the window and see if you were right. Look again for a different view of the same object by turning the page, which brings you to the next sequence.

Hoban, T. (1978). *Is it red? Is it yellow? Is it blue?* New York: Greenwillow Books.
There is no text, but the book is illustrated with beautiful photographs in vibrant colors. The author focuses on colors and concepts of shape, quantity, and direction. The author has creatively chosen what to include for the colors. For example, rather than apple for red, the author chooses a girl with a red raincoat and red umbrella. Each page is coded with color bubbles representing the colors stressed.

Hoban, T. (1982). *A, B, see!* New York: Greenwillow Books.
This is one of many highly recommended books by this author. Hoban is a talented photographer. In this book, black-and-white photograms of familiar objects from *A* to *Z* are portrayed. Photograms reveal the form or shape in white against a black background. This book shows how there is beauty and design all around us.

Hoban, T. (1983). *I read symbols.* New York: Greenwillow Books.
Colorful photographs are used to introduce the child to signs and symbols frequently seen along streets and highways.

Hoban, T. (1983). *Round and round and round.* New York: Greenwillow Books.
There is no text, but the book is illustrated with beautiful photographs in vibrant colors. The choice of examples is creative and unusual. For example, round holes in a Swiss cheese sandwich on a round bun and round ripples in water are but two of her clever examples.

Hoban, T. (1984). *Is it rough? Is it smooth? Is it shiny?* New York: Greenwillow Books.
There is no text, but the book is illustrated with beautiful photographs in vibrant colors. The author

focuses on textures and surfaces. The author has creatively chosen items such as a squashed soft drink can, caramel apples, and bales of hay. The photographs confirm the aesthetic belief that beauty is all around us.

Hughes, S. (1985). *Noisy.* New York: Lothrop, Lee & Shepard Books.
Part of a series on concepts. The story of a little girl who describes the many noises that can be heard inside and outside her house. The illustrations are charming and depict family members as real people. Children will be able to relate to these characters. The parents appear frazzled, and baby sibling always seems to have food spilled on the floor.

Hutchins, P. (1971). *Changes, changes.* New York: Macmillan.
There is no text, and illustrations tell the creative adventures of two wooden toys and their building blocks. The blocks catch on fire, convert into a fire truck, and float in the water. Children will enjoy guessing what is going to happen next. What else could they do with blocks?

Johnson, C. (1960). *A picture for Harold's room.* New York: Harper & Row.
One of a series on the adventures of Harold and his purple crayon. This one has been made into an I Can Read Book with simple words for the beginning reader. Harold thinks his room needs a picture and decides to draw one with his purple crayon. Before finishing his picture, however, Harold takes you on a journey with his purple crayon. This particular adventure includes attention to perspective when Harold draws railroad tracks that recede into the background.

Johnson, C. (1995). *Harold and the purple crayon.* New York: Harper & Row.
The story of Harold and his adventures with a purple crayon. Harold goes out for a walk and sketches some adventures. The book is small, compact, and made for small hands. The illustrations are simple, and the purple line is bold. The story resolves itself with Harold falling asleep and dropping his purple crayon.

Kampmann, L. (1971). *The children's book of painting.* New York: Van Nostrand Reinhold.
This story was originally written in German, and the story line gets a little wordy at times. It is the story of the painting adventures of two puppets, Alexander and Katinka. They experiment with watercolor, crayons, and markers. Beautiful samples of real children's art are included.

Keats, E. J. (1978). *The trip.* New York: Greenwillow Books.
The story of a boy, Louie, who is having trouble adjusting to his new move. Louie's new neighborhood is portrayed with vibrant-colored collage, paint, and pastels. Homesick, Louie makes a shoe box diorama and imagines that he flies back to see his old friends, who are dressed for Halloween. A quick fantasy flight and Louie returns to his new home just in time to go trick-or-treating with his new neighbors. A good ethnic mix of characters.

Kellogg, S. (1982). *Mystery of the stolen blue paint.* New York: Dial.
Belinda plans to paint a special blue picture but is interrupted by her cousin and his friends. She gives up and decides to pack away her art supplies. Where is the blue paint? The others do not have it. The mystery is solved when Belinda's dog Homer gives everyone a blue kiss.

Kessler, E., & Kessler, L. (1966). *Are you square?* Garden City, NY: Doubleday.
Square and round are emphasized, with other shapes introduced. The illustrations are fair, and the book relies on a strong story line.

Krauss, R. (1956). *I want to paint my bathroom blue.* New York: Harper & Row.
A boy's fantasy adventure with painting people and things different colors. Illustrated by Sendak, one of his earliest.

Kunhardt, D. (1962). *Pat the bunny.* New York: Golden Book.
A multisensory experience for very young children. Look at the pictures, listen to the words, pat the bunny, and smell the scented illustration.

Lamorisse, A. (1956). *The red balloon.* Garden City, NY: Doubleday.
A classic that still appears on television. It is the tale of a young boy, Pascal, who lives in Paris and his encounters with his magical red balloon. There are many black-and-white photographs, with only a few color ones emphasizing red.

Lionni, L. (1968). *Swimmy.* New York: Pantheon Books.
Young children love Swimmy, a small, black orphan fish who comes to save the day. Just as important are the beautiful watercolor illustrations of sea creatures and seascapes. The words have been carefully chosen and are equally beautiful.

Lionni, L. (1979). *Little blue and little yellow.* New York: Ivan Obolensky, Inc.
Depicts the adventures of torn colored paper shapes: Mama, Papa, and Child Blue. The book shows color mixing. Little Blue hugged a friend named Little Yellow and they became as one—green. The story may be a bit contrived, but it is a good introduction to color mixing and will encourage readers to use their imagination and creativity.

Lionni, L. (1985). *Colors to talk about.* New York: Pantheon.
A small, sturdy book with cardboard pages and rounded edges. It is highly recommended for older infants, toddlers, and young preschoolers. There are no words. The book relies on attractive illustrations to show the antics of colorful mice.

Lionni, L. (1991). *Matthew's dream.* New York: Knopf.
An enchanting fable about a mouse who wants to become a painter. Explores the role of art and artist in shaping our vision and expanding our dreams.

Lobel, A. (1981). *On Market Street.* New York: Greenwillow Books.
An *A*-to-*Z* picture book of old-fashioned sellers at market. Each seller is composed of the wares that he

or she sells. For example, *L* is made up solely of lollipops. The book is colorful and a creative way to discuss shapes and composition, as well as the alphabet.

Loss, J. (1974). *What is it? A book of photographic puzzles.* Garden City, NY: Doubleday.
A series of puzzles. Each one starts with a photographic close-up. Can you guess what it is? Turn the page and see it as it usually appears at normal range. Clear black-and-white photography. Challenging for both young and older children.

Lund, D. H. (1973). *The paint-box sea.* New York: McGraw-Hill.
The story of a brother and sister who explore the seashore to discover the real color of the ocean. Beautiful illustrations. Older children may be better able to relate to the older characters. Words are set in rhyme.

MacAgy, D., & MacAgy, E. (1959). *Going for a walk with a line—a step into the world of modern art.* Garden City, NY: Doubleday.
Samples of the artwork of different artists are included to show different ways that the line has been used in art.

Martin, B., Jr., (1967). *Brown bear, brown bear, what do you see?* New York: Holt, Rinehart and Winston.
Children see a variety of animals, each one a different color, looking at them. Big, bold, colorful illustrations. Children will enjoy the repetitive, catchy rhyme.

O'Neill, M. (1961). *Hailstones and halibut bones.* Garden City, NY: Doubleday.
A very highly recommended book of poetry for all the different colors. Excellent and very appropriate for young children. This book is a must for any early childhood book collection.

Phillips, R. S. (Ed.). (1978). *The great artists.* New York: Funk & Wagnalls.
A series of large paperback books on 25 artists. Each book in the series is composed of full-page reproductions with vital information concerning the artwork on the back of each. Information on each artist is in the introductory section. Prints can be removed, framed, and displayed.

Raboff, E. (1987-1988). *Art for children.* New York: Harper Collins Children's Books.
A series. Each book focuses on one artist. The books on Picasso and Chagall provide beautiful color reproductions combined with simple text.

Reiss, J. J. (1969). *Colors.* Scarsdale, NY: Bradbury Press.
Different pages focus on different colors. The pictures are large, glossy, colorful, and done with a concern for good design. Young children will enjoy the colorful shapes.

Reiss, J. J. (1974). *Shapes.* Scarsdale, NY: Bradbury Press.
Focuses on geometric shapes in the environment. Very well illustrated. Shapes are creatively combined to make different ones. Shapes are all around us.

Samton, S. W. (1985). *The world from my window.* New York: Crown Publishers.
Can serve many purposes. Focuses on numbers, colors, and poetry. The book is beautifully illustrated in vibrant colors. The numbers one through ten and corresponding objects appear as seen from one window. The story line is set in rhyme.

Sazer, N. (1976). *What do you think I saw? A nonsense number book.* New York: Pantheon Books.
Introduces the numbers one to ten while describing in rhyme the unusual things a young rhino sees on the way to the train. The book is illustrated with animals done in watercolors.

Schaefer, C. L. (1999). *The squiggle.* New York: Crown Books.
A few spare and colorful lines bring to life a preschool girl and her vivid imagination.

Shapur, F. (1972). *Round and round and square.* London: Abelard-Schuman.
Illustrated with basic shapes in bright colors. Shows how common objects like sailboats and kites are composed of simple shapes. Identifying shapes in the night and city scenes will be more difficult, since they tend to be busy.

Shaw, C. G. (1947). *It looked like spilt milk.* New York: Harper & Row.
A classic. The story of a white blob that is searching for an identity. What can it be? The book shows how it can be many things, including spilt milk. It is hoped that children will see that their own drawn or painted shapes can also be many things. Still, the author ends on a close-ended note by stating that it was a cloud rather than spilt milk. Why couldn't it be all or none of the above?

Slobodkina, E. (1968). *Caps for sale.* Reading, MA: Addison-Wesley.
A classic tale of a peddler, some monkeys, and their monkey business. Children love the suspense and antics. They also learn their colors from the peddler's checkered, gray, brown, blue, and red stacked caps.

Tabak, S. (2000). *Joseph had a little overcoat.* New York: Viking.
This is the story of a resourceful and resilient tailor who transforms his worn-out overcoat into smaller and smaller garments. The book is illustrated in a variety of media including watercolor, gouache, pencil, ink, and collage.

Tudor, T. (1978). *Five senses.* New York: Platt & Munk.
Tells the adventures of a little girl who uses all her senses on a farm. Set in the recent past. The illustrations are quite pretty, and the story may hold more appeal for girls than for boys.

Ventura, P. (1984). *Great painters.* New York: G. P. Putnam's Sons.
A resource book rather than a storybook. There is no story, but rather an explanation of artistic styles. Children may enjoy looking through this book. Not all the pictures are large enough to show to the whole class during story time.

Weisgard, L. (1956). *Treasures to see.* New York: Harcourt, Brace & World.
Depicts a trip through an art museum. The pictures are illustrations rather than photographs. The book is

dated, and the children appear as they did in the 1950s. Still, for the child who has never been to an art museum, it is a good start.

Wiesner, D. (1999). *Sector 7.* New York: Clarion Books.
This is the story of a small boy on a class trip to the Empire State building who is transported by a friendly cloud to Sector 7, a great cloud factory high in the sky. This imaginative story is illustrated with striking and dramatic watercolor illustrations that add to the element of fantasy.

Wildsmith, B. (1984). *Fishes.* London: Oxford University Press.
A close-up look at a variety of fish illustrated in a rainbow of bright colors and set against an equally colorful background. You can see the artist's initial sketches and how the paint is washed over.

Wolff, R. J. (1968). *Feeling blue.* New York: Charles Scribner's Sons.
A focus on the color blue. How do we make blue? How does blue make us feel? Where do we see blue in our world? What are the shades and tints of blue?

The book is a good introduction to one primary color. The author has also written *Hello Yellow* and *Seeing Red* with an identical format.

Yenawine, P. (1991). *Stories; colors; lines; shapes.* New York: Delacorte.
A series of four books on modern art created to help teach the basic vocabulary, including lines, colors, and shapes. Each book ends with brief background information that adults will find useful when talking with children about the paintings and sculptures reproduced in this series.

Zelinsky, P. O. (1997). *Rapunzel.* New York: Dutton.
The author retells this Grimms' folktale. The book is richly illustrated with classically beautiful illustrations including detailed oil paintings.

Zhensun, Z., & Low, A. (1991). *A young painter: The life and paintings of Wang Yani—China's extraordinary young artist.* New York: Scholastic.
Examines the life and works of Wang Yani, a Chinese girl who has received worldwide acclaim for her art. Yani began painting animals at age three.

Appendix F

Professional Organizations

Americans for the Arts
http://www.artsusa.org

ARTSEDGE
http://artsedge.kennedy-center.org

Association for Childhood Education International
www.acei.org

American Montessori Society
http://www.amshq.org

Association Montessori Internationale
http://www.montessori-ami.org

Association for Supervision and Curriculum
    Development
http://www.ascd.org/

Child Care Information Exchange
http://www.ccie.com

The Child Care Law Center
http://www.childcarelaw.org

The Children's Defense Fund
http://www.childrensdefense.org

The Children's Foundation
http://www.childrensfoundation.net

Council for Art Education, Inc.
http://www.acminet.org/

Council for Exceptional Children
Division of Early Childhood
http://www.cec.sped.org

Council for Early Childhood
Professional Recognition
http://www.cdacouncil.org

Creative Connections
http://www.creativeconnections.org

Creative Education Foundation
http://www.creativeeducationfoundation.org/

Educational Resources Information Center/Early
    Childhood Education (ERIC/ECE)
http://www.eric.ed.gov

Getty Center for Education in the Arts
http://www.getty.edu

High/Scope Educational Research Foundation
http://www.highscope.org

Innovations in Early Education
The International Reggio Exchange
http://www.mpi.wayne.edu

Kennedy Center Alliance for Arts Education Network
    (KCAAEN)
http://www.kennedy-center.org
Search for "Arts Education"
Click on "Kennedy Center: Kennedy Center Alliance for
    Arts Education Network"

National Art Education Association
http://www.naea-reston.org

National Assembly of State Arts Agencies
http://www.nasaa-arts.org

The National Association of Child Care Professionals
http://www.naccp.org

National Association for the Education of Young
    Children
http://www.naeyc.org/

National Association for Family Day Care
http://www.nafcc.org

National Association for Music Education (MENC)
http://www.menc.org

National Child Care Association
http://www.nccanet.org/

National Endowment for the Arts
Division of Education Programs
http://www.nea.gov

Save the Children, Inc.
http://www.savethechildren.org

Society for Research in Child Development
http://www.srcd.org

Southern Early Childhood Association (SECA)
http://www.southernearlychildhood.org

World Organization for Early Childhood Education
    (OMEP)
http://www.omep-usnc.org

Resources for Young Children with Special Needs

Alexander Graham Bell Association for the Deaf
http://www.agbell.org

American Association on Mental Retardation
http://www.aamr.org

American Cleft Palate Foundation
http://www.cleftline.org

American Council for the Blind (ACB)
http://www.acb.org

American Foundation of the Blind (AFB)
http://www.afb.org

American Speech-Language-Hearing Association (ASHA)
http://www.asha.org

The ARC
http://www.thearc.org

Attention Deficit Disorder Association (ADDA)
http://www.add.org

Autism Society of America
http://www.autism-society.org

Beach Center on Disability
http://www.beachcenter.org

Better Hearing Institute
http://www.betterhearing.org

Brain Injury Association
http://www.biausa.org

Children and Adults with Attention Deficit Disorders (CHADD)
http://www.chadd.org

Council for Exceptional Children (CEC)
http://www.cec.sped.org

Epilepsy Foundation of America
http://www.efa.org

ERIC Clearinghouse on Disability and Gifted Education
http://www.ericec.org

Federation for Children with Special Needs
http://www.fcsn.org

Federation of Families for Children's Mental Health
http://www.ffcmh.org

International Dyslexia Association
http://www.interdys.org

Learning Disabilities Association of America
http://www.ldanatl.org

March of Dimes Birth Defects Foundation
http://www.modimes.org

Muscular Dystrophy Association
http://www.mdausa.org

National Association for Sickle Cell Disease, Inc.
http://www.sicklecelldisease.org

National Association for the Visually Handicapped
http://www.navh.org

National Association of the Deaf
http://www.nad.org

National Coalition for Parent Involvement in Education (NCPIE)
http://www.ncpie.org

National Down Syndrome Congress
http://www.ndsccenter.org

National Down Syndrome Society
http://www.ndss.org

National Easter Seal Society
http://www.easterseals.org

National Federation of the Blind
http://www.nfb.org

National Information Center for Children and Youth with Disabilities (NICHCY)
http://www.nichcy.org

National Information Center on Deafness
Gallaudet University
http://www.gallaudet.edu

National Institute of Mental Health
http://www.nimh.nih.gov

National Institute on Child Health and Human Development
http://www.nichd.nih.gov

National Maternal & Child Health Clearinghouse
http://www.nmchc.org

National Tourette Syndrome Association
http://www.tsa-usa.org

Parents Helping Parents: The Parent-Directed Family Resource Center for Children with Special Needs
http://www.parentshelpingparents.org

Spina Bifida Association of America
http://www.sbaa.org

United Cerebral Palsy Association
http://www.ucpa.org

World Council for Gifted and Talented Children
http://www.worldgifted.org/

Zero To Three
http://www.zerotothree.org

Appendix H

National Standards for Arts Education

These standards describe what every schoolager should know and be able to do in the arts. They were developed by the Consortium of National Arts Education Associations, which includes the National Association for Music Education (MENC).

National Standards for Dance/Movement in grades K–4 include:

1. identifying and demonstrating movement elements and skills in performing dance.
2. understanding choreographic principles, processes, and structures.
3. understanding dance as a way to create and communicate meaning.
4. applying and demonstrating critical and creative thinking skills in dance.
5. demonstrating and understanding dance in various cultures and historical periods.
6. making connections between dance and healthful living.
7. making connections between dance and other disciplines.

National Standards for Music in grades K–4 include:

1. singing a varied repertoire of music, alone and with others.
2. performing a varied repertoire of music on instruments, alone and with others.
3. improvising melodies, variations, and accompaniments.
4. composing and arranging music with specified guidelines.

5. reading and notating music.
6. listening to, analyzing, and describing music.
7. evaluating music and musical performances.
8. understanding relationships between music, the other arts, and disciplines outside the arts.
9. understanding music in relation to history and culture.

National Standards for Dramatic Arts in grades K–4 include:

1. script writing by planning and recording improvisations based on personal experience and heritage, imagination, literature, and history.
2. acting by assuming roles and interacting in improvisations.
3. designing by visualizing and arranging environments for classroom dramatizations.
4. directing by planning classroom dramatizations.
5. researching by finding information to support classroom dramatizations.
6. comparing and connecting art forms by describing dramatic arts, dramatic media (film television, and electronic media), and other art forms.
7. analyzing and explaining personal preferences, and constructing meanings from classroom dramatizations and from the dramatic arts, film, television, and electronic media productions.
8. understanding context by recognizing the role of the dramatic arts, film, television, and electronic media in daily life.

National Standards for Visual Arts in grades K–4 include:

1. understanding and applying media, techniques, and processes.
2. using knowledge of structures and functions.
3. choosing and evaluating a range of subject matter, symbols, and ideas.
4. understanding the visual arts in relation to history and cultures.
5. reflecting on and assessing the characteristics and merits of their work, and the work of others.
6. making connections between visual arts and other disciplines.

Visit MENC's Web site at http://www.menc.org.

Appendix I

 Multicultural Picture Books

The following is a list of some popular children's picture books that embrace diversity.

Aardema, V. (1983). *Bringing the rain to Kapiti Plain.* (African). New York: Penguin.

Ancona, G. (1994). *The piñata maker.* (Hispanic). Orlando, FL: Harcourt.

Ancona, G. (1994). *Ricardo's day.* (Hispanic). New York: Scholastic.

Ashley, B. (1995). *Cleversticks.* (Asian-American). New York: Crown.

Bang, M. (1996). *Ten, nine, eight.* (African-American). New York: Grenwillow.

Brill, M. (1998). *Tooth tales from around the world.* (Diversity). Waterton, MA: Charlesbridge.

Brown, T. (1992). *Hello, amigos.* (Hispanic). New York: Holt.

Browne, E. (2003). *Handa's surprise.* (African). Cambridge, MA: Candlewick.

Brusca, M. (1991). *On the pampas.* (South American, Hispanic). New York: Holt.

Bunting, E. (2000). *Flower garden.* (African-American). Orlando, FL: Harcourt.

Bunting, E. (1998). *Going home.* (Hispanic). New York: HarperCollins.

Bunting, E. (1990). *How many days to America: A Thanksgiving story.* (Americana). Boston, MA: Houghton Mifflin.

Caines, J. (1984). *Just us women.* (African-American). New York: HarperCollins.

Cave, K. (2003). *One child; one seed: A South African counting book.* (African). New York: Holt.

Cheltenham Elementary School Kindergarten. (2003). *We are all alike, we are all different.* (Diversity). New York: Scholastic.

Cherry, L. (2000). *The great Kapok tree.* (Hispanic). Orlando, FL: Harcourt.

Chocolate D. M. N. (1996). *A very special Kwanzaa.* (African-American). New York: Scholastic.

Coerr, E. (2003). *Mieko and the fifth treasure.* (Japanese). New York: Penguin.

Coerr, E. (1997). *Sadako.* (Japanese). New York: Penguin.

Cohen, C. (1991). *The mud pony.* (Native American). New York: Scholastic.

Cohen, M. (2003). *Down in the subway.* (Multicultural). New York: Star Bright Books.

Cowen-Fletcher, J. (1997). *It takes a village.* (African-American). New York: Scholastic.

Crews, D. (1991). *Bigmama's.* (African-American). New York: Greenwillow.

dePaolo, T. (1991). *The legend of the Indian paintbrush.* (Native American). New York: Penguin.

Derolf, S. (1997). *The crayon box that talked.* (Diversity). New York: Random House.

Dodey, N. (1992). *Everybody cooks rice.* (Anglo-American, Multicultural). Minneapolis, MN: Lerner.

Dorros, A. (1997). *Abuela.* (Hispanic). New York: Penguin.

Dorros, A. (1999). *Isla.* (Hispanic). New York: Penguin.

Dorros, A. (2004). *Julio's Magic.* (Hispanic). New York: Harper Collins.

Dorros, A. (1997). *Radio man.* (Migrant). New York: Penguin.

Dorros, A. (1994). *Tonight is carnival.* (Hispanic). New York: Penguin.

Dotlich, R. (2002). *A family like yours.* (Multicultural). Homesdale, PA: Boyds Mill Press.

Edwards, P. (1998). *Barefoot: Escape on the underground railroad.* (African-American). New York: Harper-Collins.

Falwell, C. (1995). *Feast for 10.* (African-American). Boston: Houghton Mifflin.

Fazio, B. (1996). *Grandfather's story.* (Asian-American). Seattle, WA: Sasquatch.

Flournoy, V. (1985). *The patchwork quilt.* (African-American). New York: Dial.

Ford, J. (1996). *A Kente dress for Kenya.* (African-American). New York: Scholastic.

Fox, M. (2001). *Whoever you are.* (Diversity). Orlando, FL: Harcourt.

Friedman, I. (1987). *How my parents learned to eat.* (Asian-American, General). Boston: Houghton Mifflin.

Gonzalez, L. (1994). *The bossy gallito.* (Cuban). New York: Scholastic.

Greenfield, E. (1986). *Honey, I love.* (African-American). New York: HarperCollins.

Greenberg, P. (2002). *Oh Lord, I wish I was a buzzard.* (African-American). San Francisco: Chronicle Books.

Hartfield, C. (2002). *Me and Uncle Romie.* (African-American). New York: Dial.

Havill, J. (1987). *Jamaica's find.* (African-American). Boston: Houghton Mifflin.

Havill, J. (1990). *Jamaica tag-along.* (African-American). Boston: Houghton Mifflin.

Hays, M. (1994). *Jonathan and his Mommy.* (African-American). New York: Little, Brown & Company.

Herron, C. (1997). *Nappy hair.* (African-American). New York: Random House.

Hoffman, M. (1991). *Amazing Grace.* (African-American). New York: Dial.

Hooks, B. (2002). *Homemade love.* (African-American). New York: Hyperion.

Howard, E. (1995). *Aunt Flossie's hats.* (African-American). Boston: Houghton Mifflin.

Hubbell, P. (2003). *Black all around.* (African-American). New York: Lee & Low.

Hurwitz, J. (1993). *New shoes for Silvia.* (Hispanic). New York: William Morrow.

Isadora, R. (1994). *At the crossroads.* (African). New York: William Morrow.

Isadora, R. (1991). *Ben's trumpet.* (African-American). New York: William Morrow.

Johnson, A. (1993). *Do like Kyla.* (African-American). New York: Scholastic.

Joose, B. (1991). *Mama, do you love me?* (Native American/Alaskan). San Francisco: Chronicle Books.

Joose, B. (2001). *Stars in the darkness.* (African-American). San Francisco: Chronicle Books.

Katz, K. (2002). *The colors of us.* (Multicultural). New York: Henry Holt.

Keats, E. (1996). *The snowy day.* (African-American). New York: Viking.

Keats, E. (1976). *Whistle for Willie.* (African-American). New York: Penguin.

Keegan, M. (1999). *Pueblo girls: Growing up in two worlds.* (Multicultural). Santa Fe, NM: Clear Light Publications.

Kerley, B. (2002). *A cool drink of water.* (Multicultural). New York: National Geographic Society.

Kimmelman, L. (1996). *Hooray! It's Passover!* (Jewish-American). New York: HarperCollins.

Kleven, E. (1996). *Hooray, a pinata!* (Hispanic). New York: Penguin.

Krebs, L. (2003). *We all went on safari.* (African). Cambridge, MA: Barefoot Books.

Lawrence, J. (1995). *The great migration: An American story.* (African-American). New York: HarperCollins.

Leighton, M. (1992). *An Ellis Island Christmas.* (Immigration, Diversity). New York: Viking.

Levine, E. (1995). *I hate English.* (Asian-American, General). New York: Scholastic.

Manders, J. (2003). *Senor Don Gato.* (Hispanic). Cambridge, MA: Candlewick Press.

McGill, A. (2000). *In the hollow of your hand: Slave lullabies.* (African-American). Boston: Houghton Mifflin.

Medearis, A. (1995). *Dancing with the Indians.* (Native American). New York: Holiday House.

Miller, J. P. (2000). *We all sing with the same voice.* (Multicultural). New York: HarperCollins.

Mitchell, R. (1997). *The talking cloth.* (African-American). New York: Scholastic.

Moore, S. (2002). *Somewhere today: A book of peace.* (Multicultural, General). New York: Whitman.

Mora, P. (1997). *A birthday basket for Tia.* (Hispanic). New York: Simon & Schuster.

Mora, P. (1994). *Pablo's tree.* (Hispanic). New York: Simon & Schuster.

Morales, Y. (2003). *Just a minute.* (Hispanic). San Francisco: Chronicle Books.

Mosel, A. (1995). *Tikki, Tikki, Tembo.* (Chinese). New York: Holt.

Muth, J. J. (2003). *Stone soup.* (Diversity). New York: Scholastic.

Myers, W. D. (1996). *Harlem.* (African-American). New York: Scholastic.

Noguchi, R. & Jenks, D. (2001). *Flowers from Mariko.* (Japanese). New York: Lee & Low.

Osofsky, A. (1992). *Dreamcatcher.* (Native-American). New York: Scholastic.

Pelligrini, H. (1991). *Families are different.* (Korean, Multicultural). New York: Holiday House.

Pinkney, A. (1993). *Seven candles for Kwanzaa.* (African-American). New York: Dial.

Pinkney, S. (2000). *Shades of Black: A celebration of our children.* (African-American). New York: Scholastic.

Polacco, P. (1995). *Babushka's doll.* (Russian). New York: Simon & Schuster.

Polacco, P. (1998). *Chicken Sunday.* (Multicultural). New York: Penguin.

Polacco, P. (2001). *The keeping quilt.* (Jewish-American). New York: Simon & Schuster.

Pomeranc, M. H. (1998). *The American Wei.* (Diversity, Immigration). New York: Albert Whitman.

Riehicky, J. (1994). *Cinco de Mayo.* (Hispanic). New York: Scholastic.

Ringgold, F. (1992). *Aunt Harriet's underground railroad in the sky.* (African-American). New York: Crown.

Ringgold, F. (1996). *Bonjour, Lonnie.* (African-American). New York: Hyperion.

Ringgold, F. (1999). *Counting to Tar Beach.* (African-American). New York: Random House.

Ringgold, F. (1996). *Dinner at Aunt Connie's House.* (African-American). New York: Hyperion.

Ringgold, F. (1999). *If a bus could talk: The story of Rosa Parks.* (African-American). New York: Simon & Schuster.

Ringgold, F. (1998). *The invisible princess.* (African-American). New York: Crown.

Ringgold, F. (1995). *My dream of Martin Luther King.* (African-American). New York: Crown.

Ringgold, F. (1996). *Tar Beach.* (African-American). New York: Dell.

Robles, A. (2003). *Lakas and the Manilatown fish.* (Filipino). Berkeley, CA: Children's Book Press.

Rosa-Casanova, S. (1997). *Mama Provi and the pot of rice.* (Diversity). New York: Simon & Schuster.

Rosen, M. (1997). *Elijah's angel: A story for Chanukah and Christmas.* (Jewish, General). Orlando, FL: Harcourt.

Say, A. (1996). *El Chino.* (Hispanic). Boston: Houghton Mifflin.

Say, A. (1999). *Tea with milk.* (Asian-American). Boston: Walter Lorraine Books.

Seger, P. (1994). *Abiyoyo.* (African-American). New York: Simon & Schuster.

Simon, N. (2003). *All families are special.* (Multicultural). New York: Whitman.

Simon, N. (1999). *All kinds of children.* (Multicultural). New York: Whitman.

Soto, G. (1998). *Snapshots from a wedding.* (Mexican-American, Hispanic). New York: Penguin.

Soto, G. (1996). *Too many tamales.* (Hispanic). New York: Penguin.

Starr, M. (2001). *Alicia's happy day.* (Hispanic). New York: Bright Books.

Steptoe, J. (1987). *Mufaro's beautiful daughters.* (African). New York: William Morrow.

Stutson, C. (1996). *Prairie primer.* (Americana). New York: Penguin.

Stuve-Bodeen, S. (2003). *Babu's song.* (African). New York: Lee & Low.

Surat, M. (1990). *Angel child, dragon child.* (Vietnamese). New York: Scholastic.

Suyenaga, R. (1993). *Obon.* (Japanese-American). Lebanon, IN: Cirriculum Press.

Swamp, Chief Jake. (1997). *Giving thanks: A Native American good morning message.* (Native American). New York: Lee & Low.

Swartz, L. A. (1994). *A first Passover.* (Jewish-American). New York: Simon & Schuster.

Tarpley, N. A. (2001). *I love my hair.* (African-American). New York: Little, Brown & Co.

Tomioka, C. (1992). *Rise and shine Mariko-Chan.* (Japanese). New York: Scholastic.

Uchida, U. (1996). *The bracelet.* (Asian-American). New York: Penguin.

Udney, J. (1991). *What Mary Jo shared.* (African-American). New York: Scholastic.

Wallace, I. (1984). *Chin Chiang and the dragon's dance.* New York: Simon & Schuster.

Wells, R. (1998). *Yoko.* (Japanese). New York: Hyperion.

Williams, K. (1994). *When Africa was home.* (African-American). New York: Scholastic.

Williams, V. B. (1991). *Cherries and cherry pits.* (African-American). New York: William Morrow & Co.

Willams, V. B. (1996). *More, more more said the baby.* (Diversity). New York: Willam Morrow & Co.

Wood, D. (1996). *Northwoods cradle song from a Menominee lullaby.* (Native American). New York: Simon & Schuster.

Zamarano, A. (1999). *Let's eat.* (Spanish). New York: Scholastic.

Glossary of Key Terms

Abstract—an artistic style in which artists experimented with color and the physical properties of paint.

aesthetic attitude—an openness or spontaneity to objects and experiences.

aesthetic process/experience—active engagement with all the senses.

aesthetic response—an appreciative reaction.

aesthetic value—the result of a positive response from a person or group of people toward something.

aesthetics—a group of concepts for understanding the nature of art.

aggregate—formed when three or more diagrams are united together.

anecdote—a shortened and more focused version of the diary used in child observation.

anti-bias—a belief in equality that condemns prejudice, exclusion, discrimination, or preferential treatment.

anti-bias curriculum—an active or activist approach to challenging prejudice, stereotyping, bias, and the *isms*.

art center—a classroom area where children go to do art.

art critique—teacher facilitates an aesthetic and verbal encounter between children and a work of art.

art dialogue—verbal comments that teachers make to children concerning their art.

art dictation—a strategy that involves listening to what children have to say about their art and then neatly printing their words on the paper.

art files—a sampling or collection of an individual child's art work.

art folders—devices for storing a child's file or collection of art.

art group time—large group time when children come together to show and discuss their artistic accomplishments.

Art Idea Book—a collection of interesting pictures that serve as an inspiration for possible art subject matter.

art kiosk—a self-standing structure with three or more sides which can be used to display art.

art postcards—postcards of art reproductions used in learning games.

art specialists—one who knows about art, artists, artistic elements, and developmentally appropriate art activities.

art standards—a set of art competencies for K-12 students.

art therapy—the psychotherapeutic use of art for emotional understanding and healing.

artistic decision—time during adolescence when natural artistic development ceases unless children are given further instruction.

artistic elements—criteria used to analyze, appreciate, and judge the visual arts. Artistic elements are also the building blocks of art and can be used to talk with children about their art.

arts—literature, drama, music, dance and the visual arts.

assemblage—three-dimensional collage.

assessment—an ongoing process of documenting and recording a child's development, not to be limited to testing or equated with evaluation.

assessor—one who conducts an assessment, usually a teacher or parent. Assessment is an ongoing process of documenting and recording a child's development, not to be limited to testing or equated with evaluation.

asymmetrical (informal)—informal balance in which the objects are unevenly or unequally balanced.

atelierista—Italian for art teacher.

auditory—the sense involving hearing and listening. Auditory also refers to a learning style in which the learner learns best through speaking and listening.

balance—the result of how space is used.

baric—the sense of weight.

beliefs—principles held to be true.

bias—an attitude, belief, or feeling that results in and helps to justify unfair treatment of one's identity.

bitmapping—a system used to display drawn images on the computer screen in a painting program; a system that allows images to be moved on the screen and/or parts of images to be erased.

bodily-kinesthetic—a way of demonstrating one's intelligence through the use and control of one's bodily movements.

brain research—a line of study documenting that early experiences have a decisive impact on the architecture of the brain and on the nature and extent of adult capacities.

central processing unit (CPU)—the heart of the computer.

checklists—an observational strategy in which developmental items are identified and the observer merely indicates or checks off which items are present or absent.

child-centered—an approach to art that is unstructured and gives children much input and many choices as to how and what to make.

chromatic—the sense that allows one to identify, match, and discriminate among colors.

clay—natural substance from the earth that can be molded, sculpted, and fired in a kiln.

closed-ended—a term referring to items or questions that are conducive to conformity.

closed-ended question—a type of question in which there is one right answer.

cognitive—an explanation for artistic development which asserts that the content and style of children's art is indicative of their level of intelligence and function of conceptualization.

cognitive developmental—an explanation for child development that incorporates the best of cognitive and general developmental theories.

collage—artwork composed of different shapes or elements.

color—the visual sensation of light caused by stimulating the cones of the retina.

combine(s)—the result of two diagrams united.

complementary—colors opposite each other on the color wheel.

complimentary approach—an approach that praises children's artwork.

composition—the overall mark of success or the standard of achievement in artistic creation.

concrete operations—Piaget's third stage of cognitive development in which thinking is bound to the concrete and cannot engage in abstract thinking.

constructive play—a type of play involving building with blocks.

constructivism—a view of development based on the belief that children construct or build knowledge based on their actions on objects and their interactions with peers and adults.

constructivist education—a model of schooling based on constructivism.

content—the subject matter of a work of art.

convergent (noncreative) thinking—noncreative thinking based on coming up with the one right answer.

convergent production—coming up with the one right answer.

cool—colors including blue, green, and purple/violet, which symbolize cold or cool objects.

cooperative learning—working together when children practice language and social skills while working toward a common end.

correcting approach—an approach that attempts to correct or improve children's art.

creative movement—a type of movement that encourages children to move as they see fit as opposed to following or imitating a teacher.

creativity—the ability to see things in new ways or combine unrelated things into something new.

critical thinking—thinking that requires making decisions and judgments.

Cubism—an artistic style in which artists attempt to break their subject matter down into its component geometric or architectural shapes.

cultural differences—those qualities and practices that people use to define themselves as a cultural group.

cultural diversity—a term recognizing and accepting the influence of many cultures on society.

cultural elements—language, religion, dress, social customs, and other things that define one's culture.

cultural pluralism—view that groups should be allowed, even encouraged, to hold on to what gives them their unique identity while maintaining membership in the larger society.

culture—the attitudes, values, beliefs, customs, norms, traditions, and social habits shared by a particular group of people.

curriculum—educational program, activity, set of activities, or guidelines.

curriculum development—the process of planning activities for children on the spontaneous, short-term, and long-term basis.

dawning realism—the age during which young adolescents show a greater awareness of details in their art.

design—the overall mark of success or the standard of achievement in artistic creation.

developmentally appropriate—an activity that takes into account a child's developmental abilities, background, and individual interests.

diagrams—shapes drawn as single outline forms.

diary—a journal or ongoing account of what a child says and does.

disability—a loss or reduction of functional ability that results from an impairment.

Discipline-Based Art Education (DBAE)—a comprehensive approach to instruction and learning in art developed primarily for K-12 students.

dispositions—inclinations or habits of the mind.

divergent production—the generation of multiple responses.

diversity—an umbrella term for differences which celebrate individual uniqueness.

dramatic play—a type of play involving fantasy, imagination, or make-believe.

drawing program—a program that uses an object-oriented system to display drawn images on the computer screen; a program in which the entire drawn image must be deleted for editing.

Draw-A-Man test—a nonverbal measure of intelligence based on the drawing of a human figure.

drawing tablet—a computer screen on which the user creates bit-mapped images using a stylus or mouse.

drill and practice software—software that presents the user with an activity or question for which there is only one correct response; if the user does not choose the correct response, the software presents a series of tasks that will teach the user the correct response.

elaboration—a term characterizing thinking that is detailed.

emergent curriculum—activities that spontaneously emerge or arise as a result of children's ongoing interest in an exploration of their world.

emotional—an explanation for the development of child art that stresses that the content and style of children's art is indicative of their emotional makeup, personality, temperament, and affective state.

evaluation—the process of collecting data to make judgments that help determine whether one has successfully met one's goals and objectives.

event sampling—an observational strategy in which the observer specifies the behaviors under study and then notes when it occurs.

Expressionism—an artistic style based on an expression of the artist's emotions and feelings.

expressive arts—art, music, and movement.

Fauvism—an offshoot of Expressionism. Fauvists experimented with pure, bright colors in daring and innovative ways to express emotions.

feelings—emotions associated with a learning experience.

field trips—opportunities for children to use all their senses and gain concrete experience with people, events, and places in their local community.

flexibility—a term characterizing thinking that generates different ideas that cross categories or break boundaries.

fluency—a term characterizing thinking that generates many ideas and solutions.

Glossary of Key Terms **383**

folk arts—the expressions of members of a cultural group that are produced by individuals for the use of their group members and are made by hand rather than mass produced.

formal operations—Piaget's fourth stage of child development during which adolescents engage in abstract thinking.

formalized standardized testing—paper and pencil assessment with individual scores compared to a norm.

framing—providing a frame to "finish" a work of art.

full inclusion—an approach in which children with disabilities are placed in the same programs or classrooms and receive individualized and appropriate services alongside their nondisabled peers.

games—a type of rule-based play engaged in by older children.

general developmental—a global explanation for the development of child art that incorporates social, cultural, personality, and environmental factors as well as elements of other explanations.

gifted/gifted and talented—children of high intelligence who also demonstrate high creativity receive this label.

goal—something to strive for; a long-term aspiration.

group projects—educational activities based on children's common interests in which they can interact, support, assist, and learn from each other.

gustatory—the sense of taste.

handicap—the disadvantage caused by a disability.

holistic model of child development—a model of child development which integrates the physical, social, emotional, cognitive, and creative aspects.

hue—the name of a color.

impairment—an anatomic or functional abnormality or loss that may or may not result in a disability.

implementing—the process of carrying out an idea or putting a plan into action.

Impressionism—an artistic style in which artists painted what they perceived rather than what they knew to be there.

independence/independent—a cultural style in which individuality is valued.

individual differences—background, family, and individual variation.

ink—an opaque liquid medium usually in black with other colors available.

intellectual mediators—adults who are readily available to facilitate a child's learning.

intensity—the purity of light, e.g., bright or dull, reflected from a surface.

interdependence/interdependent—a cultural style in which family togetherness and group belongings are valued.

intermediate—the result of mixing an adjoining primary and secondary color in equal amounts.

interpersonal—intelligence is demonstrated through personal interactions with others.

intrapersonal—intelligence is demonstrated through knowing oneself.

intrinsic motivation—doing something for the sheer pleasure in doing it and in the absence of some extraneous reward.

judgmental approach—an approach that judges children's art.

kinesthetic—the sense involving a whole-body, sensory-motor muscular response.

Kinetic art—an attempt to incorporate physical movement into art by using movable parts.

knowledge—information children construct through hands-on, multisensory experiences and exploration.

lateral thinking—a way of using one's mind or mental processes that leads to creative thinking or products.

least restrictive environment—a setting that is appropriate for the child and provides the most contact possible with nondisabled children.

left hemisphere—the hemisphere of the brain housing the thinking abilities traditionally associated with school, e.g., reading, writing, and math.

line—visible mark made by an artistic tool.

literacy—knowing how to read and write.

logical-mathematical—being good at math, logical and abstract thinking, and problem solving characterizes this intelligence.

logical-mathematical knowledge—information that is constructed around the relationship of objects to each other.

mainstreaming—the placement of children with disabilities in programs having a majority of children who are not disabled.

mandala—a basic diagram and universal symbol consisting of a cross within a circle.

mandaloids—figures and objects drawn using mandalas.

mark making—a term referring to the variety of artistic marks that young children make using crayons, markers, chalk, pencils, etc.

masks—decorated items worn over or held in front of the face to hide or disguise one's identity.

mass—refers to a solid, three-dimensional body that has height, length, and width.

matting—providing an attractive border for a piece of art.

media literacy—competence in reading, analyzing, evaluating, and producing communications in a variety of media including electronic.

mixing media—combining or using more than one medium when making art.

mobile—hanging sculpture that moves.

model—an older, wiser person from whom a less experienced person learns by watching and imitating.

modes of creative expression—ways of expressing one's creativity including play, language, music, and movement.

motive—the underlying reason or purpose.

multicultural arts and crafts—providing children with activities that attempt to authentically capture the arts and crafts representing a particular culture.

multiple intelligences—a construct reflecting the belief that intelligence is not a single concept but that there are many ways of demonstrating one's intelligence. Gardner has identified eight multiple intelligences to date.

multimedia authoring tools—software used to create interactive multimedia presentations that can include text, graphics, video, audio, and animation.

multiple literacies—many ways of being considered literate and competent.

multisensory experience—an activity or experience involving many of the senses.

musical-rhythmic—demonstrating one's intelligence through singing, dancing, and making music.

narratives—a record of what an observer sees children do and hears them say.

National Standards for the Arts—the standards that address competence in the arts, in addition to providing a firm foundation for connecting arts-related concepts and facts across all art forms as well as across disciplines such as the sciences and humanities.

naturalism—a term that emphasizes the artist's attempt to make art objective and like the actual object.

naturalistic—an understanding of nature and natural phenomena characterizes this intelligence.

negative space—the space left between or surrounding subject matter, symbols, or shapes.

neutral—pigments including black and white which do not have a particular color.

Nonobjective art—abstract art pushed to the limits with no resemblance to the actual object.

non-Western art—art from non-European cultures.

objectives—the short-term bridge between long-term goals and activities.

observer—one who skillfully and unobtrusively watches children to learn more about them.

olfactory—the sense of smell.

Op art (Optical art)—an artistic style in which artists created "psychedelic" art by playing with the effects of black and white, color, figure-ground relations, and depth.

open-ended—a term referring to items or questions that are conducive to creative expression.

open-ended question—a type of question in which there is no one right answer.

open-ended software—software that allows the user to create and respond to open-ended challenges, enhancing knowledge construction.

originality—a term characterizing thinking that is unique and unusual.

painting—the process of applying paint to a surface using a hand, brush, or other tool.

painting programs—uses a bitmapping system to display images on the computer screen; lines and shapes may be edited in part or in total with an eraser tool.

papier-mâché—process of building up layers of paper that has been torn, wadded, and molded to make a three-dimensional form.

participator—one who partakes or becomes involved in the activities of another.

pattern—a mark or design that is repeated in some recurring sequence.

perception—the ability to receive sensory impressions from one's surroundings and relate them to what one knows.

perceptual—an explanation for the development of child art that stresses that the content and style of children's art reflects what they perceive rather than what they see.

physical—an explanation for the development of child art which stresses that the content, process, product, and style of children's art are indicative of their limited physical development.

physical knowledge—information about the physical properties of objects.

physical play—a type of play involving motor activity and movement.

pictorial art—the beginnings of an artistic stage in which objects drawn or painted become visually recognizable to adults.

pictorial stage—when children create objects that adults can recognize.

PIE—the cycle of curriculum development including planning, implementation, and evaluation.

planning—the proactive process of determining what and how to teach.

play—the "work" of children which is pleasurable and process-oriented.

play dough—a soft clay-type molding medium that is commercially available or can be made with common cooking ingredients.

play with natural materials—play involving water, sand, or wood.

Pointillism—an artistic style in which artists painted using small dots or points of color.

Pop art (Popular art)—an artistic style in which artists chose subject matter that was part of everyday life.

portfolio—a comprehensive collection of a child's work including samples and observational data.

positive space—the space taken up with lines, colors, shapes, and forms.

pre-operational stage—Piaget's second stage of child development during which the child attains representation and thinks in ways that are qualitatively different from adult logic or reason.

primary—red, blue, and yellow; the colors used to produce the other colors.

prints—the artistic process of making a print in which paint is applied to an object and then pressed onto paper. When the object is lifted a print results.

private speech—internalized self-talk that helps with self-guidance and self-direction in Vygotsky's sociocultural theory.

probing approach—an approach that attempts to draw from children information about their art.

process—the act of doing or being involved in an activity.

process vs. product—a comparison of the relative values of the acts associated with artistic creation and the finished products of artistic creation.

processing—discovering the physical properties of art materials and tools.

product—the tangible or finished result of processing.

Project Approach—a curriculum approach in which children are actively involved in developing long-term research-type activities into areas of personal interest.

Project Zero—Gardner's approach to art education in the early years.

pseudo-naturalistic—the stage when the art of young adolescents becomes realistic.

puppets—often three-dimensional props representing people, animals, or objects.

questioning approach—an approach that questions children about their art.

rating scales—an observational strategy in which developmental items are identified and the observer makes a judgment regarding the degree to which the item is observed in the child.

Realism—a term that emphasizes the artist's attempt to make art objective and like the actual object.

recorder—one who writes down their observations of children.

Reggio Emilia—schools found in Italy with a distinct and creative curriculum.

resist—a type of art activity in which a dried design or picture will resist a second liquid put on top of it.

right hemisphere—the hemisphere of the brain specializing in creative ways of processing information.

scaffolding—a strategy for a teacher working within a child's zone of proximal development to offer the appropriate level of support, assistance, questioning, or challenge.

schematic—the third stage according to Lowenfeld and Brittain when school-aged children achieve a form concept.

scribbles—random marks made on paper by a young child using some type of writing instrument that leaves a mark when pressure is applied. In Kellogg's stages of artistic development there are some 20 basic scribble patterns that comprise the first stage.

secondary—result of mixing two primary colors in equal amounts.

self talk—talking aloud, which Vygotsky sees as connected to what children are thinking.

sensory literacy—using all the senses to become aware of one's surroundings and experiences.

sensory motor stage—Piaget's first stage of child development during which infant thinking is limited to sensory impressions and motoric behavior.

sensory table—a large container filled with sensory-rich objects for children to explore.

sewing—an art process that uses needle, thread, or yarn.

shade—the result of adding black to any color (refers to the outside form of an object).

shape—refers to the outside form of a two-dimensional object that has length and width.

simulation software—software that allows the user to experience a computer-based model of a real-life situation.

skills—abilities or techniques that build on and apply knowledge.

social-conventional knowledge—information about daily living accepted by society.

sociocultural theory—Vygotsky's theory based on the beliefs that learning can lead development and that language plays a major role in cognitive development.

sociodramatic play—an advanced form of dramatic play that revolves around a theme with children engaging in theme-based behaviors.

software—educational programs that are run on the computer.

space—the total area defined by the size of the artist's paper or canvas.

special needs—children who are different in one or more of the areas of visual, auditory, physical, emotional, and/or cognitive functioning.

stabile—self-standing, stationary mobile.

standardized achievement testing—the use of tests that compare children's scores and thereby are a formal, less authentic way to assess what children know and can do.

sterognostic—the sense that allows one to recognize objects through tactile-muscular exploration without the aid of vision.

story songs—stories and books based on songs with a strong rhythmic component.

Structure of the Intellect—a construct viewing the intellect as consisting of three dimensions: contents, products, and operations.

studio-oriented—an approach that holds that young children should be left free to experiment with creative materials.

sun figures—human figures drawn using lines and circles.

Surrealism—or Dadaism, is an artistic style in which artists attempt to create a dreamlike world that is more intense than reality.

symmetrical (formal)—balance in which the shapes are evenly or equally balanced around some point.

tactile—the sense involving feeling and touch.

tactile-kinesthetic—a learning style in which learners use their hands and bodies to process and understand.

teachable moments—unplanned events that trigger high-interest activity and learning.

teacher-directed—an approach to art in which projects are structured and specific directions are given to ensure a recognizable product.

teacher-guided—a compromise between a teacher-directed and child-centered approach to art.

teaching style—way of teaching that is influenced by individual learning styles.

texture—the surface quality of a work of art; how it feels.

theories of artistic development—explanations for what, why, and how children create.

thermal qualities—use of certain colors conveys a sense of warmth, coolness, or the illusion of size and space.

thermic—the sense of temperature.

three-dimensional art—art with height, width, and depth.

time sampling—an observation strategy used to measure the frequency of behavior with a given period of time.

tint—the result of adding white to any color.

tokonoma—a type of aesthetic display found in traditional Japanese homes and inns.

tourist curriculum—multicultural experiences that are limited to a celebration of holidays.

troubleshooter—a role in which teachers provide encouragement and assistance to children who are artistically or creatively blocked.

types of knowledge—according to Piaget, there are three different types of knowledge: physical, social-conventional, and logical-mathematical.

types of learning—knowledge, skills, dispositions, and feelings.

_U_-shaped curve—a graphic representation of Gardner's belief that some important aspects of artistry emerge early in a child's life only to go underground during a period of middle childhood.

value—the relative lightness or darkness of a hue.

values—things that are important, valuable, worthwhile, or significant to an individual.

valuing approach—an approach that offers children value-laden comments.

verbal-linguistic—being skilled in using words defines this intelligence.

vertical thinking—learning more about something or arriving at a conventional, accepted, convergent answer.

visual—the sense involving looking and seeing. Visual also refers to a learning style in which children learn best using pictures and visual images.

visual literacy—the ability to understand and produce visual messages.

visual-spatial—the use of pictures, e.g., art and maps, characterizes this intelligence.

volume—a term that refers to a solid, three-dimensional body that has height, length, and width.

warm—colors including red, yellow, and orange that symbolize hot or warm objects.

watercolors—transparent color that comes in cake or liquid form.

weaving—a fabric art that involves a patterned in-out or over-under motion which is repeated in the alternating out-in or under-over pattern.

zone of proximal development (ZPD)—a range of skills, tasks, or abilities that a child cannot yet do alone but can accomplish with assistance from an adult or skilled peer.

References

Adams, A. (1976). *Easter egg artists.* New York: Charles Scribner's Sons.

Alexander, J. (1995, June 11). We need arts in our schools' lives, says NEA chief. *San Jose Mercury News,* A-9.

Alkema, C. J. (1971). *Art for the exceptional.* Boulder, CO: Pruett Publishing.

Alkema, C. J. (1974). *The complete crayon book.* New York: Sterling Publishing.

Alkema, C. J. (1976). *Alkema's scrap magic.* New York: Sterling Publishing.

Allen, K. E., & Cowdery, G. E. (2005). *The exceptional child: Inclusion in early childhood education* (5th ed.). Clifton Park, NY: Thomson Delmar Learning.

Alliance for Childhood. (2000). *Fool's gold: A critical look at computers in childhood.* College Park, MD: Alliance for Childhood.

Althouse, R., Johnson, M. H., & Mitchell, S. T. (2003). *The colors of learning: Integrating the visual arts into the early childhood curriculum.* New York: Teachers College Press.

Ancona, G. (1994). *The pinata maker.* San Diego, CA: Harcourt Brace.

Anderson, G. T. (2000). *An emperical comparison of the proportion of cooperative play of 4-year-old preschool children observed as they interact in four centers: Block, computer, housekeeping, and manipulative.* Alanta, GA: National Association for the Education of Young Children.

Anderson, R., Manoogian, S. T., & Reznick, J. S. (1976). The undermining and enhancing of intrinsic motivation in preschool children. *Journal of Personality and Social Psychology, 34,* 915–922.

Arnheim, R. (1973). Child art and visual thinking. In H. P. Lewis (Ed.), *Child art: The beginnings of self-affirmation* (pp. 46-72). Berkeley, CA: Diablo Press.

Ashley, B. (1992). *Cleversticks.* New York: Crown.

Balke, E. (1997). Play and the arts: The importance of the "unimportant." *Childhood Education, 73,* 355–360.

Backstein, K. (1992). *The blind men and the elephant.* New York: Scholastic.

Bang, M. (1981). *Tye May and the magic brush.* New York: Greenwillow Books.

Bang, M. (1999). *When Sophie gets angry—Really, really angry.* New York: Scholastic.

Bang, M. (1993). *Yellow ball.* New York: Penguin.

Baylor, B. (1987). *When clay sings.* New York: Atheneum/ Simon & Schuster.

Berk, L. E. (1994). Vygotsky's theory: The importance of make-believe. *Young Children,* 30–39.

Berk, L. E. (1996). *Infants, children and adolescents* (2nd ed.). Boston: Allyn & Bacon.

Berk, L. E., & Winsler, A. (1995). *Scaffolding children's learning: Vygotsky and early childhood education.* Washington, DC: NAEYC.

Blackensee, L. V. (1999). Technology tools for young learners. Larchmont, NV: Eye on Education, Inc.

Bland, J. C. (1968). *Art of the young child.* New York: Museum of Modern Art.

Blizzard, G. S. (1991). *Come look with me, enjoying art with children.* Charlottesville, VA: Thomasson-Grant.

Bodrova, E., & Leong, D. J. (1996). *Tools of the mind: The Vygotskian approach to early childhood education.* Columbus, OH: Merrill.

Bos, B. (1978). *Don't move the muffin tins: A hands-off guide to art for the young child.* Roseville, CA: Turn the Page Press.

Boutan, M. (Ed.). (1996). *Art activity packs: Matisse.* San Francisco: Chronicle Books.

Brandenberg, A. (1962). *My five senses.* New York: Thomas Y. Crowell.

Brandenberg, F. (1977). *What can you make of it?* New York: Greenwillow.

Bredekamp, S. (Ed.). (1987). *Developmentally appropriate practice in early childhood programs serving children from birth through age eight.* Washington, DC: National Association for the Education of Young Children.

Bredekamp, S. (1993). Reflections on Reggio Emilia. *Young Children, 49,* 13–17.

Bredekamp, S., & Copple, C. (1997). *Developmentally appropriate practice in early childhood programs* (rev. ed.). Washington, DC: NAEYC.

Brenner, B. (1970). *Faces.* New York: Dutton.

Brill, M. (1998). *Tooth tales from around the world.* Watertown, MA: Charlesbridge.

Brittain, W. L. (1969). Some exploratory studies of the art of preschool children. *Studies in Art Education, 10,* 14–24.

Brittain, W. L. (1979). *Creativity, art, and the young child.* New York: Macmillan.

Brookes, M. (1986). *Drawing with children.* Los Angeles: J. P. Tarcher.

Brown, M. & Brown, L.K. (1985). *The bionic bunny show.* New York: Little, Brown & Company.

Brown, T. (2005). *Someone special, just like you.* New York: Holt.

Brusca, M. (1991). *On the Pampas.* New York: Holt.

Bryan, A. (1995). *What a wonderful world.* New York: Atheneum

Bunnett, R. (1996). *Friends at school.* New York: Star Bright Books.

Bunting, E. (1998). *How many days to America: A Thanksgiving story.* New York: Clarion.

Burningham, J. (2003). *Colors.* Cambridge, MA: Candlewick.

Burns, M. (1995). *The greedy triangle.* New York: Scholastic.

Buton, L., & Kuroda, K. (1981). *Artsplay.* Reading, MA: Addison-Wesley.

Cabrera, J. (2000). *Over in the meadow.* New York: Holiday House.

Carle, E. (1973). *I see a song.* New York: Thomas Y. Crowell.

Carle, E. (2001). *Hello, red fox.* New York: Simon & Schuster.

Chaille, C., & Britain, L. (2003). *The young child as scientist.* Boston: Allyn & Bacon.

Chapman, L. H. (1978). *Approaches to art in education.* New York: Harcourt Brace Jovanovich.

Chard, S. C. (1997). *The project approach: Making curriculum come alive and managing successful projects.* New York: Scholastic.

Chase, A. E. (1962). *Famous paintings: An introduction to art.* New York: Platt & Monk.

Chenfeld, M. B. (1983). *Creative activities for young children.* New York: Harcourt Brace Jovanovich.

Chernoff, G. T. (1974). *Clay-dough play-dough.* New York: Scholastic Book Services.

Cherry, C. (1990). *Creative art for the developing child* (2nd ed.). Belmont, CA: Fearon.

Cherry, C. & Nielsen, D. M. (Ed.). (1999). *Creative art for the developing child.* New York: McGraw-Hill.

Chocolate, D. M. N. (1996). *A very special Kwanzaa.* New York: Scholastic.

Chocolate, D. M. N. (1997). *Kente colors.* New York: Walker.

Clemens, S. G. (1991). Art in the classroom: Making every day special. *Young Children, 46,* 4–11.

Clements, D. H. (1994). The uniqueness of the computer as a learning tool: Insights from research and practice. In J. L. Wright and D. D. Shade (Eds.). *Young children: Active learners in a technological age.* Washington, DC: National Association for the Education of Young Children.

Clements, D. H., & Nastasi, B. K. (1995). Computers and early childhood education. In M. Gettinger, S. N. Elliott, & T. R. Kratochwill (Eds.), *Advances in School Psychology: Preschool and Early Childhood Treatment Directions* (187–246). Hillsdale, NJ: Lawrence Erlbaum Associates.

Clements, D. H., & Sarama, J. (1998). Building blocks: Foundations for mathematical thinking, pre-kindergarten to Grade 2: Researched based materials development. National Science Foundation, grant number ESI-9730804. Available at http://www.gse.buffalo.edu/org/buildingblocks/. Buffalo, NY: State University of New York at Buffalo.

Clements, D. H., & Sarama, J. (2002). The role of technology in early childhood learning. *Teaching Children Mathematics, 8*(16), 340–343.

Cohen, M. (1980). *No good in art.* New York: Greenwillow.

Colbert, C., & Taunton, M. (1992). *Developmentally appropriate practices for the visual arts education of young children.* (NAEA Briefing Paper). Reston, VA: National Arts Education Association.

Cole, E., & Schaefer, C. (1990). Can young children be art critics? *Young Children, 45,* 33–38.

Coles, R. (1992). *Their eyes meeting the world: The drawings and paintings of children.* Boston: Houghton Mifflin.

Consortium of National Arts Education Associations. (1994). National standards for arts education. Dance, music, theatre, visual arts: What every young American should know and be able to do in the arts. Music Educators National Conference, Reston, VA.

Cook, R. E., & Armbruster, V. B. (1983). *Adapting early childhood curriculum.* St. Louis, MO: Mosby.

Cooper, E. (1997). *Country fair.* New York: Greenwillow.

Cowen-Fletcher, J. (1994). *It takes a village.* New York: Scholastic.

Crews, D. (1978). *Freight train.* New York: Greenwillow.

Crews, D. (1982). *Carousel.* New York: Greenwillow.

Crews, D. (1991). *Bigmama's.* New York: Greenwillow.

Cromwell, E. S. (2000). *Nurturing readiness in early childhood education: A whole-child curriculum for ages 2-5.* Boston: Allyn & Bacon.

Csikszentmihalyi, M. (1997, September/October). Happiness and creativity. *The Futurist.*

Cumming, R. (1979). *Just look . . . A book about paintings.* New York: Charles Scribner's Sons.

Davis, M. D., Kilgo, J. L., & Gamel-McCormick, M. (1998). *Young children with special needs: A developmentally appropriate approach.* Boston: Allyn & Bacon.

Davol, M. W. (1997). *The paper dragon.* New York: Atheneum.

Day, M. D. (1985). Evaluating student achievement indiscipline-based art programs. *Studies in Art Education, 26,* 232–240.

Day, M. D. (1999). Markers of multicultural/antibias education. *Young Children, 54,* 43–57.

Debelak, M., Herr, J., & Jacobson, M. (1981). *Creating innovative classroom materials for teaching young children.* New York: Harcourt Brace Jovanovich.

DeBono, E. (1970). *Lateral thinking: A textbook of creativity.* London: Ward Lock Educational.

Dennis, W. (1966). *Group values through children's drawings.* New York: Wiley.

de Paola, T. and Lear E. (1991). *Bonjour, Mr. Satie.* New York: Putnam.

dePaola, T. (1991). *The legend of the Indian paintbrush.* New York: Penguin.

Derman-Sparks, L. (1989). Anti-bias curriculum challenges diversity. *School Safety, 3,* 10–3.

Derman-Sparks, L., & ABC Task Force. (1989). *Anti-bias curriculum: Tools for empowering young children.* Washington, DC: NAEYC.

Derman-Sparks, L., Gutierrez, M., & Phillips, C. B. (n.d.). *Teaching young children to resist bias: What parents can do.* Washington, DC: NAEYC.

DeRolf, S. (1997). *The crayon box that talked.* New York: Random House.

Dever, M. W., & Jared, E. J. (1996). Remember to include art and crafts in your integrated curriculum. *Young Children, 51,* 69–73.

DeVries, R., & Zan, B. (1995). Creating a constructivist classroom atmosphere. *Young Children, 51,* 4–14.

Dewey, J. (1958). *Art as experience.* New York: Capricorn Books.

Diakite, B. W. (1997). *The hunterman and the crocodile: A West African folktale.* New York: Scholastic.

Dighe, J., Calormiri, Z., & Van Zutpen, C. (1998). Nurturing the language of art in children. *Young Children, 53,* 4–9.

DiLeo, J. H. (1970). *Young children and their drawings.* New York: Brunner/Mazel.

DiLeo, J. H. (1973). *Children's drawings as diagnostic aids.* New York: Brunner/Mazel.

Dimondstein, G. (1974). *Exploring the arts of children.* New York: Macmillan.

Dixon, A. (1990). *Clay.* New York: Garnett Educational Company.

Dobbs, S. M. (1998). *Learning in and through art.* Los Angeles: Getty Education Institute for the Arts.

Dodge, D. T., & Colker, L. J. (1996). *The creative curriculum for early childhood.* Washington, DC: Teaching Strategies.

Dorros, A. (1991). *Abuela.* New York: Puffin.

Dorros, A. (1991). *Tonight is carnival.* New York: Puffin.

Dorros, A. (1995). *Isla.* New York: Puffin.

Duke, L. L. (1993). Foreword. In L. Duke (Ed.), *Discipline-based art education and cultural diversity* (pp. i–iii). Santa Monica, CA: Getty Center for Education in the Arts.

Dunn-Snow, P., & D'Amelio, G. (2000). How art teachers can enhance artmaking as a therapeutic experience: Art therapy and art education. *Art Education, 53,* 46–53.

Dyson, A. H. (1982). The emergence of visible language: Interrelationships between drawing and early writing. *Visible Language, 6,* 360–381.

Dyson, A. H. (1985). Puzzles, paints, and pencils: Writing emerges. *Educational Horizons, 64,* 13–16.

Dyson, A. H. (1986). Transitions and tensions: Interrelationships between the drawing, talking, and dictating of young children. *Research in the Teaching of English, 20,* 379–409.

Dyson, A. H. (1988). Appreciate the drawing and dictating of young children. *Young Children, 43,* 25–32.

Dyson, A. H. (1989). *Multiple worlds of child writers: Friends learning to write.* New York: Teachers College Press.

Dyson, A. H. (1990). Symbol makers, symbol weavers: How children link play, pictures, and print. *Young Children, 45,* 50–57.

Early Childhood Music Summit. (2000). *Start the music.* Reston, VA: National Association for Music Education.

Eaton, M. M. (1998). *Basic issues in aesthetics.* Belmont, CA: Wadsworth.

Eberle, R. F. (1971). *Scamper: Games for imagination development.* Buffalo, NY: D.O.K. Publishers.

Edwards, B. (1979). *Drawing on the right side of the brain.* Los Angeles: J. P. Tarcher.

Edwards, C., Gandini, L., & Forman, G. (1993). *The hundred languages of children: The Reggio Emilia approach to early childhood education.* Norwood, NJ: Albex.

Edwards, C. P., & Springate, K. W. (1995). *Encouraging creativity in early childhood classrooms.* Urbana, IL: ERIC Clearinghouse on Elementary and Early Childhood Education.

Edwards, L. C. (2002). *The creative arts: A process approach for teachers and children.* Columbus, OH: Merrill.

Edwards, L. C., & Nabors, M. L. (1993). The creative artsprocess: What it is and what it is not. *Young Children,* 77–81.

Eisner, E. W. (1976). What we know about children's art—and what we need to know. In E. W. Eisner (Ed.), *The arts, human development, and education* (pp. 5–18). Berkeley, CA: McCutchan.

Eisner, E. W. (1982). *Cognition and curriculum—A basis for deciding what to teach.* New York: Longman.

Elkind, D. (2003). Thanks for the memory: The lasting value of true play. *Young Children, 58,* 46–50.

Elkind, D. (1996). Young children and technology: A cautionary note. *Young Children, 51,* 22–23.

Emberley, E. (1961). *Wing on a flea: A book about shapes.* Boston: Little, Brown.

Emberley, E. (1968). *Green says go.* Boston: Little, Brown.

Emberley, E. (1972). *Ed Emberley's drawing book: Make a world.* Boston: Little, Brown.

Emberley, E. (1973). *Drawing book of animals.* Boston: Little, Brown.

Emberley, E. (1975). *Ed Emberley's drawing book of faces.* Boston: Little, Brown.

Emberley, E. (1977). *Ed Emberley's great thumbprint drawing book.* Boston: Little, Brown.

Emberley, E. (1979). *Ed Emberley's big green drawing book.* Boston: Little, Brown.

Emberley, E. (1980). *Ed Emberley's big orange drawing book.* Boston: Little, Brown.

Emberley, E. (1981). *Ed Emberley's big purple drawing book.* Boston: Little, Brown.

Emberley, E. (1984). *Ed Emberley's picture pie: A book of circle art.* Boston: Little, Brown.

Emberley, E. (1989). *Ed Emberley's Christmas drawing book.* Boston: Little, Brown.

Emberley, E. (1991). *Ed Emberley's drawing book: Make a world.* Boston: Little, Brown.

Engel, B. S. (1995). *Considering children's art: Why and how to value their works.* Washington, DC: NAEYC.

Engel, B. S. (1996). Learning to look: Appreciating child art. *Young Children, 51,* 74–79.

Engel, D. (1989). *The little lump of clay.* New York: Morrow Jr. Books.

Epstein, A. S. (2001). Thinking about art: Encouraging art appreciation in early childhood settings. *Young Children, 56,* 38–43.

Erikson, E. H. (1963). *Childhood and society.* New York: Norton.

Fassler, J. (1991). *Howie helps himself.* New York: Albert Whitman.

Fazio, B. (1996). *Grandfather's story.* Seattle, WA: Sasquatch Books.

Feeney, S., & Moravcik, E. (1987). A thing of beauty: Aesthetic development in young children. *Young Children, 42,* 7–15.

Fiarotta, P., & Fiarotta, N. (1974). *Sticks and stones and ice cream cones.* New York: Workman Publishing Company.

Fisher, E. F. (1978). *Aesthetic awareness and the child.* Itasca, IL: F. E. Peacock.

Fisher, L. E. (1984). *Boxes! Boxes!* New York: Viking.

Florian, D. (1991). *A potter.* New York: Greenwillow.

Flux, P. (2002). *Henri Matisse.* Portsmouth, NH: Heinemann.

Fowler, V. (1982). *Paperworks.* Englewood Cliffs, NJ: Prentice-Hall.

Fox, M. (1997). *The straight line wonder.* New York: Mondo Publishing.

Fox, M. (1997). *Whoever you are.* San Diego, CA: Harcourt Brace.

Frank, M. (1976). *I can make a rainbow.* Nashville, TN: Incentive Publications.

Freeman, D. (1976). *Chalk box story.* New York: Lippincott.

Freeman, D. (1978). *Bearymore.* New York: Penguin Putnam.

Friskey, M. (1973). *What is the color of the wide, wide, world?* Chicago: Children's Press.

Furrer, P. J. (1982). *Art therapy activities and lesson plans for individuals and groups.* Springfield, IL: Charles C. Thomas.

Galin, D. (1976). Educating both halves of the brain. *Childhood Education, 53,* 17–20.

Galinsky, E. (1997). New research on the brain development of young children: Implications for families, early education and care. *CAEYC Connections,* 117–18.

Gandini, L. (1993). Fundamentals of the Reggio Emilia approach to early childhood education. *Young Children, 49,* 4–8.

Gardner, H. (1970). Children's sensitivity to painting styles. *Child Development, 41,* 813–821.

Gardner, H. (1973). *The arts and human development.* New York: Wiley.

Gardner, H. (1980). *Artful scribbles: The significance of children's drawings.* New York: Basic Books.

Gardner, H. (1990). *Art education and human development.* Los Angeles: Getty Center for Education in the Arts.

Gardner, H. (1991). *The unschooled mind.* New York: Basic Books.

Gardner, H. (1993). *Frames of mind* (10th ed.). New York: Basic Books.

Gardner, H. (1993a). *Creating minds.* New York: Basic Books.

Gardner, H. (1993b). *Multiple intelligences: The theory in practice.* New York: Basic Books.

Gardner, H. (1998). Are there additional intelligences? The case for naturalist, Spiritual, and existential intelligences. In Kane, J. (Ed.), *Education, information, and transformation.*

Gardner, H. (1999). *Intelligence reframed: Multiple intelligences for the 21st century.* New York: Basic Books.

Gardner, H., & Winner, E. (1976). How children learn . . . three stages of understanding art. *Psychology Today, 9,* 42–43.

Gargiulo, R., & Kilgo, J. L. (2005). *Young children with special needs: An introduction to early childhood special education.* (2nd ed.) Clifton Park, NY: Thomson Delmar Learning.

Garvey, C. (1990). *Play.* Enlarged edition. Cambridge, MA: Harvard University Press.

Genishi, C. (1993, October). Art, portfolios, and assessment. *Scholastic Early Childhood Today,* 67.

Gerstein, M. (2004). *The man who walked between the towers.* New York: Roaring Brook Press.

Getty Center for Education in the Arts. (1985, April). *Beyond creating: The place for art in America's schools.* A report by the Getty Center for Education in the Arts. Santa Monica, CA.

Getty Center for Education in the Arts. (1989). *Education in art: Future building.* Proceedings of a National Invitational Conference. Los Angeles.

Getz, D. (1997). *Floating home.* New York: Holt.

Getzels, J., & Jackson, P. (1962). *Creativity and intelligence.* New York: Wiley.

Ginsburg, M. (1997). *Clay boy.* New York: Greenwillow.

Golomb, C. (1974). *Young children's sculpture and drawing—a study in representative development.* Cambridge, MA: Harvard University Press.

Gonzalez-Mena, J. (1993). *The child in the family and community.* Columbus, OH: Merrill.

Gonzalez-Mena, J. (1998). *Foundations: Early childhood education in a diverse society.* Mountain View, CA: Mayfield.

Gonzalez-Mena, J. (2001). *Multicultural issues in child care.* Mountain View, CA: Mayfield.

Goodenough, F. L. (1975). *Measurement of intelligence by drawings.* New York: Arno Press.

Goodhart, P. (1997). *Row, row, row your boat.* New York: Crown.

Goodman, R. F., & Fahnestock, A. H. (2002). *The day our world changed: Children's art of 9/11.* New York: Harry N. Abrams.

Goodnow, J. (1977). *Children drawing.* Cambridge, MA: Harvard University Press.

Greenburg, P. (1999). Listening to children talk while they draw. *Young Children, 54,* 13.

Greene, R. G. (1997). *When a line bends . . . a shape begins.* Boston, MA: Houghton Mifflin.

Grifalconi, A. (1986). *The village of round and square houses.* New York: Little Brown & Company.

Grifalconi, A. (1993). *Kinda' blue.* New York: Little, Brown & Company.

Grover, M. (1996). *Circles and squares everywhere!* Orlando, FL: Harcourt.

Guilford, J. P. (1977). *Way beyond the IQ.* Buffalo, NY: Creative Education Foundation.

Hall, N. S. (1999). *Creative resources for the anti-bias classroom.* Clifton Park, NY: Thomson Delmar Learning.

Hardiman, G. W., & Zernich, T. (1981). *Art activities for children.* Englewood Cliffs, NJ: Prentice-Hall.

Harris, D. B. (1963). *Children's drawings as measures of intellectual maturity.* New York: Harcourt, Brace.

Hartley, R. E., Frank, L. K., & Goldenson, R. M. (1952). *Understanding children's play.* New York: Columbia University Press.

Haskell, L. L. (1979). *Art in the early childhood years.* Columbus, OH: Charles E. Merrill.

Haugland, S. W. (1992). Effects of computer software on preschool children's developmental gains. *Journal of Computing in Early Childhood, 3,* 15–30.

Haugland, S. W. (1999). What role should technology play in young children's learning? Part 1. *Young Children,* 26–31.

Haugland, S. W. (2000). What role should technology play in young children's learning? Part 2—early childhood classrooms in the 21st century: Using computers to maximize learning. *Young Children, 55,* 12–18.

Haugland, S. W., & Shade, D. D. (1994). Software evaluation for young children. In J. Wright & D. D. Shade (Eds.), *Young children: Active learners in a technological age* (pp. 63–76). Washington, DC: NAEYC.

Haugland, S. W., & Wright, J. L. (1997). *Young children and technology: A world of discovery.* Boston: Allyn & Bacon.

Hawkinson, J. (1974). *A ball of clay.* Chicago: Whitman.

Hawkinson, J. (1978). *Pat, swish, twist and the story of Patty Swish.* Chicago: Albert Whitman.

Healy, J. M. (1994). *Your child's growing mind.* New York: Doubleday.

Healy, J. M. (1999). *Failure to connect: How computers affect our children's minds—and what we can do about it.* New York: Simon & Schuster.

Hellan, J. R. (2000). *Rolling along: The story of Taylor and his wheelchair.* Atlanta, GA: Peachtree.

Hendrick, J. (Ed.). (1997). *First steps toward teaching the Reggio way.* Columbus, OH: Merrill.

Herberholz, B., & Hanson, L. (1990). *Early childhood art* (4th ed.). Dubuque, IA: Wm. C. Brown.

Hesse, P., & Lane, F. (2003). Media literacy starts young. *Young Children, 58,* 20–26.

Himmelman, K. (1996). *Hooray! It's Passover!* New York: HarperCollins.

Hirsch, R. A. (2004). *Early childhood curriculum.* Boston: Pearson.

Ho, M. (1996). *Hush! A Thai lullaby.* New York: Orchard.

Hoban, T. (1970). *Shapes and things.* New York: Macmillan.

Hoban, T. (1971). *Look again.* New York: Macmillan.

Hoban, T. (1974). *Circles, triangles & squares.* New York: Simon & Schuster.

Hoban, T. (1978). *Is it red? Is it yellow: Is it blue?* New York: Greenwillow.

Hoban, T. (1982). *A, B, see.* New York: Greenwillow.

Hoban, T. (1983). *I read symbols.* New York: Greenwillow.

Hoban, T. (1983). *Round and round and round.* New York: Greenwillow.

Hoban, T. (1984). *Is it rough? Is it smooth? Is it shiny?* New York: HarperCollins.

Hoberman, M. A. (1982). *A house is a house for me.* New York: Penguin Putnam.

Hoberman, M. A. (1998). *The lady with the alligator purse.* New York: Little, Brown & Company.

Hoberman, M. A. (2001). *Miss Mary Mack.* New York: Little, Brown & Company.

Hoberman, M. A. (2002). *The Eensy-Weensy spider.* New York: Little, Brown & Company.

Hoberman, M. A. (2003). *I know an old lady who swallowed a fly*. New York: Little, Brown & Company.

Hoberman, M. A. (2003). *Skip to my Lou*. New York: Little, Brown & Company.

Hoffman, M. (1991). *Amazing grace*. New York: Dial.

Hohmann, M., & Weikart, D. P. (1995). *Educating young children*. Ypsilanti, MI: High/Scope Press.

Hoover, F. L. (1961). *Art activities for the very young*. Worcester, MA: Davis Publishing.

Hughes, S. (1985). *Noisy*. New York: Lothrop, Lee & Shepard.

Humpal, M. E., & Wolf, J. (2003). Music in the inclusive environment. *Young Children, 58,* 103–107.

Hunt, M. (1995). Let there be light! Lighting up the holidays for young children. *Young Children, 51,* 79–81.

Hutchins, P. (1987). *Changes, changes*. New York: Macmillan.

Hyde, M. E. (1996). *Matisse for kids*. New York: Pelican.

Isadore, R. (1998). *Ben's trumpet*. Pine Plains, NY: Live Oak Media.

Indenbaum, V., & Shapiro, M. (1983). *The everything book for teachers of young children*. Livonia, MI: Partner Press.

Isabell, R. T., & Raines, S. C. (2003). *Creativity and the arts with young children*. Clifton Park, NY: Thomson Delmar Learning.

Jalongo, M. R. (1990). The child's right to the expressive arts: Nurturing the imagination as well as the intellect. *Childhood Education, 66,* 195–201.

Jalongo, M. R. (2003). The child's right to creative thought and expression: A position paper of the Association for Childhood Education International. *Childhood Education, 79,* 218–228.

Jalongo, M. R., & Stamp, L. N. (1997). *The arts in children's lives: Aesthetic education in early childhood*. Boston: Allyn & Bacon.

James, B. (1998). *The mud family*. London: Oxford University.

Jameson, K. (1970). *Art and the young child*. New York: Viking.

Janson, H. W., & Janson, D. J. (1984). *Janson's story of painting*. New York: Harrison House/Harry N. Abrams.

Johnson, C. (1960). *A picture for Harold's room*. New York: HarperCollins.

Johnson, C. (1981). *Harold and the purple crayon*. New York: HarperCollins.

Johnson, M. (1990). *Teach your child to draw*. Los Angeles: Lowell House.

Jonas, A. (1990). *Color dance*. New York: HarperCollins.

Jonas, A. (1997). *Watch William walk*. New York: Greenwillow.

Jones, E. (1993). The play's the thing: Style of playfulness. *Child Care Information Exchange, 18,* 28–30.

Jones, E. (1999). An emergent curriculum expert offers this afterthought. *Young Children, 54,* 16.

Jones, E, & Nimmo, J. (1994). *Emergent curriculum*. Washington, DC: NAEYC.

Jones, S. (1979). *Learning for little kids*. Boston, MA: Houghton Mifflin.

Joose, B. (1991). *Mama, do you love me?* San Francisco: Chronicle.

Joose, B. (1996). *I love you the purplest*. San Francisco: Chronicle Books.

Kaagan, S. S. (1990). *Aesthetic persuasion: Pressing the cause of arts education in American schools*. A Monograph for The Getty Center for Education in the Arts. Santa Monica, CA.

Kalman, M. (2002). *Fireboat*. New York: Penguin.

Kamii, C., & DeVries, R. (1978). *Physical knowledge in preschool education: Implications of Piaget's theory*. Englewood Cliffs, NJ: Prentice-Hall.

Kampmann, L. (1971). *The children's book of painting*. New York: Van Nostrand Reinhold.

Karnes, M. (1993). Art for children with special needs. *Scholastic Early Childhood Today, 63*.

Katz, L. (1987). What should young children be learning? *ERIC Digest*. Urbana, IL: ERIC Clearinghouse on Elementary and Early Childhood Education.

Katz, L. (1990). Impressions of Reggio Emilia preschools. *Young Children, 45,* 11–14.

Katz, L. (1994). *The project approach* (ERIC Digest, ED 368509). Urbana, Illinois: ERIC Clearinghouse on Elementary and Early Childhood Education.

Katz, L., & Chard, S. C. (1989). *Engaging children's minds: The project approach*. Norwood, NJ: Ablex.

Katz, L. G. (1987). *What should young children be learning?* Champaign, IL.: ERIC Clearinghouse on Elementary and Early Childhood Education.

Keats, E. J. (1978). *The trip*. New York: Greenwillow.

Kellogg, R. (1969). *Analyzing children's art*. Palo Alto, CA: Mayfield Publishing.

Kellogg, R. (1973). Stages of development in preschool art. In H. P. Lewis (Ed.), *Child art: The beginnings of self-affirmation*, Berkeley, CA: Diablo Press.

Kellogg, R. (1979). *Children's drawings/children's minds*. New York: Avon Books.

Kellogg, R., & O'Dell, S. (1967). *The psychology of children's art*. San Diego: CRM-Random House.

Kellogg, S. (1976). *Can I keep him?* New York: Penguin Putnam.

Kellogg, S. (1982). *Mystery of the stolen blue paint*. New York: Dial.

Kessler, E., & Kessler, L. (1966). *Are you square?* Garden City, NY: Doubleday.

Kocher, A. (1994). *Ravi's Diwali surprise*. Cleveland, OH: Modern Curriculum Press.

Kohl, M. A. (1985). *Scribble cookies and other independent creative art experiences for children*. Bellingham, WA: Bright Ring Publishing.

Koster, J. B. (1999). Clay for little fingers. *Young Children, 54,* 18–22.

Kramer, E. (1974). *Art as therapy with children*. New York: Schocken Books.

Krauss, R. (1956). *I want to paint my bathroom blue.* New York: Harper & Row.

Kristeller, J. (1994, November/December). Creating curriculum as a workshop. *Scholastic Early Childhood Today,* 58–60.

Kunhardt, D. (1962). *Pat the bunny.* New York: Golden Books.

Laden, N. (1998). *When pigasso met mootisee.* San Francisco: Chronicle Books.

Lamorisse, A. (1956). *The red balloon.* Garden City, NY: Doubleday.

Langer, S. K. (1957). *Philosophy in a new key.* Cambridge, MA: Harvard University Press.

Lankford, E. L. (1992). *Aesthetics: Issues and inquiry.* Reston, VA: National Art Education Association.

Lansing, K. M. (1969). *Art, artists, and art education.* New York: McGraw-Hill.

Lasky, L., & Mukerji, R. (1980). *Art: Basic for young children.* Washington, DC: National Association for the Education of Young Children.

Lears, L. (2003). *Ian's walk: A story about autism.* New York: Albert Whitman.

Leighton, M. (1994). *An Ellis Island Christmas.* New York: Puffin.

Lemerise, T. (1993). Piaget, Vygotsky and Logo. *The Computing Teacher, 20,* 24–28.

Lepper, M. R., & Greene, D. (1975). Turning play into work: Effects of adult surveillance and extrinsic rewards on children's intrinsic motivation. *Journal of Personality and Social Psychology, 31,* 479–486.

Lessen-Firestone, J. (1995, March). The trials of testing. *Scholastic Early Childhood Today,* 23.

LeTord, B. (1999). *A bird or two: A story about Henri Matisse.* Grand Rapids, MI: William B. Eerdmans.

Levine, E. (1989). *I hate English.* New York: Scholastic.

Lewis, H. P. (Ed.). (1973). *Child art—the beginnings of self-affirmation.* Berkeley, CA: Diablo Press.

Linder, T. W. (1983). *Early childhood special education.* Baltimore, MD: Paul H. Brooks.

Linderman, E. W., & Heberholz, D. S. (1974). *Developing artistic and perceptual awareness.* Dubuque, IA: Wm. C. Brown.

Linderman, E. W., & Linderman, M. (1984). *Arts and crafts for the classroom.* New York: Macmillan.

Lionni, L. (1968). *Swimmy.* New York: Alfred A. Knopf.

Lionni, L. (1973). *Frederick.* New York: Alfred A. Knopf.

Lionni, L. (1979). *Little blue and little yellow.* New York: Ivan Obolensky.

Lionni, L. (1985). *Colors to talk about.* New York: Alfred A. Knopf.

Lionni, L. (1991). *Matthew's dream.* New York: Knopf.

Lobel, A. (1981). *On Market Street.* New York: Greenwillow.

Loss, J. (1974). *What is it? A book of photographic puzzles.* Garden City, NY: Doubleday.

Lowenfeld, V. (1968). On the importance of early art expression. In W. L. Brittain (Ed.), *Viktor Lowenfeld speaks on art and creativity* (pp. 20–27). Washington, DC: National Art Education Association.

Lowenfeld, V., & Brittain, W. L. (1987). *Creative and mental growth.* New York: Macmillan.

Lund, D. H. (1973). *The paint-box sea.* New York: McGraw-Hill.

MacAgy, D., & MacAgy, E. (1959). *Going for a walk with a line: A step into the world of modern art.* Garden City, NY: Doubleday.

MacKinnon, D. W. (1962). The nature and nurture of creative talent. *American Psychologist, 17,* 484–495.

Maguire, A. (1999). *Special people, special ways.* Santa Monica, CA: Portunus.

Malaguzzi, L. (1993). For an education based on relationships. *Young Children, 49,* 9–12.

Martin, B. (1996). *Brown bear, brown bear.* New York: Henry Holt.

Martin, B. (1997). *Polar bear, polar bear.* New York: Henry Holt.

Martin, S. (1994). *Observation and portfolio assessment in early childhood.* Don Mills, Ontario: Addison-Wesley.

Marzollo, J. (1977). *Supertot—Creative learning activities for children from one to three and sympathetic advice for their parents.* New York: Harper & Row.

Marzollo, J. (1997). *Pretend you're a cat.* New York: Viking Penguin.

Matthews, J. C. (1997). *Computers and art education. ERIC digest* (ERIC document reproduction no. ED410180). Bloomington, IN: ERIC Clearinghouse for Social Studies/Social Science Education.

Mattil, E. L., & Marzan, B. (1981). *Meaning in children's art.* Englewood Cliffs, NJ: Prentice-Hall.

Mayhew, J. (1999). *Katie and the Mona Lisa.* New York: Scholastic.

Mayhew, J. (1999). *Katie meets the Impressionists.* New York: Scholastic.

McCorminck, L., & Feeney, S. (1995). Modifying and expanding activities for children with disabilities. *Young Children, 50,* 10–18.

McCracken, J. B. (1993). *Valuing diversity: The primary years.* Washington, DC: NAEYC.

McFee, J. K. (1970). *Preparation for art.* Belmont, CA: Wadsworth.

McFee, J. K. (1993). DBAE and cultural diversity: Some perspectives from the social sciences. In *Discipline-based art education and cultural diversity* (pp. 116–135). Santa Monica, CA: Getty Foundation for Education in the Arts.

McNeill, E., Allen, J., & Schmidt, V. (1991). *Cultural awareness for young children.* Reading, MA: Addison-Wesley.

Merberg, J., & Bober, S. (2002). *Magical day with Matisse.* San Francisco: Chronicle Books.

Meyer, D. J. (1997). *Views from our shoes: Growing up with a brother or sister with special needs.* Las Vegas, NV: Sagebrush.

Micklethwait, L. (1996). *A child's book of play in art.* New York: DK Publishing, Inc.

Millman, I. (2002). *Moses goes to a concert.* New York: Straus and Giroux.

Mitchell, R. (1997). *The talking cloth.* New York: Orchard.

Moll, P. B. (1985). *Children and scissors—a developmental approach.* Tampa, FL: Hampton Mae Institute.

Montessori, M. (1967). *The absorbent mind.* New York: Holt, Rinehart & Winston.

Morgan, G. G., & Shade, D. D. (1994). Moving early childhood education into the 21st century. In J. Wright & D. D. Shade (Eds.), *Young children: Active learners in a technological age* (pp. 135–149). Washington, DC: NAEYC.

Moyer, J. (1990). Whose creation is it, anyway? *Childhood Education, 66,* 130–131.

National Association for the Education of Young Children (NAEYC). (1991). Guidelines for appropriate curriculum content and assessment in programs serving children ages 3 through 8. *Young Children, 46,* 21–38.

National Association for the Education of Young Children (NAEYC). (1996). NAEYC position statement: Technology and young children—ages three through eight. *Young Children, 51,* 11–16.

National Standards for Arts Education. (1991). Reston, VA: National Association for Music Education.

Naumberg, M. (1973). *An introduction to art therapy.* New York: Teachers College Press.

Neely, L. P. (2001). Active for life: Developmentally appropriate movement. Practice: Children learn what they live. *Young Children, 56,* 32–37.

Neely, L. P. (2002). Practical ways to improve singing in early childhood classrooms. *Young Children, 57,* 80–85.

Neugebauer, B. (Ed.). (1987). *Alike and different—Exploring our humanity with young children.* Redmond, WA: Exchange Press.

New, R. (1990). Excellent early education: A city in Italy has it. *Young Children, 45,* 4–10.

New, R. (1993). Cultural variations on developmentally appropriate practice: Challenges to theory and practice. In C. Edwards, L. Gandini, & G. Forman (Eds.), *The hundred languages of children: The Reggio Emilia approach to early childhood education,* (pp. 215–232). Norwood, NJ: Ablex.

Newman, E. (1990, April). Yani: The brush of innocence. *Bay Area Parent,* 24–26.

Nieto, S. (1992). *Affirming diversity—The sociopolitical context of multicultural education.* White Plains, NY: Longman.

Novak, M. (1994). *Mouse TV.* New York: Orchard Books.

O'Connor, J. & Hartland, J. (2002). *Henri Matisse: Drawing with scissors.* New York: Grosset & Dunlap.

O'Neill, M. (1961). *Hailstones and halibut bones.* Garden City, NY: Doubleday.

Osofsky, A. (1992). *Dreamcatcher.* New York: Orchard.

Papert, S. (1980). *Mindstorms: Children, computers, and powerful ideas.* New York: Basic Books.

Parks, M. E. (1994). *The art teacher's desktop reference.* Englewood Cliffs, NJ: Prentice-Hall.

Parnes, S. J. (1967). *Creative behavior guidebook.* New York: Charles Scribner's Sons.

Parette, H. P., Hourcase, J. J., & Heiple, G. S. (2000). The importance of structured computer experiences for young children with and without disabilities. *Early childhood Education Journal, 27*(4), 243–250.

Parsons, M. J. (1987). Talk about a painting: A cognitive developmental analysis. *The Journal of Aesthetic Education, 21,* 37–55.

Patel, A. (2002). *On that day.* Berkeley, CA: Ten Speed Press.

Perrault, C. (1997). *Cinderella.* New York: Simon & Schuster.

Phillips, R. S. (1978). *The great artists.* New York: Funk & Wagnalls.

Piaget, J. (1953). Art education and child psychology. In E. Ziegfeld (Ed.), *Education and art* (pp. 39–56). Switzerland: UNESCO.

Piaget, J. (1962). *Play, dreams, and imitation in childhood.* New York: Norton.

Piaget, J. (1971). *Mental imagery in the child.* New York: Basic Books.

Piaget, J., & Inhelder, B. (1956). *The child's conception of space.* London: Routledge and Kegan Paul.

Piaget, J., & Inhelder, B. (1969). *The psychology of the child.* (H. Weaver, Trans.) New York: Basic Books,

Pica, R. (2004). *Experiences in movement: Birth to age 8.* (3rd ed.). Clifton Park, NY: Thomson Delmar Learning.

Pico, R. (1994). *The red comb.* New York: BridgeWater.

Pile, N. F. (1973). *Art experiences for young children.* New York: Macmillan.

Poffenberger, N. (2001). *September 11th, 2001.* Cincinatti, OH: Fun Publishing.

Polacco, P. (1988). *The keeping quilt.* New York: Simon & Schuster.

Pomeranc, M. H. (1998). *The American Wei.* Morton Grove, IL: Albert-Whitman & Company.

Raboff, E. (1987-1988). *Art for children.* New York: HarperCollins.

Raboff, E. L. (1991). *Henri Matisse.* New York: HarperCollins.

Raffi. (1990). *Baby beluga.* New York: Crown.

Raffi. (1990). *Shake my sillies out.* New York: Crown.

Raffi. (1998). *Five little ducks.* New York: Crown.

Raffi. (1998). *The wheels on the bus.* New York: Crown.

Raffi. (1999). *Down by the bay.* New York: Crown.

Reiss, J. J. (1969). *Colors.* Scarsdale, NY: Bradbury Press.

Reiss, J. J. (1974). *Shapes.* Scarsdale, NY: Bradbury Press.

Richey, D. D., & Wheeler, J. J. (2000). *Inclusive early childhood education.* Clifton Park, NY: Thomson Delmar Learning.

Riehicky, J. (1993). *Cinco de Mayo.* Chicago, IL: Children's Press.

Ringgenberg, S. (2003). Music as a teaching tool: Creating story songs. *Young Children, 58,* 76–79.

Ringgold, F. (1991). *Tar beach.* New York: Crown.

Robertson, J. (2003). *Oscar's spots.* New York: Troll.

Robles de Melendez, W., Beck, V., & Fletcher, M. (2000). *Teaching social studies in early education.* Clifton Park, NY: Thomson Delmar Learning.

Rogers, F. (2000). *Let's talk about it: Extraordinary friends.* New York: Penguin.

Rosa-Casanova, S. (1997). *Mama Provi and the pot of rice.* New York. Atheneum.

Rosenstiel, A. K., Morrison, P., Silverman, J., & Gardner, H. (1978). Critical judgement: A developmental study. *The Journal of Aesthetic Education, 12,* 95–107.

Rubin, J. A. (1978). *Child art therapy.* New York: Van Nostrand Reinhold.

Russell, I., & Waugaman, B. (1952). A study of the effect of workbook copy experiences on the creative concepts of children. Cited in V. Lowenfeld & W. L. Brittain, *Creative and mental growth.* Research Bulletin, Eastern Arts Association, *3*(1).

Sabbeth, C. (1998). *Crayons and computers: Computer art activities for kids ages 4 to 8.* Chicago Review Press.

Safford, P. L. (1989). *Integrated teaching in early childhood: Starting in the mainstream.* West Plains, NY: Longman.

Samton, S. W. (1985). *The world from my window.* New York: Crown.

Sanders, S. W. (2002). *Active for life: Developmentally appropriate movement programs for young children.* Washington, DC: National Association for the Education of Young Children.

Saracho, O. N., & Spodek, B. (Eds.). (1983). *Understanding the multicultural experience in early childhood education.* Washington, DC: NAEYC.

Say, A. (1990). *El Chino.* Boston: Houghton Mifflin.

Say, A. (1999). *Tea with milk.* Boston: Houghton Mifflin.

Sazer, N. (1976). *What do you think I saw? A nonsense number book.* New York: Pantheon.

Schaefer, C. L. (1999). *The squiggle.* New York: Crown.

Schiller, M. (1995). An emergent art curriculum that fosters understanding. *Young Children, 50,* 33–38.

Schirrmacher, R. (1980). Child art. In S. Modgil & C. Modgil (Eds.), *Toward a theory of psychological development* (pp. 733–762). Windsor, England: National Foundation for Educational Research.

Schirrmacher, R. (1986). Talking with young children about their art. *Young Children, 41,* 3–7.

Scott, L. B., May, M. E., & Shaw, M. S. (1972). *Puppets for all grades.* New York: The Instructor Publications.

Seefeldt, C. (1995). Art—A serious work. *Young Children, 45*(3), 39–45.

Seminar proceedings. (1993). *Discipline-based art education and cultural diversity.* Santa Monica, CA: J. Paul Getty Trust.

Sendak, M. (1984). *Where the wild things are.* New York: HarperCollins.

Shade, D. (1996). Software Evaluation. *Young Children, 51,* 17–21.

Shallcross, D. J. (1981). *Teaching creative behavior.* Englewood Cliffs, NJ: Prentice-Hall.

Shapur, F. (1972). *Round and round and square.* London: Abelard- Schuman.

Shaw, C. G. (1947). *It looked like spilt milk.* New York: Harper & Row.

Shaw, C. G. (1988). *It looked like spilt milk.* New York: HarperCollins.

Shore, R. (1997). *Rethinking the brain.* New York: Families and Work Institute.

Shriver, M. (2001). *What' wrong with Timmy?.* New York: Little, Brown & Company.

Silberstein-Storfer, M., & Jones, M. (1982). *Doing art together.* New York: Simon & Schuster.

Slobodkina, E. (1968). *Caps for sale.* Reading, MA: Addison-Wesley.

Small, D. (1986). *Imogene's antlers.* New York: Crown.

Smilansky, S. (1968). *The effects of sociodramatic play on disadvantaged preschool children.* New York: Wiley.

Smilansky, S. (1971). Can adults facilitate play in children? Theoretical and practical implications. Washington, DC: NAEYC.

Smith, N. R. (1982). The visual arts in early childhood education: Development and the creation of meaning. In B. Spodek (Ed.), *Handbook of research in early childhood education* (pp. 295–317). New York: Free Press.

Smith, N. R. (1983). *Experience and art. Teaching children to paint.* New York: Teachers College Press.

Smith, N., Fucigna, C., Kennedy, M., & Lord, L. (1993). *Experience and art—Teaching children to paint* (2nd ed.). New York: Teachers College Press.

Smith, R. A. (1993). Introduction to the symposium on aesthetic value and arts education. *Arts Education Policy Review, 95,* 10–12.

Smith, R. A., & Simpson, A. (1991). *Aesthetics and arts education.* Urbana and Chicago: University of Illinois Press.

Snape, M. (1991). *Boy with the square eyes.* New York: Simon & Schuster.

Sortland, B. & Elling, L. (1999). *Anna's art adventure.* Minneapolis, MN: Lerner.

Soto, G. (1997). *Snapshots from a wedding*. New York: Putnam.

Spiegel-McGill, P., Zippiroli, S., & Mistrett, S. (1989). Microcomputers as social facilitators in integrated preschools. *Journal of Early Intervention, 13*(3), 249–260.

Spier, P. (1977). *Noah's ark*. New York: Random House.

Spinelli, E. (2001). *In my new yellow shirt*. New York: Henry Holt.

Spodek, B. (1982). *Handbook of research in early childhood education*. New York: Free Press.

Spodek, B. (1993). Selecting activities in the arts for early childhood education. *Arts Education Policy Review, 94*, 11–19.

Spodek, B., Saracho, O. N., & Lee, R. C. (1984). *Mainstreaming young children*. Belmont, CA: Wadsworth.

Steig, W. (1982). *Doctor DeSoto*. New York: Scholastic.

Sternberg, R. J. (1985). *Beyond IQ*. New York: Cambridge University Press.

Sternberg, R. J. (1997). *Successful intelligence*. New York: Plume.

Sternberg, R. L. (Ed.). (2002). Models of Intelligence: International Perspectives. Washington, DC: American Psychological Association.

Sternberg, R. J., & Lubart, T. I. (1995). *Defying the crowd: Cultivating creativity in a culture of conformity*. New York: Free Press.

Stinson, K. & Betteridge, D. (1995). *Those green things*. Toronto, Ontario: Annic Press.

Stone, S. J. (1995). Wanted: Advocates for play in the primary grades. *Young Children, 50*, 45–65.

Striker, S. (1986). *Please touch—How to stimulate your child's creative development*. New York: Simon & Schuster.

Sturm, E. & Hoena, B. (Eds.). (2003). *Matisse (Masterpieces: Artists and their works)*. Mankato, MN: Capstone Press.

Stutson, C. (1996). *Prairie primer*. New York: Dutton.

Stuve-Bodeen, S. (1998). *We'll paint the octopus red*. Bethesda, MD: Woodbine House.

Suyenaga, R. (1994). *Obon*. Cleveland, OH: Modern Curriculum Press.

Swamp, Chief Jake. (1995). *Giving thanks: A Native American good morning message*. New York: Lee & Low.

Swartz, L. (1992). *A first Passover*. Cleveland, OH: Modern Curriculum Press.

Sweet, M. (2002). *Fiddle-i-fee: A farmyard song for the very young*. New York: Little, Brown & Company.

Szekely, G. (1990). An introduction to art: Children's books. *Childhood Education, 66*, 132–138.

Taback, S. (2000). *Joseph had a little overcoat*. New York: Penguin.

Taunton, M. (1984). Reflective dialogue in the art classroom: Focusing on the art process. *Art Education, 37*, 15–16.

Taunton, M., & Colbert, C. (1984). Artistic and aesthetic development: Considerations for early childhood educators. *Childhood Education, 61*, 55–63.

Thouvenelle, S. & Bewick, C. J. (1999). *Completing the computer puzzle: A guide for early childhood educators*. Boston: Pearson Education.

Topal, C. W. (1983). *Children, clay and sculpture*. Worcester, MA: Davis Publications.

Torrance, E. P. (1962). *Guiding creative talent*. Englewood Cliffs, NJ: Prentice-Hall.

Torrance, E. P. (1963a). *Creativity*. Washington, DC: National Education Association.

Torrance, E. P. (1963b). *Minnesota tests of creative thinking*. Minneapolis, MN: University of Minnesota Bureau of Educational Research.

Torrance, E. P. (1965). *Rewarding creative behavior: experiments in classroom creativity*. Englewood Cliffs, NJ: Prentice-Hall.

Torrance, E. P. (1966). *Torrance tests of creative thinking: Technical-norms manual*. Lexington, MA: Personnel Press.

Torrance, E. P. (1979). *The search for satori and creativity*. Buffalo, NY: The Creative Education Foundation.

Torrance, E. P., & Myers, R. E. (1970). *Creative learning and teaching*. New York: Harper & Row.

Tudor, T. (1978). *Five senses*. New York: Platt & Munk.

Uchida, Y. (1993). *The bracelet*. New York: Philomel.

Uhlin, D. (1979). *Art for exceptional children*. Dubuque, IA: Wm. C. Brown.

Van Alsburg, C. (1981). *Jumanji*. Boston: Houghton Mifflin.

Van Alsburg, C. (1985). *The polar express*. Boston: Houghton Mifflin.

VanHoorn, J. L., Nourot, P. M., & Scales, B. (2003). *Play at the corner of the curriculum*. New York: Prentice Hall.

Venezie, M. (1997). *Henri Matisse*. New York: Scholastic.

Ventura, P. (1984). *Great painters*. New York: G. P. Putnam's Sons.

Vygostky, L. S. (1978). *Mind and society: The development of higher psychological process*. Cambridge, MA: Harvard University Press.

Vygostky, L. S. (1980). *Mind in society*. Cambridge, MA: Harvard University Press.

Vygostky, L. S. (1986). *Thought and language*. Cambridge, MA: Harvard University Press.

Vygostky, L. S. (1987). Thinking and speech. In R. W. Rieber & A. S. Carton (Eds.), N. Minick (Trans.), *The collected works of L. S. Vygostky* (136–159). New York: Plenum.

Wachowiak, F. (1985). *Emphasis art*. New York: Harper and Row.

Walker, G. & Minnerly, D. B. (1998). *Molly meets Mona and friends: A magical day at the museum*. Bridgeport, CT: Greene Bark Press.

Wallach, M. A., & Kogan, N. (1965). *Modes of thinking in young children*. New York: Holt, Rinehart & Winston.

Walsh, E. S. (1995). *Mouse paint.* Orlando, FL: Harcourt.

Walsh, E. S. (2000). *Magic mouse.* Orlando, FL: Harcourt.

Wankelmen, W. F., Wigg, P. R., & Wigg, M. K. (1974). *A handbook of arts and crafts.* Dubuque, IA: Wm. C. Brown.

Watson, E. (1996). *Talking to angels.* Orlando, FL: Harcourt.

Weikart, D. L., Rogers, C., Adcock, C., & McClelland, D. (1971). *The cognitively oriented curriculum: A framework for preschool teachers.* Washington, DC: National Association for the Education of Young Children.

Weisgard, L. (1956). *Treasures to see.* New York: Harcourt, Brace & World.

Wellington, M. (2000). *Squeaking of art: The mice go to the museum.* New York: Penguin.

Wescott, N. B. (1991). *Peanut butter & jelly: A play rhyme.* New York: Penguin.

Whitman, C. (1998). *Bring on the blue.* New York: Abbeville Press.

Whitman, C. (1998). *Ready for red.* New York: Abbeville Press.

Whitman, C. (1998). *Yellow and you.* New York: Abbeville Press.

Wiesner, D. (1999). *Sector 7.* New York: Clarion.

Wildsmith, B. (1984). *Fishes.* London: Oxford University Press.

Wilkens, D. K. (1996). *Multiple intelligences activities (Grades K-4).* Westminster, CA: Teacher Created Materials, Inc.

Williams, G. (1969). *The rabbits' wedding.* New York: HarperCollins.

Williams, S. (1996). *I went walking.* Orlando, FL: Harcourt.

Williams, V. B. (1990). *More, more, more said the baby.* New York: Greenwillow.

Willis, J. (2000). *Susan laughs.* New York: Henry Holt.

Winn, C. M. & Walsh, D. (1996). *Box-head boy.* Minneapolis, MN: Fairview Press.

Wolf, A. D. (1984). *Mommy, it's a Renoir!* Altoona, PA: Parent-Child Press.

Wolf, A. D. (1986). *Child-size masterpieces.* Altoona, PA: Parent-Child Press.

Wolf, A. D. (1988, May/June). Hands on art. *Montessori Today.*

Wolf, A. D. (1990). Art postcards—another aspect of your aesthetics program? *Young Children, 45,* 39–43.

Wolf, J. (2000). Sharing songs with children. *National Association for the Education of Young Children, 55,* 28–30.

Wolf, J. (1994). Singing with children is a cinch! *Young Children, 49,* 20–25.

Wolff, R. J. (1968). *Feeling blue.* New York: Charles Scribner's Sons.

Wood, A. & Wood, D. (1984). *The napping house.* Orlando, FL: Harcourt.

Wood, D. (1996). *Northwoods cradle song from a Menominee lullaby.* New York: Simon & Schuster.

Wright, J. L., & Shade, D. D. (Eds.). (1993). *Young children: Active learners in a technological age.* Washington, DC: NAEYC.

Wright, S. (2003). *The arts, young children, and learning.* Boston: Allyn & Bacon.

Wright, S. K. (1994). Assessment in the arts: Is it appropriate in the early childhood years? *Studies in Art Education, 36,* 28–43.

Wright, S. K. (1997). Learning how to learn: The arts as core in an emergent curriculum. *Childhood Education, 73,* 361–365.

Yenawine, P. (1991). *Lines.* New York: Random House.

Yenawine, P. (1991). *Stories; colors; lines; shapes.* New York: Delacorte.

Yenawine, P. (2003). Jump starting visual literacy: Thoughts on image selection. Art Education, 56, 6–11.

Yolen, J. (1987). *Owl moon.* New York: Penguin.

Zelinsky, P. O. (1997). *Rapunzel.* New York: Dutton.

Zhensun, Z., & Low, A. (1991). *A young painter: The life and paintings of Wang Yani—China's extraordinary young artist.* New York: Scholastic.

Index